C0-AWI-644

Sociological Aspects
of
Drug Dependence

Editor

Charles Winick

Department of Sociology
The City College of
The City University of New York
New York, N.Y.

Published by

CRC PRESS, Inc.
18901 Cranwood Parkway · Cleveland, Ohio 44128

63346

Library of Congress Cataloging in Publication Data

Winick, Charles, 1922–
  Sociological aspects of drug dependence.

  Includes bibliographies.
  1. Drug abuse – Social aspects – Addresses, essays,
lectures. 2. Drug abuse – Treatment – Addresses, essays,
lectures. 3. Drug abuse – Study and teaching –
Addresses, essays, lectures. I. Title. [DNLM: 1. Drug
addiction. 2. Socioeconomic factors. WM270 W772s]
HV5801.W545   362.2'93   74-11692
ISBN 0-87819-057-0

    This book represents information obtained from authentic and highly regarded sources. Reprinted
material is quoted with permission, and sources are indicated. A wide variety of references are listed.
Every reasonable effort has been made to give reliable data and information, but the author and the
publisher cannot assume responsibility for the validity of all materials or for the consequences of their
use.

All rights reserved. This book, or any parts thereof, may not be reproduced in any form without
written consent from the publisher.

© 1974 by CRC Press, Inc.   .

International Standard Book Number 0-87819-057-0

Library of Congress Card Number 74-11692
Printed in the United States

DRUG DEPENDENCE SERIES – PREFACE

The enlightened World Health Organization (WHO) Expert Committee on Dependence-Producing Drugs formulated the following definition of drug dependence:

A state of periodic or chronic intoxication produced by the repeated consumption of a drug (natural or synthetic). Its characteristics include: 1) an overpowering desire or need (compulsion) to continue taking the drug and to obtain it by any means; 2) a tendency to increase the dose; 3) a psychic (psychological) and generally a physical dependence on the effects of the drug; and 4) a detrimental effect on the individual and on society.

This definition most nearly encompasses all aspects of the drug dependent condition and/or state. On this basis as well as my own research experience, the first text in this series concerning the *Chemical and Biological Aspects of Drug Dependence* was undertaken. Initially, the task of exploring all phases of drug dependence as clearly described in the WHO definition seemed impossible; however, tolerance to adversity soon developed and the texts on the *sociological, legal,* and *psychiatric aspects* of drug dependence were soon on their way to completion.

The Sociological Aspects of Drug Dependence, under the capable editorialship of Charles Winick, brings to bear in a broad manner a marvelous group of essays on the effects and interrelationship of the drug user with society, including theories, patterns of deviance, treatment, life-styles, factors related to drug dependence problems, and criminality.

Richard Bonnie and Michael Sonnenreich, editors of the *Legal Aspects of Drug Dependence*, have provided a fascinating number of pieces describing a philosophical view of the legal structure and the drug user, the interrelationship between the legal system and treatment of drug dependence, the federal and state criminal drug laws, and, finally, an exciting discussion of new and future departures in legal-drug abuse interrelationship.

Albert Kurland in the *Psychiatric Aspects of Opiate Dependence* provides insight into the clinical nature of psychogenic dependence, the personality structures, abstinence-dependence cycles, diagnostic-prognostic criteria, psychometric assessments, and an enjoyable critical evaluation of the future of psychotherapy in relation to opiate dependency dysfunctions.

It is my hope that this "Uniscience" series on drug dependence will be an authentic primary reference source of data and information for anyone with an intense interest in this drug problem.

S. J. Mulé, Ph.D.
Editor-in-Chief

PREFACE

Although there is considerable debate on the etiology and optimum treatment of drug dependence and how society should cope with it, there is no disagreement over the importance of sociological factors in its dissemination, cycles, trends, treatment and rehabilitation, prevention, and control. By "sociological," we mean those dimensions related to the conditions of our culture and society, groups and their norms, statuses, institutions and authority, social differentiation, social change, and social policy and theory.

Recent years have seen for the first time a series of significant studies of sociological elements in drug dependence. This work is so recent that there is as yet no journal or professional society specifically geared to the sociological study of drug dependence.

In the preparation of the present volume, a number of the persons conducting significant sociological studies were asked to prepare summary reports on specific nodal areas of activity, concern, and interest. The chapters have been grouped into five sections: theory; education and mass communications; some dimensions of users and prevalence; treatment and resocialization of the drug dependent; and social costs. The contributors were generally able to integrate their survey of the "state of the art" with a report on their own recent work.

Each chapter is written by a specialist and undertakes to provide an analysis of the degree of current knowledge in the specific field under discussion. Increasingly, we are recognizing that all of these aspects of drug dependence are interrelated, so that a change in any one has direct and sometimes unanticipated consequences on the others. Indeed, one of the contributions of the sociological approach has been to suggest the ways in which shifts in education or treatment approach, for example, may affect prevalence, which in turn affects policy and social costs, which then lead to modifications in theory. Many other paradigms of relationships within the field are possible.

So many areas were covered that only a multiple authorship could have provided the degree of expertise required to make the volume as valid and useful as the goals of this Uniscience Series on Drug Dependence require it to be. We hope that it will be a benchmark of our knowledge in this crucial area, as a guide to serious students of what has become an increasingly central sociological as well as social problem.

Charles Winick
New York, New York

THE EDITOR

Charles Winick, Ph.D., has been Professor of Sociology at City College and the Graduate Center, City University of New York, since 1966.

Dr. Winick has previously taught at the University of Rochester, Columbia University, and Massachusetts Institute of Technology. He was director of the program in drug dependence of the American Social Health Association from 1961 to 1966. He has been a consultant on drug dependence to and been principal investigator on projects supported by the National Institute of Mental Health, World Health Organization, American Association Against Addiction, and Commission on Marihuana and Drug Abuse, directed the Musicians' Clinic (for addicted musicians) and New York State Joint Legislative Committee on Narcotic Study, served as co-director of the Narcotic Addiction Research Project, and as secretary of the National Advisory Council on Narcotics. He has contributed more than 100 papers to the professional literature on drug dependence.

CONTRIBUTORS

Mitchell B. Balter, Ph.D.
National Institute of Drug Abuse
11400 Rockville Pike
Rockville, Maryland 20852

Edgar F. Borgatta, Ph.D.
Department of Sociology
Queens College
City University of New York
Flushing, New York 11367

Judith S. Brook, Ph.D.
Addiction Research and Treatment
Corporation Evaluation Team
Columbia University School of Social Work
622 West 113 Street
New York, New York 10025

Bruce Bullington, Ph.D.
College of Human Development
Pennsylvania State University
University Park, Pennsylvania 16902

John J. Casey, Ph.D.
Columbia Broadcasting System, Inc.
51 West 52 Street
New York, New York 10019

Carl D. Chambers, Ph.D.
Department of Epidemiology
School of Medicine
University of Miami
Miami, Florida 33157

Seymour Fiddle, J.D.
Exodus House
309 East 103 Street
New York, New York 10029

Gilbert Geis, Ph.D.
Program in Social Ecology
University of California, Irvine
Irvine, California 92664

James W. Holden, M.S.
10000 Orr Springs Road
Ukiah, California 95482

Andrew Karmen, M.A.
1486 Commonwealth Avenue
Brighton, Massachusetts 02135

Marianne T. Kleman, B.A.
Institute for Research in Social Behavior
The Claremont Hotel
Berkeley, California 94705

Monroe Lerner, Ph.D.
School of Hygiene and Public Health
Johns Hopkins University
Baltimore, Maryland 21218

Wendell R. Lipscomb, M.D.
Executive Director
Studies of Urban Research
and Community Education (SOURCE)
1713 Grove Street (Suite B)
Berkeley, California 94709

Irving F. Lukoff, Ph.D.
Director, Addiction Research and
Treatment Corporation Evaluation Team
Columbia University School of Social Work
622 West 113 Street
New York, New York 10025

Dean I. Manheimer, M.A.
Institute for Research in Social Behavior
The Claremont Hotel
Berkeley, California 94705

Glen D. Mellinger, Ph.D.
Institute for Research in Social Behavior
The Claremont Hotel
Berkeley, California 94705

Alan S. Meyer, Ph.D.
Public Education Association
20 West 40 Street
New York, New York 10018

Ron Miller, Ph.D.
Department of Sociology
Brooklyn College
City University of New York
Brooklyn, New York 11210

John G. Munns, Ph.D.
Department of Sociology
California State University, Los Angeles
Los Angeles, California 90032

George Nash, Ph.D.
Director, Drug Abuse Treatment
Information Project
Montclair State College
Upper Montclair, New Jersey 07043

David N. Nurco, D.S.W.
Maryland Psychiatric Research Center
Department of Mental Hygiene
1229 West Mount Royal Avenue
Baltimore, Maryland 21217

Edward Preble, M.A.
Department of Anthropology
New York School of Psychiatry
1 Ward's Island
New York, New York 10035

Martin Shain, M.A., Dip. Crim.
Addiction Research Foundation
33 Russell Street
Toronto 4, Ontario, Canada

Charles Winick, Ph.D.
Department of Sociology
City College and the Graduate Center
City University of New York
Convent Avenue and 138 Street
New York, New York 10031

TABLE OF CONTENTS

63346

SOCIAL COSTS

THEORY

A SOCIOLOGICAL THEORY OF THE GENESIS OF DRUG DEPENDENCE

Charles Winick

TABLE OF CONTENTS

INTRODUCTION

Many different countries have been reporting an increase in drug dependence during the last decade. In the United States, drug dependence has increased substantially since the end of World War II. It is generally accepted that from 1964 through 1969, this country experienced a heroin epidemic and that even though the number of persons newly becoming heroin users each year since 1969 has probably declined, a variety of other substances are now being used by the populations at risk.

The proliferation of drug dependence has given rise to many different explanations of its genesis, but most of them do not seem really to explain the variety of drug use situations, offer only partial clarification, or are "kinds of people" theories which have little predictive value. "Kinds of people" theories, whether psychoanalytic, psychiatric, or endocrinal, are essentially nonconfirmable because they posit the existence of certain characteristics in drug-dependent persons, but there is no way of knowing whether the characteristics antedated or were caused by the drug experience or if the characteristics are also found in nondrug users.

The huge increase in government and other institutional support for education and treatment activities connected with drug dependence has occurred in the absence of any generally accepted theory of the origins of drug dependence. Most treatment activities have been concerned with handling immediate emergency situations and providing assistance for those seeking or referred to it. Education activities have largely been conducted on an ad hoc, trial and error basis. This paper proposes a sociological theory of the origins of drug dependence that seems to fit a number of the circumstances where drug dependence has arisen in recent history and that may have some relevance to community action programs.

OTHER THEORIES

Why is a new theory of drug dependence needed? Most of the available theories help us to understand a specific situation or the use of one substance. But we now find dependence on a wide range of substances among so many different groups and even countries that a heuristic theory should improve our ability to understand the whole spectrum of dependence.

With the continuing development of new substances and the new uses to which existing substances may be part, it seems foolhardy to develop a theory of drug dependence that is linked to any one chemical. Rather, the World Health Organization definition of dependence as "a state of psychic or physical dependence or both, on a drug, arising in a person following administration of that drug on a periodic or continuous basis"[1] seems a reasonable way to approach our subject, even though the formulation is broad.

One of the most influential theories of the origins of drug dependence to be based on social dimensions is that of Lindesmith, who proposed that a person, after taking an addicting substance, must undergo withdrawal, realize the drug relieves his symptoms, take more, and interiorize society's attitudes toward the subject before he can regard himself as an addict.[2] This theory is based on the use of opiates and the withdrawal distress they occasion. Fiddle, working with young ghetto residents, has suggested that heroin users act as though they form part of a temporary social system which is a risk-discounting mechanism.[3]

Working with jazz musicians and groups of young people, Becker suggested a social learning approach to the genesis of the marihuana habit.[4] Becker's study of marihuana stressed that a user has to learn how to smoke the drug, how to recognize the drug's effects, and enjoy his sensations. A related view is that adolescent drug use is largely sociogenic and depends on a social network of friends, who introduce the drug to a youth and teach him about its use and effects.[5] An antithetical interpretation of adolescent drug use has suggested that it is a response to parental use of such psychoactive drugs as barbiturates, tranquilizers, or stimulants.[6,7]

Several other sociological and social psychological explanations have been offered to explain the beginning of drug dependence in different groups of young people. Finestone has identified the "kick" as the satisfaction of an almost existential need to heighten experience.[8] Cloward and Ohlin have popularized the concept of the addict as a double retreatist who cannot fulfill himself in either the legitimate or criminal world.[9] Chein has called attention to the adaptational aspects of heroin use for the young person in a slum environment.[10] Problem behavior theory, involving an interrelationship among personality, perceived environment, and behavior systems, has been used to predict the shift from nonuse to use of a substance among high school students.[11]

PROPOSED THEORY

The sociological theory for the genesis of drug dependence proposed in this chapter suggests that the incidence of drug dependence will be high in those groups in which there is (1) access to dependence-producing substances, (2) disengagement from negative proscriptions about their use, and (3) role strain and/or role deprivation. These factors deal with the genesis of dependence and not its continuation since the latter depends on a variety of complex circumstances.

In this paper, drugs of dependence include all psychoactive substances, including marihuana, LSD, amphetamines, barbiturates, peyote, and opiates. Dependence involves persons who are regular users. The definition of regular use involves taking the substance over a specific period of time at a specific minimal rate, and the time and rate required for regular use vary with the subject. A regular user of heroin, for example, may be defined as someone using once a day or more for at least one month.

We define a role as a set of expectations and behaviors associated with a specific position in a social system. A role strain is a felt difficulty in meeting the obligations of a role.[12] By role deprivation, we mean the reaction to the termination of a significant and cathected role relationship and loss of the occasion for the behaviors associated with a role situation.

This theory is, like the theory of differential association as an explanation of the genesis of crime,[13] a general approach which sets forth some propositions applying to all forms of drug dependence. Many other circumstances are relevant to the genesis of drug dependence, but such circumstances become relevant, it can be argued, in terms of how they affect the variables set forth in this theory. Although drug dependence for most people is probably overdetermined and based on many causal factors, one goal of science is an effort to organize knowledge systematically in a manner which will optimize prediction, rather than to develop separate interpretations for each set of variables. The situation is perhaps analogous to the wide range of suicide rates which confronted Durkheim[14] or to the seemingly random variation in the behavior of replacement troops in World War II which was identified by the U.S. Army's research branch.[15] In both cases, a theory turned out to have the capacity to bring some order into our ability to understand what had originally seemed to be a confusing situation.

SOME EXAMPLES

The ideal way to test this theory, like any theory, is to develop operational definitions of each variable, as they apply to specific populations, and then make predictions on the degree to which subgroups are likely to become drug dependent in the future. Such efforts are currently under way, but it is possible to analyze some existing information in terms of its relevance to the proposed theory. One such analysis may be made of available data on epidemics of drug dependence in other countries as well as special groups in the United States.

Foreign

In the years since World War II, Japan, Switzerland, and Sweden have had an incidence of drug dependence sufficiently high to be classified as epidemic. Drug use certainly has unique meanings for every culture, and patterns of social structure, family organization, and personality vary by society, but it may be useful to explore the relevance of these countries for our hypothesis.

The amphetamine epidemic which swept Japan between 1945 and 1955 and involved more than 2,000,000 people seems to have centered on groups which had been dislocated from their jobs and other moorings by postwar social change and on groups such as artists, Korean emigres, young male delinquents, and economically marginal persons.[16] We suggest that such persons were responding to role strain and/or deprivation. In Japan, methamphetamine was available without prescription in 1945 in large quantities, when large wartime stocks were made available to the general public. The drugs were promoted actively for their mood-elevating properties by manufacturers. The situation in Japan seems to meet the three criteria of access, freedom from negative proscriptions, and role strain and/or deprivation. Although the majority of the Japanese population did not become drug dependent, the groups which did seem to have been unusually vulnerable to role strain and/or deprivation.

When the dangers of the situation became clear, Japanese authorities acted decisively to control the availability of amphetamines, change attitudes toward their use, and assist those users who needed treatment. The enormous boom in the Japanese economy and the stabilization of the society further helped to minimize role dislocations and, thus, in terms of our hypothesis, proneness to drug dependence.

Soon after World War II, drug dependence to analgesic compounds containing phenacetin, caffeine, and a hypnotic became a severe problem in the German-speaking part of Switzerland.[17,18] Some 80% of these cases were women, who tended to fall into two groups: working housewives experiencing role strain because of the multiple demands posed by their jobs, housework, and raising children and single women who experienced role deprivation as a result of moving into urban areas from the country in order to become piecework employees of the watch and textile factories. In communities with such factories, about 1% of the population was dependent on these substances. Because Switzerland is the home of some of the world's great pharmaceutical manufacturers, the analgesic substances were not only easily available but were advertised as harmless. All three elements of our theory appear relevant to the Swiss situation.

The Swiss acted, in the early 1960s, to educate the public on the possible hazards of these substances, made access to them more difficult, and provided treatment for those already afflicted. The education and treatment effort was quite successful. By the end of 1970, it was estimated that perhaps 2,000 persons, out of a population of 6,115,000, had been investigated during the year for drug-related behavior, and the majority of these were male and relatively young (18 to 20) as compared to the older females of the 1940s and 1950s.[19]

A third foreign example is provided by Sweden, which had some 200,000 amphetamine users in 1942 to 1943.[20] The next phase in the Swedish drug problem occurred around 1959, when widespread nonmedical use of various amphetamines began again. By 1966, about 1,000 patients were being treated for drug dependence in clinics and hospitals. There is no reliable information on the role relationships of the drug-dependent persons, although they tend to be single or divorced adults, children from homes where the parents were divorced (41% as against 3% in the normal population), and others whose life situation would appear to pose problems of role strain or deprivation. There appears to have been a relative acceptance of amphetamines, which could be prescribed freely by physicians beginning in 1965, and this attitude and availability may have been a factor in Sweden's currently having an extremely serious amphetamine problem. All three prongs of our theory seem relevant to the Swedish situation. The Swedish government is only now beginning to address itself to the problem.

Examples Involving Americans

Existing studies on the existence and incidence of drug dependence, since they were not specifically conducted to measure role strain or deprivation, do not deal directly with this dimension. We can, however, infer the presence in drug-dependent persons of such role variables from secondary analysis of data collected for other purposes. For example, although the age at which a young person is allowed to work varies from state to state, we find that almost without exception it is an age at which in each state there is a peaking of incidence of new drug dependence.[21] Thus, in New York, where the young person may leave school and begin working at 16, the age of 16 has long been the single age most susceptible to experimentation with heroin. We know from studies of glue sniffers that the onset of glue sniffing seems to peak in persons who are leaving sixth grade and entering junior high school.[22] In a previous publication on the life cycle of the narcotic addict and of addiction, we have noted a heavy concentration of persons beginning drug use in their late teens and early 20s, with a drop in onset after the age of 23.[23] One reason for the heavy concentration of drug use in the years of late adolescence and early adulthood is that it is a reflection of the role strain occurring in connection with decisions about jobs, family relationships, schools, and role deprivation resulting from the loss of familiar patterns of behavior.

Ruth Benedict, many years ago, called attention to some of the potentially hazardous consequences of role discontinuity and the lack of order and sequence in the cultural training of a person moving along a life cycle.[24] People in our society have increasingly been deprived of significant role-related ritual experiences that helped in the achievement of an emotional state that could bridge the gap between old and new.[25] The role-related ritual helped to give meaning to the conclusion of one phase of the life cycle and the commencement of another, providing a sense of community and publicly affirming the subject's social and personal identity and his move from one age and status group to another. As modern American rites of passage have become more subdued, people have had a lesser identity and less opportunity to develop a sense of self. It is certainly clear that insufficiently graded sequences of role positions through which people move may be dysfunctional. We are suggesting that the dysfunction could be related to the onset of drug dependence and that it has been especially likely to occur in this country in the years since World War II.

One relatively recent situation that suggests an interpretation confirming our theory can be derived by reanalysis of the experience of the American troops in Vietnam. A study of army enlisted men who were in Vietnam from September 1970 through September 1971 concluded that approximately 35% of this group tried heroin at least once during their "hitch."[26] Fully 20% of the troops were "strung out," or dependent, on the drug during their year of service. This 20% figure does not refer to a specific point in time but is cumulative for the year.

However, when a large sample of these veterans were interviewed after their return to the United States, their heroin use had declined tremendously. Of a randomly selected sample of 451 enlisted men, less than 1% had felt themselves addicted at any time since their return. There was another sample of 469 enlisted men whose urine tests were heroin positive during their last month of service in Vietnam in September of 1971. These soldiers' heroin involvement was thus so serious that they couldn't stop using the drug even though they knew that their doing so would delay their going home. Only 7% of these soldiers had been addicted at any time since their return. Put another way, 93% of these soldiers, all of whom had been addicted in Vietnam, had ceased using heroin in the year after their return to the United States.

This study of heroin use in Vietnam was undertaken in order to determine data needed for national policy; it was not conducted in order to test any theory. However, it lends itself to interpretation in terms of our theory. While serving in Vietnam, the soldiers had (1) access to heroin, which was freely available and cost only $2.50 for a quarter gram, (2) disengagement from negative proscriptions about its use because many of the natives as well as other soldiers were already using it, and (3) severe role strain because of boredom, homesickness, uneasiness, the ambiguity of our role in Vietnam, the lack of a clearly defined "front," and the enormous opposition to the war in the United States, all of which combined to make the strain so severe that tours of duty there were limited to one year.

If we explain the genesis of the relatively high rate of Vietnam heroin use in terms of our theory, can we use the same theory to explain its relative nonresumption by the soldiers? Yes, because when they returned to this country, the soldiers came to a situation in which (1) a major law enforcement effort had made drugs relatively inaccessible and expensive, with a quarter gram of heroin costing $500, (2) there was a strong feeling of disapproval of heroin and growing acceptance of the negative proscriptions about it, and (3) much less role strain because the soldiers were out of Vietnam and usually no longer in uniform.

A theory should be able to explain negative cases, and we can also use our theory to explain why army officers serving in Vietnam were virtually uninvolved with heroin. In terms of the three prongs of our theory, army officers were (1) easily able to get heroin, (2) accepting of the conventional negative proscriptions about its use because more were careerists for whom a heroin record would have meant a serious setback to their futures, and (3) relatively unlikely to experience role strain because they were generally volunteers and service in Vietnam was almost a prerequisite for rapid promotion and later desirable staff assignments of officers. Therefore, two of the three requirements of our theory were not met, and it is not surprising that army officers largely ignored the availability of heroin, whereas enlisted men were far less likely to do so.

Any generalizations made from Vietnam experience to the drug scene in this country must be tentative because in Vietnam, heroin tended to be either sniffed or smoked rather than injected intravenously. Also, it may have been possible for some heroin users to avoid detection by "beating"

the urine test. And only an extended follow-up can identify the degree of Vietnam veterans' subsequent use of substances other than heroin. In spite of these cautions, the information currently available on this group seems to lend itself to interpretation in terms of our theory.

There are a number of studies of drug use among college students which, although they were conducted for other purposes, lend themselves to interpretation in terms of our theory. Certainly at many colleges there is a high degree of access to drugs and emancipated attitudes toward their use, which means that two out of our three conditions are met. Drug use is favored by only a minority of college students, we would argue, because they are the ones experiencing role strain and/or role deprivation. Among the contributors to role strain among the young are the current confusion over the masculine and feminine role, the decline in clothing as a participant in age-graded role expectations, the role competitiveness induced by the large numbers of young people competing for similar goals, feelings of disillusion about conventional roles associated with our involvement in Southeast Asia, loss of positive role models in mass media, consideration of the notion that many of our conventional role models in public life are ignoble or psychotic or otherwise less than admirable, and similar considerations.[27]

Suchman, in a survey of a large West Coast university, found that marihuana use was correlated positively with reading underground newspapers, negative reactions to education, respect for the "hippie" way of life, approval of getting around the law, and other dimensions of a "hang-loose" ethic,[28] which we can interpret as a special case of the larger phenomenon of role strain.

In a survey of almost 8,000 college students throughout the country, Groves found a positive correlation between marihuana, psychedelic, opium, and methedrine use and "counterculture" attitudes.[29] The latter may be interpreted as reflections of what we would consider role strain.

The recurrent finding that the incidence of drug dependence and use is higher among liberal arts than engineering students and higher among undergraduates than graduate students could be interpreted in terms of role theory.[30] The liberal arts and undergraduate student are less explicitly role-oriented and experience more role strain than the engineer-to-be or graduate student, who has made a career commitment which he is pursuing with a certain degree of comfort and awareness of what lies ahead.

Similarly, the finding that drug use is more common among students living off-campus and not with their families than among dormitory residents or students living with their families can be interpreted in terms of the greater role strain to which the off-campus students are subject.[31]

Studies of particular occupational groups with what appear to be relatively high rates of drug dependence suggest the central importance of role strain and/or deprivation. Role strain and/or deprivation were reported as a central factor in studies of physicians and nurses who are drug dependent.[32] On the other hand, the low rate of drug dependence among pharmacists and veterinarians in the past may be explained by the relative lack of role strain among them, even though they have easy access to drugs and have few negative proscriptions about them.[33] Similarly, there is hardly any drug dependence among certain medical specialties, such as dermatology and radiology, for related reasons.[34] Medical specialties which traditionally involve considerable role strain, such as psychiatry and surgery, have had a disproportionately high rate of drug dependence.[35]

Studies of jazz musicians who took drugs concluded that the occupation involved massive role strain.[36] Drug use peaked among jazz musicians at times when role deprivation threatened performers, at the time of transition from Dixieland to swing (1930–35), from swing to bop (1945–49), and from jazz to rock (1954–58).[37] Musicians who became drug users tended to be those who felt threatened by the shift from one kind of music to another. The same kind of phenomenon could be found among rock musicians as they moved from rhythm and blues (1957) to the British sound in the early 1960s to folk rock (1965) and, most recently, to "glitter rock." Those rock musicians who became drug dependent tended to be those who were most uneasy about what would happen to their ability to perform.

Groups with different kinds of cultures from the occupations noted above, like American Indians, may reflect the same basic sociological factors as other groups in which a minority becomes drug dependent. A study of Menomini Indians concluded that the members of a tribe most drawn to peyote had difficulty in developing role relationships either with the tribe or the world outside.[38]

Studies of Adolescents

There is good reason to expect that the adolescent years will be heavily complicated because of the ambiguity of the status of adolescents in our society.[39] They have lost the role of children but are not yet able to assume an adult role.

Johnston, in one of the very few studies to follow a large (2,200) sample of adolescent boys for some years, as part of the Youth in Transition study of 87 high schools, found that there was a clear and positive relationship between negative attitudes toward the Vietnam war, negative attitudes toward the government, and the use of marihuana, hallucinogens, and amphetamines.[40] We can interpret negative attitudes toward the war and government as dimensions of role strain. Seven out of ten of the respondents said they thought marihuana would be easy to obtain. Proscriptions against drug use are widely believed to be less salient among young people than other groups.

One relatively easy opportunity to test the theory has become available in recent years with the near-universal availability of marihuana. Proscriptions against its use are clearly weakening, especially among young people. All studies agree that marihuana use is still an activity in which only a minority of young people engage. The National Commission on Marihuana and Drug Abuse, in one of the very few national studies, found that 14% of young people had had experience with marihuana, but only 4% were regular users.[41] If our theory had predictive ability, we should be able to identify which young people, on the basis of role problems, would become regular marihuana users.

In order to get a direct test of the predictive ability of our theory, we developed a role inventory for adolescents. The 20 items in the inventory measure three dimensions of adolescent role:

1. The adolescent's ability to handle the options and possibilities, real and imaginary, open to him or her.
2. Positioning oneself among one's peers.
3. Handling the changes in one's body.

This role inventory was administered to 1,311 high school juniors in the Metropolitan New York area. Juniors were used because they would be unlikely to have the role adjustment problems of either seniors or entering students. Each subject also answered a number of questions about family, school, life-style, eating and drinking habits, and degree of use of a variety of psychoactive substances.

Scores on the role inventory were translated into a maximum of 100, with a relatively high score indicating comfortableness and a minimum of role conflict and/or deprivation. The students in the lowest quartile on the role inventory were regarded, in terms of our theory, as high risks in terms of use of marihuana; the other three fourths of the students were considered low risks. We found that the proportion of high risk adolescents using marihuana at least once a week or more for at least 4 weeks during the preceding year was 11%. However, only 2% of the low risk group had used marihuana once weekly or more for at least 4 weeks during the preceding year; the difference between the two groups was statistically significant (chi square = 49, with 1 df, $p < 0.001$).

This pilot study, although small in terms of numbers and confined to one part of the country, seems to provide some evidence that our theory may have predictive value.

DISCUSSION

In order to be a fully satisfactory theory, a formulation should constitute a set of interrelated propositions. This theory is modest in setting forth the proposition that incidence depends on three variables, all of which must apply if a particular subgroup is to have a relatively high rate of drug dependence.

As a generalized explanation of drug dependence, this theory does not attempt to explain specific shifts from one substance to another. Such shifts must consider the faddistic and intellectual and ideational context of drug use. Although we know that some people have shifted in recent years from heroin to amphetamines, others have left the amphetamines in favor of heroin, and some heroin users seek cocaine or illegal methadone, such changes over time can only be explained in terms of specific features of the situation. The college students of the 1960s and 1970s whose use of psychoactive drugs has occasioned so much concern represent a population different from that of the students of the 1920s and 1930s or the World War II veterans of the late 1940s. The slum youths of urban ghettoes in the 1970s are different from their counterparts in the 1950s or even 1960s. Drug-using gangs in the early 1950s are different from drug-using groups of today. And geography may contribute to trends in drug use, with the western states seeming to have developed a significant edge over other parts of the country in terms of finding and disseminating new drugs of dependence.

When we talk about access to substances, we must consider why and how different chemicals become available. Cocaine, for example, has been so expensive up to fairly recently that only someone with a large income could afford it. Successful rock musicians represented one of the few occupational groups for whom cocaine was possible. Because they could pay for it, cocaine became available to them. Substances are available to specific groups at particular times for a wide variety of reasons and not merely because supplying illegal drugs is a good business. It has been a good business for many years, but some drugs have only been available at specific times and places.

It is necessary not to adopt simplistic views of the dynamics of supply and demand and the reasons for which a drug becomes available at a particular time and in a particular state. Radicalization of a subgroup in the population, for example, will tend to be associated with greater availability of drugs to the subgroup. At the same time, the subgroup is likely to be relatively free from negative proscription about drug use.

Even though two different societies have an epidemic of drug dependence at the same time, there may be historicocultural components which are unique to each society and can help to explain why the epidemic developed when and where it did. In both France and the United States at the present time, there is a significant increase in alcohol dependence among the young, but the cultural context of the increase is quite different in each country.

Another consideration is that some students of deviant behavior have a bias against role theories because they appear to oversimplify human experiences. Most of our information and formulations about role behavior comes from studies in formal institutional settings, but drug-dependent persons are not likely to be functioning in such settings.

Any proposed theory ought to be able to explain the differential incidence of drug dependence on population subgroups in a completely sociological manner which does not rely on individual personality factors. The large number of different kinds of people who have become drug dependent makes it unlikely that they share specific personality traits. Where such personality traits have been identified, they usually apply to a wide range of activities and do not explain why persons with such traits become drug dependent rather than, for example, join the Communist party, although both the drug dependents and Communists may share the same personality characteristics.[42]

Yet another caution in relying on personality-oriented explanations is that the same behavior may be found in groups with different personality structure. The young black drug takers described in Chicago by Finestone were "cool" and "cats,"[43] whereas the young black drug users described by Chein and his colleagues in New York at around the same time were much more apathetic.[44] This difference may reflect geography, the investigator's perceptions, an actual difference between the populations, the measurements taken, or other factors.

Instead of having to say that people become drug dependent in order to meet their personality needs, we are suggesting that it is possible to locate the structural sources of role strain and deprivation within the social system. The distinction is somewhat similar to the one which Merton and Barber make in differentiating between psychological ambivalence and sociological ambivalence; psychological ambivalence centers around how the particular personality type develops a specific ambivalence and copes with it.[45] Sociological ambivalence deals with the ways in which ambivalence is likely to be built into the structure of social statuses and roles.

It ought to be possible for us to specify positions in the social structure which are more vulnerable than others to role strain and/or role deprivation. We can then specify role sets within a status which tend to place a person in a structural position of increased strain. Probably the easiest way of documenting this would be to determine the incidence of drug dependence in those structural positions which present the possibility of maximum role strain and maximum role deprivation.

In the case of physicians, for example, it is possible to locate career contingencies that are most likely to produce role strain: last year of residency, year before taking board examinations, etc. The structural source of role deprivation or its possibility would include situations such as moving into a new type of practice, failing one's specialty boards, movement of one's office, reassignment within a hospital, and change of specialty.

It might be hypothesized that all points of taking on new roles or all points of being tested for adequacy in a role are likely to be related to role strain and thus to a greater incidence of drug dependence in a group. We could also hypothesize that incompatible demands within one role, such as between two roles in the same role set, as between the entrepreneur and the humanitarian role in the physician, are likely to lead to a greater incidence of drug dependence.

We can further hypothesize that the amount of role strain is a function of various factors, so that the larger the volume of properties of a role set, the more potential role strain there might be. Similarly, we would expect role strain to be positively correlated with the ambiguity of role obligations,[46] the inconsistency of role obligations, the distribution of power and interest within the role set, the visibility of different roles within the role set, and the kind of conformity (attitudinal, behavioral, doctrinal) required by different roles within the role set.[47] Role strain would probably be more likely in role legitimation than role activation conflict situations.[48]

Once we have specified the sources of role strain in a society, we therefore should be able to specify those role situations in a society which are likely to show a high incidence of drug dependence and begin to discuss methods of reducing the strain. These methods would differ from one role to another.

Goode suggests several ways in which a person may reduce role strain: manipulation of role structure, carrying out the terms of a relationship in a manner which would reduce the strain, and changes in the structural limits and determinants of strain.[49] We may speculate that such opportunities for reducing role strain are differentially accessible to persons in different structure positions and that there will therefore be differences in the rate of turning to drugs.

Pugh has suggested that "role activation conflict" can probably be dealt with more easily than "role legitimation conflict," in which the occupant of the focal role and the members of the role set challenge the legitimacy of each other's expectations.[50]

A similar approach could be taken to situations involving role deprivation. It is relatively easy to pinpoint situations in which role deprivation may occur and to pay special attention to methods of handling the associated problems. Assuming that society continues the prevalent view that drug dependence is undesirable, it should be possible to anticipate situations likely to be related to high rates of drug dependence and to act in order to deal appropriately with them.

A role-oriented approach to prevention is likely to be more relevant than any substance orientation because there has been such an enormous increase in mixed dependencies or polydependence. As long ago as 1965, more than half of a sample of heroin addicts in New York City were polydependent.[51] In the years since 1965, there is every reason to believe that persons with mixed drug dependencies have been increasing among users and now represent a substantial majority. Concentration on high risk groups which can be identified as such in terms of role can help to minimize the hazards of gearing our community programs to specific substances.

It is likely that the most direct and immediate application of the theory is to persons whose drug of choice is heroin. Several different lines of evidence suggest that heroin users are likely to be people whose substance use is overdetermined and who have a multiplicity of problems and difficulties, whereas users of other substances are more likely to take them for specific problems.[52] Heroin users are therefore people who are especially likely to experience role difficulties. Because of its history in this country, heroin is typically regarded with caution by most people and access to it is not easy.

A role approach can help to minimize fruitless debates over whether one specific factor is more important than another in the genesis of drug dependence because role is a sufficiently dynamic concept to be able to subsume a number of other concepts. It also lends itself to operational definitions more readily than concepts such as alienation. It lends itself to comparative, cohort, and cross-cultural studies.

The role approach is consonant with modern medical thinking about the effect of stress on genesis of disease and the integration of concepts of psychosomatic disease. Medicine is moving away from allopathic treatment as it integrates the public health view of the person functioning in a specific environment.

The theory also has the possibility of permitting us to understand more about why and how people cease being drug dependent, as in the example of the American soldiers in South Vietnam cited previously. It can help us to understand the *process* by which drug dependence ceases.

The next steps in our exploration are clear. We shall attempt to develop appropriate role inventories for groups in the population other than adolescents, apply the interviews to such groups, attempt to predict their rate of drug dependence, and make appropriate modifications in our theory, on the basis of the data which are collected. It is to be hoped that the theory will be of increasing value, as it becomes less retrospective and more prospective.

Although sociologists differ on the criteria for judging theories, there is a developing consensus on what a useful theory might be. Our formulation is not yet a fully acceptable theory. It can become more acceptable with application to a variety of situations and after explicit operationalization of variables. Hopefully, it could have the potential for helping to clarify what has become a very significant social as well as sociological problem by taking account of both the "push" from the person and the "pull" of the substances.

We believe that the theory proposed herein is especially applicable to the period since World War II, during which most Americans have held conservative attitudes toward drugs. As a result of such attitudes, most drugs of dependence have, for the last several decades, carried considerable emotional loading.

It is possible that nondrug-related options will become available and salient for persons with role problems at some time in the future. If such other options emerge, appropriate changes should and will be made in the theory.

REFERENCES

1. **Eddy, N. B., Halbach, H., Isbell, H., and Seevers, M. H.,** Drug dependence: its significance and characteristics, *Bull. WHO*, 32, 721, 1965.
2. **Lindesmith, A. R.,** *Opiate Addiction,* Principia Press, Evanston, 1947.
3. **Fiddle, S.,** Some speculations in risk discounting among young ghetto heroin users, *Social Health Pap.*, 5, 16, 1970.
4. **Becker, H. S.,** Becoming a marihuana user, *Am. J. Sociol.*, 59, 235, 1953.
5. **Goode, E.,** *Drugs in American Society,* Knopf, New York, 1972, 39.
6. **Mellinger, G. H.,** Psychotherapeutic drug use among adults: a model for young drug users? *J. Drug Issues*, 1, 274, 1971.
7. **Smart, R. and Fejer, D.,** Drug use among adolescents and their parents: closing the generation gap in mood modification, *J. Abnormal Psychol.*, 79, 153, 1972.
8. **Finestone, H.,** Cats, kicks, and color, *Social Probl.*, 5, 3, 1957.
9. **Cloward, R. and Ohlin, L. E.,** *Delinquency and Opportunity,* Free Press, New York, 1960.
10. **Chein, I., Gerard, D. L., Lee, R. S., and Rosenfeld, E.,** *The Road to H,* Basic, New York, 1964.
11. **Jessor, R., Collins, M. I., and Jessor, S. L.,** On becoming a drinker, in *Nature and Nurture in Alcoholism,* Seixas, F. E., Ed., New York Academy of Sciences, New York, 1972, 199.
12. **Goode, W. J.,** A theory of role strain, *Am. J. Sociol.*, 25, 483, 1960.
13. **Sutherland, E. H.,** Development of the concept of differential association, in *The Sutherland Papers,* Cohen, A. K., Ed., Indiana University Press, Bloomington, 1956, 13.
14. **Durkheim, E.,** *Suicide: A Study in Sociology,* Free Press, New York, 1954.
15. **Merton, R. K. and Kitt, A. S.,** Contributions to the theory of reference group behavior, in *Continuities in Social Research,* Merton, R. K. and Lazarsfeld, P. F., Eds., Free Press, New York, 1950, 40.
16. **Brill, H. and Hirose, T.,** The rise and fall of a methamphetamine epidemic: Japan 1945–1955, *Semin. Psychiatr.*, 1, 179, 1969.
17. **Winick, C.,** Trends in Drug Abuse in the Post-World War II Period, unpublished paper, 1974.
18. **Kielholz, P. and Battegay, R.,** The treatment of drug addicts in Switzerland, *Compr. Psychiatr.*, 4, 225, 1963.
19. **Siegrist, H. O.,** Drug abuse in Switzerland, *Int. J. Addict.*, 7, 167, 1972.
20. **Goldberg, L.,** Drug abuse in Sweden, *U. N. Bull. Narcotics*, 20, 1, 1968.
21. **U.S. Department of Labor,** *State Child-Labor Laws,* Govt. Printing Office, Washington, D. C., 1966.
22. **Winick, C. and Goldstein, J.,** *The Glue Sniffing Problem,* American Social Health Association, New York, 1965.
23. **Winick, C.,** The life cycle of the narcotic addict and of addiction, *U. N. Bull. Narcotics*, 16, 22, 1964.
24. **Benedict, R.,** Continuities and discontinuities in cultural conditioning, *Psychiatry*, 1, 161, 1938.
25. **Winick, C.,** *The New People,* Bobbs Merrill, New York, 1969, 288.
26. **Robins, L. M.,** *A Follow-up of Vietnam Drug Users,* Special Action Office Monograph Series A, No. 1, Executive Office of the President, Washington, D.C., 1973.
27. **Winick, C.,** Some reasons for the increase in drug dependence among middle class youths, in *Sociology of Youth,* Silverstein, H., Ed., Macmillan, New York, 1973, 433.
28. **Suchman, E. A.,** The hang loose ethic and the spirit of drug use, *J. Health Social Behav.*, 9, 156, 1969.
29. **Groves, W. E.,** Students' drug use and life styles, in *Epidemiology of Drug Abuse,* Josephson, E. and Carroll, E., Eds., Winston-Wiley, Washington, D.C., 1974, in press.
30. **Marra, E. F. et al.,** *Intoxicant Drugs: Survey of Student Use, Role and Policy of the University,* SUNY at Buffalo Committee on Drugs and the Campus, Buffalo, 1967.
31. **McKenzie, J. D.,** *Trends in Marijuana Use Among Undergraduate Students at the University of Maryland,* University Counseling Center, Report 3-70, College Park, 1969.
32. **Sherlock, B. J.,** Career problems and narcotics addiction in the health profession: an exploratory study, *Int. J. Addict.*, 2, 191, 1967.
33. **Winick, C.,** Physician narcotic addicts, *Social Probl.*, 9, 174, 1961.
34. **Winick, C.,** A Follow-up Study of Narcotic Addiction Among Physicians, unpublished study, 1973.
35. **Winick, C.,** A Follow-up Study of Narcotic Addiction Among Physicians, unpublished study, 1973.
36. **Winick, C.,** The use of drugs by jazz musicians, *Social Probl.*, 7, 240, 1960.
37. **Winick, C.,** The taste of music: alcohol, drugs, and jazz, *Jazz Monthly*, 9, 8, 1962.
38. **Spindler, G.,** Personality and peyotism in Menomini Indian acculturation, *Psychiatry*, 15, 151, 1952.
39. **Coleman, J. S.,** *How Do The Young Become Adults?* Report No. 130, Center for Social Organization of Schools, Johns Hopkins University, Baltimore, 1972.
40. **Johnston, L.,** *Drugs and American Youth,* Institute for Social Research, Ann Arbor, 1973, chap. 8.
41. **Abelson, H., Cohen, R., Schrayer, D., and Rappeport, M.,** Drug experience, attitudes and related behavior among adolescents and adults, in National Commission on Marihuana and Drug Abuse, *Drug Use in America: Problem in Perspective,* Vol. 1, Part 3, Govt. Printing Office, Washington, D.C., 1973.
42. **Winick, C.,** Narcotics addiction and its treatment, *Law Contemp. Probl.*, 22, 9, 1957.
43. **Finestone, H.,** *Social Probl.*, 5, 3, 1957.
44. **Chein, I., Gerard, D. L., Lee, R. S., and Rosenfeld, E.,** *The Road to H,* Basic, New York, 1964.

45. **Merton, R. K. and Barber, E.,** Sociological ambivalence, in *Sociological Theory, Values, and Sociocultural Change,* Tiryakian, E. A., Ed., Free Press, New York, 1963, 91.

46. **Snoek, J.,** Role strain in diversified role sets, *Am. J. Sociol.,* 71, 363, 1966.

47. **Coser, R. L.,** Insulation from observability and types of social conformity, *Am. Sociol. Rev.,* 26, 28, 1961.

48. **Pugh, D.,** Role activation conflict, *Am. Sociol. Rev.,* 31, 835, 1966.

49. **Goode, W. J.,** *Am. J. Sociol.,* 25, 483, 1960.

50. **Pugh, D.,** *Am. Sociol. Rev.,* 31, 835, 1966.

51. **Abeles, H., Plew, R., Laudeutscher, I., and Rosenthal, H. M.,** Multiple-drug addiction in New York City in a selected population group, *Public Health Rep.,* 81, 685, 1966.

52. **Blum, R. H.,** *Society and Drugs,* Jossey-Bass, San Francisco, 1971.

RISK OF BEING LABELED "ALCOHOLIC":
SIGNIFICANCE OF PSYCHIATRIC STATUS AND NATIONALITY

Wendell R. Lipscomb and J. Holden

TABLE OF CONTENTS

THE PROBLEM OF DEFINING "ALCOHOLIC"

"Alcoholism" as a concept has undergone a myriad of changes throughout the history of man's relationship to alcohol. Modern research conceptions pertaining to "alcoholism" include the following: Alcohol is a drug of the depressant/tranquilizer variety rather than a magical substance inhabited by God, Satan, Truth, etc.: "alcoholism" is a form of drug abuse rather than a manifestation of possession by the devil, moral insufficiency, mental illness, etc.; the term "alcoholism" refers to a chronic process rather than to any single, discrete event or behavior.

One of the most persistent, discouraging, and confusing findings in early research attempts to study "alcoholism" and the "alcoholic" was the lack of consensus regarding the definitions of the terms being studied. In pursuit of a realistic, productive conception of "alcoholism," science has had to assault the popular reification of the term and accept the fact that "alcoholism" and "alcoholic" are merely impressive sounding, arbitrarily defined, and applied labels rather than fixed, existent, and observable realities. It soon became obvious that the criteria for the diagnosis of "alcoholism" and the criteria for labeling a person "alcoholic" were various and multitudinous; i.e., the criteria were different for different labelers. Moreover, many of the "professional" definitions were obscure, ambiguous, and unproductive. Following are some illustrative examples:

1. Alcoholism is a complex disease having physiological, psychological, and sociological implications (National Council on Alcoholism).

2. Alcoholism is a chronic behavioral disorder manifested by repeated drinking of alcoholic beverages in excess of the dietary and social uses of the community (Editor, *Quarterly Journal of Studies on Alcohol*).

3. Alcoholism represents the abnormal survival in adulthood of a need for the infantile normal experience of unitary pleasure of body and mind (prominent psychoanalyst).

4. Alcoholism is reached when certain

individuals stop bragging about how much they drink and begin to lie about how much they are drinking (American Medical Association *Archives of Industrial Health*).

    5. One becomes an alcoholic when he begins to be concerned about how activities might interfere with his drinking instead of how drinking might interfere with his activities (World Health Organization).

Early researchers were left with the choice as to which of the many conceptions or definitions was the "correct" or "best" one. Not surprisingly, within a short period of time a large body of "alcoholism" research had accumulated which was as inconsistent in its findings as it was in its definitions. This situation led to the following observation by the State of California Alcoholic Rehabilitation Commission: "Actually, the number of alcoholics in California or the United States can be estimated with only slightly more accuracy than the number of bad neighbors. Depending on the definition used and the method of its application, the number of alcoholics in California might be 100,000 or 1,000,000."

Almost without exception, however, there has been agreement among those concerned on the following points: (1) "alcoholic" and "alcoholism" are mere labels, and (2) these labels are attached to a person initially and more frequently by members of the person's community. An "alcoholic," then, is essentially a person whose use of alcohol deviates in some undesirable manner from the norms subscribed to by the labelers in the community.

A COMMUNITY-BASED DEFINITION

In 1956 the senior author submitted a study proposal to the California State Department of Public Health which suggested that "the designation of the label 'alcoholic' to a specific individual or group depends as much upon community norms and attitudes toward drinking as upon damning clinical evidence."* The overall purpose of the proposed study was "to determine in a general population those factors, conditions or states believed to be conductive ('at risk') to the labeling of 'alcoholism' or *problem drinking* and

its related social and/or medical complications."**

The investigators proposed that a definition of "alcoholic" be constructed utilizing the criteria employed by the persons who first and most frequently apply the labels to individuals, i.e., the definitions used by the community labelers.

The State Department of Public Health authorized the study of community norms, attitudes, and opinions pertaining to "alcoholism." Because of the scope of the subject and the desire to allow respondents maximal latitude in their responses, it was decided that open-ended, person-to-person interviews would be used. The central issue around which the interviews were to revolve was the study question, "Within your experience, what to you are the first evident signs that an individual is having problems associated with alcohol?" Because of time and money constraints, the number of interviews was limited to 100 to 200. The study directors decided to interview community leaders (simply defined as "the recognized head of a community organization or association"), reasoning that these individuals are the most active, sensitive, and concerned members of the community.

Using the 1950 Census data, the State of California (infamous for its high prevalence of "alcoholics") was first divided into various types of economic and geographic areas. One county from each area was chosen which was estimated to have a relatively large "alcoholic" population (utilizing the Jellinek estimation formula). A random sample was then chosen from the population of official heads of community organizations listed in professional registries, telephone books, and various community agencies which were located in the principal city of the selected counties. Of the 189 community leaders who were contacted, 107 were ultimately interviewed. Detailed accounts of the methods and findings of this study were published in 1959 and 1962.[1]

In the content analysis of the interview data, responses were first divided into those referring to the kinds of persons considered at-risk of being labeled "alcoholic" and those referring to characteristics of an "alcoholic." Within each of these sets of data, responses were further categorized on the basis of their specific content. These data are presented in Tables 1 and 2.

*Interim Report of the State Alcoholic Rehabilitation Commission, State of California, Berkeley, 1954–1957.
**Division of Alcoholic Rehabilitation, State of California, A study of community concepts and definitions, in *Alcoholism and California*, Publ. No. 1, December 1959.

TABLE 1

Kinds of Persons Considered At-risk of Being Labeled "Alcoholic"

Answers of community leaders	Percent*
Emotionally unstable persons	32
Persons with family problems	24
Persons with "bad" backgrounds	21
Regular drinkers	7
Persons who are idle or bored	6
Persons who have failed in some important area of life	5
Persons with a physical or emotional predisposition to alcohol	5
	100

*N = 189

TABLE 2

Characteristics of an "Alcoholic"

Answers of community leaders	Percent*
Have employment problems	22
Have personality difficulties	16
Drink excessively	13
Have problems with family or friends	10
Are preoccupied with alcohol	8
Have no control over their drinking	8
Have deteriorating health	7
Are dependent on effects of alcohol	6
Drink alone to protect their supply	5
All others	5
	100

*N = 189

From these findings the investigators concluded: "In general, all the categories mentioned in both sets of responses can be summarized by the phrase *persons under stress* who have serious problems because of their own emotional conflicts or because of loneliness, failure or inadequacy. Our community leaders seemed to feel that persons who learn to use alcoholic beverages to mitigate the pain generated by these conditions are those who are at risk of alcoholism."[2]

Essentially, the community leaders conceived of an "alcoholic" as a person whose nondrinking coping behaviors are insufficient in relation to the amount of stress he is experiencing and who learns to use alcohol to cope with the stress.

Chronologically, the first element of this formulation is stress. Stress is defined in the *Psychiatric Dictionary*[3] as "any interference which disturbs the functioning of the organism at any level, and which produces a situation which is natural for the organism to avoid." Stress, then, refers to the uncomfortable organismic state produced by stimuli which threaten the homeostatic functioning of the organism. Stress-producing stimuli are of manifold kinds and intensities. Moreover, a given stimulus event may be stress-producing for one person but not for another, or even stress-producing for a person at one point in time but not at another point in time. Examples of stress-producing stimuli include the loss of a loved one, an unacceptable impulse-seeking expression, financial problems, a common

cold, or, in its broadest sense, any change (desirable or undesirable) in ongoing life patterns.

A recent study[4] indicated the following to be, in rank order, the most stress-producing life change events: (1) death of spouse, (2) divorce, (3) marital separation, (4) jail term, (5) death of close family member, (6) personal injury or illness, (7) marriage, (8) fired from job, (9) marital reconciliation, and (10) retirement. Surprisingly, the authors found 90% agreement with this ordering between various age, sex, race, income, and cultural populations of adults.

Stress has a disruptive effect on an organism. In response, the organism engages in coping behaviors which seek to modify the organism and/or the environment so as to relieve the stress. In instances of prolonged stress, where the stress-producing stimulus is of a major magnitude and/or the coping behaviors are insufficiently effective, the organism's reservoir of self-protective energy, and therefore its resistance to disease and physiological dysfunction, is significantly reduced.[5]

While response to stress is instinctual, the specific coping behavior employed in response to stress is learned. Operant learning theory[6] states that when any response is closely followed by a reinforcing or desirable state of affairs (reduction of stress in the present case), the probability that the (coping) response will recur is increased. Thus, for example, a baby perceives that stress (hunger, physical discomfort) is often relieved following crying behavior and learns to cry in response to all manner of stress-producing stimuli. Each time the

17

response is emitted and followed by reinforcement, the likelihood that the response will become habitual (i.e., the habit strength of the response) increases.

As the organism matures, of course, both the types of stress-producing stimuli and the types of stress-reducing responses proliferate. The types of coping behaviors which the individual employs become multiply determined; i.e., they are chosen not only on the basis of their effectiveness at reducing stress but also according to their sociocultural acceptability, their consistency with the self-concept, their ease of execution, their concomitant consequences, etc. Examples of coping behaviors include praying, withdrawing from the stress-producing context, avoiding potential stress-producing situations, modifying or obviating the stress-producing stimulus, engaging in psychotherapy, or using tranquilizing drugs.

As we have seen, the particular coping behavior which the community leaders associate with "alcoholism" is, of course, consuming alcoholic beverages. Thus, the individual who learns to cope with stress by drinking alcohol is, by the previously discussed definition, highly at-risk of becoming or being labeled "alcoholic." This formulation is consistent with the research findings that "alcoholics" are most readily distinguished from "nonalcoholics" on the basis of their motivation to use alcohol (for personal effects rather than for social convention[7]) and their attitudes toward drinking alcohol (acceptable rather than nonacceptable as a coping behavior).[8,9]

In summary, if a person perceives the consumption of alcohol to be an acceptable and effective means of coping with stress, he is likely to respond to stress by drinking, especially to the extent that alternative coping behaviors are unavailable or are perceived as unacceptable and/or ineffective. Each time the person drinks in response to stress and has his perceptions confirmed, the habit strength of this response increases. However, the drinking of alcohol to cope with stress places the individual highly at-risk of being labeled "alcoholic" by other members of his community.

APPLICATION OF THE DEFINITION TO THE CONSTRUCTION OF A SCREENING DEVICE

The primary long-range goal of the study proposal submitted to the State of California Department of Public Health was, on the basis of the information gathered from the community leaders, " ... to conceptualize, develop and, through testing, substantiate an interviewing document (Questionnaire Screen) which on application in a general population would separate categories of presumed differential risk to the development of the alcoholism label."*

In order to make the screening device as inoffensive as possible to the respondent and because "alcoholics" are prone to defensively distort their responses to obvious and direct interviews concerning their drinking practices,[10] it was decided that the format of the screening device should be neutral in tone and nondirective in intent. The other two guidelines used in constructing the screening device were clarity and brevity.[11] The screening device ultimately took the form of a simply worded, self-administering public health questionnaire with yes-no response foils.** It was divided into six sections:

1. Items requesting the name, address, sex, age, religion, marital status, and occupation of the respondent.

2. Ten somatic dysfunctions and symptoms introduced by the phrase, "I have been bothered by ... ," which were selected from a pool of items submitted by physicians as being clinically related to worry or concern about problems.

3. Items inquiring into the respondent's use of tobacco, coffee, alcohol, and food.

4. Nine common adjustment reactions introduced by the phrase, "When you are worried or troubled do you do the following ... ," one of which was "drink or drink more alcoholic beverages."

5. Sixteen common stress-producing situations introduced by the phrase, "Have you been worried or troubled because of ...."

6. Seventeen statements indicative of personal inadequacy (e.g., loneliness, apathy, introversion) selected from available medical and

*Division of Alcoholic Rehabilitation, State of California, The development of a screening device for risk populations, in *Alcoholism and California*, Publ. No. 7, November 1961.
**A copy of the screening device is available upon request (Dr. Lipscomb).

psychological inventories and diagnostic tests and introduced by the phrase, "Are the following statements true of you?"

Several summary scores were derived from responses to the device. The number of somatic dysfunctions and symptoms checked by a respondent served as his "psychosomatic ailments score." The number of stress-producing situations checked by a respondent became his "problem situations score," and the number of inadequacy statements checked by a respondent became his "inadequacy traits score." Analyses of the results of an administration of the device to a sample of 175 urban adult "normals" (described in greater detail below) yielded a median problem situations score of 1 and a median inadequacy traits score of 2.

The next task of the study project was to determine to what extent the screening device reliably and validly separated populations into categories of risk of becoming or being labeled "alcoholic."

In this case reliability refers to response consistency; i.e., are the respondent's answers to theoretically related items and sections within the questionnaire consistent? There are several such related items and sections. As illustrated in Table 3, of the 1,525 persons to whom the device has been administered, respondents who claimed to be troubled by an above average number of problem situations (high problems group) also reported that they worried a lot more, were more often tense,

were troubled by more psychosomatic ailments, and more often drank alcohol when worried or troubled than respondents who claimed to be troubled by a below average number of problem situations (low problems group).

These same relationships obtain when comparing respondents who claimed an above average number of inadequacy traits (high inadequacy group) to respondents who claimed a below average number of inadequacy traits (low inadequacy group). Moreover, 77.9% of the high inadequacy group were also in the high problems group as compared to 43% of the low inadequacy group who also were in the high problems group. In addition, Spearman-Brown split-half reliability coefficients of 0.66 for the problem situations score and 0.80 for the inadequacy traits score have been reported.[1 2]

Validity refers to the issue of whether or not the device, in fact, does the job which it represents itself to do; i.e., does it accurately screen a general population into categories of differential risk of being labeled "alcoholic"? As with reliability, there are a number of possible approaches to the validity issue, none of which may be considered conclusive, As Cisin has pointed out, "In pursuit of the validity question, it seems appropriate to point out that what is of interest here is not the detailed accuracy of any subject's report; the uniqueness and the reproducibility of his behavior should be the problem of clinical studies, not of

TABLE 3

Selected Internal Consistency Indices

	Psychosomatic ailment score	Respondents who are "often tense" %	Respondents who "worry a lot" %	Respondents who "drink (more) when worried" %
High problems group*	3.17	55.6 (848)[†]	50.1 (764)	43.6 (665)
Low problems group	1.29	24.0 (366)	22.0 (336)	11.8 (180)
High inadequacy group	3.07	55.9 (852)	54.0 (823)	41.0 (625)
Low inadequacy group	1.20	17.8 (271)	6.0 (92)	13.1 (200)

*Respondents scoring above the medians obtained from the urban adult "normal" sample constitute the appropriate "high" groups, while the "low" groups are composed of respondents scoring at or below the appropriate medians.

[†] N = (   )

19

gross, large-scale surveys. Rather, what is of interest here is the classification of individuals into rather broad categories. Thus, the question of validity ought not to be asked about the *truthfulness* of any individual statements, but about the resultant *summary* classification of each individual."[13]

What is needed, then, is a demonstration that (1) the instrument does screen a general population into different categories and (2) the categories accurately represent the phenomena for which they are named. In the initial phases of the project, it was decided to construct categories of degree of risk of being labeled "alcoholic" which were based jointly on the problems situations score and the inadequacy traits score. Using this approach, respondents who had above average problem situations and inadequacy traits scores were placed in the "high risk" category. Respondents who had an average or below score on one of the criteria but an above average score on the other were placed in "moderate risk" categories, and respondents who had average or below scores on both criteria were placed in the "low risk" category.

While this system of classification did screen general populations into the various risk categories, there was reasonable doubt that the categories actually represented "degree of risk of being labeled 'alcoholic.'" Specifically, the data (illustrated in Figures 1 and 2) invited the following validity-related criticisms:

1. "The fact that 40% of your 'normals' are classified as high risk is, in itself, startling,"[14] especially in light of the fact that Cahalan,[15] defining "risk" in terms of a combined score for six social-psychological molar variables, has reported that 11% of his national sample were in the highest risk group.

2. Thirty-one percent of the respondents in the high risk group did not even use alcoholic beverages, which is inconsistent with the fact that the community leaders indicated that drinking practices were critical in determining whether or not they would label a person "alcoholic."

3. A respondent who had an extremely high score on one criterion but an average score on the other (e.g., a person who checked 14 problem situations and 2 inadequacy traits) would be classified as less at-risk of being labeled "alcoholic" than a person who scored one-above

average on each criterion (i.e., a person who checked 2 problem situations and 3 inadequacy traits).

Since, as previously stated, the individual who learns to cope with stress by drinking alcohol is, according to the community leaders, highly at-risk of being labeled "alcoholic," it would seem to be more appropriate and valid to construct categories of differential risk based on drinking practices. Three pieces of information relating to drinking practices are to be found from responses to the screening device: (1) Is the respondent an abstainer? (2) Is the respondent a drinker? (3) Does the respondent drink (more) when worried or troubled? Thus, three categories of risk of being labeled "alcoholic" corresponding to three types of drinking practices could be established. A respondent who reported drinking (more) in response to worry would, in this system, be highly at-risk of being labeled "alcoholic." A respondent who reported drinking alcohol, but not in response to worry or trouble, would be moderately at-risk since the drinking of alcohol is already an acceptable behavior to him. A respondent who reported being an abstainer, however, would be minimally at-risk since he is likely to consider the drinking of alcohol for any reason to be a personally unacceptable behavior.

The data from the urban adult "normal" sample, arranged according to this classification system, are depicted in Figure 3. It can be readily seen that this system was able to screen the sample into the various risk categories. Also, the proportion of respondents falling into the high risk category (13.1%) is reasonably consistent with Cahalan's findings (11%), and the proportion of abstainers in the sample is reasonably consistent with the figures reported by Maxwell,[16] Mulford and Miller[17] for Iowans, and Knupfer[18] for residents of Berkeley, California. In addition, this system precludes the classification of abstainers as high risk. Moreover, as depicted in Table 4, as risk increases the probability also increases that the respondent will have above average problems, above average inadequacy traits, or both. Essentially, this system more closely represents the criteria actually used by the community leaders in applying the label "alcoholic." In other words, the categories more accurately represent the phenomena for which they are named.

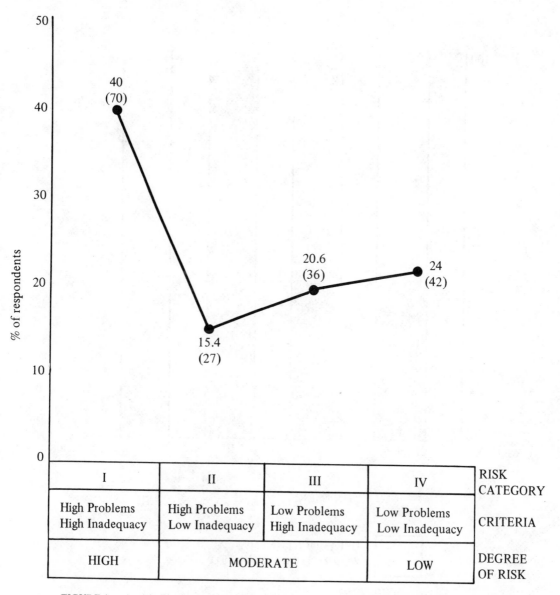

FIGURE 1.   At-risk distribution of urban adult "normal" sample (initial classification system).

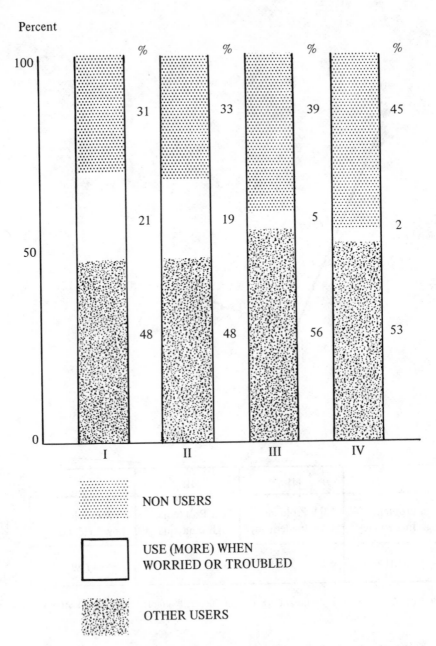

Percent

FIGURE 2. Percent of alcoholic beverage nonusers, users, and users who use (more) when worried or troubled by risk category.

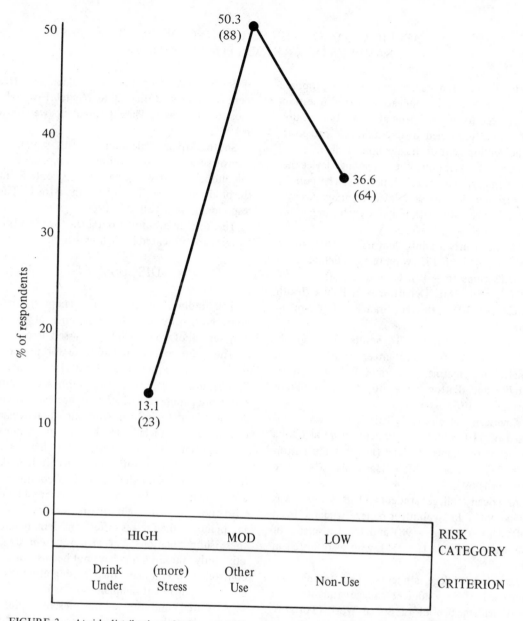

FIGURE 3.   At-risk distribution of urban adult "normal" sample (drinking practices classification system).

TABLE 4

Percentage Associations Between Risk Categories and High Problems, Traits, or Both

	Risk category					
	High		Moderate		Low	
High problems	87.0	(152)*	52.3	(92)	48.4	(85)
High traits	73.9	(129)	60.2	(105)	56.3	(99)
High both	65.2	(114)	37.5	(66)	34.4	(60)

*N = (   )

APPLICATION OF THE SCREENING DEVICE TO
SAMPLES OF VARIOUS POPULATIONS

The second long-range goal of the proposed study was "...the application of the questionnaire screen to selected general population groups, establishing presumed differential risk categories to the development of the alcoholism label."

Since its inception, the screening device has been administered to 1,525 persons. The populations from which the samples were drawn, as well as descriptive information about each sample, are presented below and in Table 5.

American urban adult "normals." This sample was composed of 175 volunteers solicited from women's clubs (n = 40), labor unions (n = 125), and California State Department of Public Health Offices (n = 10) in the San Francisco Bay Area in 1958.

American "mentally ill" adults. This sample was composed of 723 volunteer inpatients from nonalcoholic treatment programs at Atascadero (n = 677) and Patton (n = 46) California State Hospitals in 1969.

American "alcoholics." This sample was composed of 119 volunteer inpatients from alcoholic treatment programs at Napa (n = 91) and Patton (n = 28) California State Hospitals, who were tested in 1969.

American college students. This sample was composed of 112 volunteer college students from Tufts University (n = 98) and the University of Southern California (n = 15), who were tested in 1968.

Canadian college students. This sample was composed of 51 volunteer college students from the Canadian School of Social Work (Toronto, Ontario), who were tested in 1969.

Japanese college students. This sample was composed of 118 volunteer college students from colleges in Tokyo, Japan, who were tested in 1970.

Scottish "mentally ill" adults. This sample was composed of 33 volunteer patients from King's (Psychiatric) Hospital in Edinburgh, Scotland, who were tested in 1968.

South African urban adult "normals." This sample was composed of 51 volunteer inpatients in nonalcoholic medical treatment programs in Groote Schuur Hospital in Cape Town, South Africa. These respondents were tested in 1969.

Danish "alcoholics." This sample was composed of 95 volunteer inpatients in "alcoholic" treatment programs at the State Mental Hospital in Glostrup, Denmark. These respondents were tested in 1971.

South African "alcoholics." This sample was composed of 49 volunteer inpatients in "alcoholic" treatment programs in Groote Schuur Hospital in Cape Town, South Africa. These respondents were tested in 1969.

The risk distributions obtained for the various samples are presented in Figures 4 to 9.

DISCUSSION

The findings reported in this chapter must be interpreted cautiously for a number of reasons, only several of which will be discussed here.

The primary contaminating factor present in the data is sample dissimilarity (see Table 5). Specifically, age, sex, and ethnosociocultural status are parameters which have been consistently demonstrated to influence drinking practices and risk of being labeled "alcoholic." For example, youths, females, and persons of high socioeconomic status for various reasons are less likely to be labeled "alcoholic" than their counterparts, even when their drinking practices are identical with those of their counterparts. Moreover, drinking practices themselves differ considerably among these subpopulations. Yet, at the present stage of this study, these factors have not been statistically controlled to eliminate their biasing effects when comparing different sample results.

A related limitation of the present findings is the fact that the samples were not selected to be statistically or literally representative of the parent populations. Thus, for example, 94% of the American "mentally ill" adult sample were patients committed by the courts to a California state hospital for the "criminally insane" and, therefore, may or may not be representative of the parent population of American "mentally ill" adults.

As discussed earlier, risk of being labeled "alcoholic" is not simply synonymous with drinking practices as measured in this study. The present system of risk classification does not consider such important drinking practices parameters as the strength of the "drink when worried

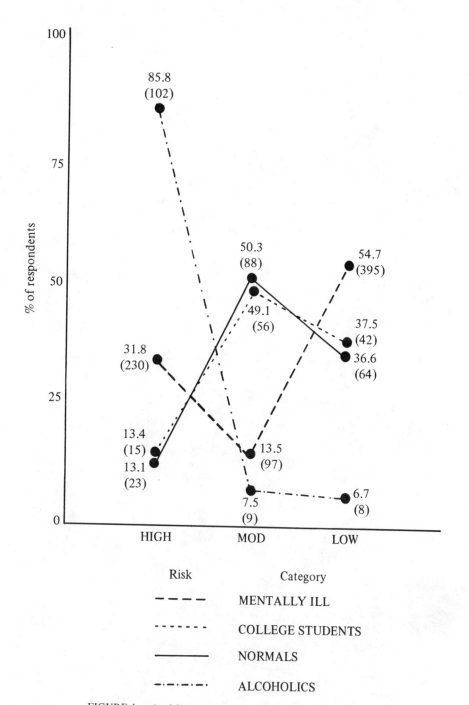

FIGURE 4.   At-risk distribution by American subpopulation.

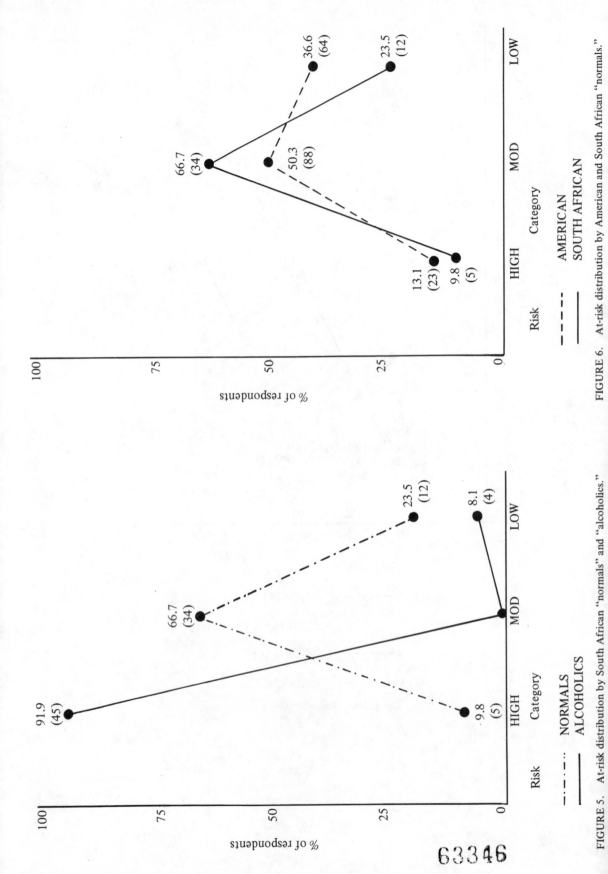

FIGURE 5. At-risk distribution by South African "normals" and "alcoholics."

FIGURE 6. At-risk distribution by American and South African "normals."

63346

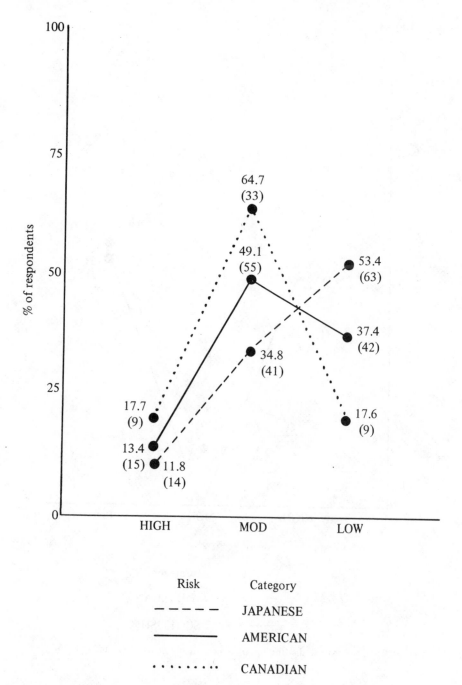

FIGURE 7. At-risk distribution by college student subpopulation.

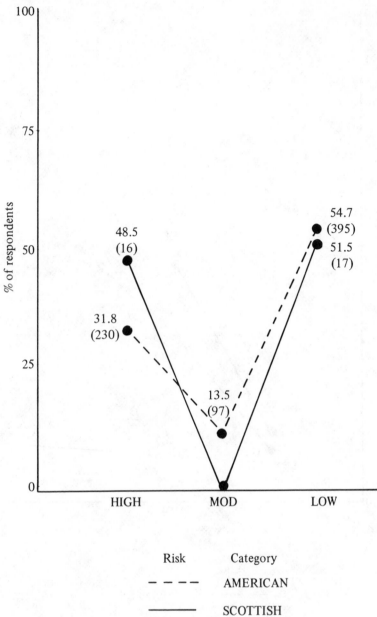

FIGURE 8.   At-risk distribution by American and Scottish "mentally ill."

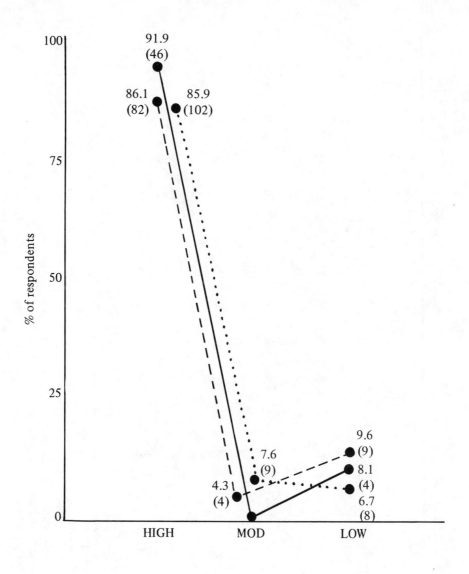

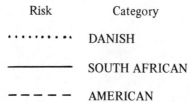

Risk   Category

·········· DANISH

————— SOUTH AFRICAN

– – – – – AMERICAN

FIGURE 9.   At-risk distribution by "alcoholic" subpopulation.

TABLE 5

Sample Characteristics in Percentages

	N=	Sex		Age		Religion				Marital Status		Occupation									
		M	F	−	+	Pr	Ca	Ot	No	M	Nm	1	2	3	4	5	6	7	8	9	10
American "normals"	175	48	52	56	44	65	21	7	7	−	−	17	3	3	1	1	2	33	8	1	31
American "mentally ill"	722	97	3	62	38	54	29	10	7	33	61	1	0	8	1	15	15	22	12	4	22
American "alcoholic"	119	91	9	17	83	60	28	4	8	82	18	4	2	4	11	24	13	12	4	0	26
American college students	112	89	11	99	1	42	22	24	12	4	96	0	0	0	0	0	0	1	0	0	99
Canadian college students	51	44	56	93	7	64	26	10	0	39	61	0	0	1	0	0	0	0	0	0	99
Japanese college students	118	5	95	99	1	3	1	27	69	99	1	0	0	0	0	0	0	0	1	0	99
Scottish "mentally ill"	33	88	12	21	79	57	33	3	7	88	12	21	25	0	9	9	9	12	3	0	12
South African "normals"	51	52	48	62	38	46	8	28	18	−	−	60	2	10	0	0	0	6	0	0	22
Danish "alcoholics"	95	99	1	30	70	82	1	1	16	71	29	9	6	5	4	7	6	15	37	3	8
South African "alcoholics"	49	86	14	36	64	64	9	6	21	−	−	23	0	2	7	25	9	23	0	0	11

KEY:

Sex: M = Male
       F = Female

Age: − = under 35
       + = over 35

Religion: Pr = Protestant
         Ca = Catholic
         Ot = Other
         No = None

Marital status: M = Married
                Nm = Not married

Occupation: 1 = Professional, technical, and kindred
             2 = Managers, officials, and proprietors
             3 = Clerical and kindred
             4 = Sales
             5 = Craftsmen, foremen, and kindred

6 = Operatives and kindred
7 = Service
8 = Laborers, except farm and mine
9 = Farmers, farm managers, and laborers
10 = None or other

or troubled" response or the relative position of this response in an individual's hierarchy of coping responses. Thus, for example, a person whose primary and habitual response to stress is the drinking of alcohol is not differentiated by the present classification system from the person who had at his disposal a number of coping responses and only on rare occasions resorts to drinking to cope with stress. Yet, surely these two individuals are differentially at-risk of being labeled "alcoholic."

These limitations notwithstanding, however, the findings do show significant differences and similarities which warrant some general observations and hypotheses.

It is immediately obvious that the risk distributions of American urban adult "normals" and American college students (Figure 4) are nearly identical. For both samples approximately one third of the respondents are abstainers. About half of the respondents in these samples drink alcohol, but not in response to stress, while an additional 13% of them drink in response to stress and are, therefore, by the present definition highly at-risk of being labeled "alcoholic." Aside from their descriptive properties, these findings suggest that the distribution of risk and drinking practices is similar on both sides of the American "generation gap"; i.e., the prevalence of accepted use and abuse of alcohol is likely, in the absence of any mitigating influence, to continue at a stable or increasing level among "middle" Americans.

The obtained distribution for the South African urban adult "normals" essentially parallels these distributions (see Figure 6). However, there are proportionally somewhat fewer abstainers (low risks), more nonstress drinkers (moderate risks) and fewer stress drinkers (high risk) in the South African sample. This suggests that alcohol use, but not abuse, is somewhat more acceptable in South Africa than in the United States.

The risk distribution of "mentally ill" Americans, however, is considerably different from those of the "normal" groups. Specifically, American "mentally ill" persons tend to either avoid or abuse alcohol, with a distinct minority using alcohol for other than coping purposes. That is, while over half of the American "mentally ill" sample are abstainers, preferring to handle stress with nondrinking (albeit ineffective) coping behaviors, over two thirds of those who drink alcohol do so to cope with stress.

The findings for the Scottish "mentally ill" sample are similar in this respect (Figure 8), suggesting that this dichotomous approach to alcohol use is not strictly an American phenomenon. The Scottish results, in fact, are even more extreme in this regard than are the American "mentally ill" findings. Specifically, *all* of the almost one half of the Scottish sample who reported using alcohol used it for coping purposes.

As may be expected, the majority of American "alcoholics" fall in the high risk group. This distribution, which also provides an index of the screening effectiveness of the device (14.2% false negatives), is almost identical to the distributions obtained from the Danish and South African "alcoholic" samples (Figure 9). Since all of these respondents were labeled "alcoholics," it seems that the criteria of labeling a person "alcoholic" and the screening effectiveness of the device are similar in all three countries.

The obtained distributions for the international college student samples (Figure 7) indicate that these groups are most readily distinguishable in terms of their proportions of abstainers. Thus, while all three samples have reasonably similar proportions of respondents in the high risk group, there are proportionally twice as many abstainers among the American college students and three times as many abstainers among the Japanese college students as among the Canadian college students. The Japanese sample is the only one of these which has more abstainers than drinkers. The drinking of alcohol is practiced by a minority (46.6%) of the Japanese college students, while the Canadian college students report the highest prevalence of drinking (82.4%).

The differences between the "alcoholic" and "normal" South African samples (Figure 5) closely parallel the differences between the corresponding American samples (Figure 4), suggesting that the differential drinking practices of "alcoholics" and "normals" are reasonably consistent across these two cultures.

Table 6 illustrates the rank-ordering of the samples within each risk category for summary purposes.

Since the primary purpose of the screening device was to sort out of a general population those persons at-risk of being labeled "alcoholic," the closing comments and generalizations regarding the data will focus on respondents who were screened by the device into the high risk category.

TABLE 6

Rank Order of Samples by Risk Category

Rank order	High risk	Moderate risk	Low risk
1	SA "alcoholic"	SA "normal"	A "mentally ill"
2	D "alcoholic"	C college student	J college student
3	A "alcoholic"	A "normal"	S "mentally ill"
4	S "mentally ill"	A college student	A college student
5	A "mentally ill"	J college student	A "normal"
6	C college student	A "mentally ill"	SA "normal"
7	A college student	A "alcoholic"	C college student
8	A "normal"	D "alcoholic"	D "alcoholic"
9	J college student	SA "alcoholic"	SA "alcoholic"
10	SA "normal"	S "mentally ill"	A "alcoholic"

Code:
SA – South African
D – Danish
A – American
C – Canadian
J – Japanese
S – Scottish

As may be seen in Figure 10, the samples of labeled "alcoholics" have the highest proportions of respondents in the high risk category. The samples having the next highest proportions of high risk respondents are the "mentally ill" samples, followed by the college student samples, and, finally, by the "normal" samples. The only exception to this pattern is that the proportion of American "normals" in the high risk category falls in between the corresponding proportions for the American and Japanese college student samples. There are two important aspects to these findings. In the first place, there are distinct "breaking" points in terms of probability of being highly at-risk of being labeled "alcoholic" between groups of labeled "alcoholics," "mentally ill," college students, and "normals" (although the latter two groups are less clearly separated from each other in this respect). Secondly, this pattern appears to exist independently of nationality.

In summary, the distributions of risk of being labeled "alcoholic," operationally defined in terms of drinking practices, are clearly different for the various psychiatric groups (i.e., "alcoholics," "mentally ill," and "normals") but are remarkably similar for psychiatrically comparable samples of various nationalities.

ACKNOWLEDGMENTS

Appreciation is expressed to the following persons who participated in the data collection for this project: J. Richard Wahl, Frank J. Vanasek, Halmuth H. Schaefer, Ernest Belden, Brendan Walsh, Daniel Glaser, Walter Clark, Stephen Williams, Griffith Edwards, Lynn Gillis, Anders Groth, Thomas Gonda.

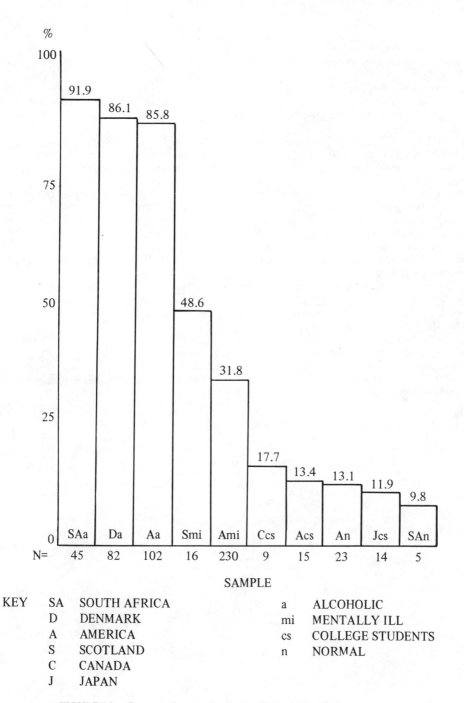

%

91.9	86.1	85.8	48.6	31.8	17.7	13.4	13.1	11.9	9.8
SAa	Da	Aa	Smi	Ami	Ccs	Acs	An	Jcs	SAn

N=   45   82   102   16   230   9   15   23   14   5

SAMPLE

KEY   SA   SOUTH AFRICA   a   ALCOHOLIC
      D   DENMARK   mi   MENTALLY ILL
      A   AMERICA   cs   COLLEGE STUDENTS
      S   SCOTLAND   n   NORMAL
      C   CANADA
      J   JAPAN

FIGURE 10.   Percent of respondents classified as high risk, by sample.

REFERENCES

1. *A Study of Community Concepts and Definitions, Part I and Part II,* Calif. State Dept. Public Health, Berkeley, 1959 and 1961.
2. Lipscomb, W. R., unpublished book, chap. 3.
3. Hinsie, L. E. and Campbell, R. J., *Psychiatric Dictionary,* Oxford University Press, New York, 1970.
4. Wyler, A. R., Masuda, M., and Holmes, T. H., Magnitude of life events and seriousness of illness, *J. Psychosoma. Med.,* 33, 115, 1971.
5. Holmes, T. H. and Masuda, M., Psychosomatic syndrome, *Psychol. Today,* p. 71, April 1972.
6. Reynolds, G. S., *A Primer of Operant Conditioning,* Scott, Foresman & Co., Glenview, Ill., 1968.
7. Mulford, H. A. and Miller, D. E., Drinking in Iowa. IV. Preoccupation with alcohol, heavy drinking and trouble due to drinking, *Q. J. Stud. Alcohol,* 21, 279, 1960.
8. Cahalan, D., Cisin, I. H., and Crossley, H. M., *American Drinking Practices: A National Survey of Behavior and Attitudes,* Monograph No. 6, Rutgers Center of Alcohol Studies, New Brunswick, N.J., 1969.
9. Knupfer, G. and Room, R., Abstainers in a metropolitan community, *Q. J. Stud. Alcohol,* 31, 108, 1970.
10. Ewing, J. A. and Rouse, B., Identifying the "Hidden Alcoholic," paper presented at the 20th Int. Congr. Alcohol and Drug Dependence, Sydney, Australia, February 2–6, 1970.
11. *The Development of a Screening Device for Risk Populations,* Publ. No. 7, Calif. State Dept. Public Health, Berkeley, 1961.
12. *The Development of a Screening Device for Risk Populations,* Publ. No. 7, Calif. State Dept. Public Health, Berkeley, 1961, 34.
13. Cisin, I. H., Community studies of drinking behavior, *Ann. N.Y. Acad. Sci.,* 107, 607, 1963.
14. Cisin, I. H., personal communication, May 1972.
15. Cahalan, D., *Problem Drinkers,* Jossey-Bass, San Francisco, 1970.
16. Maxwell, M. A., Drinking in the State of Iowa, *Q. J. Stud. Alcohol,* 13, 227, 1952.
17. Mulford, H. A. and Miller, D. E., Drinking in Iowa. I., *Q. J. Stud. Alcohol,* 20, 717, 1959.
18. Knupfer, G., *Characteristics of Abstainers,* Rep. No. 3, Division of Alcoholic Rehabilitation, Calif. State Dept. Public Health, Berkeley, 1959.

A SOCIOCULTURAL EXPLORATION OF REPORTED HEROIN USE

Irving F. Lukoff and Judith S. Brook

TABLE OF CONTENTS

INTRODUCTION

The Contemporary Drug Scene

The nature of opiate addiction in the United States has altered dramatically since evidence has been accumulated on drug users. There was, first, the shift from oral intake of morphine and related compounds to the predominance of injectable heroin.[1] But more important are the radically different populations where opiate use is now most often encountered. There is ample documentation of the shift from a predominantly white, middle-class, small-town, and largely female population of opiate users to a concentration of opiate addiction (mainly heroin) among urbanized minority group members — black, Puerto Rican, and Chicano — substantially male and generally addicted at an earlier age than previous cohorts of addicts.[2,3]

This remarkable change in the addict population directs attention to the sociocultural matrix which is associated with the very different rates of heroin use that can be observed in the urban ghettos. Too often the effort to understand addiction has been centered solely on the physiological and psychosocial aspects of drug use. Important insights concerning the addiction phenomenon itself, particularly the "learned" aspects of experimentation with heroin and other drugs, have been provided. Particularly significant is the documentation of the role peer-group processes have on induction into drug use and on the acquisition of appropriate behaviors.

Many investigators, including Becker and Goode, agree with Lindesmith that it is the ". . .social experiences during which the person acquires a conception of the meaning of the behavior, and perceptions and judgments of objects and situations, all of which make the activity possible and desirable. Thus, the motivation or disposition to engage in the activity is built up in the course of learning to engage in it and does not antedate this learning process."[4-6] These investigators tend to emphasize the unpredictability of motivational or predisposing factors by noting the vagaries and contradictions in efforts to identify such mechanisms postulated by earlier investigators.[7] However, the alternatives for understanding drug use are not bounded by a choice between predispositions, in the psychological sense on the one hand, or situational or field processes, on the other.

If we step back from the immediate situation that accompanies heroin use, there are a number of facts that direct attention to a much broader range of sociological questions. The issues we will highlight are the preconditions for heroin addiction that can assist one in understanding the very substantial variations in rates among different groups in our society, an issue that becomes lost when one focuses only on the addict and his immediate situation. Where there are substantially different rates of drug use associated with socially identified groups, an explanation is still needed at some other level than the subcultural.

Sociological explanations of drug use, and more specifically heroin use, are mainly drawn from the theories that have been developed to account for delinquent and criminal behavior. These theories tend to focus on discrete aspects of the social-cultural-psychological scene, although there are some important efforts to link together several levels of explanation. In this chapter, we will present information drawn from a survey in a high-drug-use community in order to contribute to, first, an unraveling of the importance of various factors previously identified as significant in the etiology of drug use and, second, to lay the empirical foundations for a more integrated approach to the comprehension of addiction, albeit the limitations of any one design and set of data will be underscored.

Framework for Understanding Heroin Use

A comprehensive review of the research literature on heroin addiction will not be presented; instead, we will cite only those studies that are germane to the themes examined here.

Many investigators have observed that the population of addicts often comes from areas where poverty is pervasive and endemic and from those ethnic groups that are economically the most deprived. Chein, in his pioneer studies, notes that the communities where addicts are most often observed are also the most poverty-stricken areas.[8] The Ford Foundation report, *Dealing with Drug Abuse*, also emphasizes that ". . .addicts are heavily concentrated in the poorest areas of large metropolitan areas."[9] Any ecological plotting of the location of addicts would soon confirm the consistent association of heroin addiction with ghetto communities where the assortment of social and economic ills of our cities is concentrated.

This suggests, then, that poverty may possibly play a causative role in drug use and that the use of heroin (and other drugs) may be a form of adaptation to blunt the harsh consequences of poverty. However, here one may be guilty of the ecological fallacy, wherein one assumes that poverty areas are economically and socially homogeneous.[10] Although poverty may indeed be concentrated in these communities, almost all of them contain a rich diversity of people with very different economic and social profiles. Several investigators who have carefully examined addicts and attempted to locate them in the social structures of their communities have reported, contrary to expectations, that addicts are often better educated than comparable nonaddicts from their communities, are significantly more intelligent, have histories of stable employment, and are not from the poorest segments of their communities.[11-15] There is a convergence of findings that underscores these observations from studies conducted at Lexington and Fort Worth, New York State, New York City, Chicago, and St. Louis. Vaillant observes that the members of the poorest and most deprived segments of ghetto communities, the recent migrants into the urban north, are *least likely* to be found among the addict population.[16] The findings presented in this chapter lend support to his hypothesis.

Perhaps the most subtle attempt at an explanation of heroin use is the elaboration of the Merton paradigm on anomie by Cloward and Ohlin.[17,18] These investigators identify two distinctive subsystems in lower class communities: the legitimate and illegitimate systems, each with its own "opportunity structure." According to Cloward and Ohlin, addicts are a variant of the illegitimate criminal subsystem since they eschew the more robust, aggressive activities of the illegitimate system and are, in effect, failures in both the illegitimate and legitimate systems that are available. They are "retreatists" who have abandoned the pursuit of mobility within the legitimate system as well as within the illegitimate criminal culture. Organized illegitimate criminal systems, however, are more characteristic of lower class white ethnic communities than those communities where addicts are presently concentrated.[19] It would be hard to locate a well-organized criminal culture in Puerto Rican or Chicano communities, and even in many black areas, of the dimensions that would be implied by this formulation. One study of youth gangs on the lower East Side of New York City found that gangs could not be distinguished between "bopping" ones and those that used drugs.[20] Indeed, they were synonymous at the time of their investigation. Nor does the fact that heroin is a depressant sufficiently describe the nature of the addict life-style, with the appellation of "retreatist," as the work of Preble and Finestone amply illustrates.[21,22] On the contrary, to succeed as an addict requires a constant round of activity — taking care of business — and all the resourcefulness the addict can muster in order to survive. Nor does this formulation of "failure" comport with the findings briefly cited earlier on the educational and intellectual achievement of addicts. It also fails to provide a specification of the *prior* conditions that are contributory to the movement of individuals in the same social settings toward or away from addiction: Why should addicts who, as a group, have more resourcefulness than many others in their communities be double failures?

Communities where addiction is prevalent are also recipients of large influxes of new migrants. The migrations of blacks to northern urban communities, Puerto Ricans to New York and other large cities, and Mexican-Americans from rural areas and from Mexico itself are significant elements in metropolitan areas over most of the United States. In the present study, in the community where the survey was undertaken, Bedford-Stuyvesant/Fort Greene in Brooklyn, New York, 78% of the respondents were migrants from either outside New York or the continental United States, a phenomenal proportion. Frazier, over three decades ago, in his classic study on Negro families, noted that although the migrants are often the most disorganized people in cities, it is "...the children of migrants having been bred in the slum areas of northern cities and are more sophisticated..." who contribute most heavily to crime and prostitution.[23] Vaillant documents the marked underrepresentation of migrants in the addict population of Lexington, significantly less than the native-born. The highest overrepresentation of addicts is among the offspring of migrants, of all the ethnic groups that were examined.[24] Ball also notes the preponderance of native-born in the Lexington population at levels that surpass their proportion in the communities whence they came.[25] In a study of addicts in Chicago, 68% were natives compared to only 35% of the black population.[26] The findings of Ball and Vaillant suggested the primary guiding hypothesis of this study: The greatest amount of contact with drug users occurs not among migrants but among natives in each of the four ethnic groups studied, regardless of social class status.

In this chapter, where one community is studied, respondents who report heroin use in the family and among persons they identify as friends are examined. The families and friends who were reported to use heroin may not always share the precise social attributes of the respondents who provided the information. The possible error this may introduce in classifying reported drug users (e.g., social class) is likely to be overwhelmed by the tendency of family members and persons identified as friends to share common ethnic and social characteristics. Most important, however, we can locate respondents in the community against the backdrop of nonusing respondents and follow through sets of variables in order to examine the interrelationship of sets of characteristics germane to an interconnected thesis.

In this report we first locate the families or friends of reported heroin users in the community, both in the hierarchical socioeconomic structure and among the ethnic subgroups. We endeavor to explain what we observe by linking location in the community to migratory status, i.e., whether these families are recent arrivals or natives to the region. The central thesis of this study is that migration introduces particular strains that increase the disparity between the generations, an issue we attempt to document. It is hypothesized that events such as migration introduce similar sets of responses in *all* groups, that the structural dislocations are, in a very significant way, transcultural. The ways in which particular groups accommodate to the urban environment that contribute to *rate differences* will not be closely examined in this paper.

It is our view that social-psychological themes that dwell on peer-group processes and the attendant social networks are describing the culmination of the processes we identify.[27] In the final sense, social-psychological processes, we suggest, must be preceded by sociological ones that are substantial enough to impair the legitimacy of the traditional agents of socialization and social control.

The purpose of the present study is threefold. The first aim is to locate those who report heroin use by family members and friends in the social class and ethnic group structure of the community. Second, we examine the influence of migrant-native status on social class location and on ethnic group patterns. We endeavor to demonstrate that migrant-native status is antecedent to the findings on social class location and contact with drug users and that the processes associated with migration can be observed in all ethnic groups. Third, we examine two attitude areas, attitudes toward child rearing and racial identification, that are associated with migrant-native status and with contiguity with heroin users. These serve to index the disjunction between generations that, we hypothesize, precedes increased contact with heroin users.

METHOD

Sample

The sample area is the Bedford-Stuyvesant/Fort Greene area of Brooklyn, New York, served by the Addiction Research and Treatment Corporation, a multimodality methadone maintenance program located in the community. The area is characterized by high rates of addiction. All but one of the health areas in Brooklyn identified as high addiction tracts are within the sample area, with rates in individual tracts ranging from 69.7 to 233 per 10,000, compared to an overall Brooklyn

average of 66.2, reflecting the diversity in contiguous areas within this community.

A quota sample was used to obtain 612 interviews. In the final sample, 53% of the respondents were female and 47% male, which conforms with the 1970 Census proportions. Blacks from the British West Indies and Puerto Ricans were oversampled to ensure sufficient numbers for comparative purposes. The loss of 25 booklets prior to coding some open-ended items used in this analysis, the elimination of 14 non-West Indian foreign-born blacks, as well as nonresponses to items central to the analysis reduced the sample used in this report to 568 respondents. The sample consisted of 244 American blacks, 145 British West Indians, 99 Puerto Ricans, and 80 whites. Ethnic group patterns are examined for all major themes to ensure that they are consistent with aggregative patterns.

British West Indians include persons who were born in the Caribbean Islands formerly under British suzerainty or who are the offspring of West Indian parents. There are important differences in culture between the islands in the West Indies; however, they form a cultural complex with similar patterns of slavery and postslavery social structure and economy.[28-30] Most come from Barbados, Jamaica, Bermuda, and Trinidad, with smaller numbers from Granada, the British Virgin Islands, British Guiana, and other islands. They were included because British West Indians, while they are black and many are recent immigrants, have as a group made a very different accommodation to the United States. They tend to pursue home-ownership, stress education, and are disproportionately found in the professional, business, and political leadership of the black community.[31] British West Indians share a common racial identity with American blacks, but the very different cultures and histories of these groups provide a measure of control for the identification of sociocultural processes on drug use as distinct from the accommodations blacks make to racism.

Interviews

All interviews were conducted by a team trained by the National Opinion Research Center, and interviewers were matched to the ethnic composition of the respondents. Interviews were conducted in the respondents' households with a schedule primarily composed of predetermined response categories. One set of items measuring Orientations Toward Child Rearing were open-ended, with interviewers instructed to record the exact words of respondents. Items and indexes are described when they are introduced in the following analysis. Here we will describe only a few of the more important classifications that are used in this report:

Ethnic Group. Each respondent was requested for information on his or her place of birth and that of both parents, as well as that of the spouse where this was relevant. They were also asked to identify themselves from a range of options presented to them on a card. The interviewer also noted the race of the respondent. Each respondent was classified, first on race and then, depending on place of birth of the respondent or his family of orientation, grouped into one of four categories: British West Indian, black, Puerto Rican, or white. Where a respondent was native-born but reported mixed ancestry, mainly among blacks who were descended from both West Indian and American blacks, they were grouped with the British West Indians. Whites are from several ethnic groups but were retained as a single classification because there were too few from any particular white ethnic group.

Drug Use. Toward the end of the questionnaire, each respondent was asked whether he knew anyone who used heroin. If he answered affirmatively, he was then asked, in sequence, if any of his friends had ever used heroin and, then, whether any member of his family or his relatives had ever used heroin. After these queries, the respondent was asked whether he had ever used heroin. In the following analysis, there are several ways in which this information is used: (1) Reported Family/Relative Heroin Use, which is composed of respondents who answered "yes" to the question on family use with the addition of those respondents who acknowledged they had personally used heroin. (2) Friends Reported Heroin Use is simply the proportion who reported that friends have used heroin. (3) Contiguity with Drug Users combines those who reported family/relative use and/or friends. The Contiguity Index does not distinguish those who report friends or family member use, and for some, of course, both were reported as using heroin.

Social Class. The Social Class Index is a relative ranking composed of three dichotomous items:

occupation (blue versus white collar), income (above versus below $6,000), and education (high school graduate and above versus all others). The aggregated scores were then split at approximately the median in order to have sufficient cases in each group for analysis.

Orientations Toward Child Rearing. This index was designed to identify respondents' attitudes toward child rearing. We are not identifying child-rearing practices among reported heroin users since this is precluded by the design. It is only used as an index of attitudes in an area where many investigations suggest it is an important parameter in the socialization process for both affective and cognitive behavior.[32] The particular approach taken in constructing these items and the classification scheme was influenced by Basil Bernstein and Hess and Shipman, whose works have suggested that parental behavior could be classified into three major modes: Cognitive, Imperative, and Interpersonal.[33-37] Each of these modalities has consequences for shaping the way in which children organize experience, in particular the way in which these influence cognitive processes associated with learning. In this report, however, these orientations only serve as an index to document generational differences in attitudes in one arena to which great importance is attached and where there is accumulated evidence that it is associated with important areas of social functioning.[38,39]

In the imperative case, the subject asks the child to regulate his behavior in terms of role expectation, obedience to authority, and passive compliance. In the cognitive and interpersonal instances, the parent directs the child to regulate his behavior in terms of its effects upon others as well as in terms of the future consequences of his behavior.

Each respondent was asked the following three questions:

1. Now let's take the situation where you have a 6-year-old child going to school for the first time. What would you tell him or her?

2. You find out your child of 11 or 12 is playing hooky (staying away from school without telling you). How would you handle it?

3. You notice your child's behavior has changed. You find out he has started taking drugs. What would you do?

The respondents' answers to question 1 were categorized as imperative, cognitive, or interpersonal. An imperative statement was defined as a command or unqualified injunction. Examples include:

"On the way to school, don't talk to strangers — don't take any candy from them."
"Obey the teacher."
"Be good in school, behave yourself, don't make trouble, do as you are told."

Cognitive statements provide information which contains an explanation or rationale for the rule to be observed:

"Learn everything that is taught so that one day you will finish school and have a good job."
"Going to school is very important for your future. It's a big step in your life and will help you get along in the world."

Interpersonal statements focus on interpersonal relationships between the child and his classmates and the child and his teacher:

"Try to get along with boys and girls, black and white, consider others' feelings. Try to develop good friendships with your classmates."

In question 2 and 3 the imperative approach tended to demand immediate compliance from the child who was expected to change his overt behavior without being presented with a justification for this change. These power assertive techniques included: (1) physical punishment, (2) deprivation of material objects or privileges, (3) threats of punishment, (4) verbal assaults and confirmations of the behavior problem with the authorities. Examples include:

"I would whip him or burn his feet."
"I would give him some punishment — not going to things he likes. Not letting him watch T.V., take away his allowance. I'd keep a constant watch over him."
"I'd take him to school and yell at him and hit him in front of the teacher and the class so he'd be embarrassed."

Cognitive techniques were those that attempted to determine the cause of the behavior, find a solution to the problem, or sensitize the child to the painful external consequences of the transgression. Cognitive statements were not accompanied by sanctions. For instance:

"I'd find out why and deal accordingly to change his situation. Channel his energies in a different direction."
"I would ask him why he was doing it and what drugs he was taking, what he was getting out of it. I would point out to him what drugs are harmful with the intent for the child to reflect upon his own actions and the consequences, developing the ability to think and act for himself in the interest of his personal well-being."

For each item, independent judges coded the responses and the median agreement was 90%. The particular categories are illustrated in Table 5. In this report a summary index of responses to all three items is used throughout the analysis, with respondents classified as either cognitive (including those who gave interpersonal responses) or imperative.

Racial Identification. Another indicator of changing perspectives is one's identification, how one chooses to identify oneself when presented with a choice. For whites, blacks, and British West Indians, we contrast those who select a racial identification over other possible ways of identifying themselves. It is our assumption that the choice of a racial basis for identification is also, for many, an index of a changing sense of self-concept that indicates the declining legitimacy of the connection with the parental generation. Those who are integrated into more traditional ethnic patterns, we suggest, are less likely to choose black or white; instead, they would choose more conventional forms of identification, such as Negro, West Indian, American, or various white ethnic appellations such as Italian, Jewish, etc. Puerto Ricans present a problem in that almost all chose either Puerto Rican or American, and neither choice seems to have the same impact as do more specifically racial bases of identification. There is no term for Puerto Ricans that clearly implies an altered sense of self as "Chicano" may have for Mexican-Americans. Very few Puerto Ricans are natives so that the process of altered identification may not have taken root.

FINDINGS

Background Characteristics and Reported Heroin Use

Heroin use is concentrated in urban areas. The heroin scene — the pushers, addicts, the occasional users — is, in turn, in particular neighborhoods. In the sample area, a predominantly black ghetto, there remains a small white population from a former era. The most recent additions to the community are Puerto Ricans. The blacks are composed of divergent groups, some from a long-established black community, West Indians from many Caribbean Islands, and recent migrants from the South. Poverty, while very visible, is not universally present even in "depressed" areas. There is a complex hierarchical structure, not only for ethnic composition, but on every aspect of stratification: income, education, occupation. We will first locate reported heroin users in the social structure of the community.

Thirteen percent of the respondents reported that a family member and/or relative had used heroin. These are not necessarily addicts, although the likelihood of heroin use becoming known to others in the family network suggests that heroin use was more than intermittent. We also suspect some underreporting of the actual prevalence of heroin use since it is more unlikely that individuals would report drug use where it did not exist than to deny drug use when present. Some respondents may not always have been aware of the drug-taking habits of other persons in their families, and others may have avoided answering truthfully. In other investigations where there was independent information about heroin use, through records or from urine tests, there was a very high degree of concordance between self-reports and independent confirmation.[41],[42] In the present study, only 2% of the respondents reported that they had taken heroin. Therefore, most of the respondents were reporting on other members of their families.

Three characteristics of the respondents are presented in Chart 1: education, occupation, and income. As shown in Chart 1, in each case the rates of reported heroin use by family members or relatives are directly related to the higher status of each indicator. Those with the highest educational achievement, those in white collar occupations, and those who earn more than $6,000 annually report significantly higher rates of family/relative use of heroin. When one examines a community characterized by poverty, occupations at the lowest level, and widespread disorganization and despondency, reported family/relative use is associated with the upper layers of the community social structure. These findings are at variance with explanations that direct attention to heroin use as a response to poverty and discrimination and raise serious challenge to efforts which attempt to explain the heroin epidemic in economic terms.

Ethnic Group Variations in Reported Heroin Use

The overrepresentation of particular ethnic groups in the heroin-using population is a widely observed phenomenon. In the present study, four ethnic groups who resided in the same community were examined, although each of the ethnic groups was not randomly distributed but tended to be concentrated in certain sections. All of the subjects, however, were contiguous to copping areas, and addiction was easily observed, throughout the neighborhood, even by the casual observer. The groups we examined were American-born blacks of U.S. parentage, black British West Indians, Puerto Ricans, most of whom were born on the Island, and whites, who were identified only by race and were a mixture of various white ethnic groups still residing in the area. Most individuals, even in ghetto communities, do not use heroin, so that there may be, within each of these groups, particular ways of coping with the world that may help to explain the very different rates of reported drug use.

Examination of Chart 2 indicates that the highest rate of reported heroin use is found among the Puerto Ricans (22%), whereas the lowest rates occur among the whites and British West Indians. The blacks hold an intermediate position.

These ethnic groups, however, differ not only in the cultural backgrounds they bring with them but also in their relative locations in the social class system. British West Indians and whites are overrepresented in the upper half of the social class system, blacks are almost evenly divided, and the Puerto Ricans are heavily concentrated in the lower half of the class system (note frequencies in Table 1). It is necessary, therefore, to determine whether the results observed in Chart 2 are a function of the different social class distribution of the four ethnic groups.

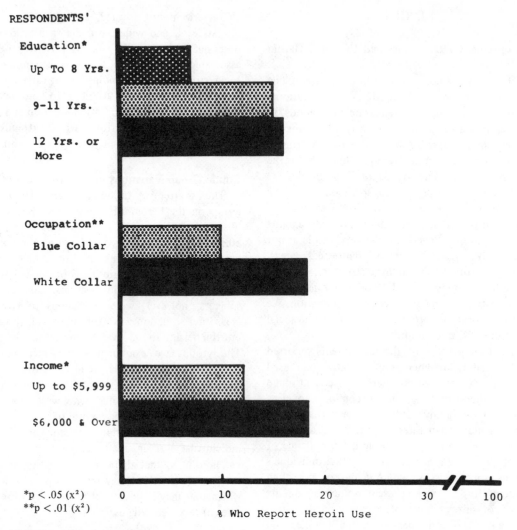

RESPONDENTS'

Education*
Up To 8 Yrs.

9-11 Yrs.

12 Yrs. or
More

Occupation**
Blue Collar

White Collar

Income*
Up to $5,999

$6,000 & Over

*p < .05 (x²)
**p < .01 (x²)

0   10   20   30   100

% Who Report Heroin Use

CHART 1. Selected background and social characteristics and percentage of respondents who report relatives or family members have used heroin.

Social Class, Ethnic Groups, and Contiguity with Drug Users

The introduction to heroin use shares with other forms of drug use a common element; namely, it is almost always introduced to the novitiate by peers. A necessary, if not always sufficient, condition for experimentation with drugs is regularized social relations with persons who use heroin.[43],[44]

In the following analysis contiguity with drug users, a combination of the responses to the questions dealing with whether the respondent has friends and/or family members or relatives who use heroin was used. A detailed description of the Contiguity Index and the composite social class score appears in the Method section. The Conti-

guity Index is more stable than the Family/Relative Index and is required for subsequent tabulation where three or four variables are simultaneously examined. In every case, both here and in subsequent sections of this paper, the patterns observed for the Contiguity Index are similar to those for the Family/Relative Index. It should be noted, however, that because of the increase in the numerator, statistical significance will be demonstrated with the Contiguity Index, where there would be too few cases with the Family/Relative Index.

Where there are adequate numbers of cases in the tables that follow, both proportions are presented. Table 1 presents the proportion of subjects in each ethnic group, within each social

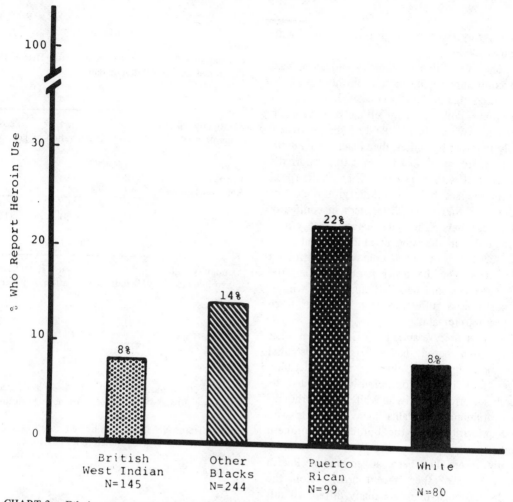

CHART 2. Ethnic group membership and percentage who report relatives or family members have used heroin. Differences as tested by $\chi^2 (0.02 > p > 0.01)$.

TABLE 1

Social Class, Ethnic Group, and Contiguity with Heroin Users*

	Social class				
	Low		High		
Ethnic group	% Contiguity with heroin users				Difference
	%	f	%	f	
White	18	(34)**	22	(46)	4
Puerto Rican	39	(70)	62	(29)	23
Black	22	(127)	42	(117)	20
British West Indian	8	(50)	16	(95)	8
Maximum % difference	31%		46%		

*Differences for ethnic groups within each social class category are significant at 0.001 level as tested by chi-square.

**Frequencies in parentheses are the base numbers for each percentage.

class category, who are high on contiguity with drug users.

As shown in Table 1, ethnicity and social class *both* contribute to the pattern on the dependent variable, contiguity with drug users. In both social class groups, rankings of the ethnic groups remain consistent, with British West Indians lowest, closely followed by whites, then blacks; the Puerto Ricans regardless of social class status report the most contact with drug users. That is, the social class differences between ethnic groups do not account for the ethnic differences in contiguity with drug users. The data suggest that ethnic groups differ in the ways in which they adapt to their social environments, even with control on social class. On the other hand, although the differences are somewhat attenuated for whites, the social class differences for the other three ethnic groups remain.

Bedford-Stuyvesant/Fort Greene, as has already been noted, has undergone substantial population shifts over the last several decades. Since 1950 it has continuously expanded its boundaries into formerly all-white neighborhoods. This community contains many migrants who come primarily from the border and southern states, as well as from the West Indies. More recently, there has been an influx of Puerto Ricans, most of them recent arrivals from the Islands. Although there are many different kinds of migrants, most of those who arrive in this community are poor, uneducated, and have few skills. As a group we would expect that recent migrants would more often be found among those who are in the lower socioeconomic stratum. This, indeed, is the case.

Migrant-Native Status and Contiguity

The subjects were also classified into migrants, first-generation, and second-generation natives and compared with respect to their reported contact with drug users for subjects under and over 30 years of age.

Since drug use is primarily an activity of younger persons, and younger respondents more often report family and friends' use of heroin, age was used as a control variable. As shown in Table 2, for the under-30 group, the migrants have the least contact with drug users, followed by the second-generation natives. The first-generation young adults report the most contact with drug users. Thus, we find an excess of reported heroin

TABLE 2

Generational Patterns in Contiguity with Heroin Users, Controlled by Age of Respondent*

Contiguity with heroin users	Under 30		
	Migrant	First generation	Second generation
None	64%	18%	47%
Friends	18	41	20
Relatives/Family	18	41	33
	100%	100%	100%
	(103)	(29)	(15)

Contiguity with heroin users	30 and Over		
	Migrant	First generation	Second generation
None	80%	74%	69%
Friends	11	13	17
Relatives/Family	9	13	14
	100%	100%	100%
	(333)	(47)	(29)

*Under 30 significant at 0.001 level as tested by chi-square; 30 and over differences are not significant.

Note: Migrants are those born outside continental U.S.A. for whites, British West Indians, and Puerto Ricans. For blacks it is all those born outside of New York, mainly border and Southern states.

use among those born in New York and more especially, the first generation, the offspring of migrants. The overrepresentation of first generation youth highlights the possible significance of exposure to two different cultures, that of their migrant parents and that of the local society. These relationships did not emerge for the subjects who are over 30 years of age. Only younger migrants show an increase in contiguity with heroin users as a function of their length of residence in the community, although this is still substantially below the rates reported for natives (data not reported here).[4][5]

The overrepresentation of natives in contiguity suggests the explanation for our earlier observation of the differential distribution of reported family/relative use and friendships with heroin users favoring those in the upper layers of the social structure. We would expect that native-born respondents would be better educated, earn more money, and have higher status occupations. This indeed is the case.

TABLE 3

Social Class, Migrant-native Status, and Contiguity with Heroin Users*

Contiguity with heroin users	Social class			
	Migrants		Natives	
	Low	High	Low	High
None	80%	72%	50%	56%
Friends	10	16	25	21
Family/Relatives	10	12	25	23
	100%	100%	100%	100%
	(245)	(199)	(32)	(88)

*Differences between social classes within migrant-native status groups are not significant. Differences between migrant-native groups holding social class constant are significant at 0.01 level as tested by chi-square.

Social Class, Migrant-Native Status, and Contiguity

The frequencies at the bottom of the columns in Table 3 reveal that migrants are more often concentrated in the lower social class, while 75% of the natives are located in the upper half of the Social Class Index. Examination of the Contiguity Index, broken down by friends and family/relative heroin use, suggests what has been taking place. Within groups classified as migrants and natives, social class differences vanish. The significant differences in contiguity are between migrants and natives, even with control on social class. These findings provide strong support for the hypothesis

that generational status, not social class, is a salient antecedent of contact with drug users.

In the last row of Table 3, 10% of lower-class migrants, compared to 12% of the higher-class ones, report heroin use by a family member or relative. Among natives, on the other hand, these proportions increase to 25% and 23%, respectively. The differences in friendships with heroin users are also substantially greater for natives than for migrants *irrespective* of social class.

In brief, the finding that those who are relatively higher in status in ghetto communities contribute disproportionately to the heroin-using population is seen to be largely a function of the differences between migrant and native status. Thus, social class differences in drug contiguity merely reflect generational mobility.

Ethnic Group, Migrant-Native Status, and Contiguity

As was previously shown, generational mobility was significantly related to contiguity with drug users for persons under 30 years of age. Ethnic differences in contact with drug users were examined with control on migrant-native status in order to determine whether ethnic differences were merely a function of different periods of immigration associated with each group. Natives and migrants are separated within each ethnic group in Table 4 and contrasted on contiguity with drug users. As shown in Table 4, the majority of whites are natives (44 versus 36), whereas for the other groups the overwhelming proportion are

TABLE 4

Ethnic Group, Migrant-Native Status, and Contiguity with Heroin Users*

Contiguity with heroin users	Ethnic group							
	White		Puerto Rican		Black		British West Indian	
	Migrant	Native	Migrant	Native	Migrant	Native	Migrant	Native
None	92%	70%	57%	17%	74%	40%	93%	67%
Friends	8	16	23	33	14	34	3	11
Family/Relatives	0	14	20	50	12	26	4	22
	100%	100%	100%	100%	100%	100%	100%	100%
	(36)	(44)	(93)	(6)	(206)	(38)	(109)	(36)

*The summary chi-square is significant at 0.001 level. Within ethnic groups differences are significant at least at 0.05 level, except for Puerto Ricans.

migrants. Only 6 of 99 Puerto Ricans are natives, while natives make up only 16% of the blacks and a slightly higher proportion of the British West Indians, 23%.

Within each ethnic group, the natives are much more likely to report both friends and kin as users of heroin. Inspection of Table 4 shows that 14% of the native whites report family or relative heroin use but none of the migrants. Among the Puerto Ricans there are too few natives for meaningful comparisons to be made, although the same trend prevails. More than twice as many native blacks, 26% compared to 12% for migrants, report family member use. For native British West Indians it is 22% in contrast to only 4% for migrants. Similar trends prevail for use of heroin by friends. When age is introduced as a control variable, the N's become very small indeed, and while younger persons consistently report more heroin-using friends and family members, the same trends prevail among both young and old (data not reported).

Whatever may be the forces that contribute to increased contiguity with heroin users, it is consistently observable within each of the four groups. The relative standing of the four groups, whether natives or migrants, is retained; i.e., whites and British West Indians are least likely to report heroin use by friends or kin. The blacks are intermediate, and the Puerto Ricans have the highest rate of contiguity. It should be noted that with so few native Puerto Ricans the comparisons are unreliable for this group. Despite the fact that Puerto Ricans are mainly a migrant population, they do have the highest rate of contiguity of the four groups in this sample. This observation and the retention of the rankings among the four groups direct attention to the particular features of the experiences of each of these groups that may be operating alongside the problems that may accompany generational differences across all of the ethnic groups.

Cultural Expressiveness: The Concomitants of Generational Change

Each ethnic group arrives with a very different cultural history and with different methods of coping with experience. For some the shift to urban environments, with the particular accommodations necessary to relate to family, work, school, and community, may, indeed, require a major alteration in the ways in which they cope

with the realities they encounter. Others arrive with cultural prescriptions that are minimally disrupted in the new environment. Some groups because of race, language, or religion may have greater difficulties in gaining access to the major institutions irrespective of the particular congruence of their prior cultural experience; nor do these difficulties vanish, in most cases, in one or two generations. Where race is also a factor the "fit" between the ethnic culture and the ability to make one's way in the community may not always be the most significant element. We would therefore expect that even over several generations there will be substantial differences in most important indicators of the way each group gains access to the resources of the community or, complementarily, fails to assimilate to the larger society.

There may also be certain underlying processes that are not necessarily unique to the particular cultural, social, or racial heritages of the groups examined in this report. We still find very different rates within the community we are examining here that are clearly parallel to the rates of heroin use found in the wider society. We have seen that within all four groups, the offspring of the migrants, particularly the first generation, are substantially more involved in friendships with heroin users and having family members and relatives who are heroin users. Therefore, it would appear to be worthwhile to explore some of the changes within the families we are examining that characterize the generations.

In this and subsequent sections, some indicators of changing perspective that are more closely associated with native status than with migrant status and are presumably relevant to contact with drug users will be explored. One indicator, described in the Method section, is Orientations Toward Child Rearing. In the present study we do not have data concerning actual child-rearing practices, but we do have information regarding the attitudes of adults concerning child rearing which should correlate with their actual child-rearing practices. Each respondent, in response to three questions that were designed to assess attitudes toward child-rearing practices, was classified as Imperative, where the thrust of the response was the imposition of sanctions, discipline, or deprivation for misconduct or, alternatively, Cognitive, wherein the responses indicated an effort to understand the behavior, increase communication, and/or direct the child to regulate his behavior in terms of the future consequences of his actions.

A second indicator of changing perspectives is one's identification, how one chooses to identify himself when presented with a choice. For whites, blacks, and British West Indians, we contrast those who select a racial identification over other possible ways of identifying themselves. The significance of identification does not have the same impact for Puerto Ricans, as noted in the Method section, possibly because they are almost all migrants.

For each of these indicators, the pattern that is associated with migrant and native status will be examined in order to determine whether this is associated with contiguity with drug users. We will ascertain whether the same process can be observed within each ethnic group to determine if the changes observed in the way native-born identify themselves and in their attitudes toward child rearing are particular to each culture or transcend cultural particularity.

Child-control Orientation, Ethnicity, Migrant-Native Status, and Contiguity

Table 5 depicts the percent of subjects whose responses were classified in each of the categories for each ethnic group in answer to each of the questions. The differences for all three questions are statistically significant. For each item the whites provide more cognitive or interpersonal responses than the other groups; however, the British West Indians are close behind, followed by the blacks; the Puerto Ricans are least likely to give cognitive answers, except for item 3. In item 3 the respondent was asked what he would do if he thought a child was using drugs.

Those with at least two responses in a particular category were classified accordingly, so that each respondent was grouped into either the Imperative or Cognitive category. The responses across the three items were aggregated into a summary index, which is used in the remainder of the analysis.

As can be seen in the column totals for Table 6, cognitive responses are not the norm for any group. The largest proportion of cognitive re-

TABLE 5

Ethnic Comparisons on Child-control Orientations

Child-control orientations	Ethnic group								
	White		Puerto Rican		Black		British West Indian		X² (Chi)
	N	%	N	%	N	%	N	%	
Question 1									
Imperative	54	67	87	88	201	82	109	75	20.34
									p < 0.001
Cognitive or interpersonal	19	24	5	5	22	9	25	17	
No answer or unclassifiable*	7	9	7	7	21	9	11	7	
Question 2									
Imperative	23	29	69	70	113	46	68	47	27.60
									p < 0.001
Cognitive	48	60	27	27	121	49	73	50	
No answer or unclassifiable*	9	11	3	3	10	4	4	3	
Question 3									
Imperative	10	12	19	19	30	12	27	19	14.40
									p < 0.05
Medical rehabilitation	25	31	46	46	124	51	53	36	
Cognitive	27	34	25	25	58	24	43	30	
No answer or unclassifiable*	18	22	9	9	32	13	22	15	

*The no answer or unclassifiable category was not used in computing the X² (Chi) values for the three questions.

TABLE 6

Ethnic Group, Child-control Orientation, and Contiguity with Heroin Users*

Contiguity with heroin users	White		Puerto Rican		Black		British West Indian	
	Imperative	Cognitive	Imperative	Cognitive	Imperative	Cognitive	Imperative	Cognitive
None	85%	63%	56%	37%	70%	59%	91%	70%
Friends/Family	15	37	44	63	30	41	9	30
	100%	100%	100%	100%	100%	100%	100%	100%
	(61)	(19)	(91)	(8)	(203)	(41)	(118)	(27)

Ethnic group

*The summary chi-square is significant at less than 0.01 level.

TABLE 7

Generational Patterns in Child-control Orientation, Controlled by Age of Respondent*

| Child-control orientation | Under 30 | | |
	Migrant	First generation	Second generation
Imperative	85%	62%	47%
Cognitive	15	38	53
	100%	100%	100%
	(103)	(29)	(15)

| Child-control orientation | 30 and Over | | |
	Migrant	First generation	Second generation
Imperative	86%	81%	83%
Cognitive	14	19	17
	100%	100%	100%
	(333)	(47)	(29)

*Under 30 significant at 0.001 level as tested by chi-square; 30 and over differences are not significant.

sponses is found among whites (24%) and the British West Indians (19%) but is fewer than one-in-ten for the other two groups. This is, of course, partly attributable to the higher social class distribution of these former groups. The results are consistent with the findings in the research literature on social class and orientations toward child rearing. Since class differences in reported drug use are a function of generational mobility, we will not present information on social class patterns, although orientation toward child control was significantly associated with social class in the expected direction (data not presented).

The paucity of cognitive responses has to be considered in evaluating the balance of the findings in this section. The central thesis concerning migratory status and ethnic groups forces an examination of these crucial variables both separately and together. Some of the cells are too small for reliable findings; however, the remarkable consistency of the data has also to be considered in justifying their presentation. Nonetheless, the subsequent analysis should be viewed with caution.

Inspection of Table 6 indicates that child-rearing orientation was significantly related to contact with drug users for the whites and British West Indians. A similar trend appeared for the blacks and Puerto Ricans. For each ethnic group,

those who are cognitive, whose attitudes favor infrequent use of punishment and rely instead on the use of explanation and reasoning, report higher rates of contiguity with drug users than those who have an imperative orientation. The summary of chi-square over the four tables is statistically significant. The same trend is observable within each group and is consistent with the thesis that the same processes may be operative for all groups. But rates of reported drug-use still differ across the groups even when orientations are held constant. Puerto Ricans and blacks still have much more contact than either British West Indians or whites, although there are substantial differences even in these latter two groups between respondents who are classified as cognitive and those who are imperative.

Table 7 presents the Child-control Orientation Index and its relation to generational patterns with control on age since reported drug use, as with identified addicts, is heavily concentrated among younger persons. In the first panel of Table 7, among those who are under 30, there is a significant increase in the number of respondents who give a cognitive response with nativity status: 15% for migrant, 38% for first-generation natives, and 53% for second generation. These differences are statistically significant beyond the 0.001 level. Unlike our earlier finding (Table 2) of an apparent decline in reported drug use for the second generation, there is, instead, an increase in cognitive responses. Among older individuals there is no observable trend toward an increase in cognitive responses. The differences in the age groups are, in part, a function of the lower education and socioeconomic status of older respondents, a significant correlate of the Orientation Index (data not presented). The Orientation Index is here viewed as an indicator of cultural disparity that weakens traditional controls. This does not preclude the probability that in successive generations this same index may have an altogether different meaning as family patterns become integrated across generations.

As the data in Table 8 show, natives, irrespective of orientation, tend to have higher rates of contiguity with heroin users so that the impact of generational patterns is not completely encapsulated in this index. Among natives, where we would expect the disparity we have described to be most significant, we see that only 36% of natives who are imperative report that friends or family members have used heroin compared to

TABLE 8

Migrant-Native Status, Orientation Toward Child Rearing, and Contiguity with Heroin Users*

| | Percent high on contiguity | | | |
| | Migrants | | Natives | |
Orientation toward child rearing	%	f	%	f
Imperative	23	(383)	36	(90)
Cognitive	26	(61)	62	(34)

*For natives differences are significant beyond 0.01 level as tested by chi-square; differences for migrants are not significant.

TABLE 9

Child-control Orientation and Contiguity with Heroin Users by Ethnic Groups and Migrant-Native Status*

		Child-control orientation			
		Imperative		Cognitive	
		% Contiguity with heroin users			
		%	f	%	f
White	Migrant	7	(30)	[17]	(6)
	Native	23	(31)	[46]	(13)
Puerto Rican	Migrant	42	(86)	[57]	(7)
	Native	[80]	(5)	[100]	(1)
Black	Migrant	26	(174)	28	(32)
	Native	52	(29)	[89]	(9)
British West Indian	Migrant	5	(93)	13	(16)
	Native	24	(25)	[55]	(11)

*p = 0.004 as tested by the binomial test for both orientation toward child control and for migrant-native differences in contiguity.

Note: Percentages in square brackets are based on fewer than 15 cases.

62% for those who are cognitively oriented. These differences are statistically significant and conform to the thesis that the changes observed in this attitude area are consistently associated with reported heroin use in the respondent's social network.

To fully test the thesis presented in this chapter, the relationship between each of our major variables will be simultaneously examined: ethnic group, migrant-native status, child-control orientations, and contiguity with heroin users. The small percentage of natives, together with the small number of cognitive responses, results in a very few cases in all too many cells. The consistency of the relationship between each of these variables, even when two of them are examined with reported heroin use, however, must also be kept in mind when examining Table 9. A test of significance which looks at trends and not at the actual magnitude of the respective proportions was used.

The data in Table 9 demonstrate that each of the patterns we have already observed persists. In all eight instances, those who are cognitively oriented also report more contact with heroin users. Again, where there is a sufficient number of cases, natives have higher rates of contact than migrants; the same trend prevails in cells with few cases. For this to occur in all eight possible contrasts by chance, the probability is 4 times in 1,000. It would, of course, be highly desirable to have these findings replicated on a much larger cohort of subjects and to link them directly to generational shifts within the family.

We observe, then, that Child-control Orientations tend to change for those born in the community, especially among younger persons.

Insofar as the cognitive mode predominates, it is conterminous with nativity status and less likely to be observed among migrants who tend to be more imperative. Concomitantly, where this is the case it is associated with increased contiguity with drug users. Still, it should be observed that relative differences are retained between ethnic groups and that natives invariably have higher rates than migrants even when orientations are held constant. Unlike our earlier observation that class differences disappeared when we examined migrant-native status, here we have to view the results as suggestive, insofar as they parallel generational patterns and are associated with increased contiguity with drug users. Nevertheless, we cannot altogether explain all the ethnic differences or completely account for the tendency for native-born to have higher rates on contiguity.

Racial Identification, Ethnicity, Migrant-Native Status, and Contiguity

A second indicator of change that accompanies generational shifts is the way respondents identify themselves, whether they select a particularistic ethnic or traditional mode of identity or one that focuses more specifically on race. In Table 10 we

TABLE 10

Migrant-native Status and Racial Identification*

Identification	Migrants	First generation	Second generation
Racial	34%	55%	61%
Other	66	45	39
	100%	100%	100%
	(444)	(78)	(44)

*p is less than 0.001 as tested by chi-square.

TABLE 11

Migrant-native Status and Racial Identification by Ethnic Groups*

	% Using racial identification			
	Migrants		Natives	
Ethnic group	%	f	%	f
White	61	(36)	71	(44)
Puerto Rican	41	(93)	17	(6)
Black	31	(206)	55	(38)
British West Indian	26	(109)	53	(36)

*The differences between migrant and native are statistically significant as tested by chi-square at less than 0.001 level.

TABLE 12

Racial Identification of Ethnic Groups and Contiguity with Heroin Users

	Identification			
	Racial		Other	
	% Report contiguity with heroin users*			
Ethnic group	%	f	%	f
White	26	(53)	7	(27)
Puerto Rican	46	(39)	45	(60)
Black	39	(84)	27	(160)
British West Indian	23	(47)	7	(98)

*Differences in contiguity significant at 0.05 level for whites, blacks, and British West Indians as tested by chi-square.

see that the tendency to select a racial category increases from 34% of migrants to 55% for first-generation and 61% for the second-generation natives. Both young and old have very similar patterns (data not presented). That is, native-born are much more likely to choose to call themselves black and white than those who were born abroad or in the South. Although we retain Puerto Ricans in this analysis, and group those who say Puerto Rican with the "racial" category, they are clearly a special case. It is our view that the choice of a racial category, whatever other significance it may have, is for many also an indication of a change in self-concept that will reduce the respondents' acceptance of traditional constraints imposed by their families.

In Table 11 are presented the percentage who use racial categories for each ethnic group, separated for migrants and natives. In each case natives are more likely to have selected a racial basis for identifying themselves. What is even more surprising, despite the increasing acceptance of black as the basis for the identification of Afro-Americans, is that the choice of a racial label, for both migrants and natives, is much more common among whites. This may be a reflection of a weakening of more traditional ethnic ties among whites or simply a response to being a remnant of a formerly white majority in a community that is now predominantly black, but this cannot be determined here.

In Table 12 for each group where racial identity is clear — whites, blacks, and British West Indians — those who avoid using a racial identification have significantly less contact with drug users. Among those who selected white, 26% report friends' or family/relative use of heroin compared to only 7% where some other form of self-identity was chosen. For blacks the difference is 39% for the racial choice compared to 27% where some other form of identification was chosen. Like whites, the discrepancy is more substantial among British West Indians, 23% versus only 7% for those who identified themselves as West Indians or Americans or chose some alternate form of identification. No differences can be observed for Puerto Ricans.

For three of our four groups, the alteration in identification is also associated with increased contiguity with heroin users. We use the choice of a racial basis for identification as an expression of a changing view of self which might be associated with a weakening of traditional forms of social control and, therefore, facilitate the tendency to conform to peer groups. The same process was observed within all age groups, although younger persons more often chose a racial basis for identification (data not presented). We still have the task of establishing whether this same process is observable for each ethnic group when we examine contiguity with heroin use for natives and migrants. As observed earlier, the consistency of the patterns with those in the previous table, where fewer variables were examined, helps to lend credence to the patterns in Table 13.

In Table 13, except for native Puerto Ricans, where racial forms of identification are used, the proportion who report contiguity with heroin users is higher; at the same time, migrants have consistently less contact with drug users than do natives. Of the possible eight contrasts on the impact of both identification and migrant status in relation to contiguity, seven of the eight contrasts are in the predicted direction, a statistically significant result.

TABLE 13

Racial Identification and Contiguity with Heroin Users for Ethnic Groups and Migrant-Native Status*

		Identification			
		Racial		Other	
		% Report contiguity with heroin users			
		%	f	%	f
White	Native	35	(31)	[15]	(13)
	Migrant	14	(22)	[0]	(14)
Puerto Rican	Native	[0]	(1)	[100]	(5)
	Migrant	47	(38)	40	(55)
Black	Native	67	(21)	53	(17)
	Migrant	30	(63)	24	(143)
British West Indian	Native	42	(19)	23	(17)
	Migrant	11	(28)	4	(81)

*p = 0.035 as tested by the binomial test for differences in racial identification and for native-migrant differences.

Note: Percentages in square brackets are based on fewer than 15 cases.

CONCLUSION

Summary of Findings

In this investigation, the distribution of re-

ported heroin use in the family and among friends in a sample of respondents selected from a ghetto community was examined. Although the subjects were not identified addicts, the findings do conform to information obtained from addicts in other investigations at many crucial junctures. By examining a sample within the community context, we were able to link a series of findings in a manner that facilitated the ordering and integration of several themes that are relevant to efforts to explain heroin use.

Reported heroin use by family members and/or relatives was obtained from subjects living in the community. Rates of reported heroin use were significantly higher among respondents who were better educated, had white collar as opposed to blue collar occupations, and who earned more money. Inspection of a community, even if it is generally one where poverty prevails, demonstrates that addicts are disproportionately drawn from the upper layers of the community.

Four major ethnic groups were identified: blacks, British West Indians (also blacks), Puerto Ricans, and whites. Ethnic differences in contact with drug users emerged: Puerto Ricans had the highest reported rate, followed by blacks, with British West Indians and whites having the lowest rates.

Since ethnic groups differ in their location in the social class system, these two variables were examined simultaneously in terms of their impact on contiguity with drug users. Despite control on social class, ethnic differences in contact with drug users were retained in the order previously described with the exception of the whites, where the SES differences were modest. There were also significant differences in contact favoring the higher social class groups. Thus, the data imply that both ethnic group membership and social class are related to contiguity with drug users.

An attempt to clarify the perplexing finding regarding the relationship between SES and reported heroin use was made. Respondents were classified as migrants, first- or second-generation natives. As might be anticipated, family and/or friend use of heroin was heavily concentrated among native-born individuals. For subjects under 30, the migrants had the least contact with drug users, followed by the second-generation natives. The first-generation young adults reported the most contact with drug users. There was only a minor and statistically insignificant increase in contiguity among native-born persons over 30 years of age. It may be inferred then, that heroin use is characteristically concentrated among young native-born individuals, and most heavily among first-generation natives.

In order to correct for the possible effects of generational mobility on relationships between social class and contact with drug users, migrant-native status was controlled. The important differences in reported kin use of heroin, and in friendships with drug users, emerged between the migrants and natives; the social class differences observed previously vanished with control on migrant-native status and were largely a function of migrant-native status. The results therefore provide strong support for the hypothesis that generational differences, *not* social class, is a salient antecedent of contact with drug users. This directs attention, then, to the significance of the migrant-native distinction itself in contributing to the likelihood individuals will be involved with heroin use.

Within each ethnic group, natives have substantially more reported kin and/or friends who have used heroin than migrants, although there are very few Puerto Rican natives in this community. Thus, the process is not confined to any one particular group but cuts across all four ethnic groups. Still, each of the groups reports rate differences in contiguity consistent with those we observed earlier so that while the migrant-native distinction contributes to substantial differences there are clearly other factors associated with the culture and experiences of these groups that are not encapsulated in this distinction.

Two indicators designed to measure changing perspectives among migrants that are associated with increasing contiguity with heroin users were used. Based on the respondent's replies to the Child Orientation Index, the subjects were classified as either Imperative or Cognitive. It should be noted that the Orientation Index is an attitude index, not a measure of actual child-rearing practices. The second indicator is Racial Identification, wherein respondents were classified on their choice of a specifically racial basis for identity, white or black, in lieu of a more traditional or national category such as Negro, West Indian, American, or more particularistic ethnic groups such as Italian, Jewish, etc. Puerto Ricans mainly chose either Puerto Rican or American and there-

fore presented a different profile than did the other groups, possibly because so few were native-born.

Ethnic groups differed significantly in the proportion who were cognitively oriented: whites and British West Indians were more often cognitive than either blacks or Puerto Ricans. In all groups the Imperative mode was more common. Contact with drug users was significantly linked with attitudes favoring the infrequent use of punishment and the use of explanation and reasoning in attempting to modify the child's behavior in the whites and British West Indians. A similar trend occurred among the blacks and Puerto Ricans. Increasing cognitive orientations were also found to be most characteristic of younger natives, those under 30. It is precisely among the native-born that cognitive orientation is linked to contiguity with reported heroin users.

When these variables are examined simultaneously, although there are several cells with insufficient numbers of cases, in every possible contrast natives report higher contiguity in every ethnic group than migrants. Moreover, whether one examines natives or migrants, where the orientation is cognitive there is a higher index value on contiguity with drug users. Although not reported here, the same relationships remain when examining younger and older respondents.

When we examine those who chose a racial basis for identification, it was found to occur more often for individuals who were native-born, increasing with each generation. Those who chose a racial basis for identification, whether whites, blacks, or British West Indians, were also significantly higher on contiguity with heroin users. When ethnic groups were sorted into natives and migrants, those who chose a racial basis for identification were consistently higher on contiguity than those who chose an alternative way to identify themselves.

In brief, these two indicators that reflect altered ways in which persons identify themselves, and in the manner in which they would cope with situations that might face children, vary with generational status. In turn, when these revised perspectives exist, there are increased reports of heroin use by friends or kin. Within each ethnic group we find similar processes at work: Native-born depart from migrants on these indicators, and when they do there is much more contiguity with heroin users among the former group. At the same time, while similar trends are observable among whites, blacks, British West Indians, and Puerto Ricans (with the exception of the latter on racial identification because there are so few native-born), there is a persistence in the relative rankings of each ethnic group no matter how the data are analyzed: Puerto Ricans are highest, followed by blacks, with British West Indians and whites having the lowest contiguity rates with family members or friends who use heroin.

Discussion

In this report we have directed attention to the significance of migrant-native status, and particularly the role of the native-born offspring of migrants, in the incidence of reported family and friends' use of heroin. The information was gathered in an urban ghetto community that, like most such neighborhoods, is characterized by a large influx of persons from outside the community. Some observers have suggested a close association between addiction and the migration of blacks and Puerto Ricans into northern cities. However, the findings reported here sustain the hypothesis that migrants have less contact with drug users than natives. Research by Vaillant and by Ball and Bates, previously cited, supports this contention. We find essentially the same processes at work in all the ethnic groups so that the significance of the disjunction between migrant and native-born residents, even if it does not altogether account for some of the rate differences between ethnic groups, would appear to be germane to the comprehension of heroin use.

We suggest that the processes we have identified are antecedent to the more specifically social-psychological processes that finally result in a particular individual's experimenting with drugs. The necessity for contact with drug users and the mechanisms of persuasion that are entailed are clearly the end of the process. However, contagion and peer-group explanations cannot account for the fact that heroin use is not a random process: Rates are high for some groups and negligible for others. Nor can reliance on social-psychological models suggest why, where drug use rates are high, all those in potential contact, the majority of the residents in communities, do not experiment with heroin. Thus, an adequate explanation of heroin use must seek out significant sociological factors that are systematically related to rate differences across groups.

Two indicators, Attitudes Toward Child-rearing Orientation and Racial Identification, highlight the importance of the disjunction between native-born and their migrant parents as vital to a comprehension of the social background that precedes contiguity with heroin users. Only then, we suggest, are peer-group processes operative, with those who deviate most from the migrant generation the likeliest targets for recruitment into heroin use. Where native-born still share the views of the migrant generation in the way they identify themselves, or in the arena of attitudes toward child control, we find a significant attenuation in the rates of contiguity with heroin users; where attitudinal changes are observed among the native-born, it is then that the highest rates occur.

A full explanation of why different rates are observed for drug use identifies social processes that transcend the particulars of a group's experiences. While the same processes operate in the same way for each ethnic group, it must also be noted, at least with the kinds of information examined here, that there remain comparative differences that are remarkably stable no matter what sets of variables are introduced. The unique social and cultural systems of each group and differences in primary group structures, most notably the family, would have to be assessed for the particularistic contributions to the phenomenon of heroin use to also finally account for *variations* in rates that are unaccounted for by the process we have identified.

If the community we have studied is unexceptional in significant ways from others where heroin use is widespread, and the findings reviewed at the beginning of this chapter would suggest this is indeed the case, efforts to link heroin use as a response to poverty and to migrants who are unprepared for the rigors of urban environments are inconsistent with the data we have presented. The communities are indeed poverty areas, and there are, in most such communities, many migrants. The fallacy is to connect some typical or modal community pattern with the behavior of specific individuals, the ecological fallacy described earlier.

Others attempt to explain heroin use as a response to status devaluation, to the "slings and arrows" of a racist society, but it is not the most disadvantaged that contribute disproportionately to the addict population. We observe the same patterns in all ethnic groups: Black West Indians are close to the behavior of whites, and even among whites the same factors emerge as important. Nor would it be a simple matter to posit a "double-failure" theory for the reasons cited earlier, and also because we would have to assume, contrary to what has been observed, that there would be persistent class differences irrespective of the migrant-native status of respondents. This is difficult to reconcile with the data reported here and reviewed earlier.

The analysis we have presented directs attention to the significance of the disjunction between the generations as a prelude to the probability of contiguity with drug users. We identified some accompaniments of this process; however, we did not, because of reliance on cross-sectional data obtained on households, provide the direct linkage between migrant parents and native-born offspring. Our findings, however, strongly suggest that the decline in family legitimacy facilitates the intrusion of other socializing agencies (mainly peer groups with divergent cultural content from the parents). Kingsley Davis has pointed out that "parent and child, in a variety of ways, find themselves enmeshed in different social contexts and possessed of different outlooks."[46] In this community, and in this era, this often means, for many, heroin use.

ACKNOWLEDGMENTS

The research on which this chapter is based was supported by Grant Numbers NI-71-046-G,NI-72-008-G, and 73-NI-99-0022-G from the United States Department of Justice, Law Enforcement Assistance Administration, to the Addiction Research and Treatment Corporation Evaluation Team through the Vera Institute of Justice and from the Addiction Research and Treatment Corporation. We gratefully acknowledge their support. The research was carried out at the Research and Demonstration Center, Columbia University School of Social Work.

The authors are also grateful for the help provided by the following individuals in the preparation of this report: Ann Scovell Gordon, who rendered valuable assistance in various aspects of this research; Takis Arsenis, who did the programming; Carol Lukoff, who coded the open-ended items; Carol LeBron and Cassandra Blunt who typed the several drafts; and Christina Cassara, who prepared the charts. The authors are indebted to Dr. David Brook and Judith Lukoff for their critical reading of this paper and for their insightful comments. We are also extremely grateful for the continual support given to us in every phase of our research effort by Beny J. Primm, M.D.

REFERENCES

1. **Ball, J. C. and Chambers, C. D.,** Overview of the problem; Terry, C. E. and Pellens, M., The extent of chronic opiate use in the United States prior to 1921, in *The Epidemiology of Opiate Addiction in the United States,* Ball, J. C. and Chambers, C. D., Eds., Charles C Thomas, Springfield, Ill., 1970, 1, 3.
2. **Ball, J. C. and Bates, W. M.,** Nativity, parentage and mobility of opiate addicts, in *The Epidemiology of Opiate Addiction in the United States,* Ball, J. C. and Chambers, C. D., Eds., Charles C Thomas, Springfield, Ill., 1970, 6.
3. **Lukoff, I. F., Quatrone, D., and Sardell, A.,** Some Aspects of the Epidemiology of Heroin Use in a Ghetto Community: A Preliminary Report, Law Enforcement Assistance Administration, U.S. Department of Justice, 1972.
4. **Lindesmith, A. R.,** Basic problems in the social psychology of addiction and a theory, in *Narcotics Addiction,* O'Donnell, J. A. and Ball, J. C., Eds., Harper & Row, New York, 1966.
5. **Goode, E.,** *The Marijuana Smokers,* Basic, New York, 1970.
6. **Becker, H. S.,** *Outsiders: Studies in the Sociology of Deviance,* Free Press, Glencoe, New York, 1963.
7. **Lindesmith, A. R.,** in *Narcotics Addiction,* O'Donnell, J. A. and Ball, J. C., Eds., Harper & Row, New York, 1966, 107.
8. **Chein, I., Gerard, D. L., Lee, R., and Rosenfeld, E.,** *The Road to H,* Basic, New York, 1964.
9. **Wald, P. M. and Hutt, P. B.,** The drug abuse survey project: summary of findings, conclusions and recommendations, in *Dealing with Drug Abuse: A Report to the Ford Foundation,* Praeger, New York, 1972, 4.

10. Robinson, W. S., Ecological correlations and the behavior of individuals, *Am. Sociol. Rev.*, XV, 351, 1950.
11. Ball, J. C. and Chambers, C. D., Eds., in *The Epidemiology of Opiate Addiction in the United States*, Charles C Thomas, Springfield, Ill., 1970, 11.
12. Abrams, A., Gagnon, J. H., and Levine, J. J., Psychosocial aspects of drug addiction, *Am. J. Public Health*, 58, 2142, 1968.
13. Chambers, C. D., An Assessment of Drug Use in the General Population, Special Report No. 1, New York State Narcotics Addiction Control Commission, May 1971.
14. Robins, L. N. and Murphy, G. E., Drug use in a normal population of young negro men, *Am. J. Public Health*, 57, 1580, 1967.
15. Lukoff, I. F., Quatrone, D., and Sardell, A., Some Aspects of the Epidemiology of Heroin Use in a Ghetto Community: A Preliminary Report, Law Enforcement Assistance Administration, U.S. Department of Justice, 1972.
16. Vaillant, G. E., Parent-child cultural disparity and drug addiction, *J. Nervous Mental Dis.*, 142(6), 534, 1966.
17. Merton, R. K., Social structure and anomie, in *Social Theory and Social Structure*, Merton, R. K., Free Press, New York, 1957, 131.
18. Cloward, R. and Ohlin, L., *Delinquency and Opportunity: A Theory of Delinquent Gangs*, Free Press, New York, 1960.
19. Whyte, W., *Street Corner Society*, University of Chicago Press, Chicago, 1943.
20. Lerman, P., Argot, symbolic deviance and subcultural delinquency, *Am. Sociol. Rev.*, 32(2), 209, 1967.
21. Preble, E. and Casey, J. J., Jr., Taking care of business: the heroin user's life on the street, *Int. J. Addict.*, 4, 1, 1969.
22. Finestone, H., Cats, kicks and color, *Social Probl.*, 5(1), 3, 1957.
23. Frazier, E. F., *The Negro Family in the United States*, University of Chicago Press, Chicago, 1939, 223.
24. Vaillant, G. E., *J. Nervous Mental Dis.*, 142(6), 534, 1966.
25. Ball, J. C. and Chambers, C. D., Eds., in *The Epidemiology of Opiate Addiction in the United States*, Charles C Thomas, Springfield, Ill., 1970.
26. Abrams, A., Gagnon, J. H., and Levine, J. J., *Am. J. Public Health*, 58, 2142, 1968.
27. Kandel, D., Interpersonal Influences on Adolescent Drug Use, paper presented at Conference on Epidemiology of Drug Use, Puerto Rico, February 1973.
28. Lowenthal, D., Race and color in the West Indies, *Daedelus*, 96(2), 580, 1967.
29. Lowenthal, D., *West Indian Societies*, Oxford University Press, New York, 1972.
30. Rubin, V., Ed., *Caribbean Studies: A Symposium*, University College of the West Indies, 1957.
31. Reid, Ira de A., *The Negro Immigrant: His Background, Characteristics and Social Adjustment, 1899–1937*, AMS Publishers, New York, 1939.
32. Bronfenbrenner, U., Socialization and social class through time and space, in *Readings in Social Psychology*, Maccoby, E. E., Newcomb, L. M., and Hartley, E. L., Eds., Holt, New York, 1958, 400.
33. Bernstein, B., *Class, Codes and Control: Theoretical Studies Towards a Sociology of Language*, Vol. I, Paladin, 1973, 33.
34. Hess, R. D. and Shipman, V., Early experience and the socialization of cognitive modes in children, *Child Dev.*, 34, 869, 1965.
35. Hess, R. D. and Shipman, V., Cognitive elements in maternal behavior, in *Minnesota Symposium in Child Psychology*, Vol. I, Hill, J. P., Ed., University of Minnesota Press, Minnesota, 1967.
36. Hess, R. D. and Shipman, V., Maternal influences upon early learning: the cognitive environments of urban pre-school children, in *Early Education*, Hess, R. D. and Bear, R. M., Eds., Aldine, Chicago, 1968.
37. Shipman, V. and Hess, R. D., Early experience in the socialization of cognitive modes in children: a study of urban negro families, paper presented at Fifth Annual Conference of the Family and Society at Merrill-Palmer Institute, April 1966.
38. Glueck, S. and Glueck, E., *Family Environment and Delinquency*, Houghton Mifflin, Boston, 1962.
39. Healy, W. and Bronner, A., *New Light on Delinquency and Its Treatment*, Yale University Press, New Haven, 1936.
40. Jessor, S. L. and Jessor, R., Maternal ideology and problem behavior, *Dev. Psychol.*, 10, 246, 1974.
41. Robins, L. N. and Murphy, G. E., *Am. J. Public Health*, 57, 1580, 1967.
42. Robins, L. N., *A Follow-up Study of Vietnam Drug Users*, Special Action Office monograph, Interim Final Report, Series A1, April 1973.
43. Ball, J. C. and Chambers, C. D., Eds., in *The Epidemiology of Opiate Addiction in the United States*, Charles C Thomas, Springfield, Ill., 1970.
44. de Alarcon, R., The spread of heroin use in the community, *Bull Narcotics*, 21(3), 17, 1969.
45. Lukoff, I. F., Quatrone, D., and Sardell, A., Some Aspects of the Epidemiology of Heroin Use in a Getto Community: A Preliminary Report, Law Enforcement Assistance Administration, U.S. Department of Justice, 1972, 48.
46. Siegel, S., *Non-parametric Statistics for the Behavioral Sciences*, McGraw-Hill, New York, 1956, 68.
47. Davis, K., The sociology of parent-youth conflict, in *The Family: Its Structure and Functions*, Coser, R. L., Ed., St. Martin's Press, New York, 1964, 463.

EDUCATION AND MASS COMMUNICATIONS

SOCIOLOGY OF DRUG EDUCATION

Alan S. Meyer

TABLE OF CONTENTS

INTRODUCTION

For some 40 years, sociologists have been concerned with sociological aspects of the causes and consequences of drug abuse and with the sociology of deviant drug behavior and treatment. Because of the newness of the field, however, only a few have raised sociological questions about drug education. Yet many such issues have implications for both educational practice and sociological theory.

This brief overview of drug education in the United States from a sociological perspective focuses on three aspects of this expanding field: (1) sociocultural contexts and settings in which drug education takes place, (2) organization, goals, and roles in school drug education programs, and

(3) consequences of school drug programs. These are followed by a summary.

SOCIOCULTURAL CONTEXTS AND SETTINGS

Drug education does not take place in a vacuum. It is shaped by strong sociocultural constraints and deeply imbedded community conditions, and it takes place in a variety of formal and informal social settings. Some of these sociocultural factors themselves constitute informal but powerful processes of community drug education.

Consequently, formal efforts at drug education, which have expanded rapidly in recent years in elementary and secondary schools across the nation, constitute for the sociologist only the "tip of the iceberg" of the drug education field. An understanding of why formal education programs have emerged as they have and why discernible success has been so difficult, if not impossible, to achieve requires a systematic consideration of the major contextual factors which have influenced the organization and outcome of these efforts.

Traditional Values and Goals for Education

Despite the periodic emergence of new values and innovative goals for society's formal efforts to educate its young, traditional values and goals tend to persist and predominate. While community conflict over educational issues is widening, the primary goal of education still appears to be the socialization of students into those youthful and adult roles which dominant groups believe will insure the stability and survival of society as it is known. This traditional goal is one of social control. Continuity and conformity are central values.

However, since the requirements for successful individual and group adaptation change in response to changing social conditions, schools must also educate in the broad sense of teaching independent and critical thinking and the ability to respond nontraditionally to new circumstances. Such skills become crucial in times of rapid social and cultural change. The goal of this type of education is one of creative social change. Highly valued are rationality and innovation. Because it is "subversive" of traditional concerns with conserving the social order, this form of critical education

has been described as antagonistic to the school's socializing function.[1]

These conflicting educational goals reflect different ways of defining education. As a leading drug educator asks:

Is education training? Is it indoctrination? Is it a "snow job" to get across a certain point of view? Or is it simply the search for truth?[2]

There is at least as much disagreement about what drug education is as there is about education in general.

"Modern" drug education, however it may be defined, has been added to the schools' responsibilities during the very period that schools have been under increasing attack for failures in both traditional socialization and in education for critical thinking. This new field has developed in the midst of powerful pressures to teach and enforce traditional norms which proscribe the use of certain drugs.

Drug educators, however, have also been exposed to nontraditional pressures. In response to the attacks on traditional education, some educators and community groups are working to reform or modernize the schools by experiments in greater community control and increased student involvement in policy decisions and by innovations in school and classroom structures and techniques. Some of these changes are being fostered by drug educators. Whether they turn out to have a significant impact on education is a question for future research.

Drug Misconceptions and Misuse of Language

A second sociocultural context in which drug education programs must now operate in this country consists of profound misconceptions and pervasive misuse of language about drugs. A basic example is the political perversion of the term "drug" itself. A reasonably scientific definition, in which "drugs" denotes all chemical substances other than food and water which affect the living organism, has apparently never been learned or has been rejected by most legislators, journalists, teachers, parents, and young people.

To the detriment of clear and unbiased communication, "drugs" has generally come to refer only to illegal chemical substances. This is true in spite of the increasing lip service given to the truism that legal drugs are drugs, too. One commonly hears, even from drug educators, the misleading phrase, "alcohol, tobacco, and drugs," but rarely the correct formulation, "alcohol, tobacco, and *other* drugs." The perversion is political because the overly narrow definition of drugs was arbitrarily established by groups with the power to maintain the criminalization of unpopular drug use while protecting the use of the popular drugs of tobacco and alcohol as if they were nondrugs. The perversion is vitally relevant to drug education because it reflects a fundamental misconception which renders all but impossible a comprehensive and realistic consideration of all drug facts.

The term "narcotic" has also lost its pharmacological meaning and has become a political weapon for punishing users of marihuana and other non-narcotic drugs. One sociologist calls the term a "discrediting label" for drugs whose use is supposed to be "bad."[3] As recently as 1973, the Supreme Court of Alabama ruled that marihuana was a "hard narcotic."[4] Legal misclassifications of drugs have become the basis for commonly accepted drug myths.

Similarly, "drug abuse" is generally misused to refer to any illegal drug use and only occasionally to abuse of legal drugs. "Drug abuse," according to Goode, provides an aura of medical objectivity to those who use the term to discredit the phenomenon it arbitrarily categorizes. He concludes:

The term so structures our perceptions of the phenomenon that it is possible to see only "abusive" aspects in it .... In such ways do science and medicine become the handmaidens of morality and politics.[5]

Also, the terms "hard" and "soft" drugs are consistently used without specifying the criteria for distinguishing between them. Legal drugs, regardless of their possible hazards, are almost always omitted from the "hard" drug category.

Other deceptive terms such as "drug-free" programs provide further examples of ideologically motivated ideas based on fundamental misconceptions as to what a drug is. Only by ignoring the crucial fact that tobacco, caffeine, alcohol, and medicines are drugs can treatment staff, clients, and others use the attractive but misleading phrase, "drug-free," instead of "opiate-free" or "free from illegal drugs." The fact that such language is rarely challenged indicates how widespread and ingrained is the acceptance of this basic cultural misperception.

The constant repetition of such misconceptions and misclassifications of drugs in the daily language of professionals and public alike presents a major obstacle to effective drug education.[6] Narrow and conflicting conceptions have also been cited as major impediments to effective prevention and control of alcohol problems.[7]

Ambivalent Attitudes Towards Drugs and Drug Users

Drug education programs must work within a community climate of ambivalent and inconsistent attitudes towards drugs. On the one hand, "drug" use is opposed by many because it is seen as hazardous to health, while on the other hand, use of legal drugs such as tobacco and alcohol which can be more hazardous than some illegal drugs is often accepted and sometimes encouraged.[8]

As long as community opposition to use of certain drugs is based more on their illegal status than on their danger to the body, then preventive efforts will prove inconsistent at best or dishonest at worst whenever "facts" about drug effects are cited as reasons to abstain.

Communities are also ambivalent in their attitudes towards the users of illegal drugs. While some believe that such users are "sick" or disturbed or maladjusted, others feel that illegal drug users are "criminals." Still others believe that the use of any drug should be purely a personal decision and that users should not be seen as either sick or criminal.

It is accurate to say that the country's ambivalence as to whether opiate addiction should be perceived as a crime or a disease (or something else) has not yet been resolved. This ambivalence, which applies to use of other unpopular drugs as well, is apparent in our laws and in our attitudes and, consequently, in our educational efforts. Even the view that alcoholism is a disease – a policy-oriented diagnosis which is becoming generally accepted as a result of an intensive educational campaign by concerned private and public organizations – has recently been questioned as the most appropriate model for defining all alcoholic subpopulations. Cigarette smoking, moreover, is beginning to be referred to as an addiction, and more smokers seem likely to refer to themselves, sometimes half jokingly, as "addicts."

In view of these differences in how users of a given drug are perceived by the public, it would be instructive to find out to what extent drug educators, parents, and children agree or disagree in the way they "diagnose" users of specific drugs.

Mixed Models of Intervention: Criminalization, Medical Care, Regulation, or Education?

Different ways of diagnosing the nature of drug problems lead to different models of intervention and control. Popular views on marihuana provide an illuminating and timely example of public confusion and contradiction over appropriate diagnoses and relevant methods of treatment and prevention. Attitudes towards marihuana users are currently in a state of transition. Recent data from the National Commission on Marihuana and Drug Abuse reflect changing and inconsistent ideas about how to control marihuana use.

There is some evidence that attitudes appear to be gradually moving towards the view that personal use of this drug should be treated as a medical problem and should no longer be treated as a crime. Such a trend is suggested by the relationship of such factors as age and education to responses to a Marihuana Commission questionnaire. Groups reported to be most receptive to a predominantly medical approach rather than a mostly police or legal approach for handling the possession of marihuana are those with at least some college, women, those in the Northeast and North Central states, and young persons between 12 and 25.[9]

About half of the adults (i.e., age 18 and over) and half of the young people favored the medical model, while another 11% of each group didn't think marihuana use was worth worrying about. Only 37% of adults and 20% of youth favored the predominantly police approach of arrest, conviction, and punishment.[10]

Substantial ambivalence is suggested, however, by the contradictory finding that 72% of the above adults also favored stricter marihuana laws.[11] In other words, a sizable proportion of adults queried believed both that there should be a better way than a police approach to handling marihuana users *and* that the existing criminal penalties should be made stricter.

Those most receptive to making marihuana laws stricter were those age 50 and older, those with an 8th-grade education or less, those who live in the South, those who are less approving of youthful life-styles, and those who favor less freedom of expression generally.[12]

The model of control next most favored by adults, after stricter laws, was that of close regulation in which quality-controlled marihuana would be sold in government licensed stores. This legalization model was acceptable to about a third of all adults and to just over half of young adults, 18 to 25.[13] However, in spite of organized educational efforts to legalize marihuana and recommendations by prestigious bodies such as the Marihuana Commission itself for decriminalizing the drug, much opposition to reform of the marihuana laws remains.

In view of the wide differences between the generations in choice of intervention models for marihuana, it would be important to know how drug educators feel about the marihuana laws and what, if anything, they convey to their students about their feelings. This may be an area where students can have more of an educational impact on their teachers than vice versa.

Public and professional attitudes towards drug users and how they should be handled are contextual variables essential to a sociological understanding of drug education in at least two ways. First, these attitudes can either coincide with and buttress existing drug laws or conflict with these laws and drain them of popular support. As public approval of marihuana laws wanes and their enforcement becomes less popular, more youths are likely to lose respect for drug laws and become even more suspicious of drug educators who attempt to justify current legal distinctions.

Secondly, community attitudes towards drug users and their handling relate quite directly to drug education through the popular belief that punishment of drug users will prevent unwanted drug behavior by others. As many as 60% of the adults surveyed by the Marihuana Commission agreed that the laws against marihuana should provide stiffer penalties than they do now "because that would discourage people from using it."[14] The hypothesis that the threat of punishment deters crime, even when the crime is as pervasive as marihuana use, still has strong support among an ambivalent public.

Thus, the criminalization model is supported, in part, because of its alleged educational value in preventing illegal drug use. At the same time, the Commission reported that formal educational efforts in the school were supported as the most appropriate sources from which youth should get facts and opinions about marihuana. Both adults and youths were more likely to cite school drug booklets and programs than they were to cite any other person, experience, or setting as a proper source for such information.[15]

Another study, however, showed that while a quarter of the young people in six communities credited schools with providing most of their information about drugs (second only to friends as a primary source), only 10% said they would contact drug education programs for further drug information.[16]

While growing public support for drug education in the schools has become an important factor which legislators and school officials need to take into account, there is recurrent support among some school and community groups for keeping drug education out of the elementary grades, if not out of the schools entirely. This version of "benign neglect" holds that teachers should avoid exposing young children to drug facts because of the possibility that drug-oriented instruction may stimulate curiosity about drugs and early experimentation where neither existed before.

These mixed feelings about the value of various educational models for intervening in drug problems raise important questions for research: What is the relative accuracy and attractiveness of facts learned from drug programs and of those learned from peers and from personal experience? Under what conditions does drug information and education contribute to greater drug abuse, and under what conditions does it reduce such abuse? Finally, how have the cultural constraints of ambivalent community attitudes and punitive drug laws limited the kinds of drug information and educational strategies which have emerged?

Punitive Laws and Official Misinformation

Our drug laws are less ambivalent than our drug attitudes. They are predominantly punitive. Possession of disfavored drugs, even for personal use, is defined by our society as a crime to be punished, sometimes severely. This process of criminalizing the "deviant" use of drugs, an example of what some criminologists call "over-criminalization,"[17] appears to be a fundamental factor in determining the nature and effectiveness of drug education.

The history of how punitive public policies relating to opiates and cocaine were established by the U.S. Treasury Department despite a key contrary ruling by the Supreme Court in 1925 has

been well documented.[18] One product of this history appears to be the development of a close interdependence between a law enforcement approach to drug control and the dissemination of myths and misinformation about drugs and drug users.

A long-time analyst of drug problems described the relationship and its implications as follows:

Perhaps the most serious consequence of the punitive approach . . . is that deriving from the educational impact of such laws and their enforcement or non-enforcement. On the one hand, laws that are based on false conceptions of the dangers of drugs mislead members of the general public who have no first-hand knowledge of drug effects. In order to justify passage of such laws, distorted pictures of the drug user are created . . . . On the other hand, young persons who are aware of the falsity of some of the "evidence" cited as reasons for harsh penalties may be led to discount the very real dangers inherent in much drug use. Not only is respect for the law undermined, but valid information is rendered suspect.[19]

Another student of deviance has described how the Federal Bureau of Narcotics, acting to initiate new "morals legislation," managed an educational campaign to criminalize marihuana use, which included dissemination of misleading information to the mass media.[20] The Marihuana Tax Act was subsequently passed in 1937 "on the ground that marihuana was a highly dangerous drug inciting its users to commit crimes of violence and often leading to insanity."[21]

Since the criminalization of opiates and marihuana, misinformation about these and other illegal drugs has been widely dispensed by government agencies, private groups, mass media, and, more recently, by the schools. Common examples, among many, are the false claims that "heroin hurts the brain" and that "marihuana generally leads to heroin use."

More drug educators are becoming careful, however, to deny such myths, and the latest government materials on drugs are somewhat less biased. Nevertheless, it is likely that most drug-oriented materials and discussions continue in one way or another to be misleading and distorted. A recent study, for example, concluded that only 16 of 220 drug abuse audiovisuals available to school and community groups were scientifically and conceptually acceptable.[22]

Since a great deal of scientific information about drugs is available, how can we account sociologically for the pervasiveness of drug misinformation? In the quotation above, the writer concludes that false stereotypes of users of disapproved drugs were created to justify the passage of ill-founded laws which define the use of these drugs as a crime. Let's examine the social bases of these and other myths more closely.

In the case of opiates and marihuana, as distinct from alcohol, the prohibition of which was engineered primarily by private temperance organizations, the groups which appear to have been most active in seeking a ban on the use of these currently illegal drugs were government units responsible for enforcing tax laws. Thus, each time such a law was passed, the U.S. Treasury Department expanded its enforcement responsibilities and personnel. Its efforts as a "moral entrepreneur," in Becker's words, included serving both as a "rule creator" and a "rule enforcer."[23] It is probable that when the same individuals or groups act both as crusaders for and enforcers of morals laws, there is maximal occupational investment in protecting these laws against any moves to limit their scope or duration.

The more these laws are based on false ideas of drug dangers, the greater will be the need to employ misinformation and emotionality in appealing for obedience to the laws and in hiding their fallacious basis. In other words, myths can serve to detract attention from the inconsistencies of current punitive drug laws which, if clearly understood, would create pressures for drug law reform.

A second factor which may help to account for the emergence of drug myths and distortions in a society characterized by punitive drug laws is the fact that punitive laws are themselves based on threat as an educational strategy to control behavior. It is therefore at least not inconsistent for such a society to shift from threatening citizens with arrest and incarceration for using certain drugs to threatening students with untrue horror stories and using other scare tactics.

The introduction into the classroom of this philosophy of teaching by threat was made especially easy by the frequent selection of local law enforcement officials as early drug educators. While lip service is currently given to the slogan "scare tactics don't work," such tactics, which inevitably involve distorting the truth, tend to persist alongside laws which threaten to punish.

A third explanation of the relationship between harsh laws and misstatements of facts about drugs posits a need on the part of some drug educators to compensate for the inadvertent glamorization of those drugs which harsh laws make into "forbidden fruits." To counteract the increased attractiveness of such drugs, some educators may well exaggerate their dangers in an emotional and inconsistent fashion. Many teachers and parents might do this without any conscious realization that they are manipulating the facts in an effort to destroy the fascination that illegal drugs hold for many young people. Ironically, by overemphasizing their dangers, these authorities may have increased even more the lure of many of these drugs.[24]

Drug-oriented Cultural Themes

As if these constraints and pressures were not sufficient to discourage drug educators, there remains the difficult task of teaching about drugs to students who are daily exposed to cultural themes which encourage dependence on external sources of relief and pleasure.

The mass media bombard the public with positive evaluations of material things and urge consumers to buy more goods in a never ending pursuit of material happiness. "Try it, you'll like it," the phrase which recently found so much receptivity, seems to symbolize the successful selling of hedonistic values. If the consumer ingests too much, as he is so often urged to do, and in his suffering moans, "I can't believe I ate the whole thing," he is reminded that "relief is just a swallow away." Oral indulgence and oral self-medication become complementary aspects of a cultural emphasis on repeated oral gratification.

Advertisements for medicines, over-the-counter drugs, and recreational drugs all contribute to the maintenance of a "drug-oriented" culture. In collaboration with parts of the pharmaceutical industry, the tobacco industry, and to some extent the medical profession, the mass media appear to encourage the overuse of drugs as an instant solution to everyday discomforts.[25]

A special kind of mass media behavior warrants particular attention in this regard. That is the contradictory way in which newspapers, magazines, and television include feature stories and public service advertisements against "drug abuse" while accepting commercial ads for cigarettes or cigars.

Research is needed to test the hypothesis that many young people's rejection of drug education is conditioned, to a degree more significant than is realized, by the clear cultural message that dependency on nicotine is too widespread and profits are too substantial for the nation to take its own warnings about tobacco seriously enough to deal with it as a major form of drug abuse.[26] If cigarette smoking with its attendant risks can be rejected as an obvious example of drug abuse by adults who like its effects, many young people must ask themselves why the use of illegal drugs, with their variable risks, should not be similarly legitimized for those who find their effects pleasurable.

The cultural messages conveyed by the media thus perpetuate misconceptions about what is a drug and what is drug abuse. Systematic misuse of drug language and distortion of information, inspired by a traditional, punitive ideology which is unresponsive to changing knowledge and attitudes, breed disrespect for drug education.

Alienation, Deviant Subcultures, and Professional Polarization

Three other conditions which characterize the community-at-large appear to create special problems for those who try to educate about drugs. These are (1) the relatively large numbers of alienated youths in and out of school, (2) "criminal addict" subgroups with their own subculture, and (3) continuing struggle for control of public policy between advocates of a traditional law enforcement approach to drug abuse treatment and prevention and advocates of alternative approaches to achieving these goals.

The growing alienation of youth in affluent industrial America has been described as taking the form of a "youth culture" which rejects the culture of the adult world through rebellion or indifference but does not offer positive visions of viable alternatives.[27] Setbacks to civil rights, assassinations of moral and political leaders, and the failure of recent efforts to use the techniques of participatory democracy to stop wars and bombing and to change directions in social policy have likely contributed further to the sense of estrangement. The gross abuses of political power revealed by the Watergate investigations have increased suspicion of authority.

Alongside and merging at points with the alienated youth cultures of the 1950s, '60s, and '70s has been a "criminal addict" subculture. This protective culture emerged earlier among opiate addicts as a form of what has been called "secondary deviation"[28] in reaction to the problems created by the new public policy which began in the 1920s to define the nonmedical use of opiates as criminal behavior.

A major link between youth alienated from the dominant culture and the deviant "criminal addict" subculture of heroin addicts and other illegal drug users was provided by the federal act in 1937 which criminalized marihuana use. Alienated young people, along with those not so alienated, who later began to smoke marihuana in increasing numbers, inevitably came into contact with sellers and users of other illegal drugs and with their subcultural rationales for continued and varied drug use.

The attractiveness of illegal drug use to numerous youths in various stages of alienation or experimentation with life-styles has apparently been enhanced by the criminal status of marihuana use in combination with the availability of an antiestablishment "criminal addict" culture which helps users adapt to society's punitive reactions. Drug educators are therefore faced with powerful peer pressures and deviant subcultural support for illegal drug use as well as with the dominant culture's support for use of hazardous legal drugs.

A third condition making the task of drug education more difficult is the continued conflict between the supporters of the current criminalization approach and the supporters of a medical or decriminalization approach to treatment and prevention.[29] Although the polarization is sometimes subtle and frequently moderated by the varieties of positions and philosophies among supporters in both camps, the emotional tensions generated by those who espouse conflicting ideologies has spilled over from the treatment field into the field of drug education.

When drug educators themselves, along with other community leaders, argue about basic assumptions, approaches, and goals, students will continue to receive conflicting messages and be likely to look elsewhere for leadership. On the other hand, teachers who refuse to take a position or avoid discussing controversial drug issues may lose credibility with students and may be abdicating an important part of their responsibility as drug educators.

Social Settings for Drug Education

An educator has recently said that "our greatest

myth is the association of education with schooling."[30] Drug education, like education generally, takes place in all types of formal and informal social settings. Drug educators, in the broadest sense, include parents, teachers, siblings, friends, physicians, politicians, police, advertisers, and all others who by word or deed convey attitudes, values, or information about drugs.

Formal drug educators appreciate the primary role of the family in shaping drug behavior. Blum, for example, concludes from his studies that families, not schools, determine children's predispositions regarding drug use.[31] The vital effect of other institutions and relationships on the use of specific drugs has also been cited. Two observers of school alcohol education note that while these programs can help, the home, the church, and peer group influences will be more important.[32] The influences on alcohol use of ethnic attitudes and religious and dietary customs as transmitted by family, church, and neighborhood have been well documented.[33]

Also, it has been shown that the cigarette smoking behavior of parents and older siblings bears a strong relationship to teenage smoking.[34] It is clear that family members often serve as significant role models, with regard to drug use generally, educating by their actions at least as effectively as by their words.

Other educational settings are more impersonal and include exposures to messages from the mass media and to those conveyed by public policy. Laws criminalizing the use of certain drugs, for example, can be said to teach that those drugs are so "bad," dangerous, powerful, and perhaps so pleasurable that users must be punished and nonusers scared away. Conversely, these laws implicitly convey the misleading message that recreational drugs which are legal are therefore "good" and less dangerous than illegal ones. Other ways in which punitive laws tend to miseducate have been suggested above.

So far, this chapter has detailed some of the conditions conducive to misunderstanding and misusing drugs which drug education in the schools is expected to counteract. Let's turn now to consider how school-based programs are organized.

ORGANIZATION, GOALS, AND ROLES IN SCHOOL DRUG PROGRAMS

Sponsoring and Financing School Drug Education

States have the responsibility for education in this country. While almost all states require some alcohol instruction in the schools, only about half require general drug education programs, and only about a third have developed drug-education curricula for their school districts.[35] Much latitude is given to local districts, therefore, as to the kind of program they offer, if any.[36] Funding of most such programs appears to be primarily the responsibility of state and local governments. Nearly all the states, however, report receiving federal funds from the expanding national budgets for drug education and training.[37]

Government financing of drug education has important implications: It is likely to insure that, in general, "approved" teachers teach about certain drugs in "acceptable" fashion to "appropriate" target groups to achieve noncontroversial goals. These implications are examined further in the following sections.

Selection and Training of Teachers

In recent years, school officials have responded in several different ways to community pressures for school instruction in drugs. Many turned first to law enforcement personnel and later to ex-addicts to exhort against use of illegal drugs. Police and ex-addict teachers, having been "trained" in a "cops and robbers" approach to drug behavior, have tended to use scare techniques and to exaggerate the dangers of illicit drug use, from heroin to marihuana.

Perhaps to offset this one-sided nonmedical approach, schools have also assigned drug education to health teachers and brought in pharmacists and physicians as lecturers. Biology teachers and especially general classroom teachers are being given responsibility for presenting drug information in the context of normal classroom discussion. In many schools, particularly in and around large urban centers, drug education has been assigned to teachers or counselors selected specifically for this task.

In-service training of teachers in drug education exists in a rudimentary stage in every state, but few classroom teachers have as yet received formal training.[38] Teachers with special responsibility for drugs are more likely to have received such training, often financed with state or federal funds.[39] In some programs, they include "paraprofessionals" and ex-addicts recruited from outside the schools. At the elementary school level, drug specialists appear more likely than classroom teachers to be male.

The introduction of staff personnel from lower socioeconomic strata may provide some students from low-income neighborhoods with important role models with whom they can identify more easily. It is also reasonable to expect that, all other things being equal, a teacher whose socioeconomic status background is similar to that of his or her students would have an easier time developing with them the kind of rapport which is conducive to learning.

Research is needed to find out to what extent the socioeconomic class background as well as the sex of drug educators affects their performance in the above respects with students of similar and different class and sex backgrounds. The implications of such findings would be important for education generally.

Selection and Recruitment of Target Groups

Scarce resources in both money and personnel for special drug education programs have helped to force consideration of which target groups should receive priority. According to one educator, "drug-prone" adolescents should constitute the primary target of drug "intervention," even though childhood is acknowledged as a critical formative period.[40] Alternative targets include all students, preschool children, parents, teachers, professionals who work with young people, drug-prone adults, all adults, the general public, and the mass media. Legislators and other politicians sometimes become informal targets of educational efforts to gain support for programs or policies.

Three major sociological issues concerning targets in the schools remain to be resolved. One such issue is what are the particular drug education needs of target groups which differ by age, socioeconomic class, rural-urban residence, and race and ethnic background? Despite agreement that programs should be fitted to the characteristics of the target group, there is disagreement on the nature of programs for specific groups and on the age at which such programs should begin. While some educators are calling for an earlier start for drug programs, a few states have held that drug education should not begin before the fourth or fifth grade.[41] As for matching programs to populations, a variety of curriculum guides differentiated by grade levels have been developed but have received little evaluation. Efforts to develop audio-visual materials for minority group youth, one of the few approaches to a specific target group to be evaluated, have been described as biased and objectionable.[42]

A second issue has to do with the effect of singling out for drug education or counseling students who are illegal drug users or those who are considered "drug-prone." The question of whether such "labeling" may be premature, punitive, and help push a youth towards a deviant career deserves serious study. In some cases, such involuntary "tracking" of students on the basis of drug behavior may reinforce the invidious effects of grouping by intelligence scores or school performance — criteria which are often associated with minority socioeconomic and racial categories.

Third, how effective can drug education of children be if parents are not educated at the same time? The selection of students rather than parents as the primary target for school programs is not only a matter of convenience. It also reinforces the currently accepted misconception that drug abuse is primarily a problem of youth.[43] Even if parents were targeted along with their children, however, could either be effectively reached if molders of mass media products and lawmakers were not simultaneously educated? Raising these questions alerts us to other serious limitations inherent in the role of the schools.

Unclear and Shifting Drug Education Goals

General drug education has as its implicit goal prevention of any illegal drug use.[44] More recently, the more general goal of reducing abuse of all drugs has been explicitly enunciated. In practice, however, prevention programs usually revert to the less controversial goal of stopping all illicit drug use.[45]

Because students frequently reject the double standard inherent in this implicit goal, i.e., "legal drugs are O.K., illegal drugs are no good," and dismiss the educational efforts to achieve it as biased, a more realistic goal has been formulated: Teach young people the knowledge, attitudes, and skills to make informed and responsible decisions about the use of drugs, legal as well as illegal.

As long as their goals relate to use of all drugs, however, conscientious programs will sooner or later run into school or community opposition to their teaching that some illegal drugs could, under some circumstances, be used responsibly or that the use of tobacco or alcohol, in specific ways, constitutes greater abuse than some illegal drug use.

Objective drug information programs of this sort, aimed at fostering critical thinking and independent action, pose a direct threat to our public policy which criminalizes the use of unpopular drugs on moralistic rather than scientific grounds. This circumstance has apparently facilitated a shift towards nondrug-oriented, more "humanistic" goals. The head of a large state drug education effort said, for example, that its primary objective was not to distribute facts but to "enhance the youngster's assessment of himself, increase his humanity and make him a contributing member of his community."[46]

Education of the total human being has been rediscovered and is currently being espoused by proponents of "humanistic" education,[47] "affective" education (i.e., relating to feelings), or "confluent" education which combines affective and intellectual development.[48] Related to these comprehensive views is the concept of "value clarification" in which critical thinking is combined with clarified values to help choose among alternatives.[49]

Other examples of specific humanistic or affective goals which are being advocated by many drug educators, in addition to enhancement of self-concept, community participation, and clarification of values, include increased awareness of one's needs and feelings and the ability to express these effectively, increased sense of responsibility for oneself and others, improved communication skills, problem-solving skills, interpersonal relations skills, and ability to make independent and informed decisions, and increased participation in alternative activities and life-styles which do not involve use of "drugs."[50]

These approaches and their broad educational goals are increasingly being utilized by drug educators to replace the unrealistic goal of preventing drug use and to moderate the controversial goal of preparing young people to make informed decisions about such use. Since these programs are usually funded to combat "the" drug problem, some version of the traditional abstinence goal is usually retained along with the humanistic goal with its implications for educational reform.

Traditionally, alcohol education has been aimed at promoting abstinence in a nation that drinks. In recent years, however, a very specific version of the responsible decision-making goal has gradually emerged in alcohol education, the goal of responsible drinking for those who choose this drug.[51] While the field is still very much divided over the goals of alcohol education, that of responsible drinking is receiving increasing acceptance. In educating about the broad spectrum of drugs, however, only a few persons have begun to state publicly that a primary goal of such general drug education should be to encourage the responsible use or nonuse of all drugs, be they medicinal or recreational.[52]

It is not yet clear whether these shifts in explicit goals and strategies for drug education are more than superficial changes to achieve the traditional goal of social control over youthful deviations from adult drug values. Deitch and Jaffe caution that the transition from "scare em" to "tell it like it is" to "truly open communication with sensitivity training" may be only a series of increasingly open seductions to get students to conform to adult norms for drug behavior.[53]

They question whether the schools and the community are ready to replace the goal of control with that of "real" education. If this were done, the adults, as well as the students involved, would have to be willing to revamp their ideas and interactions as a possible result of open interchange.[54]

Roles in Drug Education: Expectations, Behavior, Role Conflicts, and Role Models

Observers have reported that teachers, students, parents, administrators, and school board members are likely to differ in their expectations as to the proper role of the teacher and of the student as well as in their view of the primary functions of education.[55] Experience in drug education suggests that such differences exist among and within these groups regarding their standards of behavior for drug educators and their students.

Should teachers tell all or just some drug facts? Should they defend or oppose "punitive" drug laws or remain neutral? Should they report illegal drug users to police and/or to parents, or should they protect the confidences of these students? These contradictory expectations reflect current value conflicts among school and community groups. It would be instructive to identify the expectations held by each of the various parties to the educational process as to how drug teachers should act in such matters.

The actual role behavior of individual teachers and students involved in drug education is influenced by the particular nature of these school and community expectations, the nature of the drug program, and the personality, background, and values of the role incumbent. Let us first consider the behavior of teachers. Depending on the program's specific goals and methods, teachers may be expected to fulfill many different role obligations. Some of these responsibilities may contradict others and cause "role conflict" within individual teachers.[56] The actual role behavior of teachers, sometimes worked out in response to such conflicts, is likely to provide students with an adult role model to emulate or reject.

In programs aimed at stopping either all drug use or illegal drug use, teachers tend to act as "moral persuaders" (i.e., "rule supporters") and as "drug information screeners." Where responsible decision-making and humanistic or affective goals are given priority, the actual role behavior of teachers is more likely to include that of "objective fact disseminator," "value clarifier," "group process facilitator," and "learner" (vis-a-vis students as teachers).

In both the preventive and the humanistic program models, drug teachers are likely to play the role first of trainee, then of trainer (of other teachers or of student leaders), of parent educator, and perhaps of curriculum developer. They also may act as counselor, confidant, and small group leader in their interactions with students.

All teachers are expected by some groups in the school and community to act as "rule enforcers" in connection with laws and school policies concerned with drugs. The degree to which they do so depends on how they resolve the role conflicts between this and other expectations.

A teacher's role as rule enforcer may require him or her to report any illegal student drug use to parents, school or health authorities, or police. Such an obligation is likely to be felt as incompatible with the obligation to be a confidant, counselor, or value clarifier. How do most drug educators minimize their role as rule enforcer? What happens when this role expectation is generally rejected by drug teachers? Contrariwise, if teachers enforce all drug laws and rules, how will this affect the achievement of drug program goals?

Which teachers enforce rules with little or no internal conflict and which ones suffer in the process?

Much could be learned by studying reactions to this and other pairs of contradictory expectations for drug educators. Such conflicting role obligations include being both an objective fact disseminator and a moral persuader and being both a member of an association of drug educators and a member of a professional teachers' association.

Another such situation, generally ignored, is the incompatibility, for drug educators, of being a cigarette smoker in school and also being either a moral persuader or a value clarifier.[57] To what extent do teachers who smoke experience this as role conflict and by what process is such a conflict avoided or resolved in favor of continued smoking? Which teachers cut down, conceal, or stop their smoking? Finally, what are the effects on their students of these various teacher smoking patterns?

Actual behavior of young people in their student roles is also influenced by existing expectations and programs and by internal values and motivations. Traditional prevention programs are likely to encourage students to act as "recipients of information" and to be relatively formal, passive, and controlled in the classroom. We would expect students in "humanistic-type" programs, on the other hand, to be relatively informal and spontaneous and more likely than prevention program students to act as critical discussants, creative participants, and active planners in drug education. In relating to their schoolmates, they should be more likely than the passive recipients in traditional programs to be peer-group leaders in drug education.

If the drug program is ambiguous or in transition, or if some teachers who are not in the program have different expectations for students than the drug teachers do, students may experience role conflict. If some teachers reward students for being passive recipients and others reward them for being critical discussants, for example, students are liable to experience such conflict. Which students are able to vary their behavior appropriately? Which ones withdraw into a passive posture, and which maintain an active critical stance in the face of contrary expectation? Researchers might also tell us when such student behavior results in changing the expectations held by teachers.

Students also behave in school in response to what is expected of them in their roles as classmate, clique member, and club or gang member in and out of school. Whichever of these or other memberships serve as positive reference groups for the student will help determine his or her behavior in response to drug education. Expectations of one's informal group may mitigate against being either a passive recipient and/or an active participant or peer-group leader.[58] The emergence of "peer-group involvement" programs is apparently a response to this reality.

The aim of some school programs thus appears to be the development of a school climate in which expectations for students held by various groups converge to reinforce desired drug attitudes and behavior, and minimize student role conflicts and "deviant" drug behavior.

Both the drug educator and the student may serve as positive or negative role models in the process of drug education. The use of peer-group leaders and of other student counselors is based on the assumption that youth can provide more effective models of drug behavior to be emulated than can teachers.

Another type of role model has been provided by the extensive use of ex-heroin addicts as drug educators. A recent study shows that many youths believe that former drug users are the most effective transmitters in drug education.[59] Serious questions have been raised, however, about the possibility that ex-addict teachers may serve so well as positive role models for some students, perhaps for those with similar backgrounds, that use of opiates may be made more attractive.[60] Unresolved differences exist as well regarding the effectiveness of athletes or other heroes as role models for different groups of young people.

Research is also needed to determine when it is what the "model" *does* rather than what he or she says about drugs that serves as the actual role behavior which is emulated. The parental act of giving up cigarettes or cutting down on alcohol apparently speaks much louder to children than words of warning given by a parent who continues to smoke or drink immoderately.

Finally, it is commonly pointed out that when drug educators exaggerate the dangers of a drug like marihuana or otherwise distort drug facts, students tend to be suspicious of all adult drug authorities and depend even more on reports of their peers, including those who use illegal drugs.[61] Peers may thus have become stronger positive role models for some students following the exposure of these students to drug education. Just how the drug educator's age, race, ethnicity, knowledgeability, and experience, as well as sex and class background, affect his or her impact on different target groups is not yet clearly understood.

CONSEQUENCES: INDIVIDUAL AND SOCIAL CHANGE

A functional analysis of drug education can usefully focus on (1) the degree to which anticipated consequences for targeted individuals and groups are achieved, (2) the nature of unanticipated consequences for these individuals and groups, and (3) the degree to which social change, whether anticipated or not, occurs in educational and other institutions.

Knowledge, Attitudes, Values, and Behavior

Major problems have prevented definitive evaluation of school drug programs. These difficulties include (1) unclear program goals, (2) inadequate design of experimental and control group studies by failure to include such safeguards as matching of subjects and of teacher types, (3) lack of measurement of intermediate and long-term changes in outcome variables, including type, frequency, and amount of all drug use, and (4) paucity of funds available for careful studies.

In the absence of systematic evaluation, observers have used clinical judgments and survey data to conclude that traditional programs, films, and materials which use "scare" and "smear" tactics aimed at deterring illegal drug use have failed.[62] The evidence generally has included data suggesting that illegal drug use has not significantly decreased and that the abuse of certain drugs appears to have increased among some groups of young people; furthermore, many students have rejected school drug programs, citing biased and exaggerated efforts to scare them as one reason for such rejection.

Regarding the effects of more objective drug education on student drug knowledge, attitudes, and behavior, the evidence is still fragmentary and inconclusive. While several studies report increased student knowledge about drugs following exposure to drug education, some also report an increased readiness to experiment with recreational drugs such as marihuana.[63] Speculation that objective drug information may lead to increased experimentation with less hazardous illegal drugs like marihuana has been given some credence by a study of Michigan junior high school students.[64]

Even "objective" evaluation of programs is clearly limited by cultural constraints. Only in terms of traditional values could an increase in marihuana experimentation accompanied by reduced heroin use be viewed as failure.[65] If changing values were to legitimize the goal of responsible use of drugs, an increase in occasional marihuana use accompanied by reduced dependency on alcohol and tobacco, as well as on heroin, might indicate a "smashing" success.

The difficult-to-measure effects of more humanistic programs on student self-concept, ability to express feelings and relate to others effectively, and on value-clarifying and decision-making skills have just begun to be studied.

Evaluation of drug education appears to offer a particularly valuable opportunity to further investigate the interrelationships among knowledge, attitudes, values, and behavior related to drugs.

Educational Change

In its second report, the National Commission on Marihuana and Drug Abuse stated its belief "that the best response which the school system can make to drug abuse is not more and better drug education, narrowly defined, but education improved generally."[66] It is just possible that drug education efforts, while seeming to fail in their original mission of reducing drug abuse, may be serving the emergent function of stimulating educational change.

One educator who feels that "the drug issue has potential to become a powerful lever for school reform"[67] believes that while fundamental institutional change is not a realistic goal for the moment, significant school modifications can be affected by drug programs. He cited such sanctuaries from normal school environments as "rap" sessions, "alternative" schools, and counseling classes and such innovations in teacher role assignments as employing nonlicensed personnel, actively involving parents, providing "positive alternatives" to drug use, and delegating to students the responsibility for running drug programs.[68]

Such changes have led to occasional tensions between ex-addicts and professional teachers[69] and between drug program staff and other teachers. More informal and open methods of communication are resisted by those in the system who feel uncomfortable without traditional structure.

Future research can determine whether these and other techniques of humanistic or affective education will spill over from drug education to the schools generally and to what extent they will persist. Similarly, whether new "professional" associations of drug educators begin to play a role in educational and drug law reform or fixate on problems of survival remains to be seen.

Changes in Public Policy

There has been little discussion by sociologists or others of the consequences of drug education for public policy. Nonetheless, the possibility has been raised by a psychiatrist that such programs "may be ineffective distractions which diminish our motivations to examine basic moral and political questions which may be at the very roots of the drug problem."[70] This suggests that traditional efforts divert energy from social programs which combat conditions giving rise to drug abuse and from possible reform of current drug laws which stimulate youthful rebellion and interest in drugs.

Humanistic programs aimed at maximizing each student's potential for constructive living, however, might be said to deal directly with basic social and psychological needs which, if unmet, might lead to "drugs." While this may be true, the psychological focus of humanistic education is likely to keep attention away from the need to reevaluate and reform drug laws. Current drug education appears to assume that individuals must be taught to adjust to public policy and that the policy must not be seriously questioned or modified.

Nevertheless, the following hypothesis about how drug education does exert pressures for divergent policy proposals should be considered. First, drug educators have begun to disseminate objective facts about marihuana to maintain a minimum of credibility with students and with young colleagues who have increasingly experimented with or heard about the drug. Second, this partial convergence of official drug information and youthful beliefs regarding marihuana has contributed to greater community tolerance for marihuana use and greater readiness to reduce the penalties for such use. Thus, drug education may have inadvertently played a part in producing a climate in which the Marihuana Commission felt free to recommend decriminalization of marihuana. Such an unanticipated result would be dysfunctional for the maintenance of our society's punitive public policy but functional for many youths and perhaps for the society at large.

It is further hypothesized that drug education may simultaneously have contributed, albeit indirectly, to an opposing climate favoring tougher drug laws and a law enforcement approach. Since drug education has not only failed to stop the use of marihuana and other drugs but has possibly encouraged such use, it is likely that advocates of a "get tough" approach are placed in a stronger position in their fight for stricter policies.

New laws permitting urinalysis of school children to detect illegal drug use and new cries for reporting student users to the police appear to exemplify such a return to fear of punishment as a better deterrent than education. This consequence would, of course, be functional for the dominant police approach. It is thus possible that drug education, at least of the informational type, has contributed to two campaigns which are working at cross purposes with respect to moving public drug policy away from a law enforcement emphasis.

Drug education as presently organized may help to preserve and sometimes strengthen the punitive approach to disapproved drug use for a more basic structural reason. So long as drug educators are directly employed by the same agencies of government (e.g., the state, city, or county) which also enforce present drug abuse control laws, not only will students suspect the truthfulness of what is presented, as two drug specialists have pointed out,[71] but the educators will also generally support existing laws.

The question can well be raised as to when drug educators have a responsibility to speak out against public policy regarding drugs if they believe the policy is an obstacle to effective education.

SUMMARY

This sociological overview of drug education focuses attention on the ways in which complex sociocultural factors (1) limit and define the contexts and settings within which drug education takes place, (2) influence the structure of formal drug education activities and interactions, and (3) determine, to a large degree, the consequences of such education. Questions are raised in each of these areas relevant to both educational and sociological concerns. Key sociological concepts include contextual constraints, social order, criminalization, deviance and deviant subcultures, social control, labeling, role and role conflict, unanticipated consequences, and social change.

Contexts and Settings

Contextual factors which place clear constraints on the design and conduct of drug education are described: Traditional educational values and goals hinder education for independent thinking and decision-making; pervasive public misconceptions about drugs, reinforced by misuse of words, contaminate communication; ambivalent community attitudes towards drugs mistake the current legal or illegal status of drugs for their health hazards; the lack of community consensus on the nature of drug problems, as illustrated by changing perceptions of marihuana, has led to a contradictory mixture of intervention models which includes incarceration, treatment, regulation, and education.

It is also suggested that punitive laws, which may make the use of illicit drugs more risky and glamorous and therefore more attractive to some youth, have generated massive doses of drug misinformation designed to deter illegal use through fear and that mass media convey cultural themes conducive to drug use, while warning against illegal drugs in ways likely to seem hypocritical to young audiences. Efforts to educate about drugs have been further undermined by a counterculture current among many alienated youths, a criminal addict subculture which provides social support and ready rationalizations for illegal drug users, and by emotion-laden disagreements among drug specialists.

Social settings for drug education, at least as important as the schools, include the family, with its particular ethnic traditions and drug use patterns, and the peer group. Mass media audiences constitute relatively impersonal settings in which drug attitudes, events, advertisements, and public policies are disseminated.

Structure of Formal Drug Education

The implications of government financing of

drug education for the selection of teachers, target groups, and program goals are considered. Teachers selected to teach about drugs have changed from police to ex-addicts and health educators and more recently to specially trained counselors, as well as classroom teachers. Target groups tend most often to be older students, and while the special needs of different age, class, and ethnic groups for different kinds of drug education are increasingly recognized, the most effective methods for reaching different groups have not yet been identified. Equally unresolved are questions about the efficacy of focusing on students labeled as drug-prone and of youth-oriented programs which fail to reach parents, advertisers, and legislators.

The shift from the negative goal of preventing illegal drug use to the humanistic goal of coping with one's feelings, thinking well of oneself, and relating responsibly to others is noted. The question is raised as to whether this major shift is only a change in the tactics of social control or a new commitment to educating for responsible social change, with all its attendant risks.

The relevance of role theory for drug education is discussed in terms of the contradictory role expectations with which drug teachers and students are each faced and the causes and consequences of actual behavior by persons in these two roles. Both situational and individual influences on such behavior are cited. Role conflict within the individual may precede and/or follow role behavior. Actual behavior in terms of both word and deed may provide a role model for drug use or nonuse to be emulated or rejected.

Consequences

Difficulties in evaluating drug education are identified. It is pointed out, for example, that the same drug education programs may be evaluated as either failing or succeeding depending on whether the criterion of success used is the traditional one of reduced illegal use or the emerging one of reduced level of abuse among all drugs used. In the absence of adequate evaluation, it is suggested that while drug education may be failing in its manifest mission of preventing drug abuse among young people, it may be producing at least superficial changes in educational methods and approaches.

Finally, the proposition is advanced that the new drug educators' contradictory responsibilities for telling the truth and upholding the law may be contributing both to the movement for drug law reform and to the maintenance of the existing punitive public policy. When, it is asked, do drug educators have a professional responsibility to oppose drug laws which they feel obstruct their efforts?

REFERENCES

1. Szasz, T., *Ideology and Insanity*, Anchor Books, Doubleday, Garden City, N.Y., 1970, 140.
2. Nowlis, H., The fog keeps rolling in, in *A Guide for the Professions . . . Drug Abuse Education*, 2nd ed., American Pharmaceutical Association, Washington, D.C., 1969, 23.
3. Goode, E., *Drugs in American Society*, Borzoi Book, Knopf, New York, 1962, 21.
4. *Drugs and Drug Abuse Newsletter*, Scope Publ., Washington, D.C., April 1972, 8.
5. Goode, E., *Drugs in American Society*, Borzoi Book, Knopf, New York, 1962, 26.
6. Brecher, E., *Licit and Illicit Drugs*, Little, Brown & Co., Boston, 1973, 525.
7. Straus, R., Alcohol and alcoholism, in *Contemporary Social Problems,* 3rd ed., Merton, R. K. and Nisbet, R., Eds., Harcourt Brace Jovanovich, New York, 1971, 269.
8. Meyer, A., Friedman, L., and Lazarsfeld, P., Motivational conflicts engendered by the on-going discussion of cigarette smoking, in *Smoking Behavior: Motives and Incentives,* V. H. Winston & Sons, Washington, D.C., distributed by Halsted Press, John Wiley & Sons, New York, 1973, 251.
9. National Commission on Marihuana and Drug Abuse, *Marihuana: A Signal of Misunderstanding, Appendix,* Vol. II, U.S. Govt. Printing Office, Washington, D.C., 1972, 915.
10. National Commission on Marihuana and Drug Abuse, *Marihuana: A Signal of Misunderstanding, Appendix,* Vol. II, U.S. Govt. Printing Office, Washington, D.C., 1972, 916.
11. National Commission on Marihuana and Drug Abuse, *Marihuana: A Signal of Misunderstanding, Appendix,* Vol. II, U.S. Govt. Printing Office, Washington, D.C., 1972, 937.

12. National Commission on Marihuana and Drug Abuse, *Marihuana: A Signal of Misunderstanding, Appendix,* Vol. II, U.S. Govt. Printing Office, Washington, D.C., 1972, 936.

13. National Commission on Marihuana and Drug Abuse, *Marihuana: A Signal of Misunderstanding, Appendix,* Vol. II, U.S. Govt. Printing Office, Washington, D.C., 1972, 930.

14. National Commission on Marihuana and Drug Abuse, *Marihuana: A Signal of Misunderstanding, Appendix,* Vol. II, U.S. Govt. Printing Office, Washington, D.C., 1972, 907.

15. National Commission on Marihuana and Drug Abuse, *Marihuana: A Signal of Misunderstanding, Appendix,* Vol. II, U.S. Govt. Printing Office, Washington, D.C., 1972, 961.

16. Macro Systems, *Evaluation of Drug Education Programs,* Vol. I, Macro Systems, New York, June 1972, 65.

17. **Kadish, S.,** The crisis of overcriminalization, in *Crisis in American Institutions,* Skolnick, J. H. and Currie, E., Eds., Little, Brown & Co., Boston, 1970, 425.

18. **King, R.,** Narcotic drug laws and enforcement policies, in *Law and Contemporary Problems,* 22, 113, Winter 1957.

19. **Clausen, J.,** Drug use, in *Contempory Social Problems,* 3rd ed., Merton, R. K. and Nisbet, R., Eds., Harcourt Brace Jovanovich, New York, 1971, 223.

20. **Becker, H.,** *Outsiders, Studies in the Sociology of Deviance,* Free Press, MacMillan, New York, 1963, 135.

21. **Lindesmith, A.,** *The Addict and the Law,* Indiana University Press, Bloomington, 1965, 228.

22. National Coordinating Council on Drug Education, *Drug Abuse Films,* 3rd ed., Washington, D.C., 1972.

23. **Becker, H.,** *Outsiders, Studies in the Sociology of Deviance,* Free Press, MacMillan, New York, 1963, 147.

24. **Brecher, E.,** *Licit and Illicit Drugs,* Little, Brown & Co., Boston, 1973, 523.

25. **Lennard, H. L., Epstein, L. J., Ransom, D. C., and Bernstein, A.,** *Mystification and Drug Misuse,* Jossey-Bass, San Francisco, 1971.

26. **Deitch, D. and Jaffe, J.,** Problems in drug abuse education: two hypotheses, in *Communication and Drug Abuse,* Wittenborn, J. R., Ed., Charles C Thomas, Springfield, Ill., 1970, 176.

27. **Keniston, K.,** *The Uncommitted: Alienated Youth in American Society,* Harcourt, Brace & World, New York, 1960.

28. **Lemert, E.,** Social structure, social control and deviation, in *Anomie and Deviant Behavior,* Clinard, M., Ed., Free Press, Glencoe, Ill., 1966, 82.

29. **Lindesmith, A.,** *The Addict and the Law,* Indiana University Press, Bloomington, 1965, 243.

30. **Cremin, L.,** in Westerhoff, J., III, An interview with Lawrence Cremin: freeing ourselves from the mythmakers, in *Perspectives on Education,* Columbia University Teachers' College, New York, Winter/Spring, 1972, 301.

31. **Blum, R.,** A new perspective on drug education, in *Grassroots* (Suppl.), Student Association for the Study of Hallucinogens, Beloit, Wis., August 1972, 6.

32. **Chafetz, M. and Demone, H.,** *Alcohol and Society,* Oxford University Press, New York, 1962, 188.

33. **Pittman, D. and Snyder, C., Eds.,** *Society, Culture and Drinking Patterns,* John Wiley & Sons, New York, 1962, 154.

34. National Clearinghouse for Smoking and Health, *Teenage Smoking,* DHEW Publ. No. (HMS) 72-7508, U.S. Govt. Printing Office, Washington, D.C., 1972, 4.

35. National Commission on Marihuana and Drug Abuse, *Marihuana: A Signal of Misunderstanding, Appendix,* Vol. II, U.S. Govt. Printing Office, Washington, D.C., 1972, 1201.

36. Drug Abuse Council, *Survey of State Drug Abuse Activities,* MS-2, Drug Abuse Council, Washington, D.C., 1972, 13.

37. Drug Abuse Council, *Survey of State Drug Abuse Activities,* MS-2, Drug Abuse Council, Washington, D.C., 1972, 14.

38. National Commission on Marihuana and Drug Abuse, *Marihuana: A Signal of Misunderstanding, Appendix,* Vol. II, U.S. Govt. Printing Office, Washington, D.C., 1972, 1201.

39. Drug Abuse Council, *Survey of State Drug Abuse Activities,* MS-2, Drug Abuse Council, Washington, D.C., 1972, 13.

40. **De Lone, R.,** The ups and downs of drug education, *Saturday Rev. Educ.,* 55, 32, December 1972.

41. National Commission on Marihuana and Drug Abuse, *Marihuana: A Signal of Misunderstanding, Appendix,* Vol. II, U.S. Govt. Printing Office, Washington, D.C., 1972, 1203.

42. National Coordinating Council on Drug Education, *Drug Abuse Films,* 3rd ed., Washington, D.C., 1972, 101.

43. **Hictor, M.,** Drugs and society, in *The Unesco Courier,* May 1973, 29.

44. **Wald, P. and Abrams, A.,** Drug education, in *Dealing with Drug Abuse: A Report to the Ford Foundation,* Praeger, New York, 1972, 124.

45. National Commission on Marihuana and Drug Abuse, *Drug Use in America: Problems in Perspective,* 2nd Report, U.S. Govt. Printing Office, Washington, D.C., 1973, 351.

46. **Sinacore, J.,** quoted in *Attack,* N.Y. State Narcotic Addiction Control Commission, 6(2), 2, Spring 1973.

47. **Weinstein, G. and Fantini, M.,** *Toward a Humanistic Education,* Praeger, New York, 1970.

48. **Brown, G.,** *Human Teaching for Human Learning: An Introduction to Confluent Education,* Viking Press, New York, 1971.

49. **Raths, L., Harmin, M., and Simon, S.,** *Values and Teaching: Working with Values in the Classroom,* Merrill, Columbus, O., 1966.

50. **Abrams, A., Dorn, N., and Woodcock, J.,** *Suggested Framework for Consideration of Drug Education Objectives for Evaluation,* 1st Int. Congr. Drug Educ., Montreux, 1973 (mimeo).

51. **Globetti, G.,** Young people and alcohol education – abstinence or moderate drinking, *Drug Forum,* 1, 269, 1972.

52. Meyer, A., Drug education in a post-Watergate world: a critique and a proposal, in *Resource Material,* 1st Int. Congr. Drug Educ., Montreux, 1973, 239.

53. Deitch, D. and Jaffe, J., in *Communication and Drug Abuse,* Wittenborn, J. R., Ed., Charles C Thomas, Springfield, Ill., 1970, 181.

54. Deitch, D. and Jaffe, J., in *Communication and Drug Abuse,* Wittenborn, J. R., Ed., Charles C Thomas, Springfield, Ill., 1970, 184.

55. Brim, O., *Sociology and the Field of Education,* Russell Sage Foundation, New York, 1958, 15.

56. Gross, N., Mason, W., and McEachern, A., *Explorations in Role Analysis,* John Wiley & Sons, New York, 1966, 246.

57. James, W., Where did we go wrong? *J. Health Phys. Educ. Recreation,* 49(9), 1972.

58. Brim, O., *Sociology and the Field of Education,* Russell Sage Foundation, New York, 1958, 63.

59. Macro Systems, *Evaluation of Drug Education Programs,* Vol. I, Macro Systems, New York, June 1972, 33.

60. Wald, P. and Abrams, A., in *Dealing with Drug Abuse: A Report to the Ford Foundation,* Praeger, New York, 1972, 135.

61. Halleck, S., The great drug education hoax, *The Progressive,* p. 30, July 1970.

62. Wald, P. and Abrams, A., in *Dealing with Drug Abuse: A Report to the Ford Foundation,* Praeger, New York, 1972, 124.

63. Wald, P. and Abrams, A., in *Dealing with Drug Abuse: A Report to the Ford Foundation,* Praeger, New York, 1972, 134.

64. Stuart, R., *Teaching Facts About Drugs: Pushing or Preventing?* University of Michigan Behavior Change Laboratories, mimeo.

65. Wald, P. and Abrams, A., in *Dealing with Drug Abuse: A Report to the Ford Foundation,* Praeger, New York, 1972, 126.

66. National Commission on Marihuana and Drug Abuse, *Drug Use in America: Problems in Perspective,* 2nd Report, U.S. Govt. Printing Office, Washington, D.C., 1973, 358.

67. De Lone, R., *Saturday Rev. Educ.,* 55, 31, December 1972.

68. De Lone, R., *Saturday Rev. Educ.,* 55, 31, December 1972.

69. Wald, P. and Abrams, A., in *Dealing with Drug Abuse: A Report to the Ford Foundation,* Praeger, New York, 1972, 138.

70. Halleck, S., *The Progressive,* p. 30, July 1970.

71. Deitch, D. and Jaffe, J., in *Communication and Drug Abuse,* Wittenborn, J. R., Ed., Charles C Thomas, Springfield, Ill., 1970, 184.

MASS COMMUNICATIONS AND DRUG DEPENDENCE

Charles Winick

TABLE OF CONTENTS

INTRODUCTION

What is the role, if any, of the media of mass communications in the sustenance and continuation of drug dependence in this country? This issue has been the subject of acrimonious charges and countercharges, litigation, political attacks, action by federal regulatory activities, and many other kinds of responses, as well as some research. The purpose of this paper is to explore what is known about the subject.

Whatever the effects of mass communications on drug dependence might be, we can assume that they are consonant with other effects of modern media. Sociologists have identified a number of functions of mass communications in our society: activation of latent predispositions, reinforcement of existing ideas, conversion to a new viewpoint, provision of information to opinion leaders who interacted with their peers, structure and definition of cultural norms, creation of new norms in areas of behavior not controlled by strong sociocultural constraints, and communication of information.[1]

Media philosopher Marshall McLuhan has suggested that drug taking is stimulated by today's media environment of instant information. He notes that the metaphor for getting high is the same phrase we employ in describing the electronic media: "turning on."[2]

We know that the typical American averages 50 hours a week of media consumption, more than is devoted to any activity except sleeping. We do not know the detailed effects of such exposure. On the assumption that Americans' commitment of such substantial amounts of their time is of possible significance, we shall discuss specific kinds of mass communications that may be relevant to drug dependence, in terms of our current state of knowledge. We shall consider books, movies, television, advertising, and popular music. Each of these will be considered in turn.

BOOKS

The audience for current fiction is extremely difficult to determine because there is no way of knowing how many copies of a specific title may be circulating via libraries, and publishers are generally reluctant to discuss how many copies of specific titles may be sold in a given time period. During the last 30 years, the availability of inexpensive paperback editions has extended the reach of many books. Sales of 5 to 10 million copies of a title are not uncommon, and each copy may have many "passalong" readers, so that popular books have now become a medium of mass communications. The 32,000 titles published each year may have a substantive effect on information and attitudes.

Fiction of the 1950s and 1960s dealt sporadically with the issue of drug use.[3] Famous novels of the time included Nelson Algren's[4] *Man with the Golden Arm*, Alexander Trocchi's[5] *Cain's Book*, and John Rechy's[6] *City of Night*, all of which presented the drug subculture sympathetically. Jack Kerouac's[7] *On the Road*, which created a literary movement, included discussions of the use of marihuana and hashish by the "beats." Such novels presented the alienation of the drug user, as did William Burroughs'[8] *Naked Lunch* and Hubert Selby's[9] *Last Exit to Brooklyn*. Jacqueline Susann's[10] *Valley of the Dolls*, probably the most commercially successful novel of the last three decades, dealt with the use of amphetamines and barbiturates ("dolls") by celebrities trying to cope with their many problems. One of her three heroines commits suicide with barbiturates, a second begins taking them to deal with her husband's adultery, and the third takes many different drugs ("two lousy little seconals are like appetizers to me").

Chester Himes'[11],[12] very popular detective novels (*Pinktoes, Cotton Comes to Harlem*) present addicts as nuisances who prey on their ghetto neighbors. A number of writers have dealt with middle-class LSD users as a reflection of larger youth unrest, e.g., Jeremy Larner[13] and Patricia Welles.[14]

Two books of nonfiction reached millions of readers with their graphic reports of young men growing up in a drug-drenched ghetto. Claude Brown[15] and Piri Thomas[16] wrote powerful autobiographies about what is involved in a young minority group member's coming of age in a ghetto where drug use is taken for granted. Many readers got a new insight into drug use among urban Blacks and Puerto Ricans after reading these searingly honest books.

Probably the single most important American poet for young people in America is Allen Ginsberg, who has become almost a mythic figure in the last two decades. His most famous poem, *Howl*, begins with a reference to the "best minds of my generation . . . looking for an angry fix."[17] The poem deals with marihuana, peyote, amphetamines, and other drugs as a way of coping with a mechanistic world. Ginsberg has a special role among youth because he has long been a spokesman for LEMAR, the Committee to Reform the Marihuana Laws.

Many books dealing with drug themes achieve wider audiences when they are made into movies or television.

FILMS

Hollywood has been interested in the use of drugs ever since the 1920s, when a number of famour stars, in their private lives, were involved in widely publicized drug use. Silent superstar Wallace Reid died in 1923 of complications from the use of morphine, and Olive Thomas committed suicide in 1920 as a result of cocaine difficulties. Silent films of the 1920s regularly presented scenes of drug use. For example, *The Sorrows of Satan* (1926), with Ricardo Cortez, Adolphe Menjou, and Mary Astor, directed by D. W. Griffith, had a scene in an opium den.

Most of the 1920s films with drug scenes used similarly exotic locales, which presumably helped to make them acceptable to the industry self-regulation office, which had been organized in 1922 under Will H. Hays.[18] Although the Production Code which was started by what became known as "the Hays office" frowned on the presentation of drug use, a number of films of the 1930s included music with drug-oriented lyrics, such as Cab Calloway's version of "Minnie the Moocher" ("she loved him though he was cokey"). A major 1933 Paramount musical extravaganza was *International House*, starring W. C. Fields,

Rudy Vallee, and Burns and Allen. The big song of the picture was "Reefer Man," which half-teased, half-praised marihuana (". . . the reefer man . . . Wall Street's frantic/ cause he won't sell the Atlantic").

Few drug-related films were made during the 1940s. But in the 1950s and 1960s several films (e.g., *A Hatful of Rain* (1957), *Monkey on My Back* (1957), *Paris Blues* (1961), *The Connection* (1961), *The Cool World* (1963), *Synanon* (1966)) dealt with narcotic addicts sympathetically. Debate over the acceptability of drug use as a film subject peaked in 1955, when *The Man With the Golden Arm*, starring Frank Sinatra and Kim Novak, was refused a Production Code seal of approval.[19] The film attracted huge audiences even though it lacked a seal, which it obtained retrospectively in 1962. The Code was liberalized in 1956, and drug use became an acceptable subject.

In 1968, the present system of classification of films by subject matter replaced the seal, and drug content in films is now routinely accepted. Such content is important for several reasons, one of which is the youth of current movie audiences.

The movie audience is young and so is the high risk population of persons who might become drug dependent. Table 1, the information in which is derived from industry sources, gives the proportion of various age groups in the United States population in 1970 and their representation among moviegoers in 1970 and 1972. It will be noted that although persons between 12 and 29 represented only 39% of the population in 1970, they accounted for 72% of movie admissions in 1970 and 73% by 1972.

Young people will seek out movies even if there are difficulties in access, although the 9,700

TABLE 1

Attendance at Movies in 1970 and 1972 by Various Age Groups in the Population

Age group	% of 1970 Movie admissions	% of 1972 Movie admissions	% in Population, 1970
12–15	16	13	10
16–20	27	30	12
21–24	16	16	8
25–29	13	14	9
30–39	12	11	14
40–49	8	10	16
50–59	6	4	13
60+	2	2	18

theaters and 4,600 drive-ins provide relatively easy access in most of the country. In a study of a representative small town in California in which the single movie was only open on weekends and where there was also a drive-in, of the sixth and tenth graders studied, approximately half (57% of the white collar, 46% of the blue collar, and 48% of the Chicano) had seen a movie in the previous month.[20]

Why do young people decide to see a specific movie? An earlier study concluded that 45% of moviegoers are influenced to see a film by its story, 18% go because of the stars, and 27% find both reasons equally important.[21] With the decline in the studio system and disappearance of long-term contracts for stars, their importance has declined while the significance of story or subject has increased. Drug use as a film theme may therefore be attractive to young people who are drug tryers, users, or potential users.

The social nature of the moviegoing situation makes it likely that a film will be discussed by the young people who no longer just "go to the movies" but rather engage in selective exposure. They choose from what is available, and the decision to go has often involved some preliminary discussion. Since most people attend movies as part of a larger context of social activity, they often discuss the film while returning home. Emotional investment in the purchase decision often may be encouraged by previous conversation with a friend or the opinion of a favorite reviewer.

Another reason for the importance of films with some drug-related content is that they may be shown on television for years after their original release. Some 13,000 feature films are currently available for television, and a film which has completed its theatrical run may attract audiences, on television, for years and perhaps even decades.

We can form some impression of the drug content of films in two ways: noting some of the most influential films of recent years and conducting a systematic content analysis of all the drug-related films in one year. All films discussed are identified by the name of the director.

Some Influential Films

One of the first major films to present attractive people taking marihuana is Michelangelo Antonioni's very influential *Blow-up* (1966). The photographer hero attends a London party where everyone is smoking marihuana. The host is so "stoned" that he pays no attention to the hero's report of a murder. When the hero reminds a girlfriend at the party that she had expected to be in Paris, she replies, "I *am* in Paris." The film presents an interesting and attractive group of young people whose marihuana use is presented as part of their life-style. The film's existential theme (e.g., what is real and what seems to be real) was consonant with some recurrent concerns of the drug culture.

In 1967, Peter Fonda starred in *The Trip*, directed by Roger Corman. Fonda plays a television official whose life is empty and who takes LSD in order to find himself. He has various pleasant experiences, after an initial panic reaction. The hero, asked if the LSD experience was worthwhile, says, "I suppose so." His life clearly has not been changed by it. Other films presenting LSD trips are Andy Warhol's *The Chelsea Girls* (1967) and Nicholas Roeg's *Performance* (1970), starring rock music superstar Mick Jagger.

A unique film by a narcotics addict about himself is Conrad Rooks's *Chappaqua* (1967). Rooks plays an American addict who escapes from a Paris clinic where he is undergoing a cure. He experiences dreamlike hallucinations which are enhanced by the music, played and composed by famed Indian sitarist Ravi Shanker. The film's cast includes drug subculture heroes, novelist William Burroughs and poet Allen Ginsberg.

In 1969, *Easy Rider* was released and immediately became one of the most important films of the post-World War II period. Starring Peter Fonda and Dennis Hopper, this movie opens with the two motorcycle riding heroes smuggling heroin over the border from Mexico. With the proceeds from the heroin sale, they buy two flashy motorcycles. They drive to New Orleans, where they share an LSD trip with two prostitutes in a cemetery. The heroes also smoke marihuana during their trip east. Although the heroes die tragically, their defiance of society is closely linked with their drug use and undoubtedly was responsible for part of the film's huge success. *Easy Rider* was probably the first serious pro-drug film. That it met the needs of the movie audience can be seen from the simple fact that it grossed $17,000,000 in the United States, having cost only $340,000 to make.

There is a type of film called the "head picture" by drug users. It provides intersensory images and enhances the drug experience, although it usually does not contain explicit drug-related material. The favorite "head film" is probably Stanley Kubrick's science fiction *2001: A Space Odyssey* (1968). The last 15 minutes of the film contain a number of vivid abstract color images which are very psychedelic. Other "head films" include the science fiction *Fantastic Voyage* (1966), the Beatles' cartoon *Yellow Submarine* (1968), and rock music films *Monterey Pop* (1968), *Woodstock* (1970), and *A Film About Jimi Hendrix* (1973).

Another enormously influential film was Gordon Parks, Jr.'s *Superfly* (1972), which added a word to the language. The title became an adjective for someone who was dressed very attractively and was especially alert. *Superfly* cost less than $500,000 to make and grossed more than $22,000,000 in the United States. Superfly is a Black cocaine peddler whose goal is to complete one more deal which will net him one million dollars. The pusher has a Rolls Royce and sees pushing drugs as a life-style which is also a realistic way of achieving the American Dream of success. The film's song "Pusherman" is a reinforcement of this message, stressing that the pusher is "making money all the time . . . I'm your doctor, your main boy." *Superfly* became the single most successful as well as controversial of the "new" Black films, and its latent identification with praise of drug selling was at the core of both the success and controversy.

A number of films have presented drug use as central to a specific kind of youth subculture. John Avildsen's *Joe* (1970) shows a hippie commune where drug use is taken for granted. In *Zabriskie Point* (1970), Antonioni presents young Americans as routinely smoking marihuana. It is such a norm that when the hero refuses a marihuana cigarette, he apologizes by saying, "No thanks — I'm on a reality trip." Hy Averback's *I Love You Alice B. Toklas* (1968) showed young people who baked brownies with marihuana.

The film *Cisco Pike* (1972), directed by Bill Norton and starring rock star Kris Kristofferson, is probably the first serious portrait of a rock musician in fiction films. He has been arrested twice for selling drugs, with a partner who is an amateur cowboy. His drug use is part of Cisco's deterioration.

Systematic Content Study

In addition to citing the very influential movies summarized above, another way of establishing drug-related content is to look at all the films released in one year. The year was 1971, during which the country became especially concerned about drug use and federal programs assumed new initiatives. As part of a larger study of media treatment of drug use and other social problems, machinery had been established for systematic scrutiny of films to be released and for detailed content study of those which appeared to be relevant.

Of the 231 feature films released during 1971 which were preliminarily screened, 89 were monitored in accordance with a preliminary coding instrument because they had some significant drug use content. By "drug" we mean psychoactive or mood-modifying substances, excluding only alcohol. By "significant," we mean substantial scene, character, or thematic relevance. "Use" encompasses recreational use through dependence and dysfunctional abuse.

Of the 89 films screened, 23 were selected for detailed analysis. At least two persons independently coded each film, codings were compared, and the relatively few differences were resolved by discussion. The films selected are listed in Table 2.

Descriptions of the Films

Twenty-one films were made in the United

TABLE 2

Films Released in 1971 with Drug-related Content

A Safe Place
Been Down So Long It Looks Like Up to Me
Carnal Knowledge
Desperate Characters
Drive, He Said
Dirtymouth
Dusty and Sweets McGee
Fortune in Men's Eyes
Fragment of Fear
French Connection
Ginger
Guess What We Learned in School Today?
I Drink Your Blood
Jennifer on My Mind
Klute
Making It
Panic in Needle Park
Puzzle of a Downfall Child
Sweet Savior
Taking Off
THX 1138
The Cop
Vanishing Point

States, one in England, and one in France. One film had received no rating from the Production Code office, one had an X rating (no children allowed), four a PG (parental guidance suggested, some material may not be suitable for preteenagers), and 17 an R (restricted, adults must accompany children under 17). None of the films was rated G (general audiences, all ages admitted). The industry's self-regulatory apparatus clearly intended that they be approached with caution by young people.

Three of the films featured superstars whose names above a title practically guarantee success (e.g., Jane Fonda, Shirley MacLaine), seven had stars of recognizable but lesser reputation (Troy Donahue, Jack Nicholson), and the other 13 included performers who were not, at the time, established (e.g., Philip Proctor, Al Pacino, Karen Black) but who have become better known because of these films.

Jerry Schatzberg (*Puzzle of A Downfall Child*, *Panic in Needle Park*) and Richard G. Sarafian (*Vanishing Point*, *Fragment of Fear*) each directed two of the films. Among the other directors were some who were very famous (e.g., Sidney Lumet, Mike Nichols). Some script writers (e.g., Erich Segal, Joan Didion) also enjoyed major reputations.

No film was a "super-budget," in excess of $2 million, but many of them were significant in terms of their sponsorship and subsequent recognition. Two films (*Klute*, *The French Connection*) figured on most lists of the best films of the year and won Academy Awards.

Most of the films were financially successful. A film which grosses two and one half times the cost of producing the negative is generally regarded as having made a profit. Of the 19 films for which such information could be obtained, 17 had taken in more than two and a half times their negative cost.

Fully one tenth (23 out of 231) of the year's feature films had some significant drug use content. No other social problem engaged such substantial attention from the movie industry during 1971. Of course, attitudes are not affected equally by all films and some of the "blockbuster" films discussed above may have more impact, but for purposes of systematic study, taking all the films of a given kind is necessary.

A number of the other 66 films monitored had scenes involving drug use which were not considered salient enough to be included in the current study. For example, the widely praised film *Sunday, Bloody Sunday* had a scene of a boy smoking marihuana and another in which London opiate addicts are waiting to get their prescriptions filled at a pharmacy, but these scenes were not significant for the film and it was not included in this study. We recognize that some degree of information and perhaps attitudes about drugs may be communicated by such scenes in other films and that the accretion of information and attitudes from them could be considerable.

Who Are the Users?

What kinds of people are represented as drug users in these movies?

In eight movies, males are the primary users. In the other 15, both males and females are presented; no films deal with female users exclusively.

Seventeen movies primarily show whites as users, and only six present Blacks, Chicanos, or Puerto Ricans. In the latter, some whites are also usually shown.

Although "hippie" is a cultural rather than socioeconomic category, it is also included here. The number of films in each category, in terms of the major identifiable affiliations of the drug users, is

Upper class	2
Middle class	12
Lower class	4
Hippie	2
Mixed	3

Thirteen films present single or unmarried users, five show married persons, and in the other five the marital status could not be ascertained.

How old are the users? There is a considerable range in age: Five films deal primarily with persons under 20, four with those from 21 to 30, six with the 31 to 40 group, one with persons over 41, and seven are concerned with mixed age groups.

A number of different user occupations are represented. The primary occupational groups identifiable in each film, and the number of films in which they appear, follow:

Student	6
Housewife	4
Prostitute	4
Pusher	3
Model	1
Physician	1

In the other four films, no categorization was possible.

Characterizing each film by the predominant type of user, we find the following:

Tryers-experimenters	3
Recreational-social users	4
Heavy users	9
Dysfunctional abusers	7

Most major drugs of dependence are represented. Five films present mixed dependencies, with the protagonists using two or more substances. In the other films substances most favored are

Marihuana	6
Heroin	5
Hallucinogens	3
Amphetamines	3
Cocaine	1

Circumstances of Use

A considerable range of settings and circumstances for drug use is found.

Seven locales are urban, five suburban, two rural, two are hippie communes, two are foreign, one takes place in the future, and four are mixed. There are two films with high school settings and two with a college background.

In six of the films, the use is primarily a solitary activity. In seven films, the user involves more than one person. Eighteen films show the user ingesting the substance, and five do not. Typical are the several closeups of a heroin addict using a hypodermic in *Panic in Needle Park*, and a demonstration of techniques of marihuana smoking in *Taking Off*.

In all but 2 of the 18 films, there is background music before, during, or after the drug ingestion is shown. Two thirds of the music related to the ingestion is rock.

Twelve films show clearly negative consequences of drug use. Thus, in *Drive, He Said*, a medical student taking drugs to beat the draft becomes so "freaked out" that he attacks a psychiatrist and his feigned insanity backfires. In *Dirtymouth*, the chief protagonist dies of an overdose at the age of 40. In *Dusty and Sweets McGee*, three of the main characters, including one young millionaire, die from drug-related causes. In two films (*Sweet Savior* and *I Drink Your Blood*), LSD is ingested by commune members who become so crazed that they engage in bizarre behavior: beheading chickens, roasting rats, and hanging the bleeding bodies of people they have killed from rafters.

Euphoria or other positive effects of drug use are shown in four films. In *Vanishing Point*, the driver-hero can drive a car for 15 hours without a rest as a result of amphetamine use. *A Safe Place* presents marihuana as the major means by which the heroine can function. Three films present complex or mixed effects of drugs. Nine of the films suggest that drugs may function as an aphrodisiac. Hippie orgiasts take LSD in *I Drink Your Blood*, and the disciples of the new messiah in *Sweet Savior* smoke marihuana before engaging in sexual activity. The 17-year-old hero of *Making It* seduces the class virgin by giving her some curry laced with marihuana. The humans of the future in *THX 1138* can make love and conceive a child only after cutting down on drug use.

Five movies satirize drug use. In *Guess What We Learned in School Today?* the marihuana smoking of suburban housewives as they sip coffee is mocked.

Of the 20 films with references to drug effects, 16 appeared to be largely accurate. The other four, however, contain substantial inaccuracies; e.g., in *Ginger*, the villain attempts to addict the heroine against her will by giving her a single injection of heroin.

Law Enforcement

Eight of the films ascribe a significant role to government law enforcement officials, with one (*Ginger*) devoted to the adventures of a woman private detective.

The police in *Fragment of Fear*, a British film, exhibit the conventional dedication traditionally associated with British officers.

Most of the American police presented, however, tend to engage in questionable activities in their pursuit of pushers. The detective in *The French Connection* is typical of other movie detectives shown, in being vicious, reckless, and oblivious to the rights of others.

For most of the law enforcement officials, their work is a crusade, in which they work very long hours. They stay with a case until it is solved, which is hardly the case in real life. Their work in movies is compressed into dramatic encounters which are relatively unlikely in real life. The actual smugglers in *The French Connection* case, for example, were captured quietly with nobody hurt. The movie climax is a police officer racing an automobile through crowded streets to catch a smuggler who is on a speeding New York subway train. Without this chase scene, the movie would not have been a major success.

Some narcotics police are zealots, but others are dishonest. Lenny Bruce, in *Dirtymouth*, is framed by Philadelphia police for possession of drugs. Several movies communicate a paranoid feeling about the corruption and inefficiency of narcotics police. The narcotics officers in *The Organization*, for example, are so corrupt that six young people tackle the crime "organization" on their own.

In five films, there is actual showing of the importer, wholesaler, and street dealer. Realities of street sales, e.g., the heroin hidden between phone booth telephone books in *Dusty and Sweets McGee*, are shown.

Attitudes Toward Drug Use

We may anticipate that exposure to these films may, in some members of the audience, affect attitudes toward drug use.

Not one of the significant characters is in treatment. Education about drugs is similarly absent. There are, however, representations of prison inmates (*Fortune in Men's Eyes*) and students and teachers (*Been Down So Long It Looks Like Up To Me*) who take psychoactive drugs.

Five films convey a glamorous attitude about drug use along with a picture of the heroin subculture, with its discontinuities and destructiveness. Three films (*Panic in Needle Park, Jennifer on My Mind*, and *Dusty and Sweets McGee*) are cautionary tracts which also convey the notion of a star-crossed relationship between romantic victims. Only *Klute* presents the heroin addict's life as horrible.

The motivations for starting drug use are not made clear in any of the films. It is something the audience is asked to accept. Even in a film with only two major characters, like *Panic in Needle Park*, it is never clear why the heroine comes to New York or what functions are served for her by heroin.

An entertainment film is not necessarily concerned with communicating insight, but it is surprising that none of the films attempted to do so. No film offers the kind of understanding of

etiology found in *The Lost Weekend* (1945), which dealt with alcoholism.

The problems posed by the street narcotics addict, often a minority group member, are treated by only a handful of films. Whites using substances other than heroin represent the dominant group presented. With students the most frequently found occupational group and marihuana the most popular substance, only one aspect of the problem is emphasized. Film makers may have felt that the movement of drug use out of the ghetto and into the middle classes was an important theme, which maximized identification for middle-class audiences as well as one which could offer attractive roles for actors. Heroin use in an inner city setting may have been seen as too "downbeat" for general audiences. Film makers could also have had difficulty in developing a fresh viewpoint toward the street addict.

Where heroin addicts are shown, the director seldom resists the temptation to present them "shooting up." Some viewers are probably horrified and turn away from such scenes while others watch in fascination.

Another uncertain contribution is that made by the aphrodisiac connotations of drug use, in more than a third of the films. Showing the drug user then engaging in sexual activity may reinforce the stereotyped connection between drugs and sex.

The films reflect a growing awareness that there is no one drug culture, but rather a number of separate groups, each using specific substances for different reasons. It is possible to identify perhaps five different types of drug dimensions in these films: youth and "anti-square," urban drug culture, police chase, losers, and hippie.

The four youth and antisquare films (*Been Down So Long It Looks Like Up to Me, Guess What We Learned in School Today?, Making It, Taking Off*) are primarily concerned with marihuana and hallucinogens, the use of which is related to personal liberation of young people, usually middle class.

Four films (*Desperate Characters, Dusty and Sweets McGee, Klute, Panic in Needle Park*) present the urban drug culture as an expression of almost helpless alienation.

A third kind of film, the police thriller (*French Connection, Ginger, The Cop, Vanishing Point*) pits the police against a group of heroin sellers, who are presented as very unscrupulous and dangerous. Most of the other films attribute drug use not to sellers but to a whole complex of reasons related to the nature and structure of our society.

A fourth kind of film (*A Safe Place, Jennifer On My Mind, Puzzle of a Downfall Child*) deals with "beautiful losers" who are essentially doomed and take marihuana and "downers" to withdraw from reality.

The fifth genre (*I Drink Your Blood, Sweet Savior*) is concerned with residents of hippie communes, using LSD and other hallucinogens to recharge their emotional batteries.

Few of these films propose any solution to the society's drug problem. It is very significant that most of the films studied, although they have significant drug content, are not *primarily* concerned with drugs. Rather, the characters are shown participating in drug interaction as a regular but not exclusive activity; e.g., Ann-Margret, in *Carnal Knowledge*, pops pills as part of her way of life, and the pills reflect but do not determine her life-style. In most of the films, the drug use is taken for granted.[22]

TELEVISION

Inasmuch as television takes up much more time than any other leisure activity of Americans, how it deals with drugs could be an important contributor to the public's level of knowledge about and attitudes toward the subject. Television can help to legitimate a problem and influence legislative and other official action, as well as have an impact on the people who are or might become the problem.

Many Americans derive part of their knowledge about a problem like drug use from television, which is an established part of a person's daily life, a habitual and routinized activity, a well-established sequence, which punctuates the day or evening, like going to school or eating.[23]

Television is the country's most important source of continuous diversion and relaxation.[24] Becaue of its central role in providing entertainment, it may also communicate attitudes, feelings, and information about drug use and users, among other subjects.

Although viewing of entertainment programs is determined by many factors, they probably do not include a strong desire for information about drug use. But it iṣ reasonable to suspect that, by identification of viewers with characters, there

may be some degree of residual learning. The learning could involve incorporation of positive values associated with some kinds of behavior and negative values linked with other behaviors, by a media version of the process of differential association.[25]

The Audience

How large is the television audience? During the last several years, 96% of the roughly 63 million households in the United States have had a television set. By 1972, color television had reached half the homes. The typical television household uses its set between 41 and 42 hours a week, of which 14 are in the evening, from 7:30 to 11 p.m. During these "prime time" hours, 57% of the sets are in use on a typical evening. The average television household has three persons, so prime time programs can attract an enormous audience.

Are particular programs being seen by high risk groups? High school students average a weekly television viewing range of 12 to 14 hours and probably represent one of the age groups most vulnerable to drug use. In recent years, increasing numbers of junior high school age children are involved in drug use.[26]

We can estimate that the average prime time program is watched by about one tenth of the male and female teenagers and the same proportion of children 6 to 11 years old.

Because a typical evening network entertainment program is part of a series, many persons probably are regular viewers of it. They are likely to have some degree of identification with the protagonists and to anticipate seeing the episodes, a summary of which is found in newspaper and television supplements.

Television viewing is far less concentrated than watching a movie in a theater. Commercials interrupt the flow of the action, and the social context of television viewing in the home often involves interruptions and distractions. The relatively small size of the television screen may make for difficulties in concentration.

Program Content

Prior to the mid-1960s, television was extremely cautious about entertainment content concerned with drugs. Some enforcement officials felt that any presentation of drug use might arouse the curiosity of susceptible young people. As the drug problem got more attention, however, by 1968, some federal officials began to ask the broadcasting industry for assistance. In 1970, President Nixon asked the networks to cooperate. Because of the lead time needed to develop a new television series, the season beginning September 1970 was the first one that could reflect the broadcasters' response. Government activities concerned with drug use began to stress treatment and rehabilitation, and law enforcement became only one element in a national strategy rather than the dominant force it had previously been.

Television's ability to deal with problems of drug use is somewhat undercut by the constraints of prime time entertainment programs. Although evening television programs are intended for an essentially adult audience, broadcasters know that younger persons may compose some part of the audience. By the rating, from G through X, received by a theatrical film, its distributors make clear the extent to which its contents are suitable for children. No such ratings are possible for television, which is under considerable pressure to have a somewhat sanitized content.

Before any network entertainment program is broadcast, its content must be approved by the department concerned with "standards and practices." This office implements the company's guidelines as well as the Television Code of the National Association of Broadcasters. A script which poses problems is discussed with its creators, and appropriate modifications are made before the program is broadcast.[27] Presumably, any drug-related content in programs is believed appropriate and in conformity with the relevant section (IV, 18) of the Code: "Narcotic addiction shall not be presented except as a vicious habit. The administration of illegal drugs will not be displayed. The use of hallucinogenic drugs shall not be shown or encouraged as desirable or socially acceptable." This paragraph, must, however, be interpreted in the light of Section I, 7, which encourages ". . . programs presenting . . . valid moral and social issues, significant controversial and challenging concepts and other subject matter involving adult themes. Accordingly, none of the provisions of this Code . . . should be construed to prevent or impede their broadcast."[28] What this means is that drug use can be presented, depending on the context.

If there is a question about how a particular program treats drug use, the problem may be referred to the central Television Code Office. In addition to the three networks (ABC, CBS, and NBC), Code membership includes 402 stations, or 59% of the country's total. Individual stations which originate programs follow the same Code procedures with respect to drug-related content as the networks. Entertainment films originally made for theaters are subject to the established screening procedures when they are purchased for television.

Entertainment programs with content related to drug use can be said to have two kinds of content: casual references and significant thematic relevance. Each is discussed below.

Casual References

Most of the casual drug references on television are to marihuana. Relatively casual references to marihuana were found on a number of late night "talk shows" and comedy programs like Laugh-In (1967–73). It is difficult to estimate the impact of such occasional brief references to marihuana. They may only be a few seconds long but could help to legitimate attitudes of acceptance toward the substance by presenting it as a feature of the cultural landscape.

There are a number of programs on which the protagonist is shown taking a tranquilizer in order to calm himself or herself. Often, such scenes are shown in an amusing manner and mock the drug taking. They may, of course, help to convey a feeling of general social acceptance toward tranquilizers.

Some performers, such as Jackie Gleason and Dean Martin, convey a feeling of having been drinking alcoholic beverages before the program goes on the air. This may be a "put on," but it is probably a reinforcement of positive attitudes toward alcohol; e.g., if a celebrity drinks, why shouldn't I? Sometimes such performers seem to be drinking during the program by calling for a drink of water but subtly communicating the belief that the colorless liquid is actually alcohol.

Systematic Content Study

Because television does not have the equivalent of the "blockbuster" films discussed above, a systematic content study can provide a fair impression of significant drug use content.

In order to determine such content, we conducted an analysis of all evening entertainment television programs with significant drug use content broadcast in prime time during the 1970–71 and 1971–72 television seasons, running from September through May. (The months from June through August are generally devoted to reruns.) During these years, government and citizens became increasingly interested in the problems of drug use. The criteria for "drug," "significant," and "use" are the same as those noted above in the discussion of films.

As part of a larger study of media treatment of drug use and other problems, machinery had been established for screening and content analyzing all network entertainment programs during this period, at the time of their original broadcast. It is certainly likely that some relevant programs were not included, although every effort was made to include all germane programs. Only first-run programs originating on networks were used.

There was little difficulty in deciding on the programs which contained relevant content. At least two persons coded each program in accordance with a coding instrument which had previously been developed and validated. Any differences in coding were resolved by discussion.

Specific Programs

The specific programs which were included in this content analysis are set forth in Table 3 below. They are given by the series title and original air date. Although most series have a separate title for each episode, e.g., the November 3, 1971, program of Mannix is called "The Glass Trap," some series have no special titles. For purposes of uniformity of presentation, each

TABLE 3

Programs with Drug-related Content Shown in 1970–71 and 1971–72 Seasons

Series	Broadcast date
Adam 12	October 17, 1970
	February 4, 1971
	March 11, 1971.
	April 1, 1971
	November 3, 1971
	January 12, 1972
	January 26, 1972
Dan August	October 7, 1970
	March 18, 1971
Hawaii Five-O	September 23, 1970
	February 29, 1972
Headmaster	September 18, 1970
Ironside	October 1, 1970
	November 12, 1970
	November 19, 1970
	March 3, 1971
	April 15, 1971
	October 19, 1971
	November 23, 1971
Mannix	January 30, 1971
	September 29, 1971
	November 3, 1971
Marcus Welby, M.D.	November 10, 1970
Mat Lincoln	October 8, 1970
	November 5, 1970
Medical Center	October 21, 1970
	February 16, 1970
Men at Law	March 31, 1971
Mission: Impossible	October 23, 1971
	December 18, 1971
	January 1, 1972
	January 22, 1972
Mod Squad	September 8, 1970
	November 17, 1970
	February 16, 1971
	February 23, 1971
	September 28, 1971
	October 19, 1971
O'Hara, United States Treasury	September 18, 1971
	October 29, 1971
	March 3, 1972
Room 222	April 7, 1971
The Bold Ones	September 20, 1970
	October 31, 1971
The D A	October 15, 1971
The FBI	November 29, 1970
	May 16, 1971
The Interns	September 25, 1970
	November 27, 1970
	December 18, 1970
The Name of the Game	September 18, 1970
	October 16, 1970
The Psychiatrist	December 14, 1970
	February 3, 1971
The Smith Family	January 20, 1971
	May 16, 1971

program is identified by the series title and the dates of relevant programs. There are 56 programs in all.

It is possible to classify each of the above programs into one of the three basic categories of nonmusical features, as follows:

Action/ adventure/ mystery	41
Medical/ psychiatric	10
Drama	5
Total	56

These 56 programs appeared over a period of 2 years, during the 39-week period from September through May. At an average of 28 per year over 39 weeks, there was a network drug-related program broadcast approximately every 9 days, if we assume that their showings were distributed reasonably regularly throughout the 2 years. This is a substantial incidence of entertainment programs on one theme, but it is only a small part of the networks' output during this period.

There were about twice as many programs during the 1970–71 season as in 1971–72. It may be that the series, in their initial response to President Nixon's request, in 1970–71 explored the situation in which drug use was relevant and that it became difficult for writers to develop fresh situations.

Television folklore holds that an entertainment program achieving less than 30% share of the possible audience will not be renewed after its initial 13-week run. Practically all of the series studied were on the air for several seasons, so they probably attracted large audiences. Even a minimally successful program reaches more people than most successful movies. Many of the programs studied already have been shown again during summer syndication reruns. As a result, they can be seen by many millions of persons in addition to their first audiences.

All three networks are represented among the 56 programs. There are 17 different regular series, 2 miniseries within a large program sequence, and 1 "television motion picture series." Most programs are 1 hour long; two are 1½ hours and one is 2 hours long; ten are ½ hour. Most programs were sponsored and thus were able to use perhaps 50 minutes of each hour for program content, because 10 minutes are for commercial messages.

The performers in these programs include some of the country's most prominent actors, e.g., Gene Barry, Theodore Bikel, Raymond Burr, Richard Conte, Broderick Crawford, Sammy Davis, Jr., Glenn Ford, Anthony Franciosa, Lee Grant, Julie Harris, Katina Paxinou, Nipsey Russell, Robert Stack, and Orson Welles.

Who Are the Users?

What kinds of persons are shown as drug users in these 56 programs? There are 21 programs with male users and the same number with females. Fourteen programs deal with both sexes.

In 39 programs, whites are the primary users. Fifteen programs have Blacks, and there is one each with Chicanos and Puerto Ricans. Programs with minority group users usually also show whites.

Most (37) programs feature middle-class persons, with 13 concerned with lower class, 1 with upper class, and 2 with hippie users. Three programs present persons from a variety of backgrounds.

Twenty-six programs deal with single and 14 with married persons. Marital status of the protagonists of 16 programs could not be determined.

The users tend to be young. Fourteen programs deal with users under 20, and one presents a 12-year-old heroin addict. Sixteen have users from 20 to 30, nine with 31 to 40, and two with the over 41 group. Fifteen deal with mixed age groups.

The primary occupational group represented by the users in each program and the number of programs in which they figure are as follows:

Student	11
Housewife	8
Entertainer	4
Prostitute	3
Pusher	2
Teacher	2
Hippie	2
Counselor	1
Athlete	1
Scientist	1
Attendant	1
Informant	1
Physician	1

In the 20 other programs, there was no identifiable occupation or so many were shown that no summary is possible.

Characterizing the programs by the primary kind of drug use shown, we find:

Tryer-experimenters	3
Recreational-social users	11
Heavy users	12
Dysfunctional abusers	24

There are six programs in which there are accidental users; e.g., a person is served food containing LSD.

A wide range of drugs is presented in the programs. Eight programs deal with mixed dependencies. In the others, the most frequently used substances can be summarized:

Heroin	25
Marihuana	7
Hallucinogens	7
Amphetamines	4
Barbiturates	4
Cocaine	1

Three of the four programs concerned with barbiturate use appeared in the 1971–72 season, during which there was an actual and substantial increase in barbiturate abuse.

Circumstances of Use

A number of settings and circumstances for drug use are found in the programs.

Twenty-five locales are clearly urban, ten suburban, and three rural. Two are hippie communes, and six are foreign. Ten cannot easily be placed.

Reflecting the medical emphasis of five of the series, eight programs are centered in clinics or hospitals. The problems and realities of security for analgesic drugs in a medical setting figure in one situation. Other unusual settings include a carnival, a naval vessel, and an orphanage.

Exigencies of plot lead to some unusual settings for drug activities. A pleasant weekend in a mountain retreat becomes a horrible nightmare for a police chief after he is stranded in a cabin with a narcotic addict who has exhausted his supply of drugs. In the same series, an elderly Armenian is forced by two of his nephews into using his tobacco shop as a cover for marihuana sales.

The established formats for television series necessarily influence the types of situation that can be presented. Thus, because there is a series about the headmaster of a private high school and one about a public high school teacher, each of these persons is involved with student drug use. There is no series about a college campus, which may help to explain why it does not figure in any program studied.

Four different programs present drug use during a party. In only seven of the other programs, however, is drug use a social activity. Most (40) programs convey it as solitary. In five programs, it is sometimes solitary and sometimes social. Where there is a social activity connected with the drug interaction, it is never a pleasurable situation, presumably in order to minimize identification on the part of viewers.

Most of the programs observe the Code prohibition against showing actual ingestion. There are two programs, however, in which there is an explicit suggestion of a person "shooting up" heroin with a hypodermic. In each case, the actual ingestion is not fully shown on camera. In the three cases where marihuana smoking is more than implied, either the scene is very brief, contributes significantly to character delineation or advancement of the plot, or the user is subsequently inferentially censured.

All five cases in which there is ingestion appear to have employed a common sense point of view on the part of the writer or director, in that there is no lingering over the activity and what is shown is not instructional. Also, background music is not used to highlight the scene. Some possible negative aspects of the relationship between drug use and music are implied in a program about a popular singer whose effort at a comeback is destroyed by her role in smuggling heroin.

Effects of Drug Use

The consequences and effects of drug use are almost uniformly presented as being personally and socially undesirable. Euphoria is not a concomitant of heroin use. Rather, the desperate urgency of the heroin addict's craving emerges clearly. One band of addicts is so frantic that they assault a physician who is trying to treat one of them. The 16-year-old host at a marihuana party dies of a heroin overdose.

Overdoses are consequences of heroin in nine programs. In one case, the overdose is responsible for the user being in critical condition, and in the other eight, the users die.

A pill-popping housewife is so confused by the substances she is taking that she cannot recall what happened on an evening during which her husband was shot. The several marihuana-related programs do not present its effect positively.

There are four times as many "freaks" seeking kicks as "heads" seeking mind expansion in these programs.[29] Few "freaks" or "heads" achieve their goals.

Where drug culture details are shown, they are ugly. A woman who believes that a friend of her family is leading a fascinating existence learns that he is a heroin addict, whose life is sordid and dangerous.

Drug use is presented as an activity which may have unpleasant repercussions long after the original experience. For example, three medical students who do not get into difficulties at the time that they give LSD to another student as a prank later find their lives in shambles. Even a scientist conducting careful research on Mexican Indians' employment of hallucinogenics almost dies as a result.

Law Enforcement

Law enforcement activities are found in the majority (38) of the programs. A broad range of functionaries is found: a male-female enforcement team, a Los Angeles radio car police team, a semiretired officer who has a special role with the San Francisco police, a youthful male-female police team, a marshal from New Mexico who is attached to the New York Police Department, a Treasury agent, a Hawaiian police team, a police lieutenant, and a private detective. One series (Name of the Game) features investigative reporters.

Law enforcement officials on television tend to be scrupulously honest. The few dishonest ones are caught and punished. In one program, a police lieutenant engages in entrapment in order to arrest a pusher who has sold marihuana to his daughter. When a colleague and a police chief discover the situation, they prefer charges against the lieutenant.

When officials of the criminal justice system err, it is sometimes on the side of being too tough. One parole officer with a narcotics caseload is tough on his clients because his sister had a bad LSD trip.

The police will go to extraordinary lengths in order to achieve their goals. In one typical episode, two Treasury agents establish a "front" business, get themselves arrested, and arrange to get out of jail, in order to develop reputations as heroin wholesalers as part of their strategy. A police chief goes to prison after heroin and "syndicate" assets are traced to him, as part of an investigation of drug pushing.

A number of programs present how the distribution of heroin relates to other illegal activities. In one situation, the "syndicate" which controls a city's prostitution and heroin traffic is trying to get a lucrative contract for garbage removal by its withholding heroin from the addicted daughter of a city councilman whose vote is needed for the contract.

The international machinery for smuggling of heroin is presented in a number of ways. In one case, a Treasury agent is tracking some heroin to a carnival in Mexico. Another program deals with the world's largest plant for converting opium to heroin, on an island off the coast of Africa.

Heroin traffickers often are involved in exotic psychiatric conditions. A man who developed catatonia after presumably witnessing his wife being murdered not only turns out to be the murderer but to have feigned catatonia. After shooting his accomplice, he falls into a genuine catatonic trance.

Nonpsychiatric conditions among drug sellers often are unusual. One heroin smuggler dies from a rare chemical given him by a tattoo parlor. Another criminal who is led to believe that he had had a heart transplant from a priest seems to behave like a priest.

The ingenuity of smugglers figures in many programs. In one, after the death of a young bride from a heroin overdose, her coffin is used to smuggle millions of dollars to Switzerland as part of a major "caper."

Law enforcement officials usually stay with a case until it is solved. They are likely to be concerned with civil rights of defendants and with established procedures for collecting and preserving evidence.

Television policemen tend to be concerned with "big" cases, which have a number of dramatic climaxes and subclimaxes. The frequently repetitive drudgery of police work is unlikely to figure in television programs, presumably because it would not contribute to a paced conflict situation.

Treatment

Current issues in treatment of the drug user are built into a number of programs. One psychiatrist must decide whether to use methadone to help an ex-addict patient on parole, even though state law prohibits parolees from taking any drugs. Another program deals with an unmarried pregnant addict who enters a research unit where young addicts get clinical tests.

A paraprofessional assists a psychiatrist and plays a major role in helping a small town to cope with an epidemic of drug abuse. The psychiatrist, who is clearly an "active therapist," encourages the ex-addict parolee to spend the night at his home after the latter has been absent from his therapy group.

When one physician finds a 16-year-old retardate ill from an overdose at a hippie commune, the head of the commune becomes frightened and takes the doctor along as a hostage. When a patient of the physician misses an encounter session, he tells her parents that she is using drugs.

When a 14-year-old girl dies of overdose, her physician looks for help at Synanon, where residents question him about his motives during a group session.

In one program, voluntary sensitivity sessions are introduced into a high school as one way of dealing with drug use, and a student is helped by the sessions to gain insight into his problem.

Most of the drug users who are in treatment succeed in doing well. Usually, the contrast between their desperate situation before the change in their lives and the new, constructive development is striking. The programs tend to convey a positive and enthusiastic impression of what can be accomplished by treatment.

The only helping professional who is presented unfavorably in the programs studied is an unscrupulous psychiatrist who runs a mental hospital and is using drugs in order to disorient a patient so that she will be unable to testify about a murder she witnessed. Otherwise, the practitioners shown are heavily and responsibly involved with the care of their patients. They provide help, if needed, for pushers and cooperate with the criminal justice system.

Some physicians run afoul of the law and become suspects in serious criminal cases. One physician is the prime suspect in the murder of the hostess at a party, but he cannot recall the situation because he had been given drugged punch.

There have been scattered reports of drug users who were assisted or encouraged in their motivation to seek treatment because of a television program which they saw. After one 1971 program (Hawaii Five-O) dealing with amphetamines, a group of 40 midwest "speed freaks" applied for treatment as a group because of the program.

Differences Between Movies and Television

The differences between the audiences for television and movies and in their procedures for control of content are probably responsible for the differences in the manner in which the two media deal with drug use.

Drug use content is studied very carefully to establish whether and what kind of editing might be required before a movie can be telecast. Some examples may convey the kinds of adjustments made in movies when they are shown over network television.

In the film *Night of the Following Day*, the original Hollywood version (rated R) showed an airline stewardess sniffing cocaine in an airplane washroom and in her home. As a result, she is in a stupor at a time when she expected to be alert and participating in a criminal scheme. The (1972) television version did not include any scenes in which the stewardess is shown sniffing cocaine. Instead, we see a shot of a hand picking up a bottle of Scotch whisky, and we subsequently see the same bottle, empty, in a sink. When the stewardess is then shown in a stupor, the implication is that her condition is attributable to heavy drinking.

In *The Eye of the Cat*, a Hollywood film which was shown (1971) on network television, the original version (rated PG) included two sequences of attractive young adults casually smoking marihuana. They are obviously deriving pleasure from doing so, their smoking is presented as an "in" activity, and details of inhalation are presented. Neither scene appeared in the version shown on network television.

If the changes noted had not been made in the two films, it is probable that they would not have been shown on a television network. In both films, ingestion of the psychoactive substance was cut because it was believed to be overly graphic and informative and might contribute to emulation on the part of some viewers. When the films were shown theatrically, the rating they received indicated their degree of nonsuitability for young people, but such gradations do not exist in television.

Each scene involving ingestion is considered in

terms of its context and relationship to the rest of the film, and some films with such contents have been shown without changes. The film version of *The Man With the Golden Arm*, which created so much furor when it was originally released in 1955, was shown uncut on network television in 1967. An uncut version of the 1966 film *Synanon* appeared on network television in 1971. Both films show a heroin user "shooting up." The networks presenting these films presumably felt that any risk of showing the drug ingestion scenes was balanced by the contribution they made to the larger themes of the films, which are concerned with rehabilitation of heroin users.

As our society makes a more direct attack on its drug problems, we may speculate that television will be presenting more of the dimensions found in theatrical movies. At this time, however, there are still substantial differences in how the two media present drug-related content. One difference is that television programs tend either to be primarily concerned with some aspect of drug use or not to refer to it at all. Although movies routinely may contain some significant content related to drug use even if they are not primarily "drug movies," such content is quite infrequent in television.

One reason for television's lack of nonsalient references to drugs is the relatively brief period of time, about 50 minutes, that is available for the average network dramatic program, which makes it difficult for the plot to diverge too far from its basic theme. Furthermore, the need to photograph a new program each week minimizes opportunities for extra sets, character actors who are not central to the action, and other dimensions of a nontelevision movie.

Another reason is the desire of network programmers not to convey a casual attitude toward drug use. To show it as a routinized and accepted part of a person's life may, it is felt, encourages some susceptible young people to become more interested in the subject.

Television tends to be more accurate in its depiction of drug effects than are movies. In only a few programs was the drug-related behavior inconsistent with what is known about the pharmacology of the substance. However, the incidence of overdose and related deaths is extraordinarily high.

Law enforcement officials on television are usually much more cautious and sensitive to the rights of others than are their movie counterparts. They tend to be more pleasant and less obsessive than movie police, perhaps because the latter's ferocity (e.g., *The French Connection*) is only experienced once by the audience. In contrast, the heroes of a television series must appear on the screen every week for months and even years. To give them larger than life qualities and anticipate that such qualities can be acceptable to audiences on a long-term basis is probably unrealistic.

Another difference is that a substantial minority of the television drama dealing with drug use is concerned with details of treatment, which gets little attention in movies. The television medium seems to thrive on a handsome young doctor (e.g., Medical Center) or an older seasoned healer (e.g., Marcus Welby, M.D.) who can focus his skills on helping a drug user, but the subject evidently poses difficulties for movie makers. Movies of recent years that have been concerned with medical settings, e.g., *Hospital* (1971), tend to be concerned with sexual and moral problems of physicians and nurses, rather than with their patients' problems.

Although we noted above the five basic kinds of drug films in recent years (youth and "antisquare," urban drug culture, police chase, losers, and hippie), the only one of these which is significantly represented on television is the police chase. It is possible that the other four types do not lend themselves to the time and content constraints of television and its need to present situations that have a clear resolution.

Attitudes Toward Drugs

What attitudes toward drug use are conveyed by these programs? In a number of programs, efforts are made to convey some of the reasons for people "turning on." Peer pressure as a dimension of drugs figures in several contexts. Thus, in one high school situation, a young man is ostracized by his fellow athletes because he will not participate in drug use in a social setting. In another high school situation, difficulties of communication between teachers and students figure in the etiology of drug use. Where ghetto drug use is presented, it tends to be a function of alienation and marginality.

In four fifths of the programs, drug use is interpreted as a reflection of a person having a certain kind of relationship to society. In the other programs, the pusher rather than society appears responsible for the start of a person's drug involvement.

A response from society is necessary because the drug user in television drama is usually in some sort of unpleasant crisis situation. If a seller, the police are likely to be cornering him. If a nonseller user, he typically is in a situation of distress.

Although a wide range of substances and kinds of users is presented in television dramas, the three underlying themes of the programs are (1) prosecution of pushers, (2) disapproval of drug use, and (3) help for the person already involved in drugs. The notion that treatment is probably the most appropriate option for a drug user is stressed. The physicians who deal with drug users tend to be very committed to their work. Like the television police who pursue a criminal until he has been caught, the healers stay with their charges until some resolution is achieved. Practically every patient shows therapeutic movement. Therapeutic communities and group psychotherapy are presented positively and favorably, perhaps because they easily lend themselves to visualization. One reason that education and prevention activities get hardly any attention is probably the difficulty of building a dramatic episode around a relatively long-term process like education. A patient in treatment can be presented as making a dramatic breakthrough or achieving an accelerated insight, but similar compression over time is difficult in an educational context.

Similarly, one reason that there are almost four times (38) as many law enforcement as treatment (10) oriented programs is probably the greater ease with which dramatic episodes can be constructed around the former. With proportionately so many programs concerned with law enforcement, it is certainly possible that some viewers may attribute more importance to the criminal justice system's role in drug use than may be warranted by reality. Also, the investigators and police in the programs always get their man or woman, which is hardly the case in a real-life situation.[30]

ADVERTISING

Although advertising has little salience and is taken for granted by most people, it is pervasive. The typical consumer pays some attention to an average of 76 advertisements a day. In a recent year (1971), this country spent $20.5 billion on advertising, or more than half of the $36.45 billion outlay for all elementary and high school education.

Approximately $350,000,000 per year is spent on advertising drugs and remedies on radio and television. Some critics argue that exposure to such messages on a continuing basis will predispose many Americans to assume that ordinary problems of living are best handled by "popping a pill."[31] The latent message of advertising for pain-killing drugs, it is argued, is that we can handle our difficulties most directly by a pill. There have been some counterarguments that drugs are abused in countries such as Israel, Denmark, and Sweden, where no drug advertising exists, and that therefore the abuse of drugs must be caused by other factors.[32]

The advertisements for drugs on the electronic media and in newspapers and magazines are for products that enable the user to deal with headaches, nervousness, insomnia, indigestion, and related problems. Some advertisements on television, it has been claimed, use multiple images to communicate a psychedelic experience and thus presumably presensitize their audiences to the attractions of drugs. It has also been argued that a user can easily make the leap from licit drugs, which are promoted by advertising, to illicit drugs.[33]

Actually, there has been an increase in the consumption of both prescription and nonprescription drugs, but the proportion of nonprescription sales has been dropping steadily since 1919, when they were 82% of all drug shipments, to 1969, when they represented 27%.[34] People are increasingly turning to physicians rather than medicating themselves. The chapter in this volume by Manheimer and his associates concludes that Americans' use of prescription drugs tends to be conservative.

One recurrent criticism of advertising is that it presents and reinforces the notion that relief may be obtained from stress by taking a pill, or "better living through chemistry." One study of youths and adults concluded, however, that advertising was the least significant media modality in terms of the stress-relief syndrome.[35]

In spite of such negative findings, a content analysis of drug advertising on television suggested that television influences attitudes, people watch television heavily and buy advertised products, there is an average of at least one drug commercial per hour, and we can assume some kind of audience effect.[36]

The television public is, of course, getting information on drug use from many other sources. Networks and stations are also running public service antidrug abuse commercials, usually 30 or 60 seconds long. It has been estimated that about 8% of all the television public service messages are devoted to drug dependence. Little reliable information is available on the impact of such antidrug abuse commercials, and considering the enormous weight of other media-disseminated drug-related content, it would be surprising if the antidrug abuse commercials could significantly counter what is being communicated by several modalities of mass communication.

POPULAR MUSIC

The largest leisure-oriented industry in America, from a financial viewpoint, is the record and tape industry, which accounts for more than $2 billion a year. Records and tapes are not only purchased for the home, but they are also regularly played over the 300 million radios owned by Americans. Popular music fans, who are primarily between 12 and 32, pay another $150 million annually to hear their favorites in concert.

Rock music is an amalgam of country and western and rhythm and blues music and has been popular for 20 years, longer than any other fashion in popular music. It accounts for 85% of all the records sold in this country in recent years. Generalizations about rock music are complicated because there are subdivisions such as folk rock, blues rock, jug rock, raga rock, acid rock, and glitter rock.

Popular music and specifically rock music have been said to have a significant role in the increase of drug dependence in this country in recent years for a number of reasons: (1) Its performers represent a drug-oriented life-style, (2) its antisocial attitudes, (3) lyrics promote drug use, (4) psychedelic texture of the music and, (5) some aspects of suppliers of music. We shall look at each of these arguments.

Drug-oriented Life-style

Because the rock stars are among the very few people with whom many young people can identify, they become, more than any previous stars in any medium, cultural heroes to be emulated. To the extent that their putative drug use is believed to be related to their achievements, the drug use may be emulated.

Actually, there have always been some popular musicians who used whatever drugs were popular at the time.[37] These musicians always represented a minority, although some were innovators of genius, e.g., Billie Holiday and Charley Parker. Some features of the jazz musicians' life were related to their use of drugs. Situational factors such as fatigue, the need to stay up late, long rides to engagements, constant travel to overnight dates, loneliness in living out of hotels, and the need to appear smiling and fresh for an audience have been mentioned by musicians as related to their drug use.

In addition to such situational factors, we found that role strain and role deprivation problems, as discussed in the author's essay on a sociological theory of drug dependence in the present volume, were significant predisposing factors in determining which musicians would become drug dependent.

Such factors could be seen with special clarity in the deaths within a relatively short time in 1970 of rock superstars Jimi Hendrix and Janis Joplin. Hendrix had been dissatisfied with a former band and with audience demand that he continue to play and perform in his old style when he died of a barbiturate overdose. Joplin had had a downturn in her popularity when she took a fatal injection of heroin.

During the 1960s, there can be little doubt that a number of young people believed that some of the famous musicians with whom they identified were using drugs. There can also be little doubt that the amount and visibility of such use declined dramatically, and more recently, stars like Sonny Bono have even made antidrug films, and a number of groups have recorded antidrug lyrics.

The pressures on rock stars are greater than the pressures on previous popular musicians. The rock stars play before bigger audiences, and their financial and other success can be greater. But the gap between the few stars and the thousands of other musicians is greater than existed in any previous kind of popular music. The Beatles, who were receiving $2.50 each in 1962 for an evening's work, had earned $100 million when the group disbanded in 1971.

Rock musicians' drug use is therefore only the

most recent example of a long tradition of popular music reflecting current drug use patterns. We can speculate that there is, in each musical era, a clear circular reinforcing relationship among five variables: the degree to which a musician feels accepted by the larger culture, his preferred drug, the degree of its acceptance by society, its effects, and the characteristics of the music he plays. This extremely schematic formulation is set forth in Table 4.

We see that in recent years, during which rock music was disapproved of by much of the larger adult society, the drug of choice among rock musicians was cocaine, a highly disapproved substance. The drug is very stimulating, and the music is high energy and stimulating. Similar interactive relationships exist for every previous kind of popular music. It would seem that drug use among musicians is therefore not a fortuitous or casual phenomenon but is related to and emerges from larger social trends.

The possible relationship between popular musicians and drug use had first been discussed in the musical community during the late 1950s, at the time of the organization of the Musicians' Clinic, a psychiatric clinic for the treatment of addicted jazz musicians.[38] The clinic was opened in New York because so many jazz musicians were then heroin dependent. The clinic's existence helped to make for a climate of opinion somewhat inhospitable to drug use among jazz musicians, but this climate had changed when the new young rock musicians began making their way and rock became not just a form of music but also a significant and widely discussed form of social philosophy in the mid-1960s. Many adults thought that the philosophy was antisocial and their perceptions were probably reinforced by the unisex appearance of some performers, e.g., the Beatles, and the scruffiness of others, e.g., Bob Dylan.

Antisocial Attitudes

Many adults assumed that rock music promoted drug use because they felt that the music was antisocial, appealed to young people, and drug use was the most conspicuous antisocial activity of youth. Whereas people of all ages enjoyed the swing music of the 1930s and 1940s, with the arrival of rock in the 1950s, the audience for popular (rock) music became splintered, with a youth subculture emerging as the primary audience.

Rock music is perhaps the first subculture sustained on the basis of a form of music. Music, like clothing and hairstyles and argot, helps to give identity to young people while isolating them.[39] Rock music has served the needs of a subculture of retreatists as well as a contraculture of rebels and an idealist group which rejects both the means and ends of society.[40] The ability of audiences to empathize with the new musicians was enhanced by the extent, unique in popular music history, to which performers often were the composers of what they were playing.

The names of a number of the rock groups were

TABLE 4

Interrelations Among Popular Music, Preferred Drug, and Degree of Acceptance

Time period and type of music	Preferred drug	Degree of acceptance of drug	Degree of acceptance of musicians	Effects of drug	Characteristics of music and representative title
1900–1930 Dixieland	Alcohol	Generally accepted	Generally accepted	Decrease in inhibitions	Loud and aggressive "Alcoholic Blues"
1930–1944 Swing	Marihuana	Marginally acceptable	Marginally acceptable	Feel more light and "swinging"	Light, "swinging" "Sweet Marijuana Brown"
1945–1954 Bop	Heroin	Disapproved	Slight	Loss of affect detachment, withdrawal	Withdrawn, detached "Dilated Pupils"
1955– Rock	Cocaine	Very disapproved	Disapproved	Stimulation, heightening	High volume and energy level "Earth Mother"

almost disorienting and determinedly unconventional. Some names selected almost at random convey the qualities of the names: Steppenwolf, The Velvet Underground, The Fugs, The Jefferson Airplane, America, Sunday's Child, Buffalo Springfield, Electric Flag, Moving Violations, Free Flowing Salt, The Animals, Ten Years After, Blind Faith, Led Zeppelin, Iron Butterfly, and Cream. These names have an almost surrealistic quality which makes the viewer aware that the music coming from the groups is likely to be for special audiences. Some observers have felt that the unusual names of many rock groups are intended to have a druglike effect, in shaking up a person's perceptions.

Lyrics Promoting Drug Use

Perhaps the greatest concern over rock music was that generated by the lyrics. The issue was joined in September 1970 when Spiro Agnew, then Vice President, cited a number of drug-related song lyrics which he felt were encouraging the use of drugs by young people. The putative effects of song lyrics on drug use by young people were translated into national policy in 1971, when the Federal Communications Commission issued an order which required all broadcasters to prescreen all records, determine their lyrics' meaning, decide whether each record promoted or glorified drug use, and decide whether the playing of the records was desirable.

As the country became aroused about what seemed to be the increase in youthful drug use, rock music became a convenient target for many persons who felt that the music was one of the causes which led young people to use drugs.

Some critics argued that the drug-related lyrics in rock music merely reflected, rather than caused, current concerns and problems. They also complained that lyrics related to the consumption of alcohol were a considerable part of previous popular music, but no objection had been made to their promotion of this most dangerous drug of dependence.

There was general agreement that rock lyrics differed from previous popular music. One study of the 1950s concluded that most popular songs of that period were concerned with dating and courtship.[44] The songs provided vehicles for expression and emulation for young people who did not yet have a vocabulary of emotion. Rock lyrics of the 1960s were less concerned with conventional courtship than with larger social themes, problems, and the role of youth in modern society.

There is a problem in determining just what the lyrics of many popular songs mean to their audiences. An adult may conduct a content analysis of lyrics, but such an analysis may not reflect how the lyrics are actually perceived by young people.

One 1972 survey of over a thousand popular songs produced 129 potential drug-related songs, with 176 apparent references to drugs.[42] A panel of seven specialists evaluated the songs' lyrics. According to their consensus, 43% of the songs dealing with marihuana favor its use, 7% are opposed, 29% describe, 21% are conjectural. None of the opiate-related songs favor their use, 67% are opposed, 23% describe, and 10% are conjectural. Songs about cocaine are regarded as 11% in favor, 50% opposed, 35% descriptive, 4% conjectural. Music concerning hallucinogens/psychedelics is 16% in favor, 16% opposed, 34% descriptive, 33% conjectural. Alcohol-related songs are 36% in favor, 36% opposed, 22% descriptive, 6% conjectural. Amphetamine-related songs are 10% in favor, 60% against, 30% descriptive. Songs about drugs in general are 9% in favor, 39% opposed, 26% descriptive, and 26% conjectural. Any such content study must also attempt to consider the impact of the "blockbuster" drug-related lyrics that may enjoy special attention.

Psychedelic Texture

One aspect of popular music is its texture, which may influence the listeners' state of mind and produce psychedelic effects which remind the listeners of previous drug experiences.[43] Previous studies had found that popular music is enjoyed because it either creates a mood, changes an undesirable mood, or sustains an already established mood.[44]

Many persons felt that there was something about the music which encouraged listeners to take drugs while enjoying it. Such popular concern about the connection between listening to music and taking drugs was fanned by two famous rock music festivals which received enormous media coverage. The Woodstock, New York, rock festival in August 1969 attracted 460,000 young people, most of whom smoked marihuana. The widespread marihuana use attracted more attention than the fact that there were only 797 bad trips, of whom

72 had to receive medical assistance. At Altamont in California, in December 1969, 300,000 youths attended a concert given by the Rolling Stones, during which a man was killed, apparently by the Hell's Angels motorcycle gang. Drug use at this festival also was widely discussed in the media.

Some Aspects of Suppliers of Music

In any exploration of the relationship of mass communications and drug dependence, the institutions of distribution and supply must be considered. Publishers, movie studios, television networks, and advertisers have a role in the manner in which and the extent to which there is drug-related content in their output. In the case of popular music, the system of supply is complicated because it includes record manufacturers, radio stations which play records, and concert bookers. Perhaps more clearly than in the case of other media modalities, it is possible to identify a number of changes which could have led to an increase in the drug-related content of the music and occurred in institutions contributing to the supply of rock music during the 1960s.[45] Three changes in the social system of music supply may have contributed to the degree of such content in popular music: radio's efforts to recover some of the audiences which had been taken over by television, the Federal Communications Commission's order that a station with both an AM and FM component had to use different program material for each, and the autonomy granted some recording artists by their contracts.

During the 1950s, television viewing was taking more and more of the time which young people had previously devoted to radio. By the 1960s, radio stations had begun a variety of promotional and other activities designed to attract audiences by offering material not available on television. As part of this effort to broaden audiences, a number of stations and disc jockeys began playing music not available on television, some of which could have been drug related.

In 1966, the Federal Communications Commission ordered that stations with an FM and AM component would have to program separately for each. In a number of cases this led some FM stations, often small and without commercials and lacking programming experience and clearly defined audiences, to become known as "underground radio." These stations, during the late 1960s, tended to be relatively emancipated in their choice of records to be played, often featuring "hard rock" and, sometimes, drug-related lyrics.

Another possible contributor to the drug climate of popular music in the 1960s was the enormous competition among record companies for the few superstars and superstar groups, whose very name on a record might be enough to make it extremely successful. Beginning in 1965 when one noted rock group was signed to a recording contract which, in effect, permitted the group to record whatever it wished, a number of other companies, in order to be competitive, offered similar contracts to other famous performers. As a result, a few companies could not fully exercise their usual gatekeeper functions, and it became easier for some groups to record drug-related music.

In these three situations, the social structure of the broadcasting and music industry itself was responsible for some unanticipated consequences of actions which were originally undertaken in order to achieve certain marketing goals. In popular music as in the other media, there is a reciprocal and complex relationship between what the suppliers provide and the consumers want.

SOME CONCLUDING REMARKS

The various forms of mass communication discussed above provide a setting against which our efforts at treatment, prevention, and control take place. This setting has, until recently, largely been ignored by students of drug dependence. We are just beginning to consider the differential impact of media on people and the complexities in determining how different people perceive and use the media and the significance of unanticipated consequences such as "boomerang effects."

On the basis of current knowledge of the subject, it would seem that mass communication may contribute to the level of the general public's information about and attitudes toward drugs and drug use. How and if some elements in the public become drug dependent, and to what extent they do so, is a function of many variables. In the case of high risk groups, their "tendency systems" must be studied as a function of their role problems and access to drugs.[46]

Of particular interest is the possible relevance of mass communications content to attitudes toward drug use. There is an established view that although controlled experiments report substantial changes in attitudes after exposure to some media, naturalistic studies usually demonstrate few changes.[47] However, it is not surprising that entertainment media may have at least as much of an effect on formal didactic audiovisual materials to which audiences may be exposed involuntarily.

Mass communications convey notions of every aspect of the country's drug dependence situation. In view of the wide range of possible impacts, mass communications deserve and require extensive and continuing scrutiny in terms of their relationships to the various degrees and types of drug dependence.

REFERENCES

1. **DeFleur, M.,** *Theories of Mass Communication,* David McKay, New York, 1970, 118.
2. **McLuhan, H. M.,** Playboy interview, *Playboy,* March 1969, 26.
3. **Taqi, S.,** Treatment of drug usage in some examples of modern English writings, *U. N. Bull. Narcotics,* 24, 17, 1971.
4. **Algren, N.,** *The Man With the Golden Arm,* Doubleday, New York, 1950.
5. **Trocchi, A.,** *Cain's Book,* Grove, New York, 1959.
6. **Rechy, J.,** *City of Night,* Grove, New York, 1960.
7. **Kerouac, J.,** *On the Road,* Viking, New York, 1957.
8. **Burroughs, W.,** *Naked Lunch,* Grove, New York, 1962.
9. **Selby, H.,** *Last Exit to Brooklyn,* Grove, New York, 1964.
10. **Susann, J.,** *Valley of the Dolls,* Bernard Geis, New York, 1966.
11. **Himes, C.,** *Pinktoes,* Putnam, New York, 1965.
12. **Himes, C.,** *Cotton Comes to Harlem,* Putnam, New York, 1966.
13. **Larner, J.,** *The Answer,* Random House, New York, 1968.
14. **Welles, P.,** *Babyhip,* Doubleday, New York, 1967.
15. **Brown, C.,** *Manchild in the Promised Land,* Macmillan, New York, 1965.
16. **Thomas, P.,** *Down These Mean Streets,* Knopf, New York, 1967.
17. **Ginsberg, A.,** *Howl,* City Lights Book Store, San Francisco, 1966.
18. **Winick, C.,** *Taste and the Censor,* Fund for the Republic, New York, 1959.
19. **Winick, C.,** Tendency systems and the effects of a movie dealing with a social problem, *J. Gen. Psychol.,* 68, 289, 1963.
20. **Lyle, J. and Hoffman, H. R.,** Children's use of television and other media, in *Television and Day to Day Life,* Rubinstein, E. A., Ed., Govt. Printing Office, Washington, D.C., 1972, 129.
21. Opinion Research Corporation, *The Public Appraises Movies,* The Corporation, Princeton, 1957.
22. **Winick, C.,** A content analysis of drug related films, in *Social Responses to Drug Use,* National Commission on Marihuana and Drug Abuse, Ed., Govt. Printing Office, Washington, D.C., 1973, 709.
23. **Glick, I. O. and Levy, S. J.,** *Living with Television,* Aldine, Chicago, 1962.
24. **Steiner, G.,** *The People Look at Television,* Knopf, New York, 1963.
25. **Sutherland, E. H. and Cressey, D. R.,** *Principles of Criminology,* Lippincott, New York, 1970.
26. **Winick, C.,** *The Narcotic Addiction Problem,* American Social Health Association, New York, 1971.
27. **Winick, C.,** Censor and sensibility, *J. Broadcasting,* 5, 117, 1961.
28. National Association of Broadcasters, *The Television Code,* The Association, Washington, D.C., 1972.
29. **Davis, F. and Munoz, L.,** Heads and freaks, *J. Health Social Behav.,* 9, 156, 1969.
30. **Winick, C.,** A content analysis of drug related network entertainment prime time programs, in *Social Responses to Drug Use,* National Commission on Marihuana and Drug Abuse, Ed., Govt. Printing Office, Washington, D.C., 1973, 698.
31. **Lennard, H. L., Epstein, L. J., Bernstein, A., and Ransom, D. C.,** *Mystification and Drug Misuse,* Jossey-Bass, San Francisco, 1971.
32. Oxtoby-Smith Company, *Why Do American Youth Use Illicit Drugs,* Report for the Proprietary Association, 1971.
33. **Berger, A. A.,** Ads and addiction, unpublished manuscript, 1971.
34. **Halberstam, M.,** Relief is sometimes a swallow away, *N. Y. Times,* July 3, 1972, 26.
35. **Ianni, F.,** Attitudes toward the relationship among stress relief, advertising, and youthful drug abuse, in *Social Responses to Drug Use,* National Commission on Marihuana and Drug Abuse, Ed., Govt. Printing Office, Washington, D.C., 1973, 612.

36. **Barcus, F. E., Goldstein, J. M., and Pinto, S. K.,** Drug advertising on television, in *Social Responses to Drug Use,* National Commission on Marihuana and Drug Abuse, Ed., Govt. Printing Office, Washington, D.C., 1973, 623.

37. **Winick, C.,** The taste of music: alcohol, drugs, and jazz, *Jazz Monthly,* 8, 8, 1962.

38. **Winick, C. and Nyswander, M.,** Psychotherapy of successful musicians who are drug addicts, *Am. J. Orthopsychiatr.,* 31, 622, 1961.

39. **Winick, C.,** *The New People,* Bobbs Merrill, New York, 1969.

40. **Nible, R.,** Some speculations on rock music, unpublished paper, 1972.

41. **Mendelsohn, H.,** *Mass Entertainment,* College and University Press, New Haven, 1966, 118.

42. **Schwartz, E. S., Feinglass, S. F., and Drucker, C.,** Popular music and drug lyrics, in *Social Responses to Drug Use,* National Commission on Marihuana and Drug Abuse, Ed., Govt. Printing Office, Washington, D.C., 1973, 718.

43. **Krippner, S.,** Influence of "psychedelic" experience on contemporary art and music, in *Hallucinogenic Drug Research,* Gamage, J. R. and Zerkin, E. L., Eds., Stash Press, Bebit, 1970, 83.

44. **Mendelsohn, H.,** *Mass Entertainment,* College and University Press, New Haven, 1966, 118.

45. **Hirsch, P.,** personal communication, June 1, 1974.

46. **Winick, C.,** *J. Gen. Psychol.,* 68, 289, 1963.

47. **Hovland, C. I.,** Reconciling conflicting results derived from experimental and survey studies of attitude change, *Am. Psychologist,* 14, 8, 1959.

SOME DIMENSIONS OF
USERS AND PREVALENCE

USE OF MOOD-CHANGING DRUGS AMONG AMERICAN ADULTS

Dean I. Manheimer, Marianne T. Kleman,
Mitchell B. Balter, and Glen D. Mellinger

TABLE OF CONTENTS

INTRODUCTION

This paper deals with the use of psychotherapeutic drugs among adults in the United States. It is based upon data obtained in intensive personal interviews from a nation-wide probability sample and from two community-wide probability samples of American adults. It thus differs from most previous studies, which have dealt mainly with physicians' or pharmacists' records of prescriptions. Although prescription records reveal a great deal about the prescribing patterns of physicians and the volume of prescriptions issued, they reveal very little about what happens after the patient leaves the physician's office and reveal nothing at all about the use of drugs that are obtained from nonmedical sources. Equally important, medical records contain little or no information about many of the attitudes, values, and other characteristics of individuals with which this study is concerned. No one set of institutional records contains information about the whole spectrum of psychotherapeutic drug use, including how drugs are used as well as how they are acquired. Only by talking directly with a sample of persons representative of an entire community or the nation as a whole is it possible to obtain broad and realistic estimates of drug use, to describe characteristic patterns of drug use, and to learn how these patterns are related to individual needs and values. Ours is the first effort, we believe, to examine in detail and in an integrated series of studies, the patterns of acquisition and use of psychotherapeutic drugs in the United States.

The nation-wide study, with which this paper is mainly concerned, is the most recent in the series of studies that are being planned and carried out jointly by the Institute for Research in Social Behavior, Berkeley, California, and the Social Research Group of The George Washington University, Washington, D.C., with the support and close collaboration of the Psychopharmacology Research Branch of the National Institute of Mental Health.* Other studies in the series include

*The study reported here was conducted under Grants MH-12591 and MH-12590. The former was awarded originally to the Family Research Center, Langley Porter Neuropsychiatric Institute, California Department of Mental Hygiene. The grant was subsequently transferred to the Institute for Research in Social Behavior, an independent, nonprofit organization, which is the successor to the Family Research Center. The latter grant was awarded to the Social Research Group of The George Washington University.

two community-based studies in the San Francisco Bay Area as well as a methodological study on the validity of survey techniques for obtaining data on psychotherapeutic drug use.

Impetus for this research program stems from the increased importance of psychotherapeutic drugs in medical practice, especially since the introduction of tranquilizers in the mid-1950s, and a corresponding need for reliable information on how they are being used.

Previous research has, of course, provided certain indicators of the volume of psychotherapeutic drug use. Balter and Levine[1] report that ". . . it is estimated that a total of 214 million prescriptions (both new and refill) for psychotherapeutic drugs were filled in U.S. drug stores during the year 1970 . . . and these 214 million prescriptions accounted for approximately 17 per cent of the total of 1.3 billion prescriptions for all drugs . . ." In the period from 1958 to 1964, the number of new prescriptions filled for psychotherapeutic drugs was increasing at a faster rate than for all other drugs. That situation was reversed, however, in the more recent period from 1964 to 1970. During this period the number of prescriptions for all other drugs filled in U.S. drug stores rose 50%, while the corresponding rate of increase for psychotherapeutic drugs was 44%.

In any case, there is growing concern that the United States is becoming an "overmedicated" society. This is a popular theme in the U.S. these days, not only in the popular press but also in professional literature.[2-4] An epidemic of drug misuse is portrayed in which untold millions of American adults have become dependent on tranquilizers, sedatives, and stimulants. Others counter with the argument that research and medical practice have demonstrated the effectiveness of psychotherapeutic drugs in alleviating human suffering and that the whole issue is confused by the legacy of "pharmacological Calvinism."[5]

In light of this controversy, we felt it was essential to begin to identify and describe existing *patterns* of psychotherapeutic drug use. How many and what kinds of Americans were using these drugs? How often, in what manner, and under what circumstances did they use them? These data should provide us with some of the tools necessary for an objective and rational evaluation of present societal practices involving psychotherapeutic drugs.

SCOPE AND METHODS

Data from the nation-wide study were obtained from personal interviews with 2,552 adults (ages 18 to 74) living in the contiguous United States. The survey was conducted during late 1970 and early 1971. Respondents were selected by rigorous probability sampling methods in order to form a cross section of American adults living in households. Probability sampling requires that interviews must be completed with a high proportion (conventionally 85%) of the specific individuals designated as eligible for inclusion in the sample. The survey met this requirement.

Interviews lasted nearly 90 minutes, on the average. Questions covered the use and source, as well as the duration and frequency of use of psychotherapeutic drugs (both prescription and nonprescription). We also asked questions about the personal and social characteristics of respondents, covering such areas as health status, extent of being troubled by psychic and somatic symptoms, characteristic ways of coping with emotional distress, medical care practices, attitudes towards psychotherapeutic drugs, general background characteristics, and personality characteristics and values. As will become apparent, we are reporting only a small portion of the available data in this paper.

Prior to conducting full-scale studies in three communities (all of which preceded the national survey), interviewing procedures were pretested for many months in order to minimize any reluctance respondents might have about discussing their use of drugs and to maximize their ability to recall drugs they had used. The pretesting demonstrated the importance of using photographic aids to help respondents recall drugs used and of establishing good rapport with them even before raising the subject of drugs. The "drug recognition chart" pictured both over-the-counter and prescription drugs, life-sized and in color.* Questions about each class of drugs were introduced by first describing the functions of the drugs in that therapeutic class (e.g., to calm down), then showing the recognition chart; only then was the

*Medical Economics, Inc. kindly gave permission to use pictures from the *Physicians' Desk Reference* in preparing the chart.

respondent asked if he had ever used any of the pills shown in the chart.

Given these refined interviewing techniques, most drug users were both willing and able to discuss their use of drugs in considerable detail. Results from the validity study conducted by the Social Research Group[6] indicated that our data on the prevalence of drug use during the past year underestimated by only a few percentage points the results that would have been obtained if there had been no underreporting or memory loss by respondents. The study also demonstrated, however, that the validity of data on drugs used more than 1 year prior to the interview was much less satisfactory. Further, the study demonstrated that estimates of the number of people using a given class of drug (e.g., minor tranquilizers) were more reliable than estimates regarding any specific drugs in the class (e.g., meprobamate). Therefore, data reported in this paper will refer to drugs used during the year preceding interview and to classes of drugs rather than specific drugs.

We define psychotherapeutic drugs as those drugs with principal or significant effects on mood, mental processes, and/or behavior and include drugs that should be obtained through a doctor's prescription (although are sometimes obtained illegally from nonmedical sources) and that could reasonably be assigned to any one of six major therapeutic classes* and drugs with similar indications that can be purchased over the pharmacy counter without a prescription. Alcohol, tobacco, coffee, and tea are not included.

The psychotherapeutic drugs prescribed most frequently in the United States are the minor tranquilizers, sedatives, hypnotics, and stimulants. Antidepressants and major tranquilizers, which are typically directed toward the treatment of more serious illnesses, are less commonly prescribed.[1] The only over-the-counter psychotherapeutic drugs are the stimulants (usually caffeine) and tranquilizers or sedatives which are advertised as calming agents or pills that help promote sleep. It should be noted that, in the United States, over-the-counter psychotherapeutic drugs contain, by law, only small dosages of psychoactive chemical substances.

PATTERNS OF USE AND ACQUISITION OF PSYCHOTHERAPEUTIC DRUGS

During the 1-year period preceding the interview (approximately the calendar year 1970), about one adult in every three had taken a psychotherapeutic drug of some type on one or more occasions. Medically prescribed drugs were taken by about one fourth (22%) of the adults, while only about half as many (12%) used over-the-counter (OTC) drugs. While these figures were not as high as some feared they would be, they revealed that a substantial minority of Americans had used a psychotherapeutic drug one or more times during 1970.

One persistent claim is that many Americans are chronic users of psychotherapeutic drugs, taking them for long periods of time or on frequent occasions. Therefore, our next question was "How often were these drugs being used and in what pattern?" Were sizeable proportions of adults taking these drugs on a daily or regular basis, or did their use tend to be more sporadic? In the national survey, all persons who used a psychotherapeutic drug (obtained either by prescription or over-the-counter) during the past year were classified for the longest period of regular daily use. Only 6% of our respondents had ever used these drugs on a regular daily basis for 6 months or more.** Other data in the study indicated that several long periods of regular daily use of psychotherapeutic drugs over a lifetime was quite rare. In short, while a sizeable proportion of adults had used psychotherapeutic drugs during the past year, relatively few had ever used these drugs on a long-term regular basis.

This finding with respect to use patterns was consistent with our data on attitudes toward psychotherapeutic drugs. Basically we found that Americans' views toward psychotherapeutic drugs were conservative. Most of the attitudinal items we

---

*Minor tranquilizers, which are sometimes referred to as anti-anxiety agents (e.g., meprobamate, chlordiazepoxide); stimulants (e.g., dextroamphetamine, deanol); hypnotics (e.g., secobarbital, glutethimide); sedatives (e.g., phenobarbital, bromisovalum); major tranquilizers, which are sometimes referred to as anti-psychotic agents (e.g., chlorpromazine, haloperidol); and antidepressants (e.g., imipramine, isocarboxazid).

**Although the classification procedure required that a person had used a psychotherapeutic drug during the past year, the period of longest use could have occurred in a prior year. Thus the number of persons who used a drug for 6 months or longer during the *past* year is smaller than the figures shown here.

used dealt with tranquilizers because this is the class of psychotherapeutic drug which is most frequently prescribed and with which people are most familiar. Although the vast majority of respondents felt that tranquilizers were effective in calming a person, most had some misgivings as well. For example, 87% felt that use of will power was preferable to taking a tranquilizer. Sizeable majorities were also concerned about the safety of tranquilizers and possible bad side effects.

Even the users of psychotherapeutic drugs tended to hold conservative views about such use. For example, 60% of those who had themselves used tranquilizing drugs felt that tranquilizers "don't really cure anything, they just cover up the real problem," and 82% still felt that will power was preferable despite their own choice. In effect, these drug users were telling us, "Yes, I've taken these drugs, but I don't really like the idea."

The extent to which people approved of the use of psychotherapeutic drugs varied considerably with the purpose for which they were being used. When asked about using medically prescribed tranquilizers in the context of work, only 13% approved of using a tranquilizer to "be even more efficient and productive," whereas 55% approved of using the drug "when someone is upset and nervous and not working as well as he should." This finding reflects an essentially moralistic judgment that it's all right for someone to use a psychotherapeutic drug if he *must*, if something is *really* bothering him, but that it is definitely *not* all right to use such a drug simply because he *wants* to or because he would like to improve an already adequate situation.

Turning now to use of psychotherapeutic drugs by demographic subgroups, we found that women were far more likely than men to take these drugs. Whereas about four in ten women used a prescription or over-the-counter psychotherapeutic drug during the past year, only about two in ten men had done so. Interestingly, almost equal proportions of men and women had used OTC psychotherapeutic drugs, indicating that the overall differential rate of use by men and women was caused solely by the fact that far more women than men had used medically prescribed psychotherapeutic drugs. Possible reasons for this difference shall be discussed later in the chapter.

When we examined the use of any psychotherapeutic drug, regardless of whether obtained by medical prescription or purchased over-the-counter, we found that the proportion of men using any such drug was relatively high for the 18- to 29-year-old group, dropped significantly in the middle years, and increased again after age 60. In contrast, use by women did not differ by age. If anything, there was a slight decline with age.

Comparing young, middle-aged, and older persons, we found marked differences in the *type* of psychotherapeutic drug predominantly used. From age 30 on, the great majority of persons using psychotherapeutic drugs obtained them from a medical source. In contrast, younger drug users typically by-passed the medical system and medicated themselves with OTC drugs. In other words, if one considers only the medically prescribed psychotherapeutic drugs, it was older rather than younger persons who were more likely to be users.

To date, we are not entirely sure that we can explain these differences. Originally we expected to find a higher proportion of older persons reporting the kinds of psychic distress that lead to the use of these drugs, but in fact just the reverse was true. Those under age 30 actually reported higher levels of psychic distress than their elders. Another possible explanation was that young persons might be less likely to go to the doctor. However, while this turned out to be true for young men, it was not true for young women. For the time being, the best explanation seems to be that young people are more willing than their elders to rely on the relatively accessible (though less potent) OTC drugs as a way of coping with psychic distress. It may be worth noting that young people were also more likely to use alcohol than older persons, although evidence to be reported in a later article suggests that alcohol may not be simply an alternative to psychotherapeutic drugs but rather may serve, to some extent, somewhat different functions.

In comparing the relative proportions of adults who drank during the previous year to those who used psychotherapeutic drugs, we found that alcohol was the "drug of choice" for American adults. More than twice as many adults drank alcohol as used psychotherapeutic drugs. And almost 20% of our sample drank on 11 or more days during the previous month. (We chose the arbitrary figure of 11 days to exclude those people who drank only on weekends, the time when most purely social drinking occurs.)

As has been well documented in other studies,[7-9] we found that men were more likely to drink alcohol and to drink alcohol more heavily than women. On the other hand, as we discussed earlier, women were more likely than men to use medically prescribed psychotherapeutic drugs.

Although a complete analysis of the underlying reasons for these differences is beyond the scope of this chapter, we know that women were at least more willing to admit to emotional distress than men, and obtaining psychotherapeutic drugs from a physician is a way of coping with emotional problems that appears to be more culturally appropriate for women. For men to do so would perhaps imply an admission of sickness, weakness, and dependency that is inconsistent with traditional American standards of masculinity. Use of alcohol does not threaten a man's masculinity, and this may partially account for men being more likely to drink than women. If men are drinking to obtain emotional relief, then perhaps we are simply seeing the reflection of alternative methods of coping with emotional distress or other problems depending on what is culturally appropriate for one's sex. Future papers resulting from this study will explore the possibility more fully.

In the results discussed so far, we have disregarded the use of prescription psychotherapeutic drugs if they were not medically prescribed. However, one of the aims of the study was to find out the extent to which prescription drugs were being obtained from nonmedical sources, that is, from family members, friends, co-workers or even the local black market. Nation-wide, very few adults reported such nonmedical sources for their drugs. Young men (under age 30) were most likely to have obtained their prescription drugs from a nonmedical source, but even in this age and sex group less than one person in ten reported doing so.

Because this kind of use was very infrequent nationally, we would like to turn now to our two community studies in California* where we found appreciably greater prevalence of the use of prescription drugs from nonmedical sources. For example, in the San Francisco study (1967–68), about 20% of the young men reported using a prescription drug obtained from a nonmedical source. This finding is not unique to the city of San Francisco, by the way, because we obtained an even higher figure in a neighboring suburban area a year or so later. These findings were consistent with results from the national study showing that use of psychotherapeutic drugs, from whatever source, was more widespread on the West Coast than elsewhere in the United States. It should be noted, however, that data from both the San Francisco and suburban study also showed that persons who used prescription psychotherapeutic drugs from a nonmedical source were much less likely to use them on a regular, continuing basis than were persons who used medically prescribed drugs.[10,11]

The San Francisco study also included a question on whether or not the respondent had ever used marijuana. We have reported elsewhere[12,13] that among persons 18 to 34 years of age living in San Francisco, about one third of the men and one fourth of the women had ever used marijuana one or more times. Further, the likelihood of a person in this age group using marijuana was higher among those who had ever used a prescription-type psychotherapeutic drug than it was among those who had not. However, closer inspection of this finding revealed that it was not use of psychotherapeutic drugs per se which mattered, but rather *how* the drugs were obtained. The distinction became apparent when we divided persons in this age group who had used prescription-type psychotherapeutic drugs into two groups: those who had obtained their drugs from a medical source and those who obtained them from a nonmedical source. In the former group, the likelihood of having used marijuana was about the same as it was among persons who had not used prescription drugs at all. But the proportion having used marijuana was very high indeed among persons who had obtained at least one prescription-type drug from a nonmedical source; three fourths of the men in this group had used marijuana as had half of the women. To view this finding in its proper perspective, however, we should point out that while the proportion using marijuana at least once was very high in this particular subgroup, the group represented a very small segment of the population.

PATTERNS OF ILLICIT DRUG USE

There is no question that use of marijuana is increasing in the United States and that this

*Both community studies were similar in scope and design to the nation-wide study. The first was conducted in San Francisco in 1967–68. The second was conducted in parts of neighboring Contra Costa County a year and one half later.

increase is viewed with alarm by growing numbers of people. We feel, however, that in this area of drug use a distinction must be made between the concept of *illicit use* and the realities of *hard-core abuse*. Without such a distinction, you must lump together all kinds of illicit drug behavior — behavior which extends from minor technical transgressions of the law up to and including physiological dependency and serious psychological involvement. In so doing, the apparent size of the problem becomes equal to the number of people who have used drugs illicitly, and, by this definition, the problem assumes overwhelming proportions.

We would like, therefore, to examine the use of marijuana in more detail, using as our data the results from our second community study in California (1969) conducted in the suburban area close to San Francisco. In the suburban study we not only asked our respondents if they had ever used marijuana (the only question asked of San Franciscans) but also how often, how recently, and when they had first tried it. As in San Francisco, we found that among persons aged 18 to 34 years, roughly one third of the men and one fourth of the women had ever used marijuana. When we examined the distribution of number of times used, however, we found that among users of marijuana, about one third of the men and one half of the women had only experimented with it, using it no more than three times. At the other end of the continuum, among the users, about a third of both men and women had used marijuana 50 or more times. Use of alcohol covers a similarly wide range, from the occasional social drinker to those who have serious drinking problems. And just as every person who has ever used alcohol cannot be viewed as an alcoholic, we feel it unwarranted to label the infrequent user of marijuana as a hard-core drug abuser. For these reasons, we are inclined to believe that reports which stress the number of persons who have *ever* used marijuana tend to give an exaggerated view of the hard-core drug abuse problem.

With respect to characteristics associated with use of marijuana, we found that use was more prevalent among persons who were unconventional in certain ways, such as those with no religious affiliation, those who have sought psychiatric help, etc. Nevertheless, the data cannot be interpreted to mean that all or even most marijuana users are socially deviant or psychologically troubled. For example, even though use of marijuana was more frequently found among those with no religious affiliation as compared to those with such affiliation, the fact remains that over three fourths of our marijuana users *did* profess a religious affiliation, which makes them quite similar, as a group, to the group who did not use marijuana. Indeed, it is obvious that as more and more persons begin using marijuana, the overall differences between marijuana users and nonusers will tend to diminish. Those who used marijuana when it was rarely used probably were quite different in their characteristics from nonusers. A finding from our suburban study illustrates this point: Among young men who first used marijuana more than 2 years prior to being interviewed, 75% were presently smoking cigarettes; among those who started less than 2 years earlier, only 45% were presently smoking cigarettes. This latter group did not differ markedly from those who had never used marijuana, among whom 36% were presently smoking cigarettes. We do not mean to imply that a drug abuse problem does not exist in the United States. Among the growing number of illicit drug users in the U.S. there is a small proportion who are heavily involved in the activity. We have evidence from a study of a large, elite university population (1971) that although a great majority of the students had used marijuana, a much smaller proportion were intensively involved with a drug or had used many different illicit drugs. This small subgroup was also found to admit to suffering emotional distress more often than their fellow student. In short, we must concern ourselves with identifying those heavily involved with illicit drugs so that we may educate and treat those who want our help.

SUMMARY

In summary, we have reported findings from three probability sample surveys of psychotherapeutic drug use conducted in two California communities and in the United States as a whole between 1967 and 1971. Results of these studies showed that a sizeable minority of Americans had used medically prescribed or over-the-counter psychotherapeutic drugs during the year prior to interview but that relatively few persons had used these drugs on a regular, continuing basis. Many more persons, by contrast, had used alcohol during the previous year, either occasionally or regularly.

These data also demonstrate that Americans, including those who used psychotherapeutic drugs, generally have distinct qualms and misgivings about the use of psychotherapeutic drugs but will condone their use as a way to cope with impaired functioning. With respect to both legally obtained and illicit drugs, we believe there is an unfortunate tendency to exaggerate the extent of the hard-core abuse problem by considering only the number of persons using drugs while ignoring the manner in which these drugs are used.

REFERENCES

1. **Balter, M. B. and Levine, J.,** Character and Extent of Psychotherapeutic Drug Usage in the United States, presented at the 5th World Congr. Psychiatr., Mexico City, November 30, 1971.
2. **Berg, R. H.,** The over-medicated woman, *McCalls,* 67, 109, September 1971.
3. **Rogers, J. N.,** Stimulus/response: drug abuse by prescription, *Psychol. Today,* 5, 16, September 1971.
4. **Lennard, H. L., Epstein, L. J., Bernstein, A., and Ransom, D. B.,** *Mystification and Drug Misuse,* Jossey-Bass, San Francisco, 1971.
5. **Klerman, G. L.,** A reaffirmation of the efficacy of psychoactive drugs: a response to Turner, *J. Drug Issues,* p. 312, October 1971.
6. **Parry, H. J., Balter, M. B., and Cisin, I. H.,** Primary levels of under-reporting psychotropic drug use (with and without the use of visual aids), *Public Opinion Q.,* 34, 582, 1970–1971.
7. **Cahalan, D., Cisin, I. H., and Crossley, H. M.,** American Drinking Practices: A National Survey of Behavior and Attitudes Related to Alcoholic Beverages, Report No. 3 of the Social Research Group, The George Washington University, Washington, D.C., 1967.
8. **Cahalan, D. and Cisin, I. H.,** American drinking practices: summary of findings from a national probability sample. I. Extent of drinking by population subgroups, *Q. J. Stud. Alcohol,* 29, 130, 1968.
9. **Knupfer, G.,** The epidemiology of problem drinking, *Am. J. Public Health,* 57, 973, 1967.
10. **Mellinger, G. D., Balter, M. B., and Manheimer, D. I.,** Patterns of psychotherapeutic drug use among adults in San Francisco, *Arch. Gen. Psychiatr.,* 25, 385, 1971.
11. **Mellinger, G. D.,** Psychotherapeutic drug use among adults: a model for young drug users? *J. Drug Issues,* p. 274, October 1971.
12. **Manheimer, D. I., Mellinger, G. D., and Balter, M. B.,** Marijuana use among urban adults, *Science,* 166, 1544, 1969.
13. **Manheimer, D. I., Mellinger, G. D., and Balter, M. B.,** Use of marijuana among an urban cross-section of adults, in *Communication and Drug Abuse,* Wittenborn, J. R., Smith, J. P., and Wittenborn, S. A., Eds., Charles C Thomas, Springfield, Ill., 1970.

PSYCHOTROPIC DRUG USE IN AMERICAN FAMILIES

Edgar F. Borgatta

TABLE OF CONTENTS

The main theme guiding the design of the research reported here was to provide a description of the current use of psychotropic drugs in American families. Drugs, for research purposes, are defined to include common pharmaceuticals, but emphasis was placed on substances that would ordinarily be classified as sleeping pills, tranquilizers, sedatives, and stimulants. Information was sought on "legitimate" use of the drugs, but the data collection was designed to provide some information on processes of informal acquisition and diffusion of drugs within families and from friends and relatives.

PSYCHOTROPIC DRUG USE

At the time this study was devised, information on psychotropic drugs used in the population was vague and relatively unresearched. In general, industry and government sources provided no information on the nature of drug use and hardly any information on the amount of pharmaceutical drugs used in the population. One effort was on the way at the Langley Porter Neuropsychiatric Institute and the Psychopharmacology Research Branch of the NIMH. This study, which focused on adults in California, is the reference point for some of our subsequent comments.[1-3] The effort of this study, here called the *California Study,* was directed to an intensive description of patterns of drug use, attitudes towards drugs, and specific knowledge about drugs and their pharmaceutical properties, rather than with the more general description of drug use as an aspect of family process, which was the aspiration of the current study. The subsequent research of this group is reported in part in this volume (see the chapter by Manheimer et al.). Differences in emphases in the studies will be noted, but some findings may warrant comparisons.

An informal estimate based on incidental findings from another study suggested that possibly fewer than 13% of the population reported using tranquilizers. In a newspaper report in 1966,

Gallup reported that 19% of men and 30% of women had ever taken tranquilizers. The form of question used in getting drug information may well influence the type of response, and this was an issue that became quite important in the development of any further study of psychotropic drug use in the population. What is a tranquilizer in the language of the respondent; This was an unknown; some respondents may think that an aspirin is a tranquilizer; others may not know that what they are taking are tranquilizers.

While the basic data on drug use was extremely vague, it was clear in analyzing the sources of information that part of the problem was the complexity of the drug industry and the related professions. At the level of public policy, drugs are controlled on the market through their means of availability. In general, psychotropic drugs that are potentially harmful in misuse require prescription by some authorized agent, particularly the physician. The concept of danger, however, is not a simple one on which there is agreement. First, many dangerous substances are not kept off the market or restricted in purchase, and many effective poisons may be purchased at the local grocery store, hardware, or drug store. Danger implies other things in this context, including misuse by self-administration for medical purposes and possible addiction. Additionally, of course, availability is controlled by public policy for quite different reasons, such as the control of profits in the drug industry, professional interests of pharmacists, physicians, and others in the health professions, and, let us say, notions of public morality.

The control of drug use through availability suggests processes whereby particular types of persons may become users of the drugs. For example, if drugs are properly related to some manifestations of illness or physical disorder, persons with the disorders would be expected to be the likely users. If certain tranquilizers are frequently prescribed for persons who have melancholia, this association should be visible in examination of characteristics of individuals in drug use, assuming the disorder is sufficiently frequent in the general population to be statistically meaningful. At the time this research was initiated, there was a reasonably based assertion of an association between the use of tranquilizers and older women in the population, but meaningful statistics were not available. Some obvious connections could be

projected between drug use and health condition, particularly with regard to mental health. Psychotropic drugs are ostensibly used for the reduction of anxiety, tension, etc. Known use in mental hospitals is directed to types of sedation and quieting that reduces the noise level. Thus, it was a reasonable assertion that on the basis of public policy and its manifestations at various levels including through professional practice, drug use would have important ramifications for persons who have mental or physical problems or who are borderline to such problems.

From the point of view of self-selection, a number of hypotheses may be advanced about who users might be. The most general concept is one that persons who are users of drugs are those who need a "crutch." These are the persons who need some form of assistance in coping with their life situations, and the forms of assistance might be activities in some cases, drugs in others, and other alternatives certainly exist. Smoking behavior, for example, may be viewed not only as providing certain kinds of gratifications but also as providing a "thing to do" to mediate conversation and other circumstances that sometimes become tense. Verbal habits that people develop similarly can provide such "crutches." Drugs are merely one variety of this category when seen as a means of reducing anxiety or tension to facilitate continued social participation by the individual.

The view of drugs as used for a "crutch" sometimes is translated into a "need" approach to explaining human behavior. The approach has many difficulties, theoretically, but sometimes it is useful for illustrative purposes. Thus, use of drugs may be viewed as a response to a need, and this implies "dependence," either in a simple physical sense or in a psychological sense. Similarly, there are needs to smoke, to overeat, and to do other things. The approach does not have explanatory power, but it aids in the description of a class of common conditions at least to the extent of implying that individuals selectively respond to their life situations.

THE SAMPLE

The target population of the sampling was adults in families, inclusively defined as adults living singly, in families, or with families. The definition suggested excluding persons who had not reached adulthood by certain criteria. For example, the idea of the adult population which is operative in the society and relatively independent as autonomous units may be contrasted to other groups, such as full-time students, who presumably may still be preparing for adult status. Since independent studies of students were in process, it was the intention of the original design to exclude students in those cases where they were encountered in the sampling. However, it was felt at the time that the sampling was devised that attempting to exclude full-time college students who were above the minimum age (18 years of age) would involve a difficult set of instructions to convey to interviewers. Thus, the exclusion was made post hoc after the data were compiled. Thirty-two students were eliminated from the study sample on this basis, representing 1.7% of the total data collection. At the other end of the age scale, for a number of complex reasons, it was decided to set the upper age of adults for the study at 55 years of age. The main reason for this was to conform to an idea of the periods of family activity that are the inclusive range of childrearing. There was an implicit feeling that beyond that period additional concepts might arise which would give the study a different flavor. It was not the intent of the research to tackle the complex problems of a gerontological study.

Corresponding to our definition of the relevant population, hospitals, nursing homes, old age homes, and other types of group quarters of an institutional nature were excluded. It was felt that any definition of the population to be sampled would involve difficulties in interpretation, but because of possible vagaries in encountering institutions and difficulties in subsequent interpretation, these were eliminated.

In short, the population was defined as adults 18 to 55 years of age, excluding persons living in group quarters and other institutional settings and excluding students unless they were the adult or senior generation in the household.

The data collection was carried out by National Analysts, Inc., who cooperated with the researcher in the development of the questionnaire and field techniques. The design required the collection of two area probability samples stratified by type of population and geographical area. The first was to represent a sample of all households in continental United States with an interview taken from a randomly selected adult within the household. The second used the same design, but a screening questionnaire was used initially with the selected respondents to ascertain whether or not they used psychotropic drugs. If the random respondent indicated that he or she did use a drug by the identification procedure used in the study, the longer questionnaire that was basic to the study was then used.

In the field operation, in the probability sampling of all households, the number of households for which listing by age was obtained was 1,151. Of these, interviews were completed with 1,022, or 88.8% of the households. The overall completion rate on the basis of the number of households containing eligible respondents was 73.0%. In the identified drug user sample, 925 persons were identified as eligible to respond to the questionnaire, and 899, or 97.2%, completed interviews. There is no analogous overall completion rate since the basis for identification as relevant for the interview was defined by the screening procedure.

In our analysis, our operating samples are somewhat reduced from the numbers indicated above. It has already been indicated that 32 respondents identified as full-time students were removed from the sample. In addition, 18 cases had to be dropped from the study because the forms were judged to have too many blanks to be interpretable. Thus, the operating totals were for 991 respondents in the probability sample of all households, and 880 in the identified drug user sample.

One serious problem arose in the field operation of this study. While the instructions were for the eligibility and the selection of the random respondent to occur by a standard procedure, some appropriate field control was omitted. The procedure to be used was for the listing of all adults in the household between the ages of 18 and 55 years of age and then selection of a random respondent on the basis of predetermined random numbers. Unfortunately, bias developed which resulted in what can be, post hoc, described as a predictable way. The 991 respondents in the probability sample include 285 males and 706 females. The identified drug user sample of 880 was split with 172 males and 708 females. This bias for overselection of females casts doubt on the validity of the sampling procedure and created some difficulties for analysis. Retrospective checks on the sampling procedures used suggested that there should be a bias in the direction found, but in the final analysis, the magnitude of the discrepancy could not be accounted for except by some doorstep modification of the screening procedures. The probable loss of control was that interviewers could manipulate the order of listing. Aside from the discomfort created when procedures are not followed exactly in a presumably scientific work, the net consequence of this discrepancy is that it became necessary to think of the study as composed of four samples, two probability samples of households, one female and one male, and two samples of identified drug users, one female and one male. In the order indicated, these will be identified in the study as FPS, MPS, FDS, and MDS, respectively.

IDENTIFICATION OF DRUG USERS

The problem of identifying users of psychotropic drugs occupied a considerable amount of research and development. Discussions with the researchers of the California Study suggested many of the difficulties associated with valid identification of drug users, and the procedures in the current study were elected along a conservative route. Drug users would be identified by recognition procedures, and, on the doorstep, respondents were asked to identify whether they had, within the past year, used any of the pills on a "Pill Card" that had pictures of pills in common use. The Pill Card actually consisted of two plates inside a plastic jacket, both visible directly through the protective plastic cover. The color reproduction was judged by the researchers to be quite good in comparison to the source of the pictures of the pills, the *Physicians' Desk Reference to Pharmaceutical Specialties and Biologicals*.[4] The reproduction did have one distortion of color, and that was a necessary consequence of the photographic procedures used. In particular, the background for the pills had a slight grayish color instead of being a pure white. There were 54 boxes showing pills on the two plates used for identification. These represented 40 major drug categories, but the additional boxes were required because of the different forms in which these drugs reach the market. In addition, two specific verbal questions were used to get at two drugs that are frequently in liquid form and thus would not be identified by the pictures of the pills. These are meprobamate and phenobarbital. In getting information, after

the identification of a drug in use, the next question asked how long it had been since the drug had been taken. This was followed by a question on dosage. All this information was gathered on the "Selection and Call Report Form" prior to going on to the main body of the questionnaire, where the detailed information on drug use was recorded.

For the probability sample of all households, there were 1,151 cases where the household listing was obtained. This stage of contact may be taken as a standard for at least one purpose of comparison. Of this group, about 11.2% were lost, as indicated earlier, with regard to the final interview. In the final interview information we accumulated, 195 females and 48 males reported using drugs, a total of 243 persons, or 21.1% of the total number of households listed.

A comparable figure is available for the identified drug users. In this case, the number of households where listings were obtained was 6,743. Corresponding to this, the screening provided data for 708 females and 172 males identified as drug users, or a total of 880 persons. The comparable percentage is 13.1% for the identified drug users, the second stage of the data collection, a figure that is considerably lower than that of the probability sample of all households. Thus, again there are questions about the actual operation of the field procedures. It would appear that, on the doorstep, the screening procedures for the second stage involved more arbitrary rejection of respondents, with a greater loss of persons who were drug users; possibly interviewers did not take the same care to establish the information in the second stage of data collection. It should be noted that with reference to sample dwelling units selected, the percentage of household listings obtained was almost identical in comparing the probability sample of all households and the sample of identified drug users.

Table 1 provides the distribution of respondents by total number of drugs used, as reported in the survey. In the FPS, 27.6% reported using one or more drugs, and in the MPS, 16.8% reported using one or more drugs. By way of comparison, the California Study, which collected data in a different way, reported that 29% of their respondents had used psychotropic drugs (stimulants, sedatives, or tranquilizers) in the past 12 months. The California Study provided additional comparative data from a national survey indicating

40 Major Drug Representatives by Categories and Trade Names

Category	Single	Mixed	Multiple
Major psycholeptics	Thorazine Compazine Sparine Stelazine Mellaril	Combid	Eskatrol
Minor psycholeptics	Atavax Librium Valium	Librax	
Substituted diols	Meprobamate Equanil Miltown Deprol Meprospan	Equagesic	
Major antidepressives	Elavil Tofranil		
MAO inhibitors	Nardil Marplan Parnate		
Minor antidepressives	Preludin Dexedrine Ritalin	Edrisal	Dexamyl Ambar
Barbiturate sedatives	Phenobarbitol Butisol Sodium	Donnatal Tedral Fiorinal	
Barbiturate sleeping pills	Nembutal Seconal Amytal		Tuinal
Nonbarbiturate sleeping pills	Doriden Noludar Placidyl		

that 24% reported using at least one of the three types of drugs within the last 12 months. If the data from the current study are standardized to make the proportion of males in the probability sample of all households the same as that of the California Study, then the rate for the current study would be 22.4% reporting use of the drugs within the past 12 months. As we have noted, our procedures of data collection are known to be conservative, and this may account for the low figure in our study. Still, in comparison to the national study mentioned in conjunction with the California Study, the difference is not substantial. We should note that because of slight differences in definitions, the data are not exactly compar-

able, but to detail the differences probably would overemphasize the value of the comparison.

An additional figure is reported on Table 1, the percentage of users of two or more drugs, based on the total number of users in the sample. If the data collection procedures were exactly the same for the probability sample of all households and the sample of identified drug users, the percentages for the two females and for the two males should be the same. This does not turn out to be the case, and the percentages in the probability samples are higher. Again, this discrepancy suggests a need for caution in subsequent interpretation. In the two parallel comparisons, the percentage of users who use two or more drugs is higher for the female

TABLE 1

Distribution of Respondents by Number of Drugs Used*

Total number of drugs used	FPS No.	%	FDS No.	%	MPS No.	%	MDS No.	%
0	511	72.4	–	–	237	83.2	–	–
1	118	16.7	462	65.3	32	11.2	126	73.3
2	43	6.1	154	21.8	10	3.5	30	17.4
3	18	2.5	56	7.9	4	1.4	9	5.2
4	9	1.3	17	2.4	–	–	4	2.3
5	1	0.1	8	1.1	1	0.4	2	1.2
6	4	0.6	9	1.3	–	–	–	–
7	2	0.3	–	–	–	–	1	.6
8	–	–	1	0.1	–	–	–	–
9	–	–	1	0.1	1	0.4	–	–
Total	706		708		285		172	
Total number of users	195	27.6	708	100.0	48	16.8	172	100.0
Users of 2 or more	77	10.9	246	34.7	16	5.6	46	26.7
Users of 2 or more as percent of total number of users	41.6		34.7		33.3		26.7	

*If we were testing hypotheses, correlations would be statistically significant in a one-tailed test with approximately the following magnitudes: For N = 706 or 708, $|r| \geq 0.064$; for N = 285, $|r| \geq 0.099$; for N = 172, $|r| \geq 0.126$, with Alpha = 0.05.

than the male samples. This is consistent with the California Study where an alternate indicator, the percentage of frequent users, showed the rate for females almost twice that of males. While data are not presented here, in our study, alternate measures of rate of use suggest that females use more psychotropic drugs, and more often, but the findings are by no means as dramatic as suggested in the California Study.

The distribution of respondents by type of drug use is indicated in Table 2. While there is some variation in the profile of percentages, differences are not too easily interpreted. The one difference that does appear to be substantial is a higher use of the Minor Psycholeptics by females. Parallel differences occur for Substitute Diols and Major Antidepressives, but the latter are kinds of differences that exist with an enormous question mark in a backburner reference file of trivial differences that might possibly have some meaning.

BACKGROUND CHARACTERISTICS AND DRUG USE

If it is the expectation that background charac-

teristics in the usual sociological categories will be of great importance in determining who is and who is not a psychotropic drug user, there will be some disappointment in the findings of this study. Indeed, the relative lack of differences on the basis of background characteristics counteracts in part some of the discomfort created by the sampling discrepancies already noted. Comparing the FPS to the FDS and the MPS to the MDS, no interpretable differences in mean responses occurred for such variables as employment status, income, educational attainment, location, value of, or type of housing, and marital status (married vs. nonmarried). Examining correlations with number of drugs used, possibly one could become interested in a further look at the relationship of employment status to drug use. No relationship appears between race and drug use, but differences did occur in the proportion of white persons in the samples. While 81% were white in both probability samples, 88% were white in the identified drug users. No corresponding relationship between number of psychotropic drugs used and race was found in either of the probability samples, which might be expected on the basis of the mean differences in the samples. Again, possibly some subtle interviewer bias on the doorstep crept in. However, it should be recognized that the percentage of white persons in the identified drug user sample is actually closer to what one would expect on the basis of probability sampling of all households.

Table 3 presents data corresponding to the above observations, but, in addition, data on *Quick Word Test* scores are indicated.[5] Since some question has arisen on the adequacy of education information to represent one aspect of the socioeconomic status variables, it was decided to utilize an efficient verbal ability test in conjunction with the interview. The findings associated with the *QWT*, however, presented no information substantially different from that already available from the education variable.

While the California Study based its analysis on frequent drug users, it should be noted that it also reported that neither income nor education is very highly related to frequent use of psychotropic drugs. Indeed, in looking over the published data from the California Study, it appears that there is little relationship between background characteristics and frequent drug use, with two

TABLE 2

Distribution of Respondents by Type of Drug Used

Drug type	FPS No.	%	FDS No.	%	MPS No.	%	MDS No.	%
Major psycholeptics	37	19.0	109	15.4	9	18.7	29	16.9
Minor psycholeptics	60	30.8	247	34.9	11	22.9	45	26.2
Substitute diols	62	31.8	186	26.3	14	29.2	42	24.4
Major antidepressives	11	5.6	33	4.7	1	2.1	4	2.3
MAO inhibitors	5	2.6	21	3.0	0	–	2	1.2
Minor antidepressives	42	21.5	117	16.5	8	16.7	33	19.2
Barbiturate sedatives	49	25.1	203	28.7	16	33.3	49	28.5
Barbiturate sleeping pills	23	11.8	69	9.7	6	12.5	12	7.0
Nonbarbiturate sleeping pills	12	6.2	39	5.5	3	6.2	9	5.2
Total number of users	195		708		48		172	

TABLE 3

Background and Drug Use

	Correlation to no. of drugs used				Mean			
	FPS	FDS	MPS	MDS	FPS	FDS	MPS	MDS
Marriage (no, yes)	−0.05	−0.02	−0.10	0.03	0.76	0.77	0.81	0.76
Religious service attendance (often to never)	0.05	0.02	−0.01	0.18	1.71	1.92	2.22	2.30
Education	0.02	0.01	0.06	−0.14	3.84	3.87	4.00	3.98
Now working for pay (yes, no)	0.05	0.02	0.13	0.24	1.58	1.62	1.07	1.10
Worked for pay in last 3 years (yes, no)	0.05	0.03	0.04	0.21	1.38	1.42	1.02	1.08
Apartment vs. house	−0.02	0.04	−0.01	0.01	1.76	1.78	1.76	1.82
Rent vs. own	0.02	0.01	0.02	0.02	1.64	1.65	1.66	1.68
Housing worth code	−0.01	−0.01	0.07	−0.02	0.34	0.35	0.43	0.37
Own income code	−0.03	−0.03	−0.03	−0.13	1.94	1.93	4.22	4.34
Urban to rural	−0.02	0.10	−0.08	−0.10	2.41	2.42	2.45	2.32
Race (others vs. white)	0.03	−0.01	0.02	0.04	0.81	0.88	0.81	0.88
QWT score	0.05	−0.01	0.05	0.10	29.9	31.5	29.9	30.4

possible exceptions: a higher use among the separated and divorced and a lower use among blue collar and laborer occupational categories.

The current study provided the opportunity for close scrutiny of the variables associated with income and occupational status. Three alternate systems were used to classify occupational prestige, ranging from a complex code to a simple ten-category code. Using the subsamples of currently married respondents for whom adequate computation data were available (FPS = 536; FDS = 547; MPS = 232; MDS = 131), it was possible to examine alternate indices of income and status. Thus, for example, one may examine such variables as respondent's income, spouse's income, and total income in parallel. With regard to occupations, it is possible to have the variables of own occupational prestige (taking into consideration housewife as a neutral category), spouse's occupation, highest occupation of the pair, and average of the pair. Even introducing these refinements, it would take a stretch of the imagination to find any suggestive relationships between drug use and socioeconomic indicators.

DRUG USE AND HEALTH

As this chapter moves into the examination of findings, it should be noted that data were analyzed by major categories of drugs in parallel, along with a number of indicators. In observing the large correlation matrices in parallel, it became quite evident that one indicator, the total of the number of drugs reported as used, appeared in general to have the largest correlation coefficients. While occasionally (sporadically) somewhat larger correlation coefficients were encountered for the other more refined variables, it was not possible to derive any systematic information that warrants an attempt to isolate differences in relationships by drug category. The occasional large values encountered would warrant interpretation that the relation was specific to the samples and variables involved. Since this report attempts to provide global information, these types of specific findings are not reported here, and the single indicator of "number of drugs used" is utilized.

The relationship of health to psychotropic drug use should be quite direct. Presumably, the main source of these drugs is through doctors and prescription, or at least through some agency making the drugs available when the person needs them. In the current study, there are a number of indicators that relate directly to health. The information on drug use and health is presented in Table 4, and, in general, the expected relationships are quite visible. One question is direct: "How would you rate your health during the past year?" The mean response on this question is substantially poorer for the identified drug users samples

TABLE 4

Drug Use and Health

	Correlation to no. of drugs used				Mean			
	FPS	FDS	MPS	MDS	FPS	FDS	MPS	MDS
How would you rate your health during the past year? (excellent to poor)	0.27	0.20	0.24	0.06	1.91	2.28	1.69	2.14
During the past year or so would you say that you have had: (less to more sickness than most persons your age?)	0.33	0.18	0.24	0.15	1.54	1.86	1.40	1.66
Have you been hospitalized for an accident during the last 5 years? (no, yes)	0.13	0.00	0.11	−0.01	1.05	1.06	1.11	1.13
Have you been hospitalized for sickness during the last 5 years? (no, yes)	0.22	0.12	0.15	0.12	1.29	1.45	1.18	1.40
How long ago did you see your doctor? (recently to never)	−0.11	0.00	−0.20	−0.12	3.9	3.4	4.5	3.6

than for the probability samples, and the vector of correlations between responses to this question and number of drugs used is, with minor exception, substantially positive. The following related question suggests the same findings: "During the past year or so would you say you have had more, the same, or less sickness than most persons your age?"

An alternate approach to health information has to do with the amount of hospitalization an individual has had during recent history. Two questions were directed to the hospitalization experience of the respondent, one with reference to accidents and one with reference to sickness. If a relationship between hospitalization for reasons of accident and drug use exists, it is at best miniscule. On the other hand, the relationship between drug use and hospitalization for sickness appears to be consistent with the more direct questions on health.

A third approach to the question of health has to do with the recency with which the respondent has been to see a doctor. This type of question, however, is diluted as people go to see doctors for routine checkups, shots, and other reasons as well as in response to illness. The findings for this question are not inconsistent with a hypothesis of association between ill health and drug use, but fortunately this study does not depend on this question for the isolation of this relationship.

A fourth procedure for the analysis of health and drug use is to examine the relationship of certain reported symptoms and drug use. A rather extensive list of symptoms was included in the questionnaire, and the respondent was asked to answer how often he or she was bothered by each. Table 5 presents the summary information from this approach. Examining the mean values, it is seen that the probability samples are lower than the drug user sample on a number of symptoms. These include aches and pains, nausea or stomach upset, dizziness or weak feelings, headaches, skin problems, high blood pressure, and low blood pressure. In varying degrees, the correlation between number of drugs used and the symptoms is positive, but the vectors of correlations across the four samples are not of uniform magnitudes. One symptom, colds, appears to suggest no differences

TABLE 5

Symptoms and Drug Use

About how often are you bothered by each of the following conditions:	Correlation to no. of drugs used				Mean			
	FPS	FDS	MPS	MDS	FPS	FDS	MPS	MDS
Aches and pains	0.21	0.14	0.18	0.10	2.64	2.94	2.34	2.80
Nausea or stomach upset	0.18	0.11	0.04	0.01	1.93	2.22	1.76	2.17
Dizziness or weak feelings	0.20	0.18	0.22	0.07	1.88	2.26	1.49	1.76
Headaches	0.17	0.11	0.04	0.06	2.64	2.85	2.25	2.47
Coughs	0.08	0.02	−0.04	0.00	1.91	2.05	2.05	2.12
Colds	0.04	0.02	−0.06	−0.10	2.22	2.16	2.22	2.26
Irritability or nervousness	0.28	0.22	0.28	0.03	2.86	3.45	2.20	2.78
Skin problems	0.08	0.03	−0.09	−0.09	1.60	1.73	1.36	1.58
High blood pressure	0.01	0.15	0.09	0.01	1.27	1.41	1.15	1.33
Low blood pressure	0.11	0.12	−0.02	0.02	1.44	1.51	1.16	1.19
Too much smoking	0.08	0.08	0.04	0.00	1.77	1.99	2.20	2.27
Too much drinking	0.08	−0.01	−0.07	0.02	1.25	1.24	1.53	1.49
Feeling tense or emotionally upset	0.32	0.23	0.33	−0.03	2.52	3.01	1.99	2.47
Sample size	706	708	285	172				

Note: Responses coded as: 1, never; 2, rarely; 3, occasionally; 4, frequently; 5, all the time.

at all or any relationship to drug use, and the data for coughs are only a trifle more suggestive.

Except for the last two symptoms that have been mentioned, males have lower mean values than females on the symptoms. In the case of coughs, possibly males report the symptom a bit more on the average. It should be noted that two behaviors that may be representative of problems are included in this list, too much smoking and too much drinking. For both of these, the mean values for males are higher than for females. A relationship between drug use and excessive drinking appears dubious, but there is, possibly, the suggestion of a relationship between excessive smoking and drugs used, especially for the female samples. Two additional items listed with the symptoms, "Irritability or nervousness" and "Feeling tense or emotionally upset," are discussed in the next section.

PERSONALITY CHARACTERISTICS AND DRUG USE

Much of the guesstimation about "who" uses psychotropic drugs centers on notions of personality and orientations to life. These concepts were viewed as important to the research, and thus a substantial part of the questionnaire was devoted to getting this type of information. As it happens, a number of other researchers have dealt with the problem of development of relatively efficient measures of personality characteristics, values, and moods. We speak of these as types loosely, and obviously it is hard to separate measures of value from measures of personality, so our designation here is arbitrary. In any event, we used the *S-Ident* personality form which measures six personality characteristics, a short-form version of seven values from a questionnaire, and two items each to represent the dimensions of the *Work Components Study*, a paper and pencil test designed to tap the area of orientations or motivations to work.[6,7] In addition, five items were taken from prior studies of moods that appeared particularly appropriate for this study. Reliability estimates for the various scores are found in Table 6. More detailed information can be found in the basic references. The basic data, means and correlations between the variables and number of drugs used, are presented in Table 7.

To begin the presentation of these data, it is necessary to refer back to Table 5, where two items can be interpreted as personality indicators. These items are actually not dissimilar from personality indicators and, indeed, represent the two pairs of items that constitute the Emotionality variable of the Behavioral Self-Rating Scores. As will be noted from Table 5, report of being bothered by the conditions of "Irritability or nervousness" or "Feeling tense or emotionally upset" is correlated with the number of drugs used fairly substantially for at least three of the samples. In examining the mean responses for the samples, the identified drug user samples are higher than the probability samples of all households. As an incidental observation, males have lower means than females in the parallel comparisons. Related content in the area of emotional response is found in the *S-Ident* Self-depreciation and low morale score and the *S-Ident* Lack of tension score (Table 7). Again, the correlations are in the expected direction, at least for the female samples.

Data for the single item mood indicators are also shown in Table 7, and, again, the correlations for the male samples are not of the same magnitude as for the female sample, which appear to be fairly consistent and reasonably substantial considering that these are items rather than scores.

One of the notions of the types of persons who might be users of psychotropic drugs was that they were drawn from people who have difficulty in "coping" with their life situation. From the point of view of attempting to cope, some activities may be directly related to resolution of whatever underlying problems exist; others may be merely palliatives or distractions. Presumably, the presence of difficulties in coping would be associated with certain conditions, such as anxiety, tension, and other symptoms, and these would be correlated with the palliative or distracting activities. These might include, to give one example, a correlation between an expression of tension and an activity such as smoking. Then, if tension is an underlying variable associated with smoking, and tension is also related to psychotropic drug use, the model suggests a relationship between smoking and drug use.

One major question was directed at getting information about the activities that might be classed as ways of relieving tension. The question asked how often the respondent participated in given activities, including chewing gum, drinking coffee, overeating, drinking beer, drinking wine,

TABLE 6

Cronbach Alpha Coefficients for Personality and Value Scores (Reliability Estimates)

		General sample		Drug use sample	
	No. of items	Females N = 706	Males N = 285	Females N = 708	Males N = 172
S-Ident					
Leadership	4	0.63	0.71	0.68	0.65
Impulsiveness	5	0.63	0.67	0.71	0.57
Intellectual orientation	4	0.66	0.73	0.73	0.69
Aloofness	4	0.47	0.47	0.52	0.46
Self-depreciation and low morale	6	0.80	0.80	0.81	0.79
Lack of tension	4	0.64	0.57	0.67	0.65
Values					
Adherence to authority	3	0.55	0.59	0.60	0.67
Conventional religiosity	3	0.56	0.72	0.63	0.72
Adherence to conventional sex role structure	3	0.54	0.55	0.54	0.66
Government laissez-faire	3	0.67	0.75	0.66	0.65
Cynical realism	3	0.52	0.44	0.55	0.59
Fatalism	3	0.55	0.57	0.51	0.57
Civil liberties intolerance	3	0.36	0.41	0.38	0.47
WCS					
Potential for personal challenge and development	2	0.49	0.57	0.47	0.58
Responsiveness to new demands	2	0.54	0.53	0.52	0.54
Competitiveness desirability	2	0.28	0.23	0.28	0.58
Tolerance for work pressure	2	0.60	0.59	0.61	0.59
Conservative security	2	0.17	0.51	0.31	0.57
Willingness to seek rewards in spite of uncertainty	2	0.54	0.61	0.50	0.64
Surround concern	2	0.45	0.44	0.49	0.43
Fringe benefits orientation	2	0.81	0.82	0.78	0.83

drinking cocktails or other alcoholic beverages, and drinking too much. In addition, a separate question was directed to more detailed information on smoking behavior. Table 8 indicates mean scores for the four samples on the various activities, and it can be seen that differences between the probability and identified drug user samples are trivial except in the case of amount of smoking, in which case the drug user samples have higher means. In examining the correlations between number of drugs used and the activities, the picture may be in some cases suggestive but in no way conclusive. Two of the values of the correlations between number of drugs used and amount of smoking appear in the anticipated direction, but two are zeros.

Another question used in the survey was designed to explore the notion that persons who use psychotropic drugs are likely to be users of many other things that may have some effects on the body. The idea underlying this was the expectation that there might be some hypochondriasis associated with the syndromes that lead to having psychotropic drugs as a part of the therapy. However, equally, there might be the exception that in conjunction with disorders that might require psychotropic drugs, there are conditions for which commonly available substances are appropriate. It would not be surprising to find that persons who take psychotropic drugs use aspirin, Anacin®, or other pain relievers more than those who do not. On the other hand, it could equally be possible that those on psychotropic drugs do not make use (any longer) of such medicinals.

Table 9 is suggestive on the question of reported pill use. To begin with, included in the

TABLE 7

Values, Personality Characteristics, and Drug Use

	Correlation to no. of drugs used				Mean			
	FPS	FDS	MPS	MDS	FPS	FDS	MPS	MDS
S-Ident leadership	0.01	−0.05	0.05	0.07	3.52	3.78	4.42	4.89
S-Ident impulsiveness	0.10	0.07	−0.01	0.10	14.29	14.91	14.34	14.21
S-Ident intellectual orientation	0.03	−0.02	0.09	−0.04	11.41	11.45	11.22	11.32
S-Ident aloofness	0.00	−0.01	−0.07	−0.03	11.50	11.67	11.97	11.88
S-Ident self-depreciation and low morale	0.19	0.13	0.02	0.05	20.50	21.82	19.20	19.58
S-Ident lack of tension	−0.27	−0.16	−0.13	−0.13	14.57	13.19	15.86	14.72
"I tend to be dependent on others"	0.03	−0.02	−0.02	0.02	1.73	1.92	1.62	1.56
Adherence to authority	0.04	−0.01	0.01	0.12	10.59	10.72	10.35	10.33
Conventional religiosity	−0.04	0.00	0.00	−0.03	9.54	9.67	9.06	9.30
Adherence to conventional sex role structure	−0.03	0.01	−0.08	−0.11	7.20	7.17	7.70	7.59
Government laissez-faire	−0.05	0.05	0.04	0.04	8.03	8.05	8.38	8.58
Cynical realism	−0.03	0.30	−0.10	−0.01	5.59	5.60	5.81	5.65
Fatalism	−0.01	0.10	−0.02	0.12	5.54	5.50	5.15	5.13
Civil liberties intolerance	−0.05	−0.04	0.01	0.06	7.14	7.09	7.19	6.78
Potential for personal challenge and development	0.01	0.00	0.03	0.07	7.73	7.81	8.05	8.24
Responsiveness to new demands	0.01	−0.02	0.04	0.09	7.44	7.56	7.77	7.59
Competitiveness desirability	0.02	0.00	0.03	0.07	7.11	7.19	7.62	7.90
Tolerance for work pressure	0.02	0.00	−0.04	0.09	6.06	6.13	6.45	6.56
Conservative security	−0.04	−0.02	−0.01	−0.01	7.65	7.59	7.42	7.40
Willingness to seek reward in spite of uncertainty	0.06	−0.09	0.17	−0.03	5.21	5.28	4.95	5.06
Surround concern	0.05	0.05	0.03	0.08	8.78	8.80	8.67	8.74
Fringe benefits orientation	−0.01	0.05	−0.05	0.12	8.81	8.77	8.66	8.68
Lonely	0.17	0.09	−0.02	0.16	2.41	2.57	1.92	1.94
Sluggish	0.15	0.12	0.10	−0.02	2.92	3.34	2.66	3.05
Sad	0.19	0.15	0.12	0.07	2.42	2.65	2.07	2.11
Tired	0.13	0.15	0.05	0.08	3.23	3.47	3.00	3.22
Depressed	0.17	0.20	0.14	0.07	2.37	2.69	1.98	2.05

items were two that were to serve at least as partial checks in the reliability of reporting drug use. The item "Sedatives, tranquilizers, or sleeping pills" should be correlated with reported use of psychotropic drugs, and it is clear that this is the case in all four samples. Additionally, the samples of identified drug users report on the average substantially more use than the probability samples. For the item "Stimulant drugs or 'pep' pills," on the other hand, the data are by no means as clear. There is virtually no reporting of such use, suggesting that in the language of the respondents, stimulant drugs are not the drugs that they have prescribed to.

Scanning the other items in Table 8, there appears to be some association of taking of the home remedy type medicinals and use of psychotropic drugs. The small positive correlation values in the female samples, for example, in the item "Aspirin, anacin, or other pain relievers" go in this direction. Additionally, there are generally higher mean values for the samples of identified drug users than for the probability samples. The apparent sex difference in reported use of the substances may be of interest. The male samples have somewhat smaller reported use of vitamins, laxatives, pain relievers, and the psychotropic drugs, about the same reported use on drugs for colds

TABLE 8

"Coping" Activities and Drug Use

How often do you: (once a day or more to never)	Correlation to no. of drugs used				Mean			
	FPS	FDS	MPS	MDS	FPS	FDS	MPS	MDS
Chew gum	0.06	0.02	−0.04	−0.12	2.99	3.02	3.17	3.41
Drink coffee	0.03	0.03	−0.03	0.07	1.68	1.74	1.50	1.56
Overeat	−0.02	0.03	0.08	0.12	3.32	3.27	3.30	3.38
Drink beer	−0.08	0.04	−0.10	−0.07	4.24	4.24	3.22	3.40
Drink wine	0.03	0.03	0.03	−0.06	4.42	4.43	4.37	4.22
Drink cocktails, whiskey, brandy or other alcoholic beverages	−0.10	0.02	0.05	−0.01	4.02	4.01	3.68	3.70
Drink too much (alcoholic beverages)	−0.05	0.03	0.02	−0.10	4.87	4.87	4.60	4.45
About how many cigarettes a day?	0.11	0.03	−0.02	0.21	7.29	9.91	14.08	15.16

TABLE 9

Reported Pill Use and Drug Use

On the average, how frequently do you use each of the following:	Correlation to no. of drugs used				Mean			
	FPS	FDS	MPS	MDS	FPS	FDS	MPS	MDS
Vitamin pill	0.13	0.01	0.03	−0.11	2.19	2.47	1.94	2.05
Laxatives	0.03	0.10	0.09	−0.09	1.67	1.76	1.37	1.45
Aspirin, anacin, or other pain relievers	0.18	0.07	0.06	−0.01	3.07	3.27	2.80	3.02
Sedatives, tranquilizers, or sleeping pills	0.47	0.22	0.43	0.16	1.43	2.51	1.33	2.22
Anti-acids or other digestion aids	0.11	0.07	0.09	−0.09	1.58	1.91	1.70	2.29
Stimulant drugs or "pep" pills	0.10	0.14	0.14	−0.04	1.12	1.32	1.07	1.18
Antihistamines or other drugs for colds and allergies	0.14	0.00	−0.05	0.01	1.57	1.84	1.58	1.72
Sample size	706	708	285	172				

Note: Responses coded as: 1, never; 2, less than once a month; 3, about once a month; 4, about once a week; 5, once a day or more.

and allergies, but higher use reported on the item "Anti-acids or other digestion aids."

CHARACTERISTICS ATTRIBUTED TO SPOUSE AND DRUG USE

In this final section we look at the possibility that the family situation for the respondent may have something to do with drug involvement.

Obviously, not all situations of family can be examined in a sample of this type, and the focus chosen for primary consideration was the attributes of the spouse. However, to get direct responses from the spouses proved a difficulty of major proportions. To have two independent contacts would alter the proportions of the study beyond its intended scope and available budget. However, with a minor cost "Spouse Questionnaires" were left, and a limited proportion of the sample returned these subsequently. This limited return did not provide a sufficient basis to overcome the usual concerns with self-selection, and thus the basis of spouse information is through the reporting of the primary respondent, who answered a number of questions about the spouse. Thus, the responses may be indicative of things about the spouse, but equally they may be indicative (more accurately) of the respondent's perception and knowledge about the spouse. While the comparisons of these sets of data may have some utility, on the basis of the findings reported below it was decided not to introduce them here since they are complex and bear largely on other than the central issues.

The spouse's age (correlated with own, of course) does not bear any relationship to drug use. A check on age discrepancy did not reveal any relationship either. No relationship was found between drug use and reported health of the spouse. For the FPS and MPS only, there was some small correlation reported between drug use and reported use by the spouse of "Sleeping pill, tranquilizer, or sedative" ($r = 0.14$ and $r = 0.11$). Parallel to this, it was found that the direct self-report of use of such substances correlated with the report for spouses in the positive direction for all four samples with just slightly larger values. By contrast, drug use was not correlated to reported use by the spouse of stimulants, and the self-report correlated with the reported use of the spouse only at a trivial level.

Reports of disagreements with the spouse over how money should be spent, differences in attitudes toward life, amount of time spent by self or by spouse in activities such as sports, TV, hobbies, friends and relatives appeared to have no relationship to drug use. Additionally, ratings of the spouse on characteristics of friendliness, assertiveness, emotionality, or nervousness did not suggest any relationship to drug use. Finally, activities likely to be associated with the "coping" concept, including chewing gum, drinking coffee, overeating, drinking beer, wine, cocktails, drinking too much or smoking, as reported for the spouse, were not correlated with drug use.

In summary, the only thing associated with the spouse that appears to predict own drug use is reported drug use of the spouse, but in the categories of "Sleeping pill, tranquilizer, or sedative," a finding that hardly requires an extensive sociological theory for explanation.

CONCLUDING COMMENTS

The research reported here may be viewed as disappointing in not finding many strong and consistent relationships among variables. However, at least reality testing dispels speculation and unfounded theory, even though it may be more gratifying to have a long list of positive findings.

ACKNOWLEDGMENTS

Thanks are due to many in the development of this research. The initial stimulus came from David C. Glass and Orville G. Brim, Jr., at the Russell Sage Foundation. Subsequently, Mitchell B. Balter was an important source of information, and help also came from Dean I. Manheimer, Glen D. Mellinger, and Ira H. Cisin, who were engaged in relevant researches. Robert R. Evans contributed to the technical preparation of materials for field use, particularly in the development of the drug recognition plates. Medical Economics, Inc., Oradell, N.J., generously provided prints of their drug plates that were adapted to the needs of the research design with their permission. George W. Bohrnstedt negotiated many of the problems in the final design of the questionnaire as well as consulted on the study more generally. Support for the research was provided by Russell Sage Foundation, NIMH Grant MH 13445, and the University of Wisconsin Research Committee.

REFERENCES

1. **Balter, M. B. and Levine, J.,** The nature and extent of psychotropic drug usage in the United States, *Psychopharmacol. Bull.,* 5, 3, 1969.
2. **Parry, H. J., Balter, M. B., and Cisin, I. H.,** Primary levels of underreporting psychotropic drug use, *Public Opinion Q.,* 34, 582, 1970.
3. **Manheimer, D. I., Mellinger, G. D., and Balter, M. B.,** Psychotherapeutic drugs: use among adults in California, *Calif. Med.,* 109, 445, 1968.
4. *Physician's Desk Reference to Pharmaceutical Specialties and Biologicals,* Medical Economics, Inc., Oradell, N.J., 1966.
5. **Borgatta, E. F. and Corsini, R. J.,** *Quick Word Test,* Harcourt, Brace & World, New York, 1957.
6. **Borgatta, E. F., Bohrnstedt, G. W., and Ford, R. N.,** The Work Components Study (WCS): a revised set of measures for work motivation, *Multivariate Behav. Res.,* 3, 403, 1968.
7. **Borgatta, E. F.,** A short test of personality: the S-ident form, *J. Educ. Psychol.,* 63, 309, 1965.

SPECULATIONS ON A BEHAVIORAL PROGRESSION TYPOLOGY OF PLEASURE-SEEKING DRUG USE

Carl D. Chambers

TABLE OF CONTENTS

INTRODUCTION

Social and clinical investigators have long been aware that a person uses or abuses drugs within a variety of contexts depending on what these drugs do *to or for* that specific person or what that person "thinks" they will do *to or for* him. For example, the housewife who chemically copes with her role frustrations with sedatives and tranquilizers, the company executive who "increases" his efficiency and competitive effectiveness with stimulants frequently interchanged with tranquilizers, the adolescent who smokes marijuana every now and then at a party, and the heroin street addict may *all* be categorized as drug users or even as drug abusers. No one, however, is willing to assume they are all the same. To simply indicate the use, misuse, and abuse of drugs is insufficient to "type" the persons who engage in the behavior. A meaningful typology of drug users *must* focus upon the context within which this use occurs. With this in mind, I believe there will be essential agreement among investigators that most if not all drug abusers fall within one of two general categories: *self-medicators* and *pleasure seekers*.

Self-medicating oneself, usually with one or more of the legally manufactured and distributed prescription psychotropic drugs, is best framed within the context of *adaptive* behavior. While the use of these psychotropic medications certainly has personally and socially beneficial characteristics, all too often such use, even under the direction of a physician, becomes one's habitual way of responding to boredom, loneliness, frustration, stress, etc. At the present time, I do not know nor do I know anyone else who knows the content or context of the situations and experiences which "move" the individual from being functional because of the medication to becoming dysfunctional because of the use. For example, a recent study of mine to elicit such contextual information found that even the medicine misuser was unable to describe when the change occurred let alone why the change occurred.

I believe the use of drugs for their euphoric or pleasurable effects is even more complex. Such use has some of the characteristics of self-medication: Pleasure use is *sometimes* adaptive behavior; legally manufactured and distributed drugs are *sometimes* used; pleasure use *sometimes* can and does "get out-of-hand" with the user becoming personally and socially dysfunctional. There has been, however, considerably more research and clinical experience with those who use drugs for their pleasurable effects than with the self-medicators. By massaging these experiences, a *typology of pleasure seekers* based upon behavioral progressions has emerged and appears "workable."

THE PROPOSED TYPOLOGY

In this behavioral progression typology, the use of drugs for their euphoric or pleasurable effects is seen as occurring within *four* contexts. Progression from one typology category to another can be "measured" or described in terms of an increased involvement with drugs and drug users (Figure 1).

Drug Experimenters

Without question, if one measures prevalence of use, the largest group of people who use drugs for pleasure are the experimenters. They most frequently will "try" a drug a time or two in a group setting when both the psychological setting and the social setting are conducive to the "tasting" of the drug. Although an individual might experiment with a variety of drugs over a period of time, the majority of experimenters do not apparently extend the duration of frequency of this use beyond a time or two with each drug. At this level of use, drugs *do not* play a significant

role in the user's life. Drugs are being used experimentally because the "group" relates the drug effects as being pleasurable and their use as socially appropriate.

Social/Recreational Users

The second largest group of people who use drugs for pleasure are those who are the social or recreational users. These social/recreational users differ from experimenters primarily in the areas of frequency and continuity of consumption. For example, this type of user might use a drug every time he is at a party and the opportunity to do so presents itself. One might suggest that the psychological set of a social/recreational user is always conducive to using drugs and requires only an appropriate social setting to bring it about. Drugs, however, still *do not* play any significant role in the individual's life.

Committed Users

A major transition occurs among those persons whose drug use progresses beyond social and recreational use. In many respects, this transition is even greater than from experimentation to social/recreational use. The committed user has become so "involved" with drugs that they *do* play a significant role in his life. At this level of use, the individual is devoting considerable time and activity to drug-related activities. Although the committed user is still able to function, e.g., hold a job or stay in school, his proficiency and effectiveness in most areas begin to decline markedly. The committed user continues to retain control over his drug-taking behavior, but his personal and social functioning is becoming

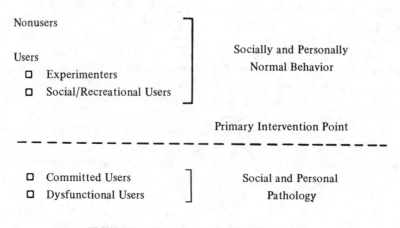

FIGURE 1.   Typology of pleasure seekers.

inversely related to the amount of time he spends involved with drug seeking and drug taking.

Dysfunctional Users

The dysfunctional user has come to the "end of the line": the street addict, the speed freak, the head, etc. Drugs have become *the* significant part of his life, and he no longer has any control over his drug-taking behavior. At this level of use, the user has become personally and socially dysfunctional and devotes all of his time and activities to drug seeking and drug taking. By the time this level of use is attained, the user has most likely been identified by one or more of the control and service agencies of the community.

From an epidemiological point of reference, it has been my experience that the *majority* of drug users in this country remain undetected and are therefore part of the *hidden* prevalence pool. For example, virtually all of the experimenters and social/recreational users who do not progress to the point of involvement where drugs become a significant part of their lives do remain "hidden." This preponderance of *hidden* over *known* users in the prevalence pools has resulted in some rather startling misconceptions about persons who use drugs for their pleasurable effects. Until quite recently, most published behavioral and characterological descriptions of users of drugs drew study cases from the pool of users *known* to either service or control agencies. Unfortunately, this bias in study cases produced the myths that "most" users of drugs were personally and socially deviant, e.g., psychopathic, criminal, etc. I would hope this chapter contributes to a more balanced understanding of drug use and drug users.

SPECULATIONS

Drugs which can produce a euphoric effect are so readily available throughout this country as to make them accessible for almost anyone who chooses to seek pleasure through their use. It would appear that experimentation with drugs begins during adolescence. The questions of *how* and *why* one gets "into" drugs are still being pursued. The first speculation I would like to play against the proposed typology deals with this issue.

Speculation #1

There has been considerable discussion among social researchers as to the relative potency of parental versus peer influences in the decision to initially experiment with drugs and to sustain this use. I am not convinced these discussions have been concluded. Nonetheless, my own research experiences lead me to suggest the following:

At least among adolescents, initial experimentation with pleasure seeking through drugs is most frequently peer initiated. I would further speculate that peers most frequently sustain the use of drugs at least through most social recreational use of drugs.

Without question, if a researcher probes through the content and context of the onset phenomena, the potency of peers providing the setting, defining the situation, providing the behavior models, and providing the drugs becomes obvious. What remains to be documented is the potency of parental influences in "setting the stage" whereby peer influences are or can be accepted or rejected.

Pleasure-seeking drug use which progresses beyond social recreational use is probably sustained more by individual perceptions and rationales than by peer influences.

At least for the present, I believe pleasure-seeking drug use can be diagramed along this dimension as follows:

Experimentation

Social/Recreational Use — Peer Initiated

Committed Use — Peer Sustained

Dysfunctional Use — Individually Sustained

Just as an aside, I believe some of the research finding differences for the *relative* potency of parental versus peer influences on the onset phenomena can be explained by differences in populations being studied. Both influences — parents who regularly use psychoactive substances themselves and peers who already have pleasure-seeking drug experience — would appear to have an influence on an individual's *choice* to experiment himself. It would not surprise me if we were to discover that the relative potency of these two influences varied by geography and along other demographic variables. In addition, I would speculate that parents, especially the female parent, who are themselves self-medicators or "chemical copers" have considerable impact on producing offspring who will also become self-medicators.

Speculation #2

There is some limited evidence to suggest that those who progress beyond the social/recreational use of drugs are the more alienated and self-estranged among our youth. I believe more involved self-sustained pleasure-seeking drug use is indeed one way with which the individual "treats" his real or perceived alienation from the mainstream of society.

The more socially alienated or self-estranged the individual is at the time drug experimentation occurs, the greater the likelihood he will become so involved with drugs that he will progress to the committed level of drug use or become dysfunctional as a result of drug use.

Unfortunately, while he perceives drugs as doing something *for* him — reducing, suppressing, or masking his feelings of alienation or self-estrangement — reality would indicate such increased involvement with drugs may serve to insure and perpetuate this alienation and estrangement.

Speculation #3

There is some limited evidence to suggest that those who progress beyond the social/recreational use of drugs are the more depressed or more anxious among our youth. As with the more alienated of our youth, I believe more involved self-sustained pleasure-seeking drug use is indeed one way with which individuals "treat" themselves for real depressions and anxieties associated with adolescent role conflicts, ambiguities, etc. There seems little doubt that some adolescents do

become clinically and measurably depressed or anxious and that individuals who become committed to drug use or become dysfunctional because of drug use most frequently have depression and anxiety pathologies. We also know the prevalence of these pathologies is greater among known drug users than among their nonusing peers in the same population. What we do *not* know is how depressed or anxious the known drug user was prior to any drug use. Nonetheless, I would speculate an association does exist.

The more depressed or anxious the individual at the time drug experimentation occurs, the greater the likelihood he will become so involved with drugs as to progress to the committed level of drug use or become dysfunctional as a result of using drugs.

Speculation #4

Although there are precious little empirical data to support it, I believe the age at which initial experimentation occurs and a constellation of variables directly associated with age have an impact on how involved an individual will become with pleasure seeking through the use of drugs. Let me state the speculation and then try to delineate the dimensions of it.

The younger the individual at the time drug experimentation occurs, the greater the likelihood he will become so involved with drugs as to progress to the committed level of drug use or become dysfunctional as a result of using drugs.

Several age-related variables seem to be operating in the decision-making processes around drug use. For example, it would appear those who are more willing to take "risks" or who are more influenced by external stimuli are more likely to decide in favor of drug experimentation. It would also appear that even among experimenters, those who are more goal directed and reality oriented are less likely to become committed to drug use or dysfunctional as a result of using drugs. I believe all these variables are age related. The older the adolescent, the less likely he will be a "risk taker," the less likely external stimuli will be his sole motivator, and the more likely he will have become goal directed and reality oriented.

If rather than trying to determine why drug users use drugs one asks nonusers why they do not use drugs, the answers one obtains are fairly consistent. Persons who do not use drugs do not believe drugs will do anything for them and indeed may "get in the way" of other things more valuable to them. In addition, there is a common reference to the "price" (social) being too high in comparison to the return.

CONCLUSION

In summary, I believe social and clinical researchers must begin to separate drug users around the behavioral content and context of this use. I, as well as others, have come to accept the "normalcy" of some pleasure-seeking experimentation and some social recreational use of drugs. I have speculated in this paper that the progression beyond social recreational use of drugs is most likely associated with the more socially alienated/self-estranged, the more depressed/anxious, the less goal directed/reality oriented, and the more risk taking/stimulus seeking among the initial experimenters.

Two things remain to be done. Empirical tests of these "hypotheses" need our immediate and vigorous attention. Once demonstrated, and I am confident they can and will be demonstrated, our prevention intervention strategies must be changed radically to reflect this awareness. For example, it seems most futile to focus our prevention efforts at the abstinence level when experimentation is normal and to be expected. What we need instead of our current prevention strategies are more effective means of dealing with adolescent personal and social role conflicts or at least strategies for nonpunitive early identification of those persons experiencing resolution difficulties. In addition, we need more realistic and adolescent-acceptable alternatives for "treating" alienation, self-estrangement, depression, and anxiety. I firmly believe *persons who become so involved with drugs as to become committed to their use or dysfunctional because of their use are system casualties who must be dealt with as individuals*. I only wish I knew how to prevent it from occurring or how to intervene in the process once it is in progress.

Some issues were not dealt with in this paper which all social and clinical researchers have encountered: persons who use drugs in order to "punish" others, the influence "good" or "bad" first experiences have on subsequent use, the retarding effect an adverse reaction may have on subsequent use, etc. No real data exist around these issues, and my own experiences have been too limited with them for any meaningful speculations. They do, however, require our attention.

At least for the present, the typology presented in this paper seems workable.

CANNABIS, ALCOHOL, AND THE FAMILY

Martin Shain

TABLE OF CONTENTS

INTRODUCTION

The concern of the study reported here was to investigate relationships between the use of drugs by students living at home and certain aspects of parental communicative, disciplinary, and attitudinal patterns.

If we limit the terms of reference of the study reported here to *drug use by students attending high school and living in intact families*, we find that most of the few studies completed to date on the relationship between drug use and communication in the family have been based on student reports of family conditions. Among these, the study by Smart, Fejer, and White[1] in Toronto demonstrates a link between grossly disrupted or broken families and drug use, while Bilodeau[2] in Montreal, introducing discipline as a variable, reports that students who see their mothers and fathers as offering "authoritarian but understanding" conditions are less frequently drug users than those who see their parents as "authoritarian and not understanding" or as "neither authoritarian nor understanding." Tec[3] reports that students in an affluent community in Eastern U.S.A. who see their families as close, warm, and offering caring control are less often drug users than those who feel more removed and distant from their families. Similar findings are reported by Streit and Oliver.[4] In a progress report from the California State Department of Education,[5] it is established that drug users report significantly less often that they would take their troubles to their parents and feel less comfortable in discussing important matters with them. None of these studies, however, squarely addresses the problem of why common antecedents produce differential results; i.e. why is it that poor communication in two similar families can produce delinquent offspring in the one and conformists in the other? Also, it is rare to find a discussion of drug use and its correlates that even tries to clarify how much of the variance in the former is explained by the latter. Two notable exceptions are studies by Smart and Fejer[6] of marihuana use among adults in Toronto and by Lavenhar et al.[7] These studies, however, do not deal with the issue in question here, namely, family correlates of student drug use. A discussion of how much variance is accounted for in these studies is a necessary prerequisite to any attempt to establish the power of such finding relative to any "explanatory" theory.

Even then, the type of data available may restrict the power of such interpretations quite severely. Most of the studies mentioned so far employ retrospective research designs, freezing reports of behavior and attitudes at one point in time. The typical mode of analysis is cross-tabulation and the use of appropriate statistical techniques such as Chi-square tests of significance. Simple correlation analysis is less common and multivariate analysis even less so. Hardly any attempts are made at longitudinal designs: Two such studies currently underway are by Annis[8] and Kandel.[9]

In the field of delinquency research, the literature abounds with "explanatory" theories frequently founded upon data which are not analyzed to the point where it is possible to see how much variance in the dependent variable (in these cases, delinquent behavior) is supposed to be explained by the study. Nonetheless, this body of literature does provide an interesting, if at times misleading, context for the present study. A debate in delinquency research which is of particular relevance here is the one between those who, in positing aspects of poor intrafamily communication as important antecedents of delinquency, argue on the one side that intervening factors are required to precipitate such deviant behavior and on the other side that the aforementioned antecedents have a direct and independent effect on delinquency. Representatives of the "intervening factor" school are Sutherland and Cressey[10] and Nye.[11] For the "independent factor" school we might select Jensen,[12] Hirschi,[13] and Briar and Piliavin.[14] Briefly, the "intervening factor" theorists argue that poor intrafamilial communication operates indirectly through other variables (such as delinquent associations) upon delinquent behavior. This is based on a belief that the dissolution of social controls within the family serves only to create a situation in which deviance *may* develop given the presence of other adverse conditions such as delinquent associations. This theory, then, deals with the "common antecedents and differential outcomes" problem by advancing the notion of intervening variables which may act differentially upon common antecedents. This view has been challenged recently by Jensen's study, the findings of which appear to indicate that poor communicative conditions have an independent and direct effect upon delinquent behavior, i.e. independent of delinquent associations. This tells us, however, that poor communicative conditions *can* have such an effect rather than that they always do. This leaves the common antecedents and differential outcomes problem unanswered.

The present study was an attempt to advance theory in the area of the family correlates of student drug use by soliciting the actual responses of parents and by employing factor analysis as a method of exploring the interactions between communication, discipline, attitudes, and drug use. It was hoped that this mode of analysis would suggest why drug use is sometimes found to be associated with poor intrafamilial conditions and sometimes not. It was not anticipated that all the answers would be obtained since, for one thing, the variables investigated were looked at selectively and, for another, certain other variables, such as peer-group associations, were left out altogether. Furthermore, factor analysis cannot answer questions of cause and effect. It can, however, *suggest* how the interaction of variables can produce different outcomes, although the investigator runs the risk of getting the chicken and egg sequence all wrong. Only longitudinal research can begin to unravel these interwoven threads.

To anticipate some of the findings, it appears that frequent communication, where it conveys the message of caring control, can operate as an insulator against student cannabis and alcohol use in the case of both boys and girls, while the converse of these conditions, especially in the case of girls, can be associated with cannabis use and higher intake of alcohol. The effect of communication appears to be an indirect one of legitimizing or not legitimizing the values, wishes, and behaviors of parents.

METHOD

The study was conducted in a school which is located in a middle-class suburb of a town of about 100,000 in southern Ontario. The school has 900 students of whom 802 filled out the questionnaire on the day of administration in January 1972. The goal of the survey was to collect three matched questionnaires per family unit. The eldest child of all the families represented in the school would fill out a questionnaire taking home two more for his or her parents. The questionnaires would then be filled out and returned via the student or returned by mail.

Homeroom teachers, who supervised the initial administration, were responsible for seeing that the questionnaires were returned. After 2 weeks, letters were sent out to those parents who had not replied with an additional request. All parents had been informed that the survey would be done by letter, and a number would have heard a radio program discussing the survey just before administration. Two days after the survey was initiated, a favorable article on the front page of a local newspaper explained the goals of the study, which was defined in terms of an ongoing community development process in which it was hoped parents would be involved. The outcome of all this was that 449 sets of questionnaires were found to be useable; i.e., we were in possession of 449 student questionnaires which had *both* parents' completed returns matched with them. This left us with 353 students who had filled out their own questionnaires whose parents did not fill out or return theirs. One hundred and sixteen of these were younger siblings who were not to take questionnaires home anyway. Analysis of the 237 student returns which should have been accompanied by those of their parents revealed that they did not differ significantly in any known way from the 449* whose parents had answered. As a group, all that can be said is that their grade averages were *slightly* lower than those of the 449 and that they show a *slightly* higher rate of drug use. Be this as it may, we are not entitled to argue from the 449 to the 237, and we are certainly not entitled to argue beyond the school and the families whose children attend it. This is so because the 449 were not a sample (we had aimed for a census), and even if they were a sample from within the school, they are not a random sample of the high school population even of the town of 100,000.

The data from the three matched questionnaires were key punched and linked by a serial number so that the resulting six cards could be treated as a unit for purposes of analysis; i.e., they permitted an easy linking of students' attitudes and behavior with those of their mothers and fathers.

Two types of analysis were reported here: cross-tabulation in brief and factor analysis in some depth. The justification offered is that each analysis seems to lend the other an additional

*This is a return of 65.45% from eligible total of 686.

perspective and each serves as a check of sorts upon the other. The perspective of factor analysis will be discussed first since it offers a more quickly grasped overview of the relationships to be discussed.

The questionnaires used in this study were basically the same for both students and parents. They dealt with attitudes toward education and drugs, perception of family warmth and closeness (students only), student perceptions of how parents would react to the discovery of their children's drug use, the parent's own estimation of their response to discovery of their offspring's drug use, drug use, and parents' reports of how much importance they attach to communication and how frequently they do certain things with their children.

The program used to perform the factor analysis was the BMD"X" system, 1972 revision. This program deals with a maximum of 198 variables. In the present investigation, the maximum represented a constraint which could be dealt with only by being somewhat selective in the entry of variables to the analysis. Exclusion was carried out on the basis of having identified variables in preliminary and tabular analysis which appeared not to differentiate within a population (i.e., students, mothers, fathers); e.g., it was found that nearly everyone endorsed certain statements, so these were omitted from the factor analysis even though the ideal would have been to leave them in. Primary factor loadings were produced in which factors were allowed to be oblique and from which were derived simple loading rotations.[15] In this report, however, considerable emphasis is placed upon discussion of unrotated factors. This raises certain major questions since an ongoing debate continues over the relative merits of rotated and unrotated factors. No technical arguments will be presented here in favor of either side of the debate. Readers are referred to technical sources for such information.[16] The decision to report unrotated factors here is based on the investigators' judgment as to their validity guided by preliminary impressions gained through cross-tabulation. In the present report, only those factors which have a bearing upon drug use are discussed since to do more would fill a volume. Below is a list of the variables which were entered into the analysis.

STUDENT VARIABLES

Age
Attitudes toward education and drugs (below) called for "strongly agree" to "strongly disagree" response.

Attitudes Toward Education
Students become arrogant the minute they get a bit of control in school affairs.

Religion is a matter to be discussed in the home, not in the school.

Morality is a matter to be discussed in the home, not in the school.

Slackening up on discipline opens the door to chaos in high shoool.

Strict rules and regulations, imposed by teachers, make school life easier in the long run.

Students learn more when they have to compete with their fellow students.

Students would prefer a school where they knew exactly what was expected of them.

A school should emphasize the teaching of skills that will enable the graduate to land high-paying jobs.

The fear of failure in school keeps students working hard.

Teachers play a more important role in the moral education of students than parents do.

Teenagers are actually happier under strict training.

Attitudes Toward Drugs
As soon as a student starts fooling around with drugs, you can expect his grade average to start dropping.

Use of some drugs, e.g., marihuana, hashish, can make leisure time more enjoyable.

The majority of young drug users come from unhappy homes.

Kids who smoke marihuana are no good for themselves or anyone else.

Drug use by the young can often be seen as a gesture of rejection of traditional society.

Regular cigarettes are more dangerous than marihuana.

People who are always turning on are basically inadequate.

Marihuana is safer than alcohol.

Drugs can be fun.

The person who smokes marihuana is almost certain to end up on hard drugs.

Drug users are often just trying to escape from the responsibility of facing reality.

There is no harm in the occasional use of marihuana.

It is no business of the school to teach students how to make moral decisions.

Teachers are better able to deal with student drug problems than parents.

Perception of Family Closeness*

Which one of the following statements best describes your family?

An exceptionally close family, finding much pleasure in each others' company and doing many things together.

A fairly close family, getting along more often than not, running smoothly, but not noted for warmth or a sense of happiness.

An indifferent family, not very concerned with each other, rarely doing things as a group; members notably cool toward each other.

An unhappy family, normally bickering and fighting or not speaking to each other; members avoid each other when possible.

Student Perception of Parents' Response to Discovery of Drug Use

If you were using drugs (other than alcohol or tobacco) and your *father* found out, how likely or unlikely do you think it is that he would respond in the following ways? (These items were repeated to gather students' perceptions of what their *mothers* would do, also.)

He would punish me
He would threaten to punish me.
He would do nothing.
He would be worried.
He would be angry.
He would discuss it with my mother.
He would discuss it with my mother and then with me.
He would confront me.
He would threaten to call the police.
He would call the police.
He would sit down with me and discuss the "dangers of drug abuse."
He would forbid me to use drugs.
He would ask me why I wanted to use drugs.
He would tell me that it is my decision to use

or not use drugs, and I must take the consequences.

He would give me an ultimatum: Either leave drugs alone or leave home.

He would try to get me to a doctor, psychiatrist, or counselor of some kind.

He would explore the risks and possible advantages of using drugs with me.

He would consider my age at the time.

He would take the kind of drugs I was using into account.

PARENT VARIABLES

In the following list, the prescript (+) indicates that this variable was entered only for fathers and the prescript (*) that this variable was entered only for mothers.

Attitudes Toward Education (instructions as for students)

It is best for a student to be told what subjects to take, rather than have him choose for himself.

+Students are not ready to handle the responsibility for their own attendance at school.

Students are responsible enough to move from class to class without a bell.

Students become arrogant the minute they get a bit of control in school affairs.

Religion is a matter to be discussed in the home, not in the school.

Morality is a matter to be discussed in the home, not in the school.

A high school can run effectively without the use of bells.

High school students are capable of living without teacher-imposed discipline.

Parents are adequately informed about what teachers do in the classroom.

Good grades are all that should really matter in school.

+The school system, as presently set up, is something to be gotten through as quickly and as quietly as possible.

Students should be free to criticize their teacher's classroom methods without its being considered a breach of discipline.

Slackening up on discipline opens the door to chaos in a high school.

*This item is an adaptation from an N.I.M.H. survey questionnaire used in New York in 1968.

The most important quality of a good teacher should be his ability to listen to what students think and feel.

+Strict rules and regulations, imposed by teachers, make school life easier in the long run.

Students should be able to run their own recreational programs.

+Students learn more when they have to compete with their fellow students.

Students should be allowed to choose their own subjects.

+The fear of failure in school keeps students working hard.

Students would rather be told what to do than have to plan courses for themselves.

+Teachers play a more important role in the moral education of students than parents do.

By the time students get to grade 13, most of them have become enthusiastic about continuing their education.

+When students are bored with school, it is mainly a result of teachers' failure to offer them sufficient challenge.

+Teenagers are actually happier under strict training.

Attitudes Toward Drugs (instructions as above)

*One of the most important aspects of drug use by young people is the sense of community and fellowship that it promotes.

Young people should be able to decide for themselves whether or not they want to use drugs.

*There is no difference between the user of alcohol and the user of drugs.

+Use of some drugs, e.g., marihuana, hashish, can make leisure time more enjoyable.

The majority of young drug users come from unhappy homes.

There is no difference between the occasional user of marihuana and the hard-core speed freak.

+Kids who smoke marihuana are no good for themselves or anyone else.

There is no difference between the person taking pep pills and the speed user.

+There is an excitement in using drugs that is difficult to match in any other activity.

+LSD can help to increase a person's awareness and self-insight.

*Teachers are better able to deal with student drug problems than parents.

Parents' Report of Own Disciplinary Practice in Hypothetical Situation

If you discovered that your teenage son or daughter (in particular, your eldest attending high school) was taking drugs, *how likely or unlikely* is it that you would respond in the following ways? Please check an answer for every statement in the following list. (5 points from very likely to extremely unlikely.)

I would threaten punishment.
I would do nothing.
I would be worried.
I would get angry.
I would discuss it with my spouse.
I would discuss it with my spouse then with my son or daughter.
I would confront my son or daughter with my knowledge.
I would threaten to call the police.
I would call the police.
I would sit down with my son or daughter and explain the dangers of drug abuse.
I would ask why he or she wanted to use drugs.
I would forbid the further use of drugs.
I would discuss it with my son or daughter telling them that it is their decision for which they must take the consequences.
I would give an ultimatum: Either leave drugs alone or leave home.
I would seek professional help for my son or daughter in the form of a doctor, psychiatrist, psychologist, guidance counselor.
I would explore the risks and possible advantages of using drugs with my son or daughter.
I would take my son's or daughter's age into account.
I would take the kind of drug involved into account.

Parents' Report on Importance Attached to Certain "Communicative Acts" and Social Standards*

How important, or unimportant, is it to you that your eldest son or daughter (attending high

---

*Some of these items are adapted from the Parental Attitude Research Instrument as adapted by Palmer et al.[17]

school): (5 points from "very important" to "of no importance")

Bring his or her friends home?
Eat dinner with you most evening of the week?
Do things with you at weekends?
Tell you what they do of an evening and at weekends.
Tell you where they are going before they go.
Talk to you about what they do with their free time outside the home.
Tell you about their thoughts and feelings.
Conform to common standards about dress (nothing really radical or way out).
Does not mix with other young people of whom you disapprove.
Try to make his or her own decisions.
Be a self-sufficent and independent person.

Parents' Report of Actual Frequency of Certain Communicative Acts

Does your eldest child (attending high school):

Tell you what he or she does of an evening and at weekends? ("always" to "rarely")
Tell you where he or she is going before going? ("always" to "rarely")
Talk to you about what he or she does with free times outside the home? ("about everything" to "about nothing")
Talk to you about his or her thoughts and feelings? ("about everything" to "about nothing")

Bring friends home? ("several times a week" to "less than once a month")
Eat dinner with you? ("several times a week" to "less than once a month")
Do things with you at weekends? ("every weekend" to "less than once a month")

Parents' Use of Drugs

During the past 6 months, how often have you taken tranquilizers (librium, valium, miltown, equanil, alarax, serax, etc.)?

RESULTS

Before analysis was conducted on the variables above, students were divided into males and females. Thus, two analyses were performed: one for male students and both their parents, the other for female students and both their parents. Six primary unrotated factors are presented below: three for boys, three for girls. In the case of the boys, the factors reported are the first, second, and fifth; in the case of the girls, the factors are the first three. The significance of this lies in the fact that the first factor describes the most comprehensive relationships discernible in the data, the following factors each accounting individually for a lesser percentage of the total variance.

In the following lists, the notation "E" means that the statement is *endorsed,* and "R" means that it is *rejected* relative to the factor in question.

CORRELATES OF THE NONUSE OF CANNABIS AND ALCOHOL

Unrotated Factor 1 for Males and Females

	Loadings	
Student Attitudes and Behavior	Males	Females
Age (younger)	0.28*	0.21*
E. Slackening up on discipline opens the door to chaos in a high school.	0.36	
E. As soon as a student starts fooling around with drugs, you can expect his grade average to start dropping.	0.30	0.32
R. Use of some drugs, e.g., marihuana, hashish, can make leisure time more enjoyable.	-0.46	-0.36

*Usually, only variables with loadings of over 0.30 are reported, but sometimes weaker loadings are given because the direction of the relationship is thought to be important.

E. Kids who smoke marihuana are no good for themselves or anyone else.	0.45	0.31
R. Regular cigarettes are more dangerous than marihuana.	−0.37	
R. Marihuana is safer than alcohol.	−0.36	
R. Drugs can be fun.	−0.40	
E. The person who smokes marihuana is certain to end up on hard drugs.	0.42	0.32
R. There is no harm in the occasional use of marihuana.	−0.47	−0.37
E. Drug users are often just trying to escape from the responsibility of facing reality.		0.30
Perception of family as close, finding pleasure in one another's company, doing many things together.	0.33	
Nonuse of marihuana or hashish.	−0.36	−0.36
Infrequent, or nonuse of alcohol.	0.30	0.23

If my father discovered that I was using drugs, he would be *most likely* to . . .

Punish me.		0.46
Get angry.		0.42
Forbid me to use drugs.		0.35
Give me an ultimatum: Leave drugs alone or leave home.		0.31

If my mother discovered that I was using drugs, she would be *most likely* to . . .

Punish me.		0.40
Get angry.		0.30

Mother's Attitudes and Behavior

E. Students become arrogant the minute they get a bit of control in school affairs.	0.40	
E. Slackening up on discipline opens the door to chaos in a high school.	0.40	0.33
E. There is no difference between the occasional user of marihuana and the hard-core speed freak.	0.30	

On discovery of my son's/daughter's drug use, I would be *most likely* to . . .

Threaten punishment.	0.31	0.41
Forbid the further use of drugs.	0.34	0.39
Get angry.		0.33
Threaten to call the police.		0.43
Call the police.		0.39

It is *most important* to me that my son/daughter . . .

Does things with me at weekends.	0.46	0.45
Tells me what he/she does of an evening and at weekends.	0.40	

Talks to me about what he/she does with his/her free time outside the home.	0.42	
Tells me where he/she is going before he/she goes.		0.30
Conforms to common standards about dress (nothing really radical or way out).	0.55	0.41
Does not mix with people of whom I disapprove.	0.43	0.37

My son/daughter . . .

Always tells me what he/she does of an evening and at weekends.	0.40	
Always tells me where he/she is going before going.	0.33	
Talks to me about everything he/she does with free time outside the home.	0.35	0.33
Talks to me about all his/her thoughts and feelings.	0.36	
Does things with us most weekends.	0.43	0.33

Father's Attitudes and Behavior

E. Students are not ready to handle the responsibility for their own attendance at school.	0.33	
E. Students become arrogant the minute they get a bit of control in school affairs.	0.35	
E. Slackening up on discipline opens the door to chaos in a high school.	0.44	0.32
E. Strict rules and regulations, imposed by teachers, make school life easier in the long run.	0.47	0.37
E. The fear of failure in school keeps students working hard.	0.35	
E. Students would rather be told what to do than have to plan courses for themselves.	0.34	
E. There is no difference between the occasional user of marihuana and the hard-core speed freak.	0.32	0.36
E. Kids who smoke marihuana are no good for themselves or anyone else.	0.37	0.37
E. Teenagers are actually happier under strict training.	0.35	0.32

On discovery of my son's/daughter's use, I would be *most likely* to . . .

Threaten punishment.	0.33	0.37
Discuss it with my spouse, then with my son/daughter.	0.34	0.35
Confront him/her.	0.32	
Forbid the future use of drugs.		0.48
Seek professional help in the form of a doctor, psychiatrist, psychologist, guidance counselor.	0.32	

Give an ultimatum: Leave drugs alone or leave home.		0.32
Get angry.		0.35
Threaten to call the police.		0.44
Call the police.		0.42

It is *most important* to me that my son/daughter . . .

Brings his/her friends home.	0.35	
Eats dinner with us most evenings.	0.36	0.38
Does things with us at weekends.	0.56	0.49
Tells me where he/she is going before going.	0.52	0.43
Talks to me about his/her free time outside the home.	0.58	0.39
Talks to me about his/her thoughts and feelings.	0.38	0.36
Conforms to common standards about dress (nothing radical, way out).	0.59	0.36
Does not mix with people of whom I disapprove.	0.45	0.46

My son/daughter . . .

Always tells me what he/she does of an evening and at weekends.	0.51	0.35
Always tells me where he/she is going before going.	0.48	
Talks to me about everything he/she does with free time outside the home.	0.57	
Talks to me about all his/her thoughts and feelings.	0.52	
Does things with me most weekends.	0.45	0.36

Summary of Male Factor 1 and Female Factor 1

These factors involve:

Males	Females
1. Age (younger)	Age (younger)
2. Anti-drug attitudes.	Anti-drug attitudes but *fewer* than in the case of boys.
3. A conservative educational attitude.	
4. Cannabis and alcohol abstinence.	Cannabis and alcohol abstinence.
5.	Perception of a punitive reaction by parents to discovery of drug use.
6. Perception of family as close, warm.	
7. Mother's conservative attitudes re: education and drugs.	Mother's conservative attitudes, but *fewer* than in the case of males.
8. Mother's *mildly* punitive response to discovery of son's drug use.	Mother's *highly* punitive response to discovery of daughter's drug use.
9. Mother's emphasis on communication with son.	Mother's emphasis on communication with daughter.
10. Mother's *very* frequent communication with son.	Mother's *fairly* frequent communication with son.

11. Father's conservative educational attitudes.
12. Father's punitive *but caring* response to discovery of son's drug use.
13. Father's emphasis on importance of communication with son.
14. Father's frequent communication with son.

Father's conservative educational attitudes (*less* in number).
Father's highly punitive *and rejecting* response to discovery of daughter's drug use.
Father's emphasis on importance of communication with daughter.
Father's frequent communication with daughter.

The factors reported above appear to describe certain conditions of family life which tend to insulate boys and girls against the use of cannabis and alcohol. In the case of boys, these conditions seem to involve more caring than is discernible in the case of girls. Parents react more severely to the idea of drug use by their daughters than to drug use by their sons, going so far as to call the police in the case of the former. The girls also perceive the likelihood of this severity. However, in both cases there appears to be strong communication between parents and children. As will be shown below, the absence of this communicative bond appears in association with cannabis and alcohol use in disciplinary conditions that do not differ very much from those described in Male and Female Factor 1. In reading the factors reported below, the reader is directed toward the relatively small loading of cannabis use for the males, which suggests that poor family situations are not as instrumental in the development of drug use in boys as they are in the case of girls. It should be noted that of all the variables reported in Factor 1 (for both males and females) age is the least important, though it has some relevance; i.e., family conditions described in the first factors will tend to be found in relation to younger students, although age is by no means the determinant of the conditions themselves.

CORRELATES OF THE USE OF CANNABIS

Unrotated Factor 2 for Males and Females

	Loadings	
Student Attitudes and Behavior	Males	Females
Age (older)		−0.22
E. Use of some drugs, e.g., marihuana, hashish, can make leisure time more enjoyable.	0.24	0.32
R. Kids who smoke marihuana are no good for themselves or anyone else.		−0.35
E. Marihuana is safer than alcohol.		0.33
E. Drugs can be fun.	0.25	0.33
R. The person who smokes marihuana is almost certain to end up on hard drugs.	−0.25	−0.38
E. There is no harm in the occasional use of marihuana.	0.33	0.45
Perception of family as distant, cold, indifferent.	−0.28	−0.41
R. Teenagers are actually happier under strict training.	−0.22	−0.31

If my father discovered that I was using drugs, he would be *most likely* to . . .

Punish me.	0.37	0.40

143

Get angry.	0.45	0.39
Call the police.	0.43	0.38
Forbid me to use drugs.		0.40
Give me an ultimatum: Either leave drugs alone or leave home.	0.39	0.38

He would be *least likely* to . . .

Discuss it with my mother and then with me.		-0.37
Ask me why I wanted to use drugs.	-0.34	-0.35
Tell me that it is my decision to use or not use drugs, and I must take the consequences.		-0.33
Explore the risks and possible advantages of using drugs with me.	-0.35	-0.30
Sit down with me and discuss the "dangers of drug abuse."	-0.44	
Take the kind of drug involved into account.	-0.30	

If my mother discovered that I was using drugs, she would be *most likely* to . . .

Threaten to punish me.	0.31	0.40
Get angry.	0.32	0.40
Threaten to call the police.	0.35	
Forbid me the further use of drugs.	0.39	

She would be *least likely* to . . .

Discuss it with my father.		-0.36
Discuss it with my father, then with me.		-0.39
Use of marihuana, hashish.	0.21	0.39
Frequent alcohol use.	-0.23	-0.27

Mother's Attitudes and Behavior

If I discovered that my son/daughter was using drugs, I would be *most likely* to . . .

Get angry.		0.31
Threaten to call the police.		0.39
Call the police.		0.34
Give an ultimatum: Leave drugs alone or leave home.		0.35
Threaten punishment.	0.35	

My son/daughter . . .

Rarely tells me where he/she is going before going.	-0.35	-0.35
Tells me about little that he/she does with free time outside the home.		-0.36
Talks to me about few of his/her thoughts and feelings.		-0.40
Rarely does things with us at weekends.	-0.35	-0.33

Father's Attitudes and Behavior

If I discovered that my son/daughter was using drugs,
I would be *most likely* to . . .

Get angry.	0.49	0.30
Call the police.	0.47	0.31
Give an ultimatum: drugs alone or leave home.	0.44	0.37

Summary of Male Factor 2 and Female Factor 2

Males	Females
	Age (older)
1.	
2. Pro-drug attitudes.	Pro-drug attitudes.
3. Perception of family as cold, distant.	Perception of family as cold, distant.
4. Perception of parents as reacting in a unilateral and very punitive way to discovery of drug use.	As for males.
5. Use of cannabis, alcohol.	Use of cannabis, alcohol.
6. Mother's threat of punishment on discovery of drug use by son.	Mother's *highly* punitive reaction to discovery of drug use.
7. Mother's shaky communication with son.	Mother's poor communication with daughter.
8. Father's highly punitive reaction to discovery of drug use.	Father's highly punitive reaction to discovery of drug use.

It must be reemphasized that Factor 2 is of less importance for male cannabis and alcohol use than it is for female use. In both cases, however, it appears to be the mother whose infrequent communication is important relative to the student's behavior.

The greater importance of poor communicative conditions for girls relative to drug use may indicate either that drug use by boys is indeed less patterned (i.e., unassociated with other significant variables) or that it is associated with variables not enquired about in this study, e.g., peer-group associations.

If the factors above exhausted the available data, it might be argued that the effect of communication on alcohol and drug use was direct; i.e., good communication is associated with cannabis and alcohol abstinence, and poor communication is associated with cannabis and alcohol use. The situation is more complicated than this, however, as Female Factor 3, below, suggests.

Unrotated Factor 3 for Females

Student Attitudes and Behavior

Loadings

E. As soon as a student starts fooling around with drugs, you can expect his grade average to start dropping. — 0.33

R. Use of some drugs, e.g., marihuana, hashish, can make leisure time more enjoyable. — −0.31

E. People who are always turning on are basically inadequate.   0.39

R. Drugs can be fun.   −0.40

E. The person who smokes marihuana is almost certain to end up on hard drugs.   0.48

E. Drug users are often just trying to escape from the responsibility of facing reality.   0.32

R. There is no harm in the occasional use of marihuana   −0.39

Nonuse of cannabis.   −0.45

Mother's Attitudes and Behavior

If I discovered that my daughter was using drugs, I would be *least likely* to . . .

Be worried.   −0.38

Discuss it with my husband, then with my daughter.   −0.42

Confront my daughter.   −0.37

Ask why she wanted to use drugs.   −0.36

It is a *matter of indifference* to me whether my daughter . . .

Brings her friends home.   −0.47

Eats dinner with us most evenings.   −0.41

Tells me where she is going before she goes.   −0.31

Talks to me about what she does with her free time outside the home.   −0.36

Tells me about her thoughts and feelings.   −0.33

Father's Attitudes and Behavior

E. Morality is a matter to be discussed in the home, not in the school.   0.31

E. Young people should be able to decide for themselves whether or not they want to use drugs.   0.32

E. LSD can help to increase a person's awareness and self-insight.   0.34

If I discovered that my daughter was using drugs, I would be *most likely* to . . .

Do nothing.   0.33

Take the kind of drug involved into account.   0.31

It is a *matter of indifference* to me whether my daughter . . .

Brings her friends home.   −0.35

Eats dinner with us most evenings.   −0.30

Summary of Female Factor 3

1. Anti-drug attitudes of female students.
2. Cannabis abstinence.
3. Mothers' and fathers' *indifferent* reaction to the discovery of their daughters' drug use.
4. Mothers' and fathers' indifference to the importance of communication with their daughters.
5. Fathers' *openness* to certain forms of drug use.

The existence of this factor certainly disturbs any hope of a neat, linear relationship between drug use and poor communication since in this case we find the reverse to be true: Factor 3 unequivocally links *nonuse* of cannabis with *poor* communication, although the existence of the latter in this instance is indicated only by parental expressions of indifference rather than by their reports of actually infrequent communication. Therefore, it is suggested that communication, or the lack of it, has an indirect effect upon adolescent drug use in this sample. It appears that communication serves to legitimize parental attitudes and behavior in the eyes of the students. Where, for example, parental attitudes are opposed to drug use and favor strong external control of adolescents by school and parents, students are more likely to conform to these attitudes themselves where good communication exists within the family. Where it does not exist, but given the same parental attitudinal and disciplinary patterns, it is more likely that adolescents will react against their parents' wishes and ideals. Such reactions may sometimes take the form of cannabis use. This much can be argued from Factors 1 and 2 for males and females. Factor 3 for females provides an example of rebellion in an unexpected direction. The process may be one in which failure to communicate dissolves the legitimacy of parental values in the eyes of the daughter who responds to the situation by valuing the opposite of what her parents seem to value. In this case it leads to the nonuse of cannabis as a rejection of the fathers' values which appear to condone drug use. The only way to test this interaction of communication, discipline, attitudes, and drug use properly, however, is by longitudinal research.

How important are these factors in clarifying the correlates of cannabis and alcohol use by students?

Male Factor 1 involves 13% of the variance in the cannabis use variable compared with 4.4% in Factor 2.* Between them, these factors account for an unimposing 17.4% of the variance in the cannabis variable. In the present study, only one more factor for the males had any statistical relevance to cannabis use, namely, Factor 5, below.

*Approximation of variance of a variable in a given factor is given by the square of its loading.

Unrotated Factor 5 for Males

Student Attitudes and Behavior	Loadings	
R. Drugs can be fun.	-0.32	
R. There is no harm in the occasional use of marihuana.	-0.31	
Nonuse of cannabis.	-0.34	

Parent Attitudes	Mother	Father
E. Students are responsible enough to move from class to class without a bell.	0.43	0.39
E. A high school can run effectively without the use of bells.	0.46	0.32

E. High school students are capable of living without teacher imposed discipline.	0.44	0.34
E. The most important quality of a good teacher should be his ability to listen to what students think and feel.	0.33	N.S.
E. Students should be allowed to choose their own subjects.	0.43	N.S.

Clearly the relationship between nonuse of drugs and parental attitudes in this factor is one that does not involve communication and discipline at all (unless by default). Thus, the 11.6% of the variance of the cannabis variable absorbed in this factor emanates from a source which has little or no bearing on the relationships discussed so far. If we are to speculate about the associations sketched by Factor 5, we might hypothesize that something about the familial conditions created by the expression of the parents' values described therein reduces the students' need for involvement with drugs. Possibly the family represents a more meaningful reference point for the student in this situation than does the drug-using peer group.

Male Factors 1, 2, and 5 involve 29% of the variance of cannabis use in this sample. The communality of this variable is 67%, i.e., the amount of variance absorbed by all the factors taken together. The difference (67 minus 29) is absorbed in insignificant fractions across the remaining factors. The unique variance (100 minus 67) is the variance that is totally unexplained by the study, in this case 33%. Thus, about as much is usefully explained for the use of cannabis by males in this sample (29%) as remains totally unexplained (33%). Perhaps nothing more remains to be explained, or, more likely, other influences have been ignored.

The three female factors reported here were the first three printed out. The variance of the cannabis variable involved in the three factors is 12.96%, 15.1%, and 20.25%, a total of 48.3%. Cannabis use is not significantly involved in any other female factor. The communality of this variable is 68.8%. It would appear that more of the variance in cannabis use is explicable in the context of the questions asked by this survey in the case of girls than it is in the case of boys. This is consistent with the earlier suggestion that more variance in cannabis use by boys is either unpatterned or associated with variables not inquired about in this study; e.g., peer-group associations

may be more important for boys than for girls. It is worth noting in relation to the point just made that 18.3% of the variance in the alcohol variable for girls is patterned in the first three factors. Alcohol use appears significantly for the males in Factors 1 and 2 to the extent of 14% of its variance. The communality of the alcohol use variable for the girls is only 46.6% and 52.5% for the boys. This means that much more of the variance in alcohol use in this sample is left unexplained or unaccounted for by the analysis as is patterned within it. It would seem that alcohol use is either more unpatterned than cannabis use, or it is to a greater extent than cannabis use associated with variables untouched by this study. One possibility is that since alcohol use is extremely common among adolescents (68% of the 449 students), it is less likely to be "patterned" than cannabis use, which is more deviant (statistically) and more likely at this point in time to be associated with special conditions of one kind or another.

Nonetheless, it is important to note that the use or nonuse of alcohol follows the direction of loadings for the use or nonuse of cannabis in the factors above, although usually in a weaker fashion. This suggests that the conditions of family life which tend to predispose students toward or insulate them from the use of cannabis are of significance also in the case of alcohol use.

THE PERSPECTIVE OF TABULAR ANALYSIS

This section attempts to clarify the foregoing to the extent that it associates actual numbers of people with the attitudes and behavior patterned by factor analysis. Cross-tabulation was done before factor analysis in order to assess the usefulness of performing the latter. The composite "student drug attitude" variable which was constructed for purposes of tabular analysis bears a great deal of similarity to the drug attitudes which cluster in the factors reported in this paper. Therefore, it seems reasonable to use the results of cross-tabulating this composite variable with selected other characteristics in order to give readers a better idea of what proportions of the sample are likely to be involved in any given factor. This is a guide and not a translation process, but it may help to bring factor analysis findings down to earth.

The "Student Drug Attitude Variable"

1. Young people should be able to decide for themselves whether or not they want to use drugs.
2. Use of some drugs, e.g., marihuana, hashish, can make leisure time more enjoyable.
3. Drugs can be fun.
4. There is an excitement in using drugs that is difficult to match in any other activity.
5. There is no harm in the occasional use of marihuana.
6. As soon as a student starts fooling around with drugs, you can expect his grade average to start dropping.
7. Kids who smoke marihuana are no good for themselves or anyone else.
8. The person who smokes marihuana is almost certain to end up on hard drugs.

Students were broken into three groups, depending on their total score (maximum 8).

Group I   Score 0–2 inc. 228 (50.78%) – unfavorable attitudes.
Group II   Score 3–5 inc. 142 (31.63%) – "middle of the road."
Group III Score 6–8 inc. 79 (17.59%) – favorable attitudes.

Comparison with Mothers' and Fathers' Drug Attitudes

	Mothers	Fathers
Group I Scores 0–2 inc.	412 (91.96%)	388 (87%) – unfavorable.
Group II Scores 3–5 inc.	35 (7.81%)	55 (12.33%) – "middle of the road."
Group III Scores 6–8 inc.	1 (0.22%)	3 (0.67%) – favorable.

Agreement with the first five statements and disagreement with the second three statements were considered as indications of favorable attitudes toward the use of cannabis and possible certain other "soft" drugs. Cross-tabulation of the groups defined relative to the 8 items with the 22 other items in the section of the questionnaire from which the former were derived suggested strongly that the items differentiate best in the realm of "soft" drug attitudes (i.e., LSD, MDA, cannabis) and not at all in the realm of "hard" drug attitudes (speed, heroin, etc.).

Selected Characteristics of Student Drug Attitude Groups

A small sample of the tables generated in tabular analysis is presented here in the hope that they will give the reader a better idea of *how many* people may be associated with some of the patterns described by factor analysis. Generally, the tabular data point in the same direction as

factor analysis, but since the students were not divided by sex in the former, the findings are more gross.

Drug Use

There is a clear relationship between favorable drug attitudes and drug use in the case of marihuana and alcohol. Group III report 62.34% marihuana use since the term began as opposed to 0.88% in Group I. Group III report 94.28% alcohol use since the term began, as opposed to 53.98% in Group I.

Although use of other drugs is not reported with great frequency, their use is almost exclusively the domain of Group III, although Group II is sometimes involved. Table 1 summarizes the relative drug use of the three groups.

It can be seen that MDA has some importance, as does LSD. Glue, speed, and heroin appear to play a minor role in this pattern of attitudes and behavior related to drug use.

TABLE 1

Student Drug Attitudes and Drug Use

	Group I (unfavorable)				Group II (middle of the road)				Group III (favorable)			
	Yes		No		Yes		No		Yes		No	
Drug	No.	%	No.	%	No.	%	No.	%	No.	%	No.	%
Marihuana	2	0.88	225	99.12	18	12.68	124	87.32	48	62.34	29	37.6
Opium	1	0.44	226	99.56	1	0.70	141	99.30	8	10.39	69	89.6
LSD	0	0.00	227	100.00	3	2.11	139	97.89	13	16.88	64	83.1
MDA	0	0.00	227	100.00	2	1.41	140	98.59	16	21.05	60	78.9
Heroin, cocaine, morphine	0	0.00	227	100.00	1	0.70	141	99.30	4	5.19	73	94.8
Glue/other solvents	0	0.00	227	100.00	2	1.41	140	98.59	1	1.30	76	98.7
Speed	0	0.00	227	100.00	0	0.00	142	100.00	3	3.95	73	96.0
Other stimulants	1	0.44	226	99.56	5	3.52	137	96.48	9	11.69	68	88.3
Barbiturates	0	0.00	227	100.00	2	1.41	140	98.59	7	9.09	70	90.9
Tranquilizers	1	0.44	226	99.56	3	2.13	138	97.87	10	12.99	67	87.0
Alcohol	122	53.98	104	46.02	114	80.28	28	19.72	73	94.81	4	5.1

Perception of Family

Group I (unfavorable to drug use) are most likely to see their families as exceptionally close, finding much pleasure in each other's company and doing many things together (59.28%) (see Table 2). Most of the remainder of Group I (35.29%) see their families as fairly close, getting along more often than not, running smoothly, but not noted for warmth or a sense of happiness. Group III demonstrates another pattern. This group are most likely to see their families as no more than fairly close (52.63%). Only 27.63% of Group III see their families as being exceptionally close, while 15.79% report that the members of their families are indifferent, not very concerned with one another, rarely do things as a group, and are notably cool toward one another. In Group I, only 3.62% report family life in this way (p < 0.001).

Communication with Father

It will be seen from Tables 3 and 4 that the differences in patterns of communication evident from factor analysis are differences of frequency. More fathers of Group I students (unfavorable) than of Group III students are told what their offspring do at evenings and weekends and are told about their children's thoughts and feelings. The differences, of course, are not absolute. Some Group III fathers enjoy very frequent interaction with their sons and daughters while some Group I fathers do not. Usually, however, the differences are between "always" and "sometimes" rather than between "always" and "never" or "everything" and "nothing."

COMMENTS

It is difficult to locate the present study within the tenets of either of the delinquency theories described in the introduction. The principal difficulty lies in the sex differentiation that is an essential part of the study's findings. In the case of the boys, it seems at first sight that the factor which involves *nonuse* of drugs and *strong* family communication falls within the "intervening variable" interpretation of deviance since the first factor apparently describes conditions which tend to *insulate* them against drug use, yet the second factor suggests only a weak link between poor communication and drug use. Thus, it might be argued that the dissolution of familial controls is not enough and that another set of variables (such as deviant associations) intervenes to draw boys into drug use. Of course, an alternative theory would be that in a sample of this kind (i.e., "normal" students attending school and living in intact families) cannabis use is largely unpatterned. In the case of the girls, however, a converse to the nonuse of drugs and strong communication

TABLE 2

Student Drug Attitudes and Perception of Family

	Very close		Fairly close		Indifferent		Unhappy		Row total	% of Total	No response
Group I (unfavorable)	131	59.28	78	35.29	8	3.62	4	1.81	221	50.92	7
Group II	66	48.18	57	41.61	11	8.03	3	2.19	137	31.57	5
Group III (favorable)	21	27.63	40	52.63	12	15.79	3	3.95	76	17.51	3
Column total	218		175		31		10		434		
% of Column total		50.23		40.32		7.14		2.30			

6 d.f.
$x^2 = 28.82$
$p < 0.001$

TABLE 3

Student Drug Attitudes and Frequency with which Father Hears What Son or Daughter Does on Evenings and Weekends

	Always		Sometimes		Never		Row total	% of Total	No response
Group I	163	72.12	62	27.43	1	0.44	226	50.90	2
Group II	89	63.57	49	35.00	2	1.43	140	31.53	2
Group III	38	48.72	40	51.28	0	0	78	17.57	1
Column total	290		151		3		444		
% of Column total		65.32		34.01		0.68			

4 d.f.
$x^2 = 19.34$
$p < 0.001$

TABLE 4

Student Drug Attitudes and Frequency with which Son or Daughter Talks to Father about Feelings

	About everything		About some things		About nothing		Row total	% of Total	No response
Group I	64	28.32	161	41.24	1	0.44	226	50.90	2
Group II	17	12.14	120	85.71	3	2.14	140	31.53	2
Group III	12	15.38	63	80.77	3	3.85	78	17.57	1
Column total	93		344		7		444		
% of Column total		20.95		77.48		1.58			

4 d.f.
$x^2 = 19.34$
$p < 0.001$

pattern does exist, together with another factor still which, when all the factors are taken together, indicates that poor intrafamilial communication can have an *inverse* relationship with drug use in the presence of certain other attitudinal and disciplinary conditions offered by parents. This study, then, adds to existing literature on intrafamilial communication and drug use in that it suggests (1) an important sex differential, (2) an interaction between drug use, communication, discipline, and attitudes, in which communication seems to serve a "legitimizing" role in the transmission of parental values, and (3) a consequent, partial explanation for the "common antecedents and differential outcome" problem.

At this point, however, a proviso should be made concerning the comparison of this study's findings with those of students of delinquency. It is perhaps unfair and unwise to locate the present study of cannabis and alcohol use in the context of studies which are concerned with behavior which is more generally considered by young people to be unacceptable, e.g., theft and other delinquent acts. It may also be unwise to look for patterns where none exist. Whereas in the case of fairly serious delinquencies, e.g., breaking and entering on numerous occasions, it may be useful to look for correlates in the offender's family life (or elsewhere), it may be less useful to look for correlates of behavior that are widely accepted (at least within the younger segment of the population), e.g., alcohol use among teenagers. Cannabis use perhaps falls between the two examples above in terms of acceptability to young people. Therefore, one might expect cannabis use to be less patterned than thieving but more patterned than alcohol use. In fact, this is the general direction in which the findings of this study do point: The frequency of alcohol use does seem to be associated, though not as strongly, with the same conditions as is marihuana use. In both cases more of their variance is unexplained than explained by this study. We have referred to the conditions of family life described herein as "common" antecedents for purposes of the "differential outcome" problem, yet this is really quite presumptuous

when we consider the possible range of meanings which could be associated with a given "communicative" act. When we are pleased to think that we are comparing families with similar "communicative" conditions, we could be easily wrong in making such equations. Study of this field relative to drug use, at least in intact families, is very much in its infancy.

The problems inherent in correlational and retrospective studies, namely, the difficulty of making causal inferences, can be partly overcome by longitudinal research designs. There is no study of this kind to the author's knowledge in the field of drug use and family conditions, although some exist in the field of delinquency, e.g., West.[18] Such a design is badly needed to sort out further the seemingly complex relationships between drug use, communication, discipline, and attitudes discussed in this paper, as well as to inspect the relative functions of the family and the peer group in the adoption of drug use.

Studies of drug use have, of course, concerned themselves both with family correlates (as in the examples above) and with peer group associations, e.g., Goode[19] and Becker.[20] But it is unusual for those who stress the importance of the family to take much notice of those who emphasize the peer group in the etiology of drug use. These studies, then, contribute little to the understanding of the interactive effects of these sets of variables.

This section would be failing in even a cursory review of the relevant literature if it did not mention a group of studies which are not easy to reconcile with the theories presented so far. These studies concern the apparently strong likelihood that parents who use drugs themselves are more likely than nonusing parents to have children who use drugs.[21]

Whether children use drugs in imitation of their parents or whether they use illegal drugs to hurt their parents who are seen as hypocritical in opposing cannabis use but using harmful drugs themselves is problematic. This is another set of variables which should be investigated in the context of those mentioned above by means of longitudinal studies.

REFERENCES

1. **Smart, R. G., Fejer, D., and White, J.,** The extent of drug use in Metropolitan Toronto schools: a study of changes from 1968 to 1970, *Addictions,* 18, 1, 1971.

2. **Bilodeau, L.,** Drug use among the students in the secondary schools and CEGEPS on Montreal Island, 1969 and 1971, *O.P.T.A.T.,* 1971.

3. **Tec, N.,** Family and differential involvement with marihuana: a study of suburban teenagers, *J. Marriage Family,* 32, 656, 1970.

4. **Streit, F. and Oliver, H. G.,** The child's perception of his family and its relationship to drug use, *Drug Forum,* I, 283, 1972.

5. California State Dept. of Education, A Study of More Effective Education Relative to Narcotics, Other Harmful Drugs and Hallucinogenic Substances, Progress Report, 1970 (mimeo).

6. **Smart, R. G.,** Marihuana use among adults in Toronto, *Br. J. Addict.,* 68, 117, 1973.

7. **Lavenhar, M. et al.,** A survey of drug abuse in six suburban New Jersey high schools. II. Characteristics of drug users and non-users, in *Student Drug Surveys,* Einstein, S. and Allen, S., Eds., Baywood, New York, 1972.

8. **Annis, H.,** A Longitudinal Study of Students in Timmins, Progress Report, Addiction Research Foundation, Toronto, 1972.

9. **Kandel, D.,** Family Processes in Adolescent Drug Use; Progress Report, Biometrics Res. N.Y. State Dept. Mental Hyg. Div. Sociomed. Sci. Dept. Psychiatr., Columbia University, Grant MH-19079, October, 1971.

10. **Sutherland, E. and Cressey, D.,** *Principles of Criminology,* 7th ed., Lippincott, Philadelphia, 1966.

11. **Nye, I.,** *Family Relationships and Delinquent Behaviour,* John Wiley & Sons, New York, 1958.

12. **Jensen, G.,** Parents, peers and delinquent action: a test of the differential association perspective, *Am. J. Sociol.,* 78, 562, 1972.

13. **Hirschi, T.,** *Causes of Delinquency,* University of California Press, Berkeley, 1969.

14. **Briar, S. and Piliavin, I.,** Delinquency, situational inducements, and commitments to conformity, *Social Probl.,* 13, 35, 1965.

15. **Jennrick, R. and Sampson, P.,** Rotation for simple loadings, *Psychometrika,* 31, 313, 1966.

16. **Rummel, R. J.,** Understanding factor analysis, *J. Conflict Resolution,* 11, 444, 1968.

17. **Palmer, T., Pearson, J., and Haire, S.,** Parental attitude research instrument adapted, in *Selected Instruments Used in the Group Home Project,* State of California, Human Relations Agency, Department of the Youth Authority, Fall 1969.

18. **West, D. J.,** *Present Conduct and Future Delinquency,* Heinemann, London, 1969.

19. **Goode, E.,** Multiple drug use among marihuana smokers, *Social Probl.,* 17, 48, 1969.

20. **Becker, H.,** Marijuana use and the social context, *Social Probl.,* 3, 35, 1955.

21. **Smart, R. G. and Fejer, D.,** Drug use among adolescents and their parents: closing the generation gap, *J. Abnormal Psychol.,* 79, 153, 1972.

DRUG DEPENDENCE AMONG NURSES

Charles Winick

TABLE OF CONTENTS

INTRODUCTION

This chapter deals with nurses who are drug dependent. The great public, governmental, and professional concern for the young or military narcotic addict and the drug-dependent person who contributes to urban crime has not, so far, led to a parallel interest in the situation of the older drug-dependent person, such as the nurse, who already has a vocation and a place in the community. "Drugs in industry" programs are just beginning to consider such persons.

The emergence of methadone maintenance as a significantly available treatment approach has, among other effects, led to the emergence of a considerable number of older persons who were opiate dependent and who had been able to conceal their drug problems for many years, including some nurses.

How many drug-dependent nurses are there and how large a proportion of the total number of nurses do they represent? There are, as of 1968, 613,188 nurses in the United States, of whom 65.3% work in institutional settings.[1]

An early attempt to extrapolate the number of nurses who became opiate addicts in the United States during 1962 concluded that a very conservative estimate would be 338, which is roughly equivalent to the number of nurses graduated each year from 13 average-size schools of nursing.[2] The rate of *known* meperidine (Demerol®) addiction among nurses in recent years has been 176 per 100,000, which is over 100 times greater than the rate in the general population. It is likely that the actual rate is substantially greater than the known rate.

It may be relevant to compare the incidence of drug dependence among physicians. (There are, as of 1968, 313,559 physicians in the United States.) A very conservative estimate of the number of physicians newly addicted to opiates during 1961 is 268, roughly equivalent to the yearly output of three average-size medical schools.[3]

Some physicians and nurses are probably dependent on a variety of substances other than meperidine and other opiates, but reliable information on the range and incidence or prevalence of such dependence is not available. Available indicators suggest that the order of magnitude of drug dependence among nurses and physicians is perhaps around 1%, although confirmation of any prevalence figure is difficult.

In view of the critical shortage of nurses and the importance of learning more about career contingencies that may be related to drug dependence, the present study was undertaken as a follow-up to previous reports on drug use by jazz musicians and physicians, the only noninstitutionalized occupational groups whose drug dependence has been documented.[4,5]

PROCEDURE

Ideally, we would take a large population of nurses who were still in training, obtain information about their backgrounds, administer various psychological tests and role and other inventories, and then follow them up for several decades. We would also apply the same procedure to a control group of women in other occupations in order to see the extent to which nursing poses special career problems and whether there is differential self-selection for nursing.

Another optimal procedure would be to obtain a sample of drug-dependent nurses and then compare them with a control group of nurses of the same age, career line, marital status, and geographic location, but who were not drug dependent, in order to determine whether the latter group experienced similar problems. If they had had similar problems, why one group became drug dependent while another did not might be analyzed, especially if longitudinal data were developed. Pending the availability of such longitudinal studies, the present study is offered as a contribution toward clarification of some of the parameters of drug dependence among nurses.

Interviews were conducted in New York, New Jersey, and Connecticut, with 195 nurses who either were or had been drug dependent at some point during a period of 7 years prior to the interview.

Every subject interviewed had used a mood-modifying substance at least daily for at least 3 months. The substances primarily used by the interviewees were meperidine (Demerol) 81%, morphine and other opiates 6%, barbiturates 10%, and others 3%.

Access to the nurses was obtained through a variety of non-law enforcement sources. Some (16%) of the nurses were or had been in treatment. Other nurses (30%) were part of a larger group of persons hospitalized for reasons other than drug dependence but whose previous drug use had been reported as part of the taking of the patients' history and which was being interviewed in order to obtain information on "unknown" addicts who function successfully in the "square world" and are not known to the authorities. The rest of the nurses (54%) interviewed were approached through noninstitutional sources.

DESCRIPTION OF INTERVIEWEES

The nurses interviewed were all female, ranging in age from 21 to 62 and averaging 43. Thirty-two percent were married, 16% were divorced, and 26% had children. One percent were Black and 99% White. Fifty-five percent were Protestant, 38% Catholic, 2% Jewish, and no information on religion could be obtained from 5%. None had been involved professionally in any research or treatment activity involving drug dependence. The typical nurse interviewed was at least as successful as the average nurse in terms of income, upward mobility, and general professional activity. Eighty-nine percent had completed 3-year programs, 2% had college baccalaureate degrees, and 9% had some college level courses. All the women were interviewed at some time subsequent to 1963.

These nurse addicts were not inadequate or marginal workers, in terms of work functioning. Practically all the nurses interviewed felt that they were and had been functioning professionally on an effective level.

The interviews averaged 2 hours. Each respondent was asked to discuss her career, beginning with her first interest in medicine and nursing. Questions were asked about early life, youth interests, health career history and inspirations, drug use, and family situation. The interviewer took notes on the nurses' comments which were content-analyzed into various content categories, which are summarized below.

SUBSTANCES USED

Meperidine is so popular because some nurses are allergic to, or throw up after using, morphine or codeine. Meperidine seldom has such side effects. One typical nurse began by taking 2 cc., quickly reached a level of 3 or 4 doses a day, and built up to 30 cc. a day in a period of 3 months. A narcotic with rapid onset of action and short duration, such as meperidine, is more subject to abuse than one with gradual onset and long duration, such as morphine.

Meperidine was more readily available to the nurses than other drugs and carried less stigma than was connected with other opiates. The nurses tended to believe that signs of meperidine use would be less visible to others than might be the case with other substances. A number of nurses did not fully appreciate the drug's addictive properties and felt that it would be easier to discontinue using it than any of the other opiates. It is less hypotensive than other opiates.

Meperidine is so readily available in hospitals because a postoperative patient who is in pain traditionally gets around 50 to 100 mg of the drug every 4 hours depending on his age, weight, height, and degree of pain. The dosage is continued for several days. It is also relatively cheap (about $2.50 for 30 cc., with 50 mg/cc.).

Many hospitals are so concerned about the possibility of a nurse taking drugs intended for patients that they have set up elaborate security procedures. Typically, the key to the narcotics cabinet is carried by the nurse in charge of the section, rather than kept in a drawer, and is signed for by the nurse in charge of the next shift. Narcotics are the responsibility of the nurse in charge of a shift. A nurse with the responsibility for narcotics may be called a "medication nurse" even if she is not a supervisor. The nurse who is going off duty and the one coming on duty cooperate in counting the narcotics supply and signing the record in many hospitals.

Some state health departments recommend that meperidine be made available in individual dose ampules, which have to be broken open for each administration. The only way a nurse or other functionary can divert such an ampule to her own use is to take it all herself.

It is probably easier for a nurse than a physician to get access to drugs in a hospital because the nurse or even a nurse's aide usually does the actual administration of drugs to a patient. The nurse usually has full access to the hospital pharmacy, to which a physician may not be readily admitted. A nurse is likely to be a more recognizable functionary of a hospital than a physician, who may be one of many with part-time "attending" privileges. She usually spends large blocks of time in the hospital, in contrast to the physician, who may only appear to visit his own patients. Even in very sophisticated teaching hospitals, the needs of the patient are so paramount that his requests for a pain-killing substance are usually honored promptly by the staff on duty at a nursing station, and the staff enjoys great latitude in dispensing such substances, provided that adequate records are maintained.

DRUG-TAKING PROCEDURES

Three fifths of the nurses tended to administer drugs to themselves at home, 8% were likely to do so while on duty, and 32% administered drugs both while working and at home, depending on the situation. Those who took drugs on duty generally went to a closet or bathroom in order to do so.

Some nurses (2%) were so eager that they sometimes took the injection through the cloth of their uniform. One woman, working with elderly terminal patients, said that she placed her own arm behind the patient's skin. The needle would go through the patient's skin and into the nurse's arm at the other end.

The drug-dependent nurse uses a variety of subterfuges to get greater access to drugs. She may ask for the shift from midnight to 8:00 A.M. or 11:00 P.M. to 7:00 A.M. These shifts, although "quiet," are not ordinarily very attractive to others. A nurse who requests such a shift, "after I have put my children to sleep," will probably get it. The night nurse prefers such duty not only because there is a skeleton staff but also because a patient usually receives sedation before going to sleep and is unlikely to require additional drugs. The night nurse who asks for narcotics may not have to divert any to the patient because she can chart the dosages and not administer them. The nurse may also give the patient part of the amount she takes from the narcotics cabinet and keep the rest for herself. The nurse may replace meperidine with distilled water or replace morphine with milk sugar. Sometimes a nurse reports that drugs have been lost or spilled.

Some nurses used considerable ingenuity in getting equipment for injections. One nurse used to leave the hospital and go to a garbage can outside, in which disposable syringes were placed after polio vaccine had been injected to patients.

Other nurses sought private duty cases, which obtained drugs from a local pharmacy via a doctor's prescription. A nurse on such duty has greater freedom in obtaining drugs than is possible in a hospital setting. She is in an advantageous position to divert drugs because the patient is hardly likely to know or remember the strength of the substance that he receives. She can also tell a doctor that her patient requires more drugs. The private duty nurse may have a patient who has a PRN prescription, which is indefinitely renewable. In severe chronic illnesses, many physicians write such prescriptions. The nurse may seek out terminal patients, who often require large quantities of narcotics.

Other nurses seek posts at nursing homes where there are elderly patients who have chronic diseases which require pain-killing preparations quite frequently. The complaints of such patients that they are not free of pain, despite medication, are probably less likely to lead to investigation than would be the case in a hospital.

DISCIPLINARY ACTION

One nurse, working in the same hospital for 5 years, was able to sustain her drug dependence without being discovered. Likelihood of discovery depends on the strictness with which the hospital maintains narcotics records. Someone who keeps her own record is relatively unlikely to be discovered until an independent check is conducted. The average nurse whose dependence had been discovered was forced to leave employment after 16 months because of the situation. Approximately two fifths of those interviewed had never been forced to leave any place of employment because of difficulties related to drug dependence. An employer who discovers that a nurse is drug dependent is required, in most states, to report her to the state licensing board.

Typically, a state licensing board places such a nurse on probation for a period of time but cautions her that the next offense means loss of license. The suspension may be for as much as a year or two, depending on the circumstances and whether she will be participating in a program of rehabilitation. Boards are much more likely to be severe with a nurse whose drug use harmed a patient than with one who has falsified records.

Boards only hear about such cases from hospitals and other employing institutions, and a hospital may not wish to report an addict nurse. If she is reported, the hospital might be unwilling to provide evidence. Hospitals often prefer to dismiss a drug-dependent nurse quietly rather than get undesirable publicity. Some may feel sorry for her, not wish to cause trouble, and record her departure "for health reasons." A nurse can generally find a new position with a minimum of difficulty. It is likely that some 42% of nurses leave or change positions each year, although precise official figures on job mobility are not available. The exchange of letters of reference is so time consuming that a nurse may work in a hospital for several months before her previous record comes to light. The nursing shortage is severe, and there may not be opportunity for full scrutiny of the background of nurses being hired.

During 1968, the last year for which full information is available, 35 state licensing boards took some disciplinary action against a total of 188 nurses. Of these 188 cases, 67 involved violation of the narcotics laws and 24 involved narcotic addiction.[6] The action taken in the 188 cases included probation (53), revocation of license (73), refusal to new license (30), suspension (25), voluntary surrender of license (24), and refusal to grant initial license.

When a state board reports some disciplinary action taken against a nurse to another state board, the response of the latter may cover a wide range. Some states record the information on a card file, others check to see if the person has registered, and some regard the information for intramural use only. Other states report the information to all hospital administrators. When a nursing board discovers that a nurse whose license has been revoked or suspended is working in the state, some disciplinary action is likely to be taken.

COMPARISON WITH STREET ADDICTS

The nurses differed from the typical street narcotic addict in a number of ways. Most urban street addicts are much younger than the nurses, come from lower socioeconomic status families, and they usually do not have a conventional vocation. None of the nurses had adolescent problems which had brought them to the attention of the law. For most street addicts, intravenous injection is the preferred method of administration, probably because it provides almost instant gratification and has a sexual dimension. Only 10% of the nurses preferred the intravenous route, 22% took drugs orally, and 68% took them intramuscularly.

It is likely that such a relatively small proportion of nurses took drugs intravenously because a "flash" or "rush" or immediate, concentrated feeling was less important than the easing, adaptational effect or escape possible via the oral or muscular route. Also, the sexual component of drug use was probably much less important for the nurses than for the younger male street addicts for whom the needle and its manipulation probably have considerable sexual loading.

The preference for intramuscular techniques of injection may reflect some gender as well as socioeconomic differences. Many female addicts prefer an intramuscular technique in order to avoid vein "tracks" and also for cosmetic reasons. Those with work problems could be seeking a plateau effect which will enable them to cope with the anxiety, uneasiness, and other difficulties they experience while working.

Although money with which to buy drugs is an important part of the life of the street addict, it is not usually a matter of consequence for the nurse, who can obtain drugs on the job. Nurse addicts do not profit financially from their use of drugs. They make no effort to seek out other users. The only shared drug habit was found in two nurses who had lived together for 8 years. Their emotional relationship with each other had antedated their drug use.

There appears to be no proselyting on the part of drug addicts. Two of the nurses interviewed were married to physicians, but neither made any effort to interest him in the habit. In fact, both women tried to conceal their drug use from their husbands.

The street addict tends to prefer heroin, while the nurse is likely to prefer meperidine. The street addict is often a member of a large subculture of other drug users, which may have a jargon and procedures of its own. Street addicts usually learn about drugs from their peers, with whom they continue to associate. Nurses generally begin drug use on their own. They seldom "graduate" to opiates, as the street addict often does. Nurses are also far less likely to be polydependent.

Perhaps the most direct difference between the street addicts of today and drug-dependent nurses is that not one of the latter who was dependent on methadone could be found, although illegal methadone is regularly used by a substantial proportion of the street addicts in many large cities. It is possible that the therapeutic connotations of methadone, as a substance used in the treatment of addiction, are such that it is simply not consonant with the requirements of the drug-dependent nurse.

REASONS FOR DRUG USE

An effort was made in the interview to reconstruct the circumstances and situations in which drug use began. The reasons were then coded into a number of categories. The total number of reasons came to over 100% because the typical respondent cited a number of factors related to the beginning of drug use, which appears to have been overdetermined.

The reasons for taking drugs noted below represent the recollection of the respondents. The lack of a control group makes it difficult for us to know how representative these problems are of all nurses.

Another consideration is that in an interview situation dealing with an emotionally freighted situation, it is probably easier for respondents to emphasize specific events and occurrences rather than more long-term factors which may be difficult to verbalize or recall or even be aware of. There also could be an unconscious self-justificatory element in any discussion by a drug user of the circumstances surrounding the onset of her habit, even if the discussion is nonthreatening.

The reasons cited by the nurses for their beginning drug use are set forth in Table 1, in percent.

Some comments on each of the reasons may help to convey their situational qualities.

TABLE 1

Reasons Cited by Nurses for Onset of Drug Use, in Percent

Fatigue	37
Ailments	34
Family terminations	19
Quarrels	18
Ambivalence	11
Insomnia	11
Magical thinking	7
Age benchmark	7
Retirement	6
Misinformation	5
Alcohol	2
Total	157

Fatigue (37%). A frequent reason for beginning drug use is fatigue. "I work so hard and I am so tired that I must have something to keep me going," said one nurse. Another observed that, "I began working double shifts at the hospital and just couldn't keep up with it. I could barely keep my eyes open. So I began taking drugs and it did help me a lot in accomplishing my job."

Many nurses appear to have had a workload which they experienced as so difficult and onerous that completing it in terms of the unit of work, e.g., the shift or the day, seemed next to impossible. They tried to accomplish as much as they could in the time available but found themselves overworked and fatigued.

Fatigue seems to have been a response to a wide variety of situations and demands. In many cases, the nurse was unable to deal directly with some problems on the job. Some deferred a decision by working more, longer, and harder, as a result of which they were increasingly tired and began to take drugs to cope with fatigue.

Ailments (34%). A number of nurses had some ailment for which they did not want to consult a doctor but for which they felt analgesics would be desirable. They would take some medication, which helped them, and then they would take more on another occasion and continue to increase the frequency of the dosage.

Such nurses complained of ailments such as migraine headaches or menstrual pains. The nurses felt that a physician would not do much for such conditions and that self-medication could be helpful.

One nurse with varicose veins, for which she rejected surgery, was in considerable pain. She took meperidine regularly, taking about 50 mg each day. "If I didn't take it, I wouldn't be able to keep up with my job, which required a lot of walking." She took the drug for 3 years and was only detected because the children in her neighborhood found several discarded and empty syringes near her home.

The nurse with varicose veins was atypical in that she had a localized and clearly identifiable symptom. Most of the nurses had vaguer complaints which appeared to have a considerable psychosomatic component.

Termination of a family relationship (19%). One nurse of 49 noted, "The only thing I had that was important was my daughter. I really had no other interest, discussed everything with her. My daughter and I kept having more and more trouble and finally she got her own apartment and moved out. I was taking morphine, not much, but when she left I really began to feel there was nothing left for me. I had nobody to talk to and I began taking morphine regularly." This woman is typical of several others who are somewhat similar to embezzlers who had what they defined as an unsharable problem.[7] This nurse had a symbiotic relationship with her daughter which was central to her. When it appeared to have ended, she saw herself as having an insoluble problem.

Several other respondents dated the onset of drug use from the loss of some significant relationship, usually by death. The death or serious illness of a husband was cited by a number of the respondents as an important element in the onset of drug use.

Quarrels (18%). Some of the nurses began using drugs as an immediate aftermath of a quarrel with someone with whom their relationship was becoming difficult because of role strain. One nurse had a "deep dish quarrel" with her husband. "I felt terrible after we had a long fight about whether we should move closer to my job, but I didn't want to go back and continue it. I thought that I could calm myself with some Demerol. I did, and the next time we quarreled, I tried it again."

Other nurses found themselves quarreling with doctors and colleagues because of a conflict between the nurses' conception of what her role ought to be and the demands and urgencies of the work situation. They would take a drug to calm themselves after the quarrel, find the drug soothing, and try it the next time there was a similar eruption.

"My job's become unbearable," said one nurse. "I had four different chiefs, all of whom were after me practically every day. Doctors would come in whom I had never seen before and begin barking orders at me and yelling and complaining that a particular item of equipment was not available. One particular doctor kept pushing me around, and we used to fight all the time. I began taking Demerol to calm down after each fight, then every night. I found myself doing things that I knew were wrong, and I was doing them over and over again. And the situation was so difficult that I had to go on that way. I was not important enough to change things."

Most of the quarrels seemed to be reflections of situations in which the nurse felt herself under more pressure than she could deal with. The quarrel stemmed from the pressure situation, which the nurse could not handle.

Ambivalence (11%). In a number of the nurses, drug use began around the time that a nurse was about to move into another or different kind of responsibility, usually a promotion to a better job situation. A common thread ran through the stories of most of these nurses: ambivalence about nursing and frustration at having to leave the bedside situation in favor of ascending the bureaucratic career ladder in the direction of supervision.

This kind of change in the job from an interpersonal situation in which the provision of emotional succorance to patients was important to a more scientific and administrative kind of responsibility seemed to awaken latent role conflicts in these women, none of whom had graduated from a 4-year program which presumably would have prepared them for administrative work. They typically had ambivalent feelings about becoming nurses before they entered the profession but had functioned effectively within it. The tremendous demand for nurses facilitated getting work and made it difficult for the nurse to think about doing other kinds of work for which she would have had to be retrained.

In a few of these cases, there was inadequate resolution of a conflict between the demands of a family situation and of work. The nurse tended to temporize, avoiding doing anything, became increasingly anxious, and began drug use as one way of handling the anxiety. Most of the nurses who

had ambivalent responses tended not to have considered other options available in their role conflicts.

Insomnia (11%). Insomnia was cited by a number of nurses as a reason for their beginning the use of drugs. The insomnia usually was related to a problem of role conflict, in personal life or on the job.

A number of nurses were depressed about their ability to cope with the conflicting strains of their job and would be so tired that they could not sleep. "I was completely limp with fatigue at the end of a day," said one nurse, "yet I couldn't fall asleep. I began taking barbiturates to force myself to sleep, and after a few months I couldn't stop taking them."

Magical thinking (7%). Some of the nurses engaged in magical thinking about the drug they used. Because of their professional role, they believed that they could take the drug without becoming addicted. One said, "Narcotics to me were something out of a Charlie Chan movie. I never thought I'd get hooked. I figured I could stop at any time." Perhaps because they used analgesic substances regularly in connection with their work, they tended to have a feeling of emancipation about these substances. "I handled these drugs so often I figured that I would know just where to stop," said one 40-year-old woman.

Reaching a specific age (7%). A number of the nurses began drug use as they approached a specific age which had a special meaning for them, especially in late middle age. "One day I looked around and realized I was 55 and had no interests and very few friends. I got more depressed and felt awful. My job had been everything to me, but it was becoming less interesting. I began to be bored on the job, which had never happened to me before. In order to help me over this bad time, I took a small amount of Demerol. It really helped me when I felt lonely. And then I tried it again, to tide me over, and I kept taking it."

Retirement (6%). For some nurses who have had a reasonably fulfilling career but do not have sufficient emotional anchorages in their family and nonwork interpersonal relations, drug use seems to have begun in connection with self-medication of various symptoms and illnesses which became more urgent as retirement became a more immediate reality.

One 63-year-old nurse had experienced intermittent pain from phlebitis for almost 20 years.

She began taking various substances for her condition only around the age of 60, as she became preoccupied with her ability to function until retirement and with what she would do after she retired. The phlebitis had not become significant to her until retirement became more immediate.

Another nurse said, "I have always had trouble with my back, but I was so busy working I never really had time to think about it. When I was one year away from retirement, either it got worse or I just became more worried about it and began thinking about how it would feel once. I left working and had all day to myself. I took some morphine to take care of the pain and it helped me a lot and before I knew it I was really only getting through the day with the help of morphine." A previous pilot study found that such problems relating to the meaning of retirement were important in addiction among the health professions.[8]

Misinformation (5%). Some of the nurses were not adequately informed about the addiction potential of meperidine. They believed that meperidine has only mild addicting potential, similar to codeine's, so that addiction was not a major risk. Some older nurse addicts were familiar with early studies which concluded that meperidine had a lesser addiction liability than morphine. Although the nurses were all aware that their self-medication with controlled substances was illegal, few knew the exact laws involved or the penalties they provided.

Alcohol (2%). A small proportion of the nurses had some experience with problem drinking before they began using other substances. One nurse had been drinking fairly steadily and heavily for 12 years, during which she functioned successfully on the job. The smell of alcohol on her breath ultimately led to difficulties, and she began using barbiturates. She was able to continue to work for a number of years while regularly on barbiturates.

There was no significant difference between the reasons for the beginning of drug use among those nurses who are or were in treatment (16%) and those who had never been in a treatment situation (84%). The nurses in treatment did not have a longer period of dependence, a more severe habit, or less family anchorages. Their getting into treatment appeared to be a function of chance as much as any of the sociological dimensions which might have appeared to be relevant.

There was also no significant difference between those nurses whose drug use had been discovered by their superiors or institutions and those who had remained undetected in terms of the reasons for onset, in terms of the genesis of their drug use. Only nurses who were working in institutional settings, however, had gone into treatment situations; not one of the private duty nurses had entered treatment, presumably because of the lack of institutional pressures on them to do so.

Because the nurse tends to work as a member of a team rather than as an individual practitioner, we might speculate that group belongingness and support would operate to minimize drug dependence among nurses. That so many nurses seem to be drug takers may reflect the nature of the work group in which they participate.

None of the subjects was a member of a religious order. It is possible that the group cohesion expected of a religious functionary could have operated to reduce the likelihood of drug dependence in nurses working within a religious context. Such persons might also be operating under more constraints in terms of living conditions and privacy.

COMPARISON OF NURSES WITH PHYSICIANS

It may be of interest to compare the drug-dependent nurses with the addicted physicians studied previously.[9] Table 2 gives the comparative importance, in percent, to each group of various reasons for starting drug use.

There are more reasons, proportionately, for physicians (216%) becoming drug dependent than for nurses (157%) to do so. We may speculate that it takes more pressure and/or problems experienced by physicians as compared with nurses to lead to drug dependence.

In both physicians and nurses, fatigue/overwork was the most important single reason for the beginning of drug dependence and ailments represented the second most frequent factor. Magical thinking and omnipotence fantasies were four times as frequent among physicians than among nurses, and alcohol was eight times as frequent.

Level of aspiration (24%) and effects on mood (21%), which were significant among physicians as reasons for starting drug use, did not figure at all among nurses.

Nurses cited specific kinds of interpersonal

TABLE 2

Comparison of Reasons for Starting Drug Use Among
Physicians and Nurses

Nurses		Physicians	
Fatigue	37	Overwork	41
Ailments	34	Ailments	36
Family terminations	19	Magical thinking	32
Quarrels	18	Marital difficulties	31
Ambivalence	11	Level of aspiration	24
Insomnia	11	Mood effects	21
Magical thinking	7	Alcohol	17
Age benchmark	7	Insomnia	11
Retirement	6	Age	3
Misinformation	5		
Alcohol	2		
Total	157		216

problems (family terminations 19% and quarrels 18%), whereas such difficulties did not figure among the addicted physicians' concerns. The physicians' marital difficulties (31%) were, however, much more deep rooted than the nurses' problems with spouses, which tended to be much more diffuse and not at all as salient.

Nurses had a number of problems connected with age (age benchmark 7% and retirement 6%) that do not figure among physicians because the latter can presumably function effectively at almost any age, whereas nurses are bound by the retirement requirements of the institutions for which so many work..

The nurses interviewed differed from addict physicians previously interviewed in several other ways.[10] In general, career problems seemed to be more important for the physicians than the more generalized interpersonal problems which affected the nurses. The physicians had more occupational options, in terms of what they might do with their professional training.

Nurses were likely to be much more depressed than the physicians. They also demonstrated more ambivalence and uncertainty about their functioning on the job. The ambivalence may be related, to some extent, to the work situation of the nurse, which is emotionally freighted as a result of the issues of life and death latent in health care. Because of the anxiety of patients and their families, it is difficult for the nurse to manifest anxiety. Beginning a pattern of drug use could be one way of dealing with such anxiety.

The concept of relative deprivation may help to clarify some nurses' feelings.[11] They can see physicians subject to analogous pressures but enjoying much larger incomes, greater upward mobility, a seemingly less stringent system of accountability, unquestioned authority, and an ability to disengage themselves from a situation as soon as they complete their professional obligations. On such dimensions, judging from our interviews, the nurse often feels that she is working as hard or harder than the doctor but is experiencing much relative deprivation.

DISCUSSION

None of the nurses had parents whose use of alcohol or other drugs had been significant, at least in terms of the nurses' ability to recall the situation. None had been involved in close relationships with peers who had been drug users. Explanation of the reasons for the drug dependence of the nurses interviewed must therefore draw on constructs other than those usually cited to account for drug dependence among the young.

It is suggested that the author's sociological theory of the genesis of drug dependence proposed elsewhere in this volume can be constructively used in order to group the specific reasons cited by the nurses for the onset of their drug dependence into a smaller number of analytic categories. We proposed that drug dependence will be high in groups with (1) access to drugs, (2) disengagement from negative proscriptions about their use, and (3) role strain and/or deprivation.

The nurses interviewed all were in situations in which they had access to drugs. It is possible to group the reasons cited by the nurses for the genesis of their drug use into those related to their having neutralized injunctions against drug use and those related to role strain and/or deprivation.

A substantial proportion (48%) of the nurses' reasons for the onset of their drug dependence could be attributed to their disengagement from negative proscriptions about drugs. It is suggested that the nurses' freedom from conventional negative proscriptions was a significant factor in their medicating themselves for their ailments (34%), engaging in magical thinking about drugs (7%), acting on the basis of misinformation about drugs (5%), or switching from alcohol (2%). This emancipation about drugs did not, however, extend to other areas of social and interpersonal attitudes, and the great majority of the nurses had constricted and conventional views of such matters. A previous study of 90 nurse patients at the Federal narcotics hospital at Lexington concluded, on the basis of psychological test data, that the patients viewed themselves as asexual and measured very high on impulse control.[12]

It is suggested that the largest single contributor to the onset of drug use among nurses could be role strain, which the nurses experienced in the form of fatigue (37%), quarrels (18%), ambivalence (11%), and insomnia (11%), which contributed to and reflected role strain. By role strain we mean a felt difficulty in fulfilling role obligations, which may be personal and/or professional.[13]

Role strain is probably especially likely among nurses because of the multiplicity of their roles, which pose difficult and contradictory demands. In contrast, a field such as pharmacy presents relatively predictable and established role demands. A pharmacist is likely to have a reasonably explicit notion of his daily work, and his expectations will tend to be met. This is probably the simplest explanation of the relatively small number of pharmacist addicts, although they have maximum access to narcotic drugs of any occupational group.

Role strain is particularly likely if a person is deeply involved in his role, and it is one which requires a substantial level of performance on a continuing basis. Nursing is such a field because it requires its practitioners to provide services for whatever patients seek help from them.

The unmarried nurse is particularly vulnerable to the pressures of role strain because she cannot rely on husband and/or children as sources of support. For such a woman, regression to a role as family member is not available, although she is often symbolically required to be a maternal figure in dealings with patients.

Although role strain might be expected to be especially common among persons working as directors of nursing services, no such functionaries were in the sample interviewed, although there was a determined effort to find at least one drug-dependent nursing administrator. The kind of commitment involved in becoming a supervisor probably requires sufficient coming to terms with the problems of the job and one's own personal difficulties, so that drug dependence would be relatively unlikely.

More of the nurses interviewed had worked in small rather than large hospitals. It is possible that small hospitals were overrepresented because their nurses tend to work harder and have a larger role range than those in large hospitals, with their greater specialization and division of labor.

Related to role strain as an important contributor to the beginning of drug use is role deprivation, by which we mean termination of a significant role relationship, as expressed in several different kinds of situations: termination of a family relationship (19%), negative feelings about reaching an age which was perceived by the nurse as an important benchmark (7%), and retirement (6%).

Almost all of the nurses for whom role deprivation tended to be significantly involved in their drug dependence were over 40. It would seem that role deprivation is more important for older nurses, but role strain is more centrally related to the reasons for the commencement of drug use among the younger nurses.

This formulation permits us to relate the genesis of drug use among nurses to its genesis among other groups. It also may help us in speculating on the likelihood of future trends. One trend working against an increase in drug dependence among nurses in the future is that private duty work in hospitals has become less available because of the development of intensive care units, which can accommodate a number of patients and offer a wide range of technical and professional services. For young nurses, the range of role strain may be reduced as the profession becomes increasingly rationalized and specialized.

A countervailing force is the participation by some student nurses, especially in urban centers, in the generally relaxed attitude toward mood modification by the use of chemical substances that is found in many colleges. Some student nurses participate in casual use of drugs for recreational and/or social purposes to a much greater extent than did previous generations. It is possible, therefore, that as they grow older, today's student nurses will feel more free to explore drug use. Although none of the nurses studied began drug use in nursing school, it is possible that the next generation of nurses will be different in this respect.

In spite of the very special nature of the nurse's occupation and her special relationship to chemical substances, trends of nurses' drug use in the future will necessarily reflect the larger social patterns of relationships to mood-modifying substances. Perhaps even more important is the possibility that any subgroup in the population which has a high degree of role strain, role deprivation, and disengagement from negative proscriptions about drugs will also tend to have a high incidence of drug dependence. If, in addition to these three dimensions, there is the additional one of access to these substances, we may anticipate a very high incidence of drug dependence. Such a formulation may be useful in identifying groups in the population at particular points in the social structure where appropriate prophylactic measures could be taken. The nurse's relationship to drug dependence is thus only an application of general principles which are relevant to all occupational groups.

REFERENCES

1. American Nurses Association, *Facts About Nursing,* The Association, New York, 1968.
2. Garb, S., Narcotic addiction in nurses and doctors, *Nursing Outlook,* 13, 31, 1965.
3. Winick, C., Physician narcotic addicts, *Social Probl.,* 9, 174, 1961.
4. Winick, C., Use of drugs by jazz musicians, *Social Probl.,* 7, 240, 1960.
5. Winick, C., *Social Probl.,* 9, 174, 1961.
6. American Nurses Association, personal communication, December 21, 1970.
7. Cressey, D. R., *Other People's Money,* Free Press, New York, 1953.
8. Sherlock, B. J., Career problems and narcotics addiction in the health professions, *Int. J. Addict.,* 2, 191, 1966.
9. Winick, C., *Social Probl.,* 9, 174, 1961.
10. Winick, C., *Social Probl.,* 9, 174, 1961.
11. Merton, R. K. and Kitt, A. S., Contributions to the theory of reference group behavior, in *Continuities in Social Research,* Merton, R. K. and Lazarsfeld, P. F., Eds., Free Press, New York, 1950, 40.
12. Poplar, J. F., Characteristics of nurse addicts, *Am. J. Nursing,* 69, 117, 1969.
13. Goode, W. J., A theory of role strain, *Am. J. Sociol.,* 25, 483, 1960.

TREATMENT AND RESOCIALIZATION OF THE DRUG DEPENDENT

TOWARDS A SOCIOLOGY OF METHADONE MAINTENANCE*

Ron Miller

TABLE OF CONTENTS

*I would like to thank Rita Seiden Miller, Alice Sardell, and Charles Winick for their assistance in the preparation of this chapter.

INTRODUCTION

During the past decade, the methadone maintenance approach to the rehabilitation of heroin addicts has emerged from an accidental laboratory treatment for two heroin addicts into the dominant treatment modality for heroin addiction. In 1974, over 75,000 heroin addicts were enrolled in methadone treatment programs in the United States. Moreover, the use of a synthetic, addictive narcotic — methadone — to eliminate dependence on another addictive narcotic — heroin — may have committed a substantial number of methadone-maintained patients to a lifetime of continued methadone medication and treatment program contact. Thus, methadone maintenance is now and will be for an indeterminate time period a major treatment/rehabilitation force in contemporary American society.

The purpose of this chapter is to advance the sociological understanding of methadone maintenance. The analysis is divided into three parts: First, I will trace the historical development of maintenance since a sociological analysis of this treatment modality must be placed in the sociohistorical context of its evolution (I will focus on methadone in the United States, although some programs exist in other countries[1]); second, I will elaborate upon the sociological implications of the historical development of maintenance; finally, I will speculate on the future of methadone maintenance.

THE HISTORY OF
METHADONE MAINTENANCE

Nineteenth-century America: A Dope Fiend's Paradise[2]

Nineteenth-century America has been described as a "dope fiend's paradise." Opium was legally sold at low prices throughout the country and was even grown in several American states. Morphine, the active ingredient in opium, was isolated early in the century; it came into common use during the Civil War to combat the pain of war injuries (all of the opiates — opium, morphine, heroin — act as analgesics and hypnotics besides their more commonly publicized euphoriant effects). Heroin, an acetyl-compound of morphine, was first marketed near the end of the century. All these opiates and pharmaceutical preparations containing them were freely available through physi-

cians, pharmacies, grocery and general stores, by mail order, and in numerous patent medicines.[3] Widespread adoption resulted from their low cost, legal availability, and medicinal properties.

The demographic characteristics of 19th- and 20th-century opiate "addicts" showed that 60% were women, many were over 40 years old, and most were from the middle and upper classes.[4] Although numerical estimates are hazardous, one source argues that by 1913 there were 782,118 addicts in the United States.[5] It is important to note that even given this maximum estimate of the number of opiate addicts, opiates taken daily in large doses by addicts were not a social menace in the 19th century and were not perceived as a menace.[6] Nevertheless, the expansion of opium smoking and the free market economy for opium, morphine, and heroin purchase were not viewed positively by all segments of American society. First, anti-Chinese ideology on the West Coast resulted in demands for restrictions on opium smoking. Second, medical concern evolved over the widespread (and not physician-controlled) availability of these addictive medicines. Third, a strong prohibitionist sentiment in the 19th century opposed the use of opiates as well as the use of alcohol. These concerns resulted in legislative attempts to control the use and distribution of the opiates. San Francisco prohibited opium smoking in smoking dens in 1875; Congress began raising the tariff on opium in 1883 and by 1909 prohibited the importation of smoking opium. In 1906, the Pure Food and Drug Act was passed against patent-medicine lobby opposition and required that medicines containing opiates had to be so labeled. Finally, the United States joined in the 1912 Hague Convention designed to control narcotic traffic internationally and to encourage domestic control as well.

The Harrison Act of 1914

The preceding discussion of opiate addiction in 19th- and early 20th-century America has been presented as background to the Harrison Act of 1914. Prior to this act, the system of opiate distribution was only minimally regulated and controlled. Large numbers of Americans were addicted to the opiates, but they were largely middle class, "responsible" citizens. The Harrison Act of 1914 was presented to Congress as a way to control the distribution of opiates in compliance with American international obligations under the

Hague Convention. Since Congress has constitutional authority to regulate interstate commerce, the act was entitled:

An Act to provide for the registration of, with collectors, of internal revenue, and to impose a special tax upon all persons who produce, import, manufacture, compound, deal in, dispense, sell, distribute, or give away opium or coca leaves, their salts, derivatives, or preparations, and for other purposes.

The Harrison Act coincided with the medical profession's efforts to gain control over the marketing of heroin, opium, and morphine; the act prohibited sale of over-the-counter preparations containing opiates and appeared to place the addict under the medical guidance of physicians. However, a pattern of selective interpretation by the Narcotics Bureau of some Supreme Court decisions resulted in the de facto implementation of the Harrison Act so as to take jurisdiction over opiate addicts away from the physician and to solidly entrust addict jurisdiction to the criminal justice system. Physicians became wary of treating addicts when some colleagues were arrested for providing opiates to addicts; the medical profession quickly disassociated itself from the addict.

Three alternatives were open to pre-Harrison opiate addicts: (1) They could totally discontinue opiate use; (2) they could switch to barbituates under physician control (this seems to have been the response for females); or (3) they could choose to continue narcotic use.[7] This latter group, because they could not obtain legal opiates, became transformed into the criminal opiate addict who has plagued American society ever since. This criminalization of addiction was accomplished by 1924; the Harrison Act had created a new criminal class and an addict subculture.[8]

Heroin Addiction Treatment 1914–1963

The treatment of heroin addiction from the passage of the Harrison Act until the early 1960s can be summarized briefly: a quickly aborted medical maintenance plan, imprisonment for criminal offenses, supervised withdrawal (detoxification) from heroin after heroin became the major illicit drug in the 1920s, attempts to rehabilitate the addict through personality reorganization, and the beginning of a civil (as opposed to criminal) commitment approach by the law enforcement establishment. All were relatively unsuccessful in their attempt to combat heroin addiction.

The rapid separation of the physician from the opiate addict after 1915 resulted in a federal decision to open government-regulated narcotic treatment clinics under medical supervision; over 40 were opened by 1920 to 1921, and they seem to have been relatively successful heroin maintenance clinics, although differences of opinion clearly exist.[9] In any event, some medical opposition, local public pressure, and law enforcement pressure combined to close them by 1924. Medical help was denied to addicts; the criminalization process was complete.

After 1924, the criminal justice approach to heroin addiction treatment dominated the American drug scene. Imprisonment for possession and sale of illicit narcotics and for drug-related offenses was the dominant treatment modality. Addicts, of course, suffered from withdrawal symptoms when imprisoned and often relapsed to drug abuse and criminal behavior when released. The criminal justice approach of legal punishment (along with attempts to limit importation of heroin) was unsuccessful. Heroin addiction was transformed from a moral problem prior to the Harrison Act to a major social, legal, and criminal problem by the 1960s.

While nontreatment and narcotic maintenance were regarded as unsatisfactory solutions, it was not until 1935 that imprisonment of heroin addicts began to be complemented by or replaced with medical detoxification, withdrawal from heroin addiction. In that year, the first United States Public Health Service Hospital was opened in Lexington, Kentucky to detoxify voluntarily or involuntarily committed addicts in a prisonlike medical facility; a second unit was opened a few years later at Fort Worth. The Lexington experience confirmed the addictive power of heroin; patients/inmates tended to return for further detoxifications, and the majority continued a pattern of addiction and criminal behavior, even though about two fifths ultimately abstained after years of relapse.[10-12] Medical detoxification was made considerably easier after World War II with the introduction of methadone, a synthetic narcotic with morphinelike properties invented by the German chemical industry. Methadone eliminated the withdrawal symptoms in morphine-heroin addicts deprived of their opiates (this is known as cross-tolerance of narcotics); thus, methadone was used to *detoxify* heroin addicts by giving them gradually *decreasing doses* of methadone. In the

1950s, the increased incidence of heroin addiction resulted in the establishment of other detoxification facilities (with psychological support services), such as Riverside Hospital and Manhattan General Hospital in New York City, the major center of heroin addiction during these years. Their experiences parallel the Lexington results: recidivism, readmission, and continued criminal activities among treated addicts.[13] Some addicts ultimately achieved an abstinent state, but the majority became readdicted soon after release.

The failure of the legal approach to eliminate addiction and the failure of the detoxification modality resulted in the development of a new concept of heroin addiction treatment in the late 1950s, the therapeutic community. Synanon took a social-psychological approach to addiction, basing its treatment philosophy on the belief that addiction results from an underlying personality disturbance; therefore, reorganization of that personality is necessary.[14,15] Synanon's residential community emphasized that addicts had to help themselves combat heroin addiction; the emphasis was upon group therapy and peer social pressure by ex-addicts and current addicts to effect the needed social-psychological transformation. The goal was heroic: addicts helping themselves to combat the evil forces of addiction. The results have been uninspiring: About 10% of Synanon members stayed abstinent for 2 years, and the abstinence rate is inflated by the exclusion of large numbers of admissions who "split" prior to formal inclusion in Synanon statistics.[16]

The therapeutic community concept, despite unimpressive quantitative results, produced major qualitative changes in increasingly visible and articulate ex-addicts. Even "splittees" were impressed by the social-psychological power of the group living experience, and many emulated the Synanon model in other parts of the United States.[17] The therapeutic community has been forcefully presented by its proponents. The emphasis is upon restructuring the defective personality structure of addicts. "A drug addict is an extremely emotionally immature person. He has never grown up, he has never been transformed from the boy of his childhood days to a responsible, mature adult."[18] Group therapy and encounter sessions are designed to complete the truncated maturation of the addict.

The therapeutic community movement was a powerful factor in continuing to mold public attitudes to value drug abstinence as the goal of rehabilitative treatment. For many addicts who struggled to become and remain drug-free, a zealous, semireligious, almost fanatical faith in the virtues of the drug-free state was communicated to the public. "Since ex-addicts obviously know what drug addiction is all about, their views are widely respected by those who are less knowledgeable."[19] Yet, despite the impressive oratorical skills of therapeutic community graduates, and despite the vivid impressions they leave upon outsiders who visit them, the drug-free residential approach has not been quantitatively successful in its rehabilitative efforts. Individuals have undergone impressive personal transformations, but the programs are selective in the patients they accept, there is a very rapid rate of "splitting" from the program, program graduates are often employed in running the therapeutic communities, and the few who leave after completing treatment are likely to return to the use of drugs.[20]

Another recent approach to the treatment of heroin addiction is civil commitment. In 1961, the State of California formally instituted civil commitment as a logical and humanitarian alternative to criminal imprisonment. Instead of being imprisoned, addicts were remanded to civil facilities reminiscent of moderate security prisons and given large-scale group therapy and close supervision. The results paralleled other program experiences: 33% seemed abstinent after 1 year, and the number dropped to 16% 3 years after release.[21] A New York State program of similar intent and structure was initiated in 1966 and had similar results.[22]

In summary, the treatment of heroin addiction from 1914 to 1963 stressed the goal of abstinence in the rehabilitation process. Imprisonment, medical detoxification, civil commitment, and the therapeutic community all sought the return of the addict to a drug-free existence. Moreover, the drug-free ideology was brilliantly elaborated upon in the late 1950s and early 1960s. All the evaluative studies, however, showed that success in achieving and maintaining permanent abstinence occurred for only a small percentage of patients.[23] On the other hand, the maintenance approach (giving addicts opiates on a continuous basis to prevent withdrawal and to eliminate the need for illegal supplies) was only briefly attempted and then rapidly disbanded and publicly discredited in 1924. Indeed, in 1963, a joint statement of the

American Medical Association's Council on Mental Health and the National Academy of Sciences' National Research Council on Narcotics and Medical Practice jointly issued an attack upon the maintenance concept: *"Continued administration of narcotic drugs solely for the maintenance of dependence is not a bona fide attempt at cure nor is it ethical treatment except in . . . unusual circumstances . . ."*[24]

The Heroin Epidemic of the 1960s

The criminalization of heroin addiction under the Harrison Act's interpretation by the Narcotics Bureau and the failure of abstinence treatment modalities provide the historical backdrop to the emergence of methadone maintenance as a treatment for heroin addiction. One more factor needs to be added, however: the explosion of public concern over the heroin epidemic in the 1960s. In terms of public visibility, heroin addiction was not a major concern from the mid-1920s to the mid-1950s, except possibly for the "propaganda" campaign instituted by the Federal Bureau of Narcotics in the 1930s to similarly criminalize marijuana.[25] During the late 1950s and throughout the 1960s, on the other hand, public visibility of heroin addiction increased exponentially. The mass media noted the rapid increase in the number of heroin addicts and strongly associated the addict with the increase in crime plaguing urban America. Estimates of the numbers of heroin addicts reflected this "national obsession"[26] with the heroin epidemic. The Federal Bureau of Narcotics' (soon to be relabeled the Bureau for Narcotics and Dangerous Drugs) 1950 nonsystematic estimate was 50,000; by the end of the next decade, they realized the need to systemize addict estimates and computed estimates of 315,000 in 1969 and 524,000 in 1970.[27] The national epidemic of heroin abuse is particularly clear for Washington, D.C. The commitment of known addicts to the D.C. jail rose gradually from about 50 cases in 1958 to about 150 cases a year from 1958 through 1966. Beginning in 1967, there was a dramatic rise to 450 cases in 1968 and to an annual rate of 1,400 by February 1969. Moreover, "there was a sudden, sharp increase from about 13,000 reported . . . offenses in the first six months of 1966 to about 36,000 in the last six months of 1969 . . . the most persuasive hypothesis is that there was a sudden epidemic of heroin addiction in Washington which led to both the increased commitment rates of narcotic offenders at the jail and the parallel increase in reported . . . crimes."[28] The heroin addiction and crime epidemic of the 1960s became a major social and political issue. The public sought relief from the plight of crime and the seemingly endless spiral of addiction.

The Methadone Maintenance Accident

Increasing public concern with heroin addiction and criminal behavior was reflected in increased political and professional concern with these social problems. In November 1963, Dr. Vincent P. Dole, a metabolic disorders research physician and professor at the prestigious Rockefeller Institute in New York City, received a grant to explore new ways to treat narcotics addiction. Among the materials read by Dr. Dole was Dr. Marie Nyswander's study, *The Drug Addict as Patient.*[29] The two soon met and then collaborated on a study of the metabolism of heroin addicts. The initial plan was to maintain two hard-core criminal addicts on morphine, in a manner similar to the British treatment of morphine addiction.

The morphine maintenance results were disastrous; the two patients were practically immobile, sitting most of the time in front of a television set waiting for the next shot of morphine. Dole and Nyswander then decided to terminate this phase of the study; to prevent withdrawal, they intended to use decreasing doses of methadone, following standard detoxification procedures. Since the two patients were on high doses of morphine, they were placed on equivalently large doses of methadone. Some discomfort on the patients' part resulted in still higher doses of methadone.

Dole and Nyswander soon noticed that dramatic alterations in patient behavior and appearance immediately occurred. One addict started to paint industriously, and the other wanted to get his high school equivalency diploma. The patients were *maintained* on *high doses* of methadone, and the pattern of improvements continued. Moreover, Dole and Nyswander discovered that methadone medication in high and continuous doses prevented narcotic hunger and, most importantly, prevented supplementary doses of heroin from giving the addicts a euphoriant high; they labeled it the methadone *blockade.*[30]

This serendipitous laboratory observation changed the course of heroin addiction treatment in the United States. Besides eliminating the craving for heroin and establishing the blockade, methadone had other qualities which made it an ideal maintenance narcotic. First, it could be given orally in high doses, and, secondly, it lasted 24 hr on one high dose administration (heroin was usually injected and always of short duration). Side effects (constipation, excessive sweating, and some reduction in sexual drive) were minimal compared to the apparent rehabilitative influence on patients.[31,32] Not surprisingly, Dole and Nyswander cautiously began trying methadone maintenance treatment with other heroin addicts.

Cautious Expansion

Dole and Nyswander treated only a few more patients by February 1965. Continued success with these patients led to a major commitment by New York City in June 1965 for $1,380,000 and a large-scale test of an "apparent treatment breakthrough."[33] An independent evaluation committee was simultaneously created to monitor and judge the effectiveness of this new treatment modality.

An article published in the prestigious *Journal of the American Medical Association* in August 1965 brought widespread attention to the methadone maintenance approach. Dole and Nyswander noted that in 22 patients orally stabilized with methadone hydrochloride, marked improvement occurred in terms of employment, education, and family reconciliation.[34] Subsequent articles proclaimed the anti-euphoriant effects of methadone[35] and the utility of treating heroin addiction as a metabolic disease by preventing narcotic hunger resulting from the long-term physiological effects of heroin.[36]

Despite this emphasis on the anti-euphoriant effects of methadone maintenance and its appropriateness as a treatment for a metabolic disorder, opposition to methadone maintenance quickly crystallized. The drug-free therapeutic communities attacked maintenance as merely substituting one addictive drug with another, longer-lasting addictive drug.[37] In addition, they felt that acceptance of methadone maintenance would lead to a societal acceptance of drug use and an increase in the numbers addicted to narcotics. The Federal Bureau of Narcotics' opposition to methadone maintenance was based on similar objections, as well as the feeling that indefinite narcotic maintenance was inappropriate medical treatment. As a result of the dominance of the drug-free

orientation in America, methadone maintenance expanded cautiously, seeking to maintain its protection as a research program. Perhaps it was allowed to expand at all only because the concern over the heroin/crime epidemic was so politically explosive that the antimethadone majority could not eliminate a program that had demonstrated some clinical effectiveness. Methadone maintenance remained a small program in New York and a small program in similar clinical research programs in Illinois and Philadelphia.[38-42]

Evaluation, Vietnam, SAODAP, and Rapid Expansion

A dominant factor in the rapid expansion of methadone maintenance has been the optimistic evaluation reports issued by research committees formed to objectively evaluate the effectiveness of this controversial program for heroin addicts. Perhaps the decisive evaluation in the history of methadone maintenance was the 1968 evaluation of the Dole-Nyswander program by the Evaluation Unit of Columbia University's School of Public Health. Published in the *Journal of the American Medical Association* in December 1968, this evaluation gave strong research support to the Dole-Nyswander approach to heroin addiction. As presented in the evaluation, the major conclusions were

1. Of 871 patients admitted to the program by March 31, 1968, 86% remained in treatment — an exceptionally high retention rate for a drug addiction treatment program.

2. For 544 men who had been in treatment at least 3 months, employment improvement has been continuous: While only 28% were employed prior to admission, after 5 months 45% were employed and after 24 months 85% were employed.

3. Substantial decrease in arrests occurred for Dole-Nyswander patients. Compared to a contrast group admitted for detoxification, rearrests were down sharply for those who remained in treatment.

4. None of the patients remaining in care became readdicted to heroin, and repeated use of other drugs was 11% amphetamines or barbiturates, 5% chronic alcohol.[43]

Although there has been considerable criticism of the methods and statistical procedures of the report (and equally strong defense of its conclusions[44]), the impression clearly remained that methadone maintenance retained heroin addicts in treatment and improved their post-program arrest and employment history. Subsequent reports by the committee over the name of the research director, Dr. Frances Gearing, confirmed the 1968 conclusions,[45-50] as did research reports on other methadone programs.[51-53] These positive evaluations undoubtedly stimulated expansion of methadone maintenance, as did the growing public fear over the heroin epidemic. In New York City alone, the methadone maintenance patient load was over 12,000 by October 1970.[54]

The expansion of methadone maintenance and the apparent success in addict rehabilitation appear to have provided the impetus for the federal government to issue plans to regulate methadone use. After 6 years of inactivity in the face of widely publicized methadone use in maintenance programs,[55] the Food and Drug Administration and the Bureau of Narcotics and Dangerous Drugs issued plans on June 11, 1970 which formally defined methadone for maintenance as an investigational new drug (I.N.D.).[56] Methadone maintenance was viewed as a research technique which showed "promise" in management and rehabilitation but which also had significant potential for abuse. The regulations went into effect on April 2, 1971. By then, however, public and professional concern over the heroin epidemic had increased enormously. The problem of widespread drug abuse among members of the United States Armed Forces serving in Vietnam startled the nation in early 1971. "The emotion-laden issue of an unpopular war was coupled with. . .panic in some parts of the United States at the thought that thousands of Vietnam veterans, addicted to inexpensive high quality opiates in Southeast Asia, would return to this country and be forced into lives of crime to support expensive narcotic habits."[57] By the summer of 1971, President Nixon had called the situation a "national emergency" and said that "America's Public Enemy Number 1 is drug abuse." He called for the creation of a top-level office, the Special Action Office for Drug Abuse Prevention of the Executive Office (SAODAP), to coordinate national programs dealing with drug abuse.

The director of SAODAP, Dr. Jerome H. Jaffe, had been Chief of the Drug Abuse Program of the Illinois Department of Public Health, a "multi-modal" program emphasizing detoxification, therapeutic communities, narcotic antagonists, and methadone maintenance. Under SAODAP stimulus, treatment programs expanded rapidly; in June 1971, 36 programs existed, while 2 years later more than 400 were funded. The expansion occurred for all treatment modalities, not just methadone maintenance.[58] Part of the expansion was due to the criminal justice system's decision to use treatment programs (especially methadone maintenance) for narcotics offenders on parole and probation and as an acceptable prearraignment alternative for arrestees dependent on narcotics. On the national level, the number of methadone maintenance patients rose sharply to 56,000 in spring 1972, 65,000 in October 1972, and 73,000 in February 1973.[59]

Clinic Procedures

The growth of methadone maintenance in this period was paralleled by a shift in intake and operational procedures. The original research program selection criteria sought to make the population fairly homogeneous in addiction history. The intake criteria were (1) age between 20 and 40 (50 by the third year), (2) a 4-year history of mainlining heroin, (3) repeated failures in other programs, (4) no mixed drug or alcohol dependencies, (5) no medical complications or psychotic behavior patterns, and (6) no legal compulsion. After an initial period accepting men only, females were also accepted.[60]

The original Dole-Nyswander research on methadone maintenance stabilization was structured into three phases:[61]

Phase I. Initial stabilization of selected addicts occurred on an inpatient basis during the first 3 to 4 years of the program. Over a 6-week period, the patient was slowly built up to a blockade dosage of 80 to 120 mg of methadone. The patient was given a series of supportive services (medical and dental care plus therapy, counseling, and vocational guidance) by both professional counselors and an ex-addict, longer-term methadone maintenance patient (termed the research assistant) who was expected to provide much of the needed emotional support for the new patient.

Phase II. After in-hospital stabilization, patients were assigned to an outpatient unit where they reported each weekday to drink their medication in front of a nurse, to give a urine specimen, and to receive continued assistance as desired. On weekends, they were allowed to self-medicate themselves at home. After a period of successful program functioning (no legal problems, no urine specimens positive for heroin, etc.), the patient reduced his in-clinic medication visits and was able to take home more and more methadone-in-Tang® (imitation orange juice).

Phase III. In phase III, after a successful 1-year minimum as an outpatient, the patient was considered to be a stable and socially productive member of the community who could be treated as an ordinary medical patient. These patients came to the clinic only once a week.

Modifications on these treatment procedures were stimulated by innovations in Philadelphia and Illinois, including outpatient induction of patients, treating patients with medical, multiple drug, or behavioral problems, and using a low dosage methadone maintenance program (eliminating "narcotic hunger" but not reaching the narcotic blockade").[62-64] Age limits were lowered to 18 in some programs, and most had no maximum age restriction. Large waiting lists resulted in rapid expansion of public and private maintenance programs.

Diversion and Governmental Reassertion

The issue of the diversion of methadone to "illicit" purposes had always been a major concern of both the Bureau of Narcotics and Dangerous Drugs and methadone program administrators. Since patients had supplies of methadone that they could take home, and since methadone was a narcotic capable of inducing euphoriant effects in an individual who had not taken a high amount of narcotics before (in medical terminology, was not tolerant), the rapid expansion of methadone programs presaged a rapid expansion of a methadone "black market" and a wave of accidental methadone poisoning of children whose parents/guardians had methadone supplies at home. From late 1971 (after the Vietnam heroin panic had subsided) through early 1973, the methadone diversion problem became a national concern. Stories appeared in the mass media about the easy availability of methadone on the streets, sold by methadone patients for money to purchase heroin, and the use of methadone as the primary addictive drug for teenage drug abusers.[65-66]

Methadone was, in fact, readily divertible to illicit purposes because most methadone patients had up to a week's methadone medication on a take-home basis. One study found that of 95 still-active heroin addicts, 96% had been offered "street" methadone and 56% had purchased some.[67] The implications of the diversion problem were immediately apparent. Dr. Peter Bourne of SAODAP noted that diversion was the greatest threat to the continued existence of methadone maintenance: "Both clinically and in a broader social sense it [diversion] represents the achilles heel of our entire effort."[68] Because of the furor over methadone diversion, the Boston methadone maintenance program shifted to a 7-day-a-week clinic attendance structure. The program directors felt that because of the Boston City Council threats in spring 1972, ". . . the choice seemed to be between no methadone maintenance program at all for the City of Boston or a methadone maintenance treatment program which operated with a 'no-take-home' policy."[69]

The methadone diversion crisis served as the vehicle for the reassertion of stricter governmental (especially Bureau of Narcotics and Dangerous Drugs) control over methadone maintenance programs. Dr. Jaffe discussed the federal government's concern over diversion at the Fourth National Conference on Methadone, January 10, 1972. He informed the audience that new guidelines were being prepared to control methadone medication more responsibly and to prevent methadone diversion.[70] The regulations were proposed in April 1972 and after strenuous opposition were instituted on December 15, 1972, 6 months after the proposed July 1972 implementation; in fact, full implementation occurred only by March 15, 1973. In general, the new regulations increased the control of the Food and Drug Administration and the Bureau of Narcotics and Dangerous Drugs over all methadone programs. Some specific points worth noting are

1. Methadone maintenance programs were told that patients must attend clinics daily (6 days a week) for their first 3 months; after 3 months of acceptable behavior and urine results, patients could reduce their visits to three times a week (with a maximum 2-day home supply) only when they were employed, in school, or a homemaker. Clients showing progressive rehabilitation after 2 years on the program could reduce visits to twice a week, with a 3-day take-home supply.

2. Methadone maintenance programs were now formally labeled as treatment programs in

view of the tremendous public health and social problems associated with the use of heroin and the demonstrated usefulness of methadone in treatment. However, rather than shift to the typical status of NDA (new drug application, with unrestricted distribution to physicians and pharmacies), an unusual combination of IND (the investigational new drug research status) and NDA was being used; thus,

3. Methadone supplies were being withdrawn from general pharmacies and would be only shipped to accredited programs and accredited hospital pharmacies; a new closed system of distribution was to be established, under which any diversion or misuse could immediately be stopped at the source of supply.[71]

In short, methadone maintenance had emerged to full-fledged governmental acceptance as an effective drug in the treatment of heroin addiction, but federal control over the programs was expanded and clinic procedures (daily or twice-a-week visits) were altered by the new federal regulations. Expansion and diversion had resulted in the reassertion of the federal government's role in the treatment of heroin addiction.

Methadone Maintenance: 1974

In one decade, methadone maintenance became the dominant treatment modality for the treatment of heroin addiction in the United States. The best available estimates are that over 75,000 patients were enrolled in methadone maintenance programs in 1974.[72] In fact, the rapid expansion of maintenance vacancies outstripped the number of addicts seeking assistance. In New York City, for example, there were almost 6,000 vacant methadone maintenance slots in December 1973.[73] On a national level, the heroin addiction epidemic appears to have subsided.[74,75] In November and December 1973 it was reported that narcotic-related crimes had decreased and that there had been "... a decline in the rate of new addiction across the country. In New York, it has been cut by 30 per cent since 1972, and in Washington, D.C., the number of new treated addicts in 1972 was 100, down from a peak of 2,700 in 1969."[76]

Thus, a program which took root and expanded rapidly during the heroin epidemic of the 1960s and the Vietnam heroin panic of 1971 had treatment vacancies when the heroin addiction epidemic receded. And, for better or for worse, the addictive properties of methadone and the emphasis upon social rehabilitation as opposed to abstinence may have committed thousands of patients and their programs to a lifetime of methadone dependence. Methadone maintenance has become, in effect, the most massive, longest-term commitment to rehabilitation ever attempted in the United States.

SOCIOLOGICAL IMPLICATIONS OF THE HISTORY OF METHADONE MAINTENANCE

The preceding historical discussion has been presented in order to provide a framework in which a sociological analysis of methadone maintenance may be understood. The growth of methadone maintenance took place within a cultural climate that had previously emphasized a criminal justice approach to controlling heroin addiction as well as a strong moral commitment to drug-free abstinence as the preferred rehabilitative outcome for heroin addicts. Methadone maintenance evolved during a period of national obsession with the heroin epidemic, the crime explosion, and the Vietnam panic. In this section, I will elaborate upon six sociological themes that emerge from my historical analysis: (1) the relationship of *ideology* and treatment, (2) methadone maintenance as *tertiary deviance*, (3) the continuing *conflict* between *medical* and *criminal justice* attempts to *control* narcotic addiction treatment, (4) the *potential for governmental control of patients* through methadone maintenance programs, (5) the *sociology* of *evaluation*, including the relationship of methadone maintenance to the life cycle analysis of narcotic addiction careers, and (6) *organizational* and *professional* issues in maintenance programs. My comments in each subsection are meant to be suggestive, not definitive.

Ideology and Treatment

In the historical evolution of methadone maintenance, moral and ideological themes emerged as central issues of debate and discussion. (Indeed, moral issues have dominated social reactions to heroin addiction, in general.) Ever since the initial publicity over maintenance, methadone proponents and opponents have been involved in a bitter ideological debate. In this subsection I will examine three sociological issues in this clash of ideologies: (1) the nature of the drug-free critique of methadone maintenance, (2) the development of a rehabilitation ideology by the proponents of methadone maintenance as a post hoc response to the drug-free critique, and (3) the lack of such an ideological commitment to maintenance by methadone patients.

The Drug-free Critique

Strong moral condemnation of methadone maintenance by advocates of drug-free rehabilitation derives much of its support from basic American attitudes strongly " ... rooted in a tradition that placed great value on abstinence, will power, postponement of gratification, and self-control, as well as a strong moral taboo against any drugs that alter moods or weaken individual self-mastery."[77] Concepts of legitimate pleasure in America exclude the euphoriant effects of morphine and heroin.[78] "Since methadone is a substitute for the pleasure of indulgence in heroin, its use must be equally wrong ...."[79]

The moral condemnation of methadone maintenance involves several interrelated critiques. First, critics argue that the genesis of drug addiction is individual psychological disturbance, a character defect, an inadequate personality. Methadone maintenance is seen as treating the symptoms of the disorder (the narcotic addiction) and failing to address the basic underlying psycho-emotional problems. By continuing drug dependence, methadone is viewed as preventing meaningful therapy. Dr. Judianne Densen-Gerber, director of Odyssey House in New York, has noted: "Methadone is a lie."[80] Second, the drug-free critics of methadone maintenance argue that the drug addiction problem is hardly solvable by substituting a legal narcotic, methadone, for illegal heroin. Methadone is just another addictive drug, not a solution to the drug addiction problem.[81] Permanent dependence upon methadone is viewed as a cure worse than the original addiction to heroin: Methadone is seen as a more potent, more addictive, and more difficult drug to withdraw from than heroin.

A third critique within the antimaintenance ideology is the implications of narcotic therapy for the society as a whole. Henry Lennard and his associates have stressed the dangers of utilizing drugs to combat drug abuse. Their major fear is that the current widespread use of drugs to solve personal problems (in 1971, 202 million legal

prescriptions were filled for psychoactive drugs — stimulants, sedatives, tranquilizers, antidepressants)[82] will only be exacerbated by the use of methadone to combat heroin addiction. Lennard, Epstein, and Rosenthal noted that methadone maintenance may be a prime example of how offering inexpensive solutions to a problem that is not well understood may lead to far more serious consequences than the original problem posed. Methadone reinforces the popular idea that drugs are magical answers to complex human and social problems. "Methadone permits the illusion of a solution."[83]

Finally, drug-free critics of methadone maintenance argue that methadone may create rather than cure addicts: First, diversion of methadone can create addicts whose primary addiction is to methadone, not heroin; second, methadone may inadvertently be given to individuals without "real" addictive histories and may, thereby, foster and accelerate the addictive process.

In summary, the ideological commitment of the drug-free critics of methadone maintenance has been reflected in a series of criticisms: (1) Maintenance treats the symptoms of addiction, not the underlying social-psychological disturbances involved; (2) a legal addiction is an unacceptable substitute for illegal addiction; (3) the methadone illusion encourages the nation to presume that human problems can be solved by chemical means; (4) methadone diversion will create a series of street addicts whose primary addiction is to methadone; and (5) premature methadone maintenance will transform individuals on the margins of an addiction career into a permanent addictive dependence. The drug-free ideology incorporates into its values and moral norms a commitment to rehabilitation that is both violated by and attacked by the chemotherapeutic technique of methadone maintenance.

The Methadone Rehabilitation Ideology

In the face of continual criticism, the proponents of methadone maintenance have been forced to develop a post hoc rehabilitation ideology. The original Dole-Nyswander theory of addiction stressed that addiction to heroin caused a metabolic imbalance which resulted in the physiological craving for narcotics which often resulted in relapse; partial corroboration for this view was seen in the Lexington research studies which showed that a "secondary abstinence" syndrome of physiological abnormalities occurred several months after detoxification was complete.[84-86] Therefore, methadone enabled addicts to begin rehabilitation by preventing secondary abstinence, drug hunger, and readdiction. This medical theory of the readdiction process was soon elaborated into a medical model of methadone treatment, with methadone compared to the use of insulin to control diabetes.[87,88]

This medical model of therapy was recently extended and significantly shifted by Dole and Nyswander. In an aggressive criticism of the abstinence ideology, they noted that abstinence before rehabilitation had repeatedly failed in the past 100 years for all but a minority of narcotic addicts. Placing a higher value on abstinence than on the patient's ability to function as a normal member of society was dysfunctional. To them, "The real revolution of the methadone era was its emphasis on rehabilitation rather than detoxification."[89] In methadone maintenance programs, detoxification was a possible final stage after social rehabilitation was complete.

Nonideological Methadone Patients

Despite this thesis that rehabilitation was much more important than abstinence, and despite the gradual adoption of this rehabilitation ideology by some program directors, I would hypothesize that the vast majority of methadone maintenance patients are largely nonideological in their views about maintenance. They accept treatment without accepting an ideological commitment to strong promaintenance attitudes, beliefs, and values. Indeed, one of the most vivid impressions that I have of several ex-addicts hired as interviewers for a research project[90] was the ideological furor of the therapeutic community graduates compared to the nonideological stance of the interviewers on methadone maintenance. The drug-free interviewers compared concepts (each therapeutic community has its own concept of addiction and treatment) during informal conversations; the methadone maintenance patients compared dosages and talked of eventual detoxification. While the interviewers on maintenance rejected the contention (politely presented) that they were "methadone addicts" — a typical drug-free derogation of maintenance patients which has received considerable public adoption — they adhered to the drug-free perspective that ultimate rehabilita-

tion necessitated withdrawal from methadone and the achievement of a stable drug-free life.

A recent study by Brown et al. provides more systematic, quantitative support for the thesis that methadone maintenance patients accept the drug-free perspective that abstinence is preferable to prolonged maintenance on methadone. Studying the attitudes of abstinent and methadone clients at the multimodality Narcotics Treatment Administration in Washington, D.C., Brown et al. noted that from a list of 300 adjectives, different combinations of characteristics were used to characterize addicts using heroin, addicts on methadone, and addicts abstinent of all drugs. While both methadone and abstinent addicts were seen as more responsible, conscientious, pro-social-achievement, and understanding of others than addicts still on heroin (seen as aggressive, antisocial), both methadone and abstinent clients see abstinent individuals as functioning more effectively and more maturely than those on methadone. "These results suggest that methadone maintenance is not yet fully accepted as a long-term treatment device ... even by those clients asking to be placed on methadone."[91]

The apparent acceptance of the drug-free rehabilitation concept by methadone patients underscores the lack of a treatment-specific ideology among methadone maintenance patients. Several sociologists have cited anecdotal instances where drug-free ex-addicts have socially ostracized and confronted methadone patients.[92,93] The topic of abstinent-methadone maintenance patient interaction would, therefore, be an interesting study in the sociology of ideology. The preceding discussion forces me to hypothesize, however, that the acceptance of the drug-free ideology by maintenance patients may effectively disarm the drug-free advocate and serve to minimize conflict and confrontation. Despite the development of a rehabilitation ideology by Dole and Nyswander, methadone maintenance patients appear to have adopted many of the attitudes regarding abstinence that have been forcefully presented by the drug-free community.

Tertiary Deviance

The success of the drug-free ideological community in stigmatizing patients on methadone maintenance as methadone "addicts" and in discrediting methadone has created an interesting sociological phenomenon. Rather than being defined as a moral rehabilitation ideology, methadone maintenance has been transformed into a special state of deviance. I have chosen to coin a new term, *tertiary deviance,* to describe this phenomenon.

The dominant sociological perspective on deviance, labeling theory, has stressed the importance of societal reactions to deviance as the crucial sociological variable. Howard Becker notes that the traditional view defines deviance as the violation of agreed-upon rules and then searches for factors in the personalities and life situations of the rule-breaker to explain their deviance. Becker notes that this perspective ignores the crucial fact about deviance: "...that *social groups create deviance by making rules whose infraction constitutes deviance...* The deviant is one to whom the label has successfully been applied; deviant behavior is behavior that people so label."[94] This labeling theory focuses upon the "moral entrepreneurs" of society who create deviance by enacting laws and who control deviance by enforcing these rules.

The concepts of primary and secondary deviation derive from this notion of the societal labeling of deviance. The terms distinguish between performing the deviant act (primary deviation) and the development of a deviant social role and subculture (secondary deviation) as a result of the need to defend oneself from or adapt to the societal response to the original deviant behavior.[95,96] The implications of the concept of primary and secondary deviance for narcotics addiction can best be understood in terms of our prior discussion of the Harrison Act of 1914. Before 1914, there were apparently hundreds of thousands of primary deviants, individuals addicted to a drug that was not morally acceptable in the society. But they functioned as individuals addicted to opiates, not as a special subculture of addicts. The passage of the Harrison Act and its interpretation by the Narcotics Bureau, the societal reaction which effectively criminalized the deviant behavior, resulted in secondary deviance. Since narcotics were no longer freely and legally available, one type of pre-1914 addicts developed a social role and career as criminal addicts, a secondary deviance pattern which shifted their self-image and their behavior patterns to a criminal subgroup identity. Thus, labeling theorists emphasize that social reactions which force secondary deviation serve to alter profoundly the

implications of the primary deviance.[97] The socially undesirable effects of drug addiction, especially the criminal behavior of addicts, are attributed by labeling theorists to the punitive reaction of American criminal justice authorities to physical addiction. The British policy of dispensing heroin through the medical system is contrasted with the American system; the British reaction did not result in secondary deviance by addicts.[98] Thus, for the most part, the British have not developed the secondary deviation addiction syndrome: the development of an addict subculture, criminal behavior by addicts, public fear of criminal assault, and widespread police corruption. The American pattern of criminalizing addiction created the secondary deviant addict subculture, created a new class of criminals, and created a need for rehabilitation/treatment programs for addiction. The predominant emphasis was upon the elimination of primary deviance: the well-publicized government effort to control addiction at its source in poppy fields and heroin-processing laboratories. When the heroin, crime, and Vietnam crises of the 1960s catapulted the effects of secondary deviation to the forefront of public concern, methadone maintenance became a politically viable response to the addiction problem. Nevertheless, the drug-free ideology that had dominated American values prior to the 1960s defined methadone maintenance as a pragmatically acceptable but ideologically deviant rehabilitative therapy.

I have chosen to label methadone maintenance, in this perspective, as tertiary deviance. I define tertiary deviance as the societal solution to social problems which takes the form of concentrating upon eliminating or minimizing the negative effects of secondary deviance as opposed to prior efforts to eliminate primary deviance. Tertiary deviance involves the legalization of behavior that had previously been viewed as immoral in an attempt to prevent the apparently widespread destructive behavior resulting from secondary deviation patterns. Tertiary deviance implies, however, that the societal legitimization of the new behavior patterns is incomplete; the solution to secondary deviation abuses is made both legitimate and illegitimate simultaneously. Moreover, the stigmatization of tertiary deviance solutions (such as methadone maintenance) indicates that the original ideological debate over the primary deviation has not been resolved; thus, tertiary deviance solutions almost automatically guarantee that ideological debate will continue and that the tertiary solution will remain under assault·by interested moral entrepreneurs. A major focus in this ideological debate will be the contention (by opponents of the tertiary solution) that legalization of the behavior will create *de novo* deviants: individuals whose deviance is encouraged and fostered by the availability of tertiary deviant behavior. Thus, tertiary deviance solutions will be portrayed by moral absolutists as contributing to an increase in deviant behavior by eliminating the social stigma previously unconditionally attached to the primary deviance. Finally, the semilegitimate semistigmatized existence of the tertiary deviance solution must create ambivalent attitudes among both providers and users (and even defenders) of the solution.

The methadone maintenance solution to the heroin addiction problem in America is a prime example of the tertiary deviance solution both in its genesis and its implications. First, methadone maintenance of heroin addicts became acceptable as a treatment modality only when the destructive effects of heroin secondary deviation became evident in the early 1960s; public concern focused on the problem of crime, public fear of criminal assault, and widespread police corruption due to the economics of the heroin black market. Ten years earlier, I would speculate, methadone maintenance would have been rejected as a treatment modality precisely because public concern was focused upon preventing primary deviation. Second, legitimization of maintenance is incomplete. Methadone maintenance is seen by many Americans as rehabilitation without honor. Third, the drug-free ideological community continues to focus upon primary deviation (narcotic addiction) as the "real" concern for society; methadone maintenance is accused of just being "another addiction." The problem of methadone creating new narcotics addicts is continually stressed in the ideological attack upon maintenance therapy.

Finally, the semistigmatized existence of methadone maintenance results in widespread ambivalence towards this tertiary deviance solution to the social problems of heroin addiction. The general society is ambivalent towards maintenance clients: Are they cured or are they still addicts? Community opposition to methadone maintenance programs (especially in "transition" neighborhoods) must be understood in the light of this societal ambivalence.[99] Program therapists (both ex-addict and nonaddict counselors) are often ambivalent about the utility of methadone maintenance as a final phase of rehabilitation. In their study of the Washington, D.C. NTA program, Brown et al. noted that even staff members saw "... the addict abstinent from all drugs as a more effective and capable person than ... the addict using methadone."[100] Patients are similarly ambivalent. While they reject the "addict" label, they still view total drug abstinence as morally superior. Nelkin describes the maintenance patient as a marginal man, isolated from his/her own communities and stigmatized by the larger society as a threat to the social order.[101]

The ambivalent reaction to methadone maintenance because of its tertiary deviance status has resulted in a state of cognitive and social dissonance for methadone patients. To resolve this dissonant state, either (1) methadone must be redefined positively as a beneficial rehabilitation ideology, or (2) methadone patients must ultimately detoxify from methadone in order for rehabilitation to be complete. The latter resolution appears to be most likely. The new concept for treatment appears to be "methadone-to-abstinence," an approach that emphasizes recruitment of addicts into an initial methadone stabilization level followed as soon as possible by ultimate abstinence. The December 1972 FDA regulations emphasize the ultimate goal of drug freedom for all methadone maintenance patients.[102] Thus, detoxification from methadone maintenance has been a major theme at the National Conference on Methadone Treatment, with most programs citing some success in detoxifying methadone patients but also major problems.[103-106] The outlook is for expansion of detoxification efforts in methadone maintenance programs, along with increased program emphasis upon maintaining contacts with the detoxified patient.

As a solution to the problems of secondary deviation, the semideviant status of methadone maintenance presents numerous problems to patients and staff. Methadone maintenance is not unique in this respect, however, since a recent theme in America's recent reaction to societal deviance has been the emphasis upon redressing problems of secondary deviation, that is, the creation and legalization of tertiary deviance solutions to social problems. Just as methadone maintenance has emerged as the solution to the secondary deviation effects related to heroin addiction, so too have (a) legalized abortions been advocated as the solution to the horrors and criminal aspects of illegal abortions and (b) off-track betting been presented as the solution to the profits, power, and moral corruption of organized crime's control of illegal gambling operations. So too in the future, I hypothesize, will the secondary deviation horrors of prostitution — venereal disease, assaults upon customers, tax evasion, and support of other illegal activities — result in the tertiary deviant solution of the legalization of houses-of-leisure. All of these tertiary deviant solutions will be faced with the same problems: semistigmatized legitimation, continual ideological attack by proponents of eliminating the primary deviation, criticisms that they create *de novo* deviants and add to the problem of moral decay in society, and the ambivalent perspectives of providers and consumers. Given their status as tertiary deviance solutions, all will face continual assaults upon their right to exist.

Medical versus Criminal Justice Control of Addiction

A third major sociological theme that emerges from the history of methadone maintenance is the continuing conflict between the medical and criminal justice (legal) approaches to the control of heroin addiction. The methadone maintenance treatment modality was a late arrival in this clash of perspectives, which had been a major issue in American history since the Harrison Act. Most scholars agree that after the passage of the Harrison Act, the control over the treatment of heroin addiction was vested in the federal government; the guiding perspective was a criminal justice emphasis on rigorous enforcement of laws with increasing penalties for violations.[107]

This jurisdictional triumph by the criminal justice system over the medical establishment from 1914 to the 1960s must be seen as part of a broader historical conflict between the major institutions of society to shape human behavior and control social deviance. Thus, Freidson has noted that even in the 19th century, medicine was a relatively unimportant societal institution, humble before the power of religion and law. Beginning in the 19th century, however, medical science began to emerge as a powerful rival to law and religion. More and more human behaviors

were seen as resulting from causes beyond human choice and self-control; the category of illness expanded rapidly in the 19th and 20th centuries, with more and more behavior patterns, e.g., hysteria, obsessive compulsive neurosis, depression, added to the concept of illness. "The increasing emphasis on the label of illness, then, has been at the expense of the labels of both crime and sin and has been narrowing the limits if not weakening the jurisdictions of the traditional control institutions of religion and law."[108]

Thus, the post-Harrison Act loss of medical control over heroin addiction was an atypical historical development. By the 1920s the public image of the addict was that of " . . . a willful degenerate, a hedonistic thrill seeker in need of imprisonment and stiff punishment. Curiously enough, at the same time the public view of many medical afflictions, such as leprosy, epilepsy, and insanity . . . came to be regarded as strictly medical problems rather than as signs of immorality and depravity."[109]

The dominance of the criminal justice perspective post-1914 has been debated in numerous treatises on heroin addiction. Most view criminal justice dominance as an unexpected result of a revenue act (the Harrison Act) which was designed to develop an orderly, physician-controlled distribution system for opiates.[110] Recently, Kramer has argued that the Narcotic Division of the Treasury Department desired control of addiction and organized the Hague Convention in 1912 in order to be able to stress international obligations as a reason to pass the Harrison Act.[111] Before and after the law was passed, editorials in the *Journal of the American Medical Association* repeatedly reaffirmed the physician's right to prescribe narcotics for addicted patients. These editorials ceased after the Treasury Department announced on May 11, 1915 that physician prescriptions for addicts must show decreasing doses over time or the physician would be presumed to be violating the law. Over the next few years Treasury Department orders became more restrictive until it became a prosecutable offense to prescribe any narcotics whatever to an unhospitalized addict.[112]

Physicians had lost the opportunity to prescribe for, and thereby treat, addicts. While hospital treatment was permitted, there were virtually no hospital facilities. A breach was made between the addict and the physician. Moreover, between 1914 and 1938, about 25,000 physicians were arrested for supplying opiates, and 5,000 actually went to jail.[113]

Justification for the Narcotic Division's actions came from some early Supreme Court decisions since the Harrison Act left the status of addicts almost completely indeterminate. In *U.S. v. Jin Fuey Moy*, the Supreme Court in 1915 ruled that possession of smuggled drugs by an addict was a violation of the Harrison Act. This decision forced the addict to go to the physician as the only legal source of supply. In *Webb v. U.S.* in 1919, the Court ruled that prescribing drugs for addicts had to be for the purpose of curing him of the habit and was in violation of the law if the prescription was issued to keep the addict comfortable by maintaining his customary use. In the 1920 Jin Fuey Moy case, the Court again ruled that a doctor could not legitimately prescribe drugs to maintain an opiate addict. Finally, the Behrman case in 1922 was resolved by the Court ruling that physicians could not prescribe drugs for an addict regardless of the physician's purpose.[114]

In addition, the post-Harrison Act narcotic clinics were being closed at the same time that these legal decisions were being made. The clinics' "failure" was widely advertised to galvanize popular sentiment against the medical approach towards addiction and in favor of a punitive police policy.[115] The medical profession cooperated with the criminal justice system in eliminating physician control of addicts when the House of Delegates of the American Medical Association adopted a resolution in the face of de facto loss of control by the medical establishment which called ambulatory treatment of narcotic addiction an unsatisfactory treatment of addiction, whether practiced by the private physician or by the narcotic clinics.[116]

Advocates of the medical control of addiction point to the next year, 1925, as the vindication of the appropriateness of the medical model of treating addiction. Dr. Charles O. Linder of Seattle was arrested and convicted of criminal violation of the law for giving an addict-police informer four tablets of morphine and cocaine. In 1925, Linder was exonerated by the U.S. Supreme Court in an unanimous decision. The court indicated that the previous cases had involved flagrant abuse, reiterated that the Harrison Act was a revenue measure, and added a strongly worded defense of the medical control of addiction.

Almost all analysts of the Linder decision agree that while it provided the support for a medical reassertion of control over narcotic addiction, the case had practically no effect.[117] It was simply ignored by the Federal Bureau of Narcotics. From the 1920s to the early 1960s, the criminal justice model of controlling addiction through imprisonment and the assumed deterrent effect of criminal prosecution remained the dominant institutional response to addiction. Various medical and sociological sources continued to argue that this legalistic approach was futile and that medical management of addiction was necessary. For example, the New York State Medical Association, the New York Academy of Medicine, and the Medical Society of the County of New York all proposed variants of programs designed to place the addict under medical supervision. However, these appeals were to no avail.

These events preceded the heroin epidemic of the late 1960s, the public panic over crime in the streets, and the fear of the return of thousands of addicted Vietnam veterans. All combined with the timely appearance of methadone maintenance to alter the balance in the medical vs. legal debate over the control of addiction. It is my thesis that the existence and growth of methadone maintenance has shifted much of the control over addiction back to medical authorities and has thereby reaffirmed the historical expansion of medical control of deviance that began in the 19th century. Nevertheless, I also feel that the semi-legitimate, tertiary deviant status of methadone maintenance prevents total dominance by the medical profession and, indeed, has already allowed the criminal justice institution to reassert its authority to control narcotic addiction.

The discovery of the rehabilitative power of methadone maintenance and its rapid expansion through 1973 reasserted medical prerogatives in the control of addiction in at least three ways. First, it forced the criminal justice system to implicitly admit the failure of its premethadone maintenance policy of controlling drug addiction. Second, methadone maintenance programs have invariably been directed and controlled by physicians. Third, and perhaps most significantly, the Dole-Nyswander theory of addiction as a metabolic disease was the first medical-physiological theory of addiction ever to receive public attention and support. Although still an unproven hypothesis, the theory strongly challenges the rights of the criminal justice system to treat a medical disease. The critics of the metabolic disease theory, including prominent physician-critics,[118] have consistently misunderstood the importance of the metabolic disease concept and the demonstration of physiological secondary abstinence in providing support to the contention of the institution of medicine that addiction is a disease, treatable by physicians.

Despite the early opposition by the Bureau of Narcotics and Dangerous Drugs to methadone maintenance,[119],[120] by 1970 a firm commitment to the medical-health model of treating addiction had taken root; politicians who had been critical of methadone maintenance " . . . began to clamor for increased numbers of methadone programs, demanding that they be established in every community where drug abuse existed."[121] More and more politicians began to move from the law enforcement approach to the public health approach.[122]

Although the medical model appears to be in ascendancy at this time, the struggle between the medical and legal institutions is far from over. The controversy over diversion which culminated in the 1972 FDA-BNDD regulations indicates how tenuous is the medical institution's control of addiction. The 1972 regulations provide that:

1. Methadone will not be given unqualified approval as a NDA (New Drug Application) but will be maintained under a dual NDA and IND (Investigational New Drug) status. This is a novel form of control by the Food and Drug Administration; no other drug had previously been assigned to utilize both the IND and the NDA procedure concurrently.

2. Methadone was withdrawn from nonhospital pharmacies for its previously acceptable use for detoxification, analgesic, and antitussive (cough medicine) purposes.

3. Methadone *detoxification* programs and procedures were now included under FDA-BNDD control.

4. Methadone maintenance was defined by administrative fiat. "If methadone is administered for more than 3 weeks, the procedure is considered to have progressed from detoxification or treatment of the acute withdrawal symptoms to that of methadone maintenance even if the goal is eventual withdrawal."[123]

5. Finally, the government reasserted its right to determine the appropriate methods for the medical treatment of addicts. In the April 1972 proposed requirements, the FDA noted that a section of the Comprehensive Drug Abuse Prevention and Control Act of 1970 requires the Secretary of Health, Education and Welfare (after appropriate consultation) to determine the appropriate methods for medical treatment of narcotic addiction.[124]

After promulgating the December 1972 regulations concerning dosage (100 mg was the new maximum recommended dosage), urine testing (morphine weekly, methadone, barbiturates, amphetamines monthly), procedures on take-home medication days, etc., the government partially resolved the ambiguity in the Harrison Act which left undefined the concept of professional practice in treating addicts. "The conditions established . . . constitute a determination of the appropriate methods of professional practice in the medical treatment of narcotic addiction of various classes of narcotics addicts with respect to the use of methadone . . . ."[125] The conflict of medical and legal perspectives has not been resolved and will probably continue to exist as long as drug addiction is an American social problem.

A cautionary paragraph needs to be added at this point. My discussion of the conflict between the medical and legal perspectives over the control of narcotic addiction should not be viewed as presenting these two alternatives as the only possible alternatives to addiction control, nor should my criticism of the legal approach be interpreted as fealty to the medical approach. I do not agree with Lindesmith's contention that " . . . power now being exercised by legislators, lawyers, judges, prosecutors, and policemen must be transferred to the medical profession."[126] The medical profession's claims to jurisdiction over narcotic addiction should not be assumed to be more valid than the legal profession's claims. All claims to control of addiction must be viewed as part of the century-old institutional competition to shape behavior and control deviance. Eliot Freidson has noted in this regard that "medicine is a moral enterprise like law and religion seeking to uncover and control things that it considers undesirable."[127] Thomas Szasz, a maverick psychiatrist, has gone further. He views addiction as a moral problem and opposes medicine's paternalistic attitude towards addicts, a paternalism Szasz sees as the ultimate consequence of medicine's continuing quest for monopolization of drug ("medicine") dispensing power. Szasz feels that individuals should have the right to self-medication, the right to freely shape their own behavior; none of society's institutions need to control the individual's right to private self-intoxification.[128] Szasz's views do have historical support, not so incidentally; the free market right to private intoxification with opiates existed prior to the Harrison Act's assertion of both medical and legal claims to control opiates.

The Role of Government: Social Control Through Methadone Maintenance?

The discussion of the medical versus legal/criminal justice/governmental control of narcotic addiction intentionally polarized these two alternative and sometimes competitive perspectives. In this subsection, I will discuss the sociological implications of a detente between the criminal justice system and the medical-public health system which has arisen out of the frustrations with the ineffectiveness of the criminal justice system prior to methadone maintenance.[129] Because of this detente, there is a potentially exponential increase in the federal government's control over addicts who have had criminal justice encounters.

The Radical Critique

The radical, militant black critique of methadone programs forms the backdrop for this issue of control through maintenance. Several ideas are interwoven in this radical critique. First, methadone maintenance is viewed as a pacification (hence, official avoidance) of underlying social and economic problems of the under class of society, a group traditionally exploited by the ruling class. This is similar to the drug-free critique that methadone treats symptoms; in this case, the underlying causes are political and economic, not individual pathologies. Heroin addicts are the casualties of an economic system that does not function and does not deal with people's basic needs of housing, medical care, and employment. " . . . To offer methadone as a means of controlling the problem of heroin addiction is not to deal with the political and economic roots of why the problem exists in the first place."[130] The solution to the addiction problem is not methadone but a fundamental transformation of American society.

Second, methadone programs are seen as part of the white Establishment's plan to hold potential revolutionaries in submission. This desire for submission is often viewed as racist in origin.[131] Richard Freeman, co-chairman of the Fifth Methadone Conference, noted, "Under the guise of politics, under the heat of emotionalism, under the displaced issue of professionalism versus para-professionalism, there lurks our seemingly eternal nemesis — racism."[132] Fourth, methadone maintenance is seen as chemical warfare; it is considered a variant of traditional submission through narcotics with the state as sole pusher and supplier.[133] Finally, maintenance is viewed as a police device to control blacks, Puerto Ricans, and Chicanos through addiction to methadone. The methadone patient must come to the clinic repeatedly and indefinitely to get his addictive medication; this enables the police to always know where the addict will be in the future. In addition, many programs require the patient's picture on an identification card.

The Boston and New York Cases

Two well-publicized efforts of police officials to intervene at maintenance clinics indicate that the radical fears of control through methadone are not idle imaginings. In Boston, 3 weeks after the maintenance program opened in August 1970, state policemen from the Narcotics Division wanted to inspect clinic records due to a complaint that methadone was being improperly administered to patients.[134] The program physician refused their request, and during further negotiations between the police and the physician, the police established an "undercover" video-tape camera in a bread truck outside the clinic to film patients coming to the clinic. The ultimate solution was a police decision to "take no further action" in the face of a potentially protracted public debate over the confidentiality issue. Nevertheless, patients recognized the potential for police access to program records; applications dropped sharply after the police visit and rose again only after the police ended their surveillance.

In New York, the implications of potential control through methadone maintenance are similarly apparent. During the week of June 5, 1972, a New York City Police Department detective appeared at one of the city maintenance clinics (under the ultimate control of the Health Services Administration) and asked to view photographs of all male Negro clients.[135] The officer was investigating a homicide and wanted to show the photographs to a witness who claimed to have seen the suspect being treated at the clinic. The request was refused. A subpoena was soon served on Dr. Robert G. Newman, a city official in charge of the program. He refused to produce the photographs, was found guilty by the New York Supreme Court of contempt of court, and was sentenced to 30 days in jail.

The Appellate Division upheld the subpoena but modified it by directing that the witness view the photographs in the presence of Dr. Newman (or his designate); only the one identified picture (if so identified) would be shown to the police or prosecutor. Since this decision did not establish the principle of absolute confidentiality, Newman made a second appeal to the New York Court of Appeals which reversed the decision on the basis of federal confidentiality laws and said that Dr. Newman had the right to withhold the photograph even in the face of a court order. The United States Supreme Court refused to review the case, thereby upholding the claim to the confidentiality of program records.[136]

The importance of this litigation over confidentiality of records lies in the fact that the case is not atypical. Intense interest has been focused on methadone patient records since many have outstanding criminal warrants and almost all had criminal behavior involvement.[137] The potential for control through methadone maintenance exists because the methadone patient " ... does *not* retain the option of simply discontinuing treatment whenever he feels threatened by the likelihood of impending or actual breach of confidentiality. He must return to the clinic for his daily medication."[138]

Criminal Justice Utilization of MMTP

The presentation of both the radical critique of methadone maintenance and the Newman position on patient confidentiality must be considered in the perspective of the criminal justice system: criminal behavior must be punished, and criminals must be pursued, arrested, indicted, and convicted. The Newman litigation has demonstrated a major sociological theme in the history of methadone maintenance: the potential for criminal justice control of tens of thousands of narcotics abusers through methadone maintenance, even in programs not under direct criminal justice control and

supervision. The sociological issue of control through a rehabilitation modality is even more pronounced in criminal justice sponsored programs.

The widely publicized effectiveness of methadone maintenance in treating addicts and reducing arrests and the political sensitivity of crime control in contemporary American society have been the major factors in the growth of the criminal justice system's interest in maintenance. Prior attempts at drug-free civil commitment of addicts have largely been ineffective: in California, in New York State, and nationally beginning in 1966 with the Narcotics Addiction Rehabilitation Act (NARA). Moreover, probation and parole systems have had their problems in achieving their goal of preventing further criminal behavior. After early opposition and skepticism, the criminal justice system has moved closer and closer to wide-scale utilization of methadone maintenance programs as the preferred (pragmatically, not ideologically) treatment modality for criminal narcotic addicts.

Two examples will be briefly summarized. Herman Joseph of the New York City Office of Probation has noted the approximately 80% relapse rate in probation/parole programs prior to 1965. He has argued that success under methadone maintenance has been striking;[139-141] in a probation plan, of 900 addicts admitted to treatment from February 1970 to November 1972, only 10.5% had been rearrested and 82% remained in treatment. Probationers and parolees were placed in methadone clinics cosponsored with traditional maintenance centers or placed in the traditional maintenance programs without direct probation/parole supervision. Joseph concluded that the model of a probation department working in conjunction with medical centers in the treatment of hard-core addicts can easily be adopted with modifications by agencies throughout the country.

A second model is the pre-trial diversion plan of the Narcotics and Treatment Administration of Washington, D.C., a program that includes abstinence and detoxification as alternatives to maintenance. The program originated within the city's criminal justice system when a 1969 study showed that 45% of all persons admitted to jail had heroin-morphine traces in their urine. This study sensitized the government to the implications and scope of the heroin epidemic and the imperative for meaningful treatment. An experimental halfway house program was soon replaced by the multimodal NTA in February 1970.[142] The close connection between NTA and the D.C. court system resulted in a preindictment program where arrested offenders are "voluntarily" given urine tests under medical privilege (offenders who refuse to give urine samples are so identified to the arraignment judge). Offenders with positive heroin samples are often ordered by the judge to receive medical intake at NTA (self-identifying addicts are immediately offered NTA treatment); the offender is then enrolled in one of the multimodal programs, often methadone maintenance, as a voluntary patient. This treatment-diversion process is completed as an alternative to possible criminal arraignment and prosecution. If the NTA patient fails to report for 7 consecutive days, program officials notify the bail agency, the U.S. attorney, and the defense counsel. Dogoloff (then Deputy Director of NTA) and Gumpper viewed this process as a possible ticket out of the criminal justice system for some addicts despite some reservations about the ethics of treating an essentially involuntary patient.[143]

This pre-trial diversion of addict offenders has become a dominant theme of the criminal justice system on the local, state, and federal level. The national Treatment Alternatives to Street Crime is a program closely modeled on the NTA experience. (Dr. Robert Dupont, former director of NTA, was the second director of SAODAP.) CASC will undoubtedly expand the numbers of addict offenders diverted prior to arraignment, trial, and incarceration into drug addiction treatment programs, especially methadone maintenance.

The issues surrounding this expansion of the criminal justice system into methadone maintenance are ideologically complex. First of all, criticism of involuntary treatment of patients in a medical treatment program is widespread. Compulsory treatment was seen as violating the principles of liberty and the guarantee of protection under the criminal justice laws.[144] Thus, the 1972 regulations insist that methadone maintenance treatment program patients be voluntary. While some program directors feel that medical discretion on modality choice means volition, Newman has noted: "When a policeman, a judge, a parole board, or a probation officer present an individual with the choice of methadone maintenance or prison, this is encompassed by my definition of unequivocal compulsion."[145] Second, there is debate over who should operate maintenance

clinics for criminal justice referred patients, the criminal justice system or the medical profession. With the criminal justice system in charge, control through methadone is maximized; with the medical center-clinic model, the physician serves as a surrogate control agent for society and the courts.[146] This problem is dramatized by the reactions possible to patient violation of program rules (e.g., using heroin). A voluntary patient is expelled; an involuntary patient may be sent to prison. Thus, while Dr. Newman argues that the criminal justice system should run their own programs and not use medical centers "as control agents for society,"[147] Dr. John Kramer notes that when methadone maintenance is part of a parole or probation program, information on patient behavior (e.g., urine results) is available to the criminal justice control system.[148]

From the perspective of society, this control of human behavior is a desirable alternative to readdiction, criminal behavior, and rearrest. From the perspective of the individual, control through maintenance limits his or her freedom and liberty. From the perspective of the sociologist, it is clear that methadone maintenance was acceptable to America because of the control potential of this treatment modality. It is not surprising that a program developed under medical auspices and proclaimed as an antireaddiction, anticrime rehabilitative technique should be adopted by that institution societally impowered to control criminal behavior. That the physician is then confronted with the unpleasant task of being a social control agent of society is similarly not surprising. The issue under controversy remains: Who defines the rules for controlling the deviance?

Sociology of Evaluation

The vast majority of studies indicates that methadone maintenance is a highly effective rehabilitation technique; almost all confirm the original 1968 evaluation of the first 4 years of the Dole-Nyswander program findings that (1) 86% of 871 patients admitted by March 31, 1968 remained in treatment, (2) employment for 544 men in the program for 3 months jumped from 28% prior to admission to 85% after 24 months, (3) a substantial decrease in arrests occurred for those remaining in treatment, and (4) none of the patients still in treatment were readdicted to heroin and repeated use of other drugs was 11% on amphetamines/barbiturates and 5% chronic alcohol.[149] Later studies by Dr. Gearing reaffirmed this early conclusion, continually documenting the power of maintenance to retain patients and reduce their arrests and drug abuse.[150-152] The impact of the Gearing evaluations (and many corroborating studies) has been the expansion of methadone maintenance.[153] Given the importance of these evaluations, therefore, four aspects of evaluation will be emphasized: (1) retention rates, (2) employment, (3) continued drug abuse, and (4) arrest rates.

Retention Rates

The original Gearing studies overestimate the power of methadone to retain heroin addicts in treatment by calculating retention rates regardless of the length of time the clients had been in the program. Thus, the late arrivals in treatment had been in the program only a few months prior to retention rate calculation. Better estimates of methadone's retention power come from later reports by Gearing; the dropout rate is approximately 15% in the first year, and 2 to 5% each year thereafter.[154] Of the first 1,000 patients admitted from 1964 to 1968, 66% were in treatment as of December 31, 1972.[155] Similar results were found in other studies: Jaffe found a 73% retention rate over 1 year,[156] Newman and Kagen found the rate to be 76% over 1 year and 65% over 2 years.[157] Dupont found a 74% retention rate over 1 year,[158] and Dale and Dale found 63% retention after 8 months.[159] Given program and city variations, the effective methadone retention rate is approximately 75% the first year with continuous attrition thereafter.

A comparative perspective can best be obtained by comparing methadone retention to the retaining power of other programs. The NTA program in Washington, D.C. found that methadone maintenance had the best retention rate of all treatment modalities; after 6 months retention rates were 74% for high dose (60 mg plus) maintenance, 31% for low dose maintenance, 14% for abstinence programs, 39% for detoxification programs.[160] The best indication of methadone's potential to retain patients is seen in a still-in-progress study by Bale et al.; heroin addicts were randomly assigned to methadone maintenance or to one of several therapeutic communities; 69% of those assigned to maintenance accepted the referral compared to 32% of those assigned to the therapeutic community.[161]

The retention power of methadone maintenance is impressive; it enables the program staff to aid in the rehabilitation process. Much of the explanation of this retention power is probably physiological — methadone is addictive.[162] Thus, retention is not meaningful in itself. If retention is important, it is important as an indication of the potential of methadone to rehabilitate addicts as measured by employment, continued drug abstinence, and crime-arrest reduction.

Employment

The evaluation studies of maintenance programs have not focused upon employment data; drug use and crime arrests are much more central evaluative concerns. Moreover, the studies focus on those who remain in the program, showing that those who stay in the program tend to become employed. Gearing shows that of 389 patients originally unemployed or illicitly active from the 1964 to 1968 cohort and remaining in treatment as of December 1972, 75% were employed, were in training programs, or were homemakers; for 271 patients who were originally "socially productive" on admission and stayed active, 92% were still socially productive.[163] Ignoring program dropouts leaves the statistically unwary with the impression that maintenance rehabilitates over three quarters of addicts. A critic could take the Gearing data and conclude that of 640 applicants from 1964 to 1968 who were not socially productive at admission, only 46% were shown to be employed in December 1972 (this makes the weak assumption that all dropouts are unemployed). This is still an apparently successful rehabilitation effort, but not as striking as Gearing's reports appear to indicate. Moreover, Brown's data show that for patients remaining in treatment, there is no difference in employment rates for the different modalities.[164]

My remarks are not meant to be disparaging of maintenance, but rather to indicate that we do not have very firm data on the impact of maintenance upon employment history, nor do we have any randomized control groups with which to compare results. The paucity of data on unemployment is especially surprising given the continuous comments of program staff that employment is the key to rehabilitation and that their biggest problems are unemployed, long-term patients. In brief, the employment history of maintenance patients is a neglected area in the sociology of work.

Drug Abuse

Since American values oppose recreational, pleasure-seeking drug use, urine testing to detect continued drug abuse has been a prominent aspect of evaluation studies. The drugs of concern are heroin — patients may sell some of their methadone for heroin or may use a high dosage of methadone to override the blockade[165] — and alcohol-amphetamines-barbiturates-cocaine which are not affected by the use of methadone. Gearing's data report minimal heroin use (about 2%),[166] heavy alcohol abuse by 8%, and amphetamines-barbiturates-cocaine 10%.[167] Most of the other studies report higher rates (and all studies use different reporting procedures, unwittingly making comparisons difficult): Chambers and Taylor report that for those in treatment at least 6 months, 35% had some heroin positive urines, 11% barbiturates, 14% amphetamines;[168] Taylor, Chambers and Dembo note that 18.5% used cocaine prior to awareness that this drug was included in urine tests;[169] Brown et al. noted of those in treatment for 6 months, about half had some illicit drugs in their urine;[170] and Dale and Dale noted that after 8 months, heroin or quinine (supposedly indicating heroin use) positive results were found for 50% of the clients.[171] Thus, drug use continues for many patients on methadone maintenance.[172]

Arrests and Crime

Perhaps the key area in the evaluation in methadone maintenance evaluation is the apparent reduction in criminal behavior because of methadone maintenance intervention in the criminal careers of addicts. More than any other topic, crime reduction was the basis of the acceptance and expansion of methadone maintenance. The Gearing studies stress the definite decline in criminal behavior as measured by arrests, once again studying only those who stayed in the program; the original 1968 data showed that for those in the program 6 to 11 months, 11% were arrested, while for those in the program over 2 years, less than 1% were arrested.[173] Subsequent reports show a pattern of declining arrests for those staying in the program, compared to an increasing arrest pattern for those discharged for cause (about 30% arrested) and an intermediate pattern for voluntary withdrawals.[174] Similar reductions in arrest rates have been documented in many research studies; for drug abusers staying on the program, arrests drop sharply.[175-179] Study after study supports this contention, usually comparing arrests immediately prior to program entrance with post-program entrance.

The major critic of methadone's apparent reduction in crime has been Irving Lukoff, evaluating ARTC, a maintenance program in Brooklyn, New York. Lukoff argues that the studies of arrest records of methadone patients have suffered from several methodological weaknesses: (1) Patients who stay in the program had fewer pre-program arrests than those who left, so focusing on still active patients overemphasizes the effects of maintenance on less difficult patients; (2) arrest decrease occurs for drug purchase — possession — and sale and not for assaultive crime, felonies, and larceny; (3) the year prior to program entrance shows an increase in arrests and thus exaggerates program impact; (4) arrest rates for his program are much higher than the Gearing reports; and (5) the arrest reduction is most likely to occur for older patients and not for younger patients.[180] Thus, arrest rate reduction and the impact of methadone maintenance seem to be related to the age of addicts remaining in the program, and a simple link between maintenance treatment and arrest reduction is misleading.

The Life Cycle of Addiction

Evaluations of methadone maintenance in terms of retention, employment, drug use, and arrest histories must be viewed within the life cycle approach to the careers of drug addicts. Several addiction researchers have noted that the careers of drug addicts can be divided into various career stages; while the labels differ, most life cycle theories stress periods of initial use and experimentation, chronic use, criminal behavior, arrests, self-identification as an addict, attempts at abstinence: self-detoxification, medical detoxification, and rehabilitation treatment program enrollment, renewed use of heroin, and possibly total and permanent abstinence.[181-183] The career is viewed as dynamic, involving " . . . spurts, reverses, periods of quiescence and lateral movement, from starting drug use to stopping to starting again and stopping, a sequence is relatively fast and at other times it may be relatively slow or involve no movement."[184]

One aspect of this life cycle of addiction requires special attention: Winick's thesis of the "maturing out" process of deaddiction. Winick examined Federal Bureau of Narcotics records to examine those addicts known to be active in 1955 for whom no record of addiction had been reentered by 1960; Winick found the group of 7,234 addicts were clustered according to age:

Maturing out of addiction is the name we can give to the process by which the addict stops taking drugs, as the problems for which he originally began taking drugs became less salient and less urgent, if our hypothesis is correct . . .

How many and what proportion of addicts mature out of addiction . . . approximately two-thirds of our sample . . . It would thus seem possible to speculate that addiction may be a self-limiting process for perhaps two-thirds of addicts.[185]

Subsequent studies indicated that perhaps about one third of addicts seemed to become abstinent on their own after years of addiction, abstinence efforts, and readdiction.[186-188]

The implications of the "maturing out" thesis for the evaluation of the effectiveness of methadone maintenance programs are difficult to assess. Let me indicate the complexity of the issue by posing currently unanswerable research questions pertaining to the four evaluation areas previously discussed. The retention studies mostly indicate that retention in programs increases with increasing patient age; the average age of all methadone patients is over 30. Does methadone maintenance retain in treatment those addicts who normally would have matured out of addiction? Has maintenance slowed the maturation process or accelerated it by providing a stabilization period and rehabilitative services? In this respect, does the detoxification-from-methadone stage represent a medically supervised parallel to the ultimate abstinence resolution? Thus, do detoxification "failures" represent cases of premature efforts to abstain, in the sense of the traditional failures on the road to abstinence? Finally, how has methadone maintenance changed the potential early abstinence career choices of young drug abusers?

Regarding employment, do the employment successes reflect an adjustment that would have occurred anyway for maturing out addicts, or does methadone maintenance accelerate employment rehabilitation through its legitimized training and placement services? On the other hand, does eligibility for welfare short-circuit total rehabilitation? Regarding drug-use on methadone, does this reflect a shift in the maturation process by

forming a subculture of methadone patients who provide social support for drug "cheating" (a support that might not have existed under traditional maturation circumstances)? From the perspective of the drug-free critique of maintenance, does methadone dispensation reinforce the drug abuser's view that drugs can solve personal and social problems?

Finally, regarding arrests and crime, how does crime reduction represent the effects of the maturing out process? Lukoff's critique of most arrest studies argues that the age of patients in most programs is skewed toward older addicts. "It is necessary to entertain the view that much of the improvement is a function of age with the changes wrought by maturation playing a significant role."[189] Is Lukoff correct: Is methadone maintenance's apparent arrest reduction power a function of the maturing out process? Or has maintenance radically short-circuited the years of criminal behavior and arrests that would have preceded maturation? Has maintenance reduced crime and arrests for addicts who otherwise would have remained in the addict subculture?

I have conveyed the inconclusive state of the evaluation of methadone maintenance programs when viewed from a sociological perspective, as well as the apparent program successes when viewed from a political-criminal justice-pragmatic perspective. Methadone maintenance seems to work, but how? The program retains a high proportion of applicants and reduces their arrests while increasing their employability, but how do these rehabilitative successes relate to the maturing out hypothesis of drug addiction? In short, how has methadone maintenance altered the history of drug addiction and deaddiction in the United States? The research studies of methadone maintenance programs have largely ignored the relationship of methadone maintenance effectiveness and the life cycle of addiction. Nevertheless, the apparent effectiveness of the program (ignoring the unanswered questions I posed) has resulted in a rapid expansion of a program, about which we know little.

Organizational and Professional Issues

The research questions I have posed about the relationship of the life cycle of addiction careers to the social rehabilitative effects of methadone maintenance are far from the only unanswered sociological questions about methadone maintenance. In fact, I think it is fair to conclude that there has been little sociological research (as contrasted with research by sociologists) on methadone maintenance. There are many other areas that require careful sociological analysis: (1) the impact of maintenance as a rehabilitative technique upon family life and family structure,[190,191] (2) sex role patterns in methadone maintenance rehabilitation, (3) the life-styles, generational differences, and subcultures of methadone maintenance patients, and (4) the relationship of methadone maintenance, social class, and social mobility. All of these represent major sociological topics; all represent relatively unexplored areas in the sociology of methadone maintenance.

Before concluding this chapter, I will briefly outline some potential topics for research within one sociological framework: the sociological analysis of bureaucratic organizations and the professions. The historical evolution of maintenance programs makes these areas especially fertile for sociological investigation.

First, comparative organizational research projects could be designed to analyze the impact of different organizational structures upon program functioning. The rapid expansion of methadone programs has resulted in radically different types of methadone maintenance program structures. At the minimum, the following organizational types exist: large clinics under medical center auspices, small clinics under medical center control, large clinics run by governmental agencies, criminal justice maintenance facilities under TASC/probation/parole programs, methadone maintenance residential facilities,[192,193] private practitioner outpatient clinics, methadone dispensation in factories,[194] and maintenance programs which are part of multimodal treatment centers. All these structural variations have their own treatment milieu, treatment philosophies, staffing patterns, and bureaucratic structure. Analysis is possible of the effects of large vs. small, public vs. nonpublic, criminal justice vs. noncriminal justice, single modality vs. multimodality, large city vs. small city programs in terms of level of bureaucratization, treatment philosophy, patient interaction patterns, and program impact upon retention, employment, drug use, and arrests of clients. Since all programs must adhere to the 1972 federal regulations on dosage, medication distribution patterns, urinalysis, intake procedures, etc., such a

comparative analysis would also allow determination of the relative effects upon program structure of federal regulations versus program history and sponsorship.

Second, the concept of professional-bureaucratic conflict[195] could be used to analyze the role of physicians, nurses, and counselors within an organizational structure shaped (in part) by federal administrative regulations. What role do physicians play within the methadone bureaucracies? What adjustments do they make to bureaucratic-federal regulations? What professional prerogatives do they exercise in these bureaucracies? Does the professional vs. bureaucratic dilemma vary in large as opposed to small clinics, public vs. private clinics, etc.?

Third, the marginal profession position of program counselors (usually college graduates) and research assistants/ex-addicts makes the methadone maintenance clinics fertile grounds for analyzing the processes of professional socialization, new career genesis, and professional/paraprofessional interaction. The potential conflict of the counselor and the research assistant/ex-addict counselor has been noted in at least one clinic.[196] Case studies of physician-nurse-counselor-assistant interaction would be especially valuable analyses of professional interaction. Finally, the interaction of staff and clients could be an extension of the study of professionalism and professional interaction.[197] With whom do the patients interact? What is the patient view of physicians, nurses, counselors, and assistants? In short, the historical evolution of methadone maintenance has resulted in organizational and professional structural elements that invite sociological analysis. Multi-organizational program models, multiprofessional and paraprofessional staffing patterns, and the complexity of federal regulations have combined to shape an interesting and analytically challenging organizational-professional-governmental complex.

IMPLICATIONS FOR THE FUTURE

In this chapter, I have traced the history of methadone maintenance in the United States and then discussed six major sociological implications of this history: (1) the relationship of ideology and treatment which highlights the debate between advocates of drug-free therapy and advocates of the Dole-Nyswander medical-rehabilitation-before-abstinence ideology, (2) the continuing problems of methadone maintenance as a tertiary deviance solution to the problems caused by the criminalization of addiction, (3) the dispute between the medical establishment and the criminal justice establishment for control of heroin addiction treatment programs, (4) the potential problems caused by the addictive nature of methadone which allows for indefinite social control of deviant individuals through methadone maintenance, (5) the sociological weaknesses in the evaluation studies of maintenance which have separated evaluation of this program from the broader theme of the life cycle of heroin addiction careers, and (6) some potential sociological research issues within the framework of the sociology of organizations and the professions.

At this point, it seems appropriate to make some speculative remarks about the future of methadone maintenance. First, I would speculate that although maintenance appears to be well established as a treatment program (75,000 patients, governmental commitment, public acceptance in the face of heroin-crime fears), I think the future history of methadone maintenance will display an intensification of the ideological debate over its nonabstinence treatment approach. The diversion of methadone to "illicit" purposes will continue to be a subject of contention, as will the "creation of a generation of addicts primarily addicted to methadone." I doubt that these ideological comments will really contest the existence of the methadone establishment. On the other hand, I feel that if any long-term harmful side effects of methadone maintenance are discovered, methadone maintenance will be under heavy assault and may disappear as quickly as the early 20th century heroin maintenance clinics. I am not predicting that these side effects will be discovered, but I am predicting major readjustments if they are isolated.

Second, I think it will become increasingly clear to the public that methadone is not a panacea for America's drug abuse problems. Not all heroin abusers will seek methadone maintenance treatment; indeed, only a minority may be attracted to its offer of rehabilitation.[198] Moreover, heroin is currently being replaced as the primary addictive drug by a shift to multiple drug use by young abusers who use cocaine, amphetamines, barbiturates, hypnotics, and alcohol in addition to sporadic heroin use.[199,200] Methadone maintenance programs may be modified to treat these multiple abusers (if I interpret the intent of the 1972 FDS regulations properly) since they are organizationally amenable to rapid shift in focus. The issue of multiple drug abuse will probably be the drug problem of the 1970s.

Predicting the future of a treatment modality that went from an accidental discovery in 1963 to over 75,000 patients in 1974 is hazardous. The drug scene shifts so rapidly that the future of methadone maintenance is susceptible to rapid, major alterations. Some indication of the rapid change potential for the drug scene can be seen in the recent BNDD restriction of the distribution of barbiturates.[201] Barbiturates are addictive and even more dangerous physiologically than heroin, but their ready availability through physicians has prevented the development of a barbiturate secondary deviation syndrome. Indeed, the situation parallels pre-Harrison Act opiate use: *"Exactly the same types of people who use narcotics in 1900 are now using barbiturates —* middle-aged, middle-class, white women with various quasi-medical, largely emotional problems that (they feel) can be solved by taking a drug."[202] Is the BNDD action the first step towards criminalizing barbiturate addiction and creating the same kinds of secondary deviation problems that resulted from the punitive interpretation of the Harrison Act? Will history repeat itself? Let me add a personal opinion: I hope not. I really do not want to write a paper 10 years from today titled "The Adaptation of Methadone Maintenance Programs to Treatment of Barbiturate Addicts: The Aftermath of the Criminalization of Barbiturate Addiction."

REFERENCES

1. **Brill, L.,** The international experience: a survey of maintenance programs, in *Methadone: Experiences and Issues,* Chambers, C. D. and Brill, L., Eds., Behavioral Publ., New York, 1973, 327.
2. **Brecher, E. M. et al.,** *Licit and Illicit Drugs,* Little, Brown & Co., Boston, 1972, 3.
3. **Terry, C. E. and Pellens, M.,** *The Opium Problem,* Bureau of Social Hygiene, New York, 1928, and Patterson Smith, Montclair, N.J., 1970.
4. **Brecher, E. M. et al.,** *Licit and Illicit Drugs,* Little, Brown & Co., Boston, 1972, chap. 3.
5. **Glaser, F. B. et al.,** The treatment of narcotic addiction in Philadelphia: yesterday, today, and tomorrow, *Philadelphia Med.,* 67, 613, 1971.
6. **Brecher, E. M. et al.,** *Licit and Illicit Drugs,* Little, Brown & Co., Boston, 1972, 42.
7. **Goode, E.,** *Drugs in American Society,* Knopf, New York, 1972, 193.
8. **Goode, E.,** *Drugs in American Society,* Knopf, New York, 1972, 194.
9. **Lindesmith, A. R.,** *The Addict and the Law,* Indiana University Press, Bloomington, 1971, 138.
10. **Hunt, G. H. and Odoroff, M. E.,** Follow-up study of narcotic drug addicts after hospitalization, *Public Health Rep.,* 77, 41, 1962.
11. **Duvall, H., Locke, B., and Brill, L.,** Follow-up study of narcotics addicts five years after hospitalization, *Public Health Rep.,* 78, 185, 1963.
12. **Vaillant, G. E.,** A twelve-year follow-up of New York narcotic addicts. I. The relation of treatment to outcome, *Am. J. Psychiatr.,* 122, 727, 1966.
13. **Trussel, R. E.,** Treatment of narcotics addicts in New York City, *Int. J. Addict.,* 5, 347, 1970.
14. **Yablonsky, L.,** *Synanon: The Tunnel Back,* MacMillan, New York, 1967.
15. **Volkman, R. and Cressey, D. R.,** Differential association and the rehabilitation of drug addicts, *Am. J. Sociol.,* 69, 129, 1963.
16. **Brecher, E. M. et al.,** *Licit and Illicit Drugs,* Little, Brown & Co., Boston, 1972, 78. Cites Grafton, S., Ed., *Addict. Drug Abuse Rep.,* 2, 2, June 1971.
17. **Ramirez, E.,** The addiction services agency of the city of New York, in *Major Modalities in the Treatment of Drug Abuse,* Brill, L. and Lieberman, L., Eds., Behavioral Publ., New York, 1972, 43.
18. *Daytop Village* (introductory booklet), New York.
19. **Howe, L. P.,** Methadone and morality: toward a sociology of addiction, *Proc. 5th Natl. Conf. Methadone Treatment,* National Association for the Prevention of Addiction to Narcotics (NAPAN), New York, 1973, 587.
20. **Lukoff, I. F.,** Issues in the evaluation of heroin treatment, in *Epidemiology of Drug Abuse,* Josephson, E. and Carroll, E., Eds., Winston-Wiley, Washington, D.C., in press.
21. **Kramer, J. C., Bass, R. A., and Berecochea, J. E.,** Civil commitment for addicts: the California program, *Am. J. Psychiatr.,* 125, 816, 1968.
22. **Waldorf, D.,** *Careers in Dope,* Prentice-Hall, Englewood Cliffs, N.J., 1973, 115.
23. **O'Donnell, J. A.,** The relapse rate in narcotic addiction: a critique of follow-up studies, in *Narcotics,* Wilner, D. M. and Kassebaum, G. G., Eds., McGraw-Hill, New York, 1965, 226.
24. American Medical Association Council on Mental Health and the National Academy of Sciences — National Research Council's Committee on Drug Addiction and Narcotics, Narcotics and medical practice, the use of narcotic drugs in medical practice and the medical management of narcotic addicts, *JAMA,* 185, 976, 1963.
25. **Becker, H. S.,** *Outsiders: Studies in the Sociology of Deviance,* Free Press, New York, 1963, chap. 7.
26. **Meyer, R. E.,** *Guide to Drug Rehabilitation: A Public Health Approach,* Beacon, Boston, 1972, 3.
27. **Markham, J. M.,** Heroin addiction numbers game, *New York Times,* June 6, 1972, 18.
28. **Dupont, R. L.,** Urban crime and the rapid development of a large heroin addiction treatment program, *Proc. 3rd Natl. Conf. Methadone Treatment,* U.S. Govt. Printing Office, Washington, D.C., Public Health Serv. Publ. No. 2172, 115.
29. **Nyswander, M. E.,** *The Drug Addict as Patient,* Grune and Stratton, New York, 1956.
30. **Hentoff, N.,** *A Doctor Among the Addicts,* Grove Press, New York, 1968, 113.
31. **Chambers, C. D., Brill, L., and Langrod, J.,** Physiological and psychological side effects reported during maintenance therapy, in *Methadone: Experiences and Issues,* Chambers, C. D. and Brill, L., Eds., Behavioral Publ., New York, 1973, 163.
32. **Waldorf, D.,** *Careers in Dope,* Prentice-Hall, Englewood Cliffs, N.J., 1973, 119.
33. **Trussel, R. E. and Gollance, H.,** Methadone maintenance treatment is successful for heroin addicts, *Hosp. Management,* 110, 57, October 1970.
34. **Dole, V. P. and Nyswander, M. E.,** A medical treatment for diacetylmorphine (heroin) addiction: a clinical trial with methadone hydrochloride, *JAMA,* 193, 80, 1965.
35. **Dole, V. P. and Nyswander, M. E.,** Rehabilitation of heroin addicts after blockade with methadone, *N.Y. State J. Med.,* 66, 2011, 1966.
36. **Dole, V. P. and Nyswander, M. E.,** Heroin addiction — a metabolic disease, *Arch. Intern. Med.,* 120, 19, 1967.
37. **Samuels, G.,** Fighting fire with fire, *New York Times,* October 15, 1967, reprinted in *Drugs,* Arno Press, New York, 1971, 32.

38. Dole, V. P. and Nyswander, M. E., *N.Y. State J. Med.,* 66, 2011, 1966.
39. Nyswander, M. E., The methadone treatment of heroin addiction, *Hosp. Pract.,* 2, 1, 1967.
40. Methadone Maintenance Evaluation Committee, Special communication: progress report of evaluation of the methadone maintenance treatment program as of March 31, 1968, *JAMA,* 206, 2712, 1968.
41. Jaffe, J. H., Zaks, M. S., and Washington, E. N., Experience with a use of methadone in a multi-modality program for the treatment of narcotic users, *Int. J. Addict.,* 4, 481, 1969.
42. Wieland, W. F. and Chambers, C. D., A comparison of two stabilization techniques, *Int. J. Addict.,* 5, 645, 1970.
43. Methadone Maintenance Evaluation Committee, *JAMA,* 206, 2712, 1968.
44. Joseph, H. and Langrod, J., Analysis of the methadone maintenance report issued by the New York State Council on Drug Addiction (May 1969), New York State Committee Against Mental Illness, New York, 1969 (mimeo).
45. Gearing F. R., Evaluation of methadone maintenance treatment program, *Int. J. Addict.,* 5, 517, 1970.
46. Gearing, F. R., Methadone maintenance treatment program: progress report of evaluation through March 31, 1970, Columbia University School of Public Health and Administrative Medicine, New York, May 8, 1970 (mimeo).
47. Gearing, F. R., Successes and failures in methadone maintenance treatment of heroin addiction in New York City, *Proc. 3rd Natl. Conf. Methadone Treatment,* U.S. Govt. Printing Office, Washington, D.C., Public Health Serv. Publ. No. 2172, 2.
48. Gearing, F. R., MMTP: Progress report through March 31, 1971 — a five year overview, Columbia University School of Public Health and Administrative Medicine, New York, May 14, 1971 (mimeo).
49. Gearing, F. R., People versus urines, Columbia University, Division of Epidemiology, New York, January 6, 1972 (mimeo).
50. Gearing, F. R., Myth versus fact in long term methadone maintenance treatment: the community's viewpoint, *Proc. 5th Natl. Conf. Methadone Treatment,* NAPAN, New York, 1973, 452.
51. Jaffe, J. H., Zaks, M. S., and Washington, E. N., *Int. J. Addict.,* 4, 481, 1969.
52. Jaffe, J., Further experience with methadone in the treatment of narcotics users, *Int. J. Addict.,* 5, 375, 1970.
53. Williams, H. R., Low and high methadone maintenance in the out-patient treatment of the hard core heroin addict, *Int. J. Addict.,* 5, 439, 1970.
54. Newman, R. G. and Kagen, J. G., The New York City methadone maintenance treatment program after two years — an overview, *Proc. 5th Natl. Conf. Methadone Treatment,* NAPAN, New York, 1973, 794.
55. Gewirtz, P. D., Methadone maintenance for heroin addicts, in *Drug Use and Social Policy,* Sussman, J., Ed., AMS Press, New York, 1972, 400.
56. *Federal Register,* 36, 6075, April 2, 1971.
57. Patch, V. D., Raynes, A., and Fisch, A., Vietnam heroin addicts in Boston, *Proc. 4th Natl. Conf. Methadone Treatment,* National Association for the Prevention of Addiction to Narcotics (NAPAN), New York, 1972, 503.
58. Jaffe, J., Methadone maintenance and the national perspective, *Proc. 5th Natl. Conf. Methadone Treatment,* NAPAN, New York, 1973, 1414.
59. Jaffe, J., *Proc. 5th Natl. Conf. Methadone Treatment,* NAPAN, New York, 1973, 1414.
60. Langrod, J. et al., Methadone maintenance from research to treatment, in *Major Modalities in the Treatment of Drug Abuse,* Brill, L. and Lieberman, L., Eds., Behavioral Publ., New York, 1972, 107.
61. Dole, V. P., Nyswander, M. E., and Warner, A., Successful treatment of 750 criminal addicts, *JAMA,* 206, 2708, 1968.
62. Wieland, W. F. and Chambers, C. D., A comparison of two stabilization techniques, *Int. J. Addict.,* 5, 645, 1970.
63. Jaffe, J. H., Zaks, M. S., and Washington, E. N., *Int. J. Addict.,* 4, 481, 1969.
64. Williams, H. R., *Int. J. Addict.,* 5, 439, 1970.
65. Yuncker, B., Methadone: the answer? *New York Post,* January 29, 1972, 27.
66. Walters, I., *Wall Street Journal,* July 27, 1972, 1.
67. Walter, P. V., Sheridan, B. K., and Chambers, C. D., Methadone diversion: a study of illicit availability, in *Methadone: Experiences and Issues,* Chambers, C. D. and Brill, L., Eds., Behavioral Publ., New York, 1973, 171.
68. Bourne, P. G., Methadone diversion, *Proc. 5th Natl. Conf. Methadone Treatment,* NAPAN, New York, 1973, 839.
69. Patch, V. D. et al., Daily visits, "no-take-home" methadone, and seven-day-per-week operation: patient retention and employment patterns subsequent to cessation of "take-home" privileges in a methadone maintenance clinic, *Proc. 5th Natl. Conf. Methadone Treatment,* NAPAN, New York, 1973, 1276.
70. Jaffe, J. H., Methadone maintenance and the national strategy, *Proc. 4th Natl. Conf. Methadone Treatment,* NAPAN, New York, 1972, 37.
71. *Federal Register,* 37, 26790, December 15, 1972.
72. Dupont, R. L., The Future of Federal Drug Abuse Programs, speech presented at 36 Annu. Meet. Comm. Probl. Drug Dependence, Mexico City, March 11, 1974.
73. Farber, M. A., City control of methadone urged after council study, *New York Times,* December 22, 1973, 29.
74. Dupont, R. L. and Greene, M. H., Patterns of heroin addiction in the District of Columbia, *Proc. 5th Natl. Conf. Methadone Treatment,* NAPAN, New York, 1973, 786.
75. Raynes, A. et al., The heroin and barbiturate epidemic in Boston, *Proc. 5th Natl. Conf. Methadone Treatment,* NAPAN, New York, 1973, 995.
76. Malek, F. V., One that got away, *New York Times,* December 5, 1973, 47.

77. Nelkin, D., *Methadone maintenance: A Technological Fix,* George Braziller, New York, 1973, 7.
78. Simrell, E. V., History of legal and medical roles in narcotic abuse in the U.S., in *The Epidemiology of Opiate Addiction in the United States,* Ball, J. C. and Chambers, C. D., Eds., Charles C Thomas, Springfield, Ill., 1970, 22.
79. Howe, L. P., *Proc. 5th Natl. Conf. Methadone Treatment,* NAPAN, New York, 1973, 587.
80. Markham, J. M., Methadone therapy programs, *New York Times,* April 17, 1973, 30.
81. Ausubel, D. P., The Dole-Nyswander treatment of heroin addiction, *JAMA,* 195, 949, 1966.
82. Lennard, H. et al., *Mystification and Drug Abuse: Hazards in Using Psychoactive Drugs,* Harper and Row, New York, 1972, vii.
83. Lennard, H., Epstein, L. J., and Rosenthal, M. S., The methadone illusion, *Science,* 176, 883, 1972.
84. Martin, W. R. and Sloan, J. W., The pathophysiology of morphine dependence and its treatment with opioid antagonists, *Pharmakopsychiatr. Neuro-Psychopharmakol.,* 1, 259, 1968.
85. Martin, W. R. and Jasinski, D. R., Physiological parameters of morphine dependence in man — tolerance, early abstinence, protracted abstinence, *Psychiatr. Res.;* 7, 9, 1969.
86. Martin, W. R., Commentary on the second national conference on methadone treatment, *Int. J. Addict.,* 5, 545, 1970.
87. Dole, V. P. and Nyswander, M. E., *JAMA,* 193, 80, 1965.
88. Nyswander, M. E., Methadone therapy for heroin addiction: where are we? Where are we going? in *The Behavioral Effects of Drugs,* Matheson, D. W. and Davison, M. A., Eds., Holt, Rinehart & Winston, New York, 1972, 237.
89. Dole, V. P. and Nyswander, M. E., Rehabilitation of patients on methadone programs, *Proc. 5th Natl. Conf. Methadone Treatment,* NAPAN, New York, 1973, 5.
90. Miller, R. et al., *An Evaluation of the New York City Ambulatory Detoxification Program,* Center for Social Research, Graduate Center, City University of New York, New York, 1972.
91. Brown, B. S. et al., Staff and client attitudes towards methadone maintenance, *Int. J. Addict.,* 7, 254, 1972.
92. Nelkin, D., *Methadone Maintenance: A Technological Fix,* George Braziller, New York, 1973, 123.
93. Nash, G., The sociology of Phoenix House: a therapeutic community for the resocialization of narcotic addicts, *Sociological Aspects of Drug Dependence,* CRC Press, Cleveland, 1974.
94. Becker, H. S., *Outsiders: Studies in the Sociology of Deviance,* Free Press, New York, 1963, 8.
95. Lemert, E. M., *Human Deviance, Social Problems, and Social Control,* Prentice-Hall, Englewood Cliffs, N.J., 1967, 17.
96. Freidson, E., *Profession of Medicine,* Dodd, Mead & Co., New York, 1970, 218.
97. Lemert, E. M., *Human Deviance, Social Problems, and Social Control,* Prentice-Hall, Englewood Cliffs, N.J., 1967, 47.
98. Schur, E. M., *Crimes Without Victims,* Prentice-Hall, Englewood Cliffs, N.J., 1965, 152.
99. Lowinson, J. H., Langrod, J., and Berle, B., Opposition to the establishment of neighborhood drug treatment centers: a problem in community medicine and practical politics, *Proc. 4th Natl. Conf. Methadone Treatment,* NAPAN, New York, 1972, 363.
100. Brown, B. S. et al., *Int. J. Addict.,* 7, 254, 1972.
101. Nelkin, D., *Methadone Maintenance: A Technological Fix,* George Braziller, New York, 1973, 150.
102. *Federal Register,* 37, 26790, December 15, 1972.
103. Lowinson, J. H. and Langrod, J., Detoxification of long-term methadone patients, *Proc. 5th Natl. Conf. Methadone Treatment,* NAPAN, New York, 1973, 256.
104. Cushman, P., Jr. and Dole, V. P., Detoxification of well rehabilitated methadone maintained patients, *Proc. 5th Natl. Conf. Methadone Treatment,* NAPAN, New York, 1973, 262.
105. Stimmel, B., Rabin, J., and Engel, C., The prognosis of patients detoxified from methadone maintenance: a follow-up study, *Proc. 5th Natl. Conf. Methadone Treatment,* NAPAN, New York, 1973, 270.
106. Chappel, J. N., Skolnick, V. B., and Senay, E. C., Techniques of withdrawal from methadone and their outcome over six months to two years, *Proc. 5th Natl. Conf. Methadone Treatment,* NAPAN, New York, 1973, 482.
107. Simrell, E. V., in *The Epidemiology of Opiate Addiction in the United States,* Ball, J. C. and Chambers, C. D., Eds., Charles C Thomas, Springfield, Ill., 1970, 27.
108. Freidson, E., *Profession of Medicine,* Dodd, Mead & Co., New York, 1970, 249.
109. Goode, E., *Drugs In American Society,* Knopf, New York, 1972, 189.
110. DeLong, J. V., Staff paper 3: treatment and rehabilitation, in *Dealing with Drug Abuse: A Report to the Ford Foundation,* Praeger, New York and Washington, 1972, 174.
111. Kramer, J. C., A perspective on heroin; the genesis of the American system of narcotics control, in *The Yearbook of Drug Abuse,* Brill, L. and Harms, E., Eds., Behavioral Publ., New York, 1973, 281.
112. Kramer, J. C., A brief history of heroin addiction in America, in *It's So Good, Don't Even Try It Once: Heroin in Perspective,* Smith, D. E. and Gray, G. R., Prentice-Hall, Englewood Cliffs, N.J., 1972, 37.
113. DeLong, J. V., in *Dealing with Drug Abuse: A Report to the Ford Foundation,* Praeger, New York and Washington, 1972, 176.
114. Lindesmith, A. R., *The Addict and the Law,* Indiana University Press, Bloomington, 1971, 6.
115. Goode, E., *Drugs in American Society,* Knopf, New York, 1972, 192.

116. **Brill, L.,** Introductory overview – historic background, in *Methadone: Experiences and Issues,* Chambers, C. D. and Brill, L., Eds., Behavioral Publ., New York, 1973, 15.

117. **Lindesmith, A. R.,** *The Addict and the Law,* Indiana University Press, Bloomington, 1971, 11.

118. **Goldstein, A.,** The pharmacologic basis of methadone treatment, *Proc. 4th Natl. Conf. Methadone Treatment,* NAPAN, New York, 1972, 27.

119. **Buckley, T.,** The fight against drugs is in a mess, *New York Times,* March 22, 1970, reprinted in *Drugs,* Arno Press, New York, 1971, 32.

120. **Miller, D.,** Letter to editor of *Yale Law Journal,* January 6, 1969, cited in Gewirtz, P. D., in *Drug Use and Social Policy,* Sussman, J., Ed., AMS Press, New York, 1972, 400.

121. **Ramer, B. S.,** Have we oversold methadone? *Proc. 4th Natl. Conf. Methadone Treatment,* NAPAN, New York, 1972, 97.

122. **Vasconcellos, J.,** Political realities in the control of addiction, *Proc. 4th Natl. Conf. Methadone Treatment,* NAPAN New York, 1972, 17.

123. *Federal Register,* 37, 26793, December 15, 1972.

124. *Federal Register,* 37, 6940, April 6, 1972.

125. *Federal Register,* 37, 26806, December 15, 1972.

126. **Lindesmith, A. R.,** *The Addict and the Law,* Indiana University Press, Bloomington, 1971, 273.

127. **Freidson, E.,** *Profession of Medicine,* Dodd, Mead & Co., New York, 1970, 208.

128. **Szasz, T. S.,** The ethics of addiction, *Am. J. Psychiatr.,* 128, 541, 1971.

129. **Wieland, W. F. and Novack, J. L.,** A comparison of criminal justice and non-criminal justice related patients in a methadone treatment program, *Proc. 5th Natl. Conf. Methadone Treatment,* NAPAN, New York, 1973, 116.

130. Statement by the Radical Caucus, *Proc. 4th Natl. Conf. Methadone Treatment,* NAPAN, New York, 1972, 557.

131. **Brill, L.,** Opposition to methadone maintenance therapy: a study of recent sources of criticism, in *Methadone: Experiences and Issues,* Chambers, C. D. and Brill, L., Eds., Behavioral Publ., New York, 1973, 317.

132. **Freeman, R. S.** Insane approaches to drug abuse, *Proc. 5th Natl. Conf. Methadone Treatment,* NAPAN, New York, 1973, 1412.

133. **Levin, T.,** New myths about drug programs, *Social Policy,* 2, 30, 1971.

134. **Fisch, A., Patch, V. D., and Raynes, A. E.,** The negative effect of police intervention on a methadone treatment program, *Proc. 4th Natl. Conf. Methadone Treatment,* NAPAN, New York, 1972, 475.

135. **Newman, R. G. and Newman, T.,** Safeguarding confidentiality of methadone patient records, *Proc. 5th Natl. Conf. Methadone Treatment,* NAPAN, New York, 1973, 1431.

136. **Newman, R. G.,** personal communication.

137. **Newman, R. G. and Newman, T.,** *Proc. 5th Natl. Conf. Methadone Treatment,* NAPAN, New York, 1973, 1431.

138. **Newman, R. G. and Newman, T.,** *Proc. 5th Natl. Conf. Methadone Treatment,* NAPAN, New York, 1973, 1435.

139. **Joseph H.,** Court services and methadone treatment: the New York City probation program, *Proc. 3rd Natl. Conf. Methadone Treatment,* U.S. Govt. Printing Office, Washington, Public Health Serv. Publ. No 2172, 104.

140. **Joseph, H.,** Methadone maintenance treatment in probation, *Proc. 4th Natl. Conf. Methadone Treatment,* NAPAN, New York, 1972, 91.

141. **Joseph, H.,** Probation, parole and addiction treatment, *Proc. 5th Natl. Conf. Methadone Treatment,* NAPAN, New York, 1973, 920.

142. **Dogoloff, L. I. and Gumpper, M. L.,** The treatment of heroin addiction and the criminal justice system: are they compatible? *Proc. 4th Natl. Conf. Methadone Treatment,* NAPAN, New York, 1972, 101.

143. **Dogoloff, L. I, and Gumpper, M. L.,** *Proc. 4th Natl. Conf. Methadone Treatment,* NAPAN, New York, 1972, 101.

144. **Newman, R. G.,** Methadone maintenance treatment: special problems of government-controlled programs, *Proc. 3rd Natl. Conf. Methadone Treatment,* U.S. Govt. Printing Office, Washington, Public Health Serv. Publ. No 2172, 121.

145. **Newman, R. G.,** *Proc. 3rd Natl. Conf. Methadone Treatment,* U.S. Govt. Printing Office, Washington, Public Health Serv. Publ. No. 2172, 122.

146. **Maddux, J. F.,** Methadone and medical ethics, *Proc. 4th Natl. Conf. Methadone Treatment,* NAPAN, New York, 1972, 265.

147. **Newman, R. G.,** *Proc. 3rd Natl. Conf. Methadone Treatment,* U.S. Govt. Printing Office, Washington, Public Health Serv. Publ. No. 2172, 123.

148. **Kramer, J. C.,** Parole, probation, police and methadone maintenance, *Proc. 3rd Natl. Conf. Methadone Treatment,* U.S. Govt. Printing Office, Washington, D.C., Public Health Serv. No. 2172, 101.

149. Methadone Maintenance Evaluation Committee, *J.A.M.A.,* 206, 2712, 1968.

150. **Gearing, F. R.,** *Int. J. Addict.,* 5, 517, 1970.

151. **Gearing, F. R.,** *Proc. 3rd Natl. Conf. Methadone Treatment,* U.S. Govt. Printing Office, Washington, D.C., Public Health Serv. Publ. No. 2172, 2.

152. **Gearing, F. R.,** *Proc. 5th Natl. Conf. Methadone Treatment,* NAPAN, New York, 1973, 452.

153. **Lukoff, I. F.,** in *Epidemiology of Drug Abuse,* Josephson, E. and Carroll, E., Eds., Winston-Wiley, Washington, D.C., in press.

154. **Gearing, F. R.,** MMTP: Progress report through March 31, 1971 – a five year overview, Columbia University School of Public Health and Administrative Medicine, New York, May 14, 1971 (mimeo).

155. Gearing, F. R., *Proc. 5th Natl. Conf. Methadone Treatment*, NAPAN, New York, 1973, 452.
156. Jaffe, J., *Int. J. Addict.*, 5, 375, 1970.
157. Newman, R. G. and Kagan, J. G., *Proc. 5th Natl. Conf. Methadone Treatment*, NAPAN, New York, 1973, 794.
158. Dale, R. T. and Dale, F. R., The use of methadone in a representative group of heroin addicts, *Int. J. Addict.*, 8, 293, 1973.
159. Dupont, R. L., Trying to treat all the heroin addicts in a community, *Proc. 4th Natl. Conf. Methadone Treatment*, NAPAN, New York, 1972, 77.
160. Brown, B. S. et al., Impact of a large-scale narcotics treatment program: a six month experience, *Int. J. Addict.*, 8, 49, 1973.
161. Bale, R. N. et al., Methadone treatment versus therapeutic communities: preliminary results of a randomized study in progress, *Proc. 5th Natl. Conf. Methadone Treatment*, NAPAN, New York, 1973, 1027.
162. Bourne, P. G. and Slade, J. D., Why is methadone maintenance successful? *Proc. 5th Natl. Conf. Methadone Treatment*, NAPAN, New York, 1973, 1086.
163. Gearing, F. R., *Proc. 5th Natl. Conf. Methadone Treatment*, NAPAN, New York, 1973, 452.
164. Brown, B. S. et al., *Int. J. Addict.*, 8, 49, 1973.
165. Goldstein, A., *Proc. 4th Natl. Conf. Methadone Treatment*, NAPAN, New York, 1972, 27.
166. Gearing, F. R., People versus urines, Columbia University, Division of Epidemiology, New York, January 6, 1972 (mimeo).
167. Gearing, F. R., *Proc. 3rd Natl. Conf. Methadone Treatment*, U.S. Govt. Printing Office, Washington, D.C., Public Health Serv. Publ. No. 2172, 2.
168. Chambers, C. D. and Taylor, W. J. R., The incidence and patterns of drug abuse during maintenance therapy, in *Methadone: Experiences and Issues*, Chambers, C. D. and Brill, L., Eds., Behavioral Publ., New York, 1973, 121.
169. Taylor, W. J. R., Chambers, C. D., and Dembo, R., Cocaine abuse among methadone maintenance patients, East. Psychiatric Res. Assoc. Annu. Meet., New York, November 7–8, 1970 (mimeo).
170. Brown, B. S. et al., *Int. J. Addict.*, 8, 49, 1973.
171. Dale, R. T. and Dale, F. R., *Int. J. Addict.*, 8, 293, 1973.
172. Wieland, W. F., Some psychosocial aspects of barbiturate and amphetamine use during methadone maintenance, *Proc. 4th Natl. Conf. Methadone Treatment*, NAPAN, New York, 1972, 145.
173. Methadone Maintenance Evaluation Committee, *J.A.M.A.*, 206, 2712, 1968.
174. Gearing, F. R., *Proc. 3rd Natl. Conf. Methadone Treatment*, U.S. Govt. Printing Office, Washington, D.C., Public Health Serv. Publ. No. 2172, 2.
175. Newman, R. G., Bashkow, S., and Cates, M., Arrest histories before and after admission to a methadone maintenance treatment program, *Proc. 5th Natl. Conf. Methadone Treatment*, NAPAN, New York, 1973, 109.
176. Sechrest, D. E. and Dunckley, T. E., A one year follow-up of methadone patients on drug use, criminal behavior, and wages earned, *Proc. 5th Natl. Conf. Methadone Treatment*, NAPAN, New York, 1973, 1290.
177. Brown, B. S. et al., *Int. J. Addict.*, 8, 49, 1973.
178. Langrod, J. and Lowinson, J. H., The scope and nature of criminality in a group of methadone patients, *Proc. 4th Natl. Conf. Methadone Treatment*, NAPAN, New York, 1972, 95.
179. Dale, R. T. and Dale, F. R., *Int. J. Addict.*, 8, 293, 1973.
180. Lukoff, I. F., in *Epidemiology of Drug Abuse*, Josephson, E. and Carroll, E., Eds., Winston-Wiley, Washington, D.C., in press.
181. Waldorf, D., *Careers in Dope*, Prentice-Hall, Englewood Cliffs, N.J., 1973, 115.
182. Alksne, H., Lieberman, L., and Brill, L., A conceptual model of the life cycle of addiction, *Int. J. Addict.*, 2, 221, 1967.
183. Ray, M. B., The cycle of abstinence and relapse among heroin addicts, *Social Probl.*, 9, 132, 1961.
184. Winick, C., Some aspects of careers of chronic heroin users, in *Epidemiology of Drug Abuse*, Josephson, E. and Carroll, E., Eds., Winston-Wiley, Washington, D.C., in press.
185. Winick, C., Maturing out of narcotic addiction, *U.N. Bull. Narcotics*, 14, 4, 1962.
186. Vaillant, G. E., *Am. J. Psychiatr.*, 122, 727, 1966.
187. Ball, J. C. and Snarr, R. W., A test of the maturation hypothesis with respect to opiate addiction, *U.N. Bull. Narcotics*, 21, 9, 1969.
188. Snow, M. S., Maturing out of narcotic addiction in New York City, *Int. J. Addict.*, in press.
189. Lukoff, I. F., in *Epidemiology of Drug Abuse*, Josephson, E. and Carroll, E., Eds., Winston-Wiley, Washington, D.C., in press.
190. Bernstein, D. M., Methadone in the family, *Proc. 4th Natl. Conf. Methadone Treatment*, NAPAN, New York, 1972, 367.
191. Africano, A., Fortunato, M., and Padow, E., The impact of program treatment on marital unions in a methadone maintained patient population, *Proc. 5th Natl. Conf. Methadone Treatment*, NAPAN, New York, 1973, 538.
192. Jaffe, J., *Int. J. Addict.*, 5, 375, 1970.
193. Brown, E. M., The need and model for a methadone maintenance residential therapeutic community, *Proc. 5th Natl. Conf. Methadone Treatment*, NAPAN, New York, 1973, 616.

194. **Hersh, R. G. and Schoof, K. G.,** Experiences in dispensing methadone in a factory, *Proc. 5th Natl. Conf. Methadone Treatment,* NAPAN, New York, 1973, 652.

195. **Scott, W. R.,** Professionals in bureaucracies – areas of conflict, in *Professionalization,* Vollmer, H. M. and Mills, D. L., Eds., Prentice-Hall, Englewood Cliffs, N.J., 1966, 265.

196. **Wolf, K., Sall, J. F., and Moton, W. F.,** Behavioral contracting as a technique for facilitating effective professional/paraprofessional interaction, *Proc. 5th Natl. Conf. Methadone Treatment,* NAPAN, New York, 1973, 243.

197. **Vollmer, H. M. and Mills, D. L., Eds.,** *Professionalization,* Prentice-Hall, Englewood Cliffs, N.J., 1966, viii.

198. **Logan, D. G.,** Heroin maintenance clinics: does the "British system" have the answers for U.S. addiction treatment shortcomings, *Proc. 5th Natl. Conf. Methadone Treatment,* NAPAN, New York, 1973, 579.

199. **Perlez, J.,** Alcohol and methadone – new peril, *New York Post,* December 6, 1973, 32.

200. **Winick, C.,** in *Epidemiology of Drug Abuse,* Josephson, E. and Carroll, E., Eds., Winston-Wiley, Washington, D.C., in press.

201. *Federal Register,* 38, 14289, May 31, 1973.

202. **Goode, E.,** *Drugs in American Society,* Knopf, New York, 1972, 193.

THE SOCIOLOGY OF PHOENIX HOUSE:
A THERAPEUTIC COMMUNITY FOR THE RESOCIALIZATION OF NARCOTIC ADDICTS

George Nash

TABLE OF CONTENTS

INTRODUCTION

This is a report on New York's Phoenix House, the largest therapeutic community for the treatment of drug abusers in the United States. It was based on 30 months of exposure to the facility and was prepared in 1970. It is published now as a contribution to the current discussion of the relative merits and efficacy of therapeutic communities, a discussion which has been expanded by two influential reviews of the literature on therapeutic communities, both of which raised questions about the long-term impact of these facilities on the country's ability to deal with its problems of drug abuse.[1,2]

My current Drug Abuse Treatment Information Project research in New Jersey which has been based on State Police record checks of all entrants into treatment is perhaps the first check of all splitees from a program.[3] We have found that there is a considerable decline in arrests after treatment for those who stay 6 months or longer in the more effective drug-free programs, whether or not they subsequently complete the program. This is the first large-scale comparative study of drug abuse treatment that has reached positive conclusions about therapeutic communities. In New Jersey the majority of the clients in the 9 drug-free programs we studied were young, and many had not been heroin addicts. Twelve out of 13 of those 27 years of age or older were in methadone treatment. Older clients who entered drug-free treatment did not show subsequent decline in arrests.

This chapter was written in a hopeful, innocent day when optimism and exuberance permeated Phoenix House during the period of my investigation.

Phoenix House, when I knew it firsthand, was an exciting type of organization that motivated people and induced certain forms of learning and growth. Many of the elements contained therein have relevance for all types of treatment and education programs. One of the problems of attempting to describe treatment programs is that they are constantly changing. Some of these observations and criticisms were already out of date by the time they were committed to paper.

This chapter will attempt to highlight the social structural elements of New York City's Phoenix Houses for the rehabilitation of narcotic addicts. It incorporates an overview of the program based on resident responses to questionnaires, as well as personal observations of the staff of the Columbia University Bureau of Applied Social Research Narcotic Addiction study team directed by the author.[4] We conducted individual hour-long interviews with 132 male residents and 25 female residents on Hart Island and Phoenix 85th Street in the summer of 1968. The percentages given here are for the total sample of 157 residents.

BACKGROUND

Although all the residents in the Phoenix Houses are ex-drug users, the goal of the program is to do more than to prevent them from relapsing to drug use. When asked, "What things about you do you think they'll consider in deciding when you can leave here (complete the program)?" over half (59%) mentioned personal adjustment and

changes in attitudes; less than 1% mentioned the use of drugs.

Efrem Ramirez, the Puerto Rican-born existential psychiatrist, who as Commissioner of New York City's Addiction Services Agency was instrumental in starting the Phoenix House Program, believes that drug abuse is the result of a character disorder and that complete immersion in the therapeutic community can take the sociopathic personality, as he calls it, and totally reconstitute it or turn it about at a 180° angle. "The object of the program is to help the former drug users reorient their motivation, their energy, and their values to become better attuned to the prevailing social trends."

Some people have compared the intensive pressure of the therapeutic community to the type of brainwashing applied by the Chinese to prisoners of war. Dr. Ramirez described some similarities in an interview.

We subject the person to a human environment which will alter his values. There is a difference between this and what is done in China, however. First, it's voluntary. Second, there is a model position, the successful ex-addict. The addict has a *disturbed, defective personality*. The aim of our program is to straighten out his values. We are very close to the primitive Christian society. This is to an extent a forced field.

The program began modestly in New York City in the early summer of 1967 with 12 graduates of a detoxification center and a former addict as its director. The men were residents of the top floor of a tenement building, and they themselves came up with the name Phoenix House. The Phoenix House program in New York City borrows heavily from its predecessors in the field, Synanon in California and Daytop in New York City. Most of the first staff members were ex-addicts who had been in these two programs. Mitchell Rosenthal, a psychiatrist who while serving in the U.S. Navy started a unit in a Naval Hospital modeled after Synanon, joined the staff in July 1967. Dr. Rosenthal, who is called Mitch by the members of his staff, has been largely responsible for the development and the supervision of the program. Dr. Ramirez resigned in December 1968. The New York Times quoted him explaining, "I am an architect rather than an administrator." In fact, although the program expanded rapidly, it did not come close to the capacity Dr. Ramirez promised.

Phases

There are three phases to the treatment program: induction and detoxification, treatment, and eldership. The Phoenix Houses, which are the subject of this chapter, are the second phase of treatment. By the time they enter a Phoenix House, all the residents have been physically detoxified, and they have had to signify their desire to enter a Phoenix House.

The first contact with the program has usually been in one of three places: a storefront Phoenix Center which drug users can enter directly from the street or be brought to by their parents or referred to by authorities, a hospital detoxification center (Morris Bernstein Institute) in downtown Manhattan, or a prison such as Riker's Island, a facility of the New York City Department of Corrections.

In addition to eliminating physical detoxification as a problem that the therapeutic community must deal with, the induction phase also provides motivation and presocialization. The ex-drug user must demonstrate that he is interested. He must be prompt for appointments. At Riker's Island, the potential entrants had to demonstrate their interest during a long induction phase which lasted several months. Despite the fact that there is some pre-socialization, most of those who came from Riker's Island admitted that they had simply been looking for an easier place to "do time" than jail. Those coming from the outside usually thought that it would be easier for them than it turns out to be. After the treatment phase, which can last up to 18 months, the resident can earn the right to be an elder. This chapter will concentrate on the treatment phase. Whereas the treatment phase is principally aimed at getting a person to come to grips with his problems, being an elder is preparation for reentering the real world. The elder can leave the house when he wishes, and he is paid a stipend. Most work in some phase of the program during this stage.

However, eldership is still a preparatory period. Although the elder residents are given positions of responsibility working in the induction or treatment phases of the program, they themselves are subject to slightly less stringent rules than the therapeutic community. The majority of them live in treatment facilities and are expected to observe certain curfews, participate in encounters, and be a source of "strength" to their house. It is not until they have worked through a number of levels that elders become graduates and become independent. Even then, a graduate who decides to work for the program is dependent on the program.

This eldership phase can take up to a year, depending on whether a person is preparing for a job as an addiction specialist or planning to go back to the square world.

At present there are 15 Phoenix Houses with about 1,200 residents. The Phoenix Houses are of two types. There are Phoenix Houses on Hart Island, where many of the men are under criminal certification to the New York State Narcotic Addiction Control Commission. They are voluntarily there rather than at Riker's Island, but they are not volunteers. Hart Island was a former correction facility which can be reached only by a 5-minute ferry ride from the mainland. The other Phoenix Houses are former tenements or apartment buildings. Some are in high drug use areas and others are in working-class neighborhoods. The majority of the residents in each of these are volunteers in that they entered the program of their own volition. However, many were in trouble with the courts or their probation officers, and this represented the alternative to jail. The State financially supports the criminally certified residents at Hart Island. Much of the support for the other residents comes in the form of welfare payments which the residents turn over to the program.

Rules and Norms, Values and Their Enforcement

There are three principal rules in the Phoenix Houses:

1. No drugs or stimulants are allowed. This includes not only all forms of drugs but also beer, wine, and other alcoholic beverages.
2. The second rule is against violence, aggression, or acting out. Not only is fighting not allowed, but the mere threat of violence can bring censure. This rule also covers illicit sexual contact. Homosexual contact is never allowed. Heterosexual contact is allowed only when men and women in the program are considered serious about one another and ready to handle it.
3. The third rule condemns the silence of anyone who knows of an infraction of the first two rules and does not report it. This exerts pressure (to report the violation) on the resident who has violated a rule and on the resident

knowing of a violation because both parties are subject to punishment when exposed.

However, these rules only provide the foundation for an elaborate structure of norms and values which govern the daily behavior of the residents. The principal values inculcated are honesty, responsibility, and concern. When we asked the residents, "What's the best thing about this place?" 28% mentioned being surrounded by concern and trust, and another third of the residents mentioned the general atmosphere of concern. Central to the whole process is communication. The resident in the therapeutic community must learn how to give and receive communications. Not only must he be able to talk openly about his problems, but he must also be able to give intelligible commands, and he must be able to explain the expectations of the community to others, especially the newer, less experienced residents.

There is a signout board near the office of the house director, on which each resident must indicate where he is at all times. Communications are carefully regulated. During the first few months that a resident is at a Phoenix House, he may not receive phone calls or visits. After that, they are strictly *regulated.* He may not leave Phoenix House except with explicit permission. Attendance at a wide range of house meetings is mandatory.

Residents are expected not to engage in "tripping" (daydreaming) or in other forms of escape. Television watching and reading are sometimes viewed as escapism. People are expected to confront their own problems or help others rather than just pass time. Residents are also expected not to "jail" (engage in negative talk) or "bad rap" (talk negatively about) the program. They are supposed to be positive and constructive and to avoid pleasant collective recollections about their life outside.

When asked, "What did you talk with other residents about?" (the day before the interview), 67% said they talked about the program and the community; 63% said they talked about their feelings and problems. Only 24% reported that they talked about their previous life. It is a moot point to discuss whether the others who did not report talking about their previous life really do talk about it. Even the fact that they did not report doing so reflects on the norm.

The resident is told that the program is difficult and that he, just as all junkies, is an irresponsible, immature, inconsiderate, dishonest person who refused to face his problems in the past, having tried to escape from them by shooting drugs. He is told to accept the idea that drugs are bad, but he is also made aware that his drug use is merely a symptom of his underlying psychological problems. He is expected to work hard, to be responsible, and to show concern for others while being honest with himself. If all of these things seem difficult or impossible, he is told to act "as if." In other words, to act as if he were concerned, responsible, and understood what he is doing.

The question of whether or not the resident basically changes cannot be readily determined. He does *learn* to alter his behavior. In many instances he is utilizing in the therapeutic community the same skills he possessed as an addict, only now he redirects the energy into socially acceptable channels. For example, a resident in "Acquisition" must convince people on the outside to contribute goods and services to the program. He must, simply stated, manipulate people. But now the ends are acceptable.

The primary way of enforcing these rules, norms, and values is the manipulation and granting of symbols, such as prestige, esteem, and acceptance. The manipulation of symbols is contingent upon the hierarchal job system which gives high status jobs to those who demonstrate responsible behavior and demotes those who do not. Although the paid staff director is ultimately responsible for, or at least must approve, job changes, residents are also responsible to one another. A resident must obey his job supervisor (another resident) and other residents who rank higher.

In many ways life in Phoenix House is the real world in microcosm. Life is organized around the work which the residents do to keep the house functioning.

When asked, "Do you now have a regular job aside from taking care of your own personal things?" and "If yes, what job?" 41% of the residents reported themselves to be in positions of authority and responsibility. Another 10% described themselves as skilled workers. The latter often supervise and/or teach unskilled or less skilled residents. Thus, roughly half of the residents reported themselves to be in positions of authority. This estimate is corroborated by the total responses to another question: "Do you supervise any other workers?" 51% of the residents said that they did supervise other workers. Although this might appear at first glance to be a system of haves and have nots, the fact that there are no limitations on upward mobility democratizes the system. Each resident assumes that he may ultimately achieve the highest ranking resident position, that of coordinator. When asked, "Do the residents have a say in how this place is run?" 93% said yes. This percentage necessarily includes the opinions of those who did not happen to be "in the ruling class" at the time interviewed.

The director and the residents in positions of authority command both positional and personal power. It is the personality, as well as the position, of the one in charge which elicits commitment from other residents. When asked, "Do you think that there are leaders among the residents here?" 96% said yes. These people were then asked, "Would you think of the most important leader among the residents that you know of here. Don't tell me his name, but tell me something about him. Why do you think he's a leader?" Almost half of the respondents (47%) mentioned the ability to relate to others as the characteristic of the leader they had in mind. Another 38% mentioned concern for others as an attribute of the leader. Only 3% mentioned experience on the streets as an attribute of the leader. Leadership is based on what the resident has accomplished in and contributed to the program.

Personnel

The complement of one Phoenix House usually consists of about 75 residents who perform almost all the work required to keep the house going and just two paid staff members, both ex-addicts. The ex-addicts, who are paid respectable salaries, occupy the positions of director and assistant director. At Hart Island there are other paid staff members because of the size of the program there. (There is, of course, a headquarters staff that oversees the entire program.) The residents themselves are organized in an elaborate hierarchy of jobs and do the rest of the work although they receive no pay.

Now we will discuss the principal organizational features of the Phoenix Houses under the following headings: degree of institutionalization, reward and punishment, confrontation and communication, sense of community, and leadership.

DEGREE OF INSTITUTIONALIZATION

Institutionalization is the routinized subjugation which occurs in facilities designed to control behavior. This is characteristic of the prisons and mental hospitals described by Erving Goffman as "total institutions."[5] Total institutions control all aspects of the residents' behavior in a coercive manner with many negative effects on both residents and staff. The Phoenix Houses avoid many of the most negative aspects of ordinary total institutions without surrendering control. One of the best ways that this is done is through the replacement of coercion with voluntarism.

No Drabness

The average prison is gray and oppressive in appearance with bars, cells, locks, clubs, military formations, uniforms, and other earmarks of coercion. There are none of these coercive symbols or mechanisms in the Phoenix Houses. The Phoenix Houses are painted bright colors. Some of the older buildings on Hart Island, in addition to being painted bright colors, have had polka dots added to them as well. Most of the buildings have been modernized and tastefully decorated with strong colors. In the former tenements in New York City, the residents decorate their own rooms in bright colors and paint their furniture. There are murals, paintings, and signs on the walls as well as pictures of the residents. The men and women dress as neatly as their jobs will allow, and they are all dressed individualistically, as there are no uniforms. The girls' skirts are short, and the men's shirts and turtlenecks are of bright colors. Although there is a signout board and a resident watching the front door, there are no bars or clubs or military formations.

Less Staff-resident Dichotomy

One of the most prominent features of total institutions is the fact that the staff is superior and the residents are constantly reminded of their inferior status. In the Phoenix Houses there is more of a continuum because residents may eventually become directors. However, at any given time a definite authority structure exists. Because there are no professionals and so few staff members actually present in the houses, this dichotomy between staff and residents is not present in the same fashion that it is in most total institutions. The position of elder also breaks down the dichotomy. The elder occupies a position midway between the director and the resident, and elders share many of the responsibilities of the director.

In appearance, it is hard for the casual visitor to distinguish the director and the assistant director from some of the residents, except that the former are slightly more likely to wear jackets, but no more likely to wear ties. There are a number of important differences between the director and the residents. The director lives at home and has a private life, while the residents are told they must be completely open and that they have no privacy. The directors have cars and other possessions which connote achievement of middle-class status, while the residents have few possessions. However, some residents do have television sets and record players, and most have radios, wrist watches, and cigarette lighters — possessions frequently denied the residents of total institutions. The director has a large office with an imposing chair and coffee table. Both the directors and the residents who have worked their way up into supervisory positions issue orders which must be obeyed. However, the residents' decisions are much more open to review (by the director) than are those of the director. Although a director may subject himself to the review of residents by going to the residents' encounters, he is more usually subject to the jurisdiction of an area director or the Director of Treatment. The hierarchy actually extends beyond the therapeutic community and, politically, beyond the Addiction Services Agency.

The fact that the residents are busy and that they provide for themselves instead of having things done for them means that there is not the active-passive distinction that occurs when the staff does everything and the residents simply respond. The fact that the residents pool their welfare checks helps them to feel that it is their program.

Acceptance of the Norms of the Organization

Most total institutions contain two cultures, the one of the staff and the one of the residents. Very frequently the staff needs to have informers to find out what is going on with the residents. The residents in the Phoenix House usually accept the norms of the institution, and if they do not understand or accept the norms, they act as if they do. No deviant subculture is permitted. The ideology is that it is the residents' house, and therefore if a person does something negative he hurts his brothers and sisters in the program and not those who are running the institution. If a deviant subculture were to develop, it would be discussed in the encounters and spotted by the expediters, whose job it is to keep in touch with what is happening in the house. The directors and assistant directors join in encounters, and the norms and rules are discussed openly and must be justified.

A question arises as to whether the residents really accept the norms or just appear to. This is probably a moot point. The houses are structured so as to allow no deviant behavior. To engage in deviant behavior, or not to report it if one is aware of it, leads to trouble. Therefore, the residents accept the norms.

This leads to an interesting phenomenon. Residents must really trust one another before they will discuss negative aspects of the program. This leads to a type of friendship called the "bad rap buddy" with whom one can safely criticize the program. Although most of the residents in the program accept the norms, and those who are less positive about the program are subject to more peer pressure and less likely to be promoted, the acceptance is not necessarily unconditional or permanent. As one ex-resident put it: "When the guys get off the ferry from Hart Island to go on pass they change completely. Most of them would be no more likely to show concern or act responsibly than anybody else." The acceptance of the norms of the institution is situation specific. The problem of the therapeutic community is to make permanent the norms of behavior that are able to be sustained by the various mechanisms of the community.

The reasons that the norms are accepted, even if the acceptance is situation specific, are fourfold:

1. The largest pressure is exerted by peers — other residents — rather than by superiors — the staff.

2. There are rewards, both from staff and other residents, for positive behavior. There is a reward system.

3. There is a system of informants and communication which allows the staff to find out when the norms are violated.

4. The norms are enforced voluntaristically

rather than coercively. This is a more effective way of motivating people.

All of the above is not meant to imply that there is no deviant behavior or that all people are completely honest. One ex-resident said that although there were almost never any drugs circulated in the community, there was a problem about illegal sexual activity, especially homosexual activity among women. Although in his estimation the sexual deviance problem was minor, it was constant. There are other problems with residents having unauthorized possessions, especially money. Although there is deviant behavior, it never approaches the scale of such activities in most confinement institutions.

No Physical Coercion

Most total institutions rely at least implicitly on physical coercion as the final means of enforcing norms. There is no physical coercion in a Phoenix House; in fact, there is a rule against physical violence of any sort, and this applies equally to the staff and to the residents. There is an elaborate system of rewards and punishments which makes physical coercion unnecessary. In addition to the physical coercion the staff of confinement institutions uses to enforce compliance, there is coercion of another sort in these facilities. There is a good deal of violence among the residents themselves, especially in prisons. In most prisons men must demonstrate their manliness. Because the staff cannot protect them, the men must protect themselves. This causes some of the weaker, younger men to seek out older, tougher men as protectors. This protection is quite often rewarded with money, material possessions — such as cigarettes or food — or with sexual privileges. It is not infrequent for a young prisoner to have to defend himself with his fists or submit to sexual attack. In the prisoner stratification system, which is separate and independent from that enforced by the staff, a man's toughness affects his rank. Although manliness is also a virtue in Phoenix House, the prohibition against violence means a man cannot rise on the basis of his ability to fight. "You really feel protected here; there isn't any violence," said a man whose forehead bore the scars of a number of prison fights.

Voluntarism

Although most of the residents are there because they would face something worse if they were not, no one feels that he is required to stay in Phoenix House. The ultimate punishment for breaking the rules is ejection from the house. For those who have come directly from Riker's Island, the prison, this means going back to it. At the Phoenix Houses in the city, one can leave the house fairly easily at any time. At Hart Island the volunteers can leave whenever they wish, but it is more difficult for those with criminal commitments to leave. However, there are no restraints at all on the Island itself. A person on a criminal commitment who really wants to leave can either get off the Island by giving someone else's name or he can escape when he goes to the mainland for a trip to a clinic or when he leaves for other routine personal business or when he is on a pass.

In fact, however, anyone who wants to leave the community has to do a lot of talking, first to the other residents and finally to the director. Most people who want to leave are talked out of it. The ideology is that one who leaves, or "splits," will definitely go back to shooting drugs and will ultimately die.

There is a rationale for this ideology. Firstly, if the staff assumed responsibility for each splitee, each splitee would represent a personal failure for the staff member. If a staff member tried to reclaim a splitee, that is, tried to follow him and coax him to come back to the program after he split, this might encourage more residents to split, to test the concern of the staff and other residents for him. At present, a resident who splits knows that no one will be trying to find him or get him back into the program. Secondly, the morale of the other residents might easily be disturbed if they considered a splitee's chance for success as good as that of the resident remaining on the island.

Despite the fact that it is not actually easy to leave, the fact that the person is not physically restrained and is at least potentially able to leave, and faces being sent to a worse institution if he doesn't behave, gives an air of voluntarism to the institution.

No Routine Dehumanization

The residents are expected to look neat. A certain amount of individuality, such as long hair, is permitted, especially among older residents who have earned it. People are called by their proper names and not by numbers. Most of the residents know the full names of their brothers and sisters in the house. Politeness is the norm, and the femininity of women is emphasized.

Sex Integration and Visitors

Most prisons in the United States are either all male or female. Visiting, when permitted, is usually under rigidly controlled circumstances. The Phoenix Houses usually have some women residents, although the majority of the residents (by a five or ten to one ratio) are male. It is felt that one of a "dope fiend's" major "hang-ups" is the inability to deal with persons of the opposite sex. Men and women are encouraged to talk with one another, and they frequently work in close proximity. Although the women's quarters are always separated from those of the men, there is a good deal of contact at work, parties, seminars, and meals. The forming of enduring friendships between men and women residents is not discouraged, and some plan to marry after leaving the program. There are frequent parties where the girls from one Phoenix House will come to another or the men from one will go to another.

There are open houses which girlfriends, wives, and visitors from the outside are encouraged to attend. Although visitors must announce their intentions to come in advance, and new residents are not allowed visitors, and people who are thought to be negative influences are not allowed, visitors are treated quite well once they arrive. There is no searching of visitors, nor is there any prohibition against physical contact. Dancing is the feature of most of the parties. Some of the houses have a room which can be used for private get-togethers between two residents of the house who are serious about each other and have the permission of the director or between a husband who is a resident of a house and a wife who lives outside. Despite the fact that contact between the sexes is encouraged, the program is extremely moralistic in that neither heterosexual promiscuity nor any sort of homosexual activities are allowed in the house.

Contact with the Outside World

The Phoenix Houses located in high drug use areas are in close proximity to the outside world. The residents can see what is going on from the windows and can stand on the sidewalk and engage freely in conversation with outsiders. Even those on Hart Island leave fairly frequently for medical appointments and routine business. The jobs of many of the residents carry them off the Island on a regular basis.

All of the residents can look forward to passes which are of three types. First, a resident goes out on a group pass, usually to some form of entertainment such as a movie, a play, or a baseball game. A number of the newer residents are under the supervision of an older resident. Next come two-person passes, where a younger resident goes out for a weekend with an older resident. Finally, a person gets an individual pass for a weekend. Residents are not allowed to drink or to use drugs on passes and urine tests are frequently made of those returning from passes. The pass is seen as a testing experience, and the director and older residents give a lot of advice to a man before he goes out on a pass. What he did on his pass is the subject of much discussion when he returns.

When asked, "Have you ever left on a pass?" 61% of the residents interviewed reported they had been on pass. Of those we asked, "Have you ever used heroin while out on pass?" only 4% said yes.

Residents are encouraged to cultivate heterosexual friendships so they can work off their sexual frustrations while on pass.

Contributions from the Private Sector

The Phoenix Houses depend for a lot of their support upon contributions from the outside world. One of the residents' job activities is "hustling" from merchants, both in the area of the house and in the balance of New York City. Local bakeries give day-old pastries. Clothing manufacturers give seconds and discontinued merchandise. The program has set up a private foundation, The Phoenix Foundation, to enlist citizen support and to allow it to give credit for donations.

REWARD AND PUNISHMENT

The residents do almost all the work in the house, and the job structure takes the form of a sharply differentiated hierarchy in which each resident is expected to work his way up. The structure is divided into a number of separate departments, each of which ranks differently in the structure. The service department and the kitchen department are the lowest-ranking departments. Each resident starts in one of these departments, scrubbing pans or cleaning toilets.

Although the members of the service department and the kitchen department are aware that they are in the lowest-ranking departments, the heads of the departments are residents who are fairly highly ranked. They attend the department heads' regular meetings.

Some of the other departments include the building department, which helps to rehabilitate and maintain the structures, the tailor shop, which handles alterations and dry cleaning, and the community relations department, which deals with visitors and handles arrangements for residents who must go outside on personal business. The acquisition department secures donations to the program. There is a graphic arts department, which makes signs and posters for the house. There is an education department, which brings in speakers from the outside and arranges the seminars and morning meetings.

At the very top of the house structure are the coordinators and the expediters. The chief coordinator is the highest-ranking resident in the house. He makes many of the important decisions involving the day-to-day operations of the house. The expediters act as messengers and footmen for the coordinators. They take orders from the coordinators and transmit them to the members of the house. The expediter checks to make sure that things are running smoothly by going through the floors of the house and making sure that the ashtrays are empty, that nobody is sitting around moping, that nobody is resting when he is supposed to be doing a job. There are expediters on duty 24 hours a day, 7 days a week. When an expediter finds a person not doing his job, he reports it to the person's supervisor. However, the supervisor is as likely to get in trouble as is the man himself.

The names of all of the residents appear on an elaborate organization chart in the director's office which shows the makeup of all the departments as well as the names of the department heads. The resident moves up within the status hierarchy on the basis of his accomplishments in the program. Each resident is periodically rated on the basis of how good a job he is doing and how well he accepts orders. His general progress in terms of coming to know himself is also a major factor in his moving up within the status hierarchy.

An example of a fairly typical job progression is provided by Rafael, as told to one of our staff members.

Rafael started work on the service crew, cleaning the house. He stayed on the service crew for 6 weeks. From there he went to the powerhouse, carrying coal in wheelbarrows to the burner. This, he said, is the hardest job on the island. And then he added, "While it is a step up from the service crew it really is a test of your attitude." Rafael stayed at work in the powerhouse for 1 month.

From the powerhouse he went to the laundry, where he washed clothes. His stay at the laundry was for 1 month. The next job was on a building crew in the new Phoenix House III, which is the house he is now living in. He said that he did everything around the place, everything that had to be done — painting, plastering, tearing down and putting up partitions. In effect, they put the house into shape in order to house all the residents. This job lasted 2 months.

After serving on the building crew, Rafael was promoted to expediter. While Rafael was working as expediter, he was put back to the maintenance crew because of a problem with "telling persons what to do." Rafael described the event as follows:

"I told this guy to clean up the floor, and I shoulda just walked off and let him do it. But I stood over him and watched him while he did it." The same day he went down to the coordinator and said that I had pushed him. This was a lie because I had not. Well, when he told them [meaning the coordinator] they put me on the bench [this is a bench in front of the director's office of the house]. I stayed on the bench as a reprimand for nine hours. You can't talk and no smoking on the bench. Well, then they gave me a haircut. You got to stand there and take it, you know. Then they put me back to the maintenance crew.

Rafael felt that he had suffered an injustice but that he didn't handle the situation properly. "I didn't ask for a special encounter on the man for ten days." In the special encounter, the accuser admitted that he had lied about Rafael, but Rafael remained on the maintenance crew and has been there for 3 weeks. Now he is in charge of one maintenance trainee, and they are responsible for all maintenance in the house.

The changing of jobs is marked by a great deal of uncertainty. Residents are told to "seek and assume," that they are responsible for getting themselves better jobs. If a resident decides he would like to hold a given job, such as that of telephone operator, he starts hanging around and observing the telephone operator on duty. The telephone operator is also eager to move up within the hierarchy, so he will usually be quite free with advice as to how he does his job. Once the resident thinks that he is ready to assume the job, he asks for it, but he may have to wait several days or weeks for an answer. This is part of the training to accept frustration. By doing different jobs in the house and supervising others, the residents learn regular work habits which will enable them to work more satisfactorily at regular jobs on the outside.

The rewards are in the form of job promotion and passes. Punishments take the form of scolding (which is known as a haircut), loss of privilege, or job demotion, and ultimately the contract and shaved head. Although a resident may work for months to move up within the job hierarchy, one serious mistake, such as the refusal to accept an order, and he can be back on the kitchen crew washing dishes. The haircuts or scoldings are quite abusive and very explicit. The contracts are frequently harsh and humiliating. A resident who left the program and went home to his mother was forced to wear diapers for 3 days when he returned to the program and to carry big signs saying, "I'm a baby. Please help me." A resident who took something from another was forced to wear a sign saying, "I'm a thief! Don't trust me!" Contracts can be quite severe with residents being given such assignments as shining the shoes of all the other residents on the Island. Contracts run for delineated periods of time. In extreme cases a man may not only have his hair shaved, but also be forced to wear drab clothes for several weeks.

The residents are told that all drug addicts are immature and that they must learn how to deal with frustration and occasional failure and how to accept punishment. Therefore, a contract is seen as a good thing for a man, even if it was awarded unfairly. Residents are told that they have to learn how to accept frustration and authority and that they will be rated on how well they accept a contract or demotion. A senior resident who has been demoted usually finds it easier to work his way back up than does a new resident.

One of the problems of the punishment system is that there is no real system of checks and balances. The directors have the final authority, and they have the tendency to feel that they don't make mistakes. The rules are explicit and harsh. Obviously not all enforcement can be uniform. This means that some people are punished who should not be and others who should be are not.

The questions were asked, "Have you ever been punished for breaking any rules, and what did you do and how were you punished?" Of those punished, 40% were punished for violations of stated institutional rules, 42% were punished for general negative behavior within the community, and 18% were punished for misbehavior on the outside; 39% were punished through the job system, either by demotion or extra work, 29% were given verbal haircuts only, 14% were given bald heads; and 18% lost privileges.

One girl whom we interviewed in an exploratory phase of the study was demoted, and so much pressure was applied that she left the program. The charge against her was that she thought she was something special and that she was acting different. The evidence was largely that she had been singled out to be interviewed. However, she was picked to be interviewed and had not sought out the attention.

An independent ombudsman would probably help to insure the rights of people unfairly singled out for punishment. However, this arrangement would undermine the authority of the director upon which so much of the system is based.

One reason that the program works is that violation of the rules is punished. The severity of the system does lead some observers to feel that the directors are unduly harsh. This probably stems from the Synanon tradition which stresses firm and visible punishment.

However, residents do get an opportunity to complain. When asked, "Have you ever lodged a complaint with one of the staff or the people in charge here?" 65% of the residents reported that they had. The residents reported the outcomes of their complaints as follows: settled in my favor, 59%; nothing happened, 18%; something adverse, 3%; still pending, 3%; other or not stated, 17%.

There are two negative outgrowths of the reward and punishment system. First, many of those who are demoted, especially from fairly high-ranking positions, split the program rather than face the humiliation. Secondly, there is a great deal of gossip about who gets punished and who does not. The program is described to newcomers in utopian terms. This is partially responsible for their initial high motivation. When they see that rewards and punishments are made by humans and that mistakes are made, this has a disillusioning effect.

Stratification within the house is on the basis of both progress in getting to know yourself, in "getting yourself together," and on the basis of the length of time spent in the program. Those who have been there longer are considered the "strength of the house" and are expected to behave more responsibly. There is usually a good deal of consensus within the house as to how well any individual resident is doing. Not only do those who are doing better have higher-ranked jobs, but they also tend to be more popular.

CONFRONTATION AND COMMUNICATION

The major method used to reach the addict is confrontation through the encounter. It is also the battleground for releasing hostility and tension and for undermining the hierarchical structure of the community. The encounters are group-therapy-type sessions where 8 to 12 of the residents sit around in a circle and talk to and shout at each other for 3 to 4 hours. There are a number of rules in the encounters, but there are no professionals involved. The encounters are directed by the older and more aware residents who are called "strength" in the group. The participants in the encounter focus on one individual at a time, for periods ranging from ½ to 2 hours.

The encounters follow a fairly standard format. A person is usually indicted over something specific. Frequently, another resident has placed a "slip" in a box during the course of the week to complain about something that the other resident has done.

Any resident in the Phoenix House, regardless of his job function, or length of residence can "drop a slip" on any other resident whom he wishes to confront in encounters. The slip usually just contains the person's name who is writing the slip, and the name of the person he wishes to confront. For example: John Jones (writer) vs. Eugene Smith. Occasionally, the person writes what is bothering him. For example: "He doesn't know how to give directions." The latter was written by a resident about his department head.

The number of slips dropped for each encounter varies according to the tension in the house created by the directors themselves (who, according to one director, do things just to create stress) and, of course, according to individual

friction. It is rare that no slips are dropped. There are an average of 10 to 15 slips in a 70-man house. The slips are deposited in a closed box from encounter to encounter.

The assistant director and coordinator of each house is responsible for setting up groups. They may be done anywhere from 2 to 4 hours before the encounter. Each person's name is on a card so that even the setting up of groups has the oddly mixed tensions of a game and a serious clinical session. After clinical decisions have largely guided the setting up of the groups, group size has to be taken into consideration.

There are various principles used in setting up groups. Firstly, slips are not necessarily honored. That is, if the assistant director feels that a resident should have to "sit on his feeling" for awhile, he may simply discard the slip and not put the people whose names appear on the slip together. Or he may save the slip for a week and put the people together at that time. Occasionally, all the slips are discarded.

Residents are aware of who the "strength" is in each group, that is, the one or two residents who have been in the program a longer time or who hold high positions (such as coordinator). The residents do not defer to "strength" or withhold from encountering them, but one is aware of their structural control. For example, strength may decide when to take the encounter off someone if a confrontation doesn't naturally end itself, i.e., with a resolution. At least one strength resident is aware of the slips which have been dropped. If someone has dropped a slip and then remains silent, strength can confront the resident for not bringing up his problem.

Occasionally the coordinator, or assistant director, or director travels from group to group. He can walk in, sit down, and put the encounter on a specific problem or person. Yet, his visiting status does not make him invulnerable. On several cases the director or a coordinator visits a group and is confronted forcefully by the whole group about a variety of issues when he had come in to confront someone else.

The encounter frequently starts by dealing with one specific misdeed that an individual is accused of doing or simply by asking a person what is bothering him. Members of the group throw out various suggestions as to what they think may be bothering the person. Once the person starts to respond or react to a charge made by the group, a number of the group members join in and they "engross" something or blow it up all out of proportion.

After the person has started to see his error or begins to be able to talk out his problems or, as it is called in Phoenix House, once he "cops to" something, the group attempts to see what he is going to do about it. People who have had a limited amount of exposure to the attack-type of group therapy of which the encounters are an example, focus on the noise, the criticism, and the venting of aggression. These sessions are good for venting aggression, but the main thing that goes on is not shouting and arguing, but a type of reasoning and convincing. Other members of the group give long discourses about their own problems which are similar to those of the person who is being encountered.

At the end of the encounter there is a conscious effort made to "patch" the person up. If the encounter has been particularly traumatic and if the person who is encountered has "dumped out a lot of garbage" or, in other words, talked about something that he has been keeping in for a long time, he may start to cry. After the verbal help is offered by the group, the members may come up, put their arms around the person who has been reduced to tears, offer him coffee, and dry his tears. There is a great deal of compassion and understanding expressed as well as hostility and aggression vented.

The encounters are quite open and honest, and they tend to keep the residents from holding things back. The complaint of the Phoenix House people with professionals is that addicts have dealt with psychiatrists, psychologists, and social workers for many years and have learned how to "con" them and make them feel sorry for them. Ex-addicts say that you cannot con an ex-addict. The addict learns in the encounter not only by being encountered but also by watching others being encountered and by encountering others.

Negative things that come out in encounters are not held against a person; in fact, they are regarded as signs of maturity and growth. In some institutions how well one is progressing in group therapy is regarded as a major sign of progress, and the residents learn to sound sincere and as if they are really working on their problems. An attempt to sound good in an encounter in Phoenix House would probably be met with derision. There are many rules in encounters. First, no physical

violence or contact is allowed. Second, any type of language is allowed. Because profanity is not allowed in everyday activity, and because the encounters tend to be very emotional, many statements contain four-letter words. This, of course, is the type of language that is frequently used by working-class men on an everyday basis. However, the emotionality and the language of attack therapy tend to make it a shocking and surprising experience for the uninitiated, middle-class observer.

After the encounter is over, there is generally some sort of a friendly positive social gathering. All the residents from the house gather for coffee and snacks. This allows the resident who has been attacked to talk the matter over again, and it also helps to put him back together.

There are also a variety of special encounters, some of which run for longer periods of time. Sometimes, when the house is thought to have special problems, there are marathons which run for a day or more. These are very emotional and often help to crack the reserve of some who are unwilling to talk about their problems.

The encounters are entirely verbal, and thus a person has to develop a certain amount of verbal skill in order to do well. The Phoenix House program attempts to make the residents articulate communicators. In addition to the encounters, there are a number of other ways in which the Phoenix House residents learn to communicate:

1. *Morning meeting.* Because the encounters tend to be critical, morning meeting is intended to start the day off in a friendly fashion. The residents give talks, sing, and recite poetry. One presents the thought for the day. However, he must know the meaning or the intent of the phrase or poem and be able to "break it down" if requested to do so.

2. *Word for the day.* Each day a new word goes up on the bulletin board, and residents are required to learn its meaning and its message.

3. *Mock speaking engagements.* Residents get up in front of the other residents and explain the program as if they were addressing a community group on the outside about their program.

4. *Grab bag seminars.* The residents pick topics out of a hat and are forced to give ad-lib speeches.

5. *Debates.* Residents are arbitrarily assigned opposite sides in debates about such topics as the pros and cons of violence. At the end of the

debate, the participants are forced to switch sides and argue the other side.

6. *Signs.* There are many signs, posters, and paintings. They detail the organization chart and explain the philosophy of the house.

7. *Titles.* Each job in the elaborate hierarchy has its own title, such as expediter, coordinator, ram-rod. The residents learn the subtlety and specificity of language.

8. *Supervision.* As a resident moves up the complex job hierarchy within Phoenix House, he is required to supervise other workers. He is required to tell them what to do and to evaluate how well they are doing.

9. *Tours and open houses.* The residents are expected to take visitors around the house and to be able to explain the house to outsiders. At open houses and parties they are expected to be able to talk to and relate to strangers.

10. *Man-to-man talk.* One of the principal spare time activities is "rapping" (based on rapport) or talking to others in an attempt to solve problems and indoctrinate newer brothers.

Communication is seen as particularly important because as a result of their "character disorders" it is said that the drug users didn't deal with people on a man-to-man basis but rather tended to be shy and retiring. Learning how to communicate is an important element in overcoming shyness. Instruction in communication covers both substance and technique. Phoenix House residents learn to look one another in the eye when they talk, to shake hands firmly, and to talk loudly enough to be heard. They are told that all people are shy and that the best way to get people over their shyness is to talk up to them. There are a large number of residents of Puerto Rican birth or ancestry. All meetings are held in English, and those of Spanish descent are forced to speak English.

There are also other types of meetings at which problems are discussed. There are general meetings which are called for special situations, generally when one or more people have done something wrong. A general meeting of the whole of Hart Island was called the day Senator Robert F. Kennedy was shot to discuss what was wrong with society. Smaller problems are dealt with in "pull-up" sessions in the morning and evening. There are also numerous meetings of supervisors and departments. All of these help to develop the ability to communicate and serve as a means of enforcing norms.

A SENSE OF COMMUNITY

In many ways the Phoenix Houses are among the most successful integrated communities in American society. The residents are young and old, ranging from boys in their early teens to men in their sixties. There are men and women, and there are blacks, whites, and Puerto Ricans. From what we have been able to observe, there is little in the way of ethnic patternings in seating arrangements at meals. The various work departments within the houses are also integrated with none being predominantly white or black or Puerto Rican. The Phoenix House ideology is that the effects of segregation are everywhere in the world and that it has to be learned how to be dealt with. Racism on the part of either blacks or whites is seen as a "hang-up" which prevents a person from coping successfully with social reality on the outside. Through the encounters many people come face-to-face with their honest attitudes about race for the first time.

Racial barriers are not as rigid as they are in most hospitals and prisons or in society at large. Consequently, subgroups within the community do not form strictly along racial lines; people of Puerto Rican ancestry are restricted in their use of Spanish. There is, however, an encounter held in Spanish for those who are unable to express complex feelings in English. They are encouraged to learn English and advance to English encounters.

However, there is racial patterning of friendships. Furthermore, on evenings when there are no encounters, the residents are allowed to schedule other activities. There are clubs which discuss and promote black culture.

There is much more needed to have a sense of community than the mere lack of subgroups. "Concern" is one of the essential elements of a Phoenix House, and the residents show considerable concern for one another. One of the first days that I ate in the dining room, five different residents came up to me asking if I was a new resident. Each introduced himself and asked if he could tell me anything about Phoenix House. When a person is depressed or gets "in a bag," others, usually the older residents, are expected to help talk him out of it. When someone is thinking of leaving, or splitting, from the community, the other residents pitch in to try to talk him out of leaving.

There is also a great deal of friendliness and pleasantry which help to build a sense of community. The community room is attractively decorated, and soul music or hard rock can usually be heard coming from the hi-fi set. In the summer at Hart Island, the residents go down to the beach in the evening. A general feeling of friendliness prevails, which makes it clear that most of the residents like the place and like each other. Each house has a distinctive personality and a song which the residents sing at morning meetings.

Another thing that binds the community together is the fact that the older residents serve as role models. The house director and assistant director are also role models. They have really made it in that they are employed in prestigious and important visible positions. The older residents also serve as role models. The role model for one 26-year-old black who had been addicted to heroin for 11 years is one of the directors, a product of Synanon. The resident described his role model in the following terms: "He's a black, proud, upright, assured man. He's done things. He doesn't have to look for things; he's achieved it." Another black man in his late 40s has as his role model a white director, whom he describes as: "An upright cat. He's the big man. He's gone a long way."

In prisons there is no positive role model. Those who command the most respect are frequently those who are the toughest, the most defiant, or were the biggest operators on the outside. Those who have made the successful transition back to the square world are not present.

Just as the Phoenix House attempts to prevent the formation of ethnic cliques, there is an attempt made to prevent the formation of cliques based on personal favoritism. To this end, house directors and assistant directors are switched between houses and between the city and Hart Island fairly frequently. The aim of the program is to build up networks of individuals rather than specific leaders.

Another thing that helps to mold the residents into a community is the crisis-type atmosphere which exists. There is a constant stream of newcomers into the house, and they must be made aware of the rules of the community. Sometimes newcomers overbalance oldtimers, and it is felt that a house is getting too "loose." In such a situation, the screws may be tightened, and the house cut off from mail and phone calls with all passes canceled. Work may be suspended and a marathon encounter held for 24 or 48 hours to bring the residents together. There are also minor crises over people wanting to split or actually splitting or over people engaging in negative behavior while on pass or being demoted for poor performance or negative attitudes on the job. The directors are on the job both day and night, sometimes working 16-hour days. Sometimes the residents are gotten out of bed in the middle of the night to discuss a special problem.

The sense of community is also built by the fact that there are a number of shared goals. Not only are the residents trying to get somewhere in terms of rehabilitating themselves, but there is a lot of work to be done. In addition to being responsible for maintaining the community, old buildings have to be rehabilitated, supplies have to be gotten from the outside, seminars, parties, and trips have to be arranged, and there are frequent visits from important people on the outside, including local and national politicians.

Another thing that helps to build a sense of community is the physical layout. All the residents of one house live together in close proximity. They eat together and work together. At Hart Island, although the residents of the four houses work at different jobs all over the Island, departments tend to be centered in individual houses, so that all of the people working in the landscaping department live in the same house.

THE EFFECTS

The ultimate goal, of course, of all narcotic treatment programs is abstention from drugs. Phoenix Houses also attempt to restructure defective personalities. Let us comment instead on some things that many of the residents do learn.

The residents do learn how to talk up, communicate their feelings, and relate to others. They overcome their fear of talking in front of groups. They learn how to accept criticism and to realize that criticism can be positive as well as negative. They become "aware." They learn how others see them. They learn to see themselves through the eyes of others. They learn proper work habits and how to adapt themselves to changing circumstances. They learn how to accept responsibility, and they are taught that one has to strive to move up. They also learn how to accept punishment and demotion.

The residents of Phoenix Houses learn to act as concerned, sensitive individuals who learn to think beyond their own immediate problems and to care about others. They learn to know other people's problems and how to help, and they also learn that other people care about them. To an extent we were able to measure this concern throughout the questionnaire. In response to the question, "Does it matter to you if any of the other guys (girls) stay off drugs when they leave here?" 83% of the Phoenix House residents answered "Yes."

They learn leadership. As they become older residents, they learn that the new residents will look up to them and expect advice and suggestions from them. To graduate to eldership (which we will not discuss in this chapter), one has to have held a position of some responsibility in the Phoenix House. We asked the residents: "Are you yourself a leader or do you hold any position in which you tell other residents what to do?" Sixty-nine percent of our respondents reported that they themselves felt that they were such leaders.

All of the above-mentioned are positive aspects. In addition, the Phoenix Houses manage to avoid most of the negative things found in confinement institutions. Homosexuality is not tolerated, and there is little homosexual behavior. When there is, it is usually brought out into the open, and participants are reprimanded. There are apparently no drugs in the community. There is no effort devoted toward preventing escapes because the people are made to feel that they are there on a voluntary basis. In confinement institutions, a great deal of creative energy goes into preventing escapes and curtailing drugs and homosexuality. Because these problems are more successfully dealt with at the Phoenix Houses, this energy is able to be channeled into other endeavors.

One of the major problems in confinement institutions is keeping people busy. This is not a problem in the Phoenix Houses. When they are not working or attending seminars or encounters, the residents are usually talking with each other and helping to solve personal problems. There is little TV watching or card playing. In one of the Phoenix Houses we studied, only 12% of the residents said that they had watched television on the preceding day, and only 10% said that they

had played cards, dominoes, or any game of that sort on the preceding day. The question was asked, "Can you tell me about your free time in general now? Do you think you have too much time with nothing to do, too little, or just enough free time?" Almost none of the Phoenix House residents reported too much free time, while 53% said they had too little. Where the residents in many confinement facilities lie on their beds in the evenings and sleep fairly long hours, the residents in the Phoenix Houses rarely go to bed before midnight.

The residents do not engage in much negative conversation. They don't talk about their life on the outside or drug use or criminal behavior or going back to drug use. Such conversation is discouraged.

NEGATIVE ASPECTS

There are negative aspects to the program, also. The program is quite inflexible. A person who has just experimented with drugs for a short time is required to spend just about as much time in a Phoenix House as a long-term drug user. Teenagers are expected to undergo the same regimen as are older residents. The program might do better by offering different modalities of treatment for people with different backgrounds and social histories.

All persons are expected to be able to assume leadership positions. This is unrealistic for all people, regardless of social class or level of education. One girl finally split from the program after a long history of being promoted to leadership positions and then being demoted. She liked the program and had grown in awareness and ability, but she just didn't like leadership roles. Everytime she was placed in one, she performed poorly. People should be prepared to become responsible followers as well as leaders.

People with criminal commitments coming in through the city jail are required to spend a long time in the induction phase at Riker's Island. The reason they spend a long time in jail is because of the shortage of space at Hart Island. Although some people spent a year in the induction phase at Riker's Island, this does not count toward the amount of time needed in the Phoenix House prior to reentry. This discriminates against people with criminal commitments. The induction phase, although modeled after Hart Island, is not the same because it is located in the compulsory environment of a prison and run on a 9 to 5 basis instead of a 24-hour basis.

The life in the Phoenix House is actually better in some ways than real life. It can be difficult for a person who has learned how to be honest and expect instant justice to accept relating to squares. Reentry attempts to accomplish this, but these problems are frequent complaints of Synanon graduates and may be expected to be complaints of Phoenix graduates.

Learning was originally downgraded. This was in part due to the antiprofessional orientation of addict-run therapeutic communities. They felt that since the professional does not really understand the problems of the addict, his education is of relatively little value. A young man who has dropped out of high school and is still in his teens might be told that it is more important to get himself together than to return to high school as a full-time student. Steps are being made to make education more important.

There is a great deal of conformity and brainwashing. One has to conform to the requirements of the program and not seek special attention or special prominence. This leads to the question, Do the people really believe in what they're saying and doing, or do they just do it to survive?

There is the belief that the person who leaves the program will go back to drugs and probably die. This may be functional in keeping people in the program, but it also helps to assure that those who do leave, even if they have spent a number of months in the program and undergone a lot of growth, will go back to drugs. They leave as outcasts, not in good standing, and therefore they may well have trouble getting a job or staying away from their old drug contacts.

A major criticism is that people are not really prepared to resume living in the real world. As Dr. Ramirez originally envisioned it, they would all become addiction specialists, and they wouldn't have to go back to monotonous jobs. But all of life contains monotony, tedium, frustration, and inequity. To cope with this is the problem of modern life. There is no other way to learn how to get along in the real world except by doing. We have found that many of the residents make excellent progress in the first months but then become disillusioned and split. They don't know if they can make it in the real world, but they resent confinement. They feel the program has nothing

more to offer them. "You learn all the games and you get tired of them," said one talented black who split unexpectedly after 9 months in the program.

A program whereby the residents worked in the community at regular jobs but came back to the house for support and help would be much more fruitful, especially after the first few months of total immersion. Then the biggest question, "Can I make it on the outside?" would be answered instead of postponed. Instead of the residents becoming angry at the program for confining them, they would lean on it for help in dealing with the problems which would become obvious to them as they attempted to live normal, unsupported lives.

The ideas of the complete cure and the graduate probably are misleading. The position in the alcoholism field of Alcoholics Anonymous is much more realistic. The former alcoholic, even if he has not had a drink for years, considers himself an alcoholic with the potential for regression. The same is clearly the case in the field of addiction. Every one of us has the potential for becoming a drug abuser, and the person who has seriously abused drugs once has a greater potential of returning to drug abuse than does the nonuser. What mixture of psychological and physiological forces is at work can only be speculated on but is not really crucial. In the past the drug abuser learned to resort to drugs when upset. If either the temptation or the trauma is too great, he may do so again.

The staff of therapeutic communities are experts at post hoc reasoning. I have engaged in many discussions about previously successful program graduates who have reverted to drug abuse. The usual explanation offered by staff is, "He wasn't together enough. We predicted this would happen." This implies that if the person had just done enough in the therapeutic community, stayed long enough, been honest enough about his problems, reached out enough for help, and in short followed the proscription of the program while in the program, he would have made a permanent successful adjustment and not reverted to drug abuse.

Whether or not a person reverts to drug abuse is probably more dependent on what happens to him in the community after he leaves than what happened to him while in the therapeutic community. Even the strongest program success can crack under sufficient pressure. Furthermore, it is not the end of the world. Rather it is the responsibility of the person who has reverted to realize that he is human, has stumbled, needs help, and is worthy of help, and it is the responsibility of the therapeutic community to respond to the person in trouble by other than the standard practice of shaving his head and making him start the program over again from the beginning. Furthermore, programs should offer crisis intervention and the possibility of short-term residential help to those who are shaky or worried but who have not resumed drug abuse.

Actually the therapeutic community phenomenon is at the same time better and worse than it appears. It is a positive experience for the person who accepts it and truly immerses himself in it while he is there. However, the basic idea that if one simply tries long enough and hard enough then drug abuse will be permanently cured is wrong.

Therapeutic communities yield insight and new methods of behavior to those who take them seriously. Some of the strongest ex-addicts I have met in methadone maintenance programs gained their insights and strength in therapeutic communities but still reverted to drug abuse. However, psychoanalysis has shown that insight and appropriate constructive behavior can vary independently of one another.

One of the principal problems of the ex-addict who has come through a therapeutic community is that he is likely to believe that he is a fraud. Although he may be insightful, able to communicate beautifully, and skilled in the area of group process, his self-image is much more based on what he has done in the past than on what he is capable of doing. This discrepancy between what he feels he is and what he is capable of doing may make him erect a shield so that strangers will not be able to penetrate beneath the facade. His self-image will only improve after years of productive living, and even then he will worry if he feels that he is expected to be perfect or that it is impossible for him to revert to drug abuse.

The playing down of the name and personality of the ex-alcoholic that Alcoholics Anonymous does is much more constructive and adaptive

than is the situation with the ex-addict. His need to be strident about how strong he is contributes further to this gap between what he truly feels he is and the image he must project. Perhaps the more desperate situation that ex-addicts were in at the time of founding of Synanon 12 years ago explains this bravado, but it is no longer productive or necessary. The strident superiority of ex-addict therapeutic community graduates turns many people off and makes it difficult for therapeutic communities to either modify their programs or cooperate with other modalities.

The false image of invincibility that the graduates feel they are supposed to project makes it extremely difficult to help them when they do revert to drug abuse.

What about cooperation between methadone maintenance and therapeutic communities?

Some methadone maintenance program people who have attempted to cooperate with therapeutic communities have reported that such cooperation has made it extremely difficult by the superiority that the Concept (e.g., therapeutic community) people feel or project.

The idea that methadone maintenance was an undesirable temporary crutch that the former Phoenix House and Synanon people brought to the Brooklyn Methadone Maintenance Program run by the Vera Institute of Justice went a long way to undermine the program. Jerome Jaffe's program in Chicago succeeded in meshing the two modalities because it was primarily a methadone maintenance program. Because they were in the majority, the methadone maintenance people were not immobilized by the insults and superiority of the Concept people. However, the Concept people were able to function because they had a great deal to contribute to every one of the patients whether or not they were drug free or on methadone maintenance.

ACKNOWLEDGMENT

The author wishes to acknowledge the entire Drug Abuse Study staff of the Columbia University Bureau of Applied Social Research and especially Carol Grossman and Dan Waldorf.

REFERENCES

1. **DeLong, J.,** Staff paper number 3, in *Dealing with Drug Abuse,* Praeger, New York, 1972.
2. **Brecher, E. M.,** *Licit and Illicit Drugs,* Little, Brown & Co., Boston, 1972, 82. For a summary of the 2-year follow-up of Phoenix House conducted by the author, see p. 80.
3. The Drug Abuse Treatment Information Project at Montclair State College directed by the author has completed the first phase of its research and issued a report, "The Impact of Drug Abuse Treatment on Criminality: A Look at 19 Programs." It is presently studying all phases of drug abuse treatment in New Jersey.
4. For a complete description of this study, see Waldorf, D., *Careers in Dope,* Prentice-Hall, Englewood Cliffs, N.J., 1973.
5. For a description of this concept, see Goffman, E., "On the Characteristics of Total Institutions" in Symposium in Preventive and Social Psychiatry, 1957.
6. These methods by which formal organizations enforce norms were first identified by Etzioni, A., A Comparative Analysis of Complex Organizations, Free Press, Glencoe, Ill., 1961.

CRISIS AND REACTION IN FIDUCIARY FUNCTIONS: TOWARDS THE SOCIOLOGY OF THE URINE TEST

Seymour Fiddle

TABLE OF CONTENTS

TECHNOLOGY AND EX-ADDICTION: THE BACKGROUND OF THE CERTIFICATION PROBLEM

With the authentic novelty of a cultural revolution, modern science has helped invent an unnoticed social reality — the technological control over tabooed consumption. Food restrictions, clothing limitations, and restrictive covenants about housing have marked most historical societies, but such patterns, typically, have been supported by and in turn supported a magical-religious structure.

The anthropologist Mary Douglas has observed that the Biblical prescriptions on food consumption were articulated with certain needs of the Hebrews: "By rules of avoidance," she has written, "holiness was given a physical expression in every encounter with the animal kingdom and at every meal. Observance of the dietary rules would have thus been a meaningful part of the great liturgical act of recognition and worship which culminated in the sacrifice in the Temple."[1]

In other cultures we have seen "the Establishment" intervene in individual consumption by punishing hunting on private land or consuming sacred totems.[2] And it is the cliché of the 20th century North American scene that the state has sought, with painful difficulty, to control indulgence in liquor and "drugs." But only in the 1960s, so far as I know, has a society, deeply disturbed by sumptuary patterns, stimulated the perfection of a laboratory technique to discipline the pattern-followers. Only in the United States in the 1960s and 1970s has the reality of a sociopsychological status, ex-addiction, come to depend on test-tube evidence. Only here in time has a man's history come to be defined, in part at least, as a continuum of "positives" or "negatives" and produced an apparatus which starts from the human production of urine and ends in the human reaction to a set of verbal and behavioral translations of a technician's perceptions and reports. Only here has test tubery generated a severe human problem in halfway houses oriented towards abstinence.

In the 1970s there are likely to be tens of thousands of men and women — I believe I am speaking conservatively — who will be submitting their urine, routinely, under the watchful eye of an impassive other who is obliged to scrutinize this customarily private act with technical objectivity to certify that the urine to be packaged and dispatched to the laboratory did, in fact, issue from the person whose name was on the label of the bottle.

The human urine-watcher, like the urinators themselves, has become part of an evidential apparatus whose centerpiece is thin layer chromatography. What is unique about the human reality of ex-addiction, therefore, is that it is generated by a kind of state-subsidized psychochemical polygraphy, daily reporting of a person's body language to answer the question, "What drugs did you use yesterday, if any?" Naturally the urinator is also asked this question orally by some human agent who duly records his answer, but over the years there has been a tendency for organizations to rely more and more on the formalized dialogue between body (the urine language) and test tube (chemical language) which takes place under a system of rigid commands and prohibitions, delays, affirmations, denials, and identifications.

In the pages which follow I seek to trace the sociological and social-psychological aspects of this alien dialogue as it has affected the human participants in one particular abstinence-oriented program, Exodus House. I would call attention to the remarkable parallelism between this experience of technological intervention and the general experience of modern man with technology, the limits on its use and the manner in which it brings us remorselessly into the region of the impossible, where human beings are compelled to live with the necessity or at least convenience of accepting limits well below the maximum possible, on pain of suffering disastrous "feedback" or the panic of the absurd.

Since it is the staff of a program which must make decisions based on controversial laboratory results, they transform a dialogue into a polylogue, in which they rather than remote laboratory technicians must bear the pressures generated.

Leaving for the end of this chapter a closer study of larger issues, let us address ourselves to the ex-addiction which is the goal of the certification process whose problematic character is our prime subject. For the graduate of a contemporary abstinence-oriented addict rehabilitation center, the root equation is *not, "I abstain from drugs; therefore, I am an ex-addict,"* but, *"We abstain; therefore, there is ex-addiction."* For aside from the well-known fallacies in the first, Cartesian phrasing (the equivocal nature of "I" for instance), the second is the deeper social reality.[3] The man who is looking for a position in an office or explaining himself to a new girlfriend is hoping he will be accepted, not as a oddball of a "new breed" (a term used in the early 1960s), but as one of a growing mass who no longer need to use the hard drugs on which they formerly depended.

"We abstain; therefore, there is ex-addiction" is nonetheless still a claim, one shadowed by public doubt, perhaps not Descartes' hyperbolic doubt but doubt withal. The public has been subjected to a wave of information propaganda which makes a contrary assumption. The proponents of the methadone program, even in recent reticent formulations, have come to argue that whatever the long-term costs and dangers of methadone, admittedly still unknown in 1971, they will be smaller than they would be without methadone. Otherwise, so the claim runs, these thousands of maintained men and women would be stealing and dying in far greater proportions. Better a chemicalized ward of the state than a predaceous junkie seems to be the methadone program formula for their "ex-addicts."

Thus, "We abstain; therefore, there is ex-addiction" may not be taken as an uncontroversial claim. What indeed do we mean by "abstention from drugs"? Are we equating it with nonusage? Just certain drugs? Do we strive for perfection? Or will we institutionalize a range of tolerance and procedures for providing for the inevitable "slips," time-worn aspects of the alcoholic-ex-alcoholic career? To abstain from drugs, I would suggest, is an existential act marked by several dimensions, several questions asked by a person: (1) *Definition* — What do I mean by drugs? (2) *Hedonism* — Do I get pleasure from drugs? (3) *Access* — Can I obtain drugs? (4) *Need* — Do I depend upon drugs? (5)

Accountability — Must I justify my drug use to some authority or higher principle? (6) *Morality* — Do I feel I shouldn't take drugs? (7) *Image and Ideology* — Do I picture drugs and drug-taking as dangerous or harmless? Do I believe the drug laws are rational or irrational? Do I see drug addicts as sinful, criminal, sick, victimized, or just like anyone else? (8) *Praxis* — How often, if at all, do I take drugs? (9) *World Picture* — How do drugs affect my perception of time and space?

One could easily formulate a wide variety of types of ex-addicts on the basis of their answers to questions tapping these dimensions. For our purposes, however, it suffices that ultimately each ex-addict finds his own private answers to the questions and that each program staff also seeks some standard answers in setting up qualifications by which it will "certify" ex-addicts. This is the essence of what I shall call their fiduciary function. Hence the "we" in "we abstain" must be expanded to include the staff and a second formula added: "We monitor the abstinence; therefore, there is ex-addiction."

It is the staff which must, day by day, handle the contradictions and fascinations generated by the task assigned them: to help control the drug-taking epidemic. It is the staff which plays collective host to the addict population, holding out to *any* heroin-taking person the chance to enter on a unique modern adventure in which, like the young would-be knights of courtly romances, they are to prove themselves. The collective host cannot explain to the new members the peculiar periods of the therapeutic adventure and can only hope that, in time, they will come to see how some of the virtues praised, but not necessarily practiced, in the streets — courage, loyalty, and honor — can be transformed and relegitimated in a rehabilitation context. Providing an ordered world with its own elite and anguish, one key element being the urine test, the staff would help emancipate the young risk-taker from the driven yet random world of the street. By definition, the process of self-selection yields it own elite, expressed as the top group of a member hierarchy that receives its scientific but not infallible basis in that test. The whole scene — a therapeutic host, young adventurers proving themselves during an epidemic, a house with a urine test and groups in round table, and an alien laboratory form — composes a surrealistic poem, whose title, inevitably, would be *Chanson de Peste*.[4]

In the pages which follow, I am investigating one aspect of the dimension of ex-addiction, accountability, and how members and staff reacted to problems of daily urine giving and taking and to the idea of a chronology of laboratory "positives" and "negatives," each "positive" being interpreted officially as a kind of discontinuity in the narrative of a member's history. In a stabilized agency, as I shall indicate the "positives," the discontinuities are seen as disturbances which come to dominate the "narrative" of an individual's program history. The "negatives" come to be accepted as a matter of course; the "positives" are more like the gaps in a tale told to a psychoanalyst; they insist on being filled.

How they are filled in Exodus House constitutes one part of the subject matter of the following pages. How they are not fillable, how the social and cultural organization of urine-testing processes generates its own impossibilities, is another part. I shall argue that this encounter with the impossible may prove to be part of the therapeutic reality of an addiction rehabilitation center. Certainly it becomes the focus of much soul-searching and ideological work by the staff and members of Exodus House.

This analysis seeks to explore the urine-testing-and-taking process *as it was experienced* at the local level, both by the addicts who were at risk and the staff committed to make decisions on the basis of laboratory returns. Such a grassroots sociology of knowledge, be it noted, is not tethered to the issue of the truth or falsity of those returns. A biochemist might well be outraged, bemused, or amused by the folklore among the ex-addicts and addicts. He might be tempted to believe that he could "straighten out" the members of programs, its staff, the participant observer, and so on.

The sociologist, however, who is committed to the examination and analysis of the meanings of phenomena on an everyday basis and to the sources and consequences of those meanings in everyday behavior, soon learns that the existence or nonexistence of a veridical reality is only one variable affecting the course of the urine-taking-and-testing process. Rational authoritative statements will be interpreted, all too often, in the light of the actual life of the interpreter and not the biochemist's. The interpreter, be he or she a patient or staff member, may, of course, be reflecting the misconceptions of the nature of the urine-taking process. In view of the importance of objective analysis in any treatment situation, especially one involving large numbers of patients, it is regrettable that there are so many misconceptions about what is involved in urine testing.

FOUR VALIDATION MODELS

By the term *fiduciary social agent,* we mean an organization expected to certify that some body or individual(s) has successfully passed certain tests. Not all treatment organizations play this societal role. Traditional prisons claim only that prisoners are not committing crimes in prison; they do not certify that a man who has left their walls has been evaluated and found changed significantly "for the better" toward a legitimate life. At best, such punitive organizations would impressionistically certify that a man had somehow survived a peculiar discipline and "had paid the price" for the crimes of which he had been found guilty by a court.

In contrast, a modern addiction treatment program, whether oriented around the goals of abstinence or of social and personal change or of all three, gets part of its justification by certifying in a characteristic way that its "graduates" in good standing have passed a number of obstacles. They have changed and are changing in what the program defines as highly desirable ways, after going through a continuum of obstacles and rewards designed to encourage these changes. Such programs are fiduciary social agents which seek to have their certifications recognized officially by governmental agencies. I am going to argue that the certification processes continually run the risks accruing in the region of the impossible, with consequences varying according to the stability of the program itself.

The chief "claim" of abstinence certification* is that a man or woman who has undergone the program of treatment and received his or her certificate is and has been drug-free for a significantly long time, as shown by adequate evidence. There are several ways to validate a claim that someone is not using drugs: (1) behavioral model,

(2) chemical model, (3) ocular model, (4) comprehensive model.

In what might be called the *behavioral model,* a man or woman is continually under observation for a long period of time and subjected to varying degrees of interpersonal examination, one part of which is informally focused on the potentiality that he might still be involved in drugs. The Synanon movement, the ideal type of the behavioral model, refuses to employ any "artificial" chemical or physical tests to determine if a particular person, or any group of their members, is indulging in drugs of any kind. Such a model also places great faith in the capacity of ex-addicts to see whether, in fact, someone is using drugs.

A fiduciary social agent that rests its case solely on a history of close contact and the expertise of the ex-addict runs into conflict with the norms of a so-called rationalistic society demanding scientific criteria of evaluation.[5]

The pure chemical mode of certifying that a man is not using drugs occurs in some parole programs. A parolee's urine is tested at regular but infrequent intervals if a parole officer suspects his client is indulging occasionally. (Provision is made for "surprise" checks.) Nalline may be used or thin layer chromatography or any other chemical test that may issue from the chemist's brain and laboratory. Under one version of this mode, a man is not told if his urine is returned positive but is allowed to continue on parole and his urine is returned subjected to testing, the results being recorded. The hope of this submodel is that the man will voluntarily stop using after awhile. Under a second submodel, a man is told as soon as he tests positively, and what happens to him depends on a transaction between the parole department and the man. Both of these submodels blend certification and control: The same test used by the treatment agency as evidence for releasing a man from his parole conditions serves to keep him under external control on the theory it will be internalized.

The pure *chemical model* also occurs in the methadone programs where newcomers to the maintenance idea have their urine taken daily. For

---

*It appears that the Rio Piedras program in Puerto Rico, originated by Dr. E. Ramirez, instituted the idea of certification and that thanks to its intimate governmental ties was able to transform the certificate received by a successful program member into a kind of diploma, permitting its holder to enter governmental positions or to pursue courses of study, e.g., medicine, which might otherwise have been denied him because of his drug record. Theoretically there might also be a nonabstinence treatment certificate. A man in a maintenance program might pursue a course of training and treatment and, at its conclusion, receive a "certification" which would not allude to his drug maintenance needs. Or, under a changed public opinion, it might even do so. The idea of certification, in short, is not tied to a particular set of program goals.

those who stay in the program, the frequency of urine testing is diminished. Since I shall devote considerable space to the manner in which urine testing takes us into the region of the relatively impossible, I will turn to the next model.

Under the system described above, the officer does not have to rely on ocular cues alone to justify his decisions as worker in a fiduciary agency. However, in the *ocular model*, found among law enforcement agencies in the past, the parole or probation officer who determines a man's chance for freedom would have him roll up his sleeves to inspect his "tracks." If he saw any indication of a break in a man's skin, it would constitute evidence of recent drug involvement. Other criteria might be distortion of a man's eyes, the color of his skin, his general physical condition (including his weight), and the state of his clothing.

The pure ocular model has been a two-person game wherein efficiency, if any, depended on the qualities of the two persons playing it. Anyone in the addiction field knows of instances in which men were able to pass inspection for awhile through *sniffing* heroin and maintaining a small habit. On the other hand, there were occasional cases of possible injustice due to misinterpretation by an over eager officer of what he took to be evidence, especially if he had stereotypes about addicts and addiction.

But therapeutically speaking, the most serious drawback to the ocular approach, "eyeball to eyeball," is that the potential certifier became emotionally involved with his client because he was functioning as an actual controller. The pride of the evaluator, his belief in his capacity to keep from being outwitted by the "scheming addict," might easily prevent objective assessment of the facts. If the evaluator sees the patient every day in an open setting, it is unlikely that he will notice the subtle changes of occasional drug use.

The *comprehensive model* of a fiduciary social agent developed at Rio Piedras, modified at Exodus House in New York, involves pharmacological, physical, psychological, and social (interpersonal) criteria for evaluating a man's drug involvement and establishing with him a history of drug-free living. But experience shows that there is *considerable* dependence on the chemical test. I wish to explore in depth certain structural crises implicit in this model, especially as that test relates

scientific to impressionistic criteria at Exodus House.

Before moving into the residence, a man gives urine daily for 10 days or so. Once in the house, "giving it up" is a daily affair, formerly conducted under the eye of an ex-addict, presently conducted under the supervision of a nonaddict staff member. Experience has revealed that even though heroin is said to stay in a person's system for 72 hours, contemporary bags are so "weak" that alternate-day testing is unreliable. When he moves out of the house, a man continues daily testing until he reaches the highest level of the program. Then testing tapers off until it is no longer given. At that point he is *certified* if he is also gainfully employed or embarked on some long-term schooling. He is given a certificate which can be, and has been, framed and hung in a man's apartment.

However, the model is comprehensive. For months at a time a man is under observation for many hours during the day by his friends. The program calls for his attendance at meetings and sociability occasions where a variety of people, some of whom have known him when he was using drugs, will see him.

He is also given compulsory physical examinations while in the house plus batteries of tests in which his conduct under pressure can be recorded. He is part of group therapy processes in which every aspect of his life comes under group scrutiny, both by professionals and ex-addicts.

Having said all this, I must repeat that it is the urine test which is situated at the center of the model. The triadic relationship — program member, urine testing process, program staff — appears to place the middle member of the triad, and especially the laboratory, in the position of a remote, silent psychoanalyst who merely records what the urine (chemical dreams, so to speak) really says. Like the classical analyst, the laboratory focuses around a kind of incest taboo, only *this* prohibition is against drugs, and the laboratory, an invisible, inaudible human being, seeks to support the "Drug Complex," not to clarify its behavioral repercussions. The laboratory simply links bottle content to bottle label and leaves it to agencies to link the label to someone's penis (and presumably someone's current drug pattern). Unlike the Freudian, the laboratory becomes involved with penis rejection rather than penis envy.

Hence, the laboratory report cannot reflect nor depend upon the queuing up and mocking banter which precedes and accompanies urine taking; it cannot take into account the anxiety each man registers: Is his bottle sterilized? Does it bear his name? Is the bottle securely closed and safe from tampering or unnatural decomposition? It cannot know or reckon with his worry that a clerk will blunder along the line. The laboratory is a structuralist's ideal reporting the timeless truth of a man's responses to the forces to which he has been subjected.

Nonetheless, both staff and program members at times have been vexed by the manner in which the fiduciary role has been played at Exodus House. If we examine the source of their complaints, we may understand the possibilities and impossibilities of the fiduciary role in addiction treatment, first in the trust which the staff sought to elicit from program members and second in the confidence they aimed to build in the public.

THE TWO "HANG-UPS": FALSE POSITIVES AND FALSE NEGATIVES

False positives occur when a laboratory reports someone used drugs but the person named denies it or some nonchemical evidence is adduced that he did not use drugs on that date. False negatives occur when the laboratory reports no use of drugs but a person not named admits he used or there is other evidence he did. These are the principal foci of complaints about the chemical test in the comprehensive model. It is fair to say that, over the years, they have been among the most important sources of friction in the Exodus House program, especially between staff and members. As the program has become more institutionalized, these complaints have tended to lose their structural impact.

The False Positive

In an earlier publication,[6] it was noted that members of a program might play upon the ambiguities of test results, especially as these ambiguities are felt by the staff or a program. A false positive can indeed become a crisis of conscience for both staff and members alike. In

numerous staff meetings and conversations around a laboratory-reported positive, the following patterns of staff interpretation have emerged: (1) *Test Validation* — A minority of the staff already had or claimed to have had some evidence that a program member had been taking drugs. The test verified what otherwise could have been an inchoate feeling that might not be transmitted into action because of the guilty member's persuasiveness. (2) *Denial* — The positive report of the laboratory ran counter to the feeling of the majority of the staff. They were sure that there was some error. They therefore suggested rechecking.* (3) *Staff Confusion and Uncertainty* — For any of a variety of circumstances, there was no consensus or near consensus on the meaning of a laboratory report. An "A-level" member in question might be going to school and appearing only twice a week for therapy and urine at the highest level of our program. Conceivably he could be "taking off" during the rest of the week. But he was at the "highest level." It made no sense. Besides which, he could have taken off on a day which would be more than 72 hours from the urine-taking day if he really wanted to; on the other hand, he had had a "breakdown" in the course of the program, so a recheck was called for. The retest was negative, and the staff breathed easier.

But then there was the member who by 1969 had spent about a year and a half like a yoyo, going up to the program hierarchy, then taking drugs, admitting it, and falling back. He now had apparently made a complete change and was headed upward. One day his urine came back positive and remained positive on rechecking. He was able, to his satisfaction, to account for all of his time on the day in which the "shot" must have taken place. Members of the staff were with him during the period in question. The writer, his therapist, had seen no special evidence of any use of drugs nor any new problem for a man who was always wrestling with problems. His taking a drug made no sense. Still, did it ever make sense? The director, explaining his stand to the member, noted that regardless of personal feeling, he had no choice but to follow the laboratory report. The member accepted the demotion which followed and worked his way back up. But he had many

*Out of such reaction came the pattern of delaying action on a specific urine until a *bridge* had been established, meaning that Exodus House received a report of the urine on the day before and after the urine in question had been received.

confused sympathizers on the staff. The comprehensive model thus contained the seeds of contradictions between impersonal and personal evidentiary techniques.

Confusion and staff denial are the reactions which most peril the functioning of a treatment organization. They highlight the contrasting life situations of staff and members. They symbolize the reality that even as Exodus House strives to become a therapeutic community, emphasizing the goals of drug abstinence and enhanced mental health and growth, one part of the organization (the staff) not only judges the other but is also obliged to believe in the laboratory in order to reduce the chance of error. Reliance on perfection of a laboratory technique becomes one more utopian element in a therapeutic utopia.

Because of their intrinsic ambiguity, false positives lend themselves to use as factional weapons where cliques develop within an addiction treatment program. Thus, during the spring and summer of 1967, a conflict between two top Exodus House staff members resulted in now one, now the other assuming the relative and absolute reins of power. Members of each clique, including the writer, tended to interpret the laboratory results according to whether they were "in" power or "out." The "out" faction, unconsciously or consciously trying to show that the "ins" did not know how to administer the program, tended to believe that the false positives were real positives, especially for those members who had aligned with the "in." And the "ins" did the reverse. The writer recalls vividly a staff meeting in which he was outvoted on a decision to "shoot" a man down for a positive, without giving him the full benefit of the doubt. The man had antagonized the head of an opposing clique. Significantly, he did react as the writer had anticipated and left the program, ultimately becoming an ex-addict worker in a court program. During this period of anguish, the staff was asked to submit its urine as a check on the lab. When one member of a clique received a positive, each clique had a different interpretation. Whereas his clique said it was a false positive showing laboratory error, the opposing clique saw it as a true positive and evidence of his involvement in drugs.

The False Negative

The false negative is disconcerting to the staff and to the program member who has thoroughly absorbed the program ideology and looks for certification based on a history of drug-free conduct. If the laboratory continually fails to register a postive when a man has actually taken drugs, it must follow that the man has found a way to "beat the test" to "beat the system." The actualization of a magical wish, it fulfills the addict's belief that he really is superior to the squares and bewilders the staff which has come to rely upon this outside, rational, impartial authority to assist it in evaluating and "moving" members. The ingenuity of the addicted deviant expertise has traditionally been turned to snubbing bureaucratic authority. The history of these so-called false negatives illuminates how addiction treatment becomes involved in the *region of the impossible*, for it becomes factually impossible for the staff or even other program members to be sure of what actually took place in these situations.

Even before the staff at Exodus House had decided to make use of urine tests, there was evidence that where tests are designed to control conduct, some addicts try to outmaneuver them. Information from the California experience with the nalline test had come via the grapevine to the writer in 1962. He was told that the injection of salt was allegedly nullifying the nalline. Was this belief just more addict folklore? After Exodus House finished its first experimental intensive program with alternate-day urine testing (1965), the writer was told by a former member that several key members of that original program had apparently passed the test by drinking quantities of beer and urinating frequently. In addition, they had played all manners of games, being sick or claiming inability to give urine on certain days. Although the staff had believed some men were not using, he claimed they all had been and that we had been badly fooled.

In the second phase of the Exodus House program (1965–), there was a "tightening up" of the urine testing process, with great attention paid to the supervision by ex-addicts. Reports were filtering in about other programs indicating that, at least in one of them, there was a regular "piss-market" where program members would buy "clean urine" and then skillfully substitute it for their own. At Exodus House, mirrors over urinals appeared to permit the ex-addict observing urination to detect any trickery. In addition, staff members let it be known that they knew games were being played on Exodus House. As early as 1966, one man trying to get a reference from us as an "ex-addict" turned in urine in a bottle which was identical in all but one small detail to that used by the House. He was told about it indirectly and never came back, unfortunately, because he was so embarrassed at being seen through, as was his bottle. It was evident that administering a testing program to preserve a drug-free utopia entailed expensive gamesmanship on both sides.

The problem of the false negative reached what the staff considered dangerous proportions in the winter of 1967–68 when one member of the program, out of a mixture of destructive and constructive impulses, claimed that he was privy to a process that seemed to work against the test. Both he and another program member, one who at the time was in poor standing, confidentially told the writer about their "trick." One could drink a large quantity of vinegar after taking a shot, nothing more. Extra gamesmanship was alleged. The man who first used the vinegar claimed he had tried to mystify the other by pretending that secret ingredients were involved, but that was because, he said, he felt he did not want to hurt the other man by giving him the guilty knowledge.

In the months that followed, there was continual, almost ulcerating, uncertainty about the vinegar. A special meeting found previous members asking pointed questions. The director could only say the staff was seeking information from the chemists. In fact, the chemists generally derided the story as magical thinking and nonsense, counter to scientific reality. But none was prepared to make a crucial test.

Finally, an opportunity arose, or seemed to arise, in the summer of 1968. A young man in residence, J. S., left on pass and came back to say, in a very chagrined manner, that he had taken a shot that afternoon and had swallowed a large quantity of vinegar. The following day he gave his urine and then was moved out of the house for a period of time. His urine was sent to the laboratory. Days passed and, in the interim, staff members would ask or be asked by program members if the urine report had come back. One day it came back, negative! The director, making the announcement in staff meeting, declared that the men should not be told about the finding. He noted that the result at least showed that the laboratory erred on the side of fairness to the men. There was no comment by any of the staff.

Was such a negative report conclusive? No, because it so happens that a man might buy a bag of heroin which contained almost no heroin. If he had been "clean," he might get some kind of reaction, especially from its adulterant material, e.g., quinine. The test might not register the microscopic amounts, and some laboratories might not test for quinine, which could also indicate resort to drugs. Moreover, there was only the word of the man himself that he had taken a shot. There was evidence that he was looking for an excuse to move out of the house because he could not take its tensions and also wanted to be in contact with his friends on the street. He admitted that he subsequently had obtained an ounce of heroin to sell. Could it be that he lied about using heroin in order to prepare the path for his departure? In a young man of 17, such conduct would not be astonishing.

Thus, the mystery of the vinegar technique remained and seemed destined to remain in the absence of some specially arranged experiment. Here again the program found itself in the region of the impossible. It was considered impossible to check out the competing hypotheses. Interviews by formal questionnaire indicated there was some measure of uncertainty among program people about the value of the test, but none seemed ready to put the test down as complete tomfoolery. Perhaps they wished to believe there was a way to separate the men from the boys and to give a valid certification when the time was right in a man's life. When the staff experienced anxiety, the program members appeared to react, there being no way to guarantee absolute validity of a laboratory test. When, however, the staff formally underscored acceptance of the lab report as valid, and stuck to it even in "hard cases," the program members appeared to become less anxious. At least those "projecting" their uncertainties about the very idea of rehabilitation appeared to have taken heart from the staff's stabilization.

SOCIAL FACTORS GENERATING PROGRAM MEMBER UNCERTAINTY ABOUT THE URINE TEST

We have noted that the chemical test is only one element of the comprehensive model used at Exodus House. Ironically, however, in the first period of the program it was the one element generated the most conflict with the other elements. It most pointedly opened up the program to public inspection. A source of great strength, the urine test could also introduce much collective insecurity in a fiduciary agent.

Like so many addiction treatment centers, Exodus House has increasingly been supported by state funds. Even its urine-testing program has been subsidized by and accountable to the New York State Narcotic Addiction Control Commission. This has meant that changes in policy and funding for the Commission and changes in policy of the Commission have affected the urine-testing program in a manner over which the program has had little control. Thus, there was a period in the winter of 1967–68, precisely the period in which vinegar began to be used, when access to laboratories was restricted because of budgetary reduction. (In earlier years there had been a period in which laboratories closed for repairs or became inaccessible, partly, it seemed, due to political gamesmanship on the city level.*) In the summer of 1968, there was a period of several weeks before contracts between state and voluntary agencies were concluded. This immediately eliminated the use of state-sponsored urine-testing programs involving California laboratories. The director was forced to explain to the men that for some period there would not be regular urine testing but spot checks (or a Russian roulette system) with which each man would have to take his chances. There would be no "double checks" because there simply was not space available to store the urine for the time needed to make the check.

In the period after this announcement, there was a temporary rise in the anxiety level of the men in the program, as registered by the writer in his therapy group. Those who already were uncertain of the efficiency of the laboratories felt an enhanced chill: the false positive could not be checked. They were that much more at the mercy of the alien lab technician, the hired servant of the distant health bureaucracy. Some clerk errone-

ously copying the records might disrupt their lives. For all these anxieties, the Exodus House staff had no good answer. It was impossible to make a daily check on workers in a distant laboratory. If there was a credibility gap, how could it be overcome?

Reports from a remote scientific bureaucracy are received by a staff who in varying degree are in constant person-to-person interaction with the subjects of these reports. To inform a man that he has received a positive becomes a very disagreeable task, especially if the bearer of the message is not sure in his own mind of the man's reactions. By an unconscious evolution, and silent consensus, the group therapist or orientor has been asked to bring the bad news, if the occasion permits, and he does so in a group context. This tends to identify the group leader as a defender of the laboratory, as well as an element of the fiduciary system, in a way that does not necessarily further the therapeutic process.

A further paradox lies within intimacy of relationship and capacity to judge whether the program member is in fact using drugs. On the one hand, the staff member can correctly and honestly say that someone using drugs is likely to be detected by those who are constantly in contact with him. At the same time, in contradiction with that, there is the familiarity effect I have earlier noted.

Daily contact tends to lower the staff member's guard; he might not notice subtle changes in a man living in the street and coming around occasionally. One becomes biased in favor of a program member and, if candid with oneself, feels the need to supplement behavioral and ocular evidence with the impersonal chemical evidence derived from a complete, but competent, stranger. Yet it is just this kind of impersonal, outside evidence, sought from the laboratory, which has been brought into question by the history of Exodus House experience.** One seemed damned if he did and damned if he did not supplement the "human" experiences of the therapeutic community by the impersonal

*Exodus House experience with private testing firms has not been a happy one. In 1966–67 one firm produced a rash of positives on men who were considered cured of their addiction. There was some evidence that their testing methods were rather gross. At least the Exodus House staff so concluded, eventually.

**In the winter of 1967–68, the writer received rumors that other programs had been besieged by the same problem, although their professional staff might not have been aware of the attack. One city program had men going out on pass, and, allegedly, the men were getting away with using heroin because they ingested vinegar. A state program based in a local hospital was being burlesqued, it was said, by these tactics. So, too, was the methadone program. Unfortunately, there was no way to check on the existence and quantity of such addict manipulation of tests. The Quaker halfway house reported that at one point there had been a "raid" on its supplies of vinegar. Whether or not the "formula" worked, it was being used. Was there a self-fulfilling prophecy?

judgments of physical science. And a program which speaks the language of existentialist humanism and structuralism subjects its staff and members to tension between being helpful and being right, between interpersonal understanding and natural science detective work. It was in danger of breaking out into a moral crisis.

In a larger sense, it would seem, Exodus House was experiencing the limitations of its "scientific" perspective, consisting of disinterested observation, radical doubt, and stress on clarification and understanding and objectivity of tone, which were being turned by program members and staff against the scientific laboratory itself. The issue was would they ever be able to adopt a "common sense" perspective, i.e., one of fully engaged, practical participation, suspended doubt, pragmatism, and a feeling for a vivid present in a public world?[7] As we shall see, by and large this has taken place.

SOME MECHANISMS FOR MANAGING TENSIONS IN THE REGION OF THE IMPOSSIBLE

We have been examining an organization dominated by addiction specialists who have developed a "therapology," a body of knowledge producing special competence in working with addicts, as well as a vested interest in that therapology. We would predict that the problem of false positives and false negatives would be met by some fairly institutionalized ideological and behavioral mechanisms to bring the staff's own professional ideals into harmony with the realities of their work, to permit them to persist in their functioning with some degree of moral and mental balance. We would expect members gradually to adopt comparable mechanisms. *Specifically, they all would have to learn to live with the reality that it was impossible to remove some areas of doubt about the urine-testing.* These mechanisms were more apparent in early than later years thanks to the growing institutionalization and stabilization of the program.

The first, though not necessarily the most prominent, mechanism was *the appeal to the higher principle of organizational protection.* Much of the anguish recorded above had to do with the concern of staff members for the possible damage they might be doing to individual program members. Shifting the focus from the existential

implications of specific laboratory reports about specific individuals to the total value of the laboratory system for the entire program, a staff member could more easily take his emotional strain. He could admit the possibility, even the inevitability, of false positives and false negatives and still feel that a defective laboratory system was better than none at all, if such an alternative could be contemplated for a program based in the community and exposed to the addict culture.

Thus, during the spring of 1967, there were persistent grapevine reports about a New York addiction program which made a point of *not* testing its men and women but relying upon behavioral and ocular evidence alone. The reports, gradually validated by underground evidence, indicated that some of that program's ex-addicts were in fact using drugs of various kinds. Later on, in the winter of 1967–68, under the weight of a fund shortage, the same kind of ocular and behavioral evidence was used in that program to weed out those members using. Exodus House members who heard of this approach argued that an arbitrary impersonal system derived from laboratory results was preferable to an arbitrary personal system based on biased perception. The writer repeatedly heard this theme: It is impossible to run a program in the street without systematic use of the urine test. "You might as well fold up your tents and go away," said the Reverend Lynn Hageman, Exodus House Director, in one conversation.

The principle of organizational protection was invoked, unconsciously, even by those men and women who complained that a false positive might be caused by inefficiency or incompetence in the handling of urine at the Exodus House level, e.g., on the part of the urine collectors. Although they might publicly inveigh about how easy it is to pick up bottles and substitute them or how a particular ex-addict is sloppy about the way in which he supervises the men as they urinate, these men were thinking not only of themselves but also of the need to keep the system of urine testing and the therapeutic community intact. *The maintenance of the program was one of the values shared by the staff and members and permitted both segments of Exodus House to keep the disquieting laboratory reports in a comfortable perspective, thereby continuing their faith in the value of certifying addict conduct the Exodus House way.* "No matter what I personally believe," a staff member would say, "you see I've got to accept the lab report because it's the best thing we have to go on." And the program members would tend to agree if properly oriented. "I can dig it," they would say, "even though I don't like it."

The second mechanism for managing tension from disagreeable laboratory reports was to *emphasize the unreliability of the addicts generally while allowing for the reliability and sincerity of particular addicts.* For instance, the staff had passed on the observation to program members, as well as to interested outsiders, that rarely had a man who received a positive admitted it was true. This pattern of addict denial began to look ridiculous in the members' eyes because it made such a great demand on the credibility of people brought up in a civilization dominated by the scientific and technological methods. A laboratory could be wrong, probably is wrong, in a small percentage of cases, but to expect that in 99% of the alleged errors it was wrong suggested that many of the so-called false positives were *not* false and that any member making the claim was "putting the staff on." This phenomenon bolstered general faith in the laboratory so that even *plausible* addict claims boomeranged against the evidence. The pattern of denial had pushed the test disbelievers into the region of the impossible; they lost credibility.

If some men seemed to the staff, and even to program members, to have a particular interest in sowing doubt to wreck the program, staff members would be heard saying that so and so had a reason for not believing that any rehabilitation program is feasible.

Thus, one of the writer's long-time drug acquaintances came around to pay his annual visit in the spring of 1968. The conversation naturally turned to the men currently in the program. The informant, who had a steady unblemished career of using drugs, even in hospitals and occasionally even in prison, skeptically commented that Exodus House claims about its men being off drugs were exaggerated. He stoutly insisted he had evidence that some of the program members were using drugs, even pointing out one across the street. Efforts to pin him down to details of time and place failed. He alluded vaguely to ways of hiding a shot, but, on the writer's suggesting the use of beer or vinegar, he simply shook his head and would say no more.

Later the writer reported the episode in detail to the staff and a number were able to discount the alleged evidence. One argument was that this man couldn't bear the idea of others actually staying clean on the street because it would put his whole ideology in jeopardy. ("When I'm ready to go off stuff, I'll go off; I don't need a program, it can't help me.") Another staff member felt that his time periods were unreliable, that he might have been talking about how some members of the program, during periods in which they were "mobilized," had in fact taken drugs. Comparably, in therapy sessions, especially in "pretherapy," it was common to hear men agree that you really could not believe a guy who had been "shooting junk" just a few weeks before. However, this argument did not hold too well at the "upper levels."

The third mechanism for handling disagreeable laboratory reports was to *attribute their apparent defects to some administrative failure over which the laboratory had no control.* In discussing the fact that some of the men in the first experimental Exodus House program (1963 to 1965) apparently had been able to get away with using drugs, one staff member noted that urine was then collected only three times a week, on alternate days, giving ample scope for manipulation. During a joint staff-members meeting, a man admitted that some 6 months before, he had taken a shot, had given urine, and no positive had been noted. He had taken a drink of vinegar, he said. In trying to discount the effect of this man's report, staff members noted that he had given his urine during a period when, thanks to temporarily decreased access to lab facilities, much collected urine was never submitted for tests. It was likely that this man's urine was among the samples not submitted. Hence, the laboratory would not have had a chance to detect his using. For the man involved, such a mechanism would be something he would have to accept as beyond his control: the region of the impossible.

A fourth mechanism for making unpleasant laboratory reports more palatable to both staff and members was to argue that *whatever might be the temporary effects of the report on a specific individual, it could become a positive influence in the long run.*

This mechanism may also be understood as a deduction from the Exodus House existentialist handling of the utopian problem which generally takes the following shape: "The world outside is an unfair one. We at Exodus House do not pretend to be fair. We are concerned with rehabilitation, not justice. We don't believe in falsifying reports because that would be playing games with people's lives. But a false positive, if a man can adapt himself to it, can be just what he needs to mobilize his resources and come back for more. Unintentionally, it is a way of preparing him for the hard knocks and unfairnesses of the world from which, as an addict, he was trying to escape into a fool's paradise. It may be a false positive, but he can make it into an affirmative stage of his life."

Among some program members this came to be called a "therapeutic positive" if they believed it was something done intentionally by staff. Others, "paranoids," saw it as untherapeutic. But the staff itself appeared to have come to accept these situations as having an unintended benefit.

In the earlier years of urine testing, when the staff had not yet arrived at a fuller awareness of the logic of reliance on such a technique, there were times when one or more staff members suggested that a positive be ignored on the theory that the program member was doing well. In those days (and the problem persisted even as late as the present writing), up to 3 weeks might have intervened due to delays in the process. At such times, the implicit logic of *not* reporting was that it would do a man harm in the long run. This logic did not prevail.

As already indicated, this long-run thinking does not hold for false negatives. If a man had told the staff he had used, and his tested urine was negative, the effects on member morale were not likely to be deemed good. Hence, there was definite pressure to withhold such reports from program members. The long-run effects of such an organizational secret on the staff are not certain. Reports of false negatives appear to be infrequent.

A fifth mechanism, deriving from the desire to reduce chances of laboratory error, differed from those already described in that it had been translated into part of the urine-testing procedure. It took its legitimation from the chemists' claims that the urine test can detect heroin for at least 72 hours after its ingestion by a human consumer. From this it followed that if urine given on Wednesday tested positively, then urine given on the Tuesday before or the Thursday after should also have been positive.

The mechanism that evolved was called *bridging*

and consisted in arguing that if one part of the expected pattern of repeated positives did not also come back positive, the original laboratory report was in error. If, in the cited instance, Tuesday's and Thursday's urine came back negative, the lab erred. Over the history of Exodus House testing, when bridging has been used, a surprising number of positives proved to be true negatives, according to this criterion.

Resort to bridging developed as a direct result of the continual attack on the laboratory by men who denied the validity of its results and by staff members who felt there were too many puzzling positives. Those on the staff who spent an appreciable amount of their time administering the urine collection and the clerical work tended to be most uncertain about the value of bridging. More than one told the writer they thought the bridging was a "cop-out," a way of not facing the unpleasantness of having to take action which might produce adverse reactions.

Their argument was that because the heroin taken by some men was so weak, the laboratory claim for 72 hours was no longer valid. It is worth adding that where interruptions took place in the urine-testing procedures because of funding or contract problems, there was no bridging, and, as remarked above, members showed more anxiety, though staff members alluded to did not. Finally it should be added that by 1970 the bridging device had been dropped. It was evidence of the greater staff security as well as of the desire to "tighten up" the program. A positive report was a positive report, and only exceptionally was there an effort to "bridge."*

The sixth mechanism for handling laboratory report tension consisted in *expanding and deepening the staff's reliance on behavioral and ocular evidence.* In other words, *the comprehensive model was taken at its fullest value.* The pressure of the crisis in fiduciary evidence thus compelled the staff to escape the pitfalls of the pure chemical approach (with its attendant dangers of alienation from the program members) and become engaged enough to be acquainted with at least some of the men they were expected to judge on a regular basis. While, as we have seen, this produced contradictions, the overall stabilization of a program also stabilized the urine testing itself.

Such a comprehensive model tended to bring

*However, the laboratory retests all positives automatically before notifying the Exodus House staff.

the staff member back to the earlier days when addiction treatment specialists were forced to assume that an addict was probably guilty (of using drugs) until he showed behavioral evidence of innocence in the area.

A good instance of this suspicion occurred when an ex-addict in residence reported having found a corner of a cellophane bag used in the sale of heroin under some lumber in the house. The smell of vomit lingered on, and there was evidence the floor had been mopped. The residents of the house were all questioned but denied any knowledge of the affair. A number of the staff indicated their skepticism, but, as one of them put it, "You can't go around putting suspicion on anybody just because you got a feeling." Another staff member, more sure of himself, whispered to another that they should watch one particular resident who, he felt, had been wrongly permitted to stay in the house after a previous infraction.

This kind of heightened alertness to behavioral and ocular evidence of drug usage was also illustrated less than 2 months after the opening of the house in April, 1968. A member came in looking drunk, claiming to have had an excess of anisette. The director and house manager spent much time testing the man's eyes for signs of heroin use, observing him when he was alone, talking to him, etc., until they were convinced he was lying. He was sent out of the house the next day for a week's "punishment." The lab report verified their judgment.

By the winter of 1970–71, with the Exodus House residence over 2½ years old and its basic institutions stabilized, there were fewer public expressions of doubt about the laboratory validity. In 1970 there were a few conspicuously startling positives, but resulting shock waves were dealt with in therapy groups. All the men involved were "shot down" as the staff, having worked through the conflicting emotions about laboratory results, refused to debate the issue. The formula, an element of the "therapological" process, was, "There is no such thing as a false positive. You've gotten a positive. Deal with it." This was the final mechanism: *denial that a false positive was possible and requiring the member to accept the impossible*. It proved most effective.

To say there was no collective member outcry about the urine test results is not to say that all doubts had been resolved. What *had* happened was that laboratory tests had become publicly validated by staff solidarity. Thus, a belief in the staff as a whole removed the urine issue from *public debate*.

In private, however, one could still detect considerable anxiety about the tests, even to the point that some staff members felt it as "paranoia." The higher the level of the man, the more concentrated his concern about a mistake. A man at the A-level was seen scrutinizing a candy wrapper to make sure it did not contain quinine. Several members were heard to accuse staff members of "fucking with" their urine, presumably tainting it with drugs to hurt reputations. And, more than once, as I have made tea in the kitchen at Exodus House, I have dryly been asked if I want to have my urine tested because you really can't be sure the tea bag really is a *tea* bag.

Thus, the concern about the laboratory had moved from the collective public to the distributive, private level as the program had become more firmly institutionalized. Looking back at the disruptive power of conspicuously surprising "positives" in the earlier years of the program, it appeared that such power was, partly, an expression of the shakiness of a new program. The ambiguities and impossibilities in the testing process could not be contained and channeled and, indeed, were intensified by the precariousness of the program itself.

Behind the new attitude to acceptance was the overall stabilization of the program due both to external and internal forces. Externally, there were material forces which brought waiting lists to the program for the first time. By 1969 the Department of Social Services had begun to send increasing numbers of potential clients to the house, thanks to a new city directive requiring every known addict applying for assistance to attend a program. A total continuing police crackdown on the street addicts added its share of "recruits" and meant that the staff could be more independent, could insist on higher levels of conformity, and indeed, had to in order to keep from being swamped by men whose motivations had little to do with self-alteration.

In addition, the general public was becoming more concerned about drug addiction, partly, no doubt, because of the bourgeoisification of addiction in the late 1960s. The morale of any program staff is likely to be bolstered by a feeling that its work is going to be publicly noted and that it is riding the stream of history. A concrete manifestation of this public interest, of course, was the augmented public budgetary allocation to Exodus House and other voluntary programs. In 1968 to 1969 the state provided $256,110 for the program, in 1969 to 1970, $375,630, and in 1970 to 1971, $395,000.

Internally, the house management staff became more confident and developed more and stronger rules than was anticipated. In effect, a strong legalistic constitution was evolving. Again, thanks to better funding, two new workshops were added, and the number of therapists and groups also increased. The early scares about the urine test served to institute a higher priority on drug vigilance among the members. They now took abstinence and "giving up their urine" more seriously. Finally the morale of the staff, as shown during their meetings, was high.

The program structure having stabilized, urine test ambiguities and impossibilities were relatively neutralized at the private and small group level.

The mechanisms described earlier for managing tension were less frequently brought into explicit play. Either they were now incorporated in practice or had been dispensed with. "Bridging" was no longer used. A positive was a "positive." Looking back again, it would seem this was due to staff's uncertainty and members' pressure on them. The bridging mechanism had been used to take the weight off making difficult statements to one's friends. The stabilization of staff power made this feeling and this mechanism obsolescent.

In the past, the comprehensive model might have been used even when the staff was in doubt about the validity of a positive. As many staff as possible would be called in to decide what move should be made when Miss X and Mr. Y both received barbiturate positive reports. The pretherapist might recommend that one be retained in her group because she had "begun to deal," while the other member, who had generally not been responsive, ought to be moved down a level. She would ask for the reaction of others on the staff. These reactions would be given and the member evaluated as a whole, in the light of reactions toward other staff members, general appearance, attendance at meetings, etc. Such a staff session might produce a doubt about the positive, but that is the risk in any human enterprise involving interpersonal evaluation. Presently, any narcotic positive automatically results in a "shoot-down"

of one or more levels in the program regardless of staff doubt.

If the total program has been stabilized and the laboratory is no longer a viable issue, we cannot say the same for the certification to the public toward which the laboratory is a guide. I shall now argue that there are strong social and cultural forces that push this final process into the region of the impossible and thereby convert what looks like a secularized and even scientific process into a quasi-magical process. The differentiation of what I call "fiduciary styles" has tended to obscure an imminent crisis and impossibility in the certification process.

SOME SOCIOLOGICAL OBSERVATIONS OF DIFFERENT FIDUCIARY STYLES

The concept, fiduciary social agent, has been sketched out for us in Max Weber's essay on *The Protestant Sects and the Spirit of Capitalism.*[8] Weber pictured the 19th-century Protestant sects as validating their members' credit worthiness. In order to enter those sects (and entry was a "voluntary" affair), they had to pass certain tests. Such a function, he noted, had not been performed by the church-type organization into which a person was *born*. Thus, Weber saw the fiduciary process as a component of the long-term secularization and rationalization of Western life. He observed that such character certifications became part of a process of stratification since social clubs and, generally, voluntary associations, by deciding who could and who could not enter, helped put some people in the pariah category and others in the "aristocratic status groups."

In this larger context, addiction treatment agencies which are asked to, or purport to be able to, certify that men who were formerly addicts have become able to live drug-free lives really are voluntary associations sifting pariahs back into the legitimate class systems. An addict who enters such an agency is hoping for social mobility through receiving what the Protestant sects in the middle 19th century gave to their members — "The social premiums, the means of discipline, . . . and the whole organizational basis of Protestant sectarianism."[9]

Weber focused on the manner in which groups in a secularized culture certified to the character, presumably the preexisting character, of their members. Addiction treatment groups have claimed or have been asked to certify that their members' characteristics have changed at least in two significant regards: (1) that they were not using drugs at the date of certification, and (2) by implication, that they had "grown" in some regard. But, as one would predict from Weber's analysis, they had to establish this in a style which would satisfy the secular-rationalized milieu in which they function. In fact, differences in fiduciary styles for handling these demands could be understood sociologically.

The "prehistory" of Exodus House, when it was known as the East Harlem Protestant Parish Narcotics Committee, shows how a shift in program structure and composition alters its certification processes. In the very late 1950s the then director, Reverend Norman Eddy, was able to bring together a number of men who had spontaneously gone off drugs, generally on leaving prison. He formed these men into what was called a "Special Program." These were men whom he met and knew from the immediate neighborhood, so he had behavioral and ocular evidence that they were not taking heroin. They partook of marijuana in varying degrees, and many of them were heavily involved with liquor. Few, if any, had any truck with "pills."

But since the Narcotics Committee was focused on heroin, the other elements mentioned were not included in the certification promise of the community. Thus, it was that, at regular Thursday night meetings open to the public and including men actively using heroin, the Reverend Eddy would call out the names of a few men and ceremoniously give them a yellow card which vouched for their not having used heroin for 3 months, an orange card which vouched to the public for their not having used heroin for 6 months, or a white card which was given for yearly heroin abstinence. Never in this writer's memory did anyone challenge these cards during the meeting, though on one occasion a local drug addict hinted that she knew something about one ex-addict being involved in selling. (Her rumor proved to have been correct and the man received 10 years in a Federal case in 1962.)

Because both the director and the entire Narcotics Committee staff (with the exception of the writer and the psychiatrist) were local residents, there was continual inflow of information about the ex-addicts which served to control their conduct and to justify the certification process.

There was no question of relying upon scientific tests. An episode which took place at an open meeting in the summer of 1962 dramatized the differences between the sense of the Narcotics Committee on this question and that of Exodus House.

Visitors from Baltimore, coming to share experiences, attended a weekly open meeting. They were naturally asked to describe how they operated their facilities which, it developed, involved urine testing. The audience was aghast, and included in this number were the staff of the Committee who agreed they would never condone a urine test. It was demeaning to the addict. The staff running the Baltimore program had little faith in their own expertise. The idea of the test itself was certain to provoke addict countermeasures to outwit it, etc., etc.

The following seem to have been some of the sociological bases for this rejection of a natural-scientific technique: (1) the East Harlem Protestant Parish Narcotics Committee was a storefront-based program oriented around the values of face-to-face living in the open community. Relying on a laboratory meant relying on an impersonal scientific bureaucracy. (2) The self-imagery of both staff and ex-addicts rested partly on the idea that the Narcotics Committee, a pioneer group, were experts. They resented the idea that they could not, unaided, determine who was and who was not using drugs or who should and who should not be certified as an ex-addict. (3) Although there was some therapy and a considerable attempt at limited material support for some of the Special Program members, the Narcotics Committee treatment strategy was based primarily on having a man discover his own motivations and test them, as he was, against the temptations of the street. Little attempt was made to foster a drug-free milieu within which a man would learn internal controls. Therefore, there was no apparent need for a test which might give a man a sense of learning control and show if he was, in fact, under control. (4) Funding was primarily through foundations and a research grant, with minimum pressure to account for results.

In contrast, the Exodus House program of the late 1960s contained elements that fostered the use of impersonal tests: (1) This was a mixed residence and community-exposed program which emphasized both exposure to addiction and protection from it in a controlled milieu. The complexity of the result and the program demanded as much objectivity as possible. (2) Although the staff and the ex-addicts were treatment veterans and "in the vanguard," they were convinced, because of shifts in drug patterns and drug quality, that there were too many cases that could not be judged correctly by ocular and behavioral clues. (3) The treatment strategy was based on the idea that addicts could be helped to learn self-control by submitting voluntarily to constant checking. The idea of a urine test did not appear alien any longer, but instead seemed to be a useful technique. "Dealienation," so to speak, had taken place. (4) Increasingly, Exodus House funding was undertaken by state authority, so that by 1968 to 1969 the vast bulk of the budget came from Albany. Since the N.A.C.C. itself needed valid evidence of the comparative worth of different competing programs, this fact encouraged the faithful use of a test that appeared to be independent of the subjective prejudices of the people who ran the programs. It permitted the separation of treatment from evaluation, at least in theory. Moreover, Exodus House was now affiliated with the New York State Division of Vocational Rehabilitation, which, having had some unfortunate experiences with so-called ex-addicts, was inclined to look with favor on a program which could objectively show that its members were off drugs.

By contrast, Synanon continued the tradition among the older ex-addicts of refusing to rely on urine tests: (1) According to a personal communication,* it had been continually engaged in lawsuits to prevent the California authorities from "evaluating" its membership. Self-dependence and self-government by ex-addicts were the *sine qua non* of their treatment strategy. Urine tests were ideologically perceived as alien, if not dehumanizing, destructive instruments. Self-controls were built in being constantly exposed to attack and demasking within a context that rewarded desired control and punished lack of desired control. These ex-addicts did not feel the need for "unnatural" nonhuman controls. (2) Their social organization approached totalitarian absorption of the individual. Constant contact with the addicts, in an organization run along "tribal" lines, under a leader who is responsible for his people meant that any slight change in the appearance of a member was "checked out" in the course of merciless interpersonal attack and examination. (3) Synanon

was partly self-sustaining, partly dependent on foundation and even governmental help. It had resisted state money which contained the demand for urine tests. (This was one reason for the failure of a potentially lucrative contract with the City of New York.) An organization which refused to account for its activities, or to describe its success or failure statistically, was not as likely as one that does so to need to fall back on natural-scientific techniques.

The upshot was that in Synanon (1) there had been a refusal to adopt state-backed testing procedures, but (2) its ideology of keeping a man indefinitely in a Synanon role within a Synanon community *totally* bypassed the "impossible" demand imposed on other agencies: Guarantee us that he will never again use drugs. Synanon, in fact, stated that this demand cannot be met. *Hence*, it kept practically all of *its members within its fold,* which had further consequences that would take us too far afield to discuss. Comparable urine ideologies could be found in other programs.[10]

THE SCOPE OF THE FIDUCIARY COMMITMENT TO THE PUBLIC: A CASE OF AMBIGUITY

We have seen that recourse to laboratory technique to support a certification was linked to certain sociological features of the certifying organization. The demand for certification by whatever means, formal or informal, was also enhanced by the rise to prominence of ex-addiction and the ex-addict as emergent social and cultural phenomena. At the late 1960s rate of rehabilitation expansion, and assuming the continued interest of government in financing rehabilitation programs, in the 1970s thousands of men and women would be claiming, with organizational backing, that they were ex-addicts.

The reason for the need to make the claim was obvious: If a man had "squared up," then he felt he had some right, at least some moral right, to be treated on an equal plane when competing with some nonaddict for a position. Certification, as we have noted, was tied to reentry into the legitimate social class system. Over the years when the writer and other members of the Exodus House staff would argue with addicts about the feasibility of rehabilitation, one of the persistent counterargu-

*From Mr. Edward Rivera, previously connected with the Santa Monica Synanon Center.

ments was, "What's the point? If I do straighten myself out, I'm still a junkie where it counts. I still can't hold a Civil Service job; I still can't get my cabaret license back. I can't hold any job where you've got to be bonded. They just won't let you come back." In the past the only argument a professional could make was that things might be different when public opinion changed and government and private business would see their way clear to permitting proven ex-addicts to show their worth on a man-to-man basis.

Many of these men were not merely "mobility-oriented" in the sociological phrase but had an almost desperate desire to "catch up" and to "make up" for the years they had "wasted" on drugs. There was a real pressure on the part of hundreds of ex-addicts to gain recognition generally and to demonstrate, in their own particular cases, that they were in fact what they claimed to be — drug-free. And this pressure was translated in turn into each addict rehabilitation center's own claim that its certification was a valid and reliable one.

We have seen the conflict of laboratory and empirical social reality and the ambiguities of evidence that resulted from trying to certify that a man had a specific history of being drug-free. But there were more ambiguities. At bottom, what did an agency certify to? To whom did it hold out this certification? For how long? Was there need for super-agency controlling and checking on the certifiers? In short, what was the scope of the certification? Some materials from the prehistory and history of Exodus House will show the importance of these questions.

In the period from 1957 to 1962, the Reverend Norman Eddy would personally receive information from time to time that a certain job was available and that an ex-addict would be acceptable. (There were limited numbers of employers, then more so than now, willing to take risks.) However, though he and his then associate, the Reverend Lynn Hageman, were in touch with men apparently off drugs, they had to think twice about referring them. A considerable proportion of the Special Program men were off heroin but on alcohol some to the point where, despite their denial, they really were alcoholics. Many had fierce tempers and an amazing assortment of psychological quirks. What did it mean if they were sent out as *representatives* of the Narcotics Committee?

The writer sat in on many such discussions in the early years. Looking back it is clear that the Committee *had not been able to clarify the scope of its certification.* That is, it had not faced the ambiguities inherent in trying to limit its commitment to the statement: So and so has been off drugs for x years. A statement of certification must also contain information relative to the basis on which a person has stayed off drugs. In the cases referred to, the Narcotics Committee was certifying men as drug addicts who were alcohol addicts. This fact produced much agony, embarrassment, and danger on the part of both the Narcotics Committee staff and the Special Program members themselves. More than once a member, hired in good faith by an employer, would prove a refractory uncooperative worker or would keep poor hours, in part at least because of his drinking and related problems. In effect, the staff found itself in the region of the impossible, promising something that could not be fulfilled.

The idea of a Special Program gradually was abandoned after the Reverend Lynn Hageman took over the directorship in 1962, but even before the change in administration there were evidences of inner conflict and tension among the members and between staff and members, precisely because of the too-limited changes in basic life-styles, psychological and social, among some of these men and because of their skepticism about the need and feasibility to make such basic changes. Special Program members often assumed that because they were no longer using heroin they had no further need to develop.

Because of the restricted commitment he could make, the director was limited in his referrals. This problem also bedeviled the Exodus House program in its earlier phases but was not as obvious to the staff. During the first experimental program, with a rather loosely supervised urine-testing program, a job slot was filled by a man who was presumed to be off drugs and who was exposed to a weekly hour of group therapy and some individual therapy. The job as machinist's helper was very demanding, calling for long hours of travel to and from home and long hours at the job. The take-home pay, however, was high for the time (1964). After a few months the staff received calls from the employer about the program member's lateness and absences. He in turn came in to say that the job was inhuman and that all the men were up in arms because there was no protection from the union.

There was much talk among the staff at the time concerning the commitment implied in sending a man to a job. But the staff felt, in general, that the member really ought to have stuck it out, that he could have then gone to another job with experience and a reference in that trade. What the staff did not know then, though it had many indications, was that this man was probably using a quantity of heroin from time to time and that as another man who knew him said of him and other program members, "Man, they're just working addicts." The first Exodus House certifications were ambiguous because the certifiers really did not know enough about what they were certifying. A pattern of denial operated to blind the staff from seeing that it was operating in the region of the impossible.

In contrast, the Exodus House program, with a halfway house for residents and (later) a comprehensive program, actually certified that a man had very probably overcome his addiction, had been exposed to psychological treatment, and had participated in a life situation which made it highly likely that he had changed in the direction of a legitimate orientation. A certification was given to a man or woman, not only because he was drug-free but also because he was either working or going to school and had also satisfactorily completed a course of group therapy which, hopefully, permitted him to live more profitably with himself and his society, in a way he decided made sense.

Here, too, comparison with Synanon's experience is instructive. After about 2½ years of closely supervised residence in their organization, a man was certified as an ex-addict. However, this tended to be only an initial certification. As we have noted, few if any members of Synanon were encouraged to go into the community and abandon Synanon at that point. Instead they were articulated into a complex socioeconomic structure, generally working for their creature comforts and in the interests of Synanon as a whole. They assumed increasingly responsible roles and remained subject to Synanon's continuing discipline and treatment strategy. Thus, a man might actually have remained in Synanon for a lifetime if he really felt he could not function on the outside. If a man left without permission and the director evaluating him thought he had left prematurely, he

would be called a *splittee* and would be so noted in the records. A splittee was not certified. What he did had no pertinence to the Synanon record. On the other hand, the very few Synanon graduates who left the field of addiction had to make it on their own. It is not clear to the present writer that formal procedures were maintained by the mother organization to validate their graduates' specific claims. However, the total weight of Synanon propaganda and information emphasized how their graduates were changed.

Writing in the 1960s, one could expect that in future years the scope and limitations of fiduciary commitments would come up for public discussion as would the liabilities of the fiduciary agencies. One could predict that pressure to formalize standards would intermittently run into conflict with certain program approaches such as Synanon and that each agency, if it survived, would have to develop its own mechanism for balancing the ambiguities and pressures of certification against the need to experiment in new directions, as Exodus House has over the past decade.

However, by the winter of 1970–71 the question of certification was in crisis. In the late 1960s New York City's Addiction Services Agency had set up procedures to certify ex-addicts who had gone through its Phoenix Houses. Committees were formed to work out procedures by which graduates of their programs could also receive certification. However, a change of administration occurred in A.S.A., Phoenix Houses became a private organization, and after a very few of its graduates were certified, A.S.A. abruptly stopped certifying anyone. There was a rumor that at least one of the certified ex-addicts had gone back to drugs and that this was also a factor; the rumor could not be officially verified.

What was barely visible in earlier years now loomed ahead as an existential crisis for all those agencies in which ex-addicts had come to expect a reward at the final stage of their participation, that reward being a piece of paper attesting to their status as an ex-addict. They wanted it, their families wanted it, the state wanted it. The agencies themselves would have liked it. Rationality demanded it.[11]

But a nagging within had to be answered although it might be phrased differently by different people: Didn't the whole question of certification take us into the region of the impossible? A kind of limited certification was given by

Exodus House: A piece of paper said that so and so had been off drugs or had undergone a program of rehabilitation. It was *retrospective, not prospective* in nature. It left it up to those who read the document to make their own interpretations, even though the staff would believe and state their belief that the graduates would not in fact use drugs. But this was not the kind of guarantee which was increasingly sought of addiction treatment agencies. *The crisis of certification came to this: that to ask agencies to make a legal prospective certification for which they would be liable in court was to place them in the region of the impossible, and yet in one way or another, those fiduciary agencies were being asked to do that.*

Moreover, thanks to the methadone program's extraordinary popularity and the widespread impression of its enormous success, such pressures were likely to rise. The claims of 80% success, sharply reduced in some cases, gave the public evidence of a remarkable transformation formula. Put the methadone in, the heroin stays out, and the former heroin user reenters the square world. Many reports and ingenious ideological and scientific mechanisms, one could predict, would continue to be heard before the "final assessment" would permit a realistic evaluation, but the interim years would see mounting pressure on other addiction centers, especially those in utopian model aiming at the drug-free life, to come up with a secure path through the impossible and promise, almost magically, that the former addict would not ever, or at least would not in the next 5 years, take a shot. And, since conduct in the region of the impossible can produce strange results, one could only predict that the future would be unpredictable.

At the same time, the Exodus House experience has shown that once a program has secured the confidence of its members, it could even absorb the complexities of *impossible demands,* at least to a point. By expressing an authoritative voice, it might help control the risks imminent in a certification statement.

SUMMARY AND IMPLICATIONS

The Exodus House experience indicates how even a comprehensive model for drug-use control, including behavioral, ocular, and chemical techniques, tends to throw great weight on the latter. In turn, this technological formalization generates some human and humanistic objections, which produce a set of structural defenses, including ideological and intellectual mechanisms to bolster the urine test. Thanks to the program's own stabilization, these defenses became more acceptable, and overt, public uncertainty diminished in intensity. Despite this improvement, a fiduciary crisis still loomed ahead, as the public would increasingly demand a higher standard of expectation from certification than an addiction agency could guarantee.

On reflection it would appear that two intellectual trends had come to coexist uneasily within Exodus House. A person could detect a strand of *existential humanism* at staff meetings, one concerned with freeing "the authentic man" beneath the psychochemical mask, focusing on the program member's experiences, on his subjectivity, as in the cliché, mockingly repeated, "What are your *feelings?*" Statements expressing this standpoint tended to see the addicted man as a victim experiencing the play of larger forces. In the urine test controversies, this strand, while emphasizing individual responsibility and commitment, would underscore the possibility that a member's urine had been the object of some bad luck.

The other strand was a *pragmatic structuralism,* focused on the necessity for explicit and implicit structures to help control the former addict, offering him paradigms of order and direction. From this standpoint, a man's subjectivity, his bad luck, his irrationality, his so-called freedom might be considered to be *the problem.* From a structural standpoint the members needed more constraints, even more punishments for their own support and growth. Not subjectivity but objectivity was the keynote. In the case of the urine controversy, this standpoint argued for strict construction of the laboratory results; a positive was a positive. Broadly speaking, the humanistic existential position drew most of its support from the professional staff, while structural approach found advocates on both sides of the staff structure. In the history of the urine test, the structuralists won out; a strict construction prevailed. Indeed, even the failure to give a specimen came to be interpreted as a positive. But in the sense that each member had to experience the possibility and even reality of a laboratory error and that the urine test was seen as a therapeutic experience, the existentialist position showed its tenacity. The "hard" knowing of structuralism and the "soft" experiencing of existentialism coincided in this question.[12]

The relationship between the urine test and its findings and the therapy sessions dramatizes another coincidence of structuralist and existentialist thinking. The heart of Exodus House, as one form of therapeutic utopia, lay in its therapy groups and group meetings in which the speech and occasional nonverbal action of the members expressed their subjectivity. Although not quite at the limiting situations of the sensitivity training fashion or movement, Exodus House clearly relied on interpersonal and community-based interactions to help the addicted man master his impulses and formulate his own life task, if possible. This existential thrust towards responsibility by group living was crosscut, as it were, by the structural Other, the laboratory Out Yonder which, even as a man was talking in his group, was processing his urine from some previous dates, objectifying not only his private act of urination but potentially any private acts of drug-taking. Even as he affirmed himself in his group, perhaps even fighting to keep an "image," the phone might be ringing and the mail might be delivering a cryptic phase which would give the lie to what he was saying. His self-presentation was structurally undermined by this delayed information. His presentation was countered by this post-sending. He was identified, rightly or wrongly, as one who had "slipped," if the anonymous technician and clerk collaborated to challenge his autonomous lie. Thus, the existential therapy was given shape and dynamism by the structural invisible other, with whom there was no possibility of disputation or contradiction.[13]

Where there had been an error — and only a fool would deny the possibility of an error in human-related technology — therapy was wrestling with the 20th century. While this was an opportunity to shadow box, it was also an exquisite chance to grow up.

The foregoing pages also demonstrate that it is impossible to separate technical from human aspects of the urine test and that, inexorably, doubts about the mechanical aspects of the test are intensified by doubts about the program which incorporates it. I suspect that even were the test to be submitted strictly to a programmed computer, the doubts from an insecure program would be projected onto the computer itself. Thanks to the human participation in the total urine-testing process, there was a continuum of possible risks or error, accident, and intrigue.

What counted was the program member's faith or development of some near equivalent to faith, his learning that the member role required participation in therapy, vigilance about giving his urine under proper conditions, and, of course, in abstaining from drugs. Another way to describe this process is to say that, as with any other organization, institutionalization had come to Exodus House to enable it to achieve and conserve its long-term values. Certain material changes, such as new ties with the Department of Social Services and new policies which had led to its insistence that addicts belong to programs, the construction of a residence offering enhanced values to members, financial stablization due to greater participation by the state in funding voluntary programs, and, in general, a greater public interest in drug addiction, all had helped stabilize the program and given a rational basis for the members to have faith in what was happening in the house and what was happening to them in particular.

REFERENCES

1. Douglas, M., *Purity and Danger,* Penguin Books, London, 1970, 72.
2. Halevy, E., *England in 1815,* Peter Smith, New York, 1949, 237; Freud, S., The return of totemism in childhood, in *Totem & Taboo,* W. W. Norton, New York, 1939. The idea of institutionalized outlets for a taboo is embodied today in the methadone program.
3. Article on Descartes, in Edwards, P., Ed., *Dictionary of Philosophy,* Vol. 2, Free Press, New York, 1967, 343.
4. Auerbach, E., *Mimesis,* Anchor Books, New York, 1953, 107.
5. Ellul, J., *The Technological Society,* Knopf, New York, 1964, 265.
6. Fiddle, S., *Portraits from a Shooting Gallery,* Harper & Row, New York, 1966, 68.

7. Winter, G., *Elements for Social Ethic,* Macmillan, New York, 1968, 75.
8. Gerth, H. and Mills, C. W., *From Max Weber: Essays in Sociology,* Oxford University Press, New York, 1940, chap. 13.
9. Gerth, H. and Mills, C. W., *From Max Weber: Essays in Sociology,* Oxford University Press, New York, 1940, 313. See p. 322, "The sect controlled and regulated the members' conduct exclusively in the sense of formal *righteousness* and methodical asceticism."
10. Yurick, S., The political economy of junk, *Monthly Rev.,* 22, 22, December 1970. "There is, of course, a fantastic rise in the therapy market" (p. 34) and the comments throughout in what is a journalistic Marxian analysis.
11. Schutz, A., The problems of rationality in the social world, in Emmett, D. and MacIntyre, A., *A Sociological Theory and Philosophical Analysis,* Macmillan, New York, 1970, 96. "The transformation of an uncontrollable and unintelligible world into an organization which can be understood and therefore mastered."
12. The works of Claude Levi-Strauss and his followers and those associated with his "school" may be taken as representing the structuralist core. A balanced analysis and evaluation of structuralism will be found in Runciman, W., What is structuralism? *Br. J. Sociol.,* 20, 253, 1969. J. P. Sartre's work represents the existentialist position, but the recent *Critical Existentialism* by Niccola Abbagnano (Anchor Books, New York, 1969) appears to be more in the spirit of Exodus House's existentialism.
13. Edelson, M., *The Practice of Sociotherapy,* Yale University Press, New Haven, 1970, offers some interesting material on the place of contradictions in a therapeutic community. cf. Friedenberg, E. E., *The Vanishing Adolescent,* 4th ed., Beacon, Boston, 1964, 11. "The youngster who has abandoned the task of defining himself in dialectical combat with society and becomes its captive and its emissary may be no rarity, but he is a casualty."

THE USE OF EX-ADDICTS IN A REHABILITATIVE
AND EDUCATIONAL PROGRAM*

Gilbert Geis, John G. Munns, and Bruce Bullington

TABLE OF CONTENTS

INTRODUCTION

The location and/or creation of jobs for abstinent narcotic addicts represents an exceedingly difficult enterprise. For one thing, the American ideology of a second chance notwithstanding, field studies clearly indicate that the "debt" of the criminal offender to the society does not end at the prison gates on release but carries over into the employment office, where one-time offenders suffer severe discrimination in their efforts to find work.[1] On top of this, drug addiction is a frightening thing to American society today and arouses an almost hysterical response in the business world. "We need realists in business, not escapists," a corporate personnel manager has written as part of a campaign to alert his fellows against the possible infiltration of drug offenders into their offices and factories.[2] The New York Temporary State Commission to Evaluate the Drug Laws, reporting in January 1973, noted that employers make no distinction between persons addicted to drugs and those who have ended the habit or who are controlling their craving by recourse to methadone regimens. The report found almost ubiquitous discrimination against former addicts. It noted that "irrational distinctions" are drawn between "rehabilitated alcoholics and rehabilitated addicts," with the former strongly favored, and called attention to what was labeled a "Catch-22" syndrome, in terms of which employers will dismiss a former addict "ostensibly not because of his past drug history, but because he lied in his application for the job about his narcotics use."[3]

Given this kind of truculence and resistance in the employment community, it becomes highly attractive to try to create special jobs for abstinent addicts which turn their disabilities into assets and which, by a delineation of relevant qualifications,

*We want to express our appreciation to Jan Martin for her help in the typing of this chapter.

see to it that the one-time narcotic addict is the only applicant who possesses the expertise defined as necessary to secure the position.

It is against this background that there has in recent years been a proliferation of situations in which former addicts are placed in roles which somewhat resemble social work positions, are paid relatively attractive salaries, and are given the task of attempting to reduce or eliminate narcotic use in others. The prototype for such efforts obviously is Synanon, a residential facility operated by ex-addicts,[4] but the Synanon model has now been extended more daringly into enterprises which attempt to insert former addicts into more traditional kinds of community roles rather than encapsulating them in a relatively isolated, self-contained, and protective environment such as that established by Synanon.[5]

THE NARCOTICS PREVENTION PROJECT

The blueprint for the Narcotics Prevention Project, a program employing ex-addicts as rehabilitative agents, was drawn after then-Representative Adam Clayton Powell pushed a bill through Congress, Public Law 89-794, which appropriated $12.1 million for drug rehabilitation efforts in poverty areas. Los Angeles received about $900,000 of this money. The Project was placed in East Los Angeles, a predominantly Mexican-American community, because the area was familiar to the persons who wrote the funding proposal. They had only recently finished an evaluation there of a state-run halfway house for paroled addicts. The halfway house, admitting its residents on a random-assignment basis, had been shown after 3 years of data collection to have failed in its mission to reduce drug use among members of the experimental group.[6]

It was believed that the halfway house had not worked well because, among other things, state parole agents had been unable to gain adequate rapport with the house residents. Former addicts, it was hypothesized, might better be able to bring about some measurable improvement in the community's severe drug problem. The use of indigenous, peer-group personnel was thought to be particularly essential in regard to Chicano addicts since they had not yet wholly introjected the American ethos, with its emphasis on verbal introspection and its lack of respect for kinship

obligations. Thus, for instance, Chicano addicts often found it undignified to talk about their personal problems or to derogate wives and mothers, tactics deemed essential for treatment success in most of the then-current modalities. The "different" nature of the target population has been well delineated by two writers: first, Octavio Paz:

. . . the ideal of manliness is never to "crack, never to break down." Those who "open themselves up" are cowards. Unlike other people, we believe that opening oneself up is a weakness or a betrayal. The Mexican can bend, can bow humbly, can even stoop, but he cannot back down, that is, he cannot allow the outside world to penetrate his privacy.[7]

And, second, Celia Heller:

Honor . . .is tied to an inner sense of integrity which every child inherits as part of his Mexican-American birthright and which he is to guard jealously against all. It manifests itself in "extreme sensitivity to insult" displayed so often by Mexican-American youths.[8]

The Narcotics Prevention Project during its first years employed a staff of 30 former addicts (or "inactive addicts" as they have now come to be designated). These men and women were selected by a panel made up of two nonaddicts and the first two employees who had been hired. A specific requirement for a position was that the applicant had had to be drug free for at least 6 months. As a condition of employment, he had to agree to periodic urinalysis tests, on both a regular and a surprise basis.

Five years later, the number of former addicts on the NPP payroll has risen to 70, and the roster of full-fledged clients fluctuates from 350 to 500. We estimate that in the first 5 years of operation, the project has provided services to nearly 10,000 persons with drug problems.

Concomitant with the project's growth in size, the procurement of additional fundings, and the expansion of services, the ex-addicts have been placed increasingly in specialized roles. At the outset of the project, the entire former addict staff, save two supervisors and an employment specialist, were assigned as general caseworkers; at present, most have specialized duties — in legal services, education, employment, hospital casework, methadone maintenance, or supervision of ancillary aftercare programs contracted with several corrections agencies.

RATIONALE FOR THE EX-ADDICT
SOCIAL WORK ROLE

The rationale for employing former addicts in community intervention roles with practicing addicts, aside from its appeal as a means for putting otherwise hard-to-employ persons to work, involves a number of assumptions. Most prominent is the folk belief — perhaps true, perhaps not — that only a former addict is capable of dealing adequately with the rationalizations, ruses, and righteousness of a continuing addict. The practicing addict is regarded as notoriously manipulative and monumentally self-deceptive while he is using opiates, conditions which can only be clearly recognized and counteracted, it is said, by a person who has become familiar with them through his own experience. The practicing addict is also said to have a very low opinion of himself and of his ability to withstand the temptation of relapse if he were to detoxify. In this regard, the model of an employed, drug-free former addict is supposed to stand as an object lesson to the user that abstinence and social responsibility can be achieved by one such as himself.

There are, in addition, other presumed assets in the role of an ex-addict paraprofessional social worker. The steady work and the decent salary are responsive to a basic assumption in our society that unemployment and poverty are precursors of personal disorganization and criminal activity. The ex-addict job itself might also be regarded as substituting in some ways for the imperatives of heroin addiction which establish an inflexible demand for "scoring" in order to outmaneuver the physiological threat of withdrawal agony. A field-worker in the Narcotics Prevention Project expressed this ideal well in explaining the satisfaction he derives from outwitting "the system" by placing his clients in jobs they otherwise might not secure and by protecting them from parole revocation by negotiations with their agents:

Well, all the time we were using, we were hustling drugs. And we still get a kick out of hustling — still get a kick out of shucking people. And so long as we can still do it . . . to an employer, to get a client a job — that gives us *our* fix.[9]

A story this man tells to illustrate his point is worth repeating, not only for the sheer pleasure it conveys — a pleasure much like that of the salesman outfoxing a client — but also for the analogy between the new assignment of the ex-addict and his former life of drug use:

In the early days of the Project, we were confronted with all these dope fiends and no beds to put them in. So we started to go to General Hospital, where at the time they wouldn't hospitalize an addict. We have these I.D. cards that say "Narcotics Prevention Project," with our pictures on them . . . We'd come screaming up to the ambulance entrance, sort of shove everybody aside and flash our card. Only we'd cover up the "Prevention Project" with our thumb . . . Police cars would be there and we'd yell: "Get that car the hell out of the way . . ." Then we'd drag the guy into the hospital. We'd flash our cards again, and just say, "Hold this man for five days!" Five days later, we'd go and pick him up and the guy would be detoxified. That really got us our fix.[10]

The anecdote also indicates the quality of service rendered to clients by the ex-addicts. Their cavalier treatment of bureaucratic protocol and their delight in developing a repertory of inventive ways to cut through red tape reap the benefits of quick results for their clients, who would otherwise be left to fend for themselves amidst what to them seems to be a bewildering maze of social, medical, and legal agencies.

There is, expectedly, an antipathy among the staff toward the professional roles which have traditionally provided services to addicts, an antipathy, it must be said, which is often reciprocated. The resentment is based partly on class and ethnic differences, partly on the alleged condescending professional work styles. Often, however, specific conflicts emerge between professional and "street" expertise. A staff worker assigned to one of the hospitals used by the project for detoxification recalls some initial problems:

At first, we had some tough times. The medical staff was not very happy with the ex-addicts' input. But we finally got together and the patient was the one who benefited. The game used to be — the addict would wait until late at night, ring for the nurse, and pour out his life story to her. The big sell was how much pain he was in. In the morning the nurse would tell the doctor: "Poor Garcia. He's in real distress. He needs more medication." But the ex-addict counselor would intervene. He'd say, "Look, he *doesn't* need any more. He's gaming you. Please don't do it!" At first, the medical people were pretty uptight. They'd let our guy know he was playing doctor. But pretty soon, they came to realize that *nobody* is tougher on an addict than an ex-addict. You've got to be a super liar to be a dope fiend for any length of time. And all of our guys knew every game. They'd played them all. The detox took a lot less time and the patient wasn't hurt at all. That's good medicine."[11]

Another confrontation with professionals occurred with the placement of former addicts in classroom roles at several nearby junior high schools. Selected project staff members worked with health education teachers both to prepare and to help teach an expanded curriculum on narcotics and dangerous drugs. From the outset, there was a mutual resentment between teachers and ex-addicts. The teachers' natural resentment of outsiders who threatened their own position of expertise escalated when some of the former addicts demonstrated a superior ability to elicit classroom interest and rapport from the students. The ex-addicts, in turn, came to have second thoughts about the teaching profession:

One thing that did amaze me about this project is how ignorant teachers are. You know, I had always held them up there some place and thought they were really something. But they are incredibly stupid.

The views of the ex-addicts toward the classroom portion of their work were expressed to a research worker in the following terms:

We have logic on our side, in that this program is getting through to the kids. You know, we are giving them a realistic picture of drugs for the first time. The normal picture presented by the schools was hardly that. But for once, they are getting the truth and I think they know it. And if they are logical – you know, if this is the way it is – then we should be getting through to some of them. I didn't feel we had nearly enough contacts with teachers in this program. We only saw them for a brief time in the workshops during which there was usually a movie or discussion, and then in the classroom when we appeared, and there, we didn't have much time to talk with them either. I don't know if we changed their opinions very much or not.

The teachers have told me time and time again that they are lost whenever we are not appearing in the classroom with them. You know, they don't know what to do. I don't know what the hell they did before. I can imagine. But what they do now is give them busy work if we are not in the classes or something like that. And the kinds of stories these teachers tell are incredible. One teacher who was introducing me tried to tell the class that because I was very short and had taller brothers who got all the girls and I never got any girls, and therefore I shot dope. The class actually booed him when he told them that. I wasn't there at the time and the kids told me later. I had already told them my only brother was a baby and he couldn't have been taller than I was and that had not a goddam thing to do with it. Now I don't know where that guy got his information, but that was incredible. I just couldn't believe it. But I was pleased to see that the class booed him down when he did it.

You know we have gone to extremes to run ourselves into the ground in our presentations to the classes. There is an awful lot of this hero worship kind of thing, and we try to play it down as much as possible. I know I did and I know the other workers did. Yet there is still a lot of hero worship there. You know there is a whole gang of girls, for example, that came up wanting my autograph after class. They crowded around, wanted my autograph, and then they dared each other to kiss me on the cheek and things like that. They think I am very young, 18 or so. They even went so far as to get my phone number. And you know since it's not listed, that's no easy chore; and now they are bugging me. They call me all the time. And they talk, like one girl talked for two hours. Most of them are just screwing around, but one had a family problem, you know, and I tried to help her. She had a brother who was using some stuff or something. But I think what they did, they got together a bunch of girls and they called every narcotics listing in the phone book until they found someone who gave my number to them. I'd sure like to interview some of these kids. I know a number of them are really off in that bag, and they are using and they are starting down that road. All of them in those schools know somebody in that grade who is shooting heroin or who has shot heroin, and that's incredible, I think. In terms of this phone business, I finally had to get someone to answer the phone. So they don't bug me anymore. I think what we should really do is start in the first grade with this anti-narcotics education.

The specialist's observations hardly need be taken literally, nor necessarily regarded as accurate appraisals of the conditions he describes. Nonetheless, they should not be summarily dismissed. For one thing, they represent the situation as one of the workers, perhaps the most articulate member of the group, saw it. For another, they tell much about the dynamics of the school situation. Again, we have the willingness of the specialists to judge the teachers, and to put them down. While the report may tell something about the presumed "needs" of the specialists, it also tells something about the vulnerability of the teachers. Perhaps equally as noteworthy is the specialist's immediate use of "our side" in his first sentence about the program: there is "their side" and "our side," and membership in whichever group is obviously clear cut and exclusive. The truth of the remark that the addicts had made strenuous efforts to run themselves down is obvious from an examination of the transcripts of questions and answers in the classes. The insight of the specialist into the deliberate cultivation of this image is noteworthy; so too is his self-evident entrancement with the hero worship that resulted despite apparent (and obviously not very strenuous) efforts to eliminate it. From the remarks of the specialist, as well as from earlier observation by several of his colleagues, it also seems likely that it was not the pupils, not the teachers, and not the school administrators that the program had the most impact on, but rather the specialists themselves. Attended to, flattered, treated enough as an out-group to arouse compensatory efforts, and by their judgment successful in their competition with the teachers, who stood well above them in social esteem, the ex-addicts may well have been the persons who reaped the richest harvest from the experimental educational program.

OUTCOME EVALUATION

When former addicts are hired as "change agents," they are thrust into constant contact with persons behaving much as they used to, and it is seen as likely that these vivid mirror images of themselves will portray the fate awaiting the workers if they relapse and thereby will reinforce commitment to the "better way of life." It is equally possible, of course, that continuous and close association with the addict world, as part of a work assignment, can prove so unsettling that the former addict might inexorably be drawn back into drug use. These are among the unsettled issues in regard to programs employing former addicts in paraprofessional rehabilitative work. Below, we will present some of the results of our inquiry about this and related matters.

We had two major foci of evaluation. The first concerned the effect of the work upon the workers themselves and asked questions such as: Do they remain drug-free? Do they stay with the job? What kinds of problems are encountered? What kind of person fares best? The second concerned the impact of the project services upon clients, asking: Is the program successful in carrying out its mission to reduce drug addiction? What other benefits and deficits appear to follow from its form of operation?

THE EX-ADDICTS AS INTERVENTION AGENTS

We concentrated our worker investigation upon a cadre of 36 ex-addicts, the men and women employed in the Project at some time during its first year of operation. We have reported elsewhere on some aspects of their experience at a point 18 months into the Project's life,[12] here we will provide outcome information covering a 3-year period, from 1967 through 1970.

By this 36-month time only 6 of the original 36 workers remained with the Project. We located 31 of the original group. Two others had died, and three we could not find, though we gathered a good deal of information about the subsequent careers of the missing cases from friends and relatives and thereby were able to include them in our calculations.

The subsequent drug use of the workers was categorized into five major types: (1) opiate readdiction, (2) chipping, that is, sporadic or light opiate use, (3) regular pill-dropping, (4) light pill or psychedelic use, and (5) total abstinence. In Table 1, the Project workers have been placed into the category which represents their most serious form of drug behavior during the 3-year period.

There are a number of ways to interpret the information in Table 1. On the one hand, half of the ex-addicts successfully remained unaddicted; on the other hand, 78% "returned to drug use." One may make whichever statistical case one cares to. By the addicts' own standards, the "success" rate would be higher than 50% for though half became readdicted, several did so for relatively short periods and subsequently detoxified. The field-workers, in this regard, came to define success, both for themselves and for their clients, in gradual and incremental terms: using less, kicking more often, using less often, having recourse to less addictive drugs. Most viewed the occasional use of amphetamines or marihuana, for example, as unimportant and harmless.

A more certain agreement can be had regarding incarceration as a true indication of failure. Revocation of parole or new convictions were the fate

TABLE 1

Heaviest Drug Use by 36 Workers: 1967–1970

Category	Number	Percent
Opiate readdiction	18	50%
Chipping	1	3
Regular pill-dropping	1	3
Light pill or psychedelic use	8	22
Total abstinence	8	22
Totals	36	100%

of 10 (28%) of the 36 persons hired by the Project during its first year. In each of these cases, heroin use preceded arrest.

There are, then, cases which are obvious successes and others which are obvious failures. Then there is a marginal group. For our purposes, we defined success as remaining opiate-abstinent and steadily employed on a full-time basis, either with the Project or elsewhere. Thirteen cases fell into this category. Failures were defined as showing opiate use on a long-term basis and/or incarceration. Twelve cases fit into this category, including the two deceased persons, both of whom had been using opiates heavily before their death. The marginal group of 11 cases included six persons who had been readdicted for relatively short periods (the longest was 4 months) and who showed indications of continued abstinence. One such person had been rehired by the Project, though the administrators were not aware of the drug-using interlude. Another marginal case was that of an uninterviewed man who, the grapevine claimed, was not addicted but who was said to be moving in criminal circles. There was also a 67-year-old worker who had been fired for heavy drinking and a female worker who was deep into barbiturate use. All told, we thought 34 of the decisions relatively easy; the two where we had difficulty both ended up in the "marginal" category.

The classification done, it was possible to pinpoint variables that might discriminate among the outcome groups. Age made no difference. The mean age of the 36 persons was 38 years, and the average age for each of the outcome groups varied no more than 8 months from this mean. Marital status related to success, with ex-addicts living with their wives or in common-law relationships showing a much higher rate of success than their fellows; 6 of 11 fell into the success category. Criminal background (measured by mean number of previous arrests) had some minor predictive value in the anticipated direction (5.7 prior arrests for successes, 6.9 for marginals, and 7.2 for failures).

Surprisingly, both educational level and income earlier earned were negatively related to success. Notable was the fact that of the five workers with some college education, three were failures and two rated as marginal. The low numbers make interpretation of this unanticipated finding hazardous; we would only speculate that persons with fewer previous opportunities and low prospects at the time might have regarded the Project with more intense appreciation than those who were in a better position.

None of the original six Blacks and only one third of the Anglos could be rated as successful, compared to over half of the Chicanos. These figures must be examined in the light of the increasing ethnic exclusivity of the Project. The numerical dominance of Chicanos, both in the catchment area and on the staff, has led gradually (and unintentionally) to a widespread identification of the NPP as a "Chicano project." The percentage of Blacks on the staff has dropped from the original 20% to only 2% at this writing, and the Anglo percent from 31% to a current 4%. Proportions of non-Chicano clientele have dropped accordingly. We would emphasize that we attribute no part of these trends to racism; prominent among our explanations would be the considerable differences found among the Chicano, Black, and Anglo drug subcultures. These differences are naturally reflected both in the effectiveness of interethnic casework and in the rehabilitative preferences of the clients.

Another unexpected finding concerned the total failure of the women ex-addicts to stay with the project or otherwise to achieve success. At the end of the 36-month research period, all seven of the women hired by the project had left. Six are known to have returned to heavy drug use, and the seventh is strongly suspected to have done so. Despite the growth of the project staff, the number of female ex-addicts working with the project has averaged around six (at this writing, seven), which represents a proportional drop to only 9% of the total ex-addict staff. Those responsible for screening fieldworker applicants admit to a reluctance to hire women ex-addicts because of their high turnover rate.

The failure rate of women on the NPP staff is one of many indications that gender is a crucial factor to consider in any attempt either to explain or to treat drug use. Females are less likely to become addicts but, once addicted, are considered "tougher nuts to crack."[13] An explanation may lie in the fact that it takes more to push a female than a male into sharply defined deviancy such as opiate use, largely because American females are more protected and tend to be less experimental than men.[14] Under such conditions, the smaller group of women addicts tends to represent a hard-core group, more highly annealed than its male counterpart.

Among our original seven female fieldworkers, we found that their relapse appeared to be directly traceable to their experience with men, either outside the project or, more often, as part of their field-work assignments. Two cases are illustrative. In the first, a 37-year-old woman was married to a man in prison with a long history of addiction. She had been a fieldworker for 18 months and, at the time her husband was released from custody, was regarded as extremely steady and reliable. Almost immediately afterward, she took up heroin use with him and shortly thereafter was arrested for the theft of checks and equipment from the project office. Her tenure as a fieldworker, it is worth noting, represented the longest period of drug abstinence in her adult life.

A 20-year-old girl, the youngest worker on the project, had a sporadic record of previous drug use. She began dating a client whom she had met in the course of her work and soon started using drugs with him. He was subsequently arrested and imprisoned for his fourth armed robbery; the girl was also arrested and incarcerated.

Our interviews indicated that each of these seven relapses was preceded by close liaisons with male addicts. It appears that the female field-workers were almost bound at some time in their work to form or renew a close relationship with a man who was using opiates and that it became extraordinarily difficult for them to sustain the relationship without sharing in drug use, as the men demanded this behavior as a demonstration of love; otherwise, they would reject their women as cold and disapproving. This demand pattern between the sexes worked but one way, however. Male workers who formed liaisons with addicted females felt no imperative obligation to share in their drug use as a testament of affection.

SEX ROLES AND ADDICTION

These findings may be looked at in terms of sociological insights about gender and human behavior. Behavioral scientists have long emphasized the importance of cultural conditioning in the development of society's sex roles, with biological imperatives defining the limits within which a broad range of sexual patterns may occur. Ethel Albert, an anthropologist at Northwestern University, has pointed out that "every nice girl of

Western culture knows that it is the male who is the sexual aggressor, while the passive female submits with good or bad grace." But, Albert notes, if we ask about sexual aggression among certain Indian or African groups, we are apt to get a different view of the matter: "Obviously, they tell us, women are more driven by sex than men." In Central Africa, anthropological investigation indicates that "everybody knows that men are not suited by nature for hard work, that women are stronger and better workers." Americans tend to think of women as less stable emotionally than men, but in Iran it is the male who is supposed to cry easily, to prefer poetry to logic, while the woman is deemed to be practical, cool, and calculating. "Viewing humanity on a worldwide scale," Albert notes, "we find no consensus. Nature makes us male or female, but the beliefs and values of our society make us the kinds of men or women we become."[15]

Biologically, heroin use leads to the prolongation of the menstrual cycle length or to elimination of periods by the drug's action on the so-called "sexual center" of the hypothalmus.[16] In addition, children born to addicted mothers run greatly increased risks of early respiratory stress, and, thereafter, if they survive, they usually must be withdrawn from the drug.[17] Conditions such as these set the limits within which roles of the female heroin addict are played, but society ultimately determines the form such roles will take.

Available evidence suggests that there are approximately four times more male than female narcotic addicts in the United States today, a condition that contrasts sharply with that prior to the passage of the Harrison Act in 1914, when women greatly outnumbered men among addicts, largely because of the opiate content of many patent medicines routinely prescribed for "female troubles."[18] The change in sex ratios underscores the necessity to consider drugs in their social context before settling on their meaning for the individual addict. Certainly, it was enactment of the federal statute that served to reverse the sexual enumeration of addicts, not any change in the role of women or the psyches of either male or female addicts.

The possibility of prostitution as a means of supporting their drug habit may make addiction an easier path for women than it is for men. Prostitution entails fewer arrests than theft, the usual means by which men sustain their drug habits. This situation in fact is apt to arouse jealousy in male addicts. "Contempt for women is a constant theme [among male addicts]," Larner notes, "typically expressed by the remark that women addicts have it easy because they can raise money by hustling."[19] The resources available from prostitution are believed by Ellinwood to be largely responsible for the fact that female addicts differ significantly in their patterns of drug abstinence from males, who tend to cease drug use more often and to remain drug-free for shorter periods of time.[20]

In other respects, the Ellinwood investigation, conducted at the Public Health Service Hospital in Lexington, Kentucky, showed comparatively few differences among male and female addicts. They were similar in age, race, and religion and had begun drug use at the same time in their lives, though the women tended to become addicted more rapidly than the men after their initial heroin use. The most interesting differences appeared in regard to early sexual histories. Some 10% of the female patients at Lexington reported that they had been "involved sexually with their fathers," and the figure for familial sexual involvement rose to nearly one quarter of the total group when sexual behavior with the stepfather (7%), male relatives (3%), and the mother's paramour (3%) were added to the tabulation.[21] The comparisons might have been more meaningful, however, had they been drawn between similar socioeconomic groups of women rather than between male and female addicts; mother-son incest, for example, is extraordinarily rarer than father-daughter incest, not only among addicts but throughout American society.[22]

Figures on frigidity among the women at Lexington do not appear to differ significantly from those reported in other sex studies: Twenty-seven percent of the women addicts said they are frigid "at all times" and 10% that they were so "with most men." Another 30% characterized themselves as "not frigid."[23] Homosexuality seemed high among the women, with 44% indicating involvement at one time or another in such activity,[24] but it must be remembered that a considerable number of the respondents had served time in various institutions where lesbian activity tends to be ubiquitous.[25]

It is sometimes maintained that prostitution by female narcotic addicts represents a symbolic

expression of self-loathing. Larner suggests that the prostitution of one of his subjects, "like that of many other female addicts," appears to be "expressive of an almost wilful desire to annihilate her femininity."[26] Another writer maintains, in the same fashion, that prostitution and drugs are functionally interrelated, the latter serving the women as a means to "soothe their self-disgust."[27]

It should not be overlooked, however, that prostitution is an expedient method for achieving many things highly regarded in our society, most notably money and material comfort, as well as heterosexual attention and, at times, excitement, leisure, and more glamour than many females who become addicts otherwise are apt to enjoy. It is necessary, of course, for the prostitute to combat the derogation heaped upon her behavior by the moral entrepreneurs of the society, but, as has been shown by a study of the responses of prostitutes to social obloquy, there are some rather formidable stances that can be employed to this end, stances which stress, for example, social utility (prostitutes keep the rape rate down) and personal value (prostitutes, able to be at home during the day, make superior mothers).[28]

Prostitution in this sense would appear to be a reasonable means by which female addicts obtain the funds necessary to maintain their drug habit. The functional relation between drugs and prostitution can perhaps be illustrated by the story of Fat Annie, a former prostitute and madame who became a heroin supplier to other madames and to pimps. The result, as she reports it, is, "I got it all now baby. Most of it I put on my back and in my stomach. Some I spend on men. The rest goes to the bank." Annie had gone into selling heroin when she found that "many girls will do for heroin what they might never do for money." Looking at her life, Annie observes, "I have no regrets. It's a dirty world and I'm no worse than anyone else."[29] Persons more righteous than Annie might find her justification less than compelling, but we are well advised to recall the observation of Dr. James Plant, an eminent psychiatrist, reporting on a delinquent girl who had been referred to him for diagnosis:

If she has not already been getting clothes, etc., through her sexual life I expect that she will soon begin doing so. To be quite frank, I am not half so disturbed about this as I am about her realistic approach to the problem. She knows that she stammers, she knows that she is poor, and she guesses that she is illegitimate, she knows that she is dumb, and in a rather cold way she looked me in the eye and asked me whether I wouldn't do the same thing.[30]

An important psychological consequence of heroin use is the dulling of the ability to achieve orgasm, an impact that strikes both male and female addicts. The subtlety of the consequence of this condition for sexual relations is indicated by the following testimonial from a male addict:

My sex drive, before narcotics, was so great that upon intercourse with a girl, I would achieve climax almost immediately. And I noticed something. That upon taking narcotics, it killed my sex drive. But, on drugs, I was able to have sex for three, four hours at a time. Which made me feel superior over the girl. The girl was always begging me to stop, she couldn't take it, when it used to be the other way around, when I used to tell the girl, you're wearing me out, honey. I never reach a climax when I'm under the influence of narcotics but mentally, I feel that I can satisfy the woman I'm with.[31]

Not without a certain smugness, the same addict claims that "any girl that has sexual intercourse with a dope addict will never be satisfied by a normal person." He points up the consequences of this condition with a fine psychiatric malapropism: "You'd be surprised the effects when you have a few girls running after you, talking about your powers as a lady's man. It does something to your ego, and your super-ego."[32]

When both partners are addicts, however, the results are less savory, as indicated by a long-term female addict:

And horse [heroin] does affect you sexually, in a lot of ways. I mean, for instance, it's almost impossible to have an orgasm beyond eight caps. It can be done but it's very unusual . . . Bob and I are the only couple I know of whose balling didn't almost absolutely stop after they got hooked.[33]

The same addict provides testimony that the effect of heroin for a time may be of such a nature that it serves to undercut psychological inhibitions and thus facilitate sexual pleasure. "Oddly enough," she writes, "in the beginning it made it easier for me to ball. Times when I would ordinarily have been in one of these flips, if I took a little heroin I was solid."[34]

A major interpretative key to narcotic addiction among females, it appears to us, lies in the structure of amorous liaisons and romantic love in this country. A highly significant distinction between male and female drug addicts seems to reside in the finding that men are most often introduced to drugs by members of their peer group, while women are first "turned on" through the offices of boyfriends or husbands.[35]

For female addicts, there appears to exist a special appeal in heroin, one that seems to us to have been inadequately noted in the existing literature. That appeal may tell us more about the particular role of women in our society than it does about opiates. And it provides, we believe, insight into the relationship between sexual role patterning and deviant behaviors which can bring a person into the realm of medical concern.

"Men know nothing of the endless storm of being a woman," John McPartland has written. "Nothing of the final strength of a woman, of her toughness, of her unexcusing, unforgiving sense of reality. But they know the weakness of women, of their needs for cruelty and for tenderness, of their damning willingness to dream and to believe."[36]

It is in these terms, we submit, though perhaps somewhat less melodramatically, that female sexuality and heroin use might best be understood. In our society, the traditional female role is one of emotional and economic dependence. At the same time, men are believed to be omnivorously interested in sexual contact, so that the indifference of the now sexually lethargic male addict to his girlfriend or wife might reasonably be regarded by her as a testament to her personal failure and inadequacy. For the male, sharing his drug with the female may reduce his guilt and certainly will provide surcease from her sexual demands. For the female, participation in the drug ritual denotes proper sex role behavior, a demonstration of concern and sharing. Thus:

So he told me, look, you son-of-a-bitch, I'll kill you if you ever speak to me like that. You want to find out what it is? Why the hell don't you use it yourself? Try it! I have a bag here. This is heroin, you see, you black bitch, this is heroin! Try it yourself, you no-good bastard! (Weeping). It's good! Use it and you'll find out how good it is. You'll feel so good, Carmen, use it, go ahead, I'll show you how to use it.

And I ran away from him. I said, no, I'm not gonna use that; I'm not that stupid. I love you, but I'll never use that in my life, so help me God! Then every day he started talking a little more about it. Then one day I gave him my arm and he shot a little bit of stuff in my arm.

And since that time, here I am. I'm a drug addict. (Weeping). A mother of four children. Four wonderful children and wonderful set of parents.[37]

It probably need not be pointed out that it is Carmen herself who, apparently spontaneously, introduces in the third paragraph of the preceding quotation the relationship between "love" and drug use with her husband.

Thereafter, the process is almost inexorable. Women who have been addicted find it very difficult to form a satisfactory relationship with a "square" male. As one has noted: "I dated some square when I was home last year. I could fool them. They didn't have to know. But I felt that I couldn't be myself."[38] Note might be made here of the speaker's change from reference to the single person she had dated to a statement about squares as a group. Combine with her statement our finding from Los Angeles interviews with a dozen female addicts that not one believed it possible for a woman to live with an addict and herself remain drug-abstinent. Among our Los Angeles subjects, the following is a typical vignette:

Apparently pressure on Helen was accumulating steadily, and she reached her breaking point toward the end of 1968. Her husband began to go out with other women and to involve himself in militant activities about the same time. Helen evidently felt very threatened by her husband's unfaithfulness, involving, as it did, younger and prettier girls, and she recognized that one reason for his unfaithfulness was his desire to enjoy drug use with a woman.

Her feeling is that somewhere along the line she recognized that she could settle all of her marital difficulties by starting to use with her husband. In the past, they were good "running partners," and she knew that she could easily regain this tight relationship by chipping around to reduce the guilt that her drug-free living had created. So she started using, hoping to keep it within bounds. She soon became hooked, and although her marital difficulties were resolved, it was at the expense of something else, including ultimately, her freedom. Both she and her husband were arrested for six counts of armed robbery and one count of grand theft. Her husband has already been sentenced to state prison. It appears as if she will receive a lesser sentence.

Materials on the relationship between sexuality and female heroin use, then, stress that it is neither the physical nor necessarily the symbolic importance of use of heroin itself, but rather its function as a testimony to heterosexual togetherness and fidelity that often prompts its use and continuance among many female addicts. In this sense, a main thrust of this review has been an elaboration of the oft-neglected motive for drug use noted by John Clausen in his observation that "the goal need have little to do with the specific effects of the narcotic," but rather may be merely "to please a loved person."[38]

EMBOURGEOISEMENT OF THE EX-ADDICTS

Our inquiries regarding the impact of employment with the project on the ex-addicts' mobility aspirations and life-styles elicited several findings which shed light on some problems probably endemic to this type of program.[39] A major research hypothesis was that a social service job, paying a decent salary to a person who stood small likelihood of commanding such a salary in the open market, would lead the employee to take on values and behavioral patterns of "respectable" middle-class society.

There was, as the project progressed, a notable embourgeoisement among the ex-addicts, but the salaries apparently were not the reason. Almost all the workers had, at some time in the past, enjoyed incomes higher than their project salaries, either by legal or illegal means. What appear more significant are certain features of the streetworker role itself, which allowed close involvement and colleague (rather than client) interaction with a system heretofore remote and mysterious.

The project served as a laboratory for the transmission of skills which, when absent, often involve a former addict in serious difficulties. Staff members became remarkably adept at manipulating prospective employers, finding legal loopholes to avoid the reincarceration of clients, and cutting through red tape to elicit services from an array of social service agencies.

The ex-addicts' view of the competence of social workers, teachers, counselors, corrections officers, and other professionals, as we have noted above, changed considerably as the workers became involved in more or less peer interaction with such persons. Many ex-addicts expressed their revelations about the caliber of those whom they had previously held in some high esteem, and the implication for their own careers was clear:

I feel, you know, if they can make the kind of money they are making — for Chrissake I sure can go out and make money.

Thus, the contacts with professionals, the

expertise developed in varieties of social work, plus the experience with the creature comforts of their new paraprofessional work styles all led to dramatic reevaluations by the former addicts of their self-esteem and their career prospects. Two years following the inception of the project, 85% of the workers, when asked what they would like to do should the project not be refunded, replied that they wanted to work with people, to help addicts, to be social workers, or to engage in similar kinds of work. These responses were significantly different from those elicited from interviews done at the time of their original hiring. Since the termination of our formal research, at least a dozen of the former addicts have moved on to administrative positions in various social work and rehabilitative agencies. These successes in turn have fueled the aspirations of fieldworkers still with the project.

But there are other pressures inherent in the fieldworker role which impede the adoption of bourgeois styles. The ex-addicts are daily being reminded, and reminding each other, that the basis of their very effectiveness is their cultural affinity and empathy with street addicts. In the early months of the project, one of the ex-addict group leaders frequently berated the workers in terms such as the following:

I think most of you have lost that thing that makes you different from them funky professionals in treating addicts. I see a lot of you falling in the bureaucratic bag. Let's not forget that we are the ones to make this project go. Without us they have nothing. Let's start showing more concern for the addict.

Being a fieldworker, in short, enhances the distance from one's previous street life which, in turn, inhibits one's effectiveness in terms of the project's rehabilitative goals. The fieldworkers were, and have remained, critically aware of these cross-pressures and have come to accept them as another routine if frustrating dilemma of the fieldworker role.

CONSEQUENCES FOR CLIENTS

It may be enough to show that some ex-addict Project workers remained drug-abstinent who otherwise seemingly would not have done so except for the opportunity which the Project afforded them. Given the facts that most claimed a weekly drug expenditure between $200 and $300 for opiates when they were addicted and that this money was largely obtained from theft, the community might realize a sizeable savings merely by paying former addicts legitimate salaries to stay clean and legally occupied. Who is to judge that this is socially less desirable than the subsidization by purchasers of writers of toothpaste advertisements or hucksters who concoct come-ons to captivate youngsters into becoming cigarette smokers?

But such an approach really begs the issue. For one thing, the program was a mixed success in keeping its employees drug-free. For another, we have no way of knowing, absent a random-assignment design or adequate matching procedures, how many of the Project personnel would have done just as well in other jobs, or with no jobs at all. They were in some ways a select group and were approaching the age at which many addicts voluntarily abandon drug use, probably for a combination of reasons, some likely physiological (they do not get the same kick out of opiates with advancing years as they did earlier, and they may be too weary to stay with the intense pace of the drug world) and some perhaps social (they may develop a finer sense of their own mortality or they may begin to fear the longer sentences likely with several prior convictions standing against them). With equivocal data on the Project's impact on its employees, it seems particularly important to examine the consequences for clients as well as those for staff in evaluating NPP's impact and importance.

The task of determining client outcome proved for us a good deal more complicated than we had anticipated.[40] Our design called for the selection at random of 100 names from the Project files, the location of these subjects, and the determination of their past and current activity. Project records proved highly inadequate for this purpose; many files were bareboned and many contained totally inaccurate information — fictitious names, false birthdays, and nonexistent addresses. Even where complete and accurate information was available, we were often led to boarding houses or other transient residences from which the client had long since departed. Families also proved poor sources of follow-up information, for many clients were estranged from their parents, and mates, who often had smoldering grudges against them for thefts of household goods or similar depradations. Ultimately, we located 54 of the 100 persons whose names we had drawn from the Project files. Demographic comparisons indicated that the group we followed did not differ significantly from the overall client population. All interviews were conducted by ex-addicts in order to increase cooperation from the subjects, particularly since they were being asked about behaviors which, if known, could get them into legal difficulty.

The client follow-up group broke down into 44 men and 10 women. Older clients predominated; only 18% of the men, for instance, were below the age of 30, and 61% had passed their 35th birthday. As expected, almost all the clients were Mexican-Americans (despite a heavy concentration of Blacks in segments of the catchment area).

Most of the persons we interviewed had come to the Project not through its outreach efforts, which were extensive, but because they had heard about it from friends on the street. Most came because they wanted jobs; fully 41% of the sample indicated that this was the explanation for their first contact with NPP. The figure varied significantly by age, however; 67% of the 30- to 34-year-old group had sought jobs from NPP, for instance, but only 17% of the 20- to 24-year-old group.

Nineteen percent of the subjects arrived at the Project because of correctional pressures, either because their parole agent had "suggested" this course or because they were parole absconders and had heard that the NPP personnel would intervene for them with the state, trying to get the best deal possible if they agreed to give themselves up. Seventeen percent of the subjects came to the Project to detoxify, and these were mostly young persons.

Evaluative comments regarding NPP by its clients were overwhelmingly positive, despite the fact that many of the persons interviewed were contacted during trips to the correctional facilities in which they were now incarcerated. Ninety-one percent reported that they were favorably impressed with the Project, 6% would not say one way or the other, while only 2% offered negative comments. The most common observations were that the ex-addict staff members really understood drugs and drug addicts, that they knew the problems, that their advice was reasonable and sensible, and that they were not condescending or impersonal or self-righteous.

Three of the more ebullient endorsements among the many accorded convey the satisfaction that clients reported with the Project:

The Project has been a lifesaver for me. When I get into trouble, I holler "Project." Because of the Project, I've never failed a nalline test and have never been hooked. I would have been in the joint a long time ago, if not for NPP.

It's a hell of a good thing. It helped me and my wife both stay out longer than we had ever stayed out before. I usually run from the gate, but the Project made me really give it a try.

The Project's beautiful! It's a clean atmosphere. They can really understand addicts. If you're sincere, it really gives you morale and a place to go.

These verbal panegyrics are buttressed by the results of a direct question asking: Did the Project make a difference in your life? Sixty-one percent thought that it had, 30% said that it had not, and 9% were uncertain about the matter. Those who said that the Project did not help them invariably placed the blame for this failure either on themselves or on their life situation, with comments such as "The program didn't work for me, as I just wasn't ready for it," or "I would have received help if I had stayed out longer." This response pattern, incidentally, contradicts the popular notion that addicts are prone to blame everyone else but themselves for their difficulties.

Judging the consequences of the program in terms of specific measures of (1) correctional outcome, (2) employment record, and (3) drug use was done by compiling the record of the subject in each of these areas month by month during the time before he came to the Project (excluding periods of imprisonment) and then for each month thereafter (with the same exclusion). Generally, we went backward 60 months and as far forward as elapsed time since program participation allowed.

Our definitions of "success" and "failure" reflected our concern to measure behavioral change in ways sensitive to gradual and incremental developments in the addicts' biographies. The tendency of many follow-up addiction studies to define failure merely as any drug relapse neglects the vicissitudes natural to most human efforts at self-improvement, not to mention the drug rehabilitation process.

Correctional "failure" was defined as spending 10% or more time incarcerated after project intervention than prior to it. "Success," correlatively, was considered to be the reduction of one's incarcerated time by 10% or more after project contact. Ex-clients with about equal amounts of imprisonment before and after were labeled "neutral." For the sample as a whole, regarding correctional experience, 46% emerged as successful, 28% neutral, and 26% failures. Unsurprisingly, successes were more predominant among older ex-clients, reflecting the general relationship among convicts between high recidivism and youthfulness.

"Success" and "failure" regarding *drug use* were defined similarly: changes of more and less than 10% of "street time" using addictive substances. Thirty-three percent were successful (decreased use by 10% or more, post treatment), 43% neutral, and 24% failures.

In regard to *employment* (again using the 10% differential as measure of success and failure), the rates were 46% success, 26% neutral, 28% failure. Here, the failure of *any* ex-client over 45 years of age to improve on his preproject employment record seriously undercut the overall ratings. Among younger ex-clients job situations improved markedly following project intervention.

The most encouraging finding emerged when we examined differential success rates for long-term and short-term clients. In each of our three evaluation categories, the success rates of those clients with longer project tenure were exceptional. The ratios of successes to failures among those staying with the project for at least 12 months were correctional, 5 to 1; drug use, 2 to 1; employment, 5 to 1. We cannot assume, given the voluntary nature of project participation, that the project services are responsible for these statistical triumphs. But the data do lend support to the project staff's contention that, given the opportunity to work with addicts over an extended period of time, they can demonstrate their ability to effect positive behavioral change among persons often viewed as incorrigible.

CONCLUSION

There is a good deal more to an evaluation of a program such as the Narcotics Prevention Project than a compilation of numerical indices of outcome. There are always value questions relating to the proper expenditure of always scarce fiscal and human resources, and there are issues bearing upon alternative intervention methods which might have greater esthetic, political, or social appeal. There are also long-run, derivative, and cost-benefit considerations to be weighed.

Our data, therefore, can provide only qualified support for any conclusion about the utility of intervention programs using former addicts to work with practicing addicts in a community setting. What we have found is that such programs can be kept viable; that is, they can survive and grow. Turnover is apt to be pronounced, with many employees returning to drugs and some going on to better positions. The dilemma of escalating ex-addict mobility aspirations versus the necessity of maintaining empathy with clients should be anticipated. Care obviously needs to be taken in hiring so as to maximize success potentiality using evidence regarding the relationship between traits and work record. Women, in particular, probably need to be involved in such programs in more circumscribed and cloistered sorts of ways or at least provided with more support and supervision than that accorded male workers. Research efforts to discern the qualities that distinguish that minority of women who are able to cope with this type of role would be of great value.

If the temptation to define success in absolutist terms is resisted and we look instead to *improvements* in the lives of addicts, then projects of the type we have been discussing, when given the opportunity to work with addicts over an extended period of time, appear to have a considerable potential for success. Such projects, if they have the same kind of experience as the NPP, will be very much utilized and appreciated by their clientele, itself no small achievement at a time when drug addicts often feel they are treated with neglect, callousness, and condescension. In all, the research and other evidence that we have accumulated provide strong support for launching new efforts and expanding existing programs which use former addicts in drug rehabilitation.

REFERENCES

1. **Schwartz, R. D. and Skolnick, J. H.,** Two studies in legal stigma, in *The Other Side,* Becker, H. S., Ed., Free Press, New York, 1964, 103.
2. **Bitter, W., Jr.,** Drug abusers — an employment problem, *Person, J.,* 50, 858, 1971; Wilke, G., Growing use of narcotics saps industry, *N.Y. Times,* March 22, 1970; Malabre, A. L., Jr., Heroin, marijuana use by workers, applicants climb at some firms, *Wall St. J.,* May 4, 1970.
3. **Farrell, W. E.,** Big plants said to spurn ex-addicts, *N.Y. Times,* January 10, 1973.
4. **Austin, B. L.,** *Sad Nun at Synanon,* Holt, Rinehart & Winston, New York, 1970; Casriel, D., *So Fair a House,* Prentice-Hall, Englewood Cliffs, N.J., 1963; Endore, S. G., *Synanon,* Doubleday, Garden City, N.Y., 1968; Yablonsky, L., *The Tunnel Back: Synanon,* Macmillan, New York, 1965.
5. **Sternberg, D.,** Synanon house — a consideration of its implications for American corrections, *J. Crim. Law,* 54, 447, 1963.
6. **Miller, D. E., Himelson, A. N., and Geis, G.,** The East Los Angeles halfway house for felon addicts, *Int. J. Addict.,* 2, 305, 1967.
7. **Paz, O.,** *Labyrinth of Solitude,* Grove Press, New York, 1961, 29.
8. **Heller, C.,** *Mexican American Youth,* Random House, New York, 1969, 36.
9. **Real, D. and Real, J.,** Raising a new generation of addicts, *Human Behav.,* 2, 10, 1971.
10. **Real D. and Real, J.,** *Human Behav.,* 2, 10, 1971.
11. **Real, D. and Real, J.,** *Human Behav.,* 2, 11, 1971.
12. **Munns, J. G., Bullington, B., and Geis, G.,** Ex-addict streetworkers in a Mexican-American community, *Crime and Delinq.,* 16, 409, 1970.
13. **Sheehy, G.,** The female addict; tougher nuts to crack, *N.Y. Herald Tribune,* January 13, 1965, 13.
14. **Kolb, L.,** Drug addiction among women, *Proc. Am. Prison Soc.,* p. 349, 1938.
15. **Albert, E.,** The roles of women: a question of values, in *Man and Civilization,* Farber, S. M. and Wilson, R., Eds., McGraw-Hill, New York, 1963, 11.
16. **Gaulden, E. C., Littlefield, B. C., Putoff, O. E., and Sievert, A. L.,** Menstrual difficulties associated with heroin addiction, *Am. J. Obstet. Gynecol.,* 90, 155, 1964.
17. **Krause, S. O., Murray, P. M., Holmes, J. B., and Burgh, R. E.,** Heroin addiction among pregnant women and their newborn babies, *Am. J. Obstet. Gynecol.,* 75, 754, 1958.
18. **Marshall, O.,** *The Opium Habit in Michigan,* State Board of Health, Lansing, 1878, 61.
19. **Larner, J., Ed.,** *The Addict in the Street,* Grove Press, New York, 1967, 15.
20. **Ellinwood, E. H., Smith, W. E., and Vaillant, G. E.,** Narcotic addiction in males and females: a comparison, *Int. J. Addict.,* 1, 35, 1966.
21. **Ellinwood, E. H., Smith, W. E., and Vaillant, G. E.,** *Int. J. Addict.,* 1, 44, 1966.
22. **Weinberg, S. K.,** *Incest Behavior,* Citadel Press, New York, 1955.
23. **Ellinwood, E. H., Smith, W. E., and Vaillant, G. E.,** *Int. J. Addict.,* 1, 44, 1966.
24. **Ellinwood, E. H., Smith, W. E., and Vaillant, G. E.,** *Int. J. Addict.,* 1, 45, 1966.
25. **Ward, D. A. and Kassebaum, G. G.,** *Women's Prison: Sex and Social Structure,* Aldine, Chicago, 1965.
26. **Larner, J., Ed.,** *The Addict in the Street,* Grove Press, New Press, New York, 1967, 15.
27. **Sheehy, G.,** *N.Y. Herald Tribune,* January 13, 1965, 13.
28. **Jackman, N. R., O'Toole, R., and Geis, G.,** The self-image of the prostitute, in *Sexual Deviance,* Gagnon, J. H. and Simon, W., Eds., Harper & Row, New York, 1972, 133.
29. **Stern, M.,** Heroin traffickers here tell how $219,000,000 trade works, *N.Y. Times,* April 20, 1970.
30. **Rumney, J. and Murphy, J. P.,** *Probation and Social Adjustment,* Rutgers University Press, New Brunswick, N.J., 1952, 117.
31. **Larner, J., Ed.,** *The Addict in the Street,* Grove Press, New York, 1967, 109.
32. **Larner, J., Ed.,** *The Addict in the Street,* Grove Press, New York, 1967, 110.
33. **Hughes, H. M., Ed.,** *The Fantastic Lodge,* Houghton Mifflin, Boston, 1961, 128.
34. **Hughes, H. M., Ed.,** *The Fantastic Lodge,* Houghton Mifflin, Boston, 1961, 128.
35. **Sheehy, G.,** *N.Y. Herald Tribune,* January 13, 1965, 13.
36. **McPartland, J.,** *No Down Payment,* Pocket Books, New York, 1957, 259.
37. **Larner, J., Ed.,** *The Addict in the Street,* Grove Press, New York, 1967, 66.
38. **Clausen, J. A.,** Drug addiction, in *Contemporary Social Problems,* Merton, R. K. and Nisbet, R., Eds., Harcourt, Brace & World, New York, 1961, 219.
39. **Bullington, B., Munns, J. G., and Geis, G.,** Purchase of conformity; ex-narcotic addicts among the bourgeoisie, *Social Probl.,* 16, 456, 1969.
40. **Bullington, B.,** Drug Use Patterns in a Chicano Community, Ph.D. dissertation, U.C.L.A., 1974.

OCCUPATIONAL SKILLS AND LIFE-STYLES
OF NARCOTIC ADDICTS*

David N. Nurco and Monroe Lerner

TABLE OF CONTENTS

*The authors gratefully acknowledge the assistance of Mrs. Georgia Thistel and Messrs. Harry K. Shock and Lewis L. Williams, members of the study staff at the time of this research effort, and Lieutenant Leon N. Tomlin, Narcotics Unit, Baltimore City Police Department.

INTRODUCTION

This chapter is presented in two parts, with a concluding statement at its end. Part I presents the results of an investigation into vocational histories of 99 narcotic addicts and their acquisition and use of job skills. Part II focuses on a theoretical notion regarding transferability of skills narcotic addicts used in the pursuit of their addiction into socially acceptable occupations.

In Part I, we use traditional social research methodology in the conduct of our study, while in Part II we take a first step in theory development of a very tentative nature. This step must of necessity be considered tentative and awaits studies to validate various narcotic addict lifestyles as well as empirically testing the notion of transferability of "narcotic addict skills" into socially acceptable occupations.

I. A STUDY OF VOCATIONAL HISTORIES OF NARCOTIC ADDICTS

At present there is little information or understanding concerning what roles job skills play in the treatment and rehabilitation process. Although there is recognition that drug abuse is a function of societal-institutional, psychological, and personal factors, these factors have not been fully considered in either job counseling or job placement. Neither has there been an effort to consider the life-styles of addicts in job selection and placement. Too often the societal norm of "regular gainful employment" has been the focus, and not being able to fulfill this goal of the "eight-to-five" job, the addict has fallen into an unemployed status.

There are few "hard" data about which specific job skills addicts have acquired and how these can be used. Certainly, there is interest in the employment problem connected with drug abuse.[1] While the need to make vocational counseling a basic part of the treatment program and the need to involve the employer in the process of placing the addict are recognized, little is known about specific job skills and their relationship to jobs now held or later sought. Other questions might also be asked: Do addicts generally lack skills; i.e., is vocational training indicated? Do they need help in finding jobs or in being motivated? Are job opportunities available?

The present study (conducted during 1971–72) examines some of these questions and presents data collected from a sample of addicts of a limited age range. It is hoped that this initial investigation will open the way to further study of employability and job skills. In addition to providing some "hard" facts, it may find application in job counseling and thus help the addict to reenter and remain in the labor force.

Study Methods and Procedure

For the purposes of this study, plans were formulated to conduct structured interviews with 99 narcotic addicts from three separate programs for addicts in the Baltimore metropolitan area. The research design called for the study population to be all male, between the ages of 21 and 35 years, and composed of 75% Negro respondents and 25% White respondents. These criteria were adopted partly to facilitate the field work involved and, with respect to age and race, to reflect the actual population concentration of addicts in the three groups overall. However, in order to forestall any possible question about parental consent for the respondent's participation, no person under 21 years of age was interviewed.

Permission was obtained to conduct interviews with narcotic addicts from three sources: (1) a prison group from a program at the Maryland House of Correction, a prison within the Maryland correctional system, (2) a community group under mandatory supervision of the Narcotic Clinic, an abstinence program for paroled narcotic addicts, and (3) a community group voluntarily in a treatment program named Project A.D.A.P.T.

Samples of addicts were drawn from these three sources on the assumption that different types of addicts would be found in each program who might very well have different occupational patterns and job skills.

Sampling Procedure

The study sample was selected by a systematic random sampling from an alphabetical list of all narcotic addicts in the three groups described above. Taking only those within the age range of 21 through 35 years, a random sample of 33 names was drawn for each group, yielding a total study sample of 99. Each group had been stratified by race in order to ensure representative coverage

TABLE 1

Age of Respondents by Group

Age	Total No.	Total %	Prison group No.	Prison group %	Mandatory supervision group No.	Mandatory supervision group %	Voluntary treatment group No.	Voluntary treatment group %
All ages	99	100.0	33	100.0	33	100.0	33	100.0
21–23	26	26.3	1	3.0	10	30.3	15	45.5
24–26	26	26.3	9	27.3	11	33.3	6	18.2
27–29	20	20.2	11	33.3	5	15.2	4	12.1
30–32	14	14.1	9	27.3	4	12.1	1	3.0
33–35	13	13.1	3	9.1	3	9.1	7	21.2
Mean age in years	26.86		28.48		26.15		25.94	

TABLE 2

Race of Respondents by Group

Race	Total No.	Total %	Prison group No.	Prison group %	Mandatory supervision group No.	Mandatory supervision group %	Voluntary treatment group No.	Voluntary treatment group %
Both races	99	100.0	33	100.0	33	100.0	33	100.0
Black	74	74.7	25	75.7	25	75.7	24	72.7
White	25	25.3	8	24.3	8	24.3	9	27.3

in the sample of respondents.* The distributions by age, race, and education of the study sample are summarized in Tables 1, 2, and 3. Replacements within the respective samples occurred whenever a respondent was no longer in the program.** Of the original sample, five refused to participate in the interview and were also replaced.*** All respondents were voluntary, unpaid participants.

Personal and Demographic Characteristics of Respondents
General

The following narrative summarizes selected demographic and other descriptive data on all three groups combined. All were males; 75% were black and 25% were white. The average age was

26.8 years at the time of interview. Predominantly, respondents were born in the Baltimore metropolitan area (84%), and 64% reported no change in basic living arrangement up to age 18; i.e., they were raised by the same parent(s) or guardian(s) throughout that period. Of these parents, 91% were not addicted to drugs or to alcohol.

Typically, a respondent grew up with more than three siblings in the home. He attended public school and had completed the ninth grade before quitting at age 16. A majority (54%) had no juvenile court record of delinquency. The average age of first illegal drug usage was just over 16 years. Only 18% ultimately served in the armed forces.

Interestingly enough for this mainly inner-city

---

*For the year 1971, on the average the racial composition of each of the programs was as follows: Maryland House of Correction, J Dormitory, 78% black, 22% white; Narcotic Clinic, 72% black, 28% white; Project A.D.A.P.T., 75% black, 25% white.

**Each replacement was made by referring back to the program roster of men, divided by race, within the study age range. Another name was randomly drawn to replace the original name.

***All refusals were cases of unwillingness to be interviewed because the prospective respondents contended they did not have the time.

TABLE 3

Education by Group

Education highest level completed	Total		Prison group		Mandatory supervision group		Voluntary treatment group	
	No.	%	No.	%	No.	%	No.	%
All levels	99	100.0	33	100.0	33	100.0	33	100.0
Some grade school	13	13.1	5	15.2	7	21.2	1	3.0
Completed grade school	17	17.2	8	24.2	6	18.2	3	9.1
Some high school	43	43.4	14	42.4	13	39.4	16	48.5
Completed high school	19	19.2	5	15.2	7	21.2	7	21.2
Some college	5	5.1	0	0.0	0	0.0	5	15.2
Completed college	1	1.0	0	0.0	0	0.0	1	3.0
More than college	1	1.0	1	3.0	0	0.0	0	0.0

population, the place of parental birth showed wide variation. The major finding was that for the 71% of the fathers the birthplace was other than Baltimore, and for 54% of all mothers the birthplace was outside Baltimore. Thus, over half the study population was first generation, urban born. Fifty-three percent of the fathers of respondents were construction, structural, or laboring workers, and 47% of the mothers were housewives. Of those mothers engaged in gainful occupations, half were service workers. Forty-seven percent of the respondents had never been married, 26% were married at the time of interview, and 27% had been married previously.

Occupational status and community living arrangements of respondents were also recorded, and it is to be noted that for the group in prison the data reflect occupation and residence during the several months prior to incarceration. There was ample variation in the occupational data in that 22% of all respondents were unemployed and 25% were working in *construction* and *structural* jobs. Over half of the men lived with parents and relatives other than spouse; in only one case was a parent a drug abuser. For those 19% who were living with a spouse in the community, four of these spouses were drug abusers. Other adult relatives in the living arrangement were, for the most part, not drug abusers (85%). Each respondent was asked his perception of the stability of his own family of orientation, and an overwhelming majority, 90%, rated their families as stable. Predictably, for the total study population, 90% had had more than one criminal trial, and 80% had served a sentence in prison.

Group Differences

The three groups differed in several important aspects:

1. The prison group had fewer young persons.

2. The voluntary treatment group had a greater prospectus of persons at either end of the age range; between 21 to 23 and 33 to 35.

3. The voluntary treatment group was better educated; 18.2% of the group had some college, whereas no one in the mandatory supervision group and only one person (3%) in the prison group had achieved that level.

4. The prison group was much less likely than the other two groups to have been living with parent(s) or other close relatives prior to incarceration (prison group, 33.3%; mandatory supervision group, 60.6%; voluntary treatment group, 54.6%).

5. The voluntary treatment group was much less likely to have had a mother working outside the home during the formative years (up to age 18); i.e., 39% of the mothers of the voluntary

treatment group were working, versus 54% for the mandatory supervision group and 58% for the prison group. Interestingly enough, there was little difference among the groups in terms of "missing fathers."

Most of the addicts in this study population had drug-free (abstinence) periods. For about three fourths, this occurred as a consequence of their periods of incarceration, while only a minority, especially of the prison and mandatory supervision groups, attributed their abstinence to the effects of drug abuse treatment programs. Of the prison group, 35.8% saw abstinence as more likely to result from incarceration, while 80.0% of the mandatory supervision group agreed. For the voluntary treatment group, on the other hand, the opposite was true; a majority of this population (62.5%) attributed their abstinence to treatment programs.

In general, we found the voluntary treatment group to be more heterogeneous in respect to social and demographic characteristics.

Race Differences

Between black and white respondents there was some variation in profile on the following measures. Typically, the black respondents reported no change of basic living arrangement throughout childhood (75%), whereas for white respondents the figure was 40%. Current occupational status* revealed that 70% of black respondents were employed full-time as against 84% of white respondents. Other variations were average age of first illegal drug use (16.9 years for blacks, 14.9 years for whites), average age of first addiction to heroin (20.5 years for blacks, 19.3 years for whites), addiction status at the time of first voluntary community service (40% of the black respondents had been addicted and 68% of the white respondents). As a result of the first offense tried in court, 48% of the black as compared to 20% of the white respondents were confined.

In addition, a much higher percentage of white drug addicts came from fatherless homes than is true of the white population in Baltimore City in 1970, according to the U.S. Census. Among blacks no such significant difference was found. Likewise, a much higher percentage of whites reported more

than one set of parents than did blacks. On the other hand, more black fathers were born outside Baltimore and the State of Maryland. Interestingly, however, most respondents believed their family backgrounds had been stable. Very little use was made of welfare assistance by the respondents' families.

Findings

The findings presented here are addressed to several questions concerning the work-a-day world of narcotic addicts. At the present time, national attention is focused on the habilation and/or rehabilitation of this population. In order to proceed properly, several questions relating to jobs held and skills acquired by such persons must be examined. In the following pages, we will begin the exploration of these issues by examining important preliminary data in order to provide a foundation for future study.

Occupational History

This section explores the jobs held by addicts *prior* to addiction (pre-addiction) as well as *subsequent* to it (post-addiction). Because addicts typically have an erratic employment record in that they hold many jobs requiring little or no skill, periods of brief employment, i.e., jobs held for less than 90 days, have been excluded from our data analysis.

Major Occupation

Table 4 deals with our study sample's pre-addiction work history. Although nearly half (47.5%) of the total sample were unemployed before addiction, this finding must be considered in the light of the fact that the average age at addiction was only 20.5 years for blacks and 19.3 for whites. In fact, most of this group had quit school at a fairly early age, dropping out while in the 10th grade, and had the double liability of low educational level and unemployment prior to the onset of drug addiction. It is therefore not surprising that not a single respondent fell into the highest occupational category; however, the remaining categories were about equally well represented. Differences among the three treatment groups with respect to occupations pre-addiction were relatively slight, although the prison sample had relatively more respondents in the *service*

*Occupation is defined herein as regular, full-time employment for a minimum of 3 months.

TABLE 4

Distribution of Major Occupations* (Pre-addiction) by Group

Major occupation pre-addiction	Total		Prison group		Mandatory supervision group		Voluntary treatment group	
	N	%	N	%	N	%	N	%
All occupations	99	100.0	33	100.0	33	100.0	33	100.0
Professional, technical, and managerial	0	0.0	0	0.0	0	0.0	0	0.0
Clerical and sales	9	9.0	4	12.1	3	9.1	2	6.1
Service	10	10.1	6	18.2	2	6.1	2	6.1
Processing, machine trades, and bench work	12	12.2	1	3.0	6	18.2	5	15.1
Structural work	9	9.0	3	9.1	3	9.1	3	9.1
Miscellaneous	12	12.2	4	12.1	5	15.1	3	9.1
Unemployed	47	47.5	15	45.5	14	42.4	18	54.5

*Occupation is defined herein as regular, full-time employment for a minimum of 3 months.

TABLE 5

Distribution of Major Occupations* (Post-addiction) by Group

Major occupation post-addiction	Total		Prison group		Mandatory supervision group		Voluntary treatment group	
	N	%	N	%	N	%	N	%
All occupations	99	100.0	33	100.0	33	100.0	33	100.0
Professional, technical, and managerial	5	5.0	0	0.0	1	3.0	4	12.1
Clerical and sales	8	8.1	3	9.1	3	9.1	2	6.1
Service	10	10.1	6	18.2	2	6.1	2	6.1
Processing, machine trades, and bench work	16	16.2	6	18.2	5	15.1	5	15.1
Structural work	24	24.2	10	30.3	7	21.2	7	21.2
Miscellaneous	15	15.2	4	12.1	7	21.2	4	12.1
Unemployed	21	21.2	4	12.1	8	24.3	9	27.3

*Occupation is defined herein as regular, full-time employment for a minimum of 3 months.

occupations and relatively fewer in the *processing, machine trades*, and *bench work* occupations than did the remaining two treatment groups.

Subsequent to addiction, unemployment was less than half the amount it had been previously (21.2% vs. 47.5%). As may be seen from Table 5, five individuals now belonged to the highest occupational category. It is perhaps significant that four of these five were enrolled in voluntary treatment.* However, it is noteworthy that the

voluntary treatment group also reported the highest rate of unemployment. Overall, the *structural work* occupations were the most heavily represented, with nearly one fourth of the total sample falling into this occupational category.

If one considers change in occupational status pre- and post-addiction, the largest single difference appears to be in terms of decreased unemployment as noted above. In addition, an increasing number of respondents appear to have

*The reader should note that in instances where a relatively small number of cases is distributed over a relatively large number of categories, as illustrated in Tables 4 and 5, the application of formal statistical tests of significance is of questionable value. In these instances, a more purely descriptive approach has been adopted.

TABLE 6

Distribution of Longest Period of Employment by Major Occupational Category (Pre-addiction) All Groups Combined

Longest period of employment	All occu-pations		Profes-sional, etc.[1]		Clerical and sales		Service		Processing, etc.[2]		Structural work		Miscel-laneous	
	N	%	N	%	N	%	N	%	N	%	N	%	N	%
Total	99	100.0	0	100.0	9	100.0	10	100.0	12	100.0	9	100.0	12	100.0
Less than 3 months*	47	47.5					Not Applicable							
3 to 6 months	11	11.1	0	0.0**	4	44.4	1	10.0	2	16.7	2	22.2	2	16.7
7 to 12 months	17	17.2	0	0.0	4	44.4	3	30.0	4	33.3	3	33.3	3	25.0
13 to 24 months	10	10.1	0	0.0	0	0.0	2	20.0	2	16.7	1	11.2	5	41.6
More than 24 months	14	14.1	0	0.0	1	11.2	4	40.0	4	33.3	3	33.3	2	16.7

[1] Professional, technical, and managerial occupations.
[2] Processing, machine trades, and bench work occupations.
*Defined herein as unemployed.
**Percentages below the double horizontal lines are based on employed respondents only.

entered the *structural work* occupations subsequent to their addictions. The reason for this may be that many *structural work* occupations require a minimum of prior skills and work experience.

Longest Period of Employment

Turning now to the issue of continuity of employment, it will be noted from Table 6 that only 14 of the entire sample of 99 respondents had been continuously employed for 24 months or longer *prior* to their addictions. The most frequent period of continuous employment was somewhere between 7 and 12 months, with the *clerical* and *sales* group displaying perhaps the greatest degree of job instability.

In a similar vein, Table 7 indicates that 20 of the 99 respondents were continuously employed for 24 months or longer *post*-addiction. As before, the most frequent period of continuous employment was still somewhere between 7 and 12 months. In contrast to the previous table, however, Table 7 suggests that respondents in the *structural work* occupations enjoyed the greatest

degree of job stability. For example, 67% (16/24) of the *structural* workers were employed continuously for 12 months or longer as opposed to only 30% (3/10) of the *service* workers, 27% (4/15) of those in the *miscellaneous** occupations, and *none* of those engaged in *clerical and sales. It would be interesting to pursue in future investigations the relative contributions of voluntary selection (the addict's choice of occupation) and actual work environment (especially as the latter relates to personality characteristics and life-styles) in determining the degree of job stability that can be anticipated.*

Reason for Leaving Job

Closely related to the matters just discussed are the reasons given by a respondent for terminating the particular job at which he had been continuously employed for the longest period of time. Considering first the pre-addiction jobs, Table 8 reveals that exactly half of the 48 persons to whom this question applied left their jobs of their own volition, but for a wide variety of *negative*

*The present discussion of occupations and job skills includes comments on occupations classified as *miscellaneous*. As used herein, this *miscellaneous* grouping includes the following: motor freight transportation, packaging and materials handling, extraction of materials, logging, production and distribution of utilities, amusement and recreation, and graphic arts.

TABLE 7

Distribution of Longest Period of Employment by Major Occupational Category (Post-addiction) All Groups Combined

Longest period of employment	All occupations		Professional, etc.[1]		Clerical and sales		Service		Processing, etc.[2]		Structural work		Miscellaneous	
	N	%	N	%	N	%	N	%	N	%	N	%	N	%
Total	99	100.0	5	100.0	8	100.0	10	100.0	16	100.0	24	100.0	15	100.0
Less than 3 months*	21	21.2				Not Applicable								
3 to 6 months	16	16.2	1	20.0**	3	37.5	4	40.0	2	12.5	3	12.5	3	20.0
7 to 12 months	28	28.3	3	60.0	5	62.5	3	30.0	4	25.0	5	20.9	8	53.4
13 to 24 months	14	14.1	1	20.0	0	0.0	1	10.0	4	25.0	6	25.0	2	13.3
More than 24 months	20	20.2	0	0.0	0	0.0	2	20.0	6	37.5	10	41.6	2	13.3

[1] Professional, technical, and managerial occupations.
[2] Processing, machine trades, and bench work occupations.
*Defined herein as unemployed.
**Percentages below the double horizontal lines are based on employed respondents only.

TABLE 8

Distribution of Reasons for Leaving Major Occupation (Pre-addiction) by Group

Reasons for leaving	Total		Prison group		Mandatory supervision group		Voluntary treatment group	
	N	%	N	%	N	%	N	%
All reasons	99	100.0	33	100.0	33	100.0	33	100.0
Respondent initiated: positive reasons	17	17.2	7	21.2	6	18.2	4	12.1
Respondent initiated: negative reasons	24	24.2	11	33.3	10	30.3	3	9.1
Employer initiated	7	7.1	2	6.1	4	12.1	1	3.0
Not applicable: Did not leave job	4	4.0	0	0.0	0	0.0	4	12.1
Never held job for at least 3 months	47	47.5	13	39.4	13	39.4	21	63.6

reasons.* Chief among these was dissatisfaction with the work situation in one of its aspects. Interestingly enough, however, 35% (17/48) left for *positive* reasons of their own, and only 15% (7/48) of all terminations were employer initiated. Differences in any of these respects between the three treatment groups are relatively slight following adjustment for the fact that nearly twice as many respondents in the voluntary treatment group, as contrasted with the other two groups, had *never* held a job pre-addiction for as long as three months.

*Reasons for leaving that were initiated by the respondent employee were categorized as either positive or negative. Examples of *positive* reasons were to get a better job, to enter a job training program, to become self-employed, and to enter the armed forces. *Negative* reasons included conflicts with other personnel on job, drug use, incarceration, family problems, and quit for no apparent reason.

TABLE 9

Distribution of Reasons for Leaving Major Occupation (Post-addiction) by Group

Reasons for leaving	Total		Prison group		Mandatory supervision group		Voluntary treatment group	
	N	%	N	%	N	%	N	%
All reasons	99	100.0	33	100.0	33	100.0	33	100.0
Respondent initiated: positive reasons	15	15.1	4	12.1	3	9.1	8	24.2
Respondent initiated: negative reasons	41	41.5	22	66.7	12	36.4	7	21.2
Employer initiated	14	14.1	2	6.1	6	18.2	6	18.2
Not applicable: Did not leave job	13	13.1	0	0.0	4	12.1	9	27.3
Never held job for at least 3 months	16	16.2	5	15.1	8	24.2	3	9.1

Post-addiction, it was again found that over half (41/70) of the total sample who had terminated their longest-held job did so for *negative* reasons of their own. Exactly 20% (14/70) were employer initiated, and another 21% (15/70) were for voluntary reasons of a positive nature. In contrast with the pre-addiction findings of Table 8, Table 9 reveals that 9 of the 33 respondents in the voluntary treatment group, as opposed to none in the prison group and only 4 in the mandatory supervision group, had yet to terminate the job that they had held for the longest period of time. Once more, this difference among groups has important implications which relate not only to possible preexisting group differences but also to the impact of the treatment modality on the continuity of the work situation.

Current Occupational Status

In contrast with the previous discussion, the following section will deal with the respondents' current occupational status.

In the major job categories of current occupations reported (Table 10), there were apparent differences among the three subgroups in that the voluntary treatment group had more respondents in the *professional, technical,* and *managerial* category. Also of special interest is the low rate of unemployment reported by the prison group* (3%) as opposed to the mandatory supervision (27%) and the voluntary treatment (36%) groups. However, this finding may reflect some bias in that

the prison sample may have been more generous in defining their pre-prison employment status, while the other two groups were more obliged to admit to their present state of unemployment.

Review of the *miscellaneous* category revealed that a majority of these occupations involved out-of-doors employment, e.g., stevedore, truck driver, etc. If the *structural* and *miscellaneous* categories are combined to form an *outdoor occupations* category (as opposed to plant, assembly, or desk work), the following tabulation emerges:

Group	Outdoor Occupations
Prison	41%
Mandatory supervision	45%
Voluntary treatment	33%

The voluntary treatment group thus appears to be underrepresented in the *outdoor occupations*. While it has the largest percentage in the highest occupational category (4/33), it also has the largest number of unemployed (12/33).

Job Skills

In the rehabilitation of the narcotic addict, the importance of vocational training and retraining has been repeatedly emphasized. Of major importance is the question of whether or not the addict has sufficient and/or appropriate job skills for the available market. For the present study, Table 11 lists the skills of respondents by treatment group.

---

*The prison group reported occupational status for the several months prior to incarceration.

TABLE 10

Distribution of Current Occupations by Group

Current occupation	Total N	Total %	Prison group* N	Prison group* %	Mandatory supervision group N	Mandatory supervision group %	Voluntary treatment group N	Voluntary treatment group %
All occupations	99	100.0	33	100.0	33	100.0	33	100.0
Professional, technical, and managerial	7	7.1	2	6.1	1	3.0	4	12.1
Clerical and sales	5	5.0	4	12.1	0	0.0	1	3.0
Service	8	8.1	4	12.1	1	3.0	3	9.1
Processing, machine trades, and bench work	10	10.1	5	15.1	3	9.1	2	6.1
Structural work	25	25.3	11	33.4	5	15.1	9	27.3
Miscellaneous	18	18.2	6	18.2	10	30.4	2	6.1
Students	3	3.0	0	0.0	3	9.1	0	0.0
Unemployed	22	22.2	1	3.0	9	27.3	12	36.3
N/A	1	1.0	0	0.0	1	3.0	0	0.0

*The prison group reported job status for the several months immediately prior to incarceration.

TABLE 11

Distribution of Number of Job Skills Acquired by Group

Number of job skills acquired	Total N	Total %	Prison group N	Prison group %	Mandatory supervision group N	Mandatory supervision group %	Voluntary treatment group N	Voluntary treatment group %
All respondents	99	100.0	33	100.0	33	100.0	33	100.0
None	23	23.2	5	15.1	6	18.2	12	36.3
1	35	35.4	11	33.3	9	27.3	15	45.5
2	20	20.2	9	27.3	7	21.1	4	12.1
3	12	12.1	3	9.1	9	27.3	0	0.0
4	4	4.0	2	6.1	0	0.0	2	6.1
5 or more	5	5.1	3	9.1	2	6.1	0	0.0
Mean	1.53		1.85		1.82		.94	

It will be seen that the voluntary treatment group reports considerably fewer job skills on the average than either the prison or mandatory supervision groups, yet the voluntary treatment group has the most stable job history.

Job skills, as reported by the respondents, were categorized as having been acquired either by formal or informal training. Criteria for formal training included formal schooling, job training classes, and/or specific on-the-job training programs, preferably verified by some indication of specific course content and the presentation of a certificate upon completion. Informal acquisition of skills comprised specific job experience, free-time learning from associates, and/or hobby or recreational experience as gauged by practice in, as well as practical knowledge of, the skill in question. Both types of skill acquisition occurred primarily during employment, i.e., as a result of specific on-the-job training or job experience.

The distribution of skills so acquired is shown in Tables 12 and 13. Because of the volume of

TABLE 12

Distribution of Job Skills Acquired in Formal Training by Group

Job skills acquired in formal training	Total (N = 99)	Prison group (N = 33)	Mandatory supervision group (N = 33)	Voluntary treatment group (N = 33)
All job skills*	71	37	23	11
Professional, technical, and managerial	3	2	1	0
Clerical and sales	10	5	4	1
Service	12	6	4	2
Processing, machine trades, and bench work	20	11	7	2
Structural work	20	11	5	4
Miscellaneous	6	2	2	2

*Numbers in table refer to job skills, not respondents.

TABLE 13

Distribution of Job Skills Acquired in Informal Training by Group

Job skills acquired in informal training	Total (N = 99)	Prison group (N = 33)	Mandatory supervision group (N = 33)	Voluntary treatment group (N = 33)
All job skills*	82	36	24	22
Professional, technical, and managerial	3	3	0	0
Clerical and sales	11	5	5	1
Service	22	8	5	9
Processing, machine trades, and bench work	13	4	7	2
Structural work	26	14	5	7
Miscellaneous	7	2	2	3

*Numbers in table refer to job skills, not respondents.

information requested, respondents frequently had difficulty in recalling the details of their job training in relation to when they became addicted. For this reason, data were analyzed only in terms of skills formally and informally acquired, not in terms of *pre-* and *post-*addiction.

Table 12 deals with job skills acquired by formal training. A total of 71 skills were learned in this way, 20 of which had applicability to occupations in *structural* (construction and building) work. Other skills learned were chiefly related to manual work and reflect the types of training generally available in programs and schools in this geographic area. Among the treatment groups, the prison group ranked highest in the number of skills formally acquired, 37, as compared with 23 for the mandatory supervision group and only 11 for the voluntary treatment group.

For skills informally acquired, a similar pattern is in evidence. Table 13 reveals that *structural* skills constitute a large proportion of the total, particularly if these are combined with other skills related to manual work. However, for skills informally acquired, there were fewer differences among the sample groups. It is interesting to note that the voluntary treatment group acquired twice as many skills informally as formally. Again, the prison group reported the most skills acquired, 36 of 82.

Use of Skills

In addition to information as to how a skill was acquired, it is of interest to determine whether or not it was subsequently used. Tables 14 and 15 describe the use of formally and informally learned skills. Seventy-one skills were reported as having been learned formally, i.e., through special training, as compared to 82 skills which were learned informally, i.e., without benefit of a formalized training program.

Of the total 71 skills learned formally, 45 were never used, 18 were used less than 1 year, and only 8 were used for 1 year or longer. The question arises as to the reason for this lack of utilization and whether the same would be found for nonaddict groups. An encouraging fact, however, is the finding that more than half of those trained in *structural* occupations subsequently used these skills on the job. It may be that *structural* jobs are more available or that this type of work is less in conflict with the life-style of the addict.

Skills learned informally appear to have been subsequently used with a much greater frequency than those learned formally. Of 82 such skills learned, only 35 were never subsequently used. One reason may be that since many such skills were learned on the job, they would have a better chance of being subsequently utilized. Furthermore, it may be assumed that informal learning of skills is more closely related to job opportunity and job interest than is formal learning. As further support for the value of informal skill learning, 23 of 47 respondents who used their skills had been on the job for over 12 months.

Looking at the utilization of skill categories, we again find that skills relating primarily to inside occupations, i.e., *professional, clerical, service, processing,* and *bench work*, appear to be under-

TABLE 14

Distribution of Job Skills Acquired in Formal Training by Use of Skill on Job

Job skills acquired in formal training	Total	Never used	Used less than 12 months	Used 12 months or more
All job skills	71	45	18	8
Professional, technical, and managerial	3	2	0	1
Clerical and sales	10	7	2	1
Service	12	8	2	2
Processing, machine trades, and bench work	20	15	5	0
Structural work	20	9	7	4
Miscellaneous	6	3	3	0

TABLE 15

Distribution of Job Skills Acquired in Informal Training by Use of Skill on Job

Job skills acquired in informal training	Total	Never used	Used less than 12 months	Used 12 months or more
All job skills	82	35	24	23
Professional, technical, and managerial	3	0	1	2
Clerical and sales	11	5	4	2
Service	22	11	6	5
Processing, machine trades, and bench work	13	8	2	3
Structural work	26	8	8	10
Miscellaneous	7	3	3	1

utilized. Of 49 such skills learned informally, 24 were never subsequently used. However, of the 33 skills relating to primarily outside occupations; i.e., *structural* and *miscellaneous*, only 11 were not utilized. The occupations falling under the *structural* and *miscellaneous* categories include welding, painting, plastering, construction, structural work, excavating, transportation, packaging, printing, etc.

Occupations of Fathers

The following section explores possible relationships between the occupations of the respondents and those of their fathers.

Table 16 presents data pertaining to the major occupations of the fathers of all respondents. *Structural* occupations comprise the most frequently occurring category overall (35%) and together with *processing, service,* and *miscellaneous* occupations account for nearly 81% of the total. Although differences among the three treatment groups on this variable do not appear especially marked, there does seem to be a tendency for fathers of the voluntary treatment respondents to be overrepresented in the *professional* category. In a similar vein, these fathers appear to be underrepresented in the *service* and *miscellaneous* occupational categories. By and large, it would appear that the respondents in the voluntary treatment group come from families enjoying higher occupational status.

Vocational Services Received

Turning now to a brief consideration of vocational services received, it may be seen from Table 17 that comparatively few vocational services were received by any group of respondents prior to addiction. The total number of such services received was only 15 for the entire sample, and approximately half of these were in the form of counseling.

Subsequent to addiction, a total of 34 services was received by all respondents. Not only is this more than twice the number received before addiction, but it would appear from Table 18 that significant differences also now appear among the three treatment groups with respect to numbers and types of services received. These differences are largely between the voluntary treatment group on the one hand and the remaining two treatment groups on the other in that the former reported no instances of testing, vocational rehabilitation, or job training while incarcerated. All of these differences can no doubt be related to the fact that fewer voluntary treatment respondents had been incarcerated for any appreciable length of time. Perhaps more importantly, Table 18 reveals the relative lack of relevant job training received while

TABLE 16

Distribution of Major Occupations of Fathers of Respondents by Group

Major occupation of father	Total		Prison group		Mandatory supervision group		Voluntary treatment group	
	N	%	N	%	N	%	N	%
All occupations of fathers	99	100.0	33	100.0	33	100.0	33	100.0
Professional, technical, and managerial	8	8.1	0	0.0	2	6.1	6	18.2
Clerical and sales	1	1.0	0	0.0	0	0.0	1	3.0
Service	10	10.1	4	12.1	4	12.1	2	6.1
Processing, machine trades, and bench work	18	18.2	9	27.3	5	15.1	4	12.1
Structural work	35	35.3	10	30.3	9	27.3	16	48.4
Miscellaneous	17	17.2	7	21.2	8	24.3	2	6.1
Not applicable*	10	10.1	3	9.1	5	15.1	2	6.1

*This category includes data unknown and father not available.

TABLE 17

Distribution of Vocational Services Received Pre-addiction by Group

Vocational services received	Total		Prison group		Mandatory supervision group		Voluntary treatment group	
All vocational services received	15		5		4		6	
Community service								
Counseling	7	(5)*	3	(2)	0	(0)	4	(3)
Testing	2	(2)	0	(0)	1	(1)	1	(1)
Job placement	4	(2)	2	(1)	2	(1)	0	(0)
Vocational rehabilitation	1	(1)	0	(0)	0	(0)	1	(1)
Institutional service								
Job training while incarcerated	1	(1)	0	(0)	1	(1)	0	(0)
Mean	0.15		0.15		0.12		0.18	

*Bracket figures indicate number of individuals receiving services.

TABLE 18

Distribution of Vocational Services Received Post-addiction by Group

Vocational services received	Total		Prison group		Mandatory supervision group		Voluntary treatment group	
All vocational services received	34		16		13		5	
Community service								
Counseling	8	(8)*	2	(2)	4	(4)	2	(2)
Testing	4	(2)	4	(2)	0	(0)	0	(0)
Job placement	9	(9)	4	(4)	2	(2)	3	(3)
Vocational rehabilitation	7	(7)	3	(3)	4	(4)	0	(0)
Institutional service								
Job training while incarcerated	6	(6)	3	(3)	3	(3)	0	(0)
Mean	0.34		0.48		0.39		0.15	

*Bracket figures indicate number of individuals receiving services.

incarcerated even among the prison sample. Correction of such an undesirable situation should be given a higher order of priority in any enlightened correctional system with which addicts are likely to come into contact.

All community services, with the exception of those provided by Vocational Rehabilitation, were provided by several different community agencies. It is interesting to note that the Vocational Rehabilitation agency gave service to only one respondent prior to addiction and to seven individuals subsequent to addiction. Three of these were in the prison group, four in the mandatory supervision group, and none in the voluntary treatment group.

Discussion and Summary

The data presented in this section provide

important information concerning the occupational backgrounds of the addict-respondents, especially as these relate to job skills acquired, occupations of fathers, vocational services received, and, perhaps most importantly, current occupational status. It is clear that all these several aspects must be considered in the intelligent planning for the rehabilitation of any addict population.

Several major points emerge that will be briefly recapitulated. First, since addiction usually occurs at a relatively early age, the majority of addicts are unemployed before addiction or employed in relatively unskilled jobs. Addiction apparently does not preclude subsequent employment, however, and nearly 80% subsequently engage in gainful activity after addiction.

The most frequently held jobs appear to be in the *structural* category. These occupations are frequently characterized by only modest educational demands, and they typically involve physical labor out-of-doors. It may well be that these characteristics conform with the personalities and life-styles of many addicts in that addicts employed in the *structural* areas also appear to enjoy the greatest degree of job stability. Interestingly enough, termination of jobs typically appears to have been for respondent-initiated reasons rather than for employer-initiated ones.

Differences among the three treatment groups studied are frequently in evidence. Most of these differences are between the prison and mandatory supervision groups on the one hand and the voluntary treatment group on the other. For example, members of the voluntary treatment group are most likely to be employed in the higher occupational categories *or* to be unemployed altogether. They are also less likely to have acquired job skills, either formally or informally. The fathers of the voluntary treatment respondents are more likely to be drawn from the higher occupational levels. All these findings suggest a considerably higher socioeconomic status, on the average, for members of the voluntary treatment group.

A somewhat discouraging note is interjected by the fact that a majority of formally learned job skills are apparently never subsequently used. This is also true, but to a lesser extent, of job skills learned informally. Once again, the most frequently utilized job skills are those relating to the *structural work* occupations, a finding that lends

additional weight to the earlier observation that the addicts studied appear to be most comfortable in out-of-doors occupations involving physical labor. It must be remembered, of course, that both availability and accessibility of the various types of jobs and occupations may be important factors here.

Finally, the data presented suggest that very few vocational rehabilitation services were utilized either before or after addiction. Only 7 individuals out of the entire sample of 99 received vocational rehabilitation services. The implication of such a finding for the successful substitution of a viable occupational alternative to the varieties of "addict careers" is obvious. It would seem that correction of this situation should be given a high order of priority if the goal of assisting the ex-addict to become a productive member of society is ever to be reached.

II. TRANSFERABILITY OF ADDICT LIFE-STYLES INTO SOCIALLY ACCEPTABLE OCCUPATIONS

In the preceding section, the analyses have focused on the job skills learned by narcotic addicts and on the variety of jobs which they have held. From the data presented and summarized, it is clear that relatively few job skills were ever formally learned and that an even smaller number were ever subsequently utilized in legitimate, gainful occupations. For these and other reasons, it is clear that alternative avenues to the solutions of the addict employment problem must be investigated. In this section, therefore, we shall discuss the matter of "life-styles" of narcotic addicts and the potential of this concept for facilitating approaches to legitimate employment.

A brief review of the literature has yielded little information as to the specific skills possessed by narcotic addicts. While addicts often feel that they possess certain skills, employers do not typically find these applicable to existing job needs.

With regard to skills learned during periods of incarceration, any training provided is usually based on available programs and/or the needs of the correctional institution rather than upon realistic manpower requirements of the market place. Many addicts are further limited because they lack the kinds of skills necessary for those jobs that are open to them. In addition, many job skills learned are frequently different from those in keeping with the life-style of the addict. For example, one addict reported having been trained while incarcerated as a sewing machine operator; however, he practiced this skill only while in jail. Out of jail, he worked as a construction laborer.

In the course of the present section, we shall propose a preliminary conceptual model which avoids the above difficulties by addressing itself to addict life-styles in terms of their transferability to socially accepted occupations. This model endeavors to deal with the problem by moving the addict into occupations related to his life-style and personality rather than by merely teaching skills in areas where training resources, not necessarily job openings, currently happen to be available.

The Concept of Central Life Interest, or "Life-style"

The concept of central life interest refers to the single activity on which dominant emphasis is placed in the life of the individual. Feldman and Thielbar make this point succinctly when they state that ". . . . a distinct life style is evident when a single activity or interest pervades a person's other interests and unrelated activities—a drug addict is an extreme example."[2]

These authors also cite other examples of a central life interest, e.g., avid baseball fans, television enthusiasts, professional San Franciscans, astrologers, etc. However, it should be noted that many of the examples cited are not occupations but rather activities, e.g., leisure-time or deviant activities, memberships (in a group), or identifications (with some larger collectivity). The drug addict as a distinct life-style is one of several such activities cited.

What are the central life interests which tie together the major items of behavior, norms, and values to comprise a life-style and to render it distinctive? Marx believed that the individual's relationship to the means of production was the sole determinant of his pattern of consumption and, in fact, of all else that was significant in his life—his ideology (Weltanschauung), personality, etc.[3] Thus, the "objective reality" of the individual's position ultimately determined all else, although Marx later admitted the possibility of "false consciousness" perhaps playing a significant role.

Max Weber, who introduced the concept "life-style" into the sociological literature, believed that subjective elements might significantly modify Marx's "objective reality," perhaps even to the point of determining a person's life-opportunities, i.e., his chances of achieving economic reward. Clearly, there is an interaction between the objective and subjective elements, an interaction which deserves further specification. But whatever the case, both Marx and Weber were speaking essentially of the "normal" individual whose central life interest is to "earn a living" or in other ways to meet the obligations of his major social role.

The point of view taken here is that for a deviant individual, the central life interest or major social role constitutes both the deviancy itself and the pursuit of the means necessary to sustain that deviancy. This seems especially true of narcotic addicts (as opposed to alcoholics, homosexuals, sexual perverts, etc.) because of the illegal nature of their activity and the consequent enormous expense involved. It is suggested that this aspect of "objective reality" sets constraints on all other aspects of the addict's life activities, determining within broad limits at least the nature of his job, family relationships, etc.

The survival of the addict in the addictive state requires the use of all resources available to him. The active, "strung-out" addict is concerned mainly with meeting his drug needs, whether through legitimate or illegitimate means. He thus develops a life-style permitting him to exist as an addict. He may "push dope," steal, become a pimp (become a prostitute in the case of the female addict), or choose some kind of legitimate employment.

The choice of life-style and the meeting of narcotic needs is related to the amount of drugs required, length of time on drugs, and, most importantly, the basic personality, temperament, predisposition, and skills of the addict in question. Opportunity, resources, contacts, etc. also play a major role in choice of life-style. It can be assumed that life-style indicates a way of meeting needs under stress and that it provides learning experiences which may be transferable to legitimate means of "making it."

During the addiction period, the addict is mainly concerned with "feeding" his habit. Interviews with addicts who are "strung out" reaffirm this strongly. Everything in their lives is centered around the need for drugs. Money or its equivalent is used purely to meet this need. Regular meals, family life, jobs, etc. hardly exist, so all-absorbing is the use of and search for drugs.

A preliminary conceptual model may thus be developed which translates the addict's life-style, his central life interests, and his ways of existing in a deviant culture to socially acceptable occupational and career pursuits. This model proposes to use some of the skills learned during the crisis of addict survival as starting points for appropriate vocational planning and training. While the survival techniques used by the addict may largely define (or reflect) his life-style and personality, there are other aspects which must also be considered. Some of these will be considered in the following section.

Limitations of Traditional Approaches

The usual and traditional approaches to job training and/or vocational rehabilitation have serious limitations when applied to an addict population. In addition to a lack of skills, there is frequently a lack of motivation and general education as well. This is further complicated by the attitude of many employers who, rather than employ addicts, actually screen them out.

Another problem is the difficulty in developing valid criteria of aptitude, interest, and job success. Reports from industry speak to these limitations, but this problem is even greater for the addict population. Since the latter is made up largely of members of minority groups, the aforementioned problem adds to the complexity of predicting job success, etc., through the use of the usual tests, limited as they may be.[4]

Kirkpatrick et al.[5] point out that little work has been done in the development of tests for ethnically disparate personnel. The situation is further described by Porter, who writes:

A . . . . frontier area that society is pressing upon us is the problem of selection in relation to minority and culturally deprived individuals. The literature in the last two years seems almost totally devoid of work by industrial psychologists dealing with this kind of problem.[6]

In addition to the above, there is the special situation of the addicted individual who has additional handicaps and limitations. First of all, his entry into addiction may have been precipitated by another or a prior deviance, i.e., his inability to conform to the usual socially accept-

able jobs. Furthermore, the usual occupations may be of little interest to him, and he may not want to be pinned down to a regular job. Alternatively, there may be jobs he would like to hold, but he does not possess the necessary skills. Finally, certain jobs will be closed to him because of employer attitudes toward his prison record and/or addiction history.

In Part I the limited utilization of vocational programs or formal training by addicts was documented. Furthermore, the unemployment rate of addicts is much higher than that of the regular population. What skills exist are usually learned informally on the job, and few efforts appear to have been made to relate the addict's interests, needs, or abilities to available jobs.

We are suggesting, therefore, that perhaps emphasis should be placed on the former life-style of the addict in approaching the problem of job training or vocational rehabilitation. Analyses should be made of the tasks which he has performed in the pursuit of his life-style in addiction, and the skills which he has learned should be catalogued. Following this, the types and kinds of legitimate jobs, for which the addict operating in specific life-styles might be suitable, should be identified, and training programs oriented to these jobs should be developed.

Our definition of life-style encompasses the constellation of behaviors centering around the various ways in which individuals define or pursue their "central life interest." For most individuals, central life interest may be nearly synonymous with the nature of their occupations or their levels of occupational aspiration, the level of educational attainment required to pursue their present or intended future occupations, and the income or other rewards they receive from such occupations. This central life interest is also likely to determine and to be dependent on the individual's values and the ways in which he participates in various primary groups and relates to significant others.

In order to look in some detail at distinctive life-styles of narcotic addicts, including the tasks they perform in the pursuit of their addictions as well as the skills they have learned to perpetuate them, we have developed three illustrative types:* street, dealer, and "shooting gallery" addicts. After examining each type, and in accordance with our preliminary model, we shall suggest possible

*The three life-styles discussed here are by no means presented as representing all narcotic addicts; to the contrary, we have in other documents enumerated 14 distinct life-styles for the total population of narcotic addicts.

legitimate occupations for each which, of course, should be considered along with the individual's intelligence and education. The reader should be cautioned that in considering the legitimate employment of either addicts or ex-addicts, the question of criminal background should be placed in proper perspective. This pattern of behavior should be sufficiently under control so as not to interfere with legitimate job placement.

In addition to these three types, some material on life-styles is presented with reference to four additional types: the female addict, the suburban addict, the employed addict, and the addict under treatment. Unlike the procedure used in discussing the earlier three, tasks performed, skills learned, and possible legitimate occupations are *not* discussed for the additional four. They are included here, nevertheless, because of their intrinsic interest and because the same kind of framework will be used in future work analyzing these life-styles.

The Street Addict

The street addict is probably the most common of all addict life-styles. Such an individual may be defined as a heroin addict, usually unemployed and with no aspirations for continuing employment, who supports his addiction primarily through the commission of illegal acts and who has had multiple experiences with the police, the courts, and the jails.

The street addict usually begins his day with a "fix" or with a foray to obtain money, property of value, or drugs so that he may function throughout the day. He has usually been an addict for many years and is thoroughly familiar with the addict subculture. His living arrangements are likely to be cheap single rooms with very little furnishings. Most of the money he obtains goes for narcotics, with just enough left over to keep him in minimally nourishing food and cheap clothing. He moves frequently since he is often unable to pay his rent. He sells drugs occasionally if he can find a supplier who will trust him to sell rather than to use, but primarily he is a shoplifter, sneak thief, apartment house burglar, or the perpetrator of other small crimes. He will occasionally commit a felony but prefers not to do so as the risk is great. He wants nothing, least of all incarceration, to interfere with his addiction.

The street addict rarely has nonaddict friends. His family is seldom an economic resource to him, although they may provide shelter and help in other ways. He knows that he will eventually be arrested and sent to jail in the course of committing at least one crime a day and sometimes as many as three. He rationalizes his fear by telling himself that incarceration will help solve some of his problems.

Addicts frequently define one another as being either "heroin addicts" or "dope fiends." A dope fiend is a heroin addict who is held in the lowest esteem by his peers. His only concern is to obtain and take drugs, regardless of the consequences to himself or to others. He appears extremely unkempt and dissipated and prefers not to receive medical treatment regardless of his condition or the consequences. He is resigned to his situation and has no desire to do anything but to use drugs until his death from natural or other causes. He may be compared with a "skid row" alcoholic. Thus, a dope fiend is a street addict, although a street addict is not necessarily a dope fiend.

Although a street addict may actually seek treatment, frequently simply to bring his habit within his financial capabilities, he usually finds some reason not to continue and soon returns to the use of drugs. He rationalizes his behavior in many ways, frequently stating that methadone is worse than heroin, that it causes impotency leading to genocide, and that it is nothing more than an attempt by the "Establishment" to poison him.

The street addict, on the rare occasion when not involved in searching for drugs, enjoys standing on corners, in poolrooms, and in front of bars discussing drugs with other addicts. He enjoys mingling with his peers and finds it difficult to be by himself in his room. Aside from his addiction, he is afflicted with a condition sometimes known among ghetto inhabitants as "street poisoned." He feels that he must always be in the street and "on the scene" because he might otherwise miss something. During occasions of arrest, prosecution, and jail he is usually forced to relinquish his heroin habit, but upon release his desire for street action brings him again in proximity with the drug scene.

The police are not convinced that the intense drive for social mingling is independent of drug involvement. They tend to see all such behavior as just another means of expressing, through talk, buying, or selling, a preempting preoccupation with drugs.

The tasks the street addict performs and the skills he may learn are as follows:

Street Addict

Tasks Performed	Skills Learned
Meets needs in a number of ways available on street.	Be "street wise" (to survive). Know location of sources of goods to be converted to cash (drugs).
Survival through anti-social activities in keeping with deviant subculture; keep a roof over his head.	Knowledge of the law.
	Know "fences."
May include larceny, "con" games, burglary, shoplifting, mugging, purse snatching, "touting" (referral to drug source, etc.).	Learn decision making.
	Must be street wise, take risks.
	Relate to peers and sources for drugs.
May work part-time in menial jobs.	Practical knowledge of applied psychology.

The types and kinds of legitimate jobs for which the street addict might be considered under our life-style concept include messenger, salesman (usually retail), acting, and jobs which would involve contact with people in the street, e.g., survey-taking, etc. Other potential jobs include factory work, unskilled laborer, stock work, warehouseman, trucker's helper, delivery man, window washer, janitorial and porter, cab driver, painter or painter's helper.

The Dealer Addict

A day in the life of the addict who has elected to sell and distribute drugs to maintain himself and his addiction is an extremely dangerous and hectic one, although he himself may not consider it anymore dangerous than ordinary ghetto living. Of all the addict types, this individual is usually the most deeply involved in the addict subculture. Although there are many involved in the illegal sale of drugs who are not addicted, those that are addicted represent, by far, the majority. Even the nonaddicted are likely to be involved with the drug culture in that they use cocaine or barbiturates. The addict dealer is likely to be a male, roughly between the ages of 16 and 40. It is felt, within the subculture, that female dealers experience many more difficulties than do males as a

result of their inability to defend themselves against the many and varied contingencies involved in drug selling. For this reason, when selling to men they are likely to do so only in a public place and with an armed male standing by for protection. Otherwise, they sell only to other females. Females are more likely, however, to be used by male dealers for stashing the supply since, if caught, they are usually treated with greater leniency. Females are paid for this service in either drugs or money.

The addicted dealer is likely to be a hard-core heroin user for many years and to be known to the authorities for his addiction. His consumption of heroin might easily exceed $100.00 per day. Since the bartering of heroin involves a seller's market, and because the dealer is usually in constant possession of large quantities of heroin to be sold on a retail basis, he is spared the difficulties resulting from the problems of acquisition. By the time he becomes a dealer his tolerance level is likely to be high. Therefore, the sellers of heroin and other habit-forming drugs consume large quantities of their own wares. This condition is known as a "dealer's habit."

Many addicts find it difficult to secure a position as a dealer since a certain degree of trust in the addict's ability to keep his own account honest is required by the "Source." Clannishness and caution by nonaddicted wholesale drug dealers ("connections"), who are frequently involved in legitimate businesses as well and who maintain close social relationships with one another, act as controls limiting the number of retail and addicted drug dealers in a community.

Even though their mortality rate is extremely high and they suffer the loss of formerly meaningful social relationships, many addicts covet a dealership because of the tremendous profits to be made and the advantages of a steady supply. Moreover, the loss of intimate relationships does not bring aloneness. The dealer is a very popular person to all the buyers in his area, the more so because each dealer usually holds a monopoly within a certain geographical territory. Once an addict has become a dealer it is difficult to give up this role even if he so wishes. His consumption has become too large for him to finance in any other way. It is unlikely he will ever choose to engage in any other type of criminal activity, although he may be forced to do so should he lose his dealership.

The dealer of heroin purchases, on a wholesale basis, "bundles," 25 $10.00 bags of heroin for $100.00 to $150.00. (Recent manipulations by those who control the heroin economy in Baltimore, along with the recent East Coast dock strike, have forced the price of local heroin to as high as $15.00 a bag, or $200.00 a bundle.) The total net profit amounts to $100.00 to $150.00 per bundle, depending on the price per bundle paid to the "connection." It is not uncommon for established drug dealers in the ghetto to sell as many as ten bundles a day by the bag. In addition to money, the dealer accepts goods, frequently stolen, and more rarely services, especially from females. Of all the illegal money-making activities in the ghetto, his is the most lucrative.

Even though the profits are high, the risks are great, and many addicts will not sell drugs for that reason. Over and above the original cost of purchase, the dealer addict must sustain certain other expenses. Often he is forced to receive less than the price of a bag from the addict pusher. Moreover, the dealer frequently works on consignment; i.e., each time he sells drugs he pays for his *previous* purchases. This involves some ability to keep accounts. He cannot make too many mistakes without, at the very least, losing his position. He is often arrested, jailed, and bailed as many as five times before the original charge against him is settled in court. Lawyers' fees, payoffs, losses resulting from robbery, and the large quantities of drugs which he himself consumes further reduce his profits. This burden is offset somewhat by certain kinds of protection provided by the organization for which he works.

The life-style and the day-to-day activities of the drug dealer-addict have changed somewhat during the last 10 years. With the increase in the drug addict population, many have been forced to discontinue the sale of heroin from their homes or from other places known only to them and to their customers. At one time it was extremely difficult to purchase heroin from any dealer who did not know to whom he was selling; now the market is more open. With the increase in law enforcement activities directed toward the drug seller, some dealers believe it necessary to conceal as much information about themselves as possible. Some are quite reluctant to make public where they live as well as other demographic information which may be used to identify them.

The dealer confines himself for the most part to one or two particular areas when he sells drugs. He attempts to protect himself by knowing the characteristics and personality of the cop on the beat, the particular shift he works, those most likely to inform or otherwise place him in danger of arrest, and other pertinent aspects of neighborhood activity. He prefers to work with someone else, usually a woman whose only functions are to conceal the evidence on her person or to act as a lookout on his behalf. The drug dealer who does not have the protection of the organization often feels the need to carry a weapon, usually a pistol, to defend himself from the addicts with whom he deals. As a result, he is often involved in violence. Some prefer to deal at night in order to reduce the possibility of being seen and to be available to the small population of employed addicts. Others hide the sold drugs in a spot some distance from themselves and thus feel safe to deal during daylight. The drug dealer usually believes he is very familiar with the law (search and seizure, frisk laws, habeas corpus, and illegal entry). It is not until actual arrest that many discover the extent of their ignorance.

Physically, the use of drugs of unknown potency, often poorly administered under unsanitary conditions, takes its toll. Edema, especially of the hands and arms, collapsed veins, liver and kidney disorders, and abscesses plague the user. Because his consumption of heroin is usually greater and more constant than that of the nondealer addict, large quantities of "cut" (heroin dilutant, usually quinine, benita, or milk sugar) build up in his body. Moreover, he becomes uncertain of his actual tolerance level. It is possible that many drug dealers in this condition subconsciously welcome arrest, conviction, and jail, as it may be their only means of dealing with their problems.

Some of the tasks the dealer addict perform and the skills he learns are as follows:

Dealer Addict

Tasks Performed	Skills Learned
Purchases and sells narcotics.	Establishing a supply and delivery system.
Cuts supplies.	Setting up business accounting procedures.
Sets up customer network.	Developing new customers.

Works to avoid getting "busted."	Finding means of protecting "business" and self.
Works at avoiding getting "taken."	Knowledge of the law.
Develops financial resources.	

The types and kinds of legitimate jobs the dealer addict may be considered for include managing a small business, door-to-door sales, driving a taxicab, parts and inventory clerk, wholesale sales, supervisor, counselor or administrative assistant on drug program, bookkeeping and clerical, race track worker, etc.

The Shooting Gallery Addict

There is a type of addict who, because of the dangers involved in continuous money-seeking activities, chooses to support his habit by performing a service to his peers in return for money or drugs. This service involves making available to other addicts a place (usually a private home or vacant building) where they may come to administer their heroin in relative safety, away from suspicious family members, untrustworthy acquaintances, or the police. In many instances, especially when the drug user lives a considerable distance from where he has purchased his "fix," he is impatient to get "high" to avert withdrawal and to avoid being arrested for possession. He needs a safe place which is close at hand.

Another factor which contributes to the popularity of the shooting gallery is the ready availability of necessary paraphernalia (hypodermic needle and syringe). In quite a few instances, the addict who has come to the shooting gallery is either (1) a neophyte addict who has difficulty in administering heroin to himself intravenously or (2) an "old junkie" (in terms of length of drug use, not in terms of chronological age) whose veins have collapsed and retreated to the bone. In either case, there is always someone available at the gallery who will assist in administering the drug.

The life-style of the shooting gallery operator is usually less hectic than that of his customers. Customarily, his fee for allowing addicts the use of the premises is one dollar or a small amount of drugs known as a "Gee-Shot," in liquid measure about 5 cc or less. Addicts who operate an active and profitable gallery may accept part of their fees

in drugs, although money is generally preferred. Occasionally the heroin accumulates faster than the gallery addict's immediate ability to consume it. He may save it in a little bottle, mixing each contribution together in liquid form until his "fix" is due, or he may sell the excess, as do an estimated 25 to 30% of all shooting gallery operators.

The addicted shooting gallery operator may rarely leave the house, as his services are constantly in demand, especially in areas where drug activity is high. If he lives on the premises, usually those living with him are peers rather than nonaddicted relatives or friends. He usually prefers either to rent the establishment in someone else's name or to have someone rent it for him under a fictitious name in order to avoid a charge of "setting up and maintaining a common nuisance." The house in which the gallery is operated is usually in a neighborhood containing low income families, high crime rates, and neighbors who are thoroughly familiar with the ghetto philosophy of avoiding trouble by ignoring what is none of their business.

Many addicts who resist the operation of shooting galleries on a large scale are content to allow a few close and trusted friends the accommodation of their homes for the purpose of using drugs. Many employed addicts with families and responsibilities use this method to support their habits. In many cases, however, nonaddicted family members will put pressure on the addict to stop the traffic in and out of the house. In such instances, he may then turn to the formal operation of a gallery.

Shooting Gallery Addict

Tasks Performed	Skills Learned
Sets up customer network.	Establishing a "business" operation of a "treatment" center.
Provides facilities and paraphernalia.	
	Selection of customers.
Provides protected setting.	Knowledge about anatomy of clientele.
Screens customers.	
	Knowledge about drug reactions.
Prepares and administers drugs if necessary.	
	Handling of crisis situations.
Instructs in the use of drugs if necessary.	Handling of funds.

Collects payment in money or kind.	Giving service.
	Knowledge of the law.
Treats overdose cases.	

The types and kinds of legitimate jobs the shooting gallery addict might be considered for include running amusement booths at a carnival, working as a "barker," nurse's aide, hygienist, medical emergency worker, counselor or counselor's aide on drug program, dietary aide, cosmetologist, food service worker, teacher's aide, recreation worker, companion and/or housekeeper, etc.

The Female Addict

The Baltimore City female heroin addict is, for the most part, under 35 years of age. During the past 5 or 6 years there appears to have been a marked increase in heroin addiction among females in the 16 to 25 year age range.

A successful involvement in the drug addict subculture depends more on the female's mind and body than it does on her muscle. A female addict often prefers to attach herself to a male addict with whom she might live, usually in a common-law relationship. Sometimes it happens that an unaddicted female is initiated into the drug scene by the male to whom she has become attached. In either case, a reciprocal agreement is likely to exist by which she contributes to the financing of his habit in return for a degree of protection from other addicts or "customers" who may take advantage of her. Sometimes these relationships are highly rewarding and even satisfying. On the other hand, they are more likely to become an unwelcome trap for the female than for the male.

The female addict, like her male counterpart, is constantly in search of funds with which to acquire heroin, but she enjoys certain advantages in money-making. If she is already a prostitute, or prone in that direction, she has a ready source of funds for drugs. Moreover, prostitution allows her to hold a legitimate job, often as dancer or sitter in a bar, if she is so inclined. Of all the illegal activities executed by addicts in their efforts to obtain funds to support the heroin habit, prostitution is considered to involve the smallest degree of risk of arrest (and even if arrested, fines are no more than $50.00 to $100.00), while at the same time providing a steady and rather predictable income with which to purchase narcotics. On the other hand, prostitution has its disadvantages. For example, it is often true that the urgent need for drug money persuades many to become prostitutes who would otherwise shun such an occupation. Even many females who are employed prior to addiction find it difficult and uneconomical to remain employed relative to the profits found in prostitution. Moral conflicts and resulting guilt feelings may never be resolved. As her physical attractiveness declines, the prostitute is patronized by a lower class clientele and must lower her rates accordingly. Meanwhile, her habit has been steadily increasing. She must, therefore, practice her trade ever more frequently, thus augmenting the strain. A white prostitute may feel the need to live with a black dealer for protection. Such a living arrangement completes her estrangement from her own culture while enclosing her in an alien society.

One of the main factors leading to motivational change by the addict is the ever-increasing difficulty which he or she experiences in obtaining funds to purchase the ever-increasing amounts of drugs needed. Prostitution, however, is considered by many female addicts to involve a seller's market. For this reason, motivation to "kick the habit" is often never achieved while the female addict remains attractive and healthy. Shoplifting (sometimes on circuit), extortion, writing bad checks, robbery, confidence (such as flim flam and the Murphy game), and other criminal activities are committed by many female addicts as supplements to, or eventual replacements of, prostitution. It is rare to find a female addict who is not engaged in prostitution at least on a part-time basis.

While dominating the lives of many female addicts, prostitution is not the only lucrative means of supporting a habit available to women. Female addicts are used in many lower echelon positions of the drug business organization. Occasionally females are dealers, though perhaps somewhat more restricted in this activity than are their male counterparts.

A female, rarely addicted to heroin but usually taking cocaine or barbiturates, may begin work as a courier at a rather young age. Frequently she is the girlfriend of an organization member. Her job is to carry the drugs on her person from seller to buyer. The transaction may be between port city source and local buyer, in which case the courier will be carrying the drugs across state lines. Or it may be between local seller and dealer. In either case the drugs are usually prepaid so that the courier's duties are ended upon delivery. Generally she delivers the drugs to a certain prearranged locality, such as a motel room, where the buyer picks them up at a later time. All her expenses are paid and her habit, if any, maintained. In the event the drugs have not previously been paid for, the courier may have to return across state lines with as much as $30,000 on her person. Almost never is an addict trusted with this amount of money. Since, however, this type of work allows formal employment in addition to its other advantages, it is usually considered worth any risk involved. If caught, the courier faces a minimum of 20 years for possession of heroin with intent to distribute.

Especially when drugs in bundles are transferred from seller to buyer (or series of buyers) locally, a lieutenant in the organization frequently acts as courier. Seldom, however, does he wish to incur the risks of carrying the goods on his own person. Therefore, he enlists the services of a female companion. In case of arrest, his chances of conviction are low, and she would probably receive some leniency. Again, many female addicts believe the advantages of money, drug supply, and the protection of a male companion are worth the risks. Women are also frequently used as stashes by anyone in possession of large quantities of drugs.

Other related jobs for which women addicts are frequently used are those of adulterating, bagging, and bundling. Heroin will probably arrive in a given city in much greater strength than is currently being allowed on the street. It must, therefore, be "cut" with milk sugar and quinine, usually to a dosage containing 3 to 6% heroin. Each dose is then "bagged" and the bags "bundled" for delivery to the local dealer. Women are usually engaged for these tasks under the very watchful eye of a trusted lieutenant of the organization.

It is interesting to note that, although these same women may well be righteously indignant and rebellious about surveillance in legitimate employment, they are at least able to accept quite stringent surveillance in low-ranking jobs in the drug business where the consequences of failure are likely to be immediate and brutal. It would be a mistake to believe that the similarities involved in employment of any kind necessarily make skills or motivations transferable across the legal line.

The Suburban Addict

The suburban addict, whether black or white, represents an ever-growing portion of the addict population. Over a period of a few short years, many suburban areas, once totally unaffected by the drug problem, have become deeply involved with drug use. When one considers the fact that one addict is capable of contributing to the addiction of five or six other potential addicts during his involvement with drugs, the rapidity of spread is not surprising.

Marijuana is the drug most likely to initiate a suburban community into the drug scene. Three to four years later this same community will probably have a considerable problem with hardcore heroin addiction. It is not necessary to postulate a direct causal relationship between marijuana and heroin in order to explain this correlation. Probably many of the same factors that led a good proportion of the younger population to marijuana would cause others to experiment with heroin. Possibly an ongoing emotional and psychological development in the young is arrested by the use of marijuana; the escape afforded by this drug substitutes for the normal experiences of facing one's problems and solving them, of facing one's desires and obtaining, compromising, or subordinating them. Therefore, when bigger problems and more demanding desires come along, a precedent for chemical escape is set which heroin fulfills. Also, possibly the type of "drug education" received by the young in and out of suburban schools has led to a credibility gap. The young experiment with marijuana, find many of the dire predictions and admonitions of their elders unwarranted, and so consider it worth the risk to go on to other things.

In any case, suburbia, where once the extent of drug use was limited to hypochondriacal housewives, insomniacs, and tranquillizer enthusiasts, now finds itself faced with the problem of illegal drug use in its schools and on its streets. In PTA meetings throughout the country, parents, teachers, and the community are horrified at reports of drug abuse and addiction within the public school system.

The life-style of the suburban addict differs from that of the ghetto or street addict in many ways. The ghetto addict is usually first a delinquent with a juvenile or adult police record. The suburban addict may have been delinquent prior to addiction but has usually been able to avoid arrest or conviction. Possibly a higher percentage of suburban addicts began using hard drugs first and turned to crime only to support a growing habit. In either case, the suburban addict has little or no experience with law enforcement or incarceration.

It is likely that the suburban addict is a product of a middle- or upper-class environment. He has the advantage of a good education and, on the average, a more physically stable family life. The better quality of that life in terms of love, order, and wisdom, however, is questionable.

The suburban addict is less likely to be known to the authorities as being addicted to an illegal drug. He is better able to conceal his addiction as he is not automatically looked upon with suspicion.

Many times the suburban addict is not faced with the problem of supporting himself with shelter and sustenance. Obtaining funds with which to purchase his illegal drugs represents, initially, very little difficulty to him. In many instances he is employed and supports his addiction through funds obtained solely through gainful employment. His superior education and the expectations of his class make a good paying job easier to find. His family, if they know of his addiction, have the resources to help and are likely to try. His living arrangements are likely to be in the home of his parents, who, though as concerned about his welfare as any, are hesitant in their efforts to obtain services for his addiction because of embarrassment and unfamiliarity with the world of social services, courts, and police. He is likely to continue for some time to have nonaddict friends who may or may not know of his addiction.

As he becomes more involved in the use of heroin, as his tolerance for the consumption of narcotics increases, as he becomes more and more a part of an outlawed subculture, the range of choice in this addict's life steadily decreases, and eventually moral and ethical values previously attained become an impractical luxury or an irrelevant nuisance. He is then capable of committing crimes if his habit has become unsupportable by legitimate means. It may be easier for the suburbanite to stay within the range of nonviolent crime because his education, employment, social connections, and familiarity with the world of legitimate business give him a wider range of nonviolent money-making activities, legal and illegal, from which to choose. On the other hand, he is probably less experienced with personal violence on a day-to-day basis than is his ghetto counterpart and may, therefore, find violent means of money-making more difficult to commit.

His main problem, however, is locating a continuing source of heroin rather than finding funds with which to purchase this drug. Suburban addicts are likely to be multiple drug users involved in the use of marijuana, LSD, barbiturates, etc. (Suburban drug use might be said to begin as an extension of the legitimate drug culture so pervasive throughout society.) Some of these drugs can be legally obtained, and others are manufactured within the suburban community. A young suburbanite frequently begins with these milder and more readily available drugs, but the involvement with the drug scene, brought about by continued use, soon throws the user into proximity with hard drugs and encourages a growing familiarity. What once seemed strange and remote now is an everyday experience. As of today, the sources of most hard drugs remain in the unfamiliar ghetto where the young suburbanite must find connections. This may be changing, however, as dealers, seeing a new and lucrative market, or following migratory patterns currently being established, move out into the suburbs.

The Employed Addict

There exists within the addict population a growing number of individuals who are able to support themselves for a time through gainful employment. To be able to work a normal day and to find the additional time and money needed to support a heroin habit with its constantly enlarging appetite is no simple task. Most addicts never intend to become "hooked on drugs." The potential addict, in many instances, is already employed and in possession of the assets nondrug-users accumulate (clothes, automobile, bank account, etc.). This employed drug user usually begins his affair with heroin only on weekends. He prefers to sniff or skin-pop heroin in the beginning because he does not want the tell-tale marks of the drug addict on his arms. His continued employment depends on his ability to conceal his use of drugs. He is fearful that his parents, wife, employer, or acquaintances will find out about his occasional flirtations with heroin. During the pre-addiction period he may advance in using heroin once or twice a week with very little change in his life-style as an employed, nonaddicted individual. Eventually, however, he will find that his involvement has increased to daily use and later to more than once a day as his tolerance for heroin increases. At this point he will usually make his first attempt to discontinue the use of heroin. He will discover, but resist admitting to himself, that his addiction is established, and he will begin to rationalize his continued use of heroin in a way acceptable to him. The duration of this transitional period, from habitual use to recognized addiction, varies with individual personality and with the contingencies of life. During this period tremendous pressure and anxiety build up in the employed individual ever fearful of discovery not only by the police but, more probably, also by the more intimate employer. As his drug use continues and increases, so does the expense involved in supporting his habit. His salary is no longer able to meet his need, and by this time he has usually sold, pawned, or otherwise disposed of his valuable assets. He is beginning to miss days from work and is often late because of his efforts to acquire his morning fix. His coordination and ability to concentrate decline, leading to shoddy production. His wages are of almost no use to him over and above contributing to the purchase of an ever-increasing amount of heroin. His family and friends are becoming suspicious and feel that something is wrong. He is constantly borrowing but never repaying. His physical appearance is beginning to change, along with his dress and manner. It' is at this point that many employed addicts are fired or decide to quit. In many cases the reason for leaving his job is rationalized to include any excuse other than his addiction to drugs. It is extremely difficult for most addicts to remain gainfully employed on a continuous basis for an acceptable length of time.

Other employed addicts resort to crime, usually in the form of stealing or of dealing in drugs. It is not known how much is stolen by addict employees from employers annually, but the estimate is high. In New York City's garment district, where many people from ghetto areas are employed in menial-type jobs, employers believe they are losing millions of dollars a year to employed addict thieves. In many instances, the dealers of heroin seek work in commercial areas such as this, not for the purpose of gainful employment, but merely to take advantage of the demand for heroin by employed addicts in the area.

Business and industry are becoming increasingly concerned about the problem of drug addiction within the ranks of the employed. Efforts are being made by some to deal with the problem on what is considered a realistic basis. Alcoholics and drug abusers employed by private and municipal agencies (e.g., Bethlehem Steel Corporation, Continental Can Company, and the State of Maryland) are now being afforded the opportunity to receive treatment for their drug problems.

The working time schedule is an extremely important factor contributing to the employed addict's ability to satisfy the requirements of employment. Whether an employed addict is male or female, skilled or unskilled, the actual hours, not the length of time, that he is engaged in employment is the most important single factor in determining the ease or difficulty with which he is able to function as an employed but active heroin addict. It is necessary to keep in mind the fact that the employed heroin addict's ability and desire to work is dependent on satisfaction of his heroin hunger immediately when it occurs. The passage of every second of time coincides with the consumption of some quantity of heroin in the addict's system. As time goes by, anxiety increases, and the addict's ability to think of anything but obtaining his next fix decreases. Many employed heroin addicts attempt to eliminate this sort of pressure by employing a number of safeguards or "tricks." Some addicts purchase a large amount of drugs each payday intending to make them last until the next payday, thereby relieving them of the need to disrupt their work in order to secure drugs. Some addicts purchase heroin at night so that it may be available to them before they go to work the following morning. Inevitably, however, some unforeseen occurrence causes a disruption to the best-laid plans. The addict may find it almost impossible to dole out to himself quantities of drugs on such a disciplined basis. Perhaps his tolerance increases unexpectedly. The potency of heroin may decrease. More often than not the addict is unable to avoid failure in balancing the needs of employment and addiction.

It should be safe to assume that because of the discipline and motivation needed in attaining a skill with even a minimum degree of competence and of having executed this skill while engaged in gainful employment and training for the length of time necessary to differentiate the skilled employee from the unskilled, most skilled addict employees became addicted *after* they had obtained their skills. The skilled addict employee differs from the unskilled addict employee primarily in the relative ease with which he is able to obtain employment and, possibly, the considerations and latitudes which he is given by his employer if problems relating to drug addiction should occur. The value of the skilled employee to his employer is determined by the ease or difficulty in replacing him with another of equal skill from the employment market, the quality of his work in relation to the speed with which it is accomplished, and his dependability. The skilled addict employee has definite advantages over his unskilled peer as far as wages and other benefits are concerned, but these usually mean very little where the high cost of illegal drugs is considered.

Attempts are now being made, largely with the aid of drug treatment programs, to assist the employed addict to remain employed and the unemployed to obtain work. It has been recognized that certain skills are required in order to successfully matriculate through the drug scene. The question arises, can these skills be used to match addicts to legitimate employment requiring similar skills? Caution should be used in basing too many hopes on this assumption. The transition from illegitimate to legitimate pursuits involves a holistic change of being: economically (not enough low skill jobs), socially (an uncomfortable and "different" culture to face), psychologically (attitudes about one's self require radical adjustment), and emotionally (feelings of anger and rebellion are not compatible with working either for or in the Establishment).

The Addict Under Treatment

Because of the widespread increase in illegal drug use, drug abuse treatment programs have been, and are being, established in every state in the union. These programs are directed toward helping the motivated abuser or addicted individual to discontinue his illegal use of drugs. The *Directory of Resources for Drug Abusers and Their Families* lists over 20 separate facilities in Baltimore City operating expressly for the purpose of treating drug abusers who are either independently motivated or for whom treatment is a condition of parole.

There are estimated to be at least 6,000 heroin addicts in the city of Baltimore alone. Of these 6,000, less than one third are receiving treatment from recognized drug abuse programs. Because of lack of funds, lack of space, lack of qualified staff, etc., most drug abuse treatment programs are unable to accommodate every addicted individual who applies to them for assistance.

The heroin addict under treatment can be classified, for our purposes, into one of two categories: those who are motivated and those who are not motivated using criteria set by the treatment program. Addicts apply for admission to drug treatment programs for many reasons, not necessarily because they are motivated to give up their habits. Pressures from family or courts, a desire to consume still another drug (methadone) in conjunction with heroin, cocaine, or barbiturates (technically not allowed but often practiced), a decrease in the availability of heroin, or the wish to qualify for a job are probably the most common reasons.

Unfortunately, there is no foolproof way to determine true motivation within an individual. The mere acceptance of a heroin-addicted individual by a drug abuse treatment program does not preclude him from the continued use of narcotics, one of which (methadone) is frequently supplied as a part of treatment. It does, however, change even the nonmotivated addict's life-style from that of an individual who has been in constant fear of withdrawal and whose every action has been designed to stay this most uncomfortable condition, to a person who is able to satisfy his craving for drugs without paying the price demanded by the withdrawal syndrome. Most drug abuse treatment programs, employing the use of methadone as a treatment modality must, as required by law, employ various controls to determine the extent of drug use by those under treatment. However, disciplinary policies vary from permissive to quite punitive, ending in expulsion. Many addicts under treatment use drugs other than heroin which are not readily visible by thin layer chromotography (cocaine, marijuana, alcohol, and illegal methadone obtained from sources other than the maintenance program). Presumably what an addict most desires is a means of chemical assistance that allows him to retain the highs and to function normally at whatever task he chooses and that does not involve the pressures and discomforts of withdrawal. Many find an approximation to this dream in a combination of drugs that includes methadone. Many drug abuse programs assume the attitude that the mere dispensing of methadone to addicts does not necessarily or immediately show positive results, and these allow an addict a number of weeks or months to show the benefit from the treatment he is receiving. In such situations, it is hoped that motivation will come with the reduction of drug-seeking pressures. What is assured, however, is a change in life-style, due primarily to the immediate elimination of this addict's greatest and most profound fear, that of withdrawal without chemical assistance.

The relative proportions of "motivated" and "nonmotivated" patients are difficult to determine. An operational definition of "motivation," however, would include a desire (1) to stay within the law (currently requiring complete abstinence from illegal drugs) and (2) to be self-supporting. Whether or not trying to "rehabilitate" heroin addicts is a "losing battle" would depend on the statistics of "success" as defined. If an addict applies for a treatment program because of a self-motivated desire to become drug free, his chances of receiving effective aid vary from fair to good, depending on the quality of the program. If, however, his motive is anything other than a personal desire for complete abstinence, his chances of successfully using a treatment program as society intends it to be used are reduced substantially. He may, nevertheless, find it of some benefit to himself to stay in therapy.

The factors determining "success" in treatment are extremely complex. Some addicts were delinquent even prior to addiction. Presumably in this case merely eliminating the addiction will not remove the pull toward a delinquent life-style. Moreover, many addicts are sensitive to existing hypocrisy among professional helpers. As the programs (or private physicians) scrutinize their patients for signs of moral lapse, so are their values scrutinized in return. Doctors who make enormous profits from their treatment of addicts, programs that serve the needs of staff members rather than those of patients, policies overtly designed to subvert individual needs to a supposed public good all help to reinforce the amoral attitudes of addicts. Another factor influencing the possibility of effective aid is the desirability of discontinuing associations with less-motivated peers. This is nearly impossible to accomplish so long as the client remains in the same environment. Finally, he must have the psychological strengths necessary to find satisfactions, comparable to those derived from drugs elsewhere, while reconciling himself to the demands of society sufficiently to allow reasonably conforming behavior. To do so he must overcome a long-term conditioned pattern of life that involved many satisfactions as well as miseries.

CONCLUSION

This chapter has attempted to make the point that the life-styles of addicts, and their vocational histories considered in relation to these life-styles, should be studied carefully from the point of view of considering the transferability of these skills for use in socially acceptable occupations. If transferability is in fact a viable concept, and much further research is needed here, vocational rehabilitation and/or retraining programs could be designed around the results of these studies. Perhaps only in this way can the terribly important, and so far at least seemingly intractable, problem of "cure" of addiction be approached. That is, the thesis put forth here is that addiction is at least as much a social as a medical phenomenon and that any cure which relies on medical techniques alone is by its very nature foredoomed to failure. Cure must be social as well as medical, and the way to provide a "social" cure is to provide socially acceptable jobs which addicts can perform acceptably; a primary way to do this, in turn, is to provide jobs for addicts which build on, and amplify, skills which they already have learned as part of their life-styles during their careers of addiction.

REFERENCES

1. Vaillant, G. E., A twelve-year follow-up of New York narcotic addicts. II. The natural history of a chronic disease, *N. Engl. J. Med.*, 275, 573, 1966.
2. Feldman, S. and Theilbar, G., Eds., *Life Styles: Diversity in American Society*, Little, Brown & Co., Boston, 1971.
3. Gerth, H. H. and Mills, C. W., Eds., *From Max Weber: Essays in Sociology*, Oxford University Press, New York, 1946.
4. Albright, L. E. et al., in *The Use of Psychological Tests in Industry*, Howard Allen, Cleveland, 1963.
5. Kirkpatrick, J. F. et al., in *Testing and Fair Employment*, New York University, New York, 1969.

SOCIAL COSTS

NARCOTIC ADDICTION AND CRIME:
SOCIAL COSTS AND FORCED TRANSFERS

John J. Casey and Edward Preble

TABLE OF CONTENTS

INTRODUCTION

The great amount of attention and money being given to attempted solutions of the narcotic addiction problem in the United States has not originated in a public concern for the health and welfare of the nation's narcotic addicts. Rather, the demand for attention has been forced upon the country because of the social, economic, and personal costs to its citizens that result from the criminal activities of narcotic addicts.

As a health problem, narcotic addiction is relatively minor when compared with the incidence of other disorders. The estimate in this study of 80,000 opiate (primarily heroin) addicts compares to: heart and circulation disease, 14 million; alcoholism, 8 million; hearing disorders, 6 million; mental retardation, 4 million; stroke, 2 million; diabetes, 1.5 million; epilepsy, 1.5 million; Parkinson's disease, 1.5 million.

To take a comparable health disorder, alcohol addiction, the direct physical and psychological effects of which are as much if not more damaging to the individual than opiate addiction, the attention and money given to the relief of its estimated 8 million victims are much less than that given to the treatment of the estimated 80,000 narcotic addicts. In New York State, for example, there is a 4 million dollar annual state expenditure in behalf of the state's 700,000 alcoholics, as compared to a 150 million dollar expenditure for the state's 50,000 opiate addicts.

The reason for this imbalance is that the activities of alcohol addicts do not so directly and dramatically affect the well-being of other people to the extent that narcotic addiction does. It is one thing to put up with the minor annoyance of contributing a quarter to a Bowery alcoholic who needs 50 cents for a pint of wine and another to be confronted with an armed attacker who needs 50 dollars a day for heroin.

It is self-preservation, economic and bodily, which is the basic motivation in the public's concern and expenditures with regard to narcotic addiction. This study will attempt to identify the nature and extent of these social and personal costs.

The estimates in this study are based upon data from the year 1966 to 1967. The main reason for this choice is that the most comprehensive data in this field are from that year as a result of two major reports: (1) The President's Commission on Law Enforcement and Administration of Justice[1] and (2) The Small Business Administration.[2] Also, a former study by the present authors was based upon data from that year.[3]

This study is concerned exclusively with opiate (mostly heroin) addicts because they are responsible for the social and economic problems which are the subject of this paper. The first question in such a study is how many heroin addicts there are in the United States. There is no single widely accepted estimate of the number of addicts in the country (including those on the street, in jails, or in hospitals). In the time period covered in this study, estimates from responsible sources ranged from 60,000 to as high as 200,000, with the largest number of experts accepting a range between 80,000 to 100,000. Today this number range has been extended to as high as 500,000.

All national estimates are originally based on the number of addicts listed by the Federal Bureau of Narcotics, which has since become the Drug Enforcement Administration. As of December 31, 1966, 59,720 persons were listed as active narcotic addicts.[4] The FBN defined an addict as anyone who was arrested for the use of opiates or cocaine during the period 1961 to 1966. Once arrested for illegal drug use, and therefore entered on the FBN list, a person continues to be counted as an active addict until a 5-year period has elapsed during which the individual does not again come to the attention of the FBN for drug use.

The FBN list is only an approximate estimate of the total number of active addicts in the United States. There are two reasons: First, by counting a man or woman as an addict for a period of 5 years after he or she has not appeared on police rolls for a narcotic violation, the Federal Bureau of Narcotics is including some who have stopped using narcotics. This results in an overestimate of the actual number of active addicts. Secondly, by recording only those drug users who come to the attention of police officials and are in turn made known to the FBN, the Bureau underestimates the actual number of drug users because a number of addicts fail to come to the attention of the police and because some addicts who come to police attention are not reported to the FBN.

In New York State the most often quoted source for addict census data is the New York City Narcotics Register, which, although it covers only the New York City metropolitan area, is believed to contain over 90% of the opiate addicts living in the state. The Register has a much larger number of data sources for New York City than does the FBN, including the New York City Police Department, public and private social service agencies, hospitals, and private physicians. In 1966, the Narcotics Register contained approximately 41,000 unduplicated names of reported addicts. The FBN list showed 31,191 for the whole state or approximately 25% less than the number the Register had recorded for the city alone. If the ratio of underreporting in New York between the Register and the FBN held true for the rest of the country, the number of active addicts would be estimated at 80,000 to 100,000. A study by the

Hudson Institute concerning drug abuse in New York also questions the acceptance of estimates in the higher range.[5]

The figure of 80,000 addicts will be used in this study. Regardless of what is used as the final estimated number of addicts, the estimates in this paper which derive from that figure can be revised according to the methodology developed in this study.

The cost of narcotic addiction can be defined, in a general way, as the loss of well-being suffered by society as a result of the life-style of the addict. The total cost can be divided into tangible and intangible costs. The tangible costs include:

1. Losses that result from a reduction in the economic production of addicts.
2. Cost of treatment and rehabilitation of addicts.
3. Cost of addiction prevention.
4. Cost of addict premature death.
5. Cost of criminal acts related to narcotic addiction.
6. Cost of social welfare payments.

The intangible costs, which are great but largely immeasurable, include nonscaleable losses that accompany addiction, such as the fear and frustration felt by society and by victims of criminal acts committed by addicts and the frustration and despair that is felt by the addict, his family and friends. Although many of the conclusions of the study are tentative, the measurement of the social cost and transfers resulting from addiction-related crime is important for any social approach to the problem. For public policy-making purposes, the cost model used in this study for the first time provides a means to measure the social cost of crime as an overall part of a social problem, addiction. For the first time, then, a tentative estimate of the total cost and transfers from addiction-related crime can be made rather than having to rely on the usual partial cost estimates. Not only does the latter approach fail to depict accurately the nature and seriousness of the problem, but it is also likely to be used as if it were a measure of the total cost and transfers.

For the purpose of this study, only the costs of criminal activity and the related intangible costs will be considered since they are peculiarly associated with the phenomenon of narcotics addiction. The other costs — loss of production, prevention,

treatment, rehabilitation, premature deaths, social welfare payments — are associated with all forms of debilitating disorders, such as heart disease, mental retardation, stroke, and alcoholism, and they can be estimated for narcotic addiction by the modified use of existing public health studies in such areas.[6]

Until very recently, the cost of crime has been an area that has not received much attention from professional economists.[7-13]

Four types of crime can be distinguished in society according to whether they involve (1) bodily harm, (2) damage to property, (3) forced transfer of goods, or (4) illegal sale of goods or services. The term "forced transfer of goods" needs some elaboration and justification. The term "transfer" is used usually to identify a positive social action; however, it is also used to identify some negative social activities such as monopolistic or oligopolistic pricing and the raising of protective tariffs. A criminal act involving the appropriation of goods or property should be considered a forced transfer as long as an addict is considered a member of society. In the case of theft, for example, the good is passed from one member of society to another without a reduction in its actual value to society. The only way in which the value of the goods lost would be included in the final calculation of the net cost of crime would be if the addict were defined not to be a member of society. In this case the value of the goods would have been lost to society. Although an addict or any criminal may be acting outside of society's rules, there is no justification for considering him to be outside of society.

The intangible costs associated with narcotic addiction are perhaps the largest in terms of social loss. However, measurement of these costs is not possible. They result from the fear, anxiety, bewilderment, and frustration experienced by the citizens of a community with a serious narcotics problem. Small businesses, for example, which stayed open at night in order to compete with daytime chain stores, are now closing early because of the fear of nighttime robbery. People are reluctant to go out at night for recreational activities, such as the movies, for fear of being mugged or having their houses burglarized while they are gone. Theatres, concert halls, amusement parks, restaurants, and other nighttime places of entertainment and recreation are not frequented as much for the same reasons. Personnel required for evening and night-shift work, such as in hospitals, are hard to recruit because of the dangers of nighttime travel. A conversational wait of 10 minutes in a big city bank teller's line will provide one with recent accounts of robberies and thefts in the neighborhood committed by addicts. One elderly lady on New York's lower East Side was observed daily with a wagon, carrying all of her meager belongings with her on the street. When questioned about this practice, she explained that her apartment had been burglarized so many times she did not dare leave anything there when she went out. These and many other intangible costs which result from narcotic addiction are probably far greater than the tangible costs which are estimated in this study.

FORCED TRANSFER RESULTING FROM ADDICT CRIME

To estimate the dollar value of the transfers resulting from crime committed by narcotic addicts, one could survey narcotic addicts in order to determine, first, the kinds and number of crimes committed by them and, second, the total dollar value of the crimes. The first step in this process has in fact been accomplished for several groups of addicts, but the second has not. There is, however, an alternative approach to the measurement of criminal transfers committed by addicts. First, one can determine the total expenditure for narcotics by addicts, as well as for all other consumed goods and services regardless of source of income or drug supply. Secondly, one can determine how much of these expenditures were made as the result of the receipt of legitimate income and how much from the result of illegal activities and, finally, how much of the illegal income was the result of each kind of criminal activity. The data necessary for measuring the social cost of addict-related crime according to this second approach are available and therefore will be adopted in this study.

No national data are available to show what the retail dollar costs of habits for each addict were in 1966. However, one source of such data is that presented by the New York State Narcotic Addiction Control Commission for the 3,623 admissions to its program for fiscal 1968.[14] The fiscal 1968 data will be used in this study as a proxy for 1966. The group reported on is made up mostly of New York City addicts and would be somewhat representative of all urban addicts. There is no similar source of data for rural addicts. Since there is no evidence to indicate how the quantity of narcotics consumed might differ among rural and urban addicts, it is not possible to ascertain how the estimate to be made might be affected by using urban data for the rural addict population. Two other qualifications must be made concerning these data before an estimate can be made: First, the New York State statistics are representative of an institutionalized group, and there is no way of knowing whether or not the total population of addicts, or even of urban addicts, consumes narcotics in the same quantities as the institutionalized group. Another possible bias in using institutional data for the total population of addicts is that such data would tend to overstate the size of habits because addicts would not appear in the sample unless they were heavily involved with drugs.

As a first step in determining how much addicts spend on narcotics, it is necessary to estimate approximately how many of the 80,000 addicts in the country were on the street during 1966 because many addicts at any given time are in jail, prison, or in residential treatment programs. In one Arthur D. Little study, it was estimated that more than 5,000 addicts were off the street either in treatment programs or penal or other institutions (1,400 in federal prisons, 700 in hospitals run by the state or city of New York, 2,300 in California state hospitals, 900 at Lexington).[15] It was further reported that there were other addicts in state prisons, private hospitals, and the Federal facility at Fort Worth; the number of addicts in this second group was not estimated. Preble and Casey estimated that 40% of the addict group they examined were off the streets in the year 1966 to 1967.

The range of estimates therefore would be approximately the 10% of the Little report (assuming that the authors of this report expected at least 3,000 additional addicts to be in the other institutions and programs not specifically enumerated in the study) and approximately 40% for the Preble and Casey study. Since the latter study examined an extreme group of addicts in one of the most notorious narcotic-use communities in the country, it is probable that the percentage probably lies between the two. For the purposes of this study, it will be assumed that an average 20% of all addicts were off the street in 1966. This means that 64,000 addicts (80,000 less 20% or

16,000) were on the street during the year. For the immediate purposes of measuring the cost of drugs, it suffices to measure the number of male and female addicts on the street (7,680 females and 56,320 males).

One additional note is necessary before presenting the distribution of addict habit costs. It is believed that the street cost of a "bag" of narcotics in New York may be among the lowest in the country. If this is true, the use of the New York data for the rest of the country may bias the estimate of the total expenditures for drugs.

Table 1 presents the distribution of average daily habit costs for the 64,000 addicts on the street in 1966 (this distribution is separately shown for male and female addicts). To estimate the cost of narcotics for this group, the distributions of Table 1 are applied to the 7,680 female and 56,320 male addicts on the street in 1966 in Table 2.

The retail cost of drugs for the 64,000 addicts on the street is $1,791,240 per day or approximately $645 million per year. In addition to the estimated expenditures for all other addict-consumed goods and services, the $645 million

figure will be used to gain an overall estimate of the dollar value earned by addicts from illegal activities. No national data are available to indicate what percentage of personal income addicts spend on drugs as compared to all other goods and services. On the basis of limited information

TABLE 1

Sex by Reported Cost Per Day of Primary Drug (Percent)

Cost per day of primary drug	Male	Female
None	4.5%	9.3%
$1–19	41.3	28.0
20–39	32.8	34.7
40–59	12.8	12.6
60–79	5.3	8.0
80–99	1.5	3.6
100 and over	1.8	3.8
Unascertained	–	–
Total	100.0%	100.0%

From N.Y. State Narcotic Addiction Control Commission, *First Annual Statistical Report*, Albany, 1968, 15. With permission.

TABLE 2

Sex by Reported Cost Per Day of Primary Drug Used by All Addicts

Cost per day	Number of males[a,b]	Number of females[b]	Total cost of males[c]	Total cost of females[c]
None	2,533	714	$ 0	$ 0
$1–19	23,259	2,150	232,590	21,500
20–39	18,473	2,665	554,190	79,950
40–59	7,209	966	360,450	48,300
60–79	2,985	613	208,950	42,910
80–90	845	275	76,050	24,750
100 and over[d]	1,014	292	101,400	29,200
Total	56,320	7,680	$1,544,630	$246,610

Total for male and female addicts $1,791,240.

[a]This column was obtained by multiplying the percentages for males shown in Table 1 by 56,320. The column does not add to this last number due to a rounding error.

[b]This column was obtained by multiplying the percentages for females shown in Table 1 by 7,680. This column does not add to this last number due to a rounding error.

[c]These columns were obtained by multiplying first the number of males and then of females by each median of the categories shown in the first column cost per day.

[d]The median was not used in this category; rather, the number $100 was used in the calculation of the last two columns.

gathered in the preparation of the Preble and Casey study, it will be assumed that 90% of the income of an addict is spent on drugs and that 10% of it is expended on all other goods and services.[16]

Table 2 shows that all male addicts expended $1,544,630 for drugs in one day. This poses the question of how much total income was necessary from all sources to sustain these expenditures. On the basis of 90% assumption, the total income per day must approximate $1,716,255 or $626,433,070 per year.

From Table 2 it can be seen that all female addicts spent $246,610 in one day for narcotics. The total income per day necessary to support this dollar amount of habit, under the assumption that 90% of all income is spent for drugs, must approximate $247,011 per day or $100 million per year.

The next question to be answered is how much of all addict income is derived from legal as well as from illegal sources. Assuming that approximately 9 to 10% of the income of male addicts is from legal sources, they must have raised $570 million from illegal activities.[17,18] For female addicts the percent of legal income is less, probably about 1.64%.[19] Using this figure, female addicts would have an income of $98.36 million from illegal sources.

The total income needed from all illegal sources to sustain the drug habits and other consumption of all the addicts on the street was equal to approximately $668 million. To determine the social costs of crime and the social transfers resulting from these crimes, it is necessary to determine the kinds of crimes committed by each addict group.

TYPES OF ADDICT CRIME

Several studies have shown the high relationship between crime and addiction.[20-25]

The Preble and Casey study presented data on the criminal occupations of addicts.[26] The results are presented in Table 3.

LOSS ESTIMATES

Having arrived at a dollar estimate of the illegal retail value of drugs sold, at an estimate of the percentage and the number of addicts on the street in 1966 who earned their income through criminal

TABLE 3

Total Criminal Addict Population by Criminal Specialty (Percent of the Total Population)[a]

Occupation	Percentage of total criminal addict population[b]
Shoplifter	14.0%
Burglar	23.9
Seller of drugs	31.6
Armed robber	9.9
Flat-footed hustler[c]	13.2
Pimp	1.6
Prostitute	4.9

[a]The original Preble and Casey data were presented in terms of percentages of the total addict population studied, including those who worked. For use in this chapter, the data were changed to reflect only percentages of those who were criminals.
[b]The percentages do not add to 100 due to rounding error.
[c]A flat-footed hustler has no criminal specialty but is versatile in that he can successfully perform several different kinds of criminal acts.

activities, and, finally, at an estimate of the kinds of criminal acts committed by addicts, one can now make some quantitative statements about the transfers resulting from addiction and the loss in social welfare from the illegal activities connected with narcotic use.

With a knowledge of the total income needs of addicts from all illegal sources to sustain their habits, that is, $668 million, it is possible to estimate the total dollar transfer resulting from each kind of criminal specialty. To make this estimate, the following calculations are required. First, Table 3 must be used to approximate the percentage of $668 million that is earned from each criminal specialty. The total illegal income earned from each is thus equal to $668 million multiplied by the following percentages: 14% from shoplifting, 23.9% from burglary, 31.6% from the sale of drugs, 9.9% from armed robbery, 13.2% from the actions of a flat-footed hustler, 1.6% from those of a pimp, and 4.9% from prostitution.[27]

The $668 million does not represent the total transfer from addict crime; it does, however, equal the dollar amount of income received from each criminal activity. The reason for this is that some crimes do not result in the addict criminal's receiving dollars but rather goods that must be transformed into dollars in order for him to purchase narcotics. This is accomplished by selling the stolen goods to a fence in return for dollars. The most frequently quoted discount across the country is that a "fence" will pay one quarter of the current value of most items. This is the estimate that will be used here to obtain the actual value of stolen property. The total value transfer of addict crimes is thus equal to the sum of money received by addicts from their crimes plus the current value of the property stolen by addicts, which is equal, in this case, to the dollars received from the fence multiplied by four. For example, if in a robbery the addict obtained $100 in cash and $20 from the sale of stolen property to a fence, the total transfer would equal $100 + (4 × $20) or $180.

To estimate the value of the transfer that results from each type of addict criminal activity the following approach will be utilized: First, there will be a determination of what percentage of the total illegal income earned by addicts results from each kind of criminal activity. Second, with these data, the value of the transfer will be estimated using the procedure outlined above. Finally, an attempt will be made to estimate how this transfer was distributed between business and individuals.

Because there is no way to gauge directly the accuracy of the estimates made in this regard, an indirect procedure will be used. Where possible, there will be an estimate of the total dollar value of the transfers of each type of crime (committed by both addicts and nonaddicts) for all of society. These numbers will serve as a control against which to compare the addict estimates. For example, if the total dollar transfer from addict crime exceeded that estimated for all of society, there would be strong reason to believe the addict estimates were biased upward. If, however, they were 50% of the total value as some are, they would provide no guidance for accepting or rejecting these estimates.

Shoplifting

Shoplifting is a source of revenue for 14% or $93.1 million (14% × $668 million) of all the income earned from all the illegal sources. Since shoplifting results only in the theft of fenceable property, the total transfer that results is equal to $372.5 million (4 × $93.1 million). During 1967 to 1968, the Small Business Administration esti-

mated that all business lost $504 million as a result of shoplifting.[28] Throughout this study, these data will be used as proxies for those of 1966. The SBA described this estimate as surprisingly low and indicated that the most widely accepted estimate for the value of transfers from this kind of crime was $2 to 2.5 billion.[29] Comparing the $372.5 million figure to the $504 million for all of society, it would seem that the addict estimate is somewhat high; however, it could also be, given the SBA comments, that the estimate for losses from all shoplifting is low. The addict number will be accepted in this study until further data are available.

Burglary

Burglary is a crime involving unlawful entry to commit a theft, whether or not force is used. It is estimated that 23% of the $668, or $159.7 million, of all addict income derived from illegal sources is the result of burglaries. The $159.7 million figure represents the total dollars that addicts received either directly as a result of the criminal acts or by having obtained property from a burglary and then fenced the goods for dollars. To determine the dollar transfer brought about by these burglaries, it is necessary first to determine the percentage of the $159.7 million that constituted cash directly received from the crime and that which was derived from the sale of fenceable goods. If only cash was taken, the transfer involved would be equal to $159.7 million; if, instead, only fenceable goods were taken, the amount would be $693.1 million ($159.7 million × 4). There is no direct evidence on the basis of which to predict where in this range ($160 to 693 million) the actual transfer will fall. There is, however, evidence to show that in 1966 the total dollar transfer from all crimes of this type in the United States was $251 million.[30] There is other evidence that the actual dollar transfer from all crimes of this type is much larger than the $251 million indicated by the *Uniform Crime Reports*. A national survey of households conducted in 1966 showed that a total of $313 million was lost by individuals alone as the result of acts of burglary. The SBA survey for 1967 to 1968 found that business lost $958 million during that 1-year period from burglary.[31] The total loss from all burglary in society might then approximate $1.2 billion in 1966 (adding the losses from business and individuals).

This range of estimates ($160 to 693 million) of transfers resulting from addict burglary makes it appear highly unlikely that all transfers resulting from this crime were either in the form of cash or fenceable goods; therefore, the mean between the two extremes will be used. It is estimated that $400 million in the form of fenceable property and money was transferred as a result of addict burglary. Seventy-five percent of all burglaries involve business establishments. It will be assumed here that the same rate holds true for addict burglaries; therefore, 75% of $400 million, or $300 million, was transferred from business establishments; the remainder, or $100 million, was transferred from private individuals.

Armed Robbery

Armed robbery involves the taking of property by force or by threat of force. The estimate made here is for property losses only and does not include an estimate of losses due to personal injury. It is assumed further that all of the transfers resulting from armed robbery involve the loss of money. Table 3 indicates that 9.9% of the $668 million, or $66.1 million, was obtained through armed robberies by addicts. Since only money is assumed to be involved in robbery, the final transfer from addict robbery is equal to $66.1 million.

It is estimated that in 1966, the total loss resulting from the robbery of individuals was $49.4 million.[32] During 1967 to 1968 it is estimated that the total loss from business robberies was equal to $77 million. It is estimated then that the total loss (for business and private individuals) was approximately $126.4 million.[33] It appears then that addicts account for slightly over half of all the transfers from this source. It seems unreasonable to believe that over half of all transfers from robberies are brought about by addicts; further research into this problem might reveal this number to be biased in an upward direction and/or that the total loss estimate from all robberies is too low. Thirty-nine percent of all robberies are of individuals (using the $49.9 million of $126.4 million); it is assumed here that the same percentage holds true for all addict robberies. Under this assumption, $25.7 million was transferred by addict robberies from individuals, and the remainder, $40.4 million, was the result of business robberies.

The Flat-footed Hustler

The addict criminal who is a flat-footed hustler (first described by Preble and Casey) can perform at least two or more criminal specialties equally well. From unpublished data gathered for the Preble and Casey study, it is estimated that one half of the hustler's illegal operations result in cash transfers and the remainder in fenceable property. From Table 3 it can be seen that 13.2% of $668 million, or $88.2 million, is earned through this class of criminal occupations.

Since one half of the $88 million is stolen property that must be sold to a fence, the total transfer from flat-footed hustlers is equal to $220 million (½ × $88 million × 4 + $39 million). Because of the lack of national data for this addict group, there is no number against which to compare this amount of transfer. In addition, there is no exact distribution figure available to describe how this transfer was divided between business and the individual. It is assumed that a large number of addicts who are flat-footed hustlers are involved in the following criminal activities: shoplifting, burglary, and robbery. In the case of shoplifting, the entire loss is undergone by business; in the case of burglary, business sustains approximately 75% of the loss; and for robbery, business sustains 60% of the loss. As a minimum estimate, it is assumed that one half of the transfer of $220 million, or $110 million, is sustained by business.

Consumer Crime

The classification known as consumer crime includes the sale of narcotics, gambling, and prostitution. Each is characterized by the fact that it involves the voluntary purchase of an illegal service. Although consumer crimes also entail a transfer, the nature of the transfer is now, of course, different because it is not forced and because, in general, the consumer is fully aware of the illegality of the act. The first transfer value to be estimated here is that resulting from prostitution. In this category is included the 4.9% of the income received by addicts from the act itself and the 1.6% that accrues from pimping; total income received from all prostitution-related acts equals 6.5% of $668 million, or $43.4 million. Since these are all cash transfers, the full value of the transfers from prostitution equals $43.4 million. Recent estimates for prostitution-related acts have suggested much higher figures.[34] The final category of consumer crime to be considered is that of drug selling by an addict. The transfer for this type of crime is equal only to the value of the drugs the addict himself consumes. Table 3 shows that 31.6% of all illegal incomes are from drug sales. The value of transfers occurring here equals $207 million (31.6 percent × $668 million). This represents the retail value of narcotics that addict narcotic sellers could receive if they had not consumed the drugs themselves.

Summary of Transfers Resulting from Addict Crimes

Table 4 summarizes the transfers that take place as a result of addict crime and their distribution between business and individuals.

Table 4 shows that the estimated total transfer caused by all addict crime is equal to approximately $1.3 billion. Forced transfers from business are equal to approximately 63% of the total, or $822 million; forced transfers from individuals were equal to approximately $486 million.

NUMBER OF ADDICT CRIMES

It is necessary to make the cost estimates in this section to project the number of each kind of addict crime (see Table 5). For these purposes, only property crimes will be considered. The procedure to be used will be to divide the total dollar transfer from each type of crime by the average dollar value lost nationally from each crime. The result will be an estimate of the number of each type of crime committed by addicts. (The calculations are shown in Table 5).

An adjustment must be made in Table 5 for the number of each type of crime that goes unreported. For instance, it is reported that 1,652,892 burglaries were committed by addicts; however, the national averages show that only one out of every two such crimes is reported to the police.[35,36] In 1966, consequently, 826,446 addict burglaries (applying the national average to addict burglaries) were reported to the police. Similarly, in 1966 there were 260,236 addict robberies as shown in Table 5. On a national average, only one out of every two such cases is reported to the police;[37] therefore, 130,118 (out of 260,236) addict robberies were reported to the police in 1966. Finally, 2,321,428 crimes are

TABLE 4

Transfers That Are the Result of Addict Crime as Distributed Between Business Establishments and Individuals (in Millions of Dollars) (1966)

Crimes	Business	Individuals	Total
Shoplifting	$373.4	–	$ 372.4
Burglary	300.	$100.	400.
Robbery	40.4	25.7	66.1
Flat-footed hustling	110.	110.	220.
Prostitution	–	43.4	43.4
Sale of Drugs	–	207.0	207.
Total	$822.8	$486.1	$1,308.9

TABLE 5

Number of Addict Property Crimes

Crimes	Total dollar value of transfer[a]	National average dollar transferred[d] (for each crime)	Number of crimes[e]
Shoplifting	$372.4 million	$ 27[b]	13,796,296
Burglary	400.0	242[b]	1,652,892
Robbery	66.1	254[b]	260,236
Flat-footed hustling	195.0	84[c]	2,321,428

[a]See Table 3.
[b]Reference 1.
[c]The estimate used here was for larceny (including pickpocketing, purse-snatching, shoplifting, theft of autos as well as auto accessories, theft of bicycles, theft from buildings and coin-operated machines, and similar crimes).
[d]All data based on the 1965 *Uniform Crime Reports*.
[e]This number is obtained by dividing the total dollar value of transfers by the national average dollar value per crime.

shown in Table 5 as having been committed by flat-footed hustlers. There are no reliable data to show how much of the crime committed by this group goes unreported. The category of crime closest to that of the flat-footed hustler that has been discussed in the literature on underreported crime is larceny over $50. The only existing study on the subject shows the amount of under-reporting to be substantial in this category, but does not quantify the amount.[38] Until further evidence becomes available, it will be assumed that the number of underreported crimes in this category is twice that of burglary and robbery; thus, one out of four crimes committed by flat-footed hustlers would be reported to the police, with the result that 580,387 (out of 2,321,428) of the crimes come to the attention of the police.

PUBLIC AND PRIVATE EXPENDITURES FOR LAW ENFORCEMENT AND CRIMINAL JUSTICE AS WELL AS GENERAL PREVENTION OF CRIMES RELATED TO NARCOTIC ADDICTION

This section will present a measurement of the social loss resulting from the arrest, trial, incarceration, probation, and parole of addicts as well as of nonaddict narcotic traffickers. In addition, the costs of equipment services, and insurance used by business and private individuals to protect themselves against addict crime will be measured.

The calculation of the social cost of addict and nonaddict arrest, trial, incarceration, probation, and parole will be performed in two parts. The first part contains an estimate for the cost of services related to the arrest, trial, and sentencing of addicts and nonaddicts on drug charges. The second will be based on the costs of the same services provided in connection with the arrest, trial, and sentencing of addicts on nondrug charges.

The cost of police, court, and penal services incurred in the case of addicts and nonaddicts who had committed drug law violations is estimated with the aid of several special surveys. In many cases, the number of governmental units involved in each survey was limited, and the total costs are, therefore, projected from very small samples. The estimate of the full costs of the criminal justice system which result from all addict nondrug-related crime is developed using an average cost of police services index for major crimes, obtained by using data from California and the District of Columbia and the average number of each type of crime committed by addicts.

It is impossible to estimate from the given data what proportion of the total costs is to be allocated between state and local police. It is assumed, however, that the major costs are borne by local police.

Social Cost of the Criminal Justice System Related to All Narcotic Law Violations
Police

The figures included in this section are the cost of federal, state, and local law enforcement agencies involved in the apprehension of narcotic law violators. In most instances, certain police officers are assigned to special squads whose duties are completely or partially concerned with the enforcement of drug laws. In forming these estimates, no attempt was made to allocate partial costs between crimes. For example, if a police officer was involved in the investigation of both narcotic cases and gambling, the entire costs of his services were allocated to narcotics. The primary reason for this procedure lies in the difficulties that would be encountered in attempting to make any kind of determination of program allocation time between crimes.

Two federal agencies are directly involved in the enforcement of the United States narcotic laws: the Federal Bureau of Narcotics and the Bureau of Customs. In 1966 (fiscal 1967) the total cost of operations of the FBN was $5.9 million. All the Bureau's costs are going to be considered in this study as part of the social costs of addiction.

The officers of the Bureau of Customs are most directly involved in border surveillance and in the control of persons and goods entering and leaving the United States. In some sense all the Bureau's agents are involved in the control of narcotics; however, costs resulting from their border surveil-lance activities are not going to be included in the final cost totals. The only costs of the Bureau to be included are those of a few inspectors and agents who spend more than half of their operating time on drug problems. Based on this, the cost of the Customs Bureau's activities in narcotics in 1966 was $488,852, as estimated by the Office of Finance and Administration of the Bureau of Customs.

The total cost of all federal police activities in the enforcement of narcotics laws in 1966 was approximately $6.4 million.

The state estimates are based on a state by state survey conducted by the Federal Bureau of Narcotics of manpower involved in the control of narcotic violations. This survey was conducted by FBN local agents who identified the number of men involved in each state in the enforcement of narcotic laws. Some of these men were members of special drug teams; others were members of the vice squad of the highway patrol or state police; finally, some were members of special narcotics investigation units. In no way is it possible to gauge how much of the activity of these men is expended in the enforcement of narcotics laws; however, the assumption throughout this study is that those whom the FBN agents identified as narcotic investigators allocated 100% of their time to drug problems.

The estimation of the cost of this service for each state requires an estimate of the salary cost of all the manpower involved, as well as the cost of all the needed support equipment and personnel. The FBN survey provides an estimate of the absolute number of men involved in this service without giving data either on the rank of these men or on the costs of their services.

State data revealing average per capita police costs for 1966 are not readily available. What is available, however, is the average expenditure for all police personnel in the leading cities of each state. This will be used as a proxy for the state financial data.

All the necessary calculations are shown in Table 6. From the table it is evident that all states expend approximately $914,000 for narcotic law enforcement; this amount constitutes approximately one sixth of the federal government's total expenditures. As could be expected, those states with the largest narcotics problem, such as New York, Illinois, and Pennsylvania, have the largest expenditures.

The estimation of manpower involved in the enforcement of narcotic laws at the county level is developed from the same survey by the Federal Bureau of Narcotics used to form the state police

costs. The estimates of the costs for this manpower again are based on the average expenditures per enforcement personnel of a selected city of the state in which the county is located. The results of these calculations are shown in Table 7.

Although only five states had counties with special narcotic units, their total expenditures exceeded those of all state units. This fact was due, however, to the very large expenditures in New York, California, and New Jersey. The large county expenditures of California counterbalance the fact that no separate state units were shown for this state, which is known to have a very large narcotics problem.

In estimating the manpower used in the enforcement of narcotics laws at the city and town level, the same survey by the FBN used to form the state and county estimates is utilized. The estimates of the costs for this manpower again are based on the average expenditures per enforcement personnel in a selected city of the state. The results of these calculations are shown in Table 8. It reveals that the total expenditure by all cities and towns in all states for narcotics law enforcement is equal to $6,624,677. The largest expenditures are for Illinois, with $468,160 (although the table does not show it, this is largely for Chicago), and for New Jersey, with $368,280.

In summary, Table 9 shows the total expenditure by all levels of government for the enforcement of narcotics laws. These totaled approximately $15.3 million. Both the local governments and the federal government expended approximately the same amounts for the enforcement of narcotic laws. The state governments spent the least amount.

The Courts

No estimate is available to show how many trials took place of narcotics addicts or traffickers for drug law violations at the local, county, or state levels of government. The only existing government figures are for the national government. In 1966 (fiscal 1967) there were 450 federal narcotic trials; of this number 137 were court trials (without jury) and 313 were jury trials. In terms of the number of trial days, there were 233 days of court narcotic trials, and 831 jury narcotic drug trials.[39] The total cost of these trials (including the operating expenses of the courtroom, the judges and related staff salary expenses, jury costs, and public defender fees, but excluding witnesses),

TABLE 6

Total Cost of State Law Enforcement Activities

State[a]	Number of men[b]	Agency[b] if identified	Average expenditure[c]	Total cost[d]
Alabama[1]	1	State Police	$6,546	$ 6,546
Connecticut[2]	2	State Police	9,500	19,000
Florida[3]	12	Bureau of Narcotics	7,290	87,480
Illinois[4]	26		8,360	217,360
Kentucky[5]	5		6,808	34,040
Maine[6]	1		8,015	8,015
Maryland[7]	2	State Police	7,631	15,262
Michigan[8]	1	State Police	8,013	8,013
New Mexico[8 a]	5		7,179	35,895
New York[9]	23	Bureau of Narcotics	8,032	184,736
N. Carolina[10]	3	Bureau of Investigation	6,526	19,578
Oklahoma[11]	3		5,672	17,016
Pennsylvania[12]	25	Div. of Behavioral P. & D.C.	7,250	181,250
Rhode Island[13]	4	Div. of Food & Drug Control, Dept. of Health	6,344	25,376
Tennessee[14]	3		7,495	22,677
Virginia[15]	4	State Police	8,063	32,252
Total				$914,496

1. Montgomery	7. Baltimore	11. Oklahoma City
2. Hartford	8. Detroit	12. Philadelphia
3. Miami	8a. Albuquerque	13. Providence
4. Chicago	9. Rochester	14. Nashville
5. Lousiville	10. Raleigh	15 Richmond
6. The Maine figures include New Hampshire and Vermont. City used was Portsmouth, N.H.		

[a]Those states not shown are presumed not to have separate drug enforcement teams. The District of Columbia is shown under the costs of cities and towns by state for law enforcement.
[b]Source of the data was the special survey by the Federal Bureau of Narcotics.
[c]For each state, this figure represents for the selected city the total expenditure divided by the total number of enforcement employees, including civilians. The cities were selected in most cases because (1) they were known to have a narcotics problem, (2) they were the largest city, or (3) they were the state capital. Source of data: The International City Managers Association, *The Municipal Yearbook,* Chicago, 1967, 452.
[d]This figure is obtained by multiplying the number of men (column 2) by the expenditure (column 4).

List of cities whose average expenditure figures were used as a proxy for State:

is $727,000. The total cost of court trials is approximately $112,000; the cost of jury trials is approximately $615,000.[40]

Corrections

To estimate the cost of federal imprisonment for narcotic law violators, one must know the total number of days of incarceration for narcotic violations in 1966 (fiscal 1967). In this calculation it is assumed here that those prisoners who were identifiable as addicts were charged with narcotic law violations. No data are available that directly reveal this fact. What is known, however, is the actual number of narcotics violators imprisoned as

TABLE 7

Total Cost of County Law Enforcement Activities by State

State[a]	Number of men[b]	Average expenditures[c]	Total cost[d]
California[1]	94	$9,411	$ 884,634
Florida[2]	2	7,290	14,580
Maryland[3]	2	7,631	15,262
New Jersey[4]	23	8,370	192,510
New York[5]	40	8,032	327,280
Total			$1,434,266

[a]The states not shown are presumed not to have a separate narcotic unit in any of their locations.

[b]Some of these data were the special survey by the Federal Bureau of Narcotics.

[c]For each state, this figure represents for the selected city the total expenditure divided by the total number of enforcement employees, including civilian workers. The city was selected because: (1) the city was known to have a narcotics problem, (2) it was the state's largest city, or (3) it was the state capital. Source of data: The International City Managers Association, *The Municipal Yearbook,* Chicago, 1967, 452.

[d]This figure is obtained by multiplying the number of men (column 2) by the average expenditure (column 3).

List of cities:
1. Los Angeles County figures
2. Miami
3. Baltimore
4. Newark
5. Rochester

of June 30, 1966. By assuming that this level remains constant throughout the year, one can estimate the total number of addict incarceration days. As of June 30, 1966, there were 3,383 narcotic violators.[41] The total number of addict incarceration days, assuming the June 30 level remains constant throughout the year, is equal to 1,234,795 (3,383 × 365 days). The total maintenance cost per day per inmate at federal prisons is $7.67 (which includes food, clothing, medical, and administrative expenses).[42] Thus, the total cost for the 1,234,795 days of incarceration is $9,470,877 (1,234,795 × $7.67).

There is no central source of information in imprisonment by offense by state, nor do all states individually keep records in this respect. The procedure in this section was to survey a few states known to have a major drug problem. (The states were identified using the FBN list.) For each state contacted, the number of addicts incarcerated for narcotic violations as of a given date was ascertained. It is assumed here that all those prisoners

who were identifiable as addicts were charged with narcotic law violation. (There is, of course, a danger that in some states those identified as addicts were in fact users of other kinds of nonnarcotic drugs such as marijuana.) As in the last section, this number is assumed to remain constant over the year. The number of narcotic law violations then is multiplied by 365, which gives the total number of days of incarceration for those sentenced under this charge. In turn, the number of days of incarceration is multiplied by the per diem expense of incarceration, which gives the total cost of incarceration for narcotic violations. These per diem expenditures are not always equal across states. Some of the figures include prorated capital expenditures, others do not; some of the states maintain prison farms, and, therefore, their lower food costs are shown in the form of lower per diem expenditures; other states do not have to calculate with these factors. Given this total for a few states, an estimate can be arrived at for all the states. Table 10 shows that for the ten states studied and the District of Columbia, the

TABLE 8

Total Cost of City and Town Law Enforcement Activities by State

State[a]	Number of men[b]	Average expenditures[c]	Total cost[d]
Alabama, Montgomery	2	$6,546	$ 13,092
Arizona, Phoenix	8	8,471	67,768
California, Los Angeles	21	9,411	197,631
Colorado, Denver	15	8,599	98,985
Connecticut, Hartford	2	9,500	19,000
D.C., City Police Dept.			146,280
Florida, Miami	8	7,290	58,320
Georgia, Atlanta	2	7,495	14,990
Hawaii, Honolulu	4	9,445	37,780
Illinois, Chicago	56	8,360	468,160
Indiana, Indianapolis	8	6,847	54,776
Kentucky, Louisville	5	6,808	34,040
Louisiana, New Orleans	14	7,746	108,444
Maine, New Hampshire, and Vermont; Portsmouth, N.H.	4	8,015	32,060
Maryland, Baltimore City	18	7,631	137,358
Massachusetts, Police Expend.			218,210
Michigan, Detroit	19	8,013	152,247
Minnesota, Minneapolis	4	8,411	33,644
Missouri, St. Louis	9	7,919	51,271
Nebraska, Omaha	2	7,186	14,372
Nevada, Las Vegas	9	10,077	90,693
New Jersey, Newark	44	8,370	368,280
New Mexico, Albuquerque	2	7,179	14,358
New York, New York City	315	10,467	3,296,605
Ohio, Cleveland	19	7,263	137,997
Oregon, Salem	6	7,945	17,670
Pennsylvania, Philadelphia	26	7,250	188,500
S. Carolina, Columbia	2	6,462	12,924
Tennessee, Nashville	1	7,559	7,558
Texas, Houston	60	6,610	396,600
Utah, Salt Lake City	2	7,252	14,504
Virginia, Richmond	5.5	8,063	44,346
Washington, Seattle	5	8,112	40,560
Wisconsin, Milwaukee	6	5,525	21,150
Wyoming, Casper	2	6,204	14,504
Total			$6,624,677

[a]The states not shown are presumed not to have cities and towns with a separate narcotics unit.

[b]Source of much data was the special manpower survey performed by the Federal Bureau of Narcotics.

[c]For each state, this figure represents for the selected city the total expenditures divided by the total number of enforcement employees, including civilian workers. The cities were selected because they were (1) known to have a narcotics problem, (2) the state's largest city, or (3) the state capital. Source of data: The International City Managers Association, *The Municipal Yearbook,* Chicago, 1967, 452.

[d]This figure was obtained by multiplying the number of men (column 2) by the average expenditure (column 4).

total costs for all narcotics violators are approximately $18 million.

From Table 10, it is possible to project an estimate of the total cost of incarceration for all addicts for drug law violations throughout the United States. This projection will be performed by using the 1966 FBN list of known addicts by state. The assumption in this approach is that while the FBN list is not completely accurate as to the absolute number of addicts, it is approximately correct in its presentation of the relative distribution of addicts among states. It is, therefore, assumed that the distribution of addicts incarcerated is approximately the same as that given by the FBN.

Finally, it is hypothesized that the distribution of costs is proportionately related to the distribution of addicts. From this set of assumptions, the following conclusions can be drawn. First, the ten states and the District of Columbia listed in Table 10 contain 86% of the total number of addicts listed in the FBN total list. In that case the same

TABLE 9

Public Expenditures for Specialized Law Enforcement Agencies Involved in the Enforcement of the Narcotic Laws – 1966 (In millions of dollars)

Federal	$ 6.4
State	.914
County	1.434
City	6.624
	$15.376

TABLE 10

Cost of Those Incarcerated for Narcotic Violations by State – 1966

State	Number confined	Number of incarceration days	Per diem cost	Total cost
California[a]	2,054	749,710	$ 7.01	$ 5,245,467
D.C.[b]	304	110,960	10.04	1,114,038
Florida[c]	14	5,110	5.81	29,688
Illinois[d]	844	303,060	4.92	1,515,655
Maryland[e]	184	67,160	4.10	275,356
Massachusetts[f]	67	24,455	9.35	228,754
Minnesota[g]	32	11,680	5.48	64,006
New York[h]	1,073	391,645	9.68	3,791,123
Ohio[i]	343	125,195	4.77	2,597,180
Pennsylvania[j]	124	45,260	7.55	341,713
Texas[k]	660	240,900	2.56	4,936,704
Total				$18,139,666

[a]The number of persons committed and the per diem cost was as of Dec. 31, 1966. Source: Statistical Division of the Department of Corrections, Sacramento, California.

[b]These data are as of June 30, 1965 and will serve as a proxy for 1966. District of Columbia Department of Correction, *Selected Criminological Data – June 30, 1964,* June 30, 1965, Washington, D.C., 1966, Table 26. These data are as of June 30, 1965.

[c]Department of Corrections, State of Florida, Tallahassee, Florida.

[d]Illinois, Department of Corrections, *Statistical Summary Report for Illinois Penitentiary,* Springfield, June 1, 1966, 5. These data apply as of June 1, 1966. The average cost was estimated in a communication from the statistical Division of the Department of Corrctions.

[e]Department of Corrections, Maryland.

[f]Massachusetts Department of Corrections.

[g]Minnesota Department of Corrections.

[h]New York State Department of Corrections.

[i]Ohio Department of Corrections.

[j]Pennsylvania Department of Corrections.

[k]Texas Department of Corrections.

states would contain 86% of the addicts incarcerated and represent 86% of the total cost of incarceration for narcotic violations. An analysis of Table 10 shows that $18 million is the approximate cost of all incarcerations in the ten states and the District of Columbia; the $18 million represents 86% of the total cost of incarceration for all 50 states; therefore, $21 million is the total cost for all of the United States for the incarceration during 1966 of all addicts and nonaddict traffickers placed in penal institutions for violation of the narcotic laws.

In summary, Table 11 shows the total expenditures by all levels of government for the imprisonment of narcotic law violators. The total expenditures by all penal agencies approximated $30.4 million. No estimate is given in this section for city or county expenditures due to the lack of data sources. The states have in this case expended more than twice as much as the federal government.

Parole and Probation

In this section, an estimate will be made of the social cost of probation and parole for the federal

and state governments. No data will be provided for county or city governments. The estimate for the state government is based on a relatively small survey of those states known to have a large percentage of the addicts in this country. From the state data, a projection is made for all of the United States.

In 1966 (fiscal 1967), as of December 30, 1966, there were 2,890 persons on parole and probation as a result of violation of narcotic laws.[43] It will be assumed that during all of 1966 this number remained constant. During 1966 (fiscal 1967), the annual cost of parole and probation was equal to $251.85 per parolee or probationer.[44] The total cost of federal parole and probation was equal to $727,846 ($251.85 X 2,890).

The procedure for estimating state expenditures is the same as that in the federal analysis. It was first ascertained how many narcotic violators were on parole and probation for a particular date in 1966. It was then assumed that this number remained constant throughout the year. From this survey, the average annual cost per parolee or probationer also was ascertained. The total cost for each state was estimated by multiplying the total number on parole by the average annual cost for these services. (The calculations are shown in Table 12.) For all states in the study, only an estimate for the cost of parole is given since the countries and towns are usually responsible for probation services and they were not contacted as part of this study.

The total cost of parole shown for the four states in Table 12 is approximately $1.3 million. To obtain an estimate for all the states in the country, the procedure used in the last section will also be utilized. The four states shown in Table 12 contain approximately 70% of the addicts listed by the FBN in 1966. It will be assumed (as in the last section) that a similar percentage of all violations of narcotic laws and the costs of parole were sustained by these states. In that case, the $1.3 million would equal 70% of the costs of parole violators of narcotics laws for all states; the total cost of parole for all states would then be approximately equal to $1.85 million.

The total cost of parole and probation in all states is shown in Table 13 as equal to $2.6 million with the largest share ($1.85 million) borne by all states.

TABLE 11

Public Expenditures for the Imprisonment of Narcotic Law Violators – 1966 (in Millions of Dollars)

Federal	$ 9.4
State	21.0
Total	$30.4

TABLE 12

Annual Cost of Parole by State (1966)

State	Number on probation and parole	Average annual cost	Total cost of parole
California[a]	1,609	$609	$ 979,881
New York[b]	589	471	277,419
Pennsylvania[c]	274	326	89,324
Texas[d]	67	200	13,400
Total cost			$1,360,024

[a]Source: California Department of Corrections, as of December 31, 1966.
[b]Source: Bureau of Parole, Estimate and Audit Division, as of December 31, 1966.
[c]Source: Bureau of Parole, as of December 31, 1966.
[d]Source: Bureau of Parole, as of August 31, 1966.

Summary

Table 14 shows the total social costs of the criminal justice system by major expenditure category. The total cost is then equal to $49.3 million for all governments. The cost distribution is most heavily concentrated in expenditures for the operation of penal institutions (which represent more than half of the total costs).

TABLE 13

Annual Cost of Parole and Probation, All States and the Federal Government – A Summary (in Millions of Dollars)

Federal	$ .727
States	1.85
Total	$2.577

TABLE 14

Social Cost of the Criminal Justice System Related to All Narcotic Law Violations – A Summary (in Millions of Dollars)

Law Enforcement Agencies	$15.4
Courts (federal only)	.7
Penal institutions	30.4
Parole and probation	2.6
Total	$49.1

Social Cost of the Criminal Justice System Related to All Addict Nonnarcotic Law Violations[4][5]

Police

The costs in this section are estimated only for local police agencies. It is assumed that most crimes included here do not involve state or federal law enforcement agencies. In estimating the costs for local police services, the total includes the expenses of both county and city or town law enforcement agencies.

The presentation of the actual estimates will be preceded by a brief description of the data to be used in their formulation. As previously indicated, the cost estimates in this section are based on data from the District of Columbia and California. They were derived by allocating all detective costs to Index Crimes (willful homicide, forcible rape, robbery, aggravated assault, burglary, larceny of $50 and over, auto theft). Neither the costs of police patrols nor of special narcotic units are included in these estimates (the latter costs have already been estimated separately). If the cost of police patrols were included in these estimates, the

total unit costs might have increased by a factor of three. In presenting these data, the writers did not clarify how many, if any, of these costs were incurred for capital items. Although it is not clear how representative the data are for the entire country, they will be used as a proxy for a national average for local law enforcement costs.

The costs shown in Table 15 are the incremental costs for major property crimes. The incremental cost is the additional cost society will incur as the result of one more unit of crime. In estimating the losses that occur as a consequence of addict crime, what is being calculated is the incremental positive change in social welfare that would occur if addict crime did not exist. To calculate this change in social welfare, the number of addict index crimes for 1966 will be multiplied by the average police cost for each of these types of crime. This calculation is approximately correct insofar as one does not believe that if addict crime ceased to exist, the structure of police services would change dramatically. If this occurred, the marginal analysis being applied here would not be appropriate. Almost the same procedure will be used throughout this section of the chapter. The products will then be totaled in order to estimate the total cost of police services resulting from the commission of nondrug-related crimes by addicts.

Before analyzing the data in Table 15 one should note that approximately $372 million of property is transferred as a result of addict shoplifting. However, no data exist to indicate the cost for this activity. The cost of police services as estimated in Table 15 will be underestimated by the actual amount of police costs incurred in the investigation and arrest of addict shoplifters.

There is one additional factor that must be noted before proceeding with an analysis of the data in Table 15. The cost incurred for police services covers only those crimes that are reported. Society incurs no police cost for those that remain unreported. In the formation of police costs in this study, the number of reported addict crimes is used.

Table 15 indicates that local and county governments throughout the United States in 1966 spent as least $96 million for police services related to addict property crimes.

The Courts

To estimate the cost of trial of addict nondrug-related violations, the data from California and the

TABLE 15

Incremental Cost of Police Services of Addict Property Crimes

Crimes	Number of addict reported crimes[a]	Incremental cost of police services per reported crime	Total cost of crime[d]
Burglary	826,446	$37[b]	$30,578,502
Robbery	130,118	82[b]	10,669,676
Flat-footed hustling	580,357	95[c]	55,133,915
Total cost			$96,372,093

[a]Estimated previously.
[b]Blaunstein, A. and Larson, R., Models of a total criminal justice system, *Operations Res.,* 45, 210, 1969.
[c]The cost of police for larceny of over $50 was used to estimate the loss for flat-footed hustlers. Blaunstein and Larson did not report the total cost for this crime in the 1969 article. In private correspondence, they did indicate that the total cost from this crime was $100 to $150 per reported crime. Using the mean figure of $125 and assuming that 76% of the costs for this type of crime in the criminal justice system are for police services, we estimate a cost of $95 per reported crime.
[d]Column 1 × Column 2.

TABLE 16

Cost of Trial for Addict Nondrug-related Offense

Crime	Number of reported crimes[a]	Cost of trial per reported offenses	Total cost[d]
Burglary	826,446	$ 9[b]	$ 7,438,114
Robbery	130,118	34[b]	4,424,012
Flat-footed hustling	580,357	1.25[c]	725,446
Total			12,587,572

[a] Estimated previously.
[b]Blaunstein, A. and Larson, R., Models of a total criminal justice system, *Operations Res.,* 45, 210, 1969.
[c]The cost of trial for larceny of over $50 was used to estimate the cost for flat-footed hustlers. Blaunstein and Larson did not report the total cost for this crime in their 1969 article. In private correspondence, they did estimate that the total cost for this crime was $100 to $150 per reported crime. Using the mean figure of $125 and the fact that 1% of the cost for this crime in the criminal justice system is for court services, the cost of $1.25 per reported crime is estimated.
[d]Column 1 × Column 2.

District of Columbia will be used. Again the data cannot be separated to indicate the costs of state, county, or local courts. In using the data, one should remember that these costs are the incremental court costs and that they include those for personnel as well as those for certain items of fixed capital. Again it should be noted that these totals do not include all property crimes (for

example, cost of shoplifting); therefore, this cost total must be considered only a minimum.

The total cost of all trials of addicts including federal narcotics trials as shown in Table 16 is equal to $12,587,572.

Corrections

The cost of incarceration of addicts for non-

TABLE 17

The Cost of Corrections for Addict Nondrug-related Offenses

Crime	Number of reported crimes by type of crime[a]	Total penal expenditures by type of crime	Total cost by type[d]
Burglary	826,446	$87[b]	$71,902,802
Robbery	130,113	760[b]	98,888,280
Flat-footed	580,359	18[c]	10,446,426
Total			$181,237,508

[a]Estimated previously.

[b]Blaunstein, A. and Larson, R., Models of a total criminal justice system, *Operations Res.*, 45, 210, 1969.

[c]This cost was estimated by using as a proxy the cost of penal services for larceny of over $50. Blaunstein and Larson did not report the total cost for these crimes in their 1969 article. In private correspondence, they did point out that the total cost for these crimes was $100 to $150 per reported crime. Using the mean figure of $125 and the fact that 15% of the cost for this crime in the criminal justice system (see Reference 45) is for court services, one arrives at an estimate of $18 per reported crime.

[d]Column 1 × Column 2.

drug law violations is again estimated by using the marginal cost of incarceration crimes reported for California and the District of Columbia (see Table 17). Again the data include both marginal capital and personnel costs and assume a constant correctional structure. Not all crimes, nor even all property crimes, are included since shoplifting is not included in the calculation. The total must be considered as a minimum estimate of such correctional costs. Finally, the costs are not separated for local (including county) and state government.

The total cost of corrections for addicts involved in nondrug-related criminal violations for all levels of government is thus equal to $181.2 million.

Table 18 shows the total social costs of the criminal justice system by major expenditure category. The total cost is equal to $290 million for all governments.

The largest part of these costs ($181 million) is the result of addict incarceration. The second largest cost category is all law enforcement agencies.

Private Costs of Crime for Business and Individuals

There are several private costs of addict crime (both drug and nondrug law violations): the cost of employing services, equipment, or techniques to prevent its occurrence or reduce its impact, the cost of insuring against losses that these crimes

TABLE 18

Social Cost of the Criminal Justice System Related to Addict Nondrug Law Criminal Violations (In Millions of Dollars)

Law enforcement agencies	$ 96.4
Courts	12.6
Penal institutions	181.1
Total cost	$290.1

might entail, the cost of being a party or a witness in a criminal proceeding.[46]

The majority of these costs (with the possible exception of the case of witness expenses) are incurred to prevent crime that would be committed by anyone, not only addicts. It will be assumed that the ratio of the magnitude of addict violations to all crime could be used to estimate the cost of protection services and devices and insurance assumed as a result of addict crime as compared to the total purchases of such equipment and services. For example, if $100 million were lost from all crime in 1966, and if addicts caused $10 million of this loss, the ratio of addict-committed crime to all crime would equal 1/10. In turn, if business and individuals spent $10 million for prohibitive devices and services, then it is estimated that 1/10 of this $10 million, or $1 million, would have been spent to prevent addict crimes or to reduce the total dollar losses. In this section, an examination of the costs of protective devices will be followed by an analysis of the cost of insurance.

Burglar alarms, watchmen's equipment, and similar devices represent an annual cost of $120 million. Another $80 million is spent for equipment such as safes, vaults, personal wall safes, bulletproof glass, iron grills, special photographic equipment, and the like.[47] It is also true that a large number of guns and other weapons sold each year are purchased for self-protection. A recent survey indicated that 37% of all households maintain firearms for protection, and 17% of all businesses similarly keep firearms.[48]

Many businesses and residences employ private protection agencies, guards, and other special personnel to protect against crime. The Task Force Report estimated that in 1966 total wages for all such services were equal to $1 billion. After making allowances for the cost of supervising personnel and other overhead costs, the total expenditures for all types of protective services and equipment could be estimated at about $1.3 billion.[49]

The total cost of all preventive equipment and services in 1966 is, therefore, equal to $1.5 billion ($1.3 billion plus 2 billion). The question that now arises is how much of this cost is the result of addict crime. The assumption in this section is that most of these expenditures are to prevent property loss, and therefore, by being able to determine the amount of property loss from addict crime as compared to property loss from all crimes, it is possible to determine the percentage of total cost for prevention services and equipment that was incurred due to the presence of addicts in society. In 1966 all private individuals lost 1.2 billion dollars' worth of property as a consequence of all criminal activities. During the same period, loss by businesses was equal to approximately $3 billion.[50] This estimate was for 1968 and is used here as a proxy for 1966. The total loss for private individuals and business is thus equal to $4.2 billion. The total losses from addict crime during this period were equal to $1.3 billion, which is approximately 30% of the total transfer from all crime of $4.2 billion. This estimate excludes the transfers from prostitution and the sale of drugs.

The total cost of private protection equipment and services purchased as the result of addict crimes is equal to 30% of the total purchased; for 1966 this would represent 30% of $1.5 billion or

$465 million. Of interest here is how this expenditure is divided between business and private industry. The assumption is made that business and individuals are rational consumers of these services; therefore, protective services and equipment are purchased by each in relationship to their relative losses. For this estimate, the overall distribution for all crimes will be used since this is the index that each group would have used in making their purchases of this type of goods or service. In 1966, private individuals experienced approximately 25% of all losses, whereas it is estimated that 75% of the $465 (or $348 million) expended for protective goods and services was paid for by business; the remainder, or $117 million, was paid for by private individuals.

From the standpoint of the individual who purchases insurance, the premium is an immediate economic cost, incurred to protect against the risk of a greater loss. It could be called a cost due to the possibility of crime. If a crime occurs, the insured suffers no further loss because he is indemnified by the insurance company. From the standpoint of all insured individuals as a group and of society as a whole, however, the fact of insurance does not alter the amount of loss due to criminal acts. It merely distributes the loss among a large number of insured persons rather than allowing it to fall solely on the victim. This service of distribution does not come free, and those who take advantage of it must pay for it. Collectively, the cost of doing so is the overhead cost of the insurance, that is, not the amount of the premium paid but the amount of the premiums paid less the amount of the losses indemnified.[51]

The overhead cost of insurance usually is estimated at about 50% of the premiums received or about the same as the losses paid.[52] It is estimated that slightly less than one fifth of all fraudulent, dishonest, or criminal acts other than auto theft are indemnified by insurance. It should also be noted that coverage is not normally available for losses due to shoplifting and therefore is not included in the estimates of the section.

The total loss from all addict crime from business and individuals that is insurable (excluding the losses from shoplifting) is equal to $661 million. Only one fifth of this loss (assuming that the national averages apply) is covered by insurance; therefore, the total loss that is covered is equal to approximately $132 million. For this type of crime, there is an 11.6% recovery rate,[53] so that the total loss paid back by insurance companies is equal to approximately $117 million ($132 million minus $15 million, 11.6% of the total insurable loss). The cost of this insurance coverage to society is then equal to 50% of the $117 million, or $58.5 million. It is assumed here that the cost of insurance is distributed in the same way as the total losses due to addict crime since 25% of all losses to society are suffered by private individuals; 25% of $58.5 million, or $14.5 million of the social cost, is borne by individuals; and the remainder, $44 million, is sustained by business.

A Summary of Private Costs of Addict Crimes

Table 19 contains a summary of the private costs of crime. The total cost is $524 million. The largest part of this expenditure represents costs of prevention devices and services ($465 out of $524 million).

TABLE 19

Private Costs of Addict Crimes – A Summary (In Millions of Dollars)

Prevention devices and services	$465.0
Insurance	58.5
Total	$523.5

CONCLUSIONS

This study estimated the social costs of narcotic (primarily heroin) addiction due to the criminal activities of addicts. Also, it estimated the amount and source of forced transfers resulting from addiction-related crime.

Although many of the conclusions are tentative, the estimates and the approach taken in this study may be of some value to other students in the field. First, no other analysis of the costs of addiction-related crime and their distribution in society has been developed. Second, for policy purposes, the study provides a model with which an estimate of the social costs of and transfers resulting from addiction-related crimes can be developed rather than having to rely on the usual partial cost estimates. Not only does this latter

approach fail to demonstrate accurately the nature and seriousness of the problem, but it also is likely to be used as if it were a measure of the total cost. The estimation techniques applied in this study for the first time provide a means to measure the social cost of crime as an overall part of a social health problem – narcotic addiction.

The calculations only applied to those persons identified as heroin addicts. It is estimated (lacking any firm data) that there were 80,000 addicts in 1966. There are those who feel that there were twice that number of active addicts. Under the simplest set of assumptions, to gain an idea of what effect this might have, one could multiply by two (or any other factor) all costs found in Table 20. To be more precise, however, it would be necessary to reestimate each of the cost and transfer categories in the same way as has been accomplished in this study.

Each cost category is estimated by considering the year 1966 in isolation, without regard to the effects of former or later years on that year's costs. Many of the estimates were formulated under a strict set of assumptions. Where the estimates were highly speculative, the conservative figures were used.

This study began with an examination of the extent of addict committed crimes and their effects on all segments of society. In Table 20, it is shown that out of a total of $1.1 billion transferred for addict crimes, $822 million was taken from private industry and $279 million from private households (other than those of the addicts). The total social cost of addiction due to criminal activities is shown to be $862 million (Table 20). This amounted in 1966 to an annual cost of $4.45 for each U.S. resident and $22.25 for each family of five. The cost attributed to each addict is $10,775. Private industry bears the single largest share of this cost, $392 million, followed closely by state, county, and local governments with $332 million; private individuals bear costs equal to $132 million; finally, the federal government bears only $17 million of the total cost.

The intangible social and personal costs of narcotic addiction, which cannot be estimated, are probably far greater than the tangible costs accounted for here.

TABLE 20

Summary of Social Costs

| Type of cost | Total | Government expenditures | | | Private individuals and philanthropies | Reduction in tax revenues | Social insurance and public welfare | All households (except that of the addict) | Borne by addicts and their families |
| | | Federal | | State, county, and local | | | | | |
		NIMH	Other						
Tangible costs									
Cost of illegal and other undesirable behavior	$862,877,172		$17,254,000	$322,123,173	$392,000,000			$131,500,000	
Cost of crime resulting in physical injury									
Cost of crime resulting in death for the victim									
Cost of crime resulting in property damage									
Cost of crime resulting in the forced exchange of goods	813,697,173			290,197,173	392,000,000			131,500,000	
Cost of the criminal justice	290,197,173			290,197,173					
Police	96,372,093			96,372,093					
Courts	12,587,572			12,587,572					
Penal institutions	181,237,508			181,237,508					
Probation and parole									
Cost of privately owned devices and purchased services employed to prevent loss from criminal activities	523,500,000				392,000,000			131,500,000	
Protective services and equipment	465,000,000				348,000,000			117,000,000	
Insurance	58,500,000				44,000,000			14,500,000	

TABLE 20 (continued)

Type of cost	Total	Government expenditures			Private individuals and philanthropies	Reduction in tax revenues	Social insurance and public welfare	All households (except that of the addict)	Borne by addicts and their families
		Federal		State, county, and local					
		NIMH	Other						
Cost of crime resulting in the illegal sale of goods and services (narcotic law violations only)									
Cost of the criminal justice system	49,180,000		17,254,000	31,926,000					
Police	15,376,000		6,400,000	8,976,000					
Courts	727,000		727,000						
Penal institutions	30,400,000		9,400,000	21,000,000					
Probation and parole	2,577,000		727,000	1,850,000					
Cost of privately owned devices and purchased services employed to prevent addict crime and to apprehend addict criminals.									
Any cost (present or future) in caring for the victim.									
Cost of organized crime's involvement in addiction									
Transfer payments									
From	0				−822.8			−279,000,000	1,101,900,000
Shoplifting	0				−372,400,000				372,400,000
Burglary	0				−300,000,000			−100,000,000	400,000,000
Robbery	0				−40,400,000			−25,700,000	66,100,000
Flat-footed hustling	0				−110,000,000			−110,000,000	220,000,000
Prostitution	0							43,400,000	43,400,000

REFERENCES

1. U.S. President's Commission on Law Enforcement and Administration of Justice, Task Force on Assessment, *Task Force Report: Cr me and Its Impact – An Assessment,* U.S. Govt. Printing Office, Washington, D.C., 1967.
2. U.S. Small Business Administration, *Crime Against Small Business,* U.S. Govt. Printing Office, Washington, D.C., 1969.
3. Preble, E. and Casey, J. J., Taking care of business – the heroin user's life on the street, *Int. J. Addict.,* 4, 1, 1969.
4. U.S. Treasury Department, *Traffic in Opium and Other Dangerous Drugs,* U.S. Govt. Printing Office, Washington, D.C., 1966.
5. Singer, M., The vitality of mythical numbers, *The Public Interest,* 23, 3, 1971.
6. Casey, J. J., Economics of Narcotics Addiction, Ph.D. dissertation, Georgetown University, Washington, D.C., 1972.
7. Becker, G. S., Crime and punishment: an economic approach, *J. Political Econ.,* 6, 169, 1968.
8. Shelling, T. C., Economics of criminal enterprise, *The Public Interest,* 9, 61, 1967.
9. Tullock, G., The welfare costs of tariffs, monopoly and theft, *West. Econ. J.,* 5, 224, 1967.
10. Rottenberg, S., The clandestine distribution of heroin, its discovery and suppression, *J. Political Econ.,* 76, 78, 1968.
11. Seidl, J. M., Upon the Hip – A Study of the Criminal Loan-shark Industry, Ph.D. dissertation, Harvard University, Cambridge, 1968.
12. Mishan, E. J., A note on the costs of tariffs, monopolies, and thefts, *West. Econ. J.,* 3, 230, 1969.
13. Moore, M., Policy concerning drug abuse in New York State, *Economics of Heroin Distribution,* Vol. III, Hudson Institute, Croton-on-the-Hudson, 1970.
14. New York Narcotic Addiction Control Commission, Office of Planning and Coordination, *First Annual Statistical Report,* Albany, 1968.
15. Arthur D. Little, Inc., *Drug Abuse and Law Enforcement. A Report to the President's Commission on Law Enforcement and Administration of Justice,* Arthur D. Little, Inc., Cambridge, 1966.
16. Preble, E. and Casey, J. J., *Int. J. Addict.,* 4, 1, 1969.
17. O'Donnell, J. A., *Narcotic Addicts in Kentucky,* Dept. of Health, Education and Welfare, Washington, D.C., 1969.
18. Casey, J. J., Economics of Narcotics Addiction, Ph.D. dissertation, Gerogetown University, Washington, D.C., 1972.
19. Casey, J. J.,Economics of Narcotics Addiction, Ph.D. dissertation, Georgetown University, Washington, D.C., 1972.
20. Faris, R. E. L. and Dunham, H. W., *Mental Disorders in Urban Areas,* University of Chicago Press, Chicago, 1939, 170.
21. Dai, B., *Opium Addiction in Chicago,* The Commercial Press, Shanghai, 1937, 88, 189.
22. Finestone, H., Narcotics and criminality, *Law Contemp. Probl.,* 1957.
23. Chein, I., Gerard, D. L., Lee, R. S., and Rosenfeld, E., *The Road to H,* Basic, New York, 1964, 11, 57.
24. Kavaler, F., Krug, D., Amsel, Z., and Robbins, R., A commentary and annotated bibliography on the relationship between narcotic addicts and criminality, *Municipal Reference Notes,* 92, 1, 1968.
25. Moore, M., Policy concerning drug abuse in New York State, *Economics of Heroin Distribution,* Vol. III, Hudson Institute, Croton-on-the-Hudson, 1970.
26. Preble, E. and Casey, J. J., *Int. J. Addict.,* 4, 1, 1969.
27. Table 3.
28. U.S. Small Business Administration, *Crime Against Small Business,* U.S. Govt. Printing Office, Washington, D.C., 1969.
29. U.S. Small Business Administration, *Crime Against Small Business,* U.S. Govt. Printing Office, Washington, D.C., 1969.
30. U.S. Federal Bureau of Investigation, *Uniform Crime Reports,* U.S. Govt. Printing Office, Washington, D.C., 1966, 105.
31. U.S. Small Business Administration, *Crime Against Small Business,* U.S. Govt. Printing Office, Washington, D.C., 1969.
32. U.S. President's Commission on Law Enforcement and Administration of Justice, Task Force on Assessment, *Task Force Report: Crime and Its Impact – An Assessment,* U.S. Govt. Printing Office, Washington, D.C., 1967.
33. U.S. Small Business Administration, *Crime Against Small Business,* U.S. Govt. Printing Office, Washington, D.C., 1969.
34. Winick, C. and Kinsie, P., *The Lively Commerce,* Quadrangle, New York, 1972.
35. U.S. President's Commission on Law Enforcement and Administration of Justice, Task Force on Assessment, *Task Force Report: Crime and Its Impact – An Assessment,* U.S. Govt. Printing Office, Washington, D.C., 1967.
36. Inciardi, J. A. and Chambers, C. D., Unreported Criminal Involvement of Narcotic Addicts, paper presented at the Southern Sociological Society, May 1971.
37. U.S. President's Commission on Law Enforcement and Administration of Justice, Task Force Assessment, *Task Force Report: Crime and Its Impact – An Assessment,* U.S. Govt. Printing Office, Washington, D.C., 1967.
38. U.S. Presidents's Commisssion on Law Enforcement and Administration of Justice, Task Force on Assessment, *Task Force Report: Crime and Its Impact – An Assessment,* U.S. Govt. Printing Office, Washington, D.C., 1967.

39. Administration Office, U.S. Courts, Division of Procedural Studies and Statistics, Washington, D.C., 1967.
40. Administration Office, U.S. Courts, Division of Procedural Studies and Statistics, Washington, D.C., 1967.
41. U.S. Bureau of Prisons, personal communication, June 1969.
42. U.S. Bureau of Prisons, personal communication, June 1969.
43. Administration Office, U.S. Courts, Division of Procedural Studies and Statistics, personal communication, February 1968.
44. Budget Office, U.S. Bureau of Parole, personal communication, March 1968.
45. The data on the general cost of police service per index crime are presented in two publications: U.S. President's Commission on Law Enforcement and Administration of Justice, Task Force on Science and Technology, *Task Force Report: Science and Technology,* U.S. Govt. Printing Office, Washington, D.C., 1967, 53; Blaunstein, A. and Larson, R., Models of a total criminal justice system, *Operations Res.,* 45, 199, 1969.
46. U.S. President's Commission on Law Enforcement and Administration of Justice, Task Force on Assessment, *Task Force Report: Crime and Its Impact — An Assessment,* U.S. Govt. Printing Office, Washington, D.C., 1967.
47. U.S. President's Commission on Law Enforcement and Administration of Justice, Task Force on Assessment, *Task Force Report: Crime and Its Impact — An Assessment,* U.S. Govt. Printing Office, Washington, D.C., 1967.
48. **Ennis, P. H.,** Criminal victimization in the United States; a report of a national survey, *Field Surveys,* prepared for the President's Commission on Law Enforcement and Administration of Criminal Justice, U.S. Govt. Printing Office, Washington, D.C., 1967, 280.
49. U.S. President's Commission on Law Enforcement and Administration of Justice, Task Force on Assessment, *Task Force Report: Crime and Its Impact — An Assessment,* U.S. Govt. Printing Office, Washington, D.C., 1967.
50. U.S. Small Business Administration, *Crime Against Small Business,* U.S. Govt. Printing Office, Washington, D.C., 1969.
51. U.S. President's Commission on Law Enforcement and Administration of Justice, Task Force on Assessment, *Task Force Report: Crime and Its Impact — An Assessment,* U.S. Govt. Printing Office, Washington, D.C., 1967.
52. U.S. President's Commission on Law Enforcement and Administration of Justice, Task Force on Assessment, *Task Force Report: Crime and Its Impact — An Assessment,* U.S. Govt. Printing Office, Washington, D.C., 1967.
53. U.S. Small Business Administration, *Crime Against Small Business,* U.S. Govt. Printing Office, Washington, D.C., 1969.

THE HEROIN ADDICTION-STREET CRIME SYNDROME: A RADICAL CRITIQUE*

Andrew Karmen

TABLE OF CONTENTS

THE NATURE OF THE PROBLEM

Fear of crime is the number one public concern today, and alarm over drug abuse, particularly heroin addiction, ranks third.[1] Most discussions and debates on these interrelated issues are circumscribed by a narrow conceptual framework bounded by deterrence and punishment on one side and rehabilitation and social reform on the other.[2] These approaches to addiction and law-breaking share the perspective that such behavior constitutes a social problem, arising out of a rejection of the normative order on two counts: the hedonistic indulgence in forbidden narcotics and the defiant resort to illegal means. Several questionable assumptions are implicit:

1. The focus of attention and the level of analysis should be the immediate individual acts associated with drug addiction and crime, and the frame of reference should be the cultural value system, reflected in morality and law.

2. A common-sense consensus exists concerning the scope of the problems of addiction and criminality, their central aspects and their limits.

3. These twin problems incur costs or losses that are borne by society as a whole, although certain individuals or groups may pay and suffer disproportionately.

4. These social afflictions can be alleviated or even fully cured by practical measures initiated by enlightened social engineers.

An alternative approach is to consider that what are widely perceived as social problems may increasingly reveal themselves as expressions of deep-seated insoluble contradictions inherent in the existing social order. Several explicit premises follow from this:

1. An examination of drug addiction and its attendant crime must be grounded in an analysis of the basic laws of motion or predominant

*This is a revised version prepared especially for this book of a paper that appeared originally in *The Human Factor,* 12(1), 25, 1973. Reprinted by permission of the author.

tendencies characterizing the current level of development of the socioeconomic system.

2. The determination of what constitutes the definite nature and limits of the unacceptable behavior labeled addiction and crime is in the final analysis imposed by the ruling interests and powers.[3]

3. Given a recognition of opposing interests and the necessity of conflict, what is actually or potentially lost by those on one side of a relationship may be gained by those in opposite circumstances or positions.

4. "Realistic solutions" directed from above for rehabilitating addicts and deterring them from further crime are actually manipulative attempts to force individuals and groups back into compromised collaboration and rigged participation within the very same system that daily reproduces the conditions generating addiction and crime.

Without a fundamental restructuring of social relationships, addiction and crime cannot be eradicated, although temporary solutions may buy time for the system and its major beneficiaries. The problem, from the viewpoint of the vested interests, is to control the implosive potential of a narcotized populace and the explosive reality of contagious lawbreaking within acceptable, manageable limits. The problem for those genuinely concerned with ending addiction and victimization is to abolish the social conditions that foster drug abuse and crime.[4]

The latest stage of advanced industrial capitalism is marked by the dominance of giant corporate oligopolies that are the end product of the processes of accumulation, merger, and conglomeration. With the decline of competition and the rise of monopoly, fundamental social relations are altered, and the unfolding of principal contradictions takes on novel guises. Intensified attempts to rationalize the parts of an irrational whole accelerate destructive and wasteful drives inherent in the system. It is within this context that the emergence, growth, and development of an interdependent drug addiction and criminal activity epidemic (that has become entrenched in the 1970s) must be placed, in order to understand and then combat it.[5] This wholistic orientation is totally at variance with those approaches that see issues of a predominantly medical, psychological, philosophical, or educational and informational nature as primary in explaining the explosive spread of drug-

related crime. While the wholistic approach does not deny the validity or legitimacy of explanations at other levels, it does reject as insufficient the fragmented, eclectic, and discontinuous picture that emerges when isolated observations and propositions are woven together into an attempted synthesis or overview.

The heroin addiction-street crime syndrome demonstrates in a microcosm how the monopoly capitalist system works. Conversely, understanding the dictates of the socioeconomic system today, it will be shown that the drug-crime syndrome illustrates its essential features.

THE DRUG-CRIME SYNDROME

Heroin addiction is qualitatively different from dependence on methadone, barbiturates, amphetamines, or alcohol because of its socially determined character. Narcotics addicts, driven underground into a furtive and fugitive existence, must pay excessive black-market prices that compel them to commit acts of desperation that evoke harsh prosecution and persecution. Other forms of drug dependence play a similar social role, with analogous effects, except for factors resulting from intense policing.

The heroin addict's daily activities are in almost continual violation of the law. Although addiction itself is not a crime, purchasing, possessing, or selling narcotics, consorting with addicts, or being in the presence of illicit drugs or their paraphernalia are serious offenses. While some addicts are able to pay for their habit from savings or earnings, the majority, recruited disproportionately from the ranks of the poor, must resort to stealing goods or robbing people — shoplifting, pickpocketing, purse-snatching, housebreaking, auto theft, mugging, armed robbery — or prostitution or dealing drugs. Addiction integrates compulsive economic crimes into the daily pattern of buying the fix and getting high in violation of the law. This totality, of repeated heroin consumption due to physical need and street crimes stemming from impoverishment, will be termed "the drug-crime syndrome."

The relationship between addiction and crime is quite complex. For many heroin users, criminal involvement antedated addiction, but the need for money for a fix certainly boosted the rate of crime commission to a feverish pitch. Continued criminal involvement also postdates the end of addiction in some cases, indicating that lawbreaking can develop an inner dynamic of its own. However, what has been unmistakably demonstrated is that addiction multiplies the victimization of the addict and the people with whom he or she comes in contact. An arithmetic increase in addiction leads to a geometric rise in crime. The drug-crime syndrome is a self-feeding sequence of activities that takes off when the conditions nurturing drug dependence and law violation mature.

Although heroin addiction is presently deeply embedded in the social fabric, the incidence of its occurrence may stabilize or taper off in the near future. Heroin addicts can sustain variations in the potency and frequency of their dosages; they can switch to substitute drugs such as methadone or suffer through considerable spells of abstinence. Physical dependence, of course, can be overcome, but equivalent patterns of self-destructive behavior such as alcoholism are well entrenched and can absorb the slack. A linear model predicting expanding addiction, street crime, and crisis would be mechanical and ahistorical because it cannot explain how flexible social mechanisms recruit and then expel victims according to the prevailing needs of the economic system.

The drug-crime syndrome cannot be eradicated under present social conditions, but its magnitude can be indirectly controlled within limits. The external constraints against its internal dynamics depend on the quantity of heroin available, the economy's manpower needs, the political power of certain interest groups related to drugs and crime, the quality of contemporary life, the state of medical science, the impact of radical opposition movements, and the domestic and foreign policy needs of the corporate power structure.

As the drug-crime syndrome has been spreading, a parallel backlash against it by the victimized public has been unfolding. A clash has developed, and polarization is accelerating. The victims of crime blame the addicts, while the addicts tend to blame either the omnipotence of the drugs or themselves. But is it possible that both sides are actually being victimized? If so, then who is benefiting from this situation, and what interests are being served?

IMPERIALIST POLICY
AND THE OPIUM TRADE

The stage of monopoly capitalism is marked by the driving need for the multinational corporate oligopolies to export surplus capital to fresh investment outlets, to siphon off precious natural resources, to harness untapped labor forces, and to penetrate all spheres of the world market. The dynamics of imperialism have embroiled the United States in distant conflicts and counterinsurgency efforts all over the globe, either overtly, covertly, or by proxy.

It is often contended in political rhetoric that the heroin plague in the U.S. is the result of a sinister "international Communist" conspiracy, intended to subvert the nation from within by sapping its strength, destroying its will, and unleashing havoc among its youth. This argument is not backed by independent evidence, and it is, in fact, an inversion of the truth. It is precisely the most virulent anticommunist forces around the world that are involved in heroin trafficking.

Middle East opium, cultivated by poor peasants in Turkey, is refined into morphine in Iran and marketed out of Lebanon to heroin-processing laboratories in Genoa, Paris, Marseilles, Brussels, Amsterdam, Munich, and Zurich. Canada, Mexico, and Paraguay are the main western hemisphere transshipment points before the contraband reaches distributors in the U.S. The trafficking in these "free world" allies is controlled by organized crime syndicates, which could not function without the compliance of corrupt officials.

Southeast Asian opium is grown by mountain tribes in the Golden Triangle region of Burma, Laos, and Thailand. Criminal gangs, legacies of French colonialism, organize much of the traffic in opiates, in cooperation with local military units, including General Vang Pao's "Secret Meo Army," and remnants of the defeated Chinese Kuomintang forces (both financed by the C.I.A.). The South Vietnamese Air Force, the Laotian Air Force, and the C.I.A.'s Air America are part of a transportation network that supplies opiates to dealers in Saigon, Vientiane, Bangkok, Singapore, Macao, Taiwan, Hong Kong, and the Philippines. The deep involvement of the Thieu-Ky-Khiem regime in Saigon facilitated the distribution of unusually high potency heroin to the lucrative G.I. market.

Clearly, concessions in the drug trade serve as indirect subsidies granted to anticommunist elements lacking sufficient funds and popular support but engaged in military counterinsurgency adventures. This situation is not unprecedented. In Southeast Asia, the profits of the opium trade were frequently appropriated as revenue from state monopolies by repressive regimes. French intelligence agencies used narcotics trafficking to finance their covert warfare against the Viet Minh.

It is apparent that no link in the world-wide chain of heroin growing, smuggling, or selling is outside of U.S. influence, under "Communist control." On the contrary, the violence, intrigue, and corruption condoned abroad comes home to roost in the guise of the drug-crime syndrome.

THE HEROIN INDUSTRY

The logic and practices of monopoly capitalist enterprise are increasingly invading all aspects of social life. Organization within the "crime" syndicates follows the same principles as in "legitimate" business, as the art of making money is transformed into the science of profit maximization. The sheer volume of the trade, the dictates of international diplomacy, the complexity of logistics of transport and supply, the highly specialized and widely dispersed personnel required, the severe risks and the staggering profits all favor the development of regional, semipermanent, internally hierarchical syndicates operating with the conscious intent of securing, dominating, and eventually monopolizing the illegal market in narcotics.

The spread of organized crime and a rationalized division of labor develops symbiotically with the pressures of law enforcement. The activities carrying the greatest likelihood of detection and punishment are abandoned to independent entrepreneurs (growing and retail selling) and are least compensated for; the functions that are strictly financial, political, and supervisory become enveloped by protective mechanisms and yet appropriate the lion's share of the lucrative profits reaped from monopoly pricing (Figure 1).

Organized crime directly or indirectly controls 85% of the U.S. heroin trade through its financing and organizing functions.[8] The rate of profit on investment is estimated for the several levels as: importers = 300%, middlemen = 100 to 145%,

pushers = 56%.[9] Strict legal sanctions shelter the trade from open competition by deterring outside speculators, while law enforcement activities eliminate small-scale usurpers who cannot afford protection. Periodic seizures by narcotic agents provide pretexts for supply crises that inexorably lead to price increases, although the cost of pure heroin in the average heavily adulterated fix is at most a few pennies.[10] By capitalizing on these ironic consequences, crime syndicates indirectly manipulate state power to further their particular interests — in this case restricting entry, driving out competition, maintaining contrived shortages, preserving internal discipline, and controlling an exclusive franchise. The corruption of law enforcement agents and government officials provides a direct avenue to political power.[11]

Another indication of the degree of centralized control over the marketing of heroin is its relative short-term price stability. The fluctuations in supply (from confiscations, dock strikes, increased border surveillance, subsidies to buy up poppy crops, etc.) and demand (due to addicts' injection of less heroin, or use of alternative drugs such as methadone, or temporary abstinence) are attenuated at street level to the extent that even during a panic the cost of addiction remains within the realm of the possible, roughly as much as the average addict can steal in a day. Conversely, even when the streets are briefly flooded, prices do not fall low enough for very long to permit addicts to get their needed dosage by lawful means.

As monopolization of an industry proceeds, competition between producers gives way to collusion among them, but competition by them as a group against the consumer public heightens, in the form of pressures to buy more and more. This subliminal warfare is carried out through a stepped-up marketing and sales effort. But the distributors of narcotics cannot push their product, at least not by advertising it openly. Impediments against sales efforts, however, are not crucial since dope is an ideal commodity in an exchange economy. Heroin's physiologically addictive powers make advertising and marketing gim-

Overseas
Supplier → Importer → Wholesaler → Jobber → Retailer → Street Wholesaler → Street Pusher → Addict

(span of organized crime's control)

FIGURE 1. Organization of the drug trade.[7]

micks unnecessary since those who crave its effects will literally break down doors to get it. Heroin expands its own sales to those who are hooked because as tolerance builds up in the addict's body, greater dosages are needed to achieve the same high. Heroin also extends its own loyal market through the proselytizing activities of the desperate and dependent who try to entangle others in order to build up the profitable and stable local markets determining their own fate. Furthermore, there is no need for the suppliers of the product to provoke artificial dissatisfaction since junk as a nondurable commodity has built-in obsolescence; the euphoria from a fix wears off. Finally, there is little or no quality control (police estimate most street samples are 5 to 15% pure).[12] The considerable latitude in potency permits the retailing network to manipulate inventories, supplies, and prices. All sorts of adulterants are added to stretch the pure grains a long way, cutting the strength while greatly increasing the cost. There is no form of consumer protection, so many die from poisonous adulterants, unanticipated overdoses, and infections.

THE STREET CRIME INDUSTRY

There is very little concern over the disproportionately high incidence of untimely death among heroin addicts because there is callous indifference to their plight while they survive. A growing number of people have become superfluous to the system as it is presently structured. As waves of technological advances approach their culmination in automation and cybernation, dramatic productivity increases are achieved. The mechanization of unskilled and repetitious tasks "frees" many workers from the production process, only to consign them to the ranks of the "hard-core unemployed." During the competitive stage of capitalism, the reserve army of labor played a crucial role as a regulatory mechanism that functioned to keep the wage demands of workers in check while also maintaining work discipline. But in today's highly stratified labor force, the hardcore unemployed evolve into a totally dependent group who have lost their competitive link with the job market. The welfare-warfare state absorbs the surplus population it generates in several ways: People are kept out of the labor force and in school, in the armed forces (men), or in the home (women), in temporary or permanent submission

on welfare or in prisons, and on the street engaged in "crime, delinquency, and deviance." Existence as a drug addict is a sober alternative for many who are recruited to heroin from the ranks of the economically superfluous.

Polemicizing against the view that all paid jobs are socially necessary, Karl Marx wrote 100 years ago:

A philosopher produces ideas, a poet poems, a clergyman sermons, a professor compendia, and so on. A criminal produces crimes. If we look a little closer at the connection between this latter branch of production and society as a whole, we shall rid ourselves of many prejudices. The criminal produces not only crimes but also criminal law, and with this also the professor who gives lectures on criminal law and in addition to this the inevitable compendium in which the same professor throws his lectures on to the general market as "commodities" . . . .

The criminal moreover produces the whole of the police and of criminal justice, constables, judges, hangmen, juries, etc. . . . .

. . . while crime takes a part of the superfluous population off the labor market and thus reduces competition among the laborers . . . the struggle against crime absorbs another part of the population. Thus the criminal comes in as one of those natural "counterweights" which bring about a correct balance and open up a whole perspective of "useful" occupations.[13]

Incorporating and updating Marx, there is a qualitative difference in the impact of heroin addiction on the "surplus population problem" that the economic structure creates and maintains, when compared to other related life-styles in crime, delinquency, and deviance. Addiction magnifies its social consequences because of its dynamic activistic dimensions, the drug-crime syndrome. An army of thieves, fences, pushers, distributors, prostitutes, and pimps are engaged by the activities of the criminal side of the syndrome, in addition to an estimated 375,000 addicts in 1971.[14]

On the other side of this employment picture, of more importance to the functioning of the system, are the multitude of people employed in the several related aspects of coping with the severe repercussions of the drug-crime syndrome. Addiction and the crimes related to it do not create very many new types of positions, but the syndrome disproportionately augments the numbers of narcotics agents, customs inspectors, cops, judges, attorneys, guards, bail bondsmen, wardens, probation and parole officers, and legal clerks associated with the administration of the law.

The ranks of those involved in rehabilitation swell; more therapists, analysts, program administrators, researchers, criminologists, social workers, medical professionals, and technicians are needed in the public and private institutions and agencies. Finally, the drug-crime syndrome generates business for locksmiths, private guard agencies, and the manufacturers of police hardware, security equipment, and heroin paraphernalia.

The loss of an addict's capacity to do work is called foregone production. It results from the addict's shortened working life, his reduced life expectancy, and his lower productivity. The difference between the estimated annual earnings of all heroin addicts and the comparable amount the group would earn were it fully employed is put at $1,149,000,000 currently. The lifetime cost per addict, borne by himself and his family, is around $30,000, and the anticipated loss for all addicts (375,000) would be about $11,000,000,000.[15] This hypothetical loss of foregone production is often treated as a social cost borne by all of society today, along with crime control expenditures and the monetary value of addict theft. Such accounting assumes that productive jobs could be provided to addicts under existing arrangements if they were able to work more. This paper assumes precisely the reverse: The absence of productive work drove many "superfluous people" to addiction; a "surplus population " must be generated by the system as it is presently structured. Foregone production represents wasted potential, a cost directly borne today by the addicts, that could be socially salvaged only under full-employment conditions.

The absorption of people by the activities associated with the drug-crime syndrome is at the same time absolutely irrational and perfectly logical given the needs of monopoly capitalism. As more and more output is produced by less and less workers, more and more people must be engaged in other pursuits. While, on the one hand, the development of the productive forces brings out the potential for a liberation of people from the daily struggle for existence, on the other it perpetuates human degradation when fettered by the existing social relations. Since the workings of the system generate those unfortunates who are recruited to a bare existence of addiction and crime, the logic of the system demands that those who attempt to patch up the gaping social wounds be considered productive and necessary. Hence,

the drug-crime syndrome creates its own lobby within the framework of "pluralism," a group of people who have a direct vested interest in the preservation, and even expansion, of the most expensive (in terms of money and manpower) solutions to the drug-crime "problem." To the extent that their job functions would be largely unproductive and socially unnecessary in a more rational social order, their services are partially "make-work," and their employment is to some degree disguised unemployment. The ensnarement of people in addiction and crime rather than productive employment represents the waste of human resources. The involvement of people in mitigating the harmful effects of the drug-crime syndrome typifies the unavoidable misallocation of human resources the system demands.

The drug-crime syndrome is "productive" in one additional sense. In the circulation of commodities, stolen goods are not lost to consumers unless they are damaged beyond repair. Otherwise, they are salvaged and follow different channels to their ultimate destination. Theft of goods by addicts, estimated at $2.6 billion in 1971,[16] attains such proportions that for certain popular items (i.e., radios, bicycles, cameras, jewelry, etc.), secondhand recycled goods may reach a significantly extended market of people who could not afford the product at full price when new but find that "hot" merchandise at substantial discounts is within their financial means. To the extent that those who were the victims of theft replace their lost goods, the net effect of stealing and fencing on consumer industries is to increase effective demand. The drug-crime syndrome thereby serves to stimulate production and profit through what can be termed "theft-enforced obsolescence." "Theft-enforced obsolescence" contributes to boosted sales in the same way as planned obsolescence and fashion style changes, reducing the threats of overproduction and underconsumption. The redistribution of used goods to those with otherwise insufficient purchasing power counteracts the spreading awareness of relative deprivation that is so politically volatile.

Hence, the drug-crime syndrome's short-term net effects are to help stave off economic and political crises, by siphoning off the hard-core unemployed from the job market and containing them, by employing others to minister to the victims of this affliction, by stimulating production, and by more equitably dispersing consumption. The long-range consequences of these inten-sifying imbalances and irrationalities remain to be seen.

ALIENATION AND NARCOTICS

The concentration of capital and the centraliza-tion of power in the corporate oligopolies assures that the development of technology and the organization of work will conform to the dictates of profit and privilege. During periods of relative prosperity, the flexibility and material wealth of the system enables it to buy off serious challenges to its hierarchical domination and technocratic rationale by transforming qualitative demands into quantitative pleas. Workers' organizations forfeit the struggle for greater participation in decision-making and control over the work process, in favor of pay bargaining. Alienated labor, powerless over the product, dispossessed from the inaccessible means of production, fragmented and stunted by repetitious, boring tasks, intensifies to a degree unparalleled in history, precisely because work of this nature is now unnecessary and anachronistic. On-the-job use of narcotics becomes widespread in factories and offices — especially among youth employed in the dullest, dirtiest, most poorly paid tasks — in numbers approaching the proportion of older workers placated by alcohol. Although job performance is not up to par, the heroin euphoria, while it lasts, makes the undesirable chores toler-able. Hence, the social relations imposed by the system that regulate the everyday work experience generate social types particularly susceptible to the lures of physical and mental escape provided by heroin.

Since alienated labor demoralizes and dehuman-izes the majority of the subject population, con-sumption rather than production becomes empha-sized as the central social activity. The theme of pleasure and fulfillment through the consumption of material goods and services is reinforced by the development of consumer industries within the economic base. Profit-hungry enterprises, at-tempting to erode the public's will to resist through the sales effort, stretch to their limits the tendencies people have to search for satisfaction within the realm of consumption. However, the forces of commercialization can only produce alienated leisure. Consumer sovereignty is touted as autonomy and self-sufficiency. Means of escape, forgetting, and distraction are devised, packaged, and pushed on vulnerable consumers. Everyday problems are left intact, but painful awareness is deadened. The consumer-oriented society develops the preconditions for the drug-oriented society. The habituation to false comforts is paralleled by dependence on chemical comforters. Both work and consumption, the basic acts of survival, increasingly lose their inner content and meaning. Addiction, as a mode of escapism, fills this spiritual void for some.

Although socialization to the consumer society is all-pervasive, a great many cannot partake in the world of consumption. Oligopolistic enterprises are able to price commodities substantially above their costs of production, at levels where the conjunction of restricted supply and manipulated demand produce maximized profits. Monopoly control over production and pricing maintains scarcity in the midst of potential plenty. The misallocation, waste, or idleness of human and material resources perpetuates poverty, unemploy-ment, and related social afflictions. Heroin indeed becomes the "opiate" of the oppressed and ex-ploited masses by directly functioning as the one consumer item that replaces all others. Through the substitute gratifications of a fix, those who have the least stake in the social order and the most interest in restructuring it are narcotized, soothed into unconsciousness and unawareness, for as long as they can stay high.

DOMESTIC POLITICS AND THE DRUG-CRIME SYNDROME

The use of debilitating drugs as a weapon of counterinsurgency is certainly not without histori-cal precedent, from the enslavement of the Chinese people via the Opium Wars by British imperialism to the weakening of Indian resistance to American expansionism through the introduc-tion of "firewater." Today, heroin addiction physically depletes the ranks of potential activists in poor and oppressed communities. As the flood of drugs into the nation's ghettoes spills over into adjoining neighborhoods, hooking unintended vic-tims, the first serious attempts are made to contain the drug plague (and drive it back into the confines where it "belongs"). Programs that pro-mote permanent addiction to methadone (main-tenance as opposed to methadone as an aid in withdrawal) or free legal heroin (the "British System") substantiate the charge that narcotics are a tool of social control and addiction a tolerable alternative to rebellion.

There is, however, the germ of rebellion within the drug-crime syndrome. The growing insulation and isolation of the centers of power from direct confrontation with oppositional movements reflect their greater political sophistication and their ability to implement and operate institutional mechanisms to channel, deflect, contain, co-opt, or distort challenges to their rule. Under these politically frustrating conditions, addiction and crime become outlets for the "wretched of the earth" to express their pent-up resentment, anger, and aggression. On the one hand, criminal acts related to the need for money stemming from addiction embody fragmented contortions of class conflict and reflect deformations of embryonic class consciousness. The tentative rejection of capitalist rules, norms, and laws, the inarticulate expression of rage against partially perceived injustices, and the defiant groping for modes of survival in a hostile social environment are all indicative of rudimentary elements of resistance and rebellion incorporated in acts integral to the drug-crime syndrome. On the other hand, the destructive self-hatred and inwardly directed aggression (toward self or peers), the inappropriate or utterly unjust choice of victims or targets, the crude and ineffective means of redress, and the misguided reasoning behind these actions are critical shortcomings that underline the persistence of false consciousness, especially unbridled individualism. Precisely because the patterns of behavior of the drug-crime syndrome are distorted approximations of class conflict, these activities preclude the development of meaningful collective struggles.

The drug-crime syndrome particularly burdens the oppressed minorities, who suffer disproportionate addiction rates and are the principal targets for addict-related street crime. To the extent that racial discrimination limits opportunities for upward mobility, illegal avenues of financial advancement take on considerable importance and attraction. Many able youths otherwise handicapped in the competition for gainful employment accept assignments from organized crime to take their chances in the risky but well-paying field of drug dealing. Since the lower level positions in the narcotics trade require close ties with community residents and receive only modest compensation and minimal protection relative to the higher echelons of trafficking, the syndicates find it in their best business interests to become typical "equal opportunity employers." These policies only further dependence. The operations of organized crime in the heroin trade may redistribute some cash within poor neighborhoods, but on balance the ghetto is drained of internal development funds. Once again, outside exploiters bleed minority communities dry.

Laws that lump together all levels of drug traffickers in terms of penalties but are applied only to the integrated lowest echelons of the trade reflect the biases among enforcers and administrators. These practices feed racist stereotypes by giving the false impression that minority group hoodlums, not international mobsters, are in immediate control of the business.

The ineffectiveness of the legislative solution to the importation and sale of opiates has been thoroughly demonstrated for more than 50 years. The supply of harvested poppies cannot be meaningfully reduced through confiscations. The 4 or 5 tons of heroin needed by U.S. addicts each year must be ferreted out from the 100,000,000 tons of other imports, and the two or three couriers smuggling in a week's national supply must be detected from among the 4,000,000 other weekly travelers.[17]

At a time when the intervention of state power is continuously being revealed as an instrument of monopoly capital, the repercussions of the drug-crime syndrome obscure this relationship. Government agencies and programs appear to be protecting innocent people from criminals, and addicts from themselves. Despite the repeated exposure of corruption in drug law enforcement bureaus, the injurious activities associated with the syndrome drive the desperate and fearful public into the embrace and defense of the proponents of "law and order." (The Knapp Commission described as "typical" such activities of the New York Police Department as high-level officers financing heroin transactions, selling official information, and protecting narcotics dealers. In addition, it reported "numerous" instances of police connecting customers to pushers, kidnapping key witnesses to prevent them from testifying against dealers, providing armed protection for dealers, and offering to obtain "hit men" to kill potential witnesses.[18])

Nor is there any reason to believe that the Federal government under the present administration is attempting to cut down the influx of drugs into the U.S. E. Howard Hunt, a former C.I.A. official who pleaded guilty to the Watergate break-in, served as a consultant to the White House on narcotics traffic. Frank Sturgis, an anti-Castro Cuban also caught in the break-in, reportedly worked for Hunt in an undercover investigation of the illicit drug trade in South America.[19] Egil Krogh, a Nixon Administration official implicated in the Watergate-Pentagon Papers affair, helped to set up the Special Action Office for Drug Abuse Prevention and aggressively lobbied for a bill that would give the Attorney General sole authority to decide what drugs were dangerous, who could use them, and who could do research with them. Among Krogh's White House assignments was responsibility for international and national drug abuse control. His aide and liaison with the BNDD was Gordon Liddy, convicted Watergate conspirator, and his supervisor was John Ehrlichman, also implicated in the case.[20]

The public outcry against drugs and crime provides a pretext for the serious erosion of civil liberties and constitutional rights. Already in effect are the following measures: stop and frisk practices, no-knock laws, bounties for drug dealers, searching of students by teachers, electronic eavesdropping, and the widespread use of undercover narcotics agents and informers, especially on college campuses where their surveillance duties sometimes expand to include infiltration of student political groups.

The New York legislation mandating a life sentence with no chance of parole for repeated offenders in narcotics selling indicates that a cynical resort to naked suppression and political manipulation is replacing the ineffective programs of prevention and treatment currently being funded. Other legislators have pointed out that a consequence of these harsh measures will be less cooperation by arrested low-level dealers with law enforcement agencies against their former bosses, the major suppliers at the highest level of organized crime, who will now be nearly immune from prosecution. A false polarization has arisen between only two alternatives: law, order, and repression vs. breakdown, chaos, and criminal anarchy.

The misleading correlation between poverty, race, addiction, and crime gives rise to popular stereotypes that demagogic political figures and movements use as fuel to thwart progressive social change. During the contradictory stage in which prosperity and crisis coexist, the inability of the system to provide decent social services to the poor and oppressed minorities is beclouded by the drug-crime issue. By fostering ideologies that blame the victims of poverty, unemployment, and addiction for their plight, instead of the institutional mechanisms of exploitation and oppression, the system is able to play off one strata of the population against another, at the expense of unity in a common struggle for living conditions up to current potentials. False splits along ethnic, racial, generational, or life-style lines assure that the warring factions will be divided and conquered on the drug-crime issue. Only pyrrhic victories can emerge from struggles over a shrinking budget for inadequate schooling, uninhabitable housing, or ineffective treatment facilities for casualties of the heroin plague. When many people oppose social reforms and perceive suppression as the only answer to the drug-crime syndrome, then the political role of narcotics is clear.

Yet the drug-crime syndrome also lays bare the many arenas in which political struggle must be waged. The ability of the wealthy and privileged to deflect prowling addicts from their neighborhoods and sanctuaries to adjacent areas points up the operation of class privilege and differential access to resources, power, and services. The brutal treatment of captured victims of the drug-crime syndrome in the courts and jails underscores these differences. The ease with which big businesses affected by losses from theft or shoplifting by addicts pass on the cost of guards, security equipment, insurance, and lost inventories to helpless consumers dramatizes the current means for the institutionalized protection of wealth.

Most importantly, the drug-crime syndrome helps clarify the causes of the fiscal bankruptcy of the state, an issue largely forfeited up till now to the conservative taxpayer's movements. The ability of the corporate bourgeoisie to socialize the toll and consequences of capitalist production is concretized by the growing public and personal costs accruing from the expenses of the drug-abuse programs, crime prevention measures, and rehabilitative facilities. The estimated costs, directly attributable to opiate addiction, for crime control expenditures incurred by government in 1971 for courts ($27,000,000), police ($58,000,000) and corrections ($150,000,000) and for treatment ($208,000,000), research ($5,000,000), and education and prevention ($61,000,000) totaled over half a billion dollars.[21] The White House Office for Drug Abuse will receive $1,000,000,000 in appropriations over 3 years, and the Law Enforcement Assistance Administration earmarked a substantial amount of its $850,000,000 budget to projects concerning drug law violations in 1973.[22] The majority foot the bill economically, socially, and psychologically for maintaining the social relations that are in the ultimate interest of a relative few. This brings into sharp focus the central contradiction of monopoly capitalism: the social nature of production versus the private nature of appropriation; the corporate oligopolies have thus far been able to successfully avoid responsibility for the multiple dislocations and human misery they generate.

TOWARD A RADICAL PROGRAM TO COMBAT THE DRUG-CRIME SYNDROME

The drug-crime syndrome is clearly personally pressing and publicly explosive. Within limits, it "solves" certain problems of monopoly capitalism while exacerbating others. Criminal behavior (at all levels of society) underscores the irrationalities of the existing system: its driving need for expansion and empire, its perpetuation of alienated labor and its propagation of alienated leisure, its enforced relative scarcity artificially preserving deprivation, its dissipation of human potential and natural resources through waste, and its provocation of inordinate tension, hatred, and fear. Yet criminal behavior revolving around drug abuse tends to evoke only repressive political responses that stifle movements for meaningful social restructuring. As long as the drug-crime syndrome remains under the "control" (through active attempts at regulation or passive benign neglect) of the existing institutional framework, it will (in the short run, only) serve to: subsidize and thereby prop up foreign puppets, justify repressive practices, deepen reliance on the police and the state, legitimize degradation by blaming the victim, suppress oppositional movements by sapping the strength of the most oppressed, bust alliances into squabbling factions, and provide a disorganized, dependent, demoralized subpopulation of strung-out victims ripe for scapegoating or intrigue.

What can be done to further expose the contradictions and defuse the false polarizations?

1. The flow of heroin must be stopped at its sources, through subsidies to cease growing opium poppies, by financing the changeover to alternative crops, or by direct purchase and then destruction. Corrupt foreign "allies" that are behind the flood of narcotics must be dumped in response to massive public pressure.

2. Research should be oriented toward the development of a nonaddictive medical antagonist to immunize addicts against the euphoric effect of narcotics.

3. Vigilance must be maintained against the introduction of any naturally occurring or synthetic functional equivalent of heroin.

4. The responsibility for crime prevention and rehabilitation must be taken from the unavoidably corrupt and repressive law enforcement and correctional agencies by well-organized community-based political movements. People cannot rely on those who have a stake in maintaining heroin addiction to eradicate it, for they will only attempt to bring the syndrome under (their) control. Alternative institutions designed and staffed by ex-addicts and concerned others must be developed and defended against the imposition of ideological strictures. In the interim, popular control must be asserted over the police, the courts, the prisons, and the rehabilitation programs.

5. The costs for the social eradication of heroin addiction must be borne by those who profit most from this plague and who alone can afford to pay for this program: the large corporate enterprises.

6. To mobilize mass support for these measures, agitation and dramatization around the link between addiction, crime, and the workings of monopoly capitalism must be carried out by individuals and groups committed to promoting fundamental change.

REFERENCES

1. *Gallup Opinion Index*, No. 91, January 1973.
2. The connotations themselves impose ideological blinders. "Crime" is used almost synonymously with its most restricted meaning, "law and order against crime in the streets." The terms "drug abuse" or "addiction" are applied almost always to the use and dependence of illicit drugs and not to the abuse of legal drugs. For the sake of clarity and brevity, street crime in this paper will refer to acts against property or persons for rational economic gain, and addiction or drug abuse will refer specifically to physical dependence on heroin.
3. Of course, the definitions of crime are actually drawn up by the legislative and judicial branches of the government, but that in no way negates the argument made here that such definitions are imposed by the ruling interests and powers of a society.
4. This statement in no sense is meant to ignore the immediate problems that must be solved and whose ill effects must be reduced and alleviated, but the short-range corrections should not replace a long-range program. The two are not at all contradictory; in fact, they are complementary.
5. Most of the arguments developed in this paper were suggested in a most imaginative and cogent article that integrated several preexisting radical perspectives; see Yurick, S., The political economy of junk, *Monthly Rev.*, 22(7), 22, December 1970. For a more extensive analysis of the workings of monopoly capitalism, see: Sweezy, P., *The Theory of Capitalist Development*, Modern Reader, New York, 1942; Baran, P., *The Political Economy of Growth*, Prometheus, New York, 1957; Baran, P. and Sweezy, P., *Monopoly Capital*, Modern Reader, New York, 1966; Gorz, A., *Strategy for Labor*, Beacon, Boston, 1964; Mandel, E., *Marxist Economic Theory*, Vol. 2, Monthly Review Press, New York, 1971; Nicolaus, M., The crisis of late capitalism, in *The Revival of American Socialism*, Fisher, G., Ed., Oxford University Press, New York, 1971; O'Connor, J., Some contradictions of advanced U.S. capitalism, *Social Theory and Practice*, 1(1), 1, 1970.
6. Several sources amply document the following charges: McCoy, A., *The Politics of Heroin in Southeast Asia*, Harper & Row, New York, 1972; *The Opium Trail*, New England Free Press, Boston, 1973; *Heroin Traffic in Southeast Asia*, Indochina Resource Center, Washington, D.C., 1972.
7. Diagram reproduced from House Select Committee on Crime, Crime in America: Heroin Importation, Distribution, Packaging and Paraphernalia, 90th Congress, 2nd Session, U.S. Govt. Printing Office, Washington, D. C., 1970, 32.
8. *Forbes Magazine*, April 1, 1970, 22.
9. **Preble, E. and Casey, J., Jr.,** Taking care of business – the heroin user's life on the street, *Int. J. Addict.*, 4(1), 12, 1969.
10. **Brecher, E.,** *Licit and Illicit Drugs*, Little, Brown & Co., Boston, 1972, 91.
11. North American Congress on Latin America, Nixon and organized crime, *Latin America and Empire Report*, 6(8), 1972.
12. *Forbes Magazine*, April 1, 1970, 21.
13. **Marx, K.,** *Theories of Surplus Value*, Progress, Moscow, 1963, 387.
14. **McGlothlin, W., Tabbush, V., and Chambers, C.,** Alternative Approaches to Opiate Addiction Control: Costs, Benefits, and Potentials, Bureau of Narcotics and Dangerous Drugs Research Paper, June 5, 1972, 7.
15. **McGlothlin, W., Tabbush, V., and Chambers, C.,** BNDD Research Paper, June 5, 1972, A9.
16. **McGlothlin, W., Tabbush, V., and Chambers, C.,** BNDD Research Paper, June 5, 1972, A4.
17. **Brecher, E.,** *Licit and Illicit Drugs*, Little, Brown & Co., Boston, 1972, 92.
18. **Walinsky, A.,** The Knapp connection, *The Village Voice*, March 1, 1973, 71.
19. *New York Times*, January 14, 1973, 44.
20. *New York Post*, May 10, 1973, 6.
21. **McGlothlin, W., Tabbush, V., and Chambers, C.,** BNDD Research Paper, June 5, 1972, A2.
22. **Ingersoll, J.,** Director's address, *Vital Speeches*, October 15, 1972, 24.

INDEX

Drug misconceptions, 60, 61, 66, 72
  as obstacle to drug education, 61
  drug laws as source of, 66
"Drug-oriented" culture, 64
  mass media as carriers of, 64, 72
Drug-taking procedures, 157, 158
Drug use, 65, 79, 111, 116, 134, 135, 137–141, 144,
      146, 152, 250
  background characteristics, 116
  by parents, 139, 152
    studies of, 134, 135
  cultural support for legal forms of, 65, 72
  education, 117
  excessive drinking, 120
  excessive smoking, 120
  health, 118, 119
  parents' response to, 137, 138, 140, 141, 144, 146
    students' perception of, 137, 140, 144
  personality characteristics, 120
  police approach to (*see also* Marihuana use,
    criminalization of), 72
    possible effects of drug education on strengthening
      of, 72
  socioeconomic status variables, 117
  spouse, 123, 124
  subcultural support for illegal forms of, 65, 72
Drug misinformation (*see* Drug misconceptions)
Drug use as a film theme, 79
Drug users, 79
Drugs, 136, 138–141, 143, 145–147
  parents' attitudes toward (*see also* Education, parents'
    attitudes toward), 138, 140, 141, 146
  students' attitudes toward (*see also* Education, students'
    attitudes toward), 136, 139, 140, 143, 145–147
Durkheim, 5
Dysfunctional users of drugs, 129, 130

E

East Harlem Protestant Parish Narcotics Committee, 231
Eddy, Norman, 231, 233
Education, 60, 70, 84, 136–141, 148, 242
  changes in, 60, 71
  conflicting goals in, 60
  parents' attitudes toward (*see also* Drugs, parents'
    attitudes toward), 137, 138, 140, 141, 148
  students' attitudes toward (*see also* Drugs, students'
    attitudes toward), 136, 139
Employed addict, 276
Employment, 239
  jobs, 239
Employment record, 250
Endocrinal, 3
Engineering students, 7
Entertainment, 85
Entertainment programs, 87
Ethnicity, 36, 39, 41–43, 45, 47–54
  child-rearing orientation, 47–50
  contact with drug users, 36, 41–43, 45
  defined, 39
  racial identification, 51–54

Euphoria, 83
Evaluation (*see* Drug education, evaluation of)
Evaluation, 243
  "change agents", 243
Ex-addicts, 218–221, 223, 224, 226, 229, 231–234
Existential humanism, 235, 236
Exodus House, 218, 219, 221–236

F

False negatives, 222–224, 228
False positives, 222, 223, 225, 227, 228
Family (*see also* Communicative patterns, Communicative
      acts), 137, 140, 143, 150
  perception of, 137, 140, 143, 150
Family relationship, 160
Fatigue, 160
Federal Bureau of Narcotics, 284, 292–298
Federal Communications Commission, 96, 97
Female addict, 274
Fiction, 78
Fiddle, 4
Fiduciary commitment, 232–235
Fiduciary function, 219
Fiduciary social agent, 220
Film ratings, 82, 86
Films, 79–85, 91, 92
Finestone, 4, 10
"Flash", 159
Forced transfer of goods, 285–288
Foreign, 3
France, 9
"Freaks", 90
Future trends, 164

G

Gangs, 9
Generational patterns (*see also* Migrant-native status), 36,
      37, 44, 45, 49, 50, 53, 54
  child-rearing orientation, 49, 50, 53, 54
  contact with drug users, 36, 37, 44, 45
  defined, 44
  racial identification, 51–54
Geography, 9
Ghetto, 84, 92
Ghetto residents, 4
Ginsberg, Allen, 78–80
Glamorous attitude, 84
Glue sniffers, 6
Goode, 10
Graduate students, 7
Group process, aspects of, 207, 209–212
  encounter, 207, 209–212
  engross, 210
  marathon, 210, 212
Group psychotherapy, 93
Groves, 7

Psychoactive drugs, 9
Psychoactive substances, 9
Psychosomatic disease, 11
Psychotherapeutic drugs, 103–109
  acquisition of, 105–107
  patterns of use, 104–107
Psychotropic drugs, 111
Publishers, 97
Puerto Ricans, 78, 82
Pugh, 10
Pusher, 92

Q

Quarrels, 160, 161

R

Racial identification, 40, 51–54
  contact with drug users, 52, 54
  defined, 40
  ethnicity by, 51–54
  generational patterns by, 51–54
  social class differences in, 51
Radicalization, 9
Radiology, 8
Radios, 94
Reasons for drug use, 159–163
Rechy, John, 78
Record and tape industry, 94
Region of the impossible, 218–220, 223, 226, 230
Regular use, 4
Relaxation, 85
Relative deprivation, 163
Research designs, 134–136, 139–150, 152
  factor analysis, 135, 136, 139–150
    compared with tabular analysis, 148–150
  longitudinal, 134, 152
  retrospective, 134
Retirement, 161, 162
Retreatists, 95
Risk-discounting, 4
Rites of passage, 6
Rock music, 9, 81, 83, 94–97
Role behavior, 69
  of drug educators, 69
  of students in drug education, 69
Role conflict, 69
  in drug educators, 69
  in students of drug education, 69
Role expectations, 68
  for drug educators, 68, 69
  for students in drug education, 69
Role models, 69
  drug educators as, 69
  ex-addicts as, 70
  parents as, 70
  students in drug education as, 70
Roles, 4, 201–204, 207, 209, 211, 212
  bad rap buddy, 202, 204

coordinator, 203, 207, 209, 211
  expediter, 204, 207, 211
  role model, 212
  strength of the house, group, 201, 209
Role deprivation, 4, 7, 8, 11, 163–165
Role discontinuity, 6
Role inventory, 8, 11
Role obligations, 10
Role sets, 10
Role strain, 4, 6, 7, 8, 10, 163–165
"Rush", 159

S

Script writers, 82
Sedatives, 104, 105
Selby, Hubert, 78
Selective exposure, 80
Self-medicators, 127, 128, 130
  adaptive behavior, 127
Self-preservation, 284
Sex, 84
Sex differentiation, 139–148, 150, 152
  and student drug use, 139–148, 152
Sex roles and addiction, 245
  "love" and drug use, 248
Shooting gallery addict, 273
"Shooting up", 84, 89, 92
Smugglers, 90
Social change (see also Drug laws, reform of and
    Education, changes in as possible consequence of
    drug education)
Social class, 36, 39, 41–43, 45, 49, 53
  child-rearing orientation, 49, 53
  contact with drugs, 36, 41–43, 45
  defined, 39
Social control, 68
  drug education as form of, 68, 73
Social learning, 4
Social mobility, 230
Social network, 4
Social order, 60
  as traditional concern of education, 60
Social problems, 309–318
  contradictions, 309, 317, 318
  costs, losses, 309, 317, 318
  definition, 309
  radical program, 318
  "realistic solutions", 310
Social/recreational users of drugs, 128, 129, 131
Social structure, 97, 165
Social system, 10
Sociological theory, 3, 163
Southeast Asia, 7
"Splittee", 234
Status, 10
Stimulants, 4, 104, 105
Strain, 10
Street addicts, 159, 270
Street crime industry, 313
Street sales, 84